PELICAN BOOKS

RED STAR OVER CHINA

Edgar Snow was a native of Missouri who went to the Far East when he was twenty-two. Before writing *Red Star Over China* he had made his home in China for seven years, studied the country and the language, and lectured at Yenching University, where his friends included students who are among China's leaders today. In Asia he worked for the *Chicago Tribune*, the *New York Sun*, the *New York Herald Tribune*, and the *London Daily Herald*. During the Second World War he was associate editor and war correspondent of the *Saturday Evening Post*, and in the post-war era he became the *Post's* widely quoted specialist on China, India, and the U.S.S.R. He was the author of several books which include *The Battle for Asia, People on Our Side, Journey to the Beginning,* and *Red China Today: The Other Side of the River.* Edgar Snow died in 1971.

Books by Edgar Snow

EDGAR SNOW

RED STAR
OVER CHINA

—

Revised and Enlarged
Edition

PENGUIN BOOKS

Penguin Books Ltd, Harmondsworth, Middlesex, England
Penguin Books Australia Ltd, Ringwood, Victoria, Australia

—

First published in Great Britain by Victor Gollancz 1937; in the U.S.A. 1938
Revised edition published in Great Britain by Victor Gollancz 1968
This edition, with further revisions, published by Pelican Books 1972
Reprinted 1973

—

—

Made and printed in Great Britain by
Hazell Watson & Viney Ltd,
Aylesbury, Bucks

Set in Linotype Juliana

Contents

PART FOUR: GENESIS OF A COMMUNIST

PART FIVE: THE LONG MARCH

PART SIX: RED STAR IN THE NORTH-WEST

PART SEVEN: EN ROUTE TO THE FRONT

PART EIGHT: WITH THE RED ARMY

8   *Contents*

APPENDICES

The maps on pp. 10–11 and 16–17 have been redrawn for this edition and are based on the maps used in the original edition, prepared from the author's own maps of the area.

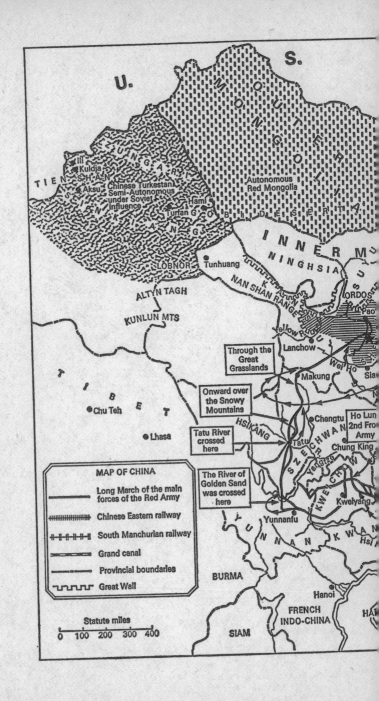

MAP OF CHINA

——————	Long March of the main forces of the Red Army
++++++++++	Chinese Eastern railway
++++++++	South Manchurian railway
=========	Grand canal
— — — —	Provincial boundaries
⌐_⌐_⌐_	Great Wall

Statute miles

0   100   200   300   400

U.   S.

OUTER MONGOLIA

Autonomous Red Mongolia

ZUNGARIA

TIEN SHAN

Ili
Kuldja
Aksu
Chinese Turkestan
Semi-Autonomous
under Soviet
influence
Turfan
Hami

GOBI DESERT

SINKIANG

INNER MU

NINGHSIA

LOBNOR   Tunhuang

NAN SHAN RANGE

KANSU

ORDOS

Pao

ALTYN TAGH

KUNLUN MTS

Yellow R.

Lanchow

Wei Ho

Sia

TIBET

Through the
Great
Grasslands

Makung

Chu Teh

Onward over
the Snowy
Mountains

Chengtu

Ho Lun
2nd Fro
Army

Lhasa

HSIKANG

Tatu River
crossed
here

Tatu

SZECHWAN

Chung King

The River of
Golden Sand
was crossed
here

Yangtze

KWEICHOW

Kweiyang

Yunnanfu

YUNNAN

KWAN

Hsi

BURMA

Hanoi

FRENCH
INDO-CHINA

HA

SIAM

S.   R.

JAPANESE
PUPPET EMPIRE

Amur River

River

Vladivostok

J A P A N

S E A

Kalgan

Peiping Tientsin
Taku   Shanhaikwan Port Arthur
Paoting HOPEI Tsingtao Chefoo Weihaiwei
Tsinan   Dairen
Taiyuan SHANTUNG
Tai Shan Kwan
Chufou

Kaifeng KIANGSU
NAN
Nanking
4th Front Army Wusch Chinkiang
ANHUI Woosung
Hankow Kiukiang Soochow Shanghai
Wuchang Nanchang Hangchow
CHEKIANG CHUSAN
Ningpo ARCHIPELAGO
Wenchow
FUKIEN

Red Capital
Central
Soviet Gov't
1934

Foochow
Chuanchow
Amoy Taiwan
(Formosa)

The 'Long March'
begins at night
16 October 1934

KWANGTUNG
Canton Swatow
Kowloon
Hong Kong
Macao
gchow wan

Seoul

Tokyo
Yokohama
Kyoto
Kobe
Shikoku
Nagasaki Kyushu

RYUKYU ISL.

P A C I F I C

O C E A N

N

YELLOW

SEA

PHILIPPINE
ISLANDS

Introduction

by Dr John K. Fairbank

Red Star Over China is a classic because of the way in which it was produced. Edgar Snow was just thirty and had spent seven years in China as a journalist. In 1936 the Chinese Communists had just completed their successful escape from South-East China to the North-West, and were embarking upon their united-front tactic. They were ready to tell their story to the outside world. Snow had the capacity to report it. Readers of the book today should be aware of this combination of factors.

Edgar Snow was born in Kansas City in 1905, his forebears having moved westward by degrees from North Carolina to Kentucky and then into Kansas Territory. In 1928 he started around the world. He reached Shanghai, became a journalist, and did not leave the Far East for thirteen years. Before he made his trip to report the Chinese Communists, he had toured through famine districts in the North-West, traversed the route of the Burma Road ten years before it was operating, reported the undeclared war at Shanghai in 1932, and become a correspondent for the *Saturday Evening Post*. He had become a friend of Mme Sun and had met numerous Chinese intellectuals and writers. Settling in Peking in 1932, he and his wife lived near Yenching University, one of the leading Christian colleges which had been built up under American missionary auspices. As energetic and wide-awake young Americans, the Snows had become widely acquainted with the Chinese student movement against Japanese aggression in late 1935. They had studied Chinese and developed a modest fluency in speaking. In addition to publishing his account of the Japanese aggression, *Far Eastern Front*, Edgar Snow had also edited a collection of translations of modern Chinese short stories, *Living China*.

Thus in the period when the Japanese expansion over Manchuria and into North China dominated the headlines, this young

American had not only reported the events of the day but had got behind them into some contact with the minds and feelings of Chinese patriotic youth. He had proved himself a young man of broad human sympathy, aware of the revolutionary stirrings among China's intellectuals, and able to meet them with some elementary use of the Chinese language. More than this, Ed Snow was an activist, ready to encourage worthy causes rather than be a purely passive spectator. Most of all, he had proved himself a zealous factual reporter, able to appraise the major trends of the day and describe them in vivid colour for the American reading public.

In 1936 he stood on the western frontier of the American expansion across the Pacific towards Asia, which had reached its height after a full century of American commercial, diplomatic, and missionary effort. This century had produced an increasing American contact with the treaty ports, where foreigners still retained their special privileges. Missionaries had pushed into the rural interior among China's myriad villages and had inspired and aided the first efforts at modernization. In the early 1930s American foundations and missionaries both were active in the movement for 'rural reconstruction', the remaking of village life through the application of scientific technology to the problems of the land. At the same time, Chinese students trained in the United States and other Western countries stood in the forefront of those modern patriots who were becoming increasingly determined to resist Japanese aggression at all costs. Western-type nationalism thus joined Western technology as a modern force in the Chinese scene, and both had been stimulated by the American contact.

Despite all these developments, however, the grievous problems of China's peasant villages had only begun to be attacked under the aegis of the new Nationalist Government at Nanking. Harassed by Japanese aggression, Chiang Kai-shek and the Kuomintang were absorbed in a defence effort which centred in the coastal treaty ports and lower Yangtze provinces, with little thought or motive for revolutionary change in the rural countryside. Meanwhile, in 1936, the Chinese Communists were known generally as 'Red bandits', and no Western observer had had direct contact with their leadership or reported it to the outside world. With the hindsight of a third of a century, it may seem to us now almost incredible that so little could have been known about Mao Tse-tung and the movement which he headed. The Chinese Communist Party had a history of fifteen years when Edgar Snow journeyed to its headquarters, but the disaster which had overtaken it in the 1920s had left it in a precarious state of weakness.

When he set out for the blockaded Red area in the North-West in June 1936, with an introduction from Mme Sun Yat-sen, he had an insight into Chinese conditions and the sentiments of Chinese youth which made him almost uniquely capable of perceiving the powerful appeal which the Chinese Communist movement was still in the process of developing. Through the good will of the Manchurian army forces at Sian, who were psychologically prepared for some kind of united front with the Communists, Snow was able to cross the lines, reach the Communist capital, then at Pao An (even further in the North-West than the later capital at Yenan), and meet Mao Tse-tung just at the time when Mao was prepared to put himself on record.

Snow came out of the blockaded Red area in October 1936, after spending four months there and taking down Mao Tse-tung's own story of his life as a revolutionist. He gave his eye-opening story to the press in articles, and finished *Red Star Over China* on the basis of his notes in July 1937.

The remarkable thing about *Red Star Over China* was that it not only gave the first connected history of Mao and his colleagues and where they had come from, but it also gave a prospect of the future of this little-known movement which was to prove disastrously prophetic. It is very much to the credit of Edgar Snow that this book has stood the test of time on both these counts – as a historical record and as an indication of a trend.

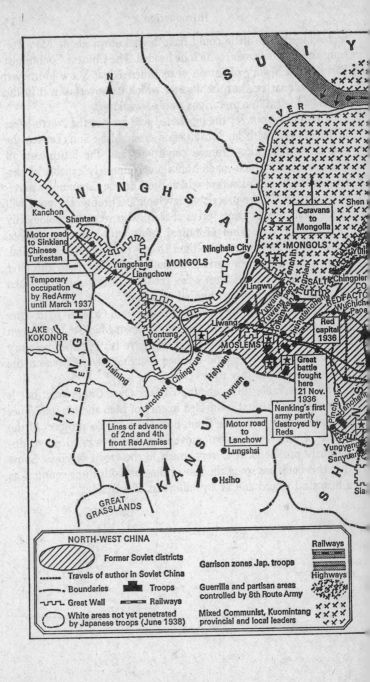

NORTH-WEST CHINA

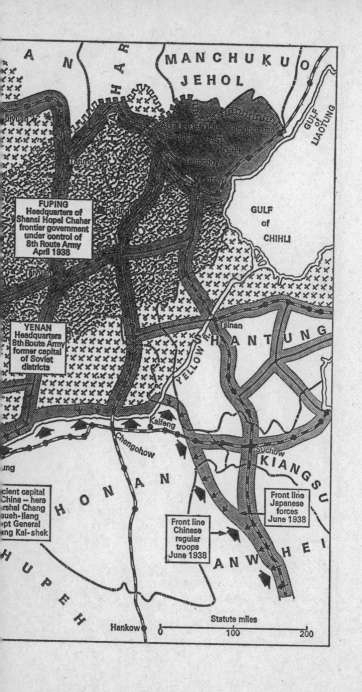

MANCHUKUO

JEHOL

CHAHAR

Taiyuan

Tatung

GULF
OF
LIAOTUNG

Shanhaikwan

HOPEI
Changchow

Tientsin

FUPING
Headquarters of
Shansi Hopei Chahar
frontier government
under control of
8th Route Army
April 1938

Fuping

HOPEI

GULF
of
CHIHLI

Taiyuan

YENAN
Headquarters
8th Route Army
former capital
of Soviet
districts

Tsinan

SHANTUNG

YELLOW RIVER

Kaifeng

Chengchow

Suchow

KIANGSU

ncient capital
China — here
arshal Chang
sueh-liang
pt General
ng Kai-shek

HONAN

Front line
Chinese
regular
troops
June 1938

Front line
Japanese
forces
June 1938

HUPEH

ANWHEI

Hankow

Statute miles

0   100   200

Preface to the Revised Edition

TRAVELS and events described in this book took place in 1936 and 1937 and the manuscript was completed in July 1937, to the sound of gunfire by Japanese troops outside the walls of Peking, where I lived. Those guns of July in China opened eight years of Sino-Japanese battle which merged with the Second World War. The same guns also heralded the ultimate Communist victory in China which profoundly altered the balance of power, both inside and outside what was formerly called 'the Communist camp'.

In time and space this report concerned an isolated fighting force in an area far removed from the West on the eve of its greatest catastrophe. The League of Nations had been destroyed when it failed to halt Japan's conquest of Manchuria in 1931-3. In 1936 the Western 'Allies' permitted Hitler, still a cardboard Napoleon, to reoccupy the Rhineland without a fight. They impotently watched Mussolini seize Ethiopia. They then imposed an arms embargo against Spain under the hypocrisy of neutralism, which denied the Republic the means to defend itself against reactionary generals led by Franco, who had the open support of thousands of imported Nazi and Fascist troops and planes. They thus encouraged Hitler and Mussolini to form an alliance ostensibly aimed at Russia but clearly intended to subjugate all of Western Europe. In 1938 Hitler was allowed to swallow Austria. He was then rewarded, by Chamberlain and Daladier, with Czechoslovakia as the price of 'peace in our time'. In compensation they soon received the Hitler-Stalin pact.

Such was the international environment of China when this journey was undertaken. Domestic conditions inside that disintegrating society are defined in the text. In 1936 I had already lived in China for seven years and I had, as a foreign correspondent, travelled widely and acquired some knowledge of the language. This was my longest piece of reportage on China. If it has enjoyed a more useful life than most journalism it is because it was not only a 'scoop' of perishable news but likewise of many facts of durable history. It won sympathetic attention also perhaps because it was a time when the Western powers, in self-interest, were hoping for a miracle in China. They dreamed of a new birth of nationalism that would keep Japan so bogged down that she would never be able to turn upon the Western colonies – her true objectives. Red Star Over China tended to show that the Chinese Communists could indeed provide that nationalist leadership needed for effective anti-Japanese resistance. How dramatically the United States' policy-making attitudes have altered since then is suggested by recalling that condensations of this report originally appeared in the Saturday Evening Post and Life magazine.

Other circumstances contributed to prolong the utility of this book. I had found Mao Tse-tung and other leaders at an especially favourable moment, in a lull between long years of battle. They gave me a vast amount of their time, and with unprecedented frankness provided more personal and impersonal information than any one foreign scribe could fully absorb. After my second visit to see Mao Tse-tung, in 1939, all the Red bases in North-West China were blockaded by Nationalist troops, in their rear, and cut off by Japanese occupation around the guerrilla areas. For another five years, while no foreign newsmen were able to reach Yenan, the Red capital, these reports remained a unique source.

Much of this work is history seen from a partisan point of view, of course, but it is history as lived by the men and women who made it. It provided not only for non-Chinese readers, but also for the entire Chinese people – including all but the Communist leaders themselves – the first authentic account of the Chinese Communist Party and the first connected story of their long struggle to carry through the most thoroughgoing social revolution in China's three millenniums of history. Many editions were published in China, and among the tens of thousands of copies of the Chinese translations some were produced entirely in guerrilla territory.

I do not flatter myself that I had much to do with imparting to this volume such lessons of international application as may be drawn from it. For many pages I simply wrote down what I was told by the extraordinary young men and women with whom it was my privilege to live at the age of thirty, and from whom I learned (or had the chance to learn) a great deal.

In 1937, when *Red Star Over China* first appeared, in England, there were practically no sources of documentation for most of the material presented here. Today many foreign China specialists – helped or led by Chinese scholars of different political colorations – have produced dozens of works of varying importance and quality. With an abundance of new information available, aided by my own and others' wisdom of hindsight, many improvements might be made in the text to minimize its limitations – and yet deprive it of whatever original value it may possess. Therefore it was my intention to leave it as first written except for corrections of typographical errors and mistakes of spelling or of factual detail. That hope has not proved wholly practicable and departures from its fulfilment are acknowledged below.

Since *Red Star Over China* was completed under conditions of war I did not have the opportunity to see or correct galley proofs of the first edition. Nor have I been able to do so with subsequent editions until now. In extenuation for one kind of mistake : my handwritten field notes contained many names previously unknown to me, and I could not always get them down in Chinese characters. Phonetic transliterations into English resulted in misspellings as judged by Wade-Giles standards. These have now been (I hope) uniformly corrected.

Aside from that kind of conformance I have widely altered former present-tense verbs to past tense in order to eliminate many seeming anachronisms and make the story more accessible to contemporary readers. Where the book quotes or paraphrases the testimony of others, the wording of the original text has generally been preserved – to avoid tampering with *a priori* historical material – even when it conflicts with more believable information now available. In a few instances where secondary material has been proved manifestly inaccurate I have cut or corrected, rather than perpetuate known errors. In either case readers may refer to the Biographical Notes or the Notes to this edition to supplement or modify some textual facts or opinions. Here and there (with a certain macabre sense of looking backwards on myself) I have reworked lines which the passage of time – or murky writing in the first instance – has made unintelligible to me. The great bulk of the volume, all the happenings, the main travel notes, interviews, and biographies – including Mao Tse-tung's – remain intact.

Such liberties as I have taken in shortening, condensing, or discarding tedious accounts of a few matters no longer of importance helped to make room for the chronology, an epilogue, new footnotes, some heretofore unpublished documents, chapter commentaries, and some fascinating lessons of history in the form of biographical sequels to the early life stories of the truly extraordinary people first introduced here. Cuts of paragraphs and even whole pages necessitated composing new transitional passages. Such 'spin-ins' are confined to knowledge available to me no later than 1937, and the same applies to page footnotes – but not to the end-of-book materials, of course.

Doubtless this tome would not have suffered (and the reader would have profited) if I had omitted several whole chapters. Revision was not easy, and I daresay someone less connected with the subject could have done it with less pain to himself and with more grace for the reader.

And so, salutations and thanks to all persons mentioned in this book for their help and permission to use their remarks and photographs, especially Mao Tse-tung; to John Fairbank, for taking one more look at these ancient spoor; to Peter J. Seybolt for a reappraisal against a background of far wider perspective than we could know in the thirties; to Enrica Collotti Pischel, for painstaking scholarship in translating into Italian and bringing up to date the 1965 edition (*Stella rossa sulla Cina*) which inspired this effort; and to Mary Heathcote, Trudie Schafer, and Lois Wheeler for assistance and encouragement in general.

Geneva, 14 February 1968   EDGAR SNOW

Preface to the Pelican Edition

AFTER the first revised and enlarged (1968) edition of this book appeared I was able to return to China (August 1970–February 1971). Now the opportunity arises to make limited modifications and additions to the text which are to be found mainly in the Notes and Appendices. One result of the Great Proletarian Cultural Revolution was to make available rich if largely still unevaluated material relating to the period originally covered by my first report. It would be impossible to incorporate in this single volume everything relevant to the subject and epoch which is now known, of course. I have had to content myself with merely indicating a few selected new sources which may assist the reader in a search for further knowledge opened by a rapidly expanding world of historical revelation.

E.S.

August 1971

Chronology of the Chinese Revolution

1. Last Days of the Monarchy

1840–42 The 'Opium Wars', during which Great Britain forcibly opens China to foreign trade. They are followed by the granting of territorial concessions and rights of inland navigation and missionary activity. The British take Hongkong.

1860 China accepts Russian annexation of eastern Siberia.

1864 Near-victorious T'ai-p'ing (Great Peace) Rebellion crushed by Sino-Manchu forces under General Tseng Kuo-fan, helped by British army regulars and mixed European and American mercenaries. Chinese revolution 'postponed sixty years'. Following French penetration and seizure of Indochina (1862), encroachments increasingly reduce the Manchu-Chinese Empire to semi-colonial status.

1866 Sun Yat-sen (founder of Kuomintang, or Nationalist Party, 1912) born in Kwantung province.

1868 Czarist Russia annexes Bokhara and begins penetration towards Chinese Turkestan.

1869 Suez Canal completed.

1870 Lenin born.

1874 Churchill born.

1879 Ch'en Tu-hsiu (first general secretary, 1921–7, of Kungch'antang, or Chinese Communist Party) born in Anhui province. Rapid expansion of French and British colonial empires in Africa.

1883–5 Franco-Chinese War. Chinese troops in Indochina, defending Peking's claim to suzerainty there, are defeated. France also acquires new territorial-political concessions in China. Britain ends China's suzerainty in Burma.

1889 Cecil Rhodes establishes British South African Company.

1893 Mao Tse-tung born in Hunan province. France extends its Indo-chinese colonial power to Laos and Cambodia.

1894–5 Sino-Japanese War. China forced to cede Taiwan (Formosa) to Japan and abandon ancient claims to suzerainty over Korea.

1898 'Hundred Days Reform' under Emperor Kuang Hsu. Empress Dowager Tz'u Hsi imprisons Kuang Hsu and returns to power, to remain real ruler till her death (1909). United States defeats Spain, takes Philippines.

1899 'Open Door' doctrine proclaimed by USA; 'equal opportunity' for foreign powers in the economic and commercial 'development' of China.

1900 So-called Boxer Rebellion. Antiforeign uprising. Allied reprisals include mass executions, crushing indemnities, new concessions, legalized foreign garrisons between Tientsin and Peking, etc. Czarist Russia takes China's port of Talien (Dairen), builds naval base (Port Arthur), acquires railway concessions across China's three north-eastern provinces (Manchuria). Mao Tse-tung works as labourer on his father's farm.

1902 Anglo-Japanese alliance.

1904–5 Russo-Japanese War. Japan gets Port Arthur, Dairen, Russia's concessions in South Manchuria (China), and additional 'rights'. Dr Sun Yat-sen forms revolutionary Alliance Society in Tokyo.

1905 First Russian Revolution.

1911 Republican revolution (the 'First Revolution') overthrows Manchu power in Central and South China. At Nanking, Sun Yat-sen declared president of provisional government, first Chinese Republic. Student Mao Tse-tung joins rebel army; resigns after six months, thinking 'revolution over'.

2. The Republic and the Warlords (1912–27)

1912 Rulers of Manchu Dynasty formally abdicate. Sun Yat-sen resigns in favour of Yuan Shih-k'ai, as president of the Republic of China. Peking is its capital. Kuomintang (Nationalists) dominates first parliament, forms cabinet. Italy takes Libya.

1912–14 Provisional constitution and parliament suspended by militarist Yuan Shih-k'ai, who becomes dictator. Japan imposes 'Twenty-one Demands', their effect to reduce China to vassal state. Yuan Shih-k'ai accepts most of the demands. Cabinet resigns. European war begins. Japan seizes Tsingtao, German colony in China. Mao first studies books by Western scholars.

1915 New Youth (Hsin Ch'ing-nien) magazine, founded by Ch'en Tu-hsiu, becomes focus of revolutionary youth, and popularizes written vernacular (*pai-hua*) language; death knell of Confucian classicism. Mao Tse-tung becomes *New Youth* contributor, under pseudonym. Yuan Shih-k'ai attempts to re-establish monarchy, with himself as emperor.

1916 Second (Republican) Revolution: overthrow of 'Emperor' Yuan Shih-k'ai by 'revolt of the generals' led by Tsai O. Nullification of Yuan's acceptance of Japan's 'Twenty-one Demands'. Era of warlords begins.

1917 Peking 'shadow government' declares war on Germany. Generalissimo Sun Yat-sen, heading separate provisional regime in Canton, also declares war. In Hunan, Mao Tse-tung becomes co-founder of radical youth group, New People's Study Society. The October Revolution occurs in Russia.

1918 End of First World War. Mao Tse-tung graduates from Hunan First Normal School, aged twenty-five. He visits Peking; becomes assistant to Li Ta-chao, librarian of Peking University. Li Ta-chao and Ch'en Tu-hsui establish Marxist study society, which Mao joins. All three later become founders of Chinese Communist Party.

1918–19 175,000 labourers sent overseas to help allies; 400 'Work-Study' student interpreters include Chou En-lai. Mao Tse-tung accompanies students to Shanghai. Back in Hunan, Mao founds *Hsiang Chiang Review*, anti-imperialist, antimilitarist, pro-Russian Revolution.

1919 May Fourth Movement. Nationwide student demonstrations against Versailles Treaty award of Germany's China concessions to Japan. Beginning of modern nationalist movement. Hungarian (Bela Kun) Communist-led social revolution suppressed.

1920 Mao Tse-tung organizes Hunan Branch of Socialist Youth Corps; among its members, Liu Shao-ch'i. Mao marries Yang K'ai-hui, daughter of his esteemed ethics professor at normal school. Mao helps found Cultural Book Study Society. League of Nations established.

1921 Chinese Communist Party formally organized at First Congress, Shanghai. Mao participates; is chosen secretary of CP of Hunan. Ts'ai Ho-sen, Chou En-lai, and others form Communist Youth League in Paris. Revolution in Mongolia.

1922 Sun Yat-sen agrees with Lenin's representative to accept Soviet aid and form united front with CCP; Communists may now hold joint membership in Kuomintang, led by Sun. Washington Conference restores Germany's colony to China.

3. Nationalist (or Great) Revolution:
Kuomintang-Communist United Front (1923–7)

1923   Agreement between Sun Yat-sen and Adolf Joffe provides basis for KMT–CCP–CPSU alliance. At Third Congress of CCP, in Canton, Mao Tse-tung elected to Central Committee and chief of organization bureau.

1924   First Congress of Kuomintang approves admission of Communists. Mao Tse-tung elected an alternate member, Central Executive Committee, Kuomintang. Lenin dies.

1925   Mao returns to Hunan, organizes peasant support for Nationalist (Liberation) Expedition. Writes his first 'classic', *Analysis of Classes in Chinese Society* (published 1926). Sun Yat-sen dies. Russian advisers choose Chiang Kai-shek as commander-in-chief. 'Universal suffrage' in Japan.

1926   Nationalist Revolutionary Expedition launched from Canton under supreme military command of Chiang Kai-shek. Mao, back in Canton, becomes deputy director Kuomintang Peasant Bureau and Peasant Movement Training Institute; he heads agit-prop department. Nationalist-Communist coalition forces conquer most of South China. Communist-led Indonesian revolution suppressed by Dutch.

4. First Communist-Nationalist Civil War (1927–37)

1927   Stalin victorious over Trotsky. In March, Mao Tse-tung publishes his *Report of an Investigation into the Peasant Movement in Hunan*; calls poor peasants 'main force' of revolution, demands confiscation of landlords' land. Thesis rejected by Communist Party Central Committee. In April, Chiang Kai-shek leads anti-Communist coup, 'beheads Party'; Communist membership reduced, by four fifths, to 10,000. Ch'en Tu-hsiu deposed as CCP secretary. Party driven underground. Mao leads peasant uprising in Hunan (August); defeated, he flees to mountain stronghold, Chingkangshan. Nanchang Uprising also defeated. Retreat to countryside. Canton (Commune) Uprising fails. P'eng P'ai leads survivors to Hailufeng and sets up Hailufeng Soviet (1927). Sukarno forms Indonesian Nationalist Party.

1928   Chiang Kai-shek establishes nominal centralized control over China under National Government (a Kuomintang, one-party dictatorship). Mao Tse-tung and Chu Teh join forces at Chingkangshan, Hunan, form first 'Red Army' of China and local soviet. Paris Peace Pact signed by the great powers, renouncing war 'as an instrument of national policy'.

1929   Mao Tse-tung and Chu Teh conquer rural territories around Juichin, Kiangsi, where a soviet government is proclaimed. Communist Politburo, dominated by Li Li-san, remains hidden in foreign-controlled Shanghai. Stock market crash in New York.

1930   Conflict between Mao's 'rural soviet movement' and Politburo leader Li Li-san, who favours urban insurrections. Red Army led by Mao and P'eng Teh-huai captures Changsha, capital of Hunan, then withdraws. Second assault on Changsha a costly failure. Li Li-san discredited by Moscow. Chiang Kai-shek launches first major offensive against the Reds. Mao Tse-tung's wife and sister executed in Changsha. Gandhi leads non-violent civil disobedience in India.

1931   Spain declares a Republic. Meeting underground in January, in Shanghai, Central Committee of CCP elects Wang Ming (Ch'en Shao-yu) general secretary and chief of Party. All-China Congress of Chinese Soviets, convened in deep hinterland of Juichin, elects Mao Tse-tung chairman of the first All-China Soviet Government, Chu Teh military commander. In September, Japan begins conquest of Manchuria; Chiang Kai-shek suspends his third 'annihilation campaign' against Red Army. End of Great Famine (1929–31) in North-West China; estimated dead, five to ten million. Wang Ming goes to Moscow. Po Ku heads Shanghai Politburo.

1932   Japan attacks Shanghai, defended by Nineteenth Route Army; unsupported by Chiang Kai-shek, it retreats to Fukien province. Chiang authorizes Tangku Truce, to end Sino–Japanese hostilities. He renews offensive against Kiangsi Soviet; Reds declare war on Japan. Police in Shanghai International Settlement help Chiang Kai-shek extirpate Red underground. Politburo chiefs Po Ku, Lo Fu, Liu Shao-ch'i, and Chou En-lai join Mao in Kiangsi Soviet. Roosevelt elected President of US.

1933   Nineteenth Route Army rebels and offers alliance to Reds, which is rejected. Chiang Kai-shek destroys Nineteenth RA, begins a new campaign against Soviet China. Hitler becomes chancellor of Germany.

1934   Second All-China Soviet Congress re-elects Mao Tse-tung chairman, but Party leadership falls to 'Twenty-eight Bolsheviks'. Red Army changes tactics and suffers decisive defeats. Main forces and party cadres retreat to West China.

1935   Politburo meets in Tsunyi, Kweichow, in January; elects Mao Tse-tung effective leader of the Party and army during Long March to North-West China. In July, Kiangsi Red forces reach Szechuan and join troops under Politburo member and Party co-founder Chang Kuo-t'ao, driven from soviet areas north of Yangtze River. In enlarged meeting of Politburo, Chang Kuo-t'ao disputes Mao's policy and leadership. Red forces divide; Mao leads southern forces into new base in North-West China, after one year of almost continuous marching, totalling 6,000 miles. (Chang Kuo-t'ao follows him a year later.) Japan demands separation of two North China provinces, under 'autonomous' regime. Japanese troops move into Chinese Inner Mongolia, set up bogus 'independent' state. Ninth December student rebellion in Peking touches off wave of anti-Japanese national patriotic activity. Italy seizes Ethiopia.

1936   Mao Tse-tung, interviewed by the author in Pao An, Shensi, tells his life story and his account of the revolution, and offers to end civil war to form a united front against Japan. Mao lectures to the Red Army University; his *On the Tactics of Fighting Japanese Imperialism* and *Strategic Problems in China's Revolutionary War* become doctrinal basis of new stage of united front against Japan. Spurning Communists' offer of a truce (first made on 1 August 1935), Chiang Kai-shek mobilizes for 'final annihilation' of Reds in North-West.

The Sian Incident, in December: Chiang Kai-shek 'arrested' by his deputy commander-in-chief, Chang Hsueh-liang, exiled Manchurian leader. Marshal Chang insists that Chiang accept national united front against Japan. Following Chiang Kai-shek's release, and undeclared truce in civil war, Kuomintang opens negotiations with CCP and its 'anti-Japanese government' based in Yenan, Shensi.

5. 'United Front' Against Japan: The Great Patriotic, or Anti-Japanese, War (1937–45)

1937   In July, Japan massively invades China. Agreement signed for joint Nationalist-Communist war of resistance against Japan. Chinese Soviet Government dissolved but continues as autonomous regional regime; Red Army becomes Eighth Route and New Fourth armies under Chiang's nominal command. Mao writes theoretical works, *On Contradiction* and *On Practice*. Italy leaves the League of Nations.

1938 Mao outlines Communists' wartime political and military ends
and means in *On the New Stage, On the Protracted War*, and
Strategic Problems in the Anti-Japanese Guerrilla War. Chang
Kuo-t'ao, expelled from the CCP, enters Kuomintang areas. Mao
becomes undisputed leader of Party. Japanese armies overwhelm
North China. Nationalists retreat to west. Communists organize
partisans far behind Japanese lines. Nazi Germany annexes
Austria and Czechoslovakia.

1939 Mao's *On the New Democracy* outlines class basis of united
front, intimates future coalition government structure. Rapid
expansion of Communist cadres and military forces. Hitler-Stalin
pact. Germany attacks Poland. With outbreak of European war,
China's struggle begins to merge with the Second World War.
Yenan blockaded by Nationalist troops.

1940–41 Breakdown of practical cooperation between Communists
and Nationalists follows Chiang Kai-shek's attack on New
Fourth Army. Ch'en Yi becomes its commander. After Pearl Harbour, Kuomintang relies on American aid while Communists
vigorously expand guerrilla areas.

1942 CCP 'rectification' campaign centres on Wang Ming and Moscow-trained 'dogmatists'; Mao's 'native' leadership enhanced.

1943 Mao Tse-tung credited (by Liu Shao-ch'i) with having 'created a
Chinese or Asiatic form of Marxism'. Attraction of 'New
Democracy' proves widespread among peasants and intellectuals;
Kuomintang morale and fighting capacity rapidly decline. Chou
En-lai claims 800,000 Party members, a half-million troops and
trained militia, in 'liberated areas' exceeding 100 million popu-
lation. Fascism collapses in Italy. By decree, Stalin abolishes the
Comintern.

1944 US Army 'observers' arrive in Yenan, Communist 'guerrilla'
capital. Allied landing in Normandy. President Roosevelt re-
elected.

1945 Seventh National Congress of CCP (April) claims Party membership of 1,200,000, with armed forces of 900,000. Germany
defeated. Russia enters Far Eastern war; signs alliance with
Chiang Kai-shek's government. Mao's report *On Coalition Government* becomes formal basis of Communist demands to end
Kuomintang dictatorship. After V-E Day, Communist-led forces
flood North China and Manchuria, competing with American-
armed Nationalists. US Ambassador Hurley flies Mao Tse-
tung to Chungking to negotiate with Chiang Kai-shek. Yalta

Pact promises Taiwan to China. Death of Roosevelt. Truman uses atomic bomb on Hiroshima. End of Second World War.

6. Second Communist-Nationalist Civil War (1946–9)

1946 Nationalists and Communists fail to agree on 'coalition government'; in June the Second Civil War, called by the Communists the War of Liberation, begins. Under Soviet Russian occupation, Eastern Europe 'goes Red'.

1947 Mao's *The Present Situation and Our Tasks* outlines strategic and tactical plans, calling for general offensive against Nationalists. Truman Doctrine proclaimed in Greece.

1948 Despite US aid to Nationalists, their defeat in Manchuria is overwhelming. Yugoslavia is expelled from Cominform, postwar successor to the Comintern.

1949 As his armies disintegrate, Chiang Kai-shek flees to Taiwan. Over the rest of China the People's Liberation Army is victorious. In March, the Central Committee of the CCP, led by Mao, arrives in Peking. Atlantic Pact (NATO) proclaimed. US 'White Paper' blames Chiang's 'reactionaries' for 'loss of China'.

7. The Chinese People's Republic (1949–   )

1949 Based on Mao's *The People's Democratic Dictatorship*, a People's Political Consultative Conference is convened, in form representing workers, peasants, intellectuals, national bourgeoisie. Chinese People's Government organized, with Mao elected chairman. On 1 October, Chinese People's Republic formally proclaimed in Peking. Mao announces foreign policy of 'leaning to one side' (towards USSR). Great Britain, Soviet Russia, Norway, The Netherlands, Sweden, Finland, Switzerland recognize the new government; the United States withdraws its diplomats from China. Mao Tse-tung leaves for Moscow – his first trip abroad. US Communist Party leaders convicted of advocating violent overthrow of the government.

1950 Mao concludes Sino-Soviet treaty of alliance; Stalin grants China $300,000,000 loan. Korean War breaks out (June) and Chinese 'Volunteers' intervene (October). India proclaims independence.

1951–2 With Soviet aid, Chinese resistance in Korea continues. American forces, barred from carrying war into China by UN and Allied policies, hold positions at Thirty-eighth Parallel in Korea. First hydrogen bomb exploded (1952) by USA.

1953 Stalin dies. Korean armistice signed. US forms alliance with

Chiang Kai-shek, making Taiwan US protectorate. Peking announces First Five-Year Plan. Soviet grants support for 156 large-scale Chinese projects. Moscow agrees to liquidate Soviet-Chinese joint enterprises and withdraw all troops from China. Rosenbergs executed in the US.

1954 Khrushchev first visits Peking. Land reform (redistribution) completed. Agricultural cooperatives lay basis for collectivization (1957). State establishes partnerships with remaining private enterprise, preliminary to complete nationalization (1957). Geneva Accords end French power in Indochina and recognize independence of Vietnam, Laos, and Cambodia. Under the influence of Secretary of State John Foster Dulles, the Eisenhower administration takes 'note' of Geneva Accords, but begins intervention in support of Ngo Dinh Diem.

1955 At Bandung Conference (twenty-nine Afro-Asian nations) China seeks broader anti-imperialist role against US and allies. China's 'foreign aid' programme competes with that of the USSR. Warsaw Pact signed by USSR and East European satellites.

1956 Khrushchev denounces Stalin at Twentieth Congress of CPSU. He proclaims end of personality cult and beginning of collective leadership. 'Hundred Flowers' period invites criticism of CCP from dissatisfied Chinese intellectuals. Hungarian revolt; Peking backs suppression. China publishes important Maoist thesis, *On the Historical Experience of the Dictatorship of the Proletariat*, acknowledging continued 'contradictions' within and between socialist states.

1957 Mao's *On the Correct Handling of Contradictions Among the People* defines limitations of criticism in relation to the Party; advances thesis of 'unity-criticism-unity' as dialectical process to isolate 'enemies of socialism' and peacefully resolve 'non-antagonistic' conflicts of interest between the state, the Party, and 'the people'. Russia agrees to supply sample atom bomb to China and help in nuclear weapons development. Sputnik launched. At November conference in Moscow, Mao discerns a 'turning point': the 'East Wind is prevailing over the West Wind'. He contends socialist forces outbalance capitalist forces. Thesis disputed by Russians. Break-up of Sino-Soviet unity begins.

1958 China announces Second Five-Year Plan. Year of the 'Great Leap Forward' and People's Communes. Peking's threat to liberate Taiwan provokes Sino-American crisis. Khrushchev withholds unconditional nuclear support for China, and Peking declines to place Chinese forces under Soviet military command. Sino-Soviet differences develop. First US space satellite launched.

1959   In the decisive Party plenum held at Lushan Mao Tse-tung has a difficult struggle to replace P'eng Teh-huai by Lin Piao as defence minister. Part of the price of his victory was, apparently, his own replacement by Lin Shao-ch'i as chairman of the government. During October anniversary celebrations Khrushchev again visits Peking, where he declares 'Imperialist war is not inevitable.' His advocacy of 'peaceful coexistence' with 'American imperialism' is sharply rejected by Chinese. China gets no A-bomb and Mao loses confidence in Khrushchev. Tibetan rebellion. Dalai Lama flees to India. During China's disputes with India and Indonesia, Khrushchev offers aid to the latter. He disparages Chinese people's communes. Castro takes power in Cuba. As US increases armed intervention, aimed to separate South Vietnam from the Republic, President Ho Chi Minh backs People's Liberation War in the South.

1960   In July, Moscow recalls all Soviet advisers from China, cancels more than 300 contracts, withdraws technical help. At Moscow international Party conference (November), Sino-Soviet 'contradictions' intensify. Chinese openly identify Khrushchev as 'revisionist'. Russians accuse Mao of seeking 'world holocaust'. Massive crop failure and industrial dislocation in China. As Sino-Indian frontier incidents grow serious, Khrushchev plays neutral role, continues economic aid to India. John F. Kennedy elected US President.

1961   At Twenty-second Soviet Party Congress in Moscow, Chou En-lai walks out when Khrushchev bans Albanian Party. Using texts from the newly published (1960) *Selected Works of Mao Tse-tung*, Vol. IV, Peking's Party press proclaims Maoist and antirevisionist theses 'true Marxism–Leninism'. Chinese replace Soviet advisers in Albania. Berlin Wall built.

1962   Sino-Soviet clashes on both state and Party levels foreshadow wide international ideological fight. Kennedy–Khrushchev duel over Cuba. When Khrushchev withdraws missiles from Cuba, Peking ridicules him for 'adventurism' and 'capitulationism'. Sino-Indian border incidents climaxed by Chinese assault, driving Indians from 35,000 square miles of territory. Chinese troops withdraw, unilaterally create 'demilitarized zone', call for peaceful negotiation. UN intervenes in the Congo.

1960–63 Following the disruption of the Chinese economy caused by dislocations during the 'Great Leap Forward', by withdrawal of Soviet aid, and by a series of natural calamities, the People's Republic slowly recovers from near-famine conditions.

1963   In final defiance of Peking's demand for a militant international 'united front against American imperialism', Moscow signs nuclear test-ban treaty with United States, makes 'peaceful co-existence' cardinal aim of Soviet foreign policy. Sino-Soviet split now reflected in intraparty cleavages in many countries. Mutual recriminations reinforced by open publication of past charges and countercharges by CCP and CPSU. Peking steps up drive for ideological leadership among 'third world' Asian–African–Latin American revolutionary forces; Moscow strives to hold following among European parties. Premier Chou En-lai visits African countries. Mao Tse-tung issues declaration calling upon 'the people of the world' to unite against American imperialism and support American Negro struggles. President Kennedy assassinated.

1964   Breakdown in Soviet-Chinese party and state relations becomes nearly complete. As France recognizes China, Communist split paralleled by Western split. Chinese offensive on two fronts – American imperialism and Soviet revisionism – has some success in dividing both camps. Two years of good harvests and new trade ties with Europe and Japan strengthen Chinese economy. Foreign Minister Ch'en Yi publicly expresses doubts concerning value of Sino-Soviet military alliance; China may no longer count on Russian aid. Mao urges Japanese socialists to recover territories lost to Russia and criticizes Soviet 'imperialism' for encroachments on Chinese territories.

After fifteen years, achievements of Chinese revolution in uniting and modernizing China widely conceded even by enemies. In rivalry with Russia, and despite exclusion from United Nations, China becomes major power with which – according to General de Gaulle – United States must negotiate in order to end war in South-East Asia. Mao Tse-tung, following a century of China's humiliation as a weak and backward nation, emerges as the first Asian political leader to attract significant world following. China explodes its first 'nuclear device'.

South Vietnamese Government, backed by the United States and badly defeated by growing forces of the National Liberation Front, verges on disintegration before pro-neutralist and pro-peace elements.

1965 President Johnson, soon after his January inauguration, moves American combat troops into Vietnam to prevent a neutralist coup in Saigon. In February he orders massive bombing of North Vietnam. Peking announces its readiness to intervene in support of the Democratic Republic of Vietnam if President Ho Chi Minh demands it, but in an interview with the author in January, Chairman Mao declares that China will not go to war against the United States unless China is directly attacked. In July, Lin Piao, China's Minister of Defence, publishes a declaration, 'Long Live the Victory of the People's War!', which calls upon the underdeveloped nations, likened to the 'rural areas of the world', to join forces against American and Western imperialism, the 'cities of the world'.

China explodes its second nuclear device.

The United Nations vote on the admission of the People's Republic ends in a 47–47 tie, with Great Britain for the first time voting in favour of seating Peking. Lacking majority support, the move is once more defeated.

1966 US forces in Vietnam approach 500,000 men, and American bombing of North Vietnam spares few targets except inner metropolitan areas of Hanoi and Haiphong. Russia sends North Vietnam aircraft, weapons, and technical personnel; China supplies small arms and food.

China launches a 'Great Proletarian Cultural Revolution' (GPCR) under Mao Tse-tung, with Lin Piao named as his 'close comrade-in-arms'. China prepares for an expected American invasion. An unprecedented purge attacks 'bourgeois' and 'revisionist' elements in the CCP. Chinese agriculture continues to improve, while scientific advances include the world's first synthesis of protein (insulin) and benzine.

1967 Great Proletarian Cultural Revolution develops into an attack on Liu Shao-ch'i, chairman of government and former first deputy Party leader, as foremost among 'those in the Party in authority who are taking the capitalist road'. Profound intraparty struggle intensifies.

As the GPCR took foreign political experts on China by complete surprise, so China's explosion of a hydrogen bomb – twenty-six months after atomic fission was achieved – nonplusses foreign military and scientific savants. The same step had taken the US more than seven years; France, after eight years of effort, had yet to test its first H-bomb.

Dean Rusk, US Secretary of State, appeals for world sympathy for Johnson's armed intervention and massive bombing in Vietnam as necessary in order to contain 'a billion Chinese armed with nuclear weapons', but no European power offers to help Rusk. China's own official policy still calls for an international agreement to destroy all nuclear weapons – an invitation ignored by the US. On 19 December, in a message to Vietnam's National Liberation Front presidium, Mao advises 'the fraternal South Vietnamese people' to 'rest assured that your struggle is our struggle'.

1968 In January the US naval reconnaissance or spy ship *Pueblo* is boarded off the North Korean coast by North Korean naval personnel and seized with its crew and officers. Public opposition to the Vietnam war and a South-East Asia policy more and more demonstrably a political failure convinces the highest ruling circles of the US that the losses of men and treasure have reached a level endangering the stability of the whole Establishment. President Johnson tacitly assumes responsibility when he announces his withdrawal from candidacy for re-election. Bombing of North Vietnam is halted and US-Vietnamese peace conversations begin in Paris. Richard Nixon is elected President with a pledge to end American involvement in war in South-East Asia.

1969 The Great Proletarian Cultural Revolution in China nears a culminating stage, following army intervention in factional disputes, the restoration of order, and break-up of Red Guard organizations dispersed to work in factory, farm, public enterprises, or at school. The CCP summons a Ninth Party Congress where a new constitution is adopted and Lin Piao is formally named 'close comrade-in-arms and successor' to Mao Tse-tung.

Economic production, interrupted by the GPCR, recovers and scores some advances. Millions of Party cadres undergo re-education in May Seventh schools where Mao Tse-tung Thought more than ever provides the scripture and guide to action for the whole nation. Party rebuilding in preparation for the adoption of a new National (Congress) constitution based on a three-way alliance of 'reliable Party cadres, representatives of mass organizations, and responsible military leaders' preoccupies political life as momentum in a production drive gains pace. Sino-Soviet border clashes increase tension; China also vigilantly watches Nixon's attempt at 'Vietnamization' of the war by US-backed

Saigon militarists and bureaucrats. Ho Chi Minh dies, and China renews assurances of solidarity with North Vietnam. Paris peace talks drag as Nixon slowly reverses the US war machine in South Vietnam.

China actively re-enters world diplomacy in a drive to establish herself as a peer of the nuclear superpowers.

1970   Lon Nol, chief of the Cambodian army, overthrows Prince Sihanouk and his leadership, and the latter sets up a regime in exile in Peking. Nixon sends Vietnamese and American troops to Lon Nol's aid but widespread criticism compels Nixon to limit US involvement. On 20 May Mao Tse-tung calls for a world united front against US imperialism, and pledges China's support to a new Hanoi–NLF (Vietcong)–Cambodia (Sihanouk)–Laos alliance. Mao declares that the danger of a new world war still exists, 'but the main trend is towards revolution'.

In Paris the US still refuses to accept Hanoi's terms which demand total and unconditional US withdrawal.

By the year end Premier Chou En-lai has concluded treaties of recognition with Canada and Italy, followed by half a dozen other powers formerly restrained by US influence. Early seating of the CPR as the sole representative of the Chinese people in the UN seems likely by not later than 1972.

1971   Nixon authorizes an 'incursion' by Vietnamese troops into Laos, heavily assisted by US logistic and air power, aimed to cut routes used by North Vietnam troops to supply Vietcong and Cambodia troops resisting Saigon-US operations. A speedy retreat from Laos demonstrates failure of Vietnamization to contain internal revolutionary forces. Under continued pressure from antiwar sentiment and mounting economic and fiscal problems in internal and world markets, Nixon speeds up withdrawal of US troops from Vietnam. In a stage-by-stage programme abandoning US 'containment of China' policy Nixon continues moves, begun in 1970, to end the trade embargo and restrictions on travels by US citizens to and from China. In April China invites a US table-tennis team to visit Peking and play there. Visas are given to US newsmen to cover that event. Mao Tse-tung's interview with the author reveals that China's policy is to reciprocate conciliatory American gestures by inviting to China some Americans from 'left, middle and centre', and Mao adds that he personally would welcome a visit by President Nixon.

The tide towards a US-China détente – with the likelihood

of the PRC taking its seat in the Security Council of the UN, and the return to China of sovereignty in the island of Taiwan – now seems irreversible. By mid-year Congress mounts ever-increasing pressure for a pledge by Nixon to withdraw all US troops from Vietnam by mid-1972 if not earlier. Revelations of the published Pentagon papers – a government-ordered report on the origins, causes, and conduct of the Vietnam adventure – fuel public opinion to an unprecedented degree and benefit Nixon by seemingly casting all blame for the Vietnam disaster on former administrations.

A Note on Chinese Pronunciation

IT is not necessary to strangle over the pronunciation of Chinese names if one observes a few simple rules in the rather arbitrary but workable Wade-Giles System of transliteration (romanization) of the language into English. Each Chinese character represents only one sound and homonyms are innumerable. Chinese is mono-syllabic, but combinations of characters in the spoken language may form a single idea or equivalent of one foreign word, and thus in a sense the spoken language is polysyllabic. Chinese sur-names come first, given names (usually two words) follow, as in Teng Hsiao-p'ing. Aspirates are represented in this book by apostrophes; they indicate a soft consonant sound. Examples:

Chi (as in Chi Chao-t'ing) is pronounced 'Gee', but *Ch'i* (as in Liu Shao-ch'i) sounds like 'Chee'. *Ch'in* is exactly our 'chin'.

Chu is like 'Jew', in Chu Teh, but *Ch'u* equals 'Chew'.

Tsung is 'dzung'; *ts'ung* with the 'ts' as in 'Patsy'.

Tai is our word sound 'die'; *T'ai* – 'tie'.

Pai is 'buy' and *P'ai* is 'pie'.

Kung is like 'Gung' (-a Din); *K'ung* with the 'k' as in 'kind'.

J is the equivalent of 'r' but roll it, as rrrun.

H before an *s*, as in *hsi*, is the equivalent of an aspirate but is often dropped, as in Sian for Hsian. One may ignore the 'h' and still be understood.

Single Chinese words are always pronounced as monosyllables. Thus: *Chiang* is not 'Chee-yi-ang' but a single sound, 'Geeang'. *Mao* is not 'May-ow' but pronounced like a cat's 'miaow' *without* the 'i'. *Chou En-lai* is 'Joe Un-lie', but the last syllable of his wife's given name, *Ying-ch'ao*, sounds like 'chow'.

Vowels in Chinese are generally short or medium, not long and flat. Thus *Tang* sounds like 'dong', never like our 'tang'. *T'ang* is 'tong'.

a as in father
e – run
eh – hen
i – see
ih – her
o – look
ou – go
u – soon

There is also a 'ü' as in German and an 'ê' as in French. I have omitted Wade's umlaut and circumflex markings, which are found in European latinizations of Chinese.

These sounds indicate Chinese as spoken in *kuo-yu*, the northern (Peking, mandarin) speech, which is now the national language, taught in all schools. Where journalism has already popularized misspellings or variants in other dialects, such as Chiang Kai-shek for Chiang Chieh-shih, etc., I have followed the familiar version.

Chinese words frequently encountered in place names are:
> *sheng* – province; *hsien* – county; *hsiang* – township; *ching* (or king) – capital; *ch'eng* – city; *ts'un* – village; *chiang* (kiang) – great river; *ho* – river; *hu* – lake; *k'ou* – mouth; *pei* – north; *nan* – south; *tung* – east; *hsi* (or *si*) – west; *chung* – central; *shan* – mountain.

Such words combine in the following examples:
> *Peking* (properly, *Pei-ching*, pronounced 'Bay-ging'), meaning 'northern capital'. Peking was renamed 'Pei-p'ing' (Peiping or, erroneously, Peping), 'northern peace' (or tranquillity), by the Kuomintang regime, which made its seat in Nanking (southern capital), but the historic name remained in general use and was formally restored in 1949.
> *Shantung* means East of the mountains.
> *Shansi* – West of the mountains.
> *Hankow* – Mouth of the Han (river).
> *Sian* – Western Peace (tranquillity).
> *Hopei* – North of the (Yellow) river.
> *Hunan* – South of the lakes.
> *Yunnan* – South of the clouds.
> *Kiangsi* – West of the river.

Part One

IN SEARCH OF RED CHINA

I

Some Unanswered Questions

DURING my seven years in China, hundreds of questions had been asked about the Chinese Red Army, the Soviets, and the Communist movement. Eager partisans could supply you with a stock of ready answers, but these remained highly unsatisfactory: How did they *know*? They had never been to Red China.

The fact was that there had been perhaps no greater mystery among nations, no more confused an epic, than the story of Red China. Fighting in the very heart of the most populous nation on earth, the Celestial Reds had for nine years been isolated by a news blockade as effective as a stone fortress. A wall of thousands of enemy troops constantly surrounded them; their territory was more inaccessible than Tibet. No one had voluntarily penetrated that wall and returned to write of his experiences since the first Chinese soviet was established in south-eastern Hunan, in November 1927.

Even the simplest points were disputed. Some people denied that there was such a thing as a Red Army. There were only thousands of hungry brigands. Some denied even the existence of soviets. They were an invention of Communist propaganda. Yet Red sympathizers extolled both as the only salvation for all the ills of China. In the midst of this propaganda and counterpropaganda, credible evidence was lacking for dispassionate observers seeking the truth. Here are some of the unanswered questions that interested everyone concerned with politics and the quickening history of the Orient:

Was or was not this Red Army of China a mass of conscious Marxist revolutionaries, disciplined by and adhering to a centralized programme and a unified command under the Chinese Communist Party? If so, what was that programme? The Communists claimed to be fighting for agrarian revolution, and against imperialism, and for soviet democracy and national emancipation. Nanking said that the Reds were only a new type of vandals and marauders led by 'intellectual bandits'. Who was right? Or was either one?

Before 1927, members of the Communist Party were admitted to the Kuomintang, but in April of that year there began a great 'purgation'. Communists, as well as unorganized radical intellectuals and thousands of organized workers and peasants, were executed on an extensive scale under Chiang Kai-shek, the leader of a Right *coup d'état* which seized power, to form a 'National Government' at Nanking. Since then it had been a crime punishable by death to be a Communist or a Communist sympathizer, and thousands had paid that penalty. Yet thousands more continued to run the risk. Thousands of peasants, workers, students, and soldiers joined the Red Army in armed struggle against the military dictatorship of the Nanking regime. Why? What inexorable force drove them on to support suicidal political opinions? What were the fundamental quarrels between the Kuomintang and the Kungch'antang? *

What were the Chinese Communists like? In what way did they resemble, in what way were they unlike, Communists or Socialists elsewhere? The tourist asked if they wore long beards, made noises with their soup, and carried homemade bombs in their briefcases. The serious-minded wanted to know whether they were 'genuine' Marxists. Did they read *Capital* and the works of Lenin? Had they a thoroughly Socialist economic programme? Were they Stalinites or Trotskyites? Or neither? Was their movement really an organic part of the World Revolution? Were they true internationalists? 'Mere tools of Moscow', or primarily nationalists struggling for an independent China?

Who were these warriors who had fought so long, so fiercely, so courageously, and – as admitted by observers of every colour, and privately among Generalissimo Chiang Kai-shek's own followers – on the whole so invincibly? What made them fight like that? What held them up? What was the revolutionary basis of their movement? What were the hopes and aims and dreams that had made of them the incredibly stubborn warriors – incredible com-

---

*The Kuomintang, or 'National People's Party', founded by Dr Sun Yatsen and others, held the hegemony of power in the so-called Great Revolution, 1923–7. The Kungch'antang, 'Share Production Party', or the Communist Party of China, founded in 1921, was the chief ally of the Kuomintang, 1923–7.

pared with the history of compromise that is China – who had endured hundreds of battles, blockade, salt shortage, famine, disease, epidemic, and finally the Long March of 6,000 miles, in which they crossed twelve provinces of China, broke through thousands of Kuomintang troops, and triumphantly emerged at last into a new base in the North-West?

Who were their leaders? Were they educated men with a fervent belief in an ideal, an ideology, and a doctrine? Social prophets, or mere ignorant peasants blindly fighting for an existence? What kind of man was Mao Tse-tung,* No. 1 'Red bandit' on Nanking's list, for whose capture, dead or alive, Chiang Kai-shek offered a reward of a quarter of a million silver dollars? † What went on inside that highly priced Oriental head? Or was Mao really already dead, as Nanking officially announced? What was Chu Teh ‡ like – the commander-in-chief of the Red Army, whose life had the same value to Nanking? What about Lin Piao,‡ the twenty-eight-year-old Red tactician whose famous Red Army Corps was said never to have suffered a defeat? Where did he come from? Who were the many other Red leaders repeatedly reported dead, only to reappear in the news – unscathed and commanding new forces against the Kuomintang?

What explained the Red Army's remarkable record of resistance for nine years against vastly superior military combinations? Lacking any industrial base, big cannon, gas, airplanes, money, and the modern techniques which Nanking had utilized in its wars against them, how had these Reds survived, and increased their following? What military tactics did they use? How were they instructed? Who advised them? Were there some Russian military geniuses among them? Who led the outmanoeuvring, not only of all Kuomintang commanders sent against them but also of Chiang Kai-shek's large and expensive staff of German advisers, headed first by General von Seeckt and later by General von Falkenhausen?

What was a Chinese soviet like? Did the peasants support it?

---

* See Part Four and Biographical Notes, hereafter BN.

† The Chinese *yuan*, then called a 'dollar' by foreigners, was worth about US $.35.

‡ See BN.

If not, what held it together? To what degree did the Reds carry out 'socialism' in districts where they had consolidated their power? Why hadn't the Red Army taken big cities? Did this prove that it wasn't a genuine proletarian-led movement, but fundamentally remained a peasant rebellion? How was it possible to speak of 'communism' or 'socialism' in China, where over 80 per cent of the population was still agrarian, where industrialism was still in infant garments – if not infantile paralysis?

How did the Reds dress? Eat? Play? Love? Work? What were their marriage laws? Were women 'nationalized', as Kuomintang publicists asserted? What was a Chinese 'Red factory'? A Red dramatic society? How did they organize their economy? What about public health, recreation, education, 'Red culture'?

What was the strength of the Red Army? Half a million, as the Comintern publications boasted? If so, why had it not seized power? Where did it gets arms and munitions? Was it a disciplined army? What about its morale? Was it true that officers and men lived alike? If, as Generalissimo Chiang announced in 1935, Nanking had 'destroyed the menace of Communist banditry', what explained the fact that in 1937 the Reds occupied a bigger single unified territory (in China's most strategic North-West) than ever before? If the Reds were finished, why did Japan demand, as the famous Third Point of Koki Hirota (Foreign Minister, 1933–6), that Nanking form an anti-Red pact with Tokyo and Nazi Germany 'to prevent the bolshevization of Asia'? Were the Reds really 'anti-imperialist'? Did they want war with Japan? Would Moscow support them in such a war? Or were their fierce anti-Japanese slogans only a trick and a desperate attempt to win public sympathy, the last cry of demoralized traitors and bandits, as the eminent Dr Hu Shih nervously assured his excited students in Peking?

What were the military and political perspectives of the Chinese Communist movement? What was the history of its development? Could it succeed? And just what would such success mean to us? To Japan? What would be the effect of this tremendous mutation upon a fifth (some said a fourth) of the world's inhabitants? What changes would it produce in world politics? In world history? How would it affect the vast British, American, and other foreign investment in China? Indeed, had the Reds any 'foreign policy' at all?

Finally, what was the meaning of the Communists' offer to form a 'national united front' in China, and stop civil war?

For some it had seemed ridiculous that not a single non-Communist observer could answer those questions with confidence, accuracy, or facts based on personal investigation. Here was a story growing in interest and importance every day; here was *the* story of China, as newspaper correspondents admitted to each other between dispatches sent out on trivial side issues. Yet we were all woefully ignorant about it. To get in touch with Communists in the 'White' areas was extremely difficult.

Communists, over whose heads hung the sentence of death, did not identify themselves as such in polite – or impolite – society. Even in the foreign concessions, Nanking kept a well-paid espionage system at work. It included, for example, such vigilantes as C. Patrick Givens, former chief Red-chaser in the British police force of Shanghai's International Settlement. Inspector Givens was each year credited with the arrest – and subsequent imprisonment or execution, after extradition from the Settlement by the Kuomintang authorities – of scores of alleged Communists, the majority of them between the ages of fifteen and twenty-five. He was only one of the many foreign sleuths hired to spy upon young Chinese radicals and hunt them down in their own country.

We all knew that the only way to learn anything about Red China was to go there. We excused ourselves by saying, '*Mei yu fa-tzu*' – 'It can't be done.' A few had tried and failed. It was believed impossible. People thought that nobody could enter Red territory and come out alive.

Then, in June 1936, a close Chinese friend of mine brought me news of an amazing political situation in North-West China – a situation which was later to culminate in the sensational arrest of Generalissimo Chiang Kai-shek, and to change the current of Chinese history. More important to me then, however, I learned with this news of a possible method of entry to Red territory. It necessitated leaving at once. The opportunity was unique and not to be missed. I decided to take it and attempt to break a news blockade nine years old.

It is true there were risks involved, though the reports later published of my death – 'killed by bandits' – were exaggerated. But against a torrent of horror stories about Red atrocities that had for many years filled the subsidized vernacular and foreign press of China, I had little to cheer me on my way. Nothing, in truth, but a letter of introduction to Mao Tse-tung, chairman of the Soviet Government.[1] All I had to do was to find him. Through what adventures? I did not know. But thousands of lives had been sacrificed in these years of Kuomintang-Communist warfare. Could one foreign neck be better hazarded than in an effort to discover why? I found myself somewhat attached to the neck in question, but I concluded that the price was not too high to pay.

In this melodramatic mood I set out.

2

Slow Train to 'Western Peace'

IT WAS early June and Peking wore the green lace of spring, its thousands of willows and imperial cypresses making the Forbidden City a place of wonder and enchantment, and in many cool gardens it was impossible to believe in the China of breaking toil, starvation, revolution, and foreign invasion that lay beyond the glittering roofs of the palaces. Here well-fed foreigners could live in their own little never-never land of whisky-and-soda, polo, tennis, and gossip, happily quite unaware of the pulse of humanity outside the great city's silent, insulating walls – as indeed many did.

And yet during the past year even the oasis of Peking had been invaded by the atmosphere of struggle that hovered over all China. Threats of Japanese conquest had provoked great demonstrations of the people, especially among the enraged youth. A few months earlier I had stood under the bullet-pitted Tartar Wall and seen 10,000 students gather, defiant of the gendarmes' clubbings, to shout in a mighty chorus: 'Resist Japan! Reject the demands of Japanese imperialism for the separation of North China from the South!'

All Peking's defensive masonry could not prevent reverberations of the Chinese Red Army's sensational attempt to march through Shansi to the Great Wall – ostensibly to begin a war against Japan for recovery of the lost territories. This somewhat quixotic expedition had been promptly blocked by eleven divisions of Generalissimo Chiang Kai-shek's crack new army, but that had not prevented patriotic students from courting imprisonment and possible death by massing in the streets and uttering the forbidden slogans: 'Cease civil war! Cooperate with the Communists to resist Japan! Save China!' *

* The 9 December 1935 student demonstration was a historic 'turning point' favourable to the Communists. Among its leaders were Huang Ching and Huang Hua. See BN.

One midnight I climbed aboard a dilapidated train, feeling a little ill, but in a state of high excitement. Excitement because before me lay a journey of exploration into a land hundreds of years and hundreds of miles removed from the medieval splendours of the Forbidden City: I was bound for 'Red China'. And a little ill because I had taken all the inoculations available. A microbe's-eye view of my bloodstream would have revealed a macabre cavalcade; my arms and legs were shot with smallpox, typhoid, cholera, typhus, and plague germs. All five diseases were prevalent in the North-West. Moreover, alarming reports had lately told of the spread of bubonic plague in Shensi province, one of the few spots on earth where it was endemic.

My immediate destination was Sianfu – which means 'Western Peace'. Sianfu was the capital of Shensi province, it was two tiresome days and nights by train to the south-west of Peking, and it was the western terminus of the Lunghai railway. From there I planned to go northward and enter the soviet districts, which occupied the very heart of Ta Hsi-pei, China's Great North-West. Lochuan, a town about 150 miles north of Sianfu, then marked the beginning of Red territory in Shensi. Everything north of it, except strips of territory along the main highways, and some points which will be noted later, was already dyed Red. With Lochuan roughly the southern, and the Great Wall the northern, extremities of Red control in Shensi, both the eastern and western Red frontiers were formed by the Yellow River. Coming down from the fringes of Tibet, the wide, muddy stream flows northward through Kansu and Ninghsia, and above the Great Wall into the province of Suiyuan – Inner Mongolia. Then after many miles of uncertain wandering towards the east it turns southward again, to pierce the Great Wall and form the boundary between the provinces of Shensi and Shansi.

It was within this great bend of China's most treacherous river that the soviets then operated – in northern Shensi, north-eastern Kansu, and south-eastern Ninghsia. And by a strange sequence of history this region almost corresponded to the original confines of the birthplace of China. Near here the Chinese first formed and unified themselves as a people, thousands of years ago.

In the morning I inspected my travelling companions and found a youth and a handsome old man with a wisp of grey beard sitting opposite me, sipping bitter tea. Presently the youth spoke to me, in formalities at first, and then inevitably of politics. I discovered that his wife's uncle was a railway official and that he was travelling with a pass. He was on his way back to Szechuan, his native province, which he had left seven years before. But he was not sure that he would be able to visit his home town after all. Bandits were reported to be operating near there.

'You mean Reds?'

'Oh, no, not Reds, although there are Reds in Szechuan, too. No, I mean bandits.'

'But aren't the Reds also bandits?' I asked out of curiosity. 'The newspapers always call them Red bandits or Communist bandits.'

'Ah, but you must know that the editors must call them bandits because they are ordered to do so by Nanking,' he explained. 'If they called them Communists or revolutionaries that would prove they were Communists themselves.'

'But in Szechuan don't people fear the Reds as much as the bandits?'

'Well, that depends. The rich men fear them, and the land-lords, and the officials and tax collectors, yes. But the peasants do not fear them. Sometimes they welcome them.' Then he glanced apprehensively at the old man, who sat listening intently, and yet seeming not to listen. 'You see,' he continued, 'the peasants are too ignorant to understand that the Reds only want to use them. They think the Reds really mean what they say.'

'But they don't mean it?'

'My father wrote to me that they did abolish usury and opium in the Sungpan [Szechuan], and that they redistributed the land there. So you see they are not exactly bandits. They have prin-ciples, all right. But they are wicked men. They kill too many people.'

Then surprisingly the greybeard lifted his gentle face and with perfect composure made an astonishing remark. '*Sha pu kou!*' he said. 'They don't kill enough!' We both looked at him flabber-gasted.

Unfortunately the train was nearing Chengchow, where I had to transfer to the Lunghai line, and I was obliged to break off the discussion. But I have ever since wondered with what deadly evidence this Confucian-looking old gentleman would have supported his startling contention. I wondered about it all the next day of travel, as we climbed slowly through the weird levels of loess hills in Honan and Shensi, and until my train – this one still new and very comfortable – rolled up to the new and handsome railway station at Sianfu.

Soon after my arrival I went to call on General Yang Hu-ch'eng,* Pacification Commissioner of Shensi province. Until a couple of years before, General Yang had been undisputed monarch of those parts of Shensi not controlled by the Reds. A former bandit, he rose to authority via the route that had put many of China's ablest leaders in office, and on the same highway he was said to have accumulated the customary fortune. But recently he had been obliged to divide his power with several other gentlemen in the North-West. For in 1935 the 'Young Marshal', Chang Hsueh-liang,* who used to be ruler of Manchuria, had brought his Tungpei (Manchurian) army into Shensi, and assumed office in Sianfu as supreme Red chaser in these parts – Vice-Commander of the National Bandit-Suppression Commission. And to watch the Young Marshal had come Shao Li-tzu,* an acolyte of Generalissimo Chiang Kai-shek. The Hon. Shao was Governor of Shensi.

A delicate balance of power was maintained between these figures – and still others. Tugging strings behind all of them was the redoubtable Generalissimo himself, who sought to extend his dictatorship to the North-West and liquidate not only the Communist-led revolution but also the troops of old Yang Hu-ch'eng and young Chang Hsueh-liang, by the simple process of using each to destroy the other – three acts of a brilliant politico-military drama the main stratagem of which Chiang evidently believed was understood only by himself. And it was that error in calculation – a little too much haste in pursuit of the purpose, a little too much confidence in his adversaries' stupidity – which was in a few months to land Chiang Kai-shek a prisoner in Sianfu, at the mercy of all three.

*See BN.

I found General Yang* in a newly finished stone mansion, just completed at a cost of $50,000. He was living in this many-chambered vault – the official home of the Pacification Commissioner – without a wife. Yang Hu-ch'eng, like many Chinese in this transitional period, was burdened with domestic infelicity, for he was a two-wife man. The first was the lily-footed wife of his youth, betrothed to him by his parents in Pucheng. The second, as vivacious and courageous a woman as Mme Chiang Kai-shek, was a pretty young mother of five children, modern and progressive, a former Communist, they said, and the girl that Yang had chosen himself. It seemed, according to the missionaries, that when he opened his new home each of his wives had presented him with the same minimum demand. Each detested the other; each had borne him sons and had the right to be legal wife; and each resolutely refused to move into the stone mansion unless the other stayed behind.

To an outsider the case looked simple: a divorce or a third wife was the obvious solution. But General Yang had not made up his mind and so he still lived alone. His dilemma was a not uncommon one in modern China. Chiang Kai-shek had faced a similar issue when he married rich, American-educated Soong Mei-ling, who as a Methodist was not prepared to accept polygamy. Chiang had finally divorced his first wife (the mother of his son Ching-kuo †) and pensioned off his two concubines. The decision was highly approved by the missionaries, who had ever since prayed for his soul. Nevertheless, this way out – a newfangled idea imported from the West – was still frowned upon by many Chinese. Old Yang, having risen from the people, was probably less concerned over the disposal of his soul than the traditions of his ancestors.

And it must not be supposed that Yang's early career as a bandit necessarily disqualified him as a leader. Such assumptions could not be made in China, where a career of banditry in early youth often indicated a man of strong character and purpose. A look at

---

*I was introduced to General Yang by Wang Ping-nan (see BN), who with his wife, Anna, was then living in Yang's home. Wang was Yang's political secretary and was chief liaison in Sian between the CCP CC and General Yang and Marshal Chang.

† See BN.

Chinese history showed that some of China's ablest patriots were at one time or another labelled bandits. The fact was that many of the worst rogues, scoundrels, and traitors had climbed to power under cover of respectability, the putrid hypocrisy of Confucian maxims, and the priestcraft of the Chinese Classics – though they had very often utilized the good strong arm of an honest bandit in doing so.

General Yang's history as a revolutionary suggested a rugged peasant who might once have had high dreams of making a big change in his world, but who, finding himself in power, looked vainly for a method, and grew weary and confused, listening to the advice of the mercenaries who gathered around him. But if he had such dreams he did not confide them to me. He declined to discuss political questions, and courteously delegated one of his secretaries to show me the city. He was also suffering from a severe headache and rheumatism when I saw him, and in the midst of his sea of troubles I was not one to insist upon asking him nettling questions. On the contrary, in his dilemma he had all my sympathy. So after a brief interview with him I discreetly retired, to seek some answers from the Honourable Governor, Shao Li-tzu.

Governor Shao received me in the garden of his spacious yamen, cool and restful after the parching heat of Sian's dusty streets. I had last seen him six years before, when he was Chiang Kai-shek's personal secretary, and at that time he had assisted me in an interview with the Generalissimo. Since then he had risen rapidly in the Kuomintang. He was an able man, well educated, and the Generalissimo had now bestowed upon him the honours of a governorship. But poor Shao, like many another civil governor, did not rule much beyond the provincial capital's grey walls – the outlying territory being divided by General Yang and the Young Marshal.

The Hon. Shao had once been a 'Communist bandit' himself. He had played a pioneer role in the Chinese Communist Party. In those days it was fashionable to be a Communist and nobody was very sure exactly what it meant, except that many bright young men were Communists. Later on he had recanted; after 1927 it had become very clear what it meant, and one could have one's head removed for it. Shao then became a devout Buddhist, and subsequently displayed no further signs of heresy. He was one of the most charming gentlemen in China.[1]

'How are the Reds getting along?' I asked him.

'There are not many left. Those in Shensi are only remnants.'

'Then the war continues?' I asked.

'No, at present there is little fighting in north Shensi. The Reds are moving into Ninghsia and Kansu. They seem to want to connect with Outer Mongolia.'

He shifted the conversation to the situation in the South-West, where insurgent generals were then demanding an anti-Japanese expedition. I asked him whether he thought China should fight Japan. 'Can we?' he demanded. And then the Buddhist governor told me exactly what he thought about Japan – not for publication – just as every Kuomintang official would then tell you his opinion of Japan – not for publication.

A few months after this interview poor Shao was to be put on the spot on this question of war with Japan – along with his Generalissimo – by some rebellious young men of Marshal Chang Hsueh-liang's army, who refused to be reasonable and take 'maybe some day' for an answer any longer. And Shao's diminutive wife – a returned student from Moscow and a former Communist herself – was to be cornered by some of the insurrectionists and make a plucky fight to resist arrest.

But Shao revealed no premonition of all this in our talk, and, an exchange of views having brought us perilously near agreement, it was time to leave. I had already learned from Shao Li-tzu what I wanted to know. He had confirmed the word of my Peking informant, that fighting had temporarily halted in north Shensi. Therefore it should be possible to go to the front, if properly arranged.

3

Some Han Bronzes

SOME six months after my arrival in Sianfu the crisis in the North-West was to explode in a manner nobody had anticipated, so that the whole world was made dramatically aware of an amazing alliance between the big army under Marshal Chang Hsueh-liang and the 'bandits' whom he had been ordered, as deputy commander-in-chief of the Communist-Suppression Forces, to destroy. But in June 1936, the outside world was still in complete ignorance of these strange developments, and even in the headquarters of Chiang Kai-shek's own Blueshirt gendarmes, who controlled the Sianfu police, nobody knew exactly what was taking place. Some 300 Communists were imprisoned in the city's jail, and the Blueshirts were hunting for more. An atmosphere of extreme tension prevailed. Spies and counterspies were everywhere.

But there is no longer any necessity to remain covert about those exciting days, with the secrets of which I was perforce entrusted, so here it can be told.

I had never seen a Red Army man before I arrived in Sianfu. The man in Peking who had written for me in invisible ink the letter addressed to Mao Tse-tung was, I knew, a Red commander, but I had not seen him. The letter had reached me through a third person, an old friend; but besides this letter I had only one hope of a connection in the North-West. I had been instructed simply to go to a hotel in Sianfu, take a room there, and await a visit from a gentleman who would call himself Wang, but about whom I knew nothing else. Nothing – except that he would arrange for me to enter the Red districts by way of the private airplane, I was promised, of Chang Hsueh-liang!

A few days after I put up in the hotel a large, somewhat florid and rotund, but strongly built and dignified Chinese, wearing a long grey silk gown, entered my open door and greeted me in excellent English. He looked like a prosperous merchant, but he introduced himself as Wang, mentioned the name of my Peking friend, and otherwise established that he was the man I awaited.

In the week that followed I discovered that Wang alone was worth the trip to Sianfu. I spent four or five hours a day listening to his yarns and reminiscences and to his more serious explanations of the political situation. He was wholly unexpected. Educated in a missionary school in Shanghai, he had been prominently identified with the Christian community, had once had a church of his own, and (as I was later to learn) was known among the Communists as Wang Mu-shih – Wang the Pastor. Like many successful Christians of Shanghai, he had been a member of the Ch'ing Pang,* and he knew everyone from Chiang Kai-shek (also a member) down to Tu Yueh-sheng, the Ch'ing Pang chieftain. He had once been a high official in the Kuomintang, but I cannot even now disclose his real name.[1]

For some time, Pastor Wang, having deserted his congregation and officialdom, had been working with the Reds. How long I do not know. He was a kind of secret and unofficial ambassador to the courts of various militarists and officials whom the Communists were trying to win over to understanding and support of their 'anti-Japanese national front' proposals. With Chang Hsueh-liang, at least, he had been successful. And here some background is necessary to illuminate the basis of the secret understanding which had at this time been reached.

Chang Hsueh-liang was until 1931 the popular, gambling, generous, modern-minded, golf-playing, dope-using, paradoxical warlord-dictator of the 30,000,000 people of Manchuria, confirmed in the office he had inherited from his ex-bandit father Chang Tso-lin by the Kuomintang Government at Nanking, which had also given him the title Vice-Commander-in-Chief of the Armed Forces of China. In September 1931, Japan set out to conquer the North-East, and Chang's reverses began. When the invasion commenced, Young Marshal Chang was in the Peking Union Hospital, below the Wall,

---

*The Ch'ing Pang, a gangster secret society, controlled the profitable traffic in opium, gambling, prostitution, kidnapping, etc., under the protection of the International Settlement and French Concession authorities. In 1927 it helped Chiang Kai-shek destroy Communist-led unions and carry out the 'Shanghai Massacre'. See Part Two, Chapter 2.

recovering from typhoid, and in no condition to meet this crisis alone. He leaned heavily on Nanking and on his blood-sworn 'elder brother', Chiang Kai-shek, the Generalissimo. But Chiang Kai-shek, who lacked adequate means to fight Japan – and the Reds – urged reliance on the League of Nations. Chang Hsueh-liang took the Generalissimo's counsel and Nanking's orders. As a result he lost his homeland, Manchuria, after only token resistance was offered by his retreating troops. Nanking propaganda had made it appear that the non-resistance policy was the Young Marshal's idea, whereas the record showed that it was the government's explicit order. The sacrifice enabled the Generalissimo to hold his own shaky regime together in Nanking and begin a new annihilation campaign against the Reds.

That was how the Manchurian troops, known in China as the Tungpei (pronounced 'Dungbei', and meaning 'North-Eastern') Army, moved south of the Great Wall into China proper. The same thing happened when Japan invaded Jehol. Chang Hsueh-liang was not in the hospital then, but he should have been. Nanking sent no support to him, and made no preparations for defence. The Generalissimo, to avoid war, was ready to see Jehol fall to Japan, too – and so it did. Chang Hsueh-liang got the blame, and docilely played the goat when somebody had to resign to appease an infuriated populace. It was Chiang or Chang – and the latter bowed and departed. He went to Europe for a year 'to study conditions'.

The most important thing that happened to Chang Hsueh-liang while he was in Europe was not that he saw Mussolini and Hitler and met Ramsay MacDonald, but it was that for the first time in several years he found himself a healthy man, cured of the dope habit. Some years before he had taken up opium, as many Chinese generals did, between battles. To break himself of the habit was not easy; his doctor assured him he could be cured by injections. He was freed of the craving for opium, all right, but when the doctor got through with him the Young Marshal was a morphine addict.

When I first met Chang at Mukden, in 1929, he was the world's youngest dictator, and he still looked fairly well. He was thin, his face somewhat drawn and jaundiced-looking, but his mind was quick and energetic, he seemed full of exuberance. He was openly anti-Japanese, and he was eager to perform miracles in driving

Japan from China and modernizing Manchuria. Several years later his physical condition was much worse. One of his doctors in Peking told me that he was spending $200 a day on 'medicine' – a special preparation of morphine which theoretically could be 'tapered off'.

But in Shanghai, just before he left for Europe, Chang Hsueh-liang began to cure himself of the drug habit. When he returned to China in 1934 his friends were pleased and amazed: he had put on weight and muscle, there was colour in his cheeks, he looked ten years younger, and people saw in him traces of the brilliant leader of his youth. He had always possessed a quick, realistic mind, and now he gave it a chance to develop. At Hankow he resumed command of the Tungpei Army, which had been shifted to Central China to fight the Reds. It was a tribute to his popularity that, despite his errors of the past, his army enthusiastically welcomed him back.

Chang adopted a new routine – up at six, hard exercise, daily drill and study, simple food and Spartan habits, and direct personal contact with the subalterns as well as officers of his troops, which still numbered about 140,000 men. A new Tungpei Army began to emerge. Sceptics gradually became convinced that the Young Marshal had again become a man worth watching, and took seriously the vow he had made on his return: that his whole life would be devoted to the task of recovering Manchuria, and erasing the humiliation of his people.

Meanwhile, Chang had not lost faith in the Generalissimo. In their entire relationship Chang had never wavered in his loyalty to the older man, whose regime he had three times saved from collapse, and in whose judgement and sincerity he placed full confidence. He evidently believed Chiang Kai-shek when he said he was preparing to recover Manchuria, and would yield no more territory without resistance. In 1935 Japan's militarists continued their aggression: the puppet regime of east Hopei was set up, part of Chahar was annexed, and demands were made for the separation of North China from the South, to which Nanking partly acquiesced. Ominous discontent rumbled among the Young Marshal's officers and men, especially after his troops were shifted to the North-West to continue to wage an unpopular civil war against the Red Army, while Japanese attrition continued almost unopposed.

After months of fighting the Reds in the South, several important realizations had come to the Young Marshal and some of his officers: that the 'bandits' they were fighting were in reality led by able, patriotic, anti-Japanese commanders; that this process of 'Communist extermination' might last for many more years; that it was impossible to resist Japan while the anti-Red wars continued; and that meanwhile the Tungpei Army was rapidly being reduced and disbanded in battles which were to it devoid of meaning.

Nevertheless, when Chang shifted his headquarters to the North-West, he began an energetic campaign against the Reds. For a while he had some success, but in October and November 1935 the Tungpei Army suffered serious defeats, reportedly losing two whole divisions (the 101st and 109th) and part of a third (110th). Thousands of Tungpei soldiers 'turned over' to the Red Army. Many officers were also taken captive, and held for a period of 'anti-Japanese tutelage'.

When those officers were released, and returned to Sian, they brought back to the Young Marshal glowing accounts of the morale and organization in the soviet districts, but especially of the Red Army's sincerity in wanting to stop civil war, unify China by peaceful democratic methods, and unite to oppose Japanese imperialism. Chang was impressed. He was impressed even more by reports from his divisions that the sentiment throughout the whole army was turning against war with the Reds, whose slogans – 'Chinese must not fight Chinese !' and 'Unite with us and fight back to Manchuria !' – were infecting the rank and file of the entire Tungpei Army.

In the meantime, Chang himself had been strongly influenced to the left. Many of the students in his Tungpei University had come to Sian and were working with him, and among these were some Communists. After the Japanese demands in Peking of December 1935, he had sent word to the North that all anti-Japanese students, regardless of their political beliefs, could find haven in Sianfu. While anti-Japanese agitators elsewhere in China were being arrested by agents of the Nanking government, in Shensi they were encouraged and protected. Some of Chang's younger officers had been much influenced by the students also, and when the captured officers returned from the Red districts and reported that open anti-Japanese mass organizations were flourishing there, and described the Reds' patriotic propaganda among the people, Chang began to think more and more of the Reds as natural allies rather than enemies.

It was at this point, early in 1936, Pastor Wang told me, that he one day called on Chang Hsueh-liang and opened an interview by declaring: 'I have come to borrow your airplane to go to the Red districts.'

Chang jumped up and stared in amazement. 'What? You dare to come here and make such a request? Do you realize you can be shot for this?'

The Pastor elaborated. He explained that he had contacts with the Communists and knew things which Chang should know. He talked for a long time about their changing policies, about the necessity for a united China to resist Japan, about the Reds' willingness to make big concessions in order to influence Nanking to resist Japan, a policy which the Reds realized they could not, alone, make effective. He proposed that he should arrange for a further discussion of these points between Chang and certain Red leaders. And to all of this, after his first surprise, Chang listened attentively. He had for some time been thinking that he could make use of the Reds: they also evidently believed they could make use of him; very well, perhaps they could utilize each other on the basis of common demands for an end to civil war and united resistance to Japan.

The Pastor did, after all, fly to Yenan, north Shensi, in the Young Marshal's private airplane. He entered Soviet China and returned with a formula for negotiation. And a short time later Chang Hsueh-liang himself flew up to Yenan, met Chou En-lai,* and after long and detailed discussion with him became convinced, according to Wang, of the Reds' sincerity, and of the sanity and practicability of their proposals for a united front.

First steps in the implementation of the Tungpei-Communist agreement included the cessation of hostilities in Shensi. Neither side was to move without notifying the other. The Reds sent several

*See BN.

delegates to Sianfu, who put on Tungpei uniforms, joined Chang Hsueh-liang's staff, and helped reorganize political training methods in his army. A new school was opened at Wang Ch'u Ts'un, where Chang's lower officers went through intensified courses in politics, economics, social science, and detailed and statistical study of how Japan had conquered Manchuria and what China had lost thereby. Hundreds of radical students flocked to Sian and entered another anti-Japanese political training school, at which the Young Marshal also gave frequent lectures. Something like the political commissar system used in Soviet Russia and by the Chinese Red Army was adopted in the Tungpei Army. Some aging higher officers inherited from the Manchurian days were sacked; to replace them Chang Hsueh-liang promoted radical younger officers, to whom he now looked for his main support in building a new army. Many of the corrupt sycophants who had surrounded Chang during his 'playboy' years were also replaced by eager and serious-minded students from the Tungpei University.

Such changes developed in close secrecy, made possible by Chang's semi-autonomy as a provincial warlord. Although the Tungpei troops no longer fought the Reds, there were Nanking troops along the Shansi-Shensi border and in Kansu and Ninghsia, and some fighting continued in those regions. No word of the truce between Chang and the Communists crept into the press. And although Chiang Kai-shek's spies in Sian knew that something was fermenting, they could get few details of its exact nature. Occasional trucks arrived in Sian carrying Red passengers, but they looked innocuous; they all wore Tungpei uniforms. The occasional departure of other trucks from Sian to the Red districts aroused no suspicion; they resembled any other Tungpei trucks setting off for the front.

It was on just such a truck, Pastor Wang confided to me soon after my arrival, that I would myself be going to the front. The journey by plane was out: too much risk of embarrassment to the Young Marshal was involved, for his American pilots might not hold their tongues if a foreigner were dumped on the front and not returned.

One morning the Pastor called on me with a Tungpei officer – or at any rate a youth wearing the uniform of a Tungpei officer –

and suggested a trip to the ancient Han city outside Sian. A curtained car waited for us in front of the hotel, and when we got in I saw in a corner a man wearing dark glasses and the Chung Shan uniform of a Kuomintang official. We drove out to the site of the old palace of the Han Dynasty,* and there we walked over to the raised mound of earth where the celebrated Han Wu Ti once sat in his throne room and 'ruled the earth'. Here you could still pick up fragments of tile from those great roofs of over 2,000 years ago.

Pastor Wang and the Tungpei officer had some words to exchange, and stood apart, talking. The Kuomintang official, who had sat without speaking during our long dusty drive, came over to me and removed his dark glasses and his white hat. I saw that he was quite young. Under a rim of thick, glossy hair a pair of intense eyes sparkled at me. A mischievous grin spread over his bronzed face, and one look at him, without those glasses, showed that the uniform was a disguise, that this was no sedentary bureaucrat but an out-of-doors man of action. He was of medium height and looked slight of strength, so that when he came close to me and suddenly took my arm in a grip of iron I winced with surprise. There was a pantherish grace about the man's movements, I noticed later, a lithe limberness under the stiff formal cut of the suit.

He put his face close to mine and grinned and fixed his sharp, burning eyes on me and held my two arms tightly in that iron grip, and then wagged his head and comically screwed up his mouth – and winked! 'Look at me!' he whispered with the delight of a child with a secret. 'Look at me! Look at me! Do you recognize me?'

I did not know what to think of the fellow. He was so bubbling over about something that his excitement infected me, and I felt foolish because I had nothing to say. Recognize him? I had never met a Chinese like him in my life! I shook my head apologetically.

He released a hand from my arm and pointed a finger at his chest. 'I thought maybe you had seen my picture somewhere,' he said. 'Well, I am Teng Fa,' he offered – '*Teng Fa!*'† He pulled back his head and gazed at me to see the effect of the bombshell.

*The illustrious Han Dynasty governed the 'Central Kingdom' for a period (202 B.C.–A.D. 220) that overlapped with the life span of the Roman Empire, with which it had some trade and cultural exchanges.
† See BN.

Teng Fa? Teng Fa ... why, Teng Fa was chief of the Chinese Red Army's Security Police. And something else, there was $50,000 on his head !

Teng danced with pleasure when he disclosed his identity. He was irrepressible, full of amusement at the situation : he, the notorious 'Communist bandit', living in the very midst of the enemy's camp, thumbing his nose at the spies that hovered everywhere. And he was overjoyed at seeing me – he literally hugged me repeatedly – an American who was voluntarily going into the 'bandit' areas. He offered me everything. Did I want his horse? Oh, what a horse he had, the finest in Red China ! His pictures? He had a wonderful collection and it was all mine. His diary? He would send instructions to his wife, who was still in the soviet areas, to give all this and more to me. And he kept his word.

What a Chinese ! What a Red bandit !

Teng Fa was a Cantonese, the son of a working-class family, and had once been a foreign-style cook on a Canton–Hongkong steamer. He had been a leader of the great Hongkong shipping strike, when he was beaten in the chest and had had some ribs broken by a British constable who did not like pickets. And then he had become a Communist, and entered Whampoa, and taken part in the Nationalist Revolution, until after 1927 he had joined the Red Army in Kiangsi.

We stood for an hour or more on that height, talking and looking down on the green-shrouded grave of an imperial city. How incongruous and yet how logical it was that this place should seem to the Communists the one rendezvous where we four could safely meet, the exact spot where, two millenniums ago, Han Wu Ti had ruled a united China, and so successfully consolidated a people and a culture from the chaos of warring states that their descendants, ever since, had been content to call themselves Sons of Han.

It was here that Teng told me who would escort me to the Red districts, how I would travel, how I would live in Red China, and assured me of a warm welcome there.

'Aren't you afraid for your head?' I asked as we drove back to the city.

'Not any more than Chang Hsueh-liang is,' he said. 'I'm living with him.'

4

Through Red Gates

WE left Sianfu before dawn, the high wooden gates of the once 'golden city' swinging open and noisily dragging their chains before the magic of our military pass. In the half-light of predawn the big army trucks lumbered past the airfield from which expeditions set out for daily reconnaissance and bombing over the Red lines.

To a Chinese traveller every mile of this road northward from Sianfu evokes memories of the rich and colourful pageant of his people. It seemed not inappropriate that the latest historical mutation in China, the Communist movement, should choose this locale in which to work out a destiny. In an hour we were being ferried across the Wei River, in whose rich valley Confucius' ancestors * developed their rice culture and formulated traditions still a power in the folk myth of rural China today. And towards noon we had reached Ts'un Pu. It was near this battlemented city that the towering and terrible figure who first 'unified' China – the Emperor Ch'in Shih Huang Ti – was born some 2,200 years ago. The Emperor Ch'in first consolidated all of the ancient frontier walls of his country into what remains today the most stupendous masonry on earth – the Great Wall of China.

Opium poppies nodded their swollen heads, ready for harvest, along the newly completed motor road – a road already deeply wrinkled with washouts and ruts, so that at times it was scarcely navigable even for our six-ton Dodge truck. Shensi had long been a noted opium province. During the great North-West Famine, which a few years before had taken a toll of 3,000,000 lives, American Red Cross investigators attributed much of the tragedy to the cultivation of the poppy, forced upon the peasants by provincial monopolies controlled by greedy warlords. The best land being devoted to the poppy, in years of drought there was a serious short-

* During 3000–551 B.C.

age of millet, wheat, and corn, the staple cereals of the North-West.

I spent the night on a clay k'ang,* in a filthy hut at Lochuan, with pigs and donkeys quartered in the next room, and rats in my own, and I'm sure we all slept very little. Next morning, a few miles beyond that city, the loess terraces rose higher and more imposing, and the country was weirdly transformed.

The wonderful loess lands, which cover much of Kansu, Shensi, Ninghsia, and Shansi provinces, account for the marvellous fertility of these regions (when there is rainfall), for the loess furnishes an inexhaustible porous topsoil tens of feet deep. Geologists think the loess is organic matter blown down in centuries past from Mongolia and from the west by the great winds that rise in Central Asia. Scenically the result is an infinite variety of queer, embattled shapes – hills like great castles, like rows of mammoth, nicely rounded scones, like ranges torn by some giant hand, leaving behind the imprint of angry fingers. Fantastic, incredible, and sometimes frightening shapes, a world configurated by a mad god – and sometimes a world also of strange surrealist beauty.

And though we saw fields and cultivated land everywhere, we seldom saw houses. The peasants were tucked away in those loess hills also. Throughout the North-West, as has been the habit of centuries, men lived in homes dug out of the hard, fudge-coloured cliffs – yao-fang, or 'cave houses', as the Chinese call them. But they were no caves in the Western sense. Cool in summer, warm in winter, they were easily built and easily cleaned. Even the wealthiest landlords often dug their homes in the hills. Some of them were many-roomed edifices, gaily furnished and decorated, with stone floors and high-ceilinged chambers, lighted through rice-paper windows opened in the walls of earth also athwart the stout, black-lacquered doors.

Once, not far from Lochuan, a young Tungpei officer, who rode beside me in the cavorting truck, pointed to such a yao-fang-ts'un – a cave village. It lay only a mile or so distant from the motor road, just across a deep ravine.

*A k'ang is a raised earthen platform built in Chinese houses, with a fireplace at one end. The flue is arranged in a maze beneath, so that it heats the clay platform, if desired.

'They are Reds,' he revealed. 'One of our detachments was sent over there to buy millet a few weeks ago, and those villagers refused to sell us a catty of it. The stupid soldiers took some by force. As they retired the peasants shot at them.' He swung his arms in an arc including everything on each side of the highway, so carefully guarded by dozens of *pao-lei* – hilltop machine-gun nests – manned by Kuomintang troops. '*Hung-fei*,' he said, 'everything out there is Red-bandit territory.'

I gazed towards the spaces indicated with keener interest, for it was into that horizon of unknown hill and upland that I intended, within a few hours, to make my way.

On the road we passed part of the 105th Division, all Manchurians, moving back from Yenan to Lochuan. They were lean and sturdy youths, most of them taller than the average Chinese soldier. At a roadside inn we stopped to drink tea, and I sat down near several of them who were resting. They were just returning from Wa Ya Pao, in north Shensi, where there had been a skirmish with the Reds. I overheard scraps of conversation between them. They were talking about the Reds.

'They eat a lot better than we do,' one argued.

'Yes – eat the flesh of the *lao-pai-hsing* !' * another replied.

'Never mind that – a few landlords – it's all to the good. Who thanked us for coming to Wa Ya Pao? The landlords! Isn't it a fact? Why should we kill ourselves for these rich men?'

'They say more than 3,000 of our Tungpei men are with them now . . .'

'Another thing on their side. Why should we fight our own people, when none of us want to fight anybody, unless it's a Japanese, eh?'

An officer approached and this promising conversation came to an end. The officer ordered them to move on. They picked up their rifles and trudged off down the road. Soon afterwards we drove away.

Early in the afternoon of the second day we reached Yenan, where north Shensi's single road fit for wheeled traffic came to an end – about 400 *li*,† more or less, south of the Great Wall. It

---

*Lao-pai-hsing, literally 'old hundred names', is the colloquial Chinese expression for the country people.

† One Chinese *li* is about a third of a mile.

was a historic town : through it, in centuries past, had come the nomadic raiders from the north, and through it swept the great Mongol cavalry of Genghis Khan, in its ride of conquest towards Sianfu.

Yenan was ideally suited for defence. Cradled in a bowl of high, rock-ribbed hills, its stout walls crawled up to the very tops. Attached to them now, like wasps' nests, were newly made fortifications, where machine guns bristled towards the Reds not far beyond. The road and its immediate environs were then held by Tungpei troops, but until recently Yenan had been completely cut off. The Reds had turned upon their enemy the blockade which the Generalissimo enforced against themselves, and hundreds reportedly had died of starvation.

The long Red siege of Yenan * had been lifted a few weeks before I arrived, but signs of it were still evident in the famished-looking inhabitants and the empty shelves or barred doors of shops. Little food was available and prices were alpine. What could be bought at all had been secured as a result of a temporary truce with the Red partisans. In return for an agreement not to take the offensive against the soviet districts on this front, the soviet peasants now sold grain and vegetables to the hungry anti-Red troops.

I had my credentials for a visit to the front. My plan was to leave the city early next morning, and go towards the 'White' lines, where the troops were merely holding their positions, without attempting any advance. Then I meant to branch off on one of the mountain lanes over which, I had been told, merchants smuggled their goods in and out of the soviet regions.

To state precisely the manner in which, just as I had hoped, I did pass the last sentry and enter no man's land, might have caused serious difficulties for the Kuomintang adherents who assisted me on my way. Suffice it to say that my experience proved once more that anything is possible in China, if it is done in the Chinese manner. For by seven o'clock next morning I had really left the last Kuomintang machine gun behind, and was walking through the thin strip of territory that divided 'Red' from 'White'.

With me was a single muleteer, who had been hired for me by a

---

* Yenan was later occupied by the Red Army and became the provisional Red capital. See Part Twelve.

Manchurian colonel in Yenan. He was to carry my scant belongings – bedding roll, a little food, two cameras and twenty-four rolls of film – to the first Red partisan outpost. I did not know whether he himself was a Red bandit or a White bandit – but bandit he certainly looked. All this territory having for several years alternately been controlled by armies of both colours, it was quite possible for him to have been either – or perhaps both.

For four hours we followed a small winding stream and did not see any sign of human life. There was no road at all, but only the bed of the stream that rushed swiftly between high walls of rock, above which rose swift hills of loess. It was the perfect setting for the blotting-out of a too inquisitive foreign devil. A disturbing factor was the muleteer's frequently expressed admiration of my cowhide shoes.

'*Tao-la!*' he suddenly shouted around his ear, as the rock walls at last gave way and opened out into a narrow valley, green with young wheat. 'We have arrived!'

Relieved, I gazed beyond him and saw in the side of a hill a loess village, where blue smoke curled from the tall clay chimneys that stood up like long fingers against the face of the cliff. In a few minutes we were there.

A young farmer who wore a turban of white towelling on his head and a revolver strapped to his waist came out and looked at me in astonishment. Who was I and what did I want?

'I am an American journalist,' I said in conformance with the instructions Wang the Pastor had given me. 'I want to see the local chief of the Poor People's League.'

He looked at me blankly and replied, '*Hai p'a!*'

Hai p'a in any Chinese I had ever heard had only one meaning: 'I'm afraid.' If he is afraid, I thought to myself, what the devil am I supposed to feel? But his appearance belied his words: he looked completely self-assured. He turned to the *lofu* and asked him who I was.

The muleteer repeated what I had said, adding a few flourishes of his own. With relief, I saw the young farmer's face soften and then I noticed that he was really a good-looking young man, with fine bronzed skin and good white teeth. He did not seem to belong to the race of timid peasants of China elsewhere. There was a challenge in his sparkling merry eyes, and a certain bravado. He slowly moved his hand away from his revolver butt and smiled.

'I am that man,' he said. 'I am the chief. Come inside and drink some hot tea.'

These Shensi hill people had a dialect of their own, full of slurred colloquialisms, but they understood *pai-hua*, or mandarin Chinese, and most of their own speech was quite comprehensible to an outlander. After a few more attempts at conversation with the chief, he began to show understanding, and we made good progress. Occasionally into our talk, however, would creep this *hai p'a* business, but for a while I was too disconcerted to ask him just *what* he feared. When I finally did probe into the matter, I discovered that *hai p'a* in the dialect of the Shensi hills is the equivalent of *pu chih-tao* in mandarin Chinese. It simply means 'don't understand'. My satisfaction at this discovery was considerable.

Seated on a felt-covered *k'ang* I told my host more about myself and my plans. In a short time he seemed reassured. I wanted to go to An Tsai – the county seat – where I then believed Soviet Chairman Mao Tse-tung to be. Could he give me a guide and a muleteer?

Certainly, certainly, he agreed, but I should not think of moving in the heat of day. The sun had already climbed to its zenith, it was really very hot, I looked tired, and, meanwhile, had I eaten? Actually I was ravenous, and without any further ceremony I accepted this invitation to a first meal with a 'Red bandit'. My muleteer was anxious to return to Yenan, and, paying him off, I bade him goodbye. It was a farewell to my last link with the 'White' world for many weeks to come. I had crossed the Red Rubicon.

I was now at the mercy of Mr Liu Lung-huo – Liu the Dragon Fire, as I learned the young peasant was called – and likewise at the mercy of his tough-looking comrades, who had begun to drift in from neighbouring *yao-fang*. Similarly clad and armed, they looked at me curiously and laughed at my preposterous accent.

Liu offered me tobacco, wine, and tea, and plied me with numerous questions. He and his friends examined with close interest, interrupted by exclamations of approval, my camera, my shoes, my woollen stockings, the fabric of my cotton shorts, and (with lengthy admiration) the zipper on my khaki shirt. The general impression seemed to prevail that, however ridiculous it might look, the ensemble evidently served its purposes well enough. I did not know just what 'communism' might mean to these men in practice, and I was prepared to see my belongings rapidly 'redistributed' – but instead I was given the foreign-guest treatment.

In an hour a vast platter of scrambled eggs arrived, accompanied by steamed rolls, boiled millet, some cabbage, and a little roast pork. My host apologized for the simplicity of the fare, and I for an inordinate appetite. Which latter was quite beside the point, as I had to punt my chopsticks at a lively pace to keep up with the good fellows of the Poor People's League.

Dragon Fire assured me that An Tsai was 'only a few steps', and though I was uneasy about it I could do nothing but wait, as he insisted. When finally a youthful guide appeared, accompanied by a muleteer, it was already past four in the afternoon. Before leaving, I ventured to pay Mr Liu for his food, but he indignantly refused.

'You are a foreign guest,' he explained, 'and you have business with our Chairman, Mao. Moreover, your money is no good.' Glancing at the bill I held out to him, he asked, 'Haven't you any soviet money?' When I replied in the negative, he counted out a dollar's worth of soviet paper notes. 'Here – you will need this on the road.'

Mr Liu accepted a Kuomintang dollar in exchange; I thanked him again, and climbed up the road behind my guide and muleteer.

Ahead of me was a narrow escape and an incident which was later to nourish the rumour that I had been kidnapped and killed by bandits. And as a matter of fact, bandits – not Red but White – were already trailing me behind those silent walls of loess.

Part Two

THE ROAD TO THE
RED CAPITAL

I

Chased by White Bandits

'DOWN with the landlords who eat our flesh !'
  'Down with the militarists who drink our blood !',
  'Down with the traitors who sell China to Japan !'
  'Welcome the United Front with all anti-Japanese armies !'
  'Long live the Chinese Revolution !'
  'Long live the Chinese Red Army !'
It was under these somewhat disturbing exhortations, em-blazoned in bold black characters, that I spent my first night in Red territory.

But it was not in An Tsai and not under the protection of any Red soldiers. For, as I had feared, we did not reach An Tsai that day, but by sunset had arrived only at a little village that nestled in the curve of a river, with hills brooding darkly on every side. Several layers of slate-roofed houses rose up from the lip of the stream, and it was on their mud-brick walls that the slogans were chalked. Fifty or sixty peasants and staring children poured out to greet my caravan of one donkey.

My young emissary of the Poor People's League decided to deposit me here. One of his cows had recently calved, he said; there were wolves in the neighbourhood, and he had to get back to his charges. An Tsai was still ten miles distant and we could not get there easily in the dark. He turned me over for safekeeping to the chairman of the local branch of the Poor People's League. Both guide and mule-teer refused any compensation for their services – either in White money or in Red.

The chairman was a youth in his early twenties who wore a faded blue cotton jacket under a brown, open face, and a pair of white trousers above a pair of leathery bare feet. He welcomed me and was very kind. He offered me a room in the village meeting house, and had hot water brought to me, and a bowl of millet. But I declined the dark, evil-smelling room and petitioned for the use of two dismantled doors. Laying these on a couple of benches, I unrolled my blankets and made my bed in the open. It was a gorgeous night, with a clear sky spangled with northern stars, and the waters in a little fall below me murmured of peace and tranquillity. Exhausted from the long walk, I fell asleep immediately.

When I opened my eyes again dawn was just breaking. The chairman was standing over me, shaking my shoulder.

'What is it?'

'You had better leave a little early. There are bandits near here, and you ought to get to An Tsai quickly.'

Bandits? He was not talking about Reds, he meant 'White bandits'. I got up without further persuasion. I did not want anything to happen to me so ridiculous as being kidnapped by White bandits in Soviet China.

White bandits were in the Kuomintang's terminology called *min-t'uan*, or 'people's corps', just as Red bandits were in soviet terminology called *yu-chi-tui*, 'roving bands' – Red partisans. In an effort to combat peasant uprisings, the *min-t'uan* forces had increasingly been organized by the Kuomintang. They functioned as an organic part of the *pao-chia* system, an ancient method of controlling the peasantry which was now being widely imposed by both the Kuomintang in China and the Japanese in Manchukuo.

Pao-chia literally means 'guaranteed armour'. One *chia* consisted of approximately ten families, with a headman supposedly elected but usually appointed by the local magistrate. One *pao* was made up of approximately ten *chia*. The combined *pao-chia* was held collectively responsbile to the district magistrate (*hsien chang*), a government appointee, for any offence committed by any member of the roughly hundred-family unit. It was the *chia* headman's duty to report any 'rebel son' in his group, otherwise he would be punished for any irregularity. By such means the Mongols and Manchus had pacified rural China – and it was not a popular means, especially among the poor.

As a measure for preventing the organization of peasant protest it was almost unbeatable. Since headmen of the *pao-chia* were nearly always rich farmers, landlords, pawnbrokers, or money-lenders – most zealous of subjects – naturally they were not inclined to 'guarantee' any tenant or debtor peasants of a rebellious turn of mind. Yet not to be guaranteed was a serious matter. An unguaranteed man could be thrown in jail on any pretext, as a 'suspicious character'.

This meant in effect that the whole peasantry was placed at the mercy of the gentry, who at any time could ruin a man by refusing to guarantee him. Among the functions of the *pao-chia*, and a very important one, was the collection of taxes for the maintenance of the *min-t'uan*, or militia. The *min-t'uan* was selected, organized, and commanded by the landlords and gentry. Its primary duties were to fight communism, to help collect rents and share-crop debts, to collect loans and interest, and to support the local magistrates' efforts to gather in the taxes.

Hence it happened that, when the Red Army occupied a territory, its first as well as its last enemy was the *min-t'uan*. For the *min-t'uan* had no base except in the landlords who paid them, and they lost that base when the Reds came in. Class war in China was best seen in the struggles between *min-t'uan* and Red partisans, for here very often was a direct armed conflict between landlords and their former tenants and debtors. *Min-t'uan* mercenaries numbered hundreds of thousands and were most important auxiliaries of the some 2,000,000 nominally anti-Red troops of China.

Now, although there was a truce between the Red Army and the Kuomintang Army on this front, attacks by the *min-t'uan* on the Red partisan brigades continued intermittently. In Sian, Lochuan, and Yenan I had heard that many landlords who had fled to these cities were now financing or personally leading the White bandits to operate in the soviet border districts. Taking advantage of the absence of the main Red forces, they made retaliatory raids into Red territory, burning and looting villages and killing peasants. Leaders were carried off to the White districts, where generous rewards were given for such Red captives by the landlords and White officers.

Interested primarily in *revanche* and quick cash returns on their adventures, the *min-t'uan* were credited with the most destructive work of the Red-White wars. I, at any rate, had no wish to test out the White bandits' 'foreign policy' on myself. Although my belongings were few, I feared that the little cash and clothing I had, together with my cameras, would prove prizes too tempting for them to overlook, if it required only the erasure of a lone foreign devil to possess them.

After hastily swallowing some hot tea and wheat cakes, I set off with another guide and muleteer contributed by the chairman. For an hour we followed the bed of the stream, occasionally passing small cave villages, where heavy-furred dogs growled menacingly at me and child sentinels came out to demand our road pass. Then we reached a lovely pool of still water set in a natural basin hollowed from great rocks, and there I saw my first Red warrior.

He was alone except for a white pony which stood grazing beside the stream, wearing a vivid silky-blue saddle-blanket with a yellow star on it. The young man had been bathing; at our approach he jumped up quickly, pulling on a sky-blue coat and a turban of white towelling on which was fixed a red star. A Mauser hung at his hip, with a red tassel dangling bravely from its wooden combination holster-stock. With his hand on his gun he waited for us to come up to him, and demanded our business from the guide.

'I have come to interview Mao Tse-tung,' I said. 'I understand he is at An Tsai. How much further have we to go?'

'Chairman Mao?' he inquired slowly. 'No, he is not at An Tsai.' Then he peered behind us and asked if I were alone. When he convinced himself that I was, his reserve dropped from him, he smiled as if at some secret amusement, and said, 'I am going to An Tsai. I'll just go along with you to the district government.'

He walked his pony beside me and I volunteered more details about myself, and ventured some inquiries about him. I learned that he was in the political defence bureau, and was on patrol duty along this frontier. And the horse? It was a 'gift' from Young Marshal Chang Hsueh-liang. He told me that the Reds had captured over 1,000 horses from Chang's troops in recent battles in north Shensi. I learned further that he was called Yao, that he was twenty-two years old, and that he had been a Red for six years.

In a couple of hours we had reached An Tsai, which lay opposite the Fu Ho, a subtributary of the Yellow River. A big town on the map, An Tsai turned out to be little but the pretty shell of its wall. The streets were completely deserted and everything stood in crumbling ruins.

'The town was completely destroyed over a decade ago by a great flood,' Yao explained. 'The whole city went swimming.'

An Tsai's inhabitants had not rebuilt the city, but lived now in the face of a great stone cliff, honeycombed with *yao-fang*, a little beyond the walls. Upon arrival we discovered, however, that the Red Army detachment stationed there had been dispatched to chase bandits, while members of the district soviet had gone to Pai Chia P'ing, a nearby hamlet, to render a report to a provincial commissioner. Yao volunteered to escort me to Pai Chia P'ing – 'Hundred Family Peace' – which we reached at dusk.

I had already been in soviet territory a day and a half, yet I had seen no signs of wartime distress, had met but one Red soldier, and a populace that universally seemed to be pursuing its agrarian tasks in complete composure. Yet I was not to be misled by appearances. I remembered how, during the Sino-Japanese War at Shanghai in 1932, Chinese peasants had gone on tilling their fields in the very midst of battle, with apparent unconcern. So that when, just as we rounded a corner to enter 'Hundred Family Peace', I heard blood-curdling yells directly above me, I was not entirely unprepared.

Looking towards the sound of the fierce battle cries, I saw, standing on a ledge above the road, in front of a row of barrack-like houses, a dozen peasants brandishing spears, pikes and a few rifles in the most uncompromising of attitudes. It seemed that the question of my fate as blockade runner – whether I was to be given the firing squad as an imperialist, or to be welcomed as an honest inquirer – was about to be settled without further delay.

I must have turned a comical face toward Yao, for he burst into laughter. '*Pu p'a*,' he chuckled. 'Don't be afraid. They are only some partisans – *practising*. There is a Red partisan school here. Don't be alarmed!'

Later on I learned that the curriculum for partisans included this rehearsal of ancient Chinese war cries, just as in the days of feudal tourneys described in one of Mao Tse-tung's favourite books, the *Shui Hu Chuan*.* And having experienced a certain frigidity

---

*Literally *The Water Margin*, a celebrated Chinese romance of the sixteenth century. Pearl Buck has translated it under the title *All Men Are Brothers*.

of spine as an unwitting subject of the technique, I could testify that it was still very effective in intimidating an enemy.

I had just sat down and begun an interview with a soviet functionary to whom Yao had introduced me in Pai Chia P'ing, when a young commander, wearing a Sam Browne belt, stumbled up on a sweating horse and plunged to the ground. He looked curiously at me. And it was from him that I heard the full details of my own adventure.

The new arrival was named Pien, and he was commandant of the An Tsai Red Guard. He announced that he had just returned from an encounter with a force of about a hundred *min-t'uan*. A little peasant boy – a 'Young Vanguard' – had run several miles and arrived almost exhausted at An Tsai, to warn them that *min-t'uan* had invaded the district. And that their leader was a really *white* bandit! – a foreign devil – *myself*!

'I at once took a mounted detachment over a mountain short cut, and in an hour we sighted the bandits,' Pien recounted. 'They were following you' – he pointed at me – 'only about two *li* behind. But we surrounded them, attacked in a valley, and captured some, including two of their leaders, and several horses. The rest escaped towards the frontier.' As he concluded his brief report, some of his command filed into the courtyard, leading several of the captured mounts.

I began to wonder if he really thought I *was* leading the *min-t'uan*. Had I escaped from Whites – who, had they seized me in no man's land, undoubtedly would have called me a Red – only to be captured by the Reds and accused of being a White?

But presently a slender young officer appeared, ornamented with a black beard unusually heavy for a Chinese. He came up and addressed me in a soft, cultured voice. 'Hello,' he said, 'are you looking for somebody?'

He had spoken in *English*!

And in a moment I learned that he was the notorious Chou En-lai.

2

The Insurrectionist[1]

AFTER I had talked for a few minutes with Chou En-lai and explained who I was, he arranged for me to spend the night in Pai Chia P'ing, and asked me to come next morning to his headquarters in a nearby village.

I sat down to dinner with a section of the communications department, which was stationed here, and met a dozen young men who were billeted in Pai Chia P'ing. Some of them were teachers in the partisan school, one was a radio operator, and some were officers of the Red Army. Our meal consisted of boiled chicken, unleavened whole-wheat bread, cabbage, millet, and potatoes, of which I ate heartily. But, as usual, there was nothing to drink but hot water and I could not touch it. I was parched with thirst.

The food was served – delivered is the word – by two nonchalant young lads wearing uniforms several sizes too large for them, and peaked Red caps with long bills that kept flapping down over their eyes. They looked at me sourly at first, but after a few minutes I managed to provoke a friendly grin from one of them. Emboldened by this success, I called to him as he went past.

'*Wei* [hey] !,' I called, 'bring us some cold water.'

The youth simply ignored me. In a few minutes I tried the other one, with no better result.

Then I saw that Li K'e-nung,* head of the communications section, was laughing at me behind his thick-lensed goggles. He plucked my sleeve. 'You can call him "little devil",' he advised, 'or you can call him "comrade" [*t'ung-chih*] – but you cannot call him *wei*! In here everybody is a comrade. These lads are Young Vanguards, and they are here because they are revolutionaries and volunteer to help us. They are not servants. They are future Red warriors.'

Just then the cold (boiled) water did arrive.

*See BN.

'Thank you,' I said apologetically, '– comrade !'

The Young Vanguard looked at me boldly. 'Never mind that,' he said, 'you don't thank a comrade for a thing like that !'

I had never before seen so much personal dignity in any Chinese youngsters. This first encounter was only the beginning of a series of surprises that the Young Vanguards were to give me, for as I penetrated deeper into the soviet districts I was to discover in these red-cheeked 'little Red devils' – cheerful, gay, energetic, and loyal – the living spirit of an astonishing crusade of youth.

It was one of those Sons of Lenin, in fact, who escorted me in the morning to Chou En-lai's headquarters. That turned out to be a bombproof hut (half cave) surrounded by many others exactly like it, in which farmers dwelt undismayed by the fact that they were in a battle area, and that in their midst was the Red commander of the Eastern Front.* The quartering of a few troops in the vicinity did not seem to have disturbed the rustic serenity. Before the quarters of Chou En-lai, for whose head Chiang Kai-shek had offered $80,000, there was one sentry.

Inside I saw that the room was clean but furnished in the barest fashion. A mosquito net hanging over the clay *k'ang* was the only luxury observable. A couple of iron dispatch boxes stood at the foot of it, and a little wooden table served as desk. Chou was bending over it reading radiograms when the sentry announced my arrival.

'I have a report that you are a reliable journalist, friendly to the Chinese people, and that you can be trusted to tell the truth,' said Chou. 'This is all we want to know. It does not matter to us that you are not a Communist. We will welcome any journalist who comes to see the soviet districts. It is not we, but the Kuomintang, who prevent it. You can write about anything you see and you will be given every help to investigate the soviet districts.'

Evidently the 'report' about me had come from the Communists' secret headquarters in Sian. The Reds had radio communication with all important cities of China, including Shanghai, Hankow, Nanking, and Tientsin. Despite frequent seizures of Red radio sets in the White cities, the Kuomintang had never succeeded in severing urban-rural Red communications for very long. According to Chou, the Kuomintang had never cracked the Red Army's codes

* Yeh Chien-ying was Chou's chief of staff. See BN.

since they first established a radio department, with equipment captured from the White troops.

Chou's radio station, a portable wireless set powered by a manually operated generator, was erected only a short distance from his headquarters. Through it he was in touch with all important points in the soviet areas, and with every front. He even had direct communication with Commander-in-Chief Chu Teh, whose forces were then stationed hundreds of miles to the south-west, on the Szechuan--Tibetan border. There was a radio school in Pao An, temporary soviet capital in the North-West, where about ninety students were being trained as radio engineers. They picked up the daily broadcasts from Nanking, Shanghai, and Tokyo, and furnished news to the press of Soviet China.

Chou squatted before his little desk and put aside his radiograms – mostly reports (he said) from units stationed at various points along the Yellow River, opposite Shansi province, the Reds' Eastern Front. He began working out a suggested itinerary for me. When he finished he handed me a paper containing items covering a trip of ninety-two days.

'This is my recommendation,' he said, 'but whether you follow it is your own business. I think you will find it an interesting journey.'

But ninety-two days! And almost half of them to be spent on foot or horseback. What was there to be seen? Were the Red districts so extensive as that? As it turned out, I was to spend much longer than he had suggested, and in the end to leave with reluctance because I had seen so little.

Chou promised me the use of a horse to carry me to Pao An, three days distant, and arranged for me to leave the following morning, when I could accompany part of the communications corps that was returning to the provisional capital. I learned that Mao Tse-tung and other soviet functionaries were there now, and Chou agreed to send a radio message to them telling of my arrival.

As we talked I had been studying Chou with deep interest; like many Red leaders, he was as much a legend as a man. Slender and of medium height, with a slight wiry frame, he was boyish in appearance despite his long black beard, and had large, warm, deep-set eyes. A certain magnetism about him seemed to derive from a combination of personal charm and assurance of command. His English was somewhat hesitant and difficult. He told me he had not used it for five years. The account below is based on notes of our conversation at that time.

Chou was born in 1899 in Huai-an, Kiangsu, in what he called a 'bankrupt mandarin family'. His mother was a native of Shaohsing, Chekiang province. Chou was given (at the age of four months) to the family of his father's young brother. The brother was about to die without issue when Chou's father, to assure him of male posterity (on the family tablets), presented him with En-lai to rear as his own son. 'My aunt became my real mother when I was a baby,' said Chou. 'I did not leave her for even one day until I was ten years old – when she and my natural mother both died.'

Chou's paternal grandfather was a scholar who served as a magistrate in Huai-an county, north Kiangsu, during the Manchu Dynasty. It was there that Chou spent his childhood, while his father, Chou Yun-liang, who had passed the imperial examinations, vainly waited for a magistry; he died while Chou was still an infant. His foster mother (whom Chou called 'mother') was highly literate, and that was not general then among officials' wives. Still more uncommon, she liked fiction and 'forbidden' * stories of past rebellions, to which she introduced Chou as a child. His early education was in a family school under a private tutor who taught classical literature and philosophy, to prepare one for official life. After his 'two mothers' died Chou was sent to live with another aunt and uncle – his father's older brother, who was also an official – in Fengtien (Mukden, Shenyang), Manchuria. He began to read illegal books and papers written or inspired by such reformists as Liang Ch'i-ch'ao.

At the age of fourteen Chou entered Nankai Middle School, in Tientsin. The monarchy had been overthrown and Chou now fully 'came under the influence of the Kuomintang' or Nationalist Party founded by Dr Sun Yat-sen. Japan had provided hospitality to Sun Yat-sen during his agitation against the monarchy. Sun still found refuge there as he prepared to overthrow corrupt warlords who had

* Thus he read most of the exciting books that also affected Mao Tse-tung as a boy. See Part Four, Chapters 1 and 2.

seized the republic. Chou himself went to Japan in 1917, the year he graduated from Nankai Middle School. While learning Japanese, Chou was an 'auditor student' at Waseda University in Tokyo, and at the University of Kyoto. He also became widely acquainted with revolution-minded Chinese students in Japan during his eighteen months there, and kept in touch, through letters and reading, with events in Peking.

In 1919 the former director of Nankai Middle School, Chang Po-ling, became chancellor of the newly organized Nankai University of Tientsin. Chou left Japan to enroll there at Chang's invitation. Meanwhile his relatives – 'a spendthrift lot', Chou called them – had become so impoverished that they could provide no support for Chou's college plans. Chang Po-ling gave Chou a job that paid enough to meet costs of tuition, lodging, and books. 'During my last two years at Nankai Middle School I had received no help from my family. I lived on a scholarship which I won as best student in my class. In Japan I had lived by borrowing from my friends. Now at Nankai University I became editor of the *Hsueh-sheng Lien-ho Hui Pao* [Students' Union Paper], which helped cover some expenses.' Chou managed to do that despite five months spent in jail in 1919, as a leader of Nankai's student rebellion which grew out of the May Fourth movement.*

During that period Chou helped to form the Chueh-wu Shih, or Awakening Society, a radical group whose members later became, variously, anarchists, Nationalists, and Communists. (One of them was Teng Ying-ch'ao,† whom Chou was to marry in 1925.) The Awakening Society existed until the end of 1920, when four of its founders, led by Chou, went to France as part of the Work-Study programme organized by Ch'en Tu-hsiu† and other Francophiles.

'Before going to France,' said Chou, 'I read translations of the *Communist Manifesto*; Kautsky's *Class Struggle*; and *The October Revolution*. These books were published under the auspices of the *New Youth* [*Hsin Ch'ing-nien*], edited by Ch'en Tu-hsiu. I also personally met Ch'en Tu-hsiu as well as Li Ta-chao† – who were to

---

*Inspired by nation-wide resistance to Japan's 'Twenty-one Demands' and to the Versailles Treaty award, to Japan, of Germany's colony in Tsingtao, China.

† See BN.

become founders of the Chinese Communist Party.' (Chou made no reference to any meeting with Mao Tse-tung at that time.)

'I sailed for France in October 1920. On the way I met many Hunanese students who were members of the Hsin-Min Hsueh-hui [the New People's Study Society], organized by Mao Tse-tung. Among these were Ts'ai Ho-sen * and his sister, Ts'ai Ch'ang,* who organized the first China Socialist Youth Corps in France in 1921. In 1922 I became a founder-member of the [Chinese] Communist Youth League and began to work full time for that organization.† After two years I went to London, where I spent two and a half months. I did not like it. Then I went to Germany and worked there for a year, helping to organize.‡ Our Communist Youth League had sent delegates to Shanghai in 1922, to request admission to the Party, formed the year before. Our petition being granted, the CYL became formally affiliated with the Party, and thus I became a Communist. Founder-members of the CYL in France who became Party members in this way included Ts'ai Ho-sen, Ts'ai Ch'ang, Chao Shih-yen, Li Fu-ch'un,* Li Li-san,* Wang Jo-fei, and the two sons of Ch'en Tu-hsiu – Ch'en Yen-nien and Ch'en Ch'iao-nien. Ch'en Yen-nien later became a ricksha puller in order to organize rickshamen in Shanghai. During the counter-revolution he was captured and badly tortured before he was killed. His brother was executed at Lunghua a year later – 1928.

'Among members of our Chinese Students' Union in France more than four hundred joined the CYL. Fewer than a hundred joined the anarchists and about a hundred became Nationalists.'

Financial support for Chinese students in France came from the Sino-French Educational Association and from Tsai Yuan-p'ei and Li Shih-tseng. 'Many old and patriotic gentlemen,' said Chou, 'privately helped us students, and with no personal political aims.'[2] Chou's own financial backer while in Europe was Yen Hsiu, a founder of Nankai University. Unlike some Chinese students, Chou did no manual labour in France, except for a brief period at the Renault plant, when he studied labour organization. After a year with a private tutor, learning the French language, he devoted

---

* See BN.
† The CYL was an outgrowth of the Socialist Youth Corps.
‡ Chu Teh was one of Chou's recruits to communism.

his entire time to politics. 'Later on,' Chou told me, 'when friends remarked that I had used Yen Hsiu's money to become a Communist, Yen quoted a Chinese proverb, "Every intelligent man has his own purposes!"'

In France, London, and Germany Chou spent three years. On his return to China he stopped briefly for instructions in Moscow. Late in 1924 he arrived in Canton, where he became Chiang Kai-shek's deputy director of the political department of Whampoa Academy. (While still in Paris Chou had been elected to the Central Executive Committee of the Kuomintang. In Canton he was also elected secretary of the Kwangtung provincial Communist Party – paradox of a strange alliance!) At Whampoa, Chou's real boss was the Russian adviser, General Vasili Bluecher,* known in Canton as Galin.

Under the skilful guidance of Galin, and of the Russians' chief political adviser, Mikhail Borodin,* Chou En-lai built up a circle of cadet disciples known as the League of Military Youth, which included Lin Piao and other future generals of the Red Army. His influence was further enhanced when, in 1925, he was appointed political commissar of the Nationalists' first division, which suppressed a revolt near Swatow – an occasion Chou utilized to organize labour unions in that port. In March 1926 Kuomintang-Communist tension resulted in Chiang's first anti-Communist blow. He succeeded in ending the practice of dual-party membership and removed many Communists from Whampoa posts. Chou En-lai remained, however, on Chiang Kai-shek's orders.

During 1926 the Northern Expedition got under way, with Chiang Kai-shek as commander-in-chief selected jointly by the Kuomintang and the Communists. Chou En-lai was ordered to prepare an insurrection and help the Nationalist Army seize Shanghai. Within three months the Communist Party had organized 600,000 workers and was able to call a general strike, but it was a fiasco. Unarmed and untrained, the workers did not know how to go about 'seizing the city'.

Underestimating the significance of the first and then of a second strike, the northern warlords cut off a number of heads but failed to halt the labour movement, while Chou En-lai learned by

*See BN.

practice 'how to lead an uprising'. Chou and such Shanghai labour leaders as Chao Tse-yen, Chao Shih-yen, Ku Shun-chang, and Lo Yi-ming now succeeded in organizing 50,000 pickets. With Mausers smuggled into the city an 'iron band' of 300 marksmen was trained, to become the only armed force these Shanghai workers had.

On 21 March 1927, the revolutionists called a general strike which closed all the industries of Shanghai. They first seized the police stations, next the arsenal, then the garrison, and after that, victory. Five thousand workers were armed, six battalions of revolutionary troops created, the warlord armies withdrew, and a 'citizens' government' was proclaimed. 'Within two days,' said Chou, 'we won everything but the foreign concessions.'

The International Settlement (jointly controlled by Britain, the US, and Japan) and the French Concession which adjoined it were never attacked during the third insurrection; otherwise the triumph was complete – and short-lived. The Nationalist Army, led by General Pai Chung-hsi, was welcomed to the city by the workers' militia. Then on 12 April the Nationalist-Communist coalition abruptly ended when Chiang Kai-shek set up a separate regime in Nanking, to lead one of history's classic counter-revolutions.

In the French Concession and the International Settlement, Chiang's envoys had secretly conferred with representatives of the foreign powers. They reached agreements to cooperate against the Chinese Communists and their Russian allies – until then also Chiang's allies. Given large sums by Shanghai's bankers, and the blessings of the foreign authorities, including guns and armoured cars, Chiang was also helped by powerful Settlement and Concession underworld leaders. They mobilized hundreds of professional gangsters. Installed in the foreigners' armoured cars, and attired in Nationalist uniforms, the gangsters carried out a night operation in coordination with Chiang's troops, moving in from the rear and other flanks. Taken by complete surprise by troops considered friendly, the militiamen were massacred and their 'citizens' government' bloodily dissolved.

And thus it happened that Chou En-lai, after a remarkably lucky escape, began his life as a fugitive from Kuomintang assassins and a leader of the revolution which finally raised the Red banner in China.

Dozens of Chou En-lai's close co-workers in the Shanghai Uprising were seized and executed. Chou estimated the toll of the 'Shanghai Massacre' at 5,000 lives.[3] He himself was captured by Chiang Kai-shek's Second Division, and General Pai Chung-hsi (later ruler of Kwangsi) issued an order for his execution. But the brother of the division commander had been Chou's student at Whampoa, and he helped Chou to escape.

The Insurrectionist fled to Wuhan * and then to Nanchang, where he helped organize the August First Uprising. Senior member of the Politburo at the time, Chou was secretary of the Front Committee that directed the uprising, which was a fiasco. Next he went to Swatow and held it for ten days against assaults from both foreign gunboats and the native troops of militarists. With the failure and defeat of the Canton Commune, Chou was obliged to work underground – until 1931, when he succeeded in 'running the blockade' and entered the soviet districts of Kiangsi and Fukien. There he was made political commissar to Chu Teh, commander-in-chief of the Red Army. Later Chou became vice-chairman of the revolutionary military council, an office he still held when I met him. There had been years of exhausting struggle in the South, and then the Long March. . . . But of Chou's further story, and of the scenes and events already mentioned, I was shortly to learn more, and in a broader context, from Mao Tse-tung and others.

Chou left me with an impression of a cool, logical, and empirical mind. In his days at Nankai (I had heard from one of his classmates there) Chou had often taken feminine leads in school plays. There was nothing effeminate about the tough, bearded, unsentimental soldier I met in Pai Chia P'ing. But there was charm – one quality in the mixed ingredients that were to make Chou Red China's No. 1 diplomat.

---

* Wuhan is the collective name for the triple cities – Hanyang, Hankow, Wuchang – at the confluence of the Han and Yangtze rivers.

3

Something About Ho Lung[1]

NEXT morning at six I set out with a squad of about forty youths of the communications corps, who were escorting a caravan of goods to Pao An.

I found that only myself, Fu Chin-kuei, an emissary from the Waichiaopu – the Reds' own 'Foreign Office' – and Li Chiang-lin, a Red commander, were mounted. It may not be precisely the word : Fu had a privileged perch on a stout but already heavily laden mule; Li Chiang-lin rode an equally overburdened ass; and I was vaguely astride the lone horse, which at times I could not be quite sure was really there at all.

My animal had a quarter-moon back and a camel gait. His enfeebled legs wobbled so that I expected him at any moment to buckle up and breathe his last. He was especially disconcerting as we crept along the narrow trails hewn from steep cliffs that rose up from the river bed we followed. It seemed to me that any sudden shift of my weight over his sunken flanks would send us both hurtling to the rocky gorge below.

Li Chiang-lin laughed down from his pyramid of luggage at my discomfiture. 'That's a fine saddle you are sitting, *t'ung-chih*, but what is that underneath it?'

At his gibe I could not resist commenting : 'Just tell me this, Li Chiang-lin, how can you fight on dogs like these? Is this how you mount your Red Cavalry?'

'*Pu-shih!* No, you will see! Is your steed *huai-la*? * Well, it's just because we have bad ones like this at the rear that our cavalry is unbeatable at the front! If there is a horse that is fat and can run, not even Mao Tse-tung can keep him from the front! Only the worn-out dogs we use in our rear. And that's how it is with everything : guns, food, clothing, horses, mules, camels, sheep –

* 'Broken' or 'useless'.

the best go to our Red fighters! If it's a horse you want, *t'ung-chih*, go to the front!'

But men? Li explained that it was easier to spare a good man from the front than a good horse.

And Commander Li was a good man, a good Bolshevik and a good storyteller. He had been a Red for ten years, and was a veteran of the Nanchang Uprising of 1927, when communism first became an independent force in China. As I rode, walked, panted and thirsted up and down the broken hills of Shensi beside Commander Li, he recounted incidents and anecdotes one after another, and sometimes, when pressed again and again, even stooped to talk about himself.

A Hunanese, Li had been a middle-school student when he joined the Kuomintang and began to take part in the Great Revolution. He must have entered the Communist Party in the early 1920s; he had worked as a labour organizer with Teng Fa in Hongkong during the great seamen's strike of 1922. He said that in 1925 he had been sent, as part of a Communist-led delegation, to see Ho Lung,* who already had a reputation as a bandit leader. Li's reminiscences are here presented as part of the Red Army legend.

'Ho Lung's men were not bandits, even then,' Li told me, as we sat resting one day beneath some trees that stood beside a cool stream. 'His father had been a leader in the Ke Lao Hui,† and Ho Lung inherited his prestige, so that he became famous throughout Hunan when still a young man. Many stories are told by the Hunanese of his bravery as a youth.

'His father was a military officer in the Ch'ing Dynasty, and one day he was invited to a dinner by his fellow officers. He took his son, Ho Lung, with him. His father was boasting of Ho Lung's fearlessness, and one of the guests decided to test it out. He fired off a gun under the table. They say that Ho Lung did not even blink!

'When we met him he had already been commissioned in the

* See BN.
† The Elder Brother Society, an ancient secret organization which fought the Manchus and was useful to Sun Yat-sen. In structure it strikingly resembled the cell system adopted by the Chinese Communist Party underground.

provincial army. He then controlled a territory through which rich opium caravans had to pass from Yunnan to Hankow, and he lived by taxing them, and did not rob the people. His followers did not rape or carouse, like the troops of many warlord armies, and he did not let them smoke opium. They kept their rifles clean. But it was the custom there to offer opium to guests. Lo Hung himself did not smoke, but when we arrived he had opium pipes and opium brought to the *k'ang*, and over these we talked about revolution.

'The head of our propaganda committee was Chou Yi-chung, a Communist, who had some family connection with Ho Lung. We talked to him for three weeks. Ho Lung had not had much education, except in military affairs, but he was not an ignorant man.

'We established a Party training school in his army, with Chou Yi-chung – who was later killed – as leader. Although it was a Kuomintang Nationalist training school, most of the propagandists were Communists. Many students entered the school and later became political leaders. Besides Ho Lung's army, the school furnished political commissioners for the Third Division, under Yuan Tso-ming, who was then commander of the Left Route Army. Yuan Tso-ming was assassinated by agents of T'ang Sheng-chih, and the Third Division was given to Ho Lung. His enlarged command was called the Twentieth Army, which became part of the main Fourth Group Army * under the Left Kuomintang general, Chang Fa-kuei.'

'What happened to Ho Lung after the Nanchang Uprising?'

'His forces were defeated. He and Chu Teh next moved to Swatow. They were defeated again. The remnant of his army went into the interior, but Ho Lung escaped to Hongkong. Later he smuggled himself to Shanghai, and then, disguised, he returned to Hunan.

'It is said of Ho Lung that he established a soviet district in Hunan with one knife. This was early in 1928. Ho Lung was in hiding in a village, plotting with members of the Ke Lao Hui, when some Kuomintang tax collectors arrived. Leading a few villagers, he attacked the tax collectors and killed them with his own knife, and then disarmed the tax collectors' guard. From this

* Part of the Nationalist-Communist Northern Expedition (1926–7) against the provincial warlords and the Peking Government.

adventure he got enough revolvers and rifles to arm his first peasants' army.'

Ho Lung's fame in the Elder Brother Society extended over all China. The Reds said that he could go unarmed into any village of the country, announce himself to the Elder Brother Society, and form an army. The society's special ritual and language were quite difficult to master, but Ho Lung had the highest 'degrees' and was said to have more than once enlisted an entire Ke Lao Hui branch in the Red Army. His eloquence as a speaker was well known in the Kuomintang. Li said that when he spoke he could 'raise the dead to fight'.

When Ho Lung's Second Front Red Army finally withdrew from the Hunan soviet districts, in 1935, its rifles were reported to number more than 40,000, and this army underwent even greater hardships in its own Long March to the North-West than the main forces from Kiangsi. Thousands died on the snow mountains, and thousands more starved to death or were killed by Nanking bombs. Yet so great was Ho Lung's personal magnetism, and his influence throughout rural China, Li said, that many of his men starved with him and died on the road rather than desert, and thousands of poor men along the route of march joined in to help fill up the dwindling ranks. In the end he reached eastern Tibet, where he finally connected with Chu Teh, with about 20,000 men – most of them barefoot, half-starved, and physically exhausted. After several months of recuperation, his troops were now on the march again, into Kansu, where they were expected to arrive in a few weeks.

'What does Ho Lung look like?' I asked Li.

'He is a big man, and strong as a tiger. He never gets tired. They say he carried many of his wounded men on the march. Even when he was a Kuomintang general he lived as simply as his men. He cares nothing about personal possessions – except horses. He loves horses. Once he had a beautiful horse that he liked very much. It was captured by some enemy troops. Lo Hung went to battle to recover that horse. He got it back!

'Although he is impetuous, Ho Lung is very humble. Since he joined the Communists he has been faithful to the Party, and has never broken Party discipline. He always asks for criticism and listens carefully to advice. His sister is much like him – a big woman, with large [unbound] feet. She has led Red troops in battle herself – and carried wounded men on her back. So has Ho Lung's wife.'

Ho Lung's hatred of the rich had become legendary in China. It was said that landlords and gentry used to flee without further ado, even from places well guarded by Nanking troops, if Ho Lung was reported as far away as 200 li – for he was famous for the swiftness of his movements.

Once Ho Lung arrested a Swiss missionary named Bosshard, and a military court 'sentenced' him to eighteen months' imprisonment for alleged espionage. The Reverend Bosshard's sentence had still not been completed when Ho Lung began the Long March, but he was ordered to move with the army. He was finally released during the march, when his sentence expired, and was given travelling expenses to Yunnanfu. Rather to most people's surprise, the Reverend Bosshard brought out few harsh words about Ho Lung. On the contrary, he was reported to have remarked, 'If the peasants knew what the Communists were like, none of them would run away.'*

It was the noon halt, and we decided to bathe in the cool, inviting stream. We got in and lay on a long, flat rock, while the shallow water rippled over us in cool sheets. Some peasants went past, driving a big cloud of sheep before them; overhead the sky was clear and blue. There was nothing but peace and beauty here, and it was that odd midday moment when the world for centuries has been like this, with only peace, beauty and contentment.

I asked Li Chiang-lin if he were married.

'I was,' he said slowly. 'My wife was killed in the South, by the Kuomintang.'

---

*Related to me by Dr Joseph F. Rock, who talked to Bosshard when he arrived in Yunnanfu.

4

Red Companions

NORTH SHENSI was one of the poorest parts of China I had seen, not excluding western Yunnan. There was no real land scarcity, but there was in many places a serious scarcity of real land – at least real farming land. Here in Shensi a peasant could own as much as 100 *mou* * of land and yet be a poor man. A landlord in this country had to possess at least several hundred *mou* of land, and even on a Chinese scale he could not be considered rich unless his holdings were part of the limited and fertile valley land, where rice and other valued crops could be grown.

The farms of Shensi could have been described as slanting, and many of them also as slipping, for landslides were frequent. The fields were mostly patches laid on the serried landscape, between crevices and small streams. The land seemed rich enough in many places, but the crops grown were strictly limited by the steep gradients, in both quantity and quality. There were few genuine mountains, only endless broken hills. Their sharp-angled shadowing and colouring changed miraculously with the sun's wheel, and towards dusk they became a magnificent sea of purpled hilltops with dark velvety folds running down, like the pleats on a mandarin skirt, to ravines that seemed bottomless.

After the first day I rode little, not so much out of pity for the languishing nag, but because everyone else marched. Li Chiang-lin was the oldest warrior of the company. Most of the others were lads in their teens, hardly more than children. One of these was nicknamed 'Lao Kou', the Old Dog, and walking with him I asked why he had joined the Reds.

He was a southerner and had come all the way from the Fukien soviet districts, on the Red Army's 6,000-mile expedition which foreign military experts refused to believe possible. Yet here was

* One Chinese *mou* is about a sixth of an acre.

Old Dog, seventeen years old, and actually looking fourteen. He had made that march and thought nothing of it. He said he was prepared to walk another 25,000 *li* if the Red Army did.

With him was a lad nicknamed Local Cousin, and he had walked almost as far, from Kiangsi. Local Cousin was sixteen.

Did they like the Red Army? I asked. They looked at me in genuine amazement. It had evidently never occurred to either of them that anyone could not like the Red Army.

'The Red Army has taught me to read and to write,' said Old Dog. 'Here I have learned to operate a radio, and how to aim a rifle straight. The Red Army helps the poor.'

'Is that all?'

'It is good to us and we are never beaten,' added Local Cousin. 'Here everybody is the same. It is not like the White districts, where poor people are slaves of the landlords and the Kuomintang. Here everybody fights to help the poor, and to save China. The Red Army fights the landlords and the White bandits and the Red Army is anti-Japanese. Why should anyone not like such an army as this?'

There was a peasant lad who had joined the Reds in Szechuan, and I asked him why he had done so. He told me that his parents were poor farmers, with only four *mou* of land (less than an acre), which wasn't enough to feed him and his two sisters. When the Reds came to his village, he said, all the peasants welcomed them, brought them hot tea and made sweets for them. The Red dramatists gave plays. It was a happy time. Only the landlords ran. When the land was redistributed his parents received their share. So they were not sorry, but very glad, when he joined the poor people's army.

Another youth, about nineteen, had formerly been an iron-smith's apprentice in Hunan, and he was nicknamed 'T'ieh Lao-hu', the Iron Tiger. When the Reds arrived in the district, he had dropped bellows, pans, and apprenticeship, and, clad only in a pair of sandals and trousers, hurried off to enlist. Why? Because he wanted to fight the masters who starved their apprentices, and to fight the landlords who robbed his parents. He was fighting for the revolution, which would free the poor. The Red Army was good to people and did not rob them and beat them like the White armies. He pulled up his trouser leg and displayed a long white scar, his souvenir of battle.

There was another youth from Fukien, one from Chekiang, several more from Kiangsi and Szechuan, but the majority were natives of Shensi and Kansu. Some had 'graduated' from the Young Vanguards, and (though they looked like infants) had already been Reds for years. Some had joined the Red Army to fight Japan, two had enlisted to escape from slavery,* three had deserted from the Kuomintang troops, but most of them had joined 'because the Red Army is a revolutionary army, fighting landlords and imperialism'.

Then I talked to a squad commander, who was an 'older' man of twenty-four. He had been in the Red Army since 1931. In that year his father and mother were killed by a Nanking bomber, which also destroyed his house, in Kiangsi. When he got home from the fields and found both his parents dead he had at once thrown down his hoe, bidden his wife good-bye, and enlisted with the Communists. One of his brothers, a Red partisan, had been killed in Kiangsi in 1935.

They were a heterogeneous lot, but more truly 'national' in composition than ordinary Chinese armies, usually carefully segregated according to provinces. Their different provincial backgrounds and dialects did not seem to divide them, but became the subject of constant good-natured raillery. I never saw a serious quarrel among them. In fact, during all my travel in the Red districts, I was not to see a single fist fight between Red soldiers, and among young men I thought that remarkable.

Though tragedy had touched the lives of nearly all of them, they were perhaps too young for it to have depressed them much. They seemed to me fairly happy, and perhaps the first consciously happy group of Chinese proletarians I had seen. Passive contentment was the common phenomenon in China, but the higher emotion of happiness, which implies a feeling of positiveness about existence, was rare indeed.

They sang nearly all day on the road, and their supply of songs was endless. Their singing was not done at a command, but was spontaneous, and they sang well. Whenever the spirit moved him,

* Really indentured labour; in those parts it amounted to slavery. Chinese used the word *ya-t'ou*, which literally means 'yoke-head'.

or he thought of an appropriate song, one of them would suddenly burst forth, and commanders and men joined in. They sang at night, too, and learned new folk tunes from the peasants, who brought out their Shensi guitars.

What discipline they had seemed almost entirely self-imposed. When we passed wild apricot trees on the hills there was an abrupt dispersal until everyone had filled his pockets, and somebody always brought me back a handful. Then, leaving the trees looking as if a great wind had struck through them, they moved back into order and quick-timed to make up for the loss. But when we passed private orchards, nobody touched the fruit in them, and the grain and vegetables we ate in the villages were paid for in full.

As far as I could see, the peasants bore no resentment towards my Red companions. Some seemed on close terms of friendship, and very loyal – a fact probably not unconnected with a recent re-division of land and the abolition of taxes. They freely offered for sale what edibles they had, and accepted soviet money without hesitation. When we reached a village at noon or sunset the chairman of the local soviet promptly provided quarters, and designated ovens for our use. I frequently saw peasant women or their daughters volunteer to pull the bellows of the fire of our ovens, and laugh and joke with the Red warriors, in a very emancipated way for Chinese women – especially Shensi women.

On the last day, we stopped for lunch at a village in a green valley, and here all the children came round to examine the first foreign devil many of them had seen. I decided to catechize them.

'What is a Communist?' I asked.

'He is a citizen who helps the Red Army fight the White bandits and the Japanese,' one youngster of nine or ten piped up.

'What else?'

'He helps fight the landlords and the capitalists!'

'But what is a capitalist?' That silenced one child, but another came forward: 'A capitalist is a man who does not work, but makes others work for him.' Oversimplification, perhaps, but I went on:

'Are there any landlords or capitalists here?'

'No!' they all shrieked together. 'They've all run away!'

'Run away? From what?'

'From our RED ARMY !'

'Our' army, a peasant child talking about 'his' army? Well, obviously it wasn't China, but, if not, what was it? Who could have taught them all this?

I was to learn who it was when I examined the textbooks of Red China and met old Santa Claus Hsu T'eh-li,* once president of a normal school in Hunan, now Soviet Commissioner for Education.

Part Three

IN 'DEFENDED PEACE'

I

Soviet Strong Man

SMALL villages were numerous in the North-West, but towns of any size were infrequent. Except for the industries begun by the Reds it was agrarian and in places semipastoral country. Thus it was quite breathtaking to ride out suddenly on the brow of the wrinkled hills and see stretched out below me in a green valley the ancient walls of Pao An, which means 'Defended Peace'.*

Pao An was once a frontier stronghold, during the Chin and T'ang dynasties, against the nomadic invaders to the north. Remains of its fortifications, flame-struck in that afternoon sun, could be seen flanking the narrow pass which once emptied into this valley the conquering legions of the Mongols. There was an inner city, still, where the garrisons were once quartered; and a high defensive masonry, lately improved by the Reds, embraced about a square mile in which the present town was located.

Here at last I found the Red leader whom Nanking had been fighting for ten years – Mao Tse-tung, chairman of the 'Chinese People's Soviet Republic', to employ the official title which had recently been adopted. The old cognomen, 'Chinese Workers' and Peasants' Soviet Republic', was dropped when the Reds began their new policy of struggle for a united front.

Chou En-lai's radiogram had been received and I was expected. A room was provided for me in the 'Foreign Office', and I became temporarily a guest of the soviet state. My arrival resulted in a phenomenal increase of the foreign population of Pao An. The other Occidental resident was a German known as Li Teh T'ung-chih [1] – the 'Virtuous Comrade Li'. Of Li Teh, the only foreign adviser ever with the Chinese Red Army, more later.

I met Mao soon after my arrival: a gaunt, rather Lincolnesque figure, above average height for a Chinese, somewhat stooped,

---

*In December 1936, the Reds occupied Yenan (Fushih), north Shensi, and the capital was transferred there. See Part Twelve.

with a head of thick black hair grown very long, and with large, searching eyes, a high-bridged nose and prominent cheekbones. My fleeting impression was of an intellectual face of great shrewdness, but I had no opportunity to verify this for several days. Next time I saw him, Mao was walking hatless along the street at dusk, talking with two young peasants and gesticulating earnestly. I did not recognize him until he was pointed out to me – moving along unconcernedly with the rest of the strollers, despite the $250,000 which Nanking had hung over his head.

I could have written a book about Mao Tse-tung. I talked with him many nights, on a wide range of subjects, and I heard dozens of stories about him from soldiers and Communists. My written interviews with him totalled about 20,000 words. He told me of his childhood and youth, how he became a leader in the Kuomintang and the Nationalist Revolution, why he became a Communist, and how the Red Army grew. He described the Long March to the North-West and wrote a classical poem about it for me. He told me stories of many other famous Reds, from Chu Teh down to the youth who carried on his shoulders for over 6,000 miles the two iron dispatch boxes that held the archives of the Soviet Government.

The story of Mao's life was a rich cross-section of a whole generation, an important guide to understanding the sources of action in China, and I have included that full exciting period of personal history, just as he told it to me.* But here my own impressions of him may be worth recording.

There would never be any one 'saviour' of China, yet undeniably one felt a certain force of destiny in Mao. It was nothing quick or flashy, but a kind of solid elemental vitality. One felt that whatever there was extraordinary in this man grew out of the uncanny degree to which he synthesized and expressed the urgent demands of millions of Chinese, and especially the peasantry. If their 'demands' and the movement which was pressing them forward were the dynamics which could regenerate China, then in that deeply historical sense Mao Tse-tung might possibly become a very great man. Meanwhile, Mao was of interest as a personality, apart from his political life, because, although his name was as

* See Part Four.

familiar to many Chinese as that of Chiang Kai-shek, very little was known about him, and all sorts of strange legends existed about him. I was the first foreign newspaperman to interview him.

Mao had the reputation of a charmed life. He had been repeatedly pronounced dead by his enemies, only to return to the news columns a few days later, as active as ever. The Kuomintang had also officially 'killed' and buried Chu Teh many times, assisted by occasional corroborations from clairvoyant missionaries. Numerous deaths of the two famous men, nevertheless, did not prevent them from being involved in many spectacular exploits, including the Long March. Mao was indeed in one of his periods of newspaper demise when I visited Red China, but I found him quite substantially alive. There were good reasons why people said that he had a charmed life, however; although he had been in scores of battles, was once captured by enemy troops and escaped, and had the world's highest reward on his head, during all these years he had never once been wounded.

I happened to be in Mao's house one evening when he was given a complete physical examination by a Red surgeon [2] – a man who had studied in Europe and who knew his business – and pronounced in excellent health. He had never had tuberculosis or any 'incurable disease', as had been rumoured by some romantic travellers. His lungs were completely sound, although, unlike most Red commanders, he was an inordinate cigarette smoker. During the Long March, Mao and Li Teh had carried on original botanical research by testing out various kinds of leaves as tobacco substitutes.

Ho Tzu-ch'en, Mao's second wife,[3] a former schoolteacher and a Communist organizer herself, had been less fortunate than her husband. She had suffered more than a dozen wounds, caused by splinters from an air bomb, but all of them were superficial. Just before I left Pao An the Maos were proud parents of a new baby girl. He had two other children by his former wife, Yang K'ai-hui,* the daughter of his favourite professor. She was killed in Changsha in 1930 at the order of General Ho Chien, warlord of Hunan province.

Mao Tse-tung was forty-three years old when I met him in 1936.

*See BN.

He was elected chairman of the provisional Central Soviet Government at the Second All-China Soviet Congress, attended by delegates representing approximately 9,000,000 people then living under Red laws.* Here, incidentally, it may be inserted that Mao Tse-tung estimated the maximum population of the various districts under the direct control of the Central Soviet Government in 1934 as follows: Kiangsi Soviet, 3,000,000; Hupeh-Anhui-Honan Soviet, 2,000,000; Hunan-Kiangsi-Hupeh Soviet, 1,000,000; Kiangsi-Hunan Soviet, 1,000,000; Chekiang-Fukien Soviet, 1,000,000; Hunan-Hupeh Soviet, 1,000,000; total, 9,000,000. Fantastic estimates ranging as high as ten times that figure were evidently achieved by adding up the entire population in every area in which the Red Army or Red partisans had been reported as operating. Mao laughed when I quoted him the figure of '80,000,000' people living under the Chinese soviets, and said that when they had that big an area the revolution would be practically won. But of course there were many millions in all the areas where Red partisans had operated.

The influence of Mao Tse-tung throughout the Communist world of China was probably greater than that of anyone else. He was a member of nearly everything – the revolutionary military committee, the political bureau of the Central Committee, the finance commission, the organization committee, the public health commission, and others. His real influence was asserted through his domination of the political bureau,† which had decisive power in the policies of the Party, the government, and the army. Yet, while everyone knew and respected him, there was – as yet, at least – no ritual of hero worship built up around him. I never met a Chinese Red who drooled 'our-great-leader' phrases,‡ I did not hear Mao's name used as a synonym for the Chinese people, but still I never met one who did not like 'the Chairman' – as everyone called him –

---

*See Mao Tse-tung et al., *Fundamental Laws of the Chinese Soviet Republic* (London, Martin Lawrence, 1934). It contains the provisional constitution of the soviets, and a statement of basic objectives during the 'bourgeois-democratic' phase of the revolution. See also Mao Tse-tung, *Red China: President Mao Tse-tung Reports on the Progress of the Chinese Soviet Republic* (London, Martin Lawrence, 1934).

† See Part Four, Chapter 6, text and note 3.

‡ See Mao Tse-tung, BN.

and admire him. The role of his personality in the movement was clearly immense.

Mao seemed to me a very interesting and complex man. He had the simplicity and naturalness of the Chinese peasant, with a lively sense of humour and a love of rustic laughter. His laughter was even active on the subject of himself and the shortcomings of the soviets – a boyish sort of laughter which never in the least shook his inner faith in his purpose. He was plain-speaking and plain-living, and some people might have considered him rather coarse and vulgar. Yet he combined curious qualities of naïveté with incisive wit and worldly sophistication.

I think my first impression – dominantly one of native shrewdness – was probably correct. And yet Mao was an accomplished scholar of Classical Chinese, an omnivorous reader, a deep student of philosophy and history, a good speaker, a man with an unusual memory and extraordinary powers of concentration, an able writer, careless in his personal habits and appearance but astonishingly meticulous about details of duty, a man of tireless energy, and a political strategist of considerable genius. It was interesting that many Japanese regarded him as the ablest Chinese strategist alive.

The Reds were putting up some new buildings in Pao An, but accommodations were very primitive while I was there. Mao lived with his wife in a two-room *yao-fang* with bare, poor, map-covered walls. He had known much worse, and as the son of a 'rich' peasant in Hunan he had also known better. The Maos' chief luxury (like Chou's) was a mosquito net. Otherwise Mao lived very much like the rank and file of the Red Army. After ten years of leadership of the Reds, after hundreds of confiscations of property of landlords, officials, and tax collectors, he owned only his blankets and a few personal belongings, including two cotton uniforms. Although he was a Red Army commander as well as chairman, he wore on his coat collar only the two red bars that are the insignia of the ordinary Red soldier.

I went with Mao several times to mass meetings of the villagers and the Red cadets, and to the Red theatre. He sat inconspicuously in the midst of the crowd and enjoyed himself hugely. I remember once, between acts at the Anti-Japanese Theatre, there was a general demand for a duet by Mao Tse-tung and Lin Piao, the twenty-eight-year-old president of the Hung Chung Ta-hsueh (Red Army University) and formerly a famed young cadet on Chiang Kai-shek's staff. Lin blushed like a schoolboy and got them out of the 'command performance' by a graceful speech, calling upon the women Communists for a song instead.

Mao's food was the same as everybody's, but being a Hunanese he had the southerner's *ai-la,* or 'love of pepper'. He even had pepper cooked into his bread. Except for this passion, he scarcely seemed to notice what he ate. One night at dinner I heard him expand on a theory of pepper-loving peoples being revolutionaries. He first submitted his own province, Hunan, famous for the revolutionaries it has produced. Then he listed Spain, Mexico, Russia, and France to support his contention, but laughingly had to admit defeat when somebody mentioned the well-known Italian love of red pepper and garlic, in refutation of his theory. One of the most amusing songs of the 'bandits', incidentally, was a ditty called 'The Hot Red Pepper'. It told of the disgust of the pepper with his pointless vegetable existence, waiting to be eaten, and how he ridiculed the contentment of the cabbages, spinach, and beans with their invertebrate careers. He ends up by leading a vegetable insurrection. 'The Hot Red Pepper' was a great favourite with Chairman Mao.

He appeared to be quite free from symptoms of megalomania, but he had a deep sense of personal dignity, and something about him suggested a power of ruthless decision when he deemed it necessary. I never saw him angry, but I heard from others that on occasions he had been roused to an intense and withering fury. At such times his command of irony and invective was said to be classic and lethal.

I found him surprisingly well informed on current world politics. Even on the Long March, it seems, the Reds received news broadcasts by radio, and in the North-West they published their own newspapers. Mao was exceptionally well read in world history and had a realistic conception of European social and political conditions. He was very interested in the Labour Party of England, and questioned me intensely about its present policies, soon exhausting all my information. It seemed to me that he found it difficult to understand why, in a country where workers were enfranchised, there was still no workers' government. I was afraid my answers did not satisfy him. He expressed profound contempt for Ramsay MacDonald, whom he designated as a *han-chien* – an archtraitor of the British people.

His opinion of President Roosevelt was rather interesting. He believed him to be anti-Fascist, and thought China could cooperate with such a man. He asked innumerable questions about the New Deal, and Roosevelt's foreign policy. The questioning showed a remarkably clear conception of the objectives of both. He regarded Mussolini and Hitler as mountebanks, but considered Mussolini intellectually a much abler man, a real Machiavellian, with a knowledge of history, while Hitler was a mere will-less puppet of the reactionary capitalists.

Mao had read a number of books about India and had some definite opinions on that country. Chief among these was that Indian independence would never be realized without an agrarian revolution. He questioned me about Gandhi, Jawaharlal Nehru, Suhasini Chattopadhyaya, and other Indian leaders I had known. He knew something about the Negro question in America, and unfavourably compared the treatment of Negroes and American Indians with policies in the Soviet Union towards national minorities. He was interested when I pointed out certain great differences in the historical background of the Negro in America and that of minorities in Russia.

Mao was an ardent student of philosophy. Once when I was having nightly interviews with him on Communist history, a visitor brought him several new books on philosophy, and Mao asked me to postpone our engagements. He consumed those books in three or four nights of intensive reading, during which he seemed oblivious to everything else. He had not confined his reading to Marxist philosophers, but also knew something of the ancient Greeks, of Spinoza, Kant, Goethe, Hegel, Rousseau, and others.

I often wondered about Mao's own sense of responsibility over the question of force, violence, and the 'necessity of killing'. He had in his youth had strongly liberal and humanistic tendencies, and the transition from idealism to realism evidently had first been made philosophically. Although he was peasant-born, he did not as a youth personally suffer much from oppression of the landlords, as did many Reds, and, although Marxism was the core of his thought, I deduced that class hatred was for him probably an intellectually acquired mechanism in the bulwark of his philosophy rather than an instinctive impulse to action.

There seemed to be nothing in him that might be called religious feeling. He was a humanist in a fundamental sense; he believed in man's ability to solve man's problems. I thought he had probably on the whole been a moderating influence in the Communist movement where life and death were concerned.

Mao worked thirteen or fourteen hours a day, often until very late at night, frequently retiring at two or three. He seemed to have an iron constitution. That he traced to a youth spent in hard work on his father's farm, and to an austere period in his school-days when he had formed a kind of Spartan club with some comrades. They used to fast, go on long hikes in the wooded hills of South China, swim in the coldest weather, walk shirtless in the rain and sleet – to toughen themselves. They intuitively knew that the years ahead would demand the capacity for withstanding great hardship and suffering.

Mao once spent a summer tramping all over Hunan, his native province. He earned his bread by working from farm to farm, and sometimes by begging. Another time, for days he ate nothing but hard beans and water – again a process of 'toughening' his stomach. The friendships he made on country rambles in his early youth were of great value to him when, some ten years later, he began to organize thousands of farmers in Hunan into the famous peasant unions which became the first base of the soviets, after the Kuomintang broke with the Communists in 1927.

Mao impressed me as a man of considerable depth of feeling. I remember that his eyes moistened once or twice when he was speaking of dead comrades, or recalling incidents in his youth, during the rice riots and famines of Hunan, when some starving peasants were beheaded in his province for demanding food from the yamen. One soldier told me of seeing Mao give his coat away to a wounded man at the front. They said that he refused to wear shoes when the Red warriors had none.

Yet I doubted very much if he would ever command great respect from the intellectual élite of China, perhaps not entirely because he had an extraordinary mind, but because he had the personal habits of a peasant. The Chinese disciples of Pareto might have thought him uncouth. Talking with Mao one day, I saw him absent-mindedly turn down the belt of his trousers and search for some guests – but then it is just possible that Pareto might have done a little searching himself if he had lived in similar circumstances. But I am sure that Pareto would never have taken off his trousers in the presence of the president of the Red Army University – as Mao did once when I was interviewing Lin Piao. It was extremely hot inside the little cave. Mao lay down on the bed, pulled off his pants, and for twenty minutes carefully studied a military map on the wall – interrupted occasionally by Lin Piao, who asked for confirmation of dates and names, which Mao invariably knew. His nonchalant habits fitted with his complete indifference to personal appearance, although the means were at hand to fix himself up like a chocolate-box general or a politician's picture of *Who's Who in China*.

Except for a few weeks when he was ill, he walked most of the 6,000 miles of the Long March, like the rank and file. He could have achieved high office and riches by 'betraying' to the Kuomintang, and this applied to most Red commanders. The tenacity with which these Communists for ten years clung to their principles could not be fully evaluated unless one knew the history of 'silver bullets' in China, by means of which other rebels were bought off.

I was able to check up on many of Mao's assertions, and usually found them to be correct. He subjected me to mild doses of political propaganda, but it was interesting compared to what I had received in non-bandit quarters. He never imposed any censorship on me, in either my writing or my photography, courtesies for which I was grateful. He did his best to see that I got facts to explain various aspects of soviet life.

2

Basic Communist Policies

WHAT were the fundamental policies of the Chinese Reds? I had a dozen or more talks on this subject with Mao Tse-tung and other leading Communists. But before one examined their policies it was necessary to have some conception of the nature of the long struggle between the Communists and Nanking. To comprehend even the recent events in the Reddening North-West one had first to look at a few facts of history, as they looked to Chinese Communists.

In the following paragraphs I have paraphrased, in part, the comments of Lo Fu (Chang Wen-t'ien),* the English-speaking general secretary of the Communist Party Politburo, whom I interviewed in Pao An.

The Chinese Communist Party was founded only in 1921 (an event reserved for more detailed discussion in a later context). It grew rapidly until 1923, when a two-party alliance was formed with Dr Sun Yat-sen's Kuomintang (commonly called the Nationalist Party). Dr Sun had independently reached an entente with the Russian Communist Party, under Lenin, which offered Sun material and political help. Neither the Kungch'antang (Chinese Communist Party) nor the Kuomintang held power at the time, but Sun was supported by provincial warlords in South China. They permitted Sun to set up a provisional all-China government in Canton, in rivalry to the Peking Government, which was backed by a coterie of northern warlords and was recognized by the foreign powers. From 1923 onward the Kuomintang was reorganized with the help of Russian political advisers, along lines of the party of Lenin. With Sun's concurrence, some members of the young Chinese Communist Party also joined the Kuomintang. Sun Yatsen was a nationalist patriot whose ambition was to recover China's

*See BN.

sovereign independence; beyond that, his concepts of social revolution (as expressed in his *Three Principles of the People*) were a vague mixture of reform capitalism and socialism. The Communists supported Sun's national independence aspirations but they aimed ultimately at a proletarian dictatorship.

Moscow had at first (1918–22) tried to advance Russian revolutionary interests in the Far East by working with the Peking warlords. In 1921–2 the Comintern reassessed the value of potential allies in China after its delegate, Henricus Sneevliet,* returned with a favourable report on the prospects of Dr Sun Yat-sen. Completely disillusioned after Western rejection of his plans (at the Washington Conference, 1921–2) for the 'international development of China', Dr Sun now welcomed Russian offers of aid extended through the Comintern's agent, Adolf Joffe. A complete reorientation of Soviet policy began with the Sun-Joffe agreement. In the Sun-Joffe joint statement (26 January 1923), which became the basis of the three-way alliance (Kuomintang–Chinese Communist–Soviet Russia), it was agreed that 'conditions do not exist here [in China] for the successful establishment of communism or socialism', while the 'chief and immediate aim of China is the achievement of national union and national independence', in the struggle for which the Chinese 'could depend on the aid of Russia'. When Mikhail Borodin arrived in Canton late in 1922, to become Sun's adviser and head of the Soviet mission, he held dual positions as a delegate of the Soviet Politburo and a delegate of the Comintern, itself already an instrument of Soviet foreign policy. (Inherent in this dualism from the outset were contradictions between Russian national interests and the interests of the Chinese Communist Party, which were never resolved.)

The durability of the alliance, as far as Chinese Communists were concerned, depended upon the continued acceptance by the Kuomintang of two major objectives. The first recognized the necessity for an anti-imperialist policy – the recovery of complete political, territorial, and economic sovereignty by revolutionary action. The second demanded an internal policy of 'antifeudalism and antimilitarism' – the overthrow of landlords and warlords, and the construction of new forms of social, economic, and political

*See Part Four, Chapter 4.

life, which both the Communists and the Kuomintang agreed must be 'democratic' in character.

'Democratic' was a word used by Dr Sun to cover his paternalistic concept of a revolution in which the 'people' or masses were to achieve 'modernization' under the 'tutelage' of his Nationalist Party. For the Communists the concept was a 'bourgeois-democratic' revolution that could be manipulated, by stages, towards socialism, under the 'hegemony' of their party. The two-party government formed at Canton consisted only of members of the Central Executive Committee of the Kuomintang – which from 1924 to 1927 included Communists. It was never more 'legal' or 'democratic' than its own organic structure. Communist membership in Kuomintang central organs was limited to one third of the total.

The Communists regarded the successful fulfilment of Dr Sun's 'bourgeois-democratic' revolution as a necessary preliminary to the socialist society later to be established. Their position in support of a 'democratic independence and liberation' movement seemed logical.

Dr Sun Yat-sen died in 1925, before the revolution was completed. Cooperation between the Kuomintang and the Kungch'antang came to an end in 1927. From the Communist viewpoint, the Nationalist Revolution could also be said to have ended then. The right wing of the Kuomintang, dominated by the new militarism, and supported by certain foreign powers, the treaty-port * bankers, and the landlords, broke away from the Left Kuomintang Government at Hankow. It formed a regime at Nanking under Chiang Kai-shek which the Communists and the majority of the Kuomintang at that time regarded as 'counter-revolutionary', that is, against the 'bourgeois-democratic revolution' itself.

The Kuomintang soon reconciled itself to the Nanking *coup d'état*,† but communism became a crime punishable by death. What the Reds conceived to be the two main points of nationalism – the anti-imperialist movement and the democratic revolution –

---

* Coastal and inland ports opened to foreign commerce by treaties imposed on China during the Opium Wars and later.

† Except for a splinter left-wing element which came to be personified by Mme Sun Yat-sen (Soong Ch'ing-ling). See BN.

were in practice abandoned. Militarists' civil wars and, later, intensive war against the rising agrarian revolution ensued. Many thousands of Communists and former peasant-union and labour leaders were killed. The unions were suppressed. An 'enlightened dictatorship' made war on all forms of opposition. Even so, quite a number of Communists survived in the army, and the Party held together throughout a period of great terrorism. In 1937, despite the expenditure of billions of dollars in civil war against them, the Red armies occupied in the North-West the largest (though sparsely populated) connected territory ever under their complete control.

Of course the Reds believed that the decade of history since 1927 had richly validated their thesis that national independence and democracy (which the Kuomintang also set as its objective) could not be achieved in China without an anti-imperialist policy externally, and an agrarian revolution internally. To see why communism steadily increased its following, especially among patriotic youth, and why at the moment it still projected upon the screen of history the shadows of great upheaval and change in the Orient, one had to note its main contentions. What were they?

First of all, the Reds argued that, after Nanking split the living forces of the revolution, China rapidly lost much ground. Compromise followed compromise. The failure to realize agrarian reforms resulted in widespread discontent and open rebellion from the rural population in many parts of the country. General conditions of poverty and distress among the rural populace seriously worsened. China now had some passable motor roads, an excellent fleet of airplanes, and a New Life movement,* but reports came in daily of catastrophes which in China were considered more or less routine. Even as I was writing this chapter, for example, the press brought this appalling news from Central and West China :

Famine conditions continue to be reported in Honan, Anhui, Shensi, Kansu, Szechuan, and Kweichow. Quite evidently the country faces one of the most severe famines of many years, and thousands have already died. A recent survey by the Szechuan Famine Relief Commission discovered that 30,000,000 people are now in the famine belt of

*Launched by Chiang in an attempt to revivify certain rules of personal behaviour based on Confucian teachings.

that province, where bark and 'Goddess-of-Mercy' earth* are being consumed by tens of thousands. There are said to be over 400,000 famine refugees in Shensi, over 1,000,000 in Kansu, some 7,000,000 in Honan, and 3,000,000 in Kweichow. The famine in Kweichow is admitted by the official Central News to be the most serious in 100 years, affecting sixty districts of the province.[1]

Szechuan was one of the provinces where taxes had been collected sixty years or more in advance, and thousands of acres of land had been abandoned by farmers unable to pay rents and outrageous loan interest. In my files were items, collected over a period of six years, showing comparable distress in many other provinces. There were few signs that the rate of frequency of these calamities was diminishing.

While the mass of the rural population was rapidly going bankrupt, concentration of land and wealth in the hands of a small number of landlords and land-owning usurers increased in proportion to the general decline of independent farming.† Sir Frederick Leith-Ross was reported to have said that there was no middle class in China, but only the incredibly poor and the very rich. Enormous taxes, the share-crop method, and the whole historical system of social, political, and economic relationships described by Dr Karl August Wittfogel as the 'Asiatic mode of production', contrived to leave the landless peasantry constantly heavily in debt, without reserves, and unable to meet such crises as drought, famine, and flood.

Mao Tse-tung, when a secretary of the Kuomintang's Committee on the Peasant Movement in 1926 (and a candidate to the Central Executive Committee of the Kuomintang),‡ supervised the collection of land statistics for areas in twenty-one provinces. He asserted that this investigation indicated that resident landlords, rich

---

* Balls of mud and straw eaten to appease hunger, and often resulting in death.

† See Bibliography for a few introductory works on land tenure in China.

‡ Mao was also deputy chief of the Kuomintang propaganda department and deputy director of its Peasant Movement Training Institute, where he lectured to many cadres who later joined him in the formation of the Red Army.

peasants, officials, absentee landlords, and usurers, about 10 per cent of the whole rural population, together owned over 70 per cent of the cultivable land in China. About 15 per cent was owned by middle peasants. But over 65 per cent of the rural population, made up of poor peasants, tenants, and farm workers, owned only from 10 to 15 per cent of the total arable land.[2]

'These statistics were suppressed after the counter-revolution,' according to Mao. 'Now, ten years later, it is still impossible to get any statement from Nanking on land distribution in China.'

The Communists alleged that rural bankruptcy had been accelerated by the Kuomintang's policy of 'non-resistance to imperialism' – in particular, Japanese imperialism. As a result of Nanking's 'no-war policy' against Japan, China had lost to Japanese invaders about a fifth of her national territory, over 40 per cent of her railway mileage, 85 per cent of her unsettled lands, a large part of her coal, 80 per cent of her iron deposits, 37 per cent of her finest forest lands, and about 40 per cent of her national export trade. Japan now controlled over 75 per cent of the total pig iron and iron-mining enterprises of what remained of China, and over half of the textile industry of China. The conquest of Manchuria also robbed China of its own best market as well as its most accessible raw materials. In 1931, Manchuria took more than 27 per cent of its total imports from other Chinese provinces, but in 1935 China could sell Manchukuo only 4 per cent of those imports. It presented Japan with the region of China best suited for industrial development – and enabled her to prevent that development and shuttle the raw materials to her own industries. It gave to Japan the continental base from which she could inexorably continue her aggression in China. Such changes, many felt, completely wiped out the benefits of any reforms that Nanking might be able to claim to its credit for generations in the future – even provided the rest of China remained intact.

And what was achieved by Nanking's nine years of war against the Reds? The North-West junta had recently summarized the results in a manifesto opposing preparations for the sixth anti-Red 'final annihilation' drive.* It reminded us that Manchuria had

*From a statement issued by the 'United Anti-Japanese Council' at the time of the Sian Incident. See Part Twelve, Chapter 2.

gone to Japan during one 'final-annihilation' drive, Shanghai had been invaded during another, Jehol had been given up during the third, East Hopei lost during still another, and the sovereignty of Hopei and Chahar provinces had been badly impaired during the fifth 'remnant-bandit extermination'.

Of course Nanking could not stop civil war as long as the Reds continued to attempt to overthrow the government by force. In April 1932, when the Chinese Soviet Republic declared war against Japan, it had offered to combine with anti-Japanese elements. Again in January 1933 it had proposed to unite with 'any armed force' in a 'united front from below'. There was no real offer, however, to compromise with Chiang Kai-shek.[3] By mid 1936 the Communists (and the Comintern) had radically changed their position. In a search for broad national unity, they included the Kuomintang and even Chiang Kai-shek. The Chinese Communist Party now promised to unite its Red Army and the soviet districts under the sovereignty of the Kuomintang Central Government, provided that the latter would agree to 'establish democratic representative government, resist Japan, enfranchise the people, and guarantee civil liberties to the masses'.[*] In other words, the Reds were ready to 'remarry' the Kuomintang if it would return to the 'bourgeois-nationalist' programme of anti-imperialism and antifeudalism. But of these two basic aims they realized that the fight for national survival was paramount, and must be conducted even at the expense of modifying the internal struggle over the land question; that class antagonisms might have to be sublimated in, certainly could not be satisfied without, the successful solution of the external struggle against Japan.

To quote Mao in his interview with me:

'The fundamental issue before the Chinese people today is the struggle against Japanese imperialism. Our soviet policy is decisively conditioned by this struggle. Japan's warlords hope to subjugate the whole of China and make of the Chinese people their colonial slaves. The fight against the Japanese invasion, the fight against Japanese economic and military conquest – these are the main

---

[*] But Mao Tse-tung had no intention, of course, as he would soon make clear to me, of surrendering either Communist-held territory or the political independence of his party to the Generalissimo.

tasks that must be remembered in analyzing soviet politics.

'Japanese imperialism is not only the enemy of China but also of all people of the world who desire peace. Especially it is the enemy of those peoples with interests on the Pacific Ocean, namely, the American, British, French, and Soviet Russian nations. The Japanese continental policy, as well as naval policy, is directed not only against China but also against those countries ...

'What do we expect from the foreign powers? We expect at least that friendly nations will not help Japanese imperialism, and will adopt a neutral position. We hope that they will actively help China to resist invasion and conquest.'

In using the word 'imperialism', the Communists sharply distinguished between Japan and friendly and nonaggressive democratic capitalist powers. Mao Tse-tung explained:

'Concerning the question of imperialism in general we observe that among the great powers some express unwillingness to engage in a new world war, some are not ready to see Japan occupy China: countries such as America, Great Britain, France, Holland, and Belgium. Then there are countries permanently under the menace of the aggressive powers, such as Siam, the Philippines, Central American countries, Canada, India, Australia, the Dutch Indies, etc. – all more or less under the direct threat of Japan. We consider them our friends and invite their cooperation ...

'So, except for Japan and those countries which help Japanese imperialism, the categories mentioned above can be organized into antiwar, anti-aggression, anti-Fascist world alliances. ... In the past, Nanking has received much help from America, England, and other countries. Most of these funds and supplies have been used in civil war. For every Red soldier killed, Nanking has slain many peasants and workers. According to a recent article by the banker Chang Nai-ch'i it has cost the Chinese people about $80,000 for every Red soldier killed by Nanking.* Such "help" therefore does not seem to us to have been rendered to the Chinese people.

'Only when Nanking determines to cease civil war and to fight against Japanese imperialism, and unites with the people's revolu-

---

*Far more civilians and 'partisans' were killed than regular Red soldiers. Mr Chang's estimate included costs of lost labour, lost crops, ruined villages and towns, ruined farmlands, etc., as well as actual military expenses.

tion to organize a democratic national defence government – only then can such help be of real benefit to the Chinese nation.'

I asked Mao whether the soviets were in favour of cancelling unequal treaties. He pointed out that many of these unequal treaties had, in effect, already been destroyed by the Japanese, especially in the case of Manchuria. But as for the future attitude of a representative government in China, he declared:

'Those powers that help or do not oppose China in her war of independence and liberation should be invited to enjoy close friendly relations with China. Those powers which actively assist Japan should naturally not be given the same treatment; for example, Germany and Italy, which have already established special relations with Manchukuo, and cannot be regarded as powers friendly to the Chinese people.

'With friendly powers, China will peacefully negotiate treaties of mutual advantage. With other powers China is prepared to maintain cooperation on a much broader scale. ... So far as Japan is concerned, China must by the act of war of liberation cancel all unequal treaties, confiscate all Japanese imperialist holdings, and annul Japan's special privileges, concessions, and influence in this country. Concerning our relations with other powers, we Communists do not advocate any measure that may place at disadvantage the world position of China in her struggle against Japanese imperialism.

'When China really wins her independence, then legitimate foreign trading interests will enjoy more opportunities than ever before. The power of production and consumption of 450,000,000 people is not a matter that can remain the exclusive interest of the Chinese, but one that must engage the many nations. Our millions of people, once really emancipated, with their great latent productive possibilities freed for creative activity in every field, can help improve the economy as well as raise the cultural level of the whole world. But the productive power of the Chinese people has in the past scarcely been touched; on the contrary, it has been suppressed – both by native militarists and Japanese imperialism.'

Finally I asked, 'Is it possible for China to make anti-imperialist alliances with democratic capitalist powers?'

'Anti-imperialist, anti-Fascist alliances,' replied Mao, 'are in the nature of peace alliances, and for mutual defence against war-making nations. A Chinese anti-Fascist pact with capitalist democracies is perfectly possible and desirable. It is to the interest of such countries to join the anti-Fascist front in self-defence ...

'If China should become completely colonized it would mean the beginning of a long series of terrible and senseless wars. A choice must be made. For itself, the Chinese people will take the road of struggle against its oppressors, and we hope also that the statesmen and people of foreign nations will march with us on this road, and not follow the dark paths laid down by the bloody history of imperialism ...

'To oppose Japan successfully, China must also seek assistance from other powers. *This does not mean, however, that China is incapable of fighting Japan without foreign help!* The Chinese Communist Party, the Soviet Government, the Red Army, and the Chinese people are ready to unite with any power to shorten the duration of this war. But if none join us we are determined to carry on alone.'

Did the Reds really imagine that China could defeat Japan's mighty war machine? I believed that they did. What was the peculiar shape of logic on which they based their assumption of triumph? It was one of dozens of questions I put to Mao Tse-tung.

3

On War With Japan[1]

ON 16 July 1936, I sat on a square, backless stool inside Mao Tse-tung's residence. It was after nine at night, 'Taps' had been sounded and nearly all lights were out. The walls and ceiling of Mao's home were of solid rock; beneath was a flooring of bricks. Cotton gauze extended halfway up windows also hollowed from stone, and candles sputtered on the square, unpainted table before us, spread with a clean red-felt cloth. Mrs Mao was in an adjoining room making compote from wild peaches purchased that day from a fruit merchant. Mao sat with his legs crossed, in a deep shelf hewn from the solid rock, and smoked a Chien Men cigarette.

Seated next to me was Wu Liang-p'ing,* a young soviet 'func-tionary' who acted as interpreter in my 'formal' interviews with Mao Tse-tung. I wrote down in full in English Mao Tse-tung's answers to my questions, and these were then translated into Chinese and corrected by Mao, who is noted for his insistence upon accuracy of detail. With the assistance of Mr Wu, the interviews were retranslated into English, and because of such precautions I believe these pages to contain few errors of reporting. They were, of course, the strictly partisan views of the leader of the Chinese Communists – views being made known to the Western world for the first time.

Wu Liang-p'ing, to whom I am indebted for much assistance in gathering material, was the son of a rich landlord in Fenghua, Chiang Kai-shek's native district in Chekiang. He had fled from there some years ago when his father, apparently an ambitious burgher, wished to betroth him to a relative of the Generalissimo. Wu was a graduate of Ta Hsia University, in Shanghai. There Patrick Givens, chief of the Criminal Investigation Department of the British-controlled police of the International Settlement, had arrested Wu Liang-p'ing. Charged with Communist activity, Wu

* See BN.

spent two years in the Settlement's Ward Road Jail. He had studied in France, England, and Russia, was twenty-six years old, and for his energetic labours as a Communist received his uniform, room, and food – the latter consisting chiefly of millet and noodles.

Mao began to answer my first question, about Communist policy towards Japan, which was this: 'If Japan is defeated and driven from China, do you think that the major problem of "foreign imperialism" will in general have been solved here?'

'Yes. If other imperialist countries do not act like Japan, and if China defeats Japan, it will mean that the Chinese masses have awakened, have mobilized, and have established their independence. Therefore the main problem of imperialism will have been solved.'

'Under what conditions do you think the Chinese people can exhaust and defeat the forces of Japan?' I asked.

He replied: 'Three conditions will guarantee our success: first, the achievement of the National United Front against Japanese imperialism in China; second, the formation of a World Anti-Japanese United Front; third, revolutionary action by the oppressed peoples at present suffering under Japanese imperialism. Of these, the central necessity is the union of the Chinese people themselves.'

My question: 'How long do you think such a war would last?'

Mao's answer: 'That depends on the strength of the Chinese People's Front, many conditioning factors in China and Japan, and the degree of international help given to China, as well as the rate of revolutionary development in Japan. If the Chinese People's Front is powerfully homogeneous, if it is effectively organized horizontally and vertically, if the international aid to China is considerable from those governments which recognize the menace of Japanese imperialism to their own interests, if revolution comes quickly in Japan, the war* will be short and victory speedily won. If these conditions are not realized, however, the war will be very long, but in the end, just the same, Japan will be defeated, only the sacrifices will be extensive and it will be a painful period for the whole world.'

---

*The Communists were already 'officially' at war with Japan, the Soviet Government having declared such a war in a proclamation issued in Kiangsi in April 1932. See *Red China: President Mao Tse-tung Reports . . .*, p. 6. (See Bibliography.)

Question: 'What is your opinion of the probable course of development of such a war, politically and militarily?'

Answer: 'Two questions are involved here – the policy of the foreign powers, and the strategy of China's armies.

'Now, the Japanese continental policy is already fixed and is well known. Those who imagine that by further sacrifices of Chinese sovereignty, by making economic, political, or territorial compromises and concessions, they can halt the advance of Japan, are only indulging in Utopian fancy. Nanking has in the past adopted erroneous policies based on this strategy, and we have only to look at the map of East Asia to see the results of it.

'But we know well enough that not only North China but the Lower Yangtze Valley and our southern seaports are already included in the Japanese continental programme. Moreover, it is just as clear that the Japanese navy aspires to blockade the China seas and to seize the Philippines, Siam, Indochina, Malaya, and the Dutch East Indies. In the event of war, Japan will try to make them her strategic bases, cutting off Great Britain, France, and America from China, and monopolizing the seas of the southern Pacific. These moves are included in Japan's plans of naval strategy, copies of which we have seen. And such naval strategy will be coordinated with the land strategy of Japan.

'Many people think it would be impossible for China to continue her fight against Japan once the latter had seized certain strategic points on the coast and enforced a blockade. This is nonsense. To refute it we have only to refer to the history of the Red Army. In certain periods our forces have been exceeded numerically some ten or twenty times by the Kuomintang troops, which were also superior to us in equipment. Their economic resources many times surpassed ours, and they received material assistance from the outside. Why, then, has the Red Army scored success after success against the White troops and not only survived till today but increased its power?

'The explanation is that the Red Army and the Soviet Government had created among all people within their areas a rocklike solidarity, because everyone in the soviets was ready to fight for his government against the oppressors, because every person was voluntarily and consciously fighting for his own interests and what he believed to be right. Second, in the struggle of the soviets the people were led by men of ability, strength, and determination, equipped with deep understanding of the strategic, political, economic, and military needs of their position. The Red Army won its many victories – beginning with only a few dozen rifles in the hands of determined revolutionaries – because its solid base in the people attracted friends even among the White troops as well as among the civilian populace. The enemy was infinitely our superior militarily, but politically it was immobilized.

'In the anti-Japanese war the Chinese people would have on their side greater advantages than those the Red Army has utilized in its struggle with the Kuomintang. China is a very big nation, and it cannot be said to be conquered until every inch of it is under the sword of the invader. If Japan should succeed in occupying even a large section of China, getting possession of an area with as many as 100 or even 200 million people, we would still be far from defeated. We would still have left a great force to fight against Japan's warlords, who would also have to fight a heavy and constant rearguard action throughout the entire war.

'As for munitions, the Japanese cannot seize our arsenals in the interior, which are sufficient to equip Chinese armies for many years, nor can they prevent us from capturing great amounts of arms and ammunition from their own hands. By the latter method the Red Army has equipped its present forces from the Kuomintang: for nine years they have been our "ammunition carriers". What infinitely greater possibilities would open up for the utilization of such tactics as won our arms for us if the whole Chinese people were united against Japan!

'Economically, of course, China is not unified. But the uneven development of China's economy also presents advantages in a war against the highly centralized and highly concentrated economy of Japan. For example, to sever Shanghai from the rest of China is not as disastrous to the country as would be, for instance, the severance of New York from the rest of America. Moreover, it is impossible for Japan to isolate all of China: China's North-West, South-West, and West cannot be blockaded by Japan.

'Thus once more the central point of the problem becomes the mobilization and unification of the entire Chinese people and the building up of a united front, such as has been advocated by the Communist Party ever since 1932.'

Question: 'In the event of a Sino-Japanese war, do you think there will be a revolution in Japan?'

Answer: 'The Japanese revolution is not only a possibility but a certainty. It is inevitable and will begin to occur promptly after the first severe defeats suffered by the Japanese Army.'

Question: 'Do you think Soviet Russia and Outer Mongolia would become involved in this war, and would come to the assistance of China? Under what circumstances is that likely?'

Answer: 'Of course the Soviet Union is also not an isolated country. It cannot ignore events in the Far East. It cannot remain passive. Will it complacently watch Japan conquer all China and make of it a strategic base from which to attack the USSR? Or will it help the Chinese people to oppose their Japanese oppressors, win their independence, and establish friendly relations with the Russian people? We think Russia will choose the latter course.

'We believe that once the Chinese people have their own government and begin this war of resistance and want to establish friendly alliances with the USSR, as well as other friendly powers, the Soviet Union will be in the vanguard to shake hands with us. The struggle against Japanese imperialism is a world task and the Soviet Union, as part of that world, can no more remain neutral than can England or America.'

Question: 'Is it the immediate task of the Chinese people to regain all the territories lost to Japanese imperialism, or only to drive Japan from North China, and all Chinese territory beyond the Great Wall?'

Answer: 'It is the immediate task of China to regain all our lost territories, not merely to defend our sovereignty south of the Great Wall. This means that Manchuria must be regained. We do not, however, include Korea, formerly a Chinese colony,* but when we have re-established the independence of the lost territories of China, and if the Koreans wish to break away from the chains of Japanese imperialism, we will extend them our enthusiastic help in their struggle for independence. The same thing applies for Taiwan

---

*Not really a 'Chinese colony' but a neighbour over whom China claimed suzerainty before her defeat by Japan in 1895.

[Formosa].² As for Inner Mongolia, which is populated by both Chinese and Mongolians, we will struggle to drive Japan from there and help Inner Mongolia to establish an autonomous state.' *

Question : 'In actual practice, how could the Soviet Government and the Red Army cooperate with the Kuomintang armies in a war against Japan? In a foreign war it would be necessary for all Chinese armies to be placed under a centralized command. Would the Red Army agree, if allowed representation on a supreme war council, to submit to its decisions both militarily and politically?'

Answer : 'Yes. Our government will wholeheartedly submit to the decisions of such a council, provided it really resists Japan.'

Question : 'Would the Red Army agree not to move its troops into or against any areas occupied by Kuomintang armies, except with the consent or at the order of the supreme war council?'

Answer : 'Yes. Certainly we will not move our troops into any areas occupied by anti-Japanese armies – nor have we done so for some time past. The Red Army would not utilize any wartime situation in an opportunist way.'

Question : 'What demands would the Communist Party make in return for such cooperation?'

Answer : 'It would insist upon waging war, decisively and finally, against Japanese aggression. In addition it would request the observance of the points advanced in the calls for a democratic republic and the establishment of a national defence government.' †

Question : 'How can the people best be armed, organized, and trained to participate in such a war?'

---

*In answer to a later question, in another interview, Mao Tse-tung made the following statement concerning Outer Mongolia :

'The relationship between Outer Mongolia and the Soviet Union, now and in the past, has always been based on the principle of complete equality. When the people's revolution has been victorious in China, the Outer Mongolian republic will automatically become a part of the Chinese federation, at its own will. The Mohammedan and Tibetan peoples, likewise, will form autonomous republics attached to the China federation.' See Appendices, Further Interviews with Mao Tse-tung, 'On the Comintern, China, and Outer Mongolia'.

† Discussed in several proclamations issued to the Kuomintang in 1935 and 1936 by the Soviet Government and the Red Army. See Part Eleven, Chapter 6.

Answer: 'The people *must* be given the right to organize and to arm themselves. This is a freedom which Chiang Kai-shek has in the past denied to them. The suppression has not, however, been entirely successful – as, for example, in the case of the Red Army. Also, despite severe repression in Peking, Shanghai, and other places, the students have begun to organize themselves and have already prepared themselves politically. But still the students and the revolutionary anti-Japanese masses have not yet got their freedom, cannot be mobilized, cannot be trained and armed. When the contrary is true, when the masses are given economic, social, and political freedom, their strength will be intensified hundreds of times, and the true power of the nation will be revealed.

'The Red Army through its own struggle has won its freedom from the militarists to become an unconquerable power. The anti-Japanese volunteers have won their freedom of action from the Japanese oppressors and have armed themselves in a similar way. If the Chinese people are trained, armed, and organized they can likewise become an invincible force.'

Question: 'What, in your opinion, should be the main strategy and tactics to be followed in this "war of liberation"?'

Answer: 'The strategy should be that of a war of manoeuvre, over an extended, shifting, and indefinite front: a strategy depending for success on a high degree of mobility in difficult terrain, and featured by swift attack and withdrawal, swift concentration and dispersal. It will be a large-scale war of manoeuvre rather than the simple positional war of extensive trench work, deep-massed lines and heavy fortifications. Our strategy and tactics must be conditioned by the theatre in which the war will take place, and this dictates a war of manoeuvre.

'This does not mean the abandonment of vital strategic points, which can be defended in positional warfare as long as profitable. But the pivotal strategy must be a war of manoeuvre, and important reliance must be placed on guerrilla and partisan tactics. Fortified warfare must be utilized, but it will be of auxiliary and secondary strategic importance.'

Here it may be inserted that this sort of strategy in general seemed to be rather widely supported also among non-Communist Chinese military leaders. Nanking's wholly imported air force provided an impressive if costly internal police machine, but few experts had illusions about its long-range value in a foreign war. Both the air force and such mechanization as had taken place in the central army were looked upon by many as costly toys incapable of retaining a role of initiative after the first few weeks, since China lacked the industries necessary to maintain and replenish either an air force or any other highly technical branch of modern warfare.

Pai Chung-hsi, Li Tsung-jen,* Han Fu-chu, Hu Tsung-nan, Ch'en Ch'eng, Chang Hsueh-liang, Feng Yu-hsiang, and Ts'ai T'ing-k'ai were among the leading Nationalist generals who seemed to share Mao's conviction that China's sole hope of victory over Japan must rest ultimately on superior manoeuvering of great masses of troops, divided into mobile units, and the ability to maintain a protracted defence over immense partisan areas.

Mao Tse-tung continued:

'Geographically the theatre of the war is so vast that it is possible for us to pursue mobile warfare with the utmost efficiency and with a telling effect on a slow-moving war machine like Japan's, cautiously feeling its way in front of fierce rear-guard actions. Deep concentration and the exhausting defence of a vital position or two on a narrow front would be to throw away all the tactical advantages of our geography and economic organization, and to repeat the mistake of the Abyssinians. Our strategy and tactics must aim to avoid great decisive battles in the early stages of the war, and gradually to break the morale, the fighting spirit, and the military efficiency of the living forces of the enemy . . .

'Besides the regular Chinese troops we should create, direct, and politically and militarily equip great numbers of partisan and guerrilla detachments among the peasantry. What has been accomplished by the anti-Japanese volunteer units of this type in Manchuria is only a very minor demonstration of the latent power of resistance that can be mobilized from the revolutionary peasantry of all China. Properly led and organized, such units can keep the Japanese busy twenty-four hours a day and worry them to death.

'It must be remembered that the war will be fought inside China. This means that the Japanese will be entirely surrounded by a hostile Chinese people. The Japanese will be forced to move in all

*See BN.

their provisions and guard them, maintaining troops along all lines of communications, and heavily garrisoning their bases in Manchuria and Japan as well.

'The process of the war will present to China the possibility of capturing many Japanese prisoners, arms, ammunition, war machines, and so forth. A point will be reached where it will become more and more possible to engage Japan's armies on a basis of positional warfare, using fortifications and deep entrenchment, for, as the war progresses, the technical equipment of the anti-Japanese forces will greatly improve, *and will be reinforced by important foreign help*. Japan's economy will crack under the strain of a long, expensive occupation of China and the morale of her forces will break under the trial of a war of innumerable but indecisive battles. The great reservoirs of human material in the revolutionary Chinese people will still be pouring men ready to fight for their freedom into our front lines long after the tidal flood of Japanese imperialism has wrecked itself on the hidden reefs of Chinese resistance.

'All these and other factors will condition the war and will enable us to make the final and decisive attacks on Japan's fortifications and strategic bases and to drive Japan's army of occupation from China.

'*Japanese officers and soldiers captured and disarmed by us will be welcomed and will be well treated. They will not be killed. They will be treated in a brotherly way. Every method will be adopted to make the Japanese proletarian soldiers, with whom we have no quarrel, stand up and oppose their own Fascist oppressors. Our slogan will be: "Unite and oppose the common oppressors, the Fascist leaders." Anti-Fascist Japanese troops are our friends, and there is no conflict in our aims.'* *

It was past two o'clock in the morning and I was exhausted, but I could see no signs of fatigue on Mao's thoughtful face. He alternately walked up and down between the two little rooms, sat down, lay down, leaned on the table, and read from a sheaf of reports in the intervals when Wu translated and I wrote. Mrs Mao also was still awake. Suddenly both of them bent over and gave an exclamation of delight at a moth that had languished beside the candle. It

*Emphasis added.

was a really lovely thing, with wings shaded a delicate apple-green and fringed in a soft rainbow of saffron and rose. Mao opened a book and pressed this gossamer of colour between its leaves.

Could such people really be thinking seriously of war?

4

$2,000,000 in Heads

THERE were many things unique about the Red Army University.

Its president was a twenty-eight-year-old army commander who (Communists said) had never lost a battle. It boasted, in one class of undergraduates, veteran warriors whose average age was twenty-seven, with an average of eight years of fighting experience and three wounds each. Was there any other school where 'paper shortage' made it necessary to use the blank side of enemy propaganda leaflets for classroom notebooks? Or where the cost of educating each cadet, including food, clothing, all institutional expenses, was less than $15 silver per month? Or where the aggregate value of rewards offered for the heads of various notorious cadets exceeded $2,000,000?

Finally, it was probably the world's only seat of 'higher learning' whose classrooms were bombproof caves, with chairs and desks of stone and brick, and blackboards and walls of limestone and clay.

In Shensi and Kansu, besides ordinary houses, there were great cave dwellings, temple grottoes and castled battlements hundreds of years old. Wealthy officials and landlords built these queer edifices a thousand years ago, to guard against flood and invasion and famine, and here hoarded the grain and treasure to see them through sieges of each. Many-vaulted chambers, cut deeply into the loess or solid rock, some with rooms that held several hundred people, these cliff dwellings made perfect bomb shelters. In such archaic manors the Red University found strange but safe accommodation.

Lin Piao, the president, was introduced to me soon after my arrival, and he invited me to speak one day to his cadets. He suggested the topic: 'British and American policies towards China.' When he arranged a 'noodle dinner' for the occasion it was too much for me, and I succumbed.

Lin Piao was the son of a factory owner in Hupeh province, and was born in 1908. His father was ruined by extortionate taxation, but Lin managed to get through prep school, and became a cadet in the famous Whampoa Academy at Canton. There he made a brilliant record. He received intensive political and military training under Chiang Kai-shek and Chiang's chief adviser, the Russian General Bluecher. Soon after his graduation the Nationalist Expedition began, and Lin Piao was promoted to a captaincy. By 1927, at the age of twenty, he was a colonel in the noted Fourth Kuomintang Army, under Chang Fa-kuei. And in August of that year, after the Right *coup d'état* at Nanking, he led his regiment to join the Twentieth Army under Ho Lung and Yeh T'ing* in the Nanchang Uprising, which began the Communists' armed struggle for power.

With Mao Tse-tung, Lin Piao shared the distinction of being one of the few Red commanders never wounded. Engaged on the front in more than a hundred battles, in field command for more than ten years, exposed to every hardship that his men had known, with a reward of $100,000 on his head, he was as yet unhurt.

In 1932, Lin Piao was given command of the First Red Army Corps, which then numbered about 20,000 rifles. It became, according to general opinion among Red Army officers, their 'most dreaded force', chiefly because of Lin's extraordinary talent as a tactician. The mere discovery that they were fighting the First Red Army Corps was said to have sometimes put a Nanking army to rout.

Like many able Red commanders, Lin had never been outside China, and spoke and read no language but Chinese. Before the age of thirty, however, he had already won recognition beyond Red circles. His articles in the Chinese Reds' military magazines, *Struggle* and *War and Revolution*, had been republished, studied, and criticized in Nanking military journals, and also in Japan and Soviet Russia. He was noted as the originator of the 'short attack' – a tactic on which General Feng Yu-hsiang had commented. To the Reds' skilful mastery of the 'short attack' many victories of the First Army Corps were said to be traceable.

With Commander Lin and his faculty I journeyed one morning a short distance beyond the walls of Pao An to the Red Army Uni-

* See BN.

versity. We arrived at recreation hour. Some of the cadets were playing basketball on the two courts set up; others were playing tennis on a court laid down on the turf beside the Pao An River, a tributary of the Yellow River. Still other cadets were playing table tennis, writing, reading new books and magazines, or studying in their primitive 'clubrooms'.

This was the First Section of the University, in which there were some 200 students. Altogether, Hung Ta, as the school was known in the soviet districts, had four sections, with over 800 students. There were also, near Pao An, and under the administrative control of the education commissioner, radio, cavalry, agricultural, and medical-training schools. There was a Communist Party school* and a mass-education training centre.

Over 200 cadets assembled to hear me explain 'British and American policies'. I made a crude summary of Anglo-American attitudes, and agreed to answer questions. It was a great mistake, I soon realized, and the noodle dinner hardly compensated for my embarrassment.

'What is the attitude of the British Government towards the formation of the pro-Japanese Hopei-Chahar Council, and the garrisoning of North China by Japanese troops?'

'What are the results of the NRA policy in America, and how has it benefited the working class?'

'Will Germany and Italy help Japan if a war breaks out with China?'

'How long do you think Japan can carry on a major war against China if she is not helped by other powers?'

'Why has the League of Nations failed?'

'Why is it that, although the Communist Party is legal in both Great Britain and America, there is no workers' government in either country?'

'What progress is being made in the formation of an anti-Fascist front in England? In America?'

'What is the future of the international student movement, which has its centre in Paris?'

---

*Tung Pi-wu was director of this Party school. (Li Wei-han and K'ang Sheng were to succeed him in that post.) Hsieh Fu-chih was one of the cadets. See BN.

'In your opinion, can Leith-Ross's visit to Japan result in Anglo-Japanese agreement on policies towards China?'

'When China begins to resist Japan, will America and Great Britain assist China or Japan?'

'Please tell us why America and Great Britain keep their fleets and armed forces in China if they are friends of the Chinese people?'

'What do the American and British workers think of the USSR?'

No small territory to cover in a two-hour question period! And it was not confined to two hours. Beginning at ten in the morning, it continued till late in the afternoon.

Afterwards I toured the various classrooms and talked with Lin Piao and his faculty. They told me something of the conditions of enrolment in their school, and showed me printed announcements of its courses, thousands of copies of which had been secretly distributed throughout China. The four sections of the academy invited 'all who are determined to fight Japanese imperialism and to offer themselves for the national revolutionary cause, regardless of class, social, or political differences'. The age limit was sixteen to twenty-eight, 'regardless of sex'. 'The applicants must be physically strong, free from epidemic diseases,' and also – rather sweeping – 'free from all bad habits'.

In practice, I discovered, most of the cadets in the First Section were battalion, regimental, or division commanders or political commissars of the Red Army,* receiving advanced military and political training. According to Red Army regulations, every active commander or commissar was supposed to spend at least four months at such study during every two years of active service.

The Second and Third Sections included company, platoon, and squad commanders – experienced fighters in the Red Army – as well as new recruits selected from 'graduates of middle schools or the equivalent, unemployed teachers or officers, cadres of anti-Japanese volunteer corps and anti-Japanese partisan leaders, and workers who have engaged in organizing and leading labour movements'. Over sixty middle-school graduates from Shansi had joined the Reds during their expedition to that province.

Classes in the Second and Third Sections lasted six months. The

*One of them was Lo Jui-ch'ing. See BN.

Fourth Section was devoted chiefly to 'training engineers, cavalry cadres, and artillery units'. Here I met some former machinists and apprentices. Later on, as I was leaving Red China, I was to meet, entering by truck, eight new recruits for the 'bandit university' arriving from Shanghai and Peking. Lin Piao told me that they had a waiting list of over 2,000 student applicants from all parts of China. At that time every cadet had to be 'smuggled' in.

The curriculum varied in different sections of Hung Ta. In the First Section political lectures included these courses: Political Knowledge, Problems of the Chinese Revolution, Political Economy, Party Construction, Tactical Problems of the Republic, Leninism and Historical Foundations of Democracy, and Political and Social Forces in Japan. Military courses included: Problems of Strategy in the War with Japan, Manoeuvring Warfare (against Japan), and The Development of Partisan Warfare in the Anti-Japanese War.

Special textbooks had been prepared for some of these courses. Some were carried clear from the soviet publishing house in Kiangsi, where (I was told) more than eight hundred printers were employed in the main plant. In other courses the materials used were lectures by Red Army commanders and Party leaders, dealing with historical experiences of the Russian and the Chinese revolutions, or utilizing material from captured government files, documents and statistics.

These courses at Hung Ta perhaps suggested a reply to the question, 'Do the Reds really intend to fight Japan?' It sufficed to show how the Reds foresaw and actively planned for China's 'war of independence' against Japan – a war which they regarded as inevitable unless, by some miracle, Japan withdrew from the vast areas of China already under the wheels of Nippon's military juggernaut.

That the Reds were fully determined to fight, and believed that the opening of the war would find them first on the front, was indicated not only in the impassioned utterances of their leaders, in grim practical schooling in the army, and in their proposals for a 'united front' with their ten-year enemy, the Kuomintang, but also by the intensive propagandizing one saw throughout the soviet districts.

Playing a leading part in this educative mission were the many companies of youths known as the Jen-min K'ang-Jih Chu-She, or

People's Anti-Japanese Dramatic Society, who travelled ceaselessly
back and forth in the Red districts, spreading the gospel of resistance and awakening the slumbering nationalism of the peasantry.

It was to one of the performances of this astonishing children's
theatre that I went soon after my first visit to the Red Army University.

5

Red Theatre

PEOPLE were already moving down towards the open-air stage, improvised from an old temple, when I set out with the young official who had invited me to the Red Theatre. It was Saturday, two or three hours before sunset, and all Pao An seemed to be going.

Cadets, muleteers, women and girl workers from the uniform and shoe factory, clerks from the cooperatives and from the soviet post office, soldiers, carpenters, villagers followed by their infants, all began streaming towards the big grassy plain beside the river, where the players were performing. It would be hard to imagine a more democratic gathering – something like old-time Chautauqua.

No tickets were sold, there was no 'dress circle', and there were no preferred seats. Goats were grazing on the tennis court not far beyond. I noticed Lo Fu, general secretary of the Politburo of the Central Committee, Lin Piao, Lin Po-chu (Lin Tsu-han), the commissioner of finance, Chairman Mao Tse-tung, and other officials and their wives scattered through the crowd, seated on the springy turf like the rest. No one paid much attention to them once the performance had begun.

Across the stage was a big pink curtain of silk, with the words 'People's Anti-Japanese Dramatic Society' in Chinese characters as well as Latinized Chinese, which the Reds were promoting to hasten mass education. The programme was to last three hours. It proved to be a combination of playlets, dancing, singing, and pantomime – a kind of variety show, or vaudeville, given unity chiefly by two central themes: anti-Nipponism and the revolution. It was full of overt propaganda and the props were primitive. But it had the advantage of being emancipated from cymbal-crashing and falsetto singing, and of dealing with living material rather than with meaningless historical intrigues that are the concern of the decadent Chinese opera.[1]

What it lacked in subtlety and refinement it partly made up by its robust vitality, its sparkling humour, and a sort of participation between actors and audience. Guests at the Red Theatre seemed actually to listen to what was said : a really astonishing thing in contrast with the bored opera audience, who often spent their time eating fruit and melon seeds, gossiping, tossing hot towels back and forth, visiting from one box to another, and only occasionally looking at the stage.

The first playlet was called *Invasion*. It opened in a Manchurian village in 1931, with the Japanese arriving and driving out the 'non-resisting' Chinese soldiers. In the second scene Japanese officers banqueted in a peasant's home, using Chinese men for chairs and drunkenly making love to their wives. Another scene showed Japanese dope peddlers selling morphine and heroin and forcing every peasant to buy a quantity. A youth who refused to buy was singled out for questioning.

'You don't buy morphine, you don't obey Manchukuo health rules, you don't love your "divine" Emperor P'u Yi,'* charged his tormentors. 'You are no good, you are an anti-Japanese bandit!' And the youth was promptly executed.

A scene in the village market place showed small merchants peacefully selling their wares. Suddenly Japanese soldiers arrived, searching for more 'anti-Japanese bandits'. Instantly they demanded passports, and those who had forgotten them were shot. Then two Japanese officers gorged themselves on a peddler's pork. When he asked for payment they looked at him in astonishment. 'You ask for payment? Why, Chiang Kai-shek gave us Manchuria, Jehol, Chahar, the Tangku Truce, the Ho-Umetsu Agreement, and the Hopei-Chahar Council without asking a single copper! And you want us to pay for a little pork!' Whereupon they impaled him as a 'bandit'.

In the end, of course, all that proved too much for the villagers. Merchants turned over their stands and umbrellas, farmers rushed forth with their spears, women and children came with their knives, and all swore to 'fight to the death' against the *Jih-pen-kuei* – the 'Japanese devils'.

The little play was sprinkled with humour and local idiom. Bursts of laughter alternated with oaths of disgust and hatred for

*See BN.

the Japanese. The audience got quite agitated. It was not just political propaganda to them, nor slapstick melodrama, but the poignant truth itself. The fact that the players were mostly youths in their teens and natives of Shensi and Shansi seemed entirely forgotten in the onlookers' absorption with the ideas presented.

The substratum of bitter reality behind this portrayal, done as a sort of farce, was not obscured by its wit and humour for at least one young soldier there. He stood up at the end, and in a voice shaking with emotion cried out: 'Death to the Japanese bandits! Down with the murderers of our Chinese people! Fight back to our homes!' The whole assembly echoed his slogans mightily. I learned that this lad was a Manchurian whose parents had been killed by the Japanese.

Comic relief was provided at this moment by the meandering goats. They were discovered nonchalantly eating the tennis net, which someone had forgotten to take down. A wave of laughter swept the audience while some cadets gave chase to the culprits and salvaged this important property of the recreation department.

Second number on the programme was a harvest dance, daintily performed by a dozen girls of the dramatic society. Barefoot, clad in peasant trousers and coats and fancy vests, with silk bandannas on their heads, they danced with good unison and grace. Two of these girls, I learned, had walked clear from Kiangsi, where they had learned to dance in the Reds' dramatic school at Juichin. They had genuine talent.

Another unique and amusing number was called the 'United Front Dance', which interpreted the mobilization of China to resist Japan. By what legerdemain they produced their costumes I do not know, but suddenly there were groups of youths wearing sailors' white jumpers and caps and shorts – first appearing as cavalry formations, next as aviation corps, then as foot soldiers, and finally as the navy. Their pantomime and gesture, at which Chinese are born artists, very realistically conveyed the spirit of the dance. Then there was something called the 'Dance of the Red Machines'. By sound and gesture, by an interplay and interlocking of arms, legs, and heads, the little dancers ingeniously imitated the thrust and drive of pistons, the turn of cogs and wheels, the hum of dynamos – and visions of a machine-age China of the future.

Between acts, shouts arose for extemporaneous singing by people in the audience. Half a dozen native Shensi girls – workers in the factories – were by popular demand required to sing an old folk song of the province, accompaniment being furnished by a Shensi farmer with his homemade guitar. Another 'command' performance was given by a cadet who played the harmonica, and one was called upon to sing a favourite song of the Southland. Then, to my utter consternation, a demand began that the *wai-kuo hsin-wen chi-che* – the foreigner newspaperman – strain his lungs in a solo of his own !

They refused to excuse me. Alas, I could think of nothing but fox trots, waltzes, *La Bohème*, and 'Ave Maria', which all seemed inappropriate for this martial audience. I could not even remember 'The Marseillaise'. The demand persisted. In extreme embarrassment I at last rendered 'The Man on the Flying Trapeze'. They were very polite about it. No encore was requested.

With infinite relief I saw the curtain go up on the next act, which turned out to be a social play with a revolutionary theme – an accountant falling in love with his landlord's wife. Then there was more dancing, a 'Living Newspaper' dealing with some late news from the South-West, and a chorus of children singing 'The International'. Here the flags of several nations were hung on streamers from a central illuminated column, round which reclined the young dancers. They rose slowly, as the words were sung, to stand erect, clenched fists upraised, as the song ended.

The theatre was over, but my curiosity remained. Next day I went to interview Miss Wei Kung-chih, director of the People's Anti-Japanese Dramatic Society.

Miss Wei was born in Honan in 1907 and had been a Red for ten years. She originally joined a propaganda corps of the political training school (where Teng Hsiao-p'ing* was director) of the Kuominchun, 'Christian General' Feng Yu-hsiang's army, but when Feng reconciled himself to the Nanking *coup d'état* in 1927 she deserted, along with many young students, and became a Communist in Hankow. In 1929 she was sent to Europe by the Communist Party and studied for a while in France, then in Moscow. A year later she returned to China, successfully ran the Kuomin-

*See BN.

tang blockade around Red China, and began to work at Juichin.

She told me something of the history of the Red Theatre. Dramatic groups were first organized in Kiangsi in 1931. There, at the famous Gorky School (under the technical direction of Yeh Chienying*) in Juichin, with over 1,000 students recruited from the soviet districts, the Reds trained about sixty theatrical troupes, according to Miss Wei. They travelled through the villages and at the front. Every troupe had long waiting lists of requests from village soviets. The peasants, always grateful for any diversion in their culture-starved lives, voluntarily arranged all transport, food, and housing for these visits.

In the South, Miss Wei had been an assistant director, but in the North-West she had charge of the whole organization of dramatics. She made the Long March from Kiangsi, one of the very few soviet women who lived through it. Theatrical troupes were created in Soviet Shensi before the southern army reached the North-West, but with the arrival of new talent from Kiangsi the dramatic art apparently acquired new life. There were about thirty such travelling theatrical troupes there now, Miss Wei told me, and others in Kansu. I was to meet many later on in my travels.

'Every army has its own dramatic group,' Miss Wei continued, 'as well as nearly every district. The actors are nearly all locally recruited. Most of our experienced players from the South have now become instructors.'

I met several Young Vanguards, veterans of the Long March, still in their early teens, who had charge of organizing and training children's dramatic societies in various villages.

'Peasants come from long distances to our Red dramatics,' Miss Wei proudly informed me. 'Sometimes, when we are near the White borders, Kuomintang soldiers secretly send messages to ask our players to come to some market town in the border districts. When we do this, both Red soldiers and White leave their arms behind and go to this market place to watch our performance. But the higher officers of the Kuomintang never permit this, if they know about it, because once they have seen our players many of the Kuomintang soldiers will no longer fight our Red Army.'

What surprised me about these dramatic 'clubs' was that,

*See BN.

equipped with so little, they were able to meet a genuine social need. They had the scantest properties and costumes, yet with these primitive materials they managed to produce the authentic illusion of drama. The players received only their food and clothing and small living allowances, but they studied every day, like all Communists, and they believed themselves to be working for China and the Chinese people. They slept anywhere, cheerfully ate what was provided for them, walked long distances from village to village. From the standpoint of material comforts they were unquestionably the most miserably rewarded thespians on earth, yet I hadn't seen any who looked happier.

The Reds wrote nearly all their own plays and songs. Some were contributed by versatile officials, but most of them were prepared by story writers and artists in the propaganda department. Several Red dramatic skits were written by Ch'eng Fang-wu, a well-known Hunanese author whose adherence to Soviet Kiangsi in 1933 had excited Shanghai. More recently Ting Ling,* China's foremost woman author, had added her talent to the Red Theatre.

There was no more powerful weapon of propaganda in the Communist movement than the Red's dramatic troupes, and none more subtly manipulated. By constant shifts of programme, by almost daily changes of the 'Living Newspaper' scenes, new military, political, economic, and social problems became the material of drama, and doubts and questionings were answered in a humorous, understandable way for the sceptical peasantry. When the Reds occupied new areas, it was the Red Theatre that calmed the fears of the people, gave them rudimentary ideas of the Red programme, and dispensed great quantities of revolutionary thoughts, to win the people's confidence. During the Reds' 1935 Shansi expedition, for example, hundreds of peasants heard about the Red players with the army, and flocked to see them.

The whole thing was 'propaganda in art' carried to the ultimate degree, and plenty of people would say, 'Why drag art into it?' Yet in its broadest meaning it was art, for it conveyed for its spectators the illusions of life, and if it was a naïve art it was because the living material with which it was made and the living men to whom it appealed were in their approach to life's problems also

*See BN.

naïve. For the masses of China there was no fine partition between art and propaganda. There was only a distinction between what was understandable in human experience and what was not.

One could think of the whole history of the Communist movement in China as a grand propaganda tour, and the defence, not so much of the absolute rightness of certain ideas, perhaps, as of their right to exist. I was not sure that they might not prove to be the most permanent service of the Reds, even if they might be in the end defeated and broken. For millions of young peasants who had heard the Marxist gospel preached by those beardless youths, thousands of whom were now dead, the old exorcisms of Chinese culture would never again be quite as effective. Wherever in their incredible migrations destiny had moved these Reds, they had vigorously demanded deep social changes – for which the peasants could have learned to hope in no other way – and they had brought new faith in action to the poor and the oppressed.

However badly they had erred at times, however tragic had been their excesses, however exaggerated had been the emphasis here or the stress there, it had been their sincere and sharply felt propagandist aim to shake, to arouse, the millions of rural China to their responsibilities in society; to awaken them to a belief in human rights, to combat the timidity, passiveness, and static faiths of Taoism and Confucianism, to educate, to persuade, and, no doubt, at times to beleaguer and coerce them to fight for 'the reign of the people' – a new vision in rural China – to fight for a life of justice, equality, freedom, and human dignity, as the Communists saw it. Far more than all the pious but meaningless resolutions passed at Nanking, this growing pressure from a peasantry gradually standing erect in a state of consciousness, after two millenniums of sleep, could force the realization of a vast mutation over the land.[2]

What this 'communism' amounted to in a way was that, for the first time in history, thousands of educated youths, stirred to great dreams themselves by a universe of scientific knowledge to which they were suddenly given access, 'returned to the people', went to the deep soil-base of their country, to 'reveal' some of their new-won learning to the intellectually sterile countryside, the dark-living peasantry, and sought to enlist its alliance in building a 'more abundant life'. Fired by the belief that a better world could be made, and that only they could make it, they carried their formula – the ideal of the commune – back to the people for sanction and support. And to a startling degree they seemed to be winning it. They had brought to millions, by propaganda and by action, a new conception of the state, society, and the individual.

I often had a queer feeling among the Reds that I was in the midst of a host of schoolboys, engaged in a life of violence because some strange design of history had made this seem infinitely more important to them than football games, textbooks, love, or the main concerns of youth in other countries. At times I could scarcely believe that it had been only this determined aggregation of youth, equipped with an Idea, that had directed a mass struggle for ten years against all the armies of Nanking. How had the incredible brotherhood arisen, banded together, held together, and whence came its strength? And why had it perhaps, after all, failed to mature, why did it still seem fundamentally like a mighty demonstration, like a crusade of youth? How could one ever make it plausible to those who had seen nothing of it?

Then Mao Tse-tung began to tell me something about his personal history, and as I wrote it down, night after night, I realized that this was not only his story but an explanation of how communism grew – a variety of it real and indigenous to China – and why it had won the adherence and support of thousands of young men and women. It was a story that I was to hear later on, with rich variations, in the life stories of many other Red leaders. It was a story people would want to read, I thought.

Part Four

GENESIS OF A COMMUNIST

Part Four

GENESIS OF A COMMUNE

I

Childhood

ON the five or six sets of questions I had submitted on different matters, Mao had talked for a dozen nights, hardly ever referring to himself or his own role in some of the events described. I was beginning to think it was hopeless to expect him to give me such details: he obviously considered the individual of very little importance. Like other Reds I met he tended to talk only about committees, organizations, armies, resolutions, battles, tactics, 'measures', and so on, and seldom of personal experience.

For a while I thought this reluctance to expand on subjective matters, or even the exploits of their comrades as individuals, might derive from modesty, or a fear or suspicion of me, or a consciousness of the price so many of these men had on their heads. Later on I discovered that that was not so much the case as it was that most of them actually did not remember personal details. As I began collecting biographies I found repeatedly that the Communist would be able to tell everything that had happened in his early youth, but once he had become identified with the Red Army he lost himself somewhere, and without repeated questioning one could hear nothing more about *him*, but only stories of the Army, or the Soviets, or the Party – capitalized. These men could talk indefinitely about dates and circumstances of battles, and movements to and from a thousand unheard-of places, but those events seemed to have had significance for them only collectively, not because they as individuals had made history there, but because the Red Army had been there, and behind it the whole organic force of an ideology for which they were fighting. It was an interesting discovery, but it made difficult reporting.

One night when all other questions had been satisfied, Mao turned to the list I had headed 'Personal History'. He smiled at a question, 'How many times have you been married?' – and the rumour later spread that I had asked Mao how many wives he had.

He was sceptical, anyway, about the necessity for supplying an autobiography. But I argued that in a way that was more important than information on other matters. 'People want to know what sort of man you are,' I said, 'when they read what you say. Then you ought also to correct some of the false rumours circulated.'

I reminded him of various reports of his death, how some people believed he spoke fluent French, while others said he was an ignorant peasant, how one report described him as a half-dead tubercular, while others maintained that he was a mad fanatic. He seemed mildly surprised that people should spend their time speculating about him. He agreed that such reports ought to be corrected. Then he looked over the items again, as I had written them down.

'Suppose,' he said at last, 'that I just disregard your questions, and instead give you a general sketch of my life? I think it will be more understandable, and in the end all of your questions will be answered just the same.'

During the nightly interviews that followed – we were like conspirators indeed, huddled in that cave over the red-covered table, with sputtering candles between us – I wrote until I was ready to fall asleep. Wu Liang-p'ing sat next to me and interpreted Mao's soft southern dialect, in which a chicken, instead of being a good substantial northern *chi*, became a romantic *ghii*, and *Hunan* became *Funan*, and a bowl of *ch'a* turned into *ts'a*, and many much stranger variations occurred. Mao related everything from memory, and I put it down as he talked. It was, as I have said, retranslated and corrected, and this is the result, with no attempt to give it literary excellence, beyond some necessary corrections in the syntax of the patient Mr Wu:

'I was born in the village of Shao Shan, in Hsiang T'an *hsien*,* Hunan province, in 1893.[1] My father's name was Mao Jen-sheng [Mao Shun-sheng], and my mother's maiden name was Wen Ch'i-mei.

'My father was a poor peasant and while still young was obliged to join the army because of heavy debts. He was a soldier for many years. Later on he returned to the village where I was born, and by saving carefully and gathering together a little money through

---

*A *hsien* roughly corresponds to a US county. It was the smallest territorial unit under the central government, and was ruled by a magistrate.

small trading and other enterprise he managed to buy back his land.

'As middle peasants then my family owned fifteen *mou* * of land. On this they could raise sixty *tan* † of rice a year. The five members of the family consumed a total of thirty-five *tan* – that is, about seven each – which left an annual surplus of twenty-five *tan*. Using this surplus, my father accumulated a little capital and in time purchased seven more *mou*, which gave the family the status of 'rich' peasants. We could then raise eighty-four *tan* of rice a year.

'When I was ten years of age and the family owned only fifteen *mou* of land, the five members of the family consisted of my father, mother, grandfather, younger brother, and myself. After we had acquired the additional seven *mou*, my grandfather died, but there came another younger brother. However, we still had a surplus of forty-nine *tan* of rice each year, and on this my father steadily prospered.

'At the time my father was a middle peasant he began to deal in grain transport and selling, by which he made a little money. After he became a 'rich' peasant, he devoted most of his time to that business. He hired a full-time farm labourer, and put his children to work on the farm, as well as his wife. I began to work at farming tasks when I was six years old. My father had no shop for his business. He simply purchased grain from the poor farmers and then transported it to the city merchants, where he got a higher price. In the winter, when the rice was being ground, he hired an extra labourer to work on the farm, so that at that time there were seven mouths to feed. My family ate frugally, but had enough always.

'I began studying in a local primary school when I was eight and remained there until I was thirteen years old. In the early morning and at night I worked on the farm. During the day I read the Confucian Analects and the Four Classics. My Chinese teacher belonged to the stern-treatment school. He was harsh and severe, frequently beating his students. Because of that I ran away from the school when I was ten. I was afraid to return home for fear of receiving a beating there, and set out in the general direction of the city, which

* About 2·5 acres, or one hectare.

† One *tan* is a *picul*, or 133⅓ pounds.

I believed to be in a valley somewhere. I wandered for three days before I was finally found by my family. Then I learned that I had circled round and round in my travels, and in all my walking had got only about eight li * from my home.

'After my return to the family, however, to my surprise conditions somewhat improved. My father was slightly more considerate and the teacher was more inclined to moderation. The result of my act of protest impressed me very much. It was a successful "strike".

'My father wanted me to begin keeping the family books as soon as I had learned a few characters. He wanted me to learn to use the abacus. As my father insisted upon this I began to work at those accounts at night. He was a severe taskmaster. He hated to see me idle, and if there were no books to be kept he put me to work at farm tasks. He was a hot-tempered man and frequently beat both me and my brothers. He gave us no money whatever, and the most meagre food. On the fifteenth of every month he made a concession to his labourers and gave them eggs with their rice, but never meat. To me he gave neither eggs nor meat.

'My mother was a kind woman, generous and sympathetic, and ever ready to share what she had. She pitied the poor and often gave them rice when they came to ask for it during famines. But she could not do so when my father was present. He disapproved of charity. We had many quarrels in my home over this question.

'There were two "parties" in the family. One was my father, the Ruling Power. The Opposition was made up of myself, my mother, my brother, and sometimes even the labourer. In the "united front" of the Opposition, however, there was a difference of opinion. My mother advocated a policy of indirect attack. She criticized any overt display of emotion and attempts at open rebellion against the Ruling Power. She said it was not the Chinese way.

'But when I was thirteen I discovered a powerful argument of my own for debating with my father on his own ground, by quoting the Classics. My father's favourite accusations against me were of unfilial conduct and laziness. I quoted, in exchange, passages from the Classics saying that the elder must be kind and affection-

*Two and two-thirds miles.

ate. Against his charge that I was lazy I used the rebuttal that older people should do more work than younger, that my father was over three times as old as myself, and therefore should do more work. And I declared that when I was his age I would be much more energetic.

'The old man continued to "amass wealth", or what was considered to be a great fortune in that little village. He did not buy more land himself, but he bought many mortgages on other people's land. His capital grew to two or three thousand Chinese dollars.*

'My dissatisfaction increased. The dialectical struggle in our family was constantly developing.† One incident I especially remember. When I was about thirteen my father invited many guests to his home, and while they were present a dispute arose between the two of us. My father denounced me before the whole group, calling me lazy and useless. This infuriated me. I cursed him and left the house. My mother ran after me and tried to persuade me to return. My father also pursued me, cursing at the same time that he commanded me to come back. I reached the edge of a pond and threatened to jump in if he came any nearer. In this situation demands and counterdemands were presented for cessation of the civil war. My father insisted that I apologize and k'ou-t'ou ‡ as a sign of submission. I agreed to give a one-knee k'ou-t'ou if he would promise not to beat me. Thus the war ended, and from it I learned that when I defended my rights by open rebellion my father relented, but when I remained meek and submissive he only cursed and beat me the more.

'Reflecting on this, I think that in the end the strictness of my father defeated him. I learned to hate him, and we created a real united front against him. At the same time it probably benefited me. It made me most diligent in my work; it made me keep my books carefully, so that he should have no basis for criticizing me.

'My father had had two years of schooling and he could read

*Mao used the Chinese term *yuan*, which was often translated as 'Chinese dollars'; 3,000 yuan in cash in 1900 was an impressive sum in rural China.

†Mao used all these political terms humorously in his explanations, laughing as he recalled such incidents.

‡Literally, to 'knock head'. To strike one's head to the floor or earth was expected of son to father and subject to emperor, in token of filial obedience.

enough to keep books. My mother was wholly illiterate. Both were from peasant families. I was the family "scholar". I knew the Classics, but disliked them. What I enjoyed were the romances of Old China, and especially stories of rebellions. I read the *Yo Fei Chuan* [the *Yo Fei Chronicles*], *Shui Hu Chuan* [*The Water Margin*], *Fan T'ang* [*Revolt Against the T'ang*], *San Kuo* [the *Three Kingdoms*], and *Hsi Yu Chi* [*Travels in the West*, the story of Hsuan Tsang's seventh-century semilegendary pilgrimage to India] while still very young, and despite the vigilance of my old teacher, who hated these outlawed books and called them wicked. I used to read them in school, covering them up with a Classic when the teacher walked past. So also did most of my schoolmates. We learned many of the stories almost by heart, and discussed and rediscussed them many times. We knew more of them than the old men of the village, who also loved them and used to exchange stories with us. I believe that perhaps I was much influenced by such books, read at an impressionable age.

'I finally left the primary school when I was thirteen and began to work long hours on the farm, helping the hired labourer, doing the full labour of a man during the day and at night keeping books for my father. Nevertheless, I succeeded in continuing my reading, devouring everything I could find except the Classics. This annoyed my father, who wanted me to master the Classics, especially after he was defeated in a lawsuit because of an apt Classical quotation used by his adversary in the Chinese court. I used to cover up the window of my room late at night so that my father would not see the light. In this way I read a book called *Sheng-shih Wei-yen* [*Words of Warning*],* which I liked very much. The author, one of a number of old reformist scholars, thought that the weakness of China lay in her lack of Western appliances – railways, telephones, telegraphs, and steamships – and wanted to have them introduced into the country. My father considered such books a waste of time. He wanted me to read something practical like the Classics, which could help him in winning lawsuits.

---

*By Chung Kuang-ying, who advocated many democratic reforms, including parliamentary government and modern methods of education and communications. His book had a wide influence when published in 1898, the year of the ill-fated Hundred Days Reform.

'I continued to read the old romances and tales of Chinese literature. It occurred to me one day that there was one thing peculiar about such stories, and that was the absence of peasants who tilled the land. All the characters were warriors, officials, or scholars; there was never a peasant hero. I wondered about this for two years, and then I analyzed the content of the stories. I found that they all glorified men of arms, rulers of the people, who did not have to work the land, because they owned and controlled it and evidently made the peasants work it for them.

'My father was in his early days, and in middle age, a sceptic, but my mother devoutly worshipped Buddha. She gave her children religious instruction, and we were all saddened that our father was an unbeliever. When I was nine years old I seriously discussed the problem of my father's lack of piety with my mother. We made many attempts then and later on to convert him, but without success. He only cursed us, and, overwhelmed by his attacks, we withdrew to devise new plans. But he would have nothing to do with the gods.

'My reading gradually began to influence me, however; I myself became more and more sceptical. My mother became concerned about me, and scolded me for my indifference to the requirements of the faith, but my father made no comment. Then one day he went out on the road to collect some money, and on his way he met a tiger. The tiger was surprised at the encounter and fled at once, but my father was even more astonished and afterwards reflected a good deal on his miraculous escape. He began to wonder if he had not offended the gods. From then on he showed more respect to Buddhism and burned incense now and then. Yet when my own backsliding grew worse, the old man did not interfere. He prayed to the gods only when he was in difficulties.

'*Sheng-shih Wei-yen* [*Words of Warning*] stimulated in me a desire to resume my studies. I had also become disgusted with my labour on the farm. My father naturally opposed me. We quarrelled about it, and finally I ran away from home. I went to the home of an unemployed law student, and there I studied for half a year. After that I studied more of the Classics under an old Chinese scholar, and also read many contemporary articles and a few books.

'At this time an incident occurred in Hunan which influenced my whole life. Outside the little Chinese school where I was studying, we students noticed many bean merchants coming back from Changsha. We asked them why they were all leaving. They told us about a big uprising in the city.

'There had been a severe famine that year, and in Changsha thousands were without food. The starving sent a delegation to the civil governor to beg for relief, but he replied to them haughtily, "Why haven't you food? There is plenty in the city. I always have enough." When the people were told the governor's reply, they became very angry. They held mass meetings and organized a demonstration. They attacked the Manchu yamen, cut down the flagpole, the symbol of office, and drove out the governor. Following this the Commissioner of Internal Affairs, a man named Chang, came out on his horse and told the people that the government would take measures to help them. Chang was evidently sincere in his promise, but the Emperor disliked him and accused him of having intimate connections with "the mob". He was removed. A new governor arrived, and at once ordered the arrest of the leaders of the uprising. Many of them were beheaded and their heads displayed on poles as a warning to future "rebels".

'This incident was discussed in my school for many days. It made a deep impression on me. Most of the other students sympathized with the "insurrectionists", but only from an observer's point of view. They did not understand that it had any relation to their own lives. They were merely interested in it as an exciting incident. I never forgot it. I felt that there with the rebels were ordinary people like my own family and I deeply resented the injustice of the treatment given to them.

'Not long afterwards, in Shao Shan, there was a conflict between members of the Ke Lao Hui,* a secret society, and a local landlord. He sued them in court, and as he was a powerful landlord he easily bought a decision favourable to himself. The Ke Lao Hui members were defeated. But instead of submitting, they rebelled against the landlord and the government and withdrew to a local mountain called Liu Shan, where they built a stronghold. Troops were sent against them and the landlord spread a story that they had sacri-

*The same society to which Ho Lung belonged.

ficed a child when they raised the banner of revolt. The leader of the rebels was called P'ang the Millstone Maker. They were finally suppressed and P'ang was forced to flee. He was eventually captured and beheaded. In the eyes of the students, however, he was a hero, for all sympathized with the revolt.

'Next year, when the new rice was not yet harvested and the winter rice was exhausted, there was a food shortage in our district. The poor demanded help from the rich farmers and they began a movement called "Eat Rice Without Charge".* My father was a rice merchant and was exporting much grain to the city from our district, despite the shortage. One of his consignments was seized by the poor villagers and his wrath was boundless. I did not sympathize with him. At the same time I thought the villagers' method was wrong also.

'Another influence on me at this time was the presence in a local primary school of a "radical" teacher. He was "radical" because he was opposed to Buddhism and wanted to get rid of the gods. He urged people to convert their temples into schools. He was a widely discussed personality. I admired him and agreed with his views.

'These incidents, occurring close together, made lasting impressions on my young mind, already rebellious. In this period also I began to have a certain amount of political consciousness, especially after I read a pamphlet telling of the dismemberment of China. I remember even now that this pamphlet opened with the sentence: "Alas, China will be subjugated!" It told of Japan's occupation of Korea and Taiwan, of the loss of suzerainty in Indochina, Burma, and elsewhere. After I read this I felt depressed about the future of my country and began to realize that it was the duty of all the people to help save it.

'My father had decided to apprentice me to a rice shop in Hsiang T'an, with which he had connections. I was not opposed to it at first, thinking it might be interesting. But about this time I heard of an unusual new school and made up my mind to go there, despite my father's opposition. This school was in Hsiang Hsiang *hsien*, where my mother's family lived. A cousin of mine was a student there and he told me of the new school and of the changing conditions in "modern education". There was less emphasis on the

*Literally 'Let's eat at the Big House', that is, at the landlord's granary.

Classics, and more was taught of the "new knowledge" of the West. The educational methods, also, were quite "radical".

'I went to the school with my cousin and registered. I claimed to be a Hsiang Hsiang man, because I understood that the school was open only to natives of Hsiang Hsiang. Later on I took my true status as a Hsiang T'an native when I discovered that the place was open to all. I paid 1,400 coppers here for five months' board, lodging, and all materials necessary for study. My father finally agreed to let me enter, after friends had argued to him that this "advanced" education would increase my earning powers. This was the first time I had been as far away from home as fifty *li*. I was sixteen years old.

'In the new school I could study natural science and new subjects of Western learning. Another notable thing was that one of the teachers was a returned student from Japan, and he wore a false queue. It was quite easy to tell that his queue was false. Everyone laughed at him and called him the "False Foreign Devil".

'I had never before seen so many children together. Most of them were sons of landlords, wearing expensive clothes; very few peasants could afford to send their children to such a school. I was more poorly dressed than the others. I owned only one decent coat-and-trousers suit. Gowns were not worn by students, but only by the teachers, and none but "foreign devils" wore foreign clothes. Many of the richer students despised me because usually I was wearing my ragged coat and trousers. However, among them I had friends, and two especially were my good comrades. One of them is now a writer, living in Soviet Russia.*

'I was also disliked because I was not a native of Hsiang Hsiang. It was very important to be a native of Hsiang Hsiang and also important to be from a certain district of Hsiang Hsiang. There was an upper, lower, and middle district, and lower and upper were continually fighting, purely on a regional basis. Neither could become reconciled to the existence of the other. I took a neutral position in this war, because I was not a native at all. Consequently all three factions despised me. I felt spiritually very depressed.

'I made good progress at this school. The teachers liked me,

* Hsiao San (Emi Siao). See Bibliography.

especially those who taught the Classics, because I wrote good essays in the Classical manner. But my mind was not on the Classics. I was reading two books sent to me by my cousin, telling of the reform movement of K'ang Yu-wei. One was by Liang Ch'i-ch'ao,* editor of the *Hsin-min Ts'ung-pao* [*New People's Miscellany*]. I read and reread those books until I knew them by heart. I worshipped K'ang Yu-wei and Liang Ch'i-ch'ao, and was very grateful to my cousin, whom I then thought very progressive, but who later became a counter-revolutionary, a member of the gentry, and joined the reactionaries in the period of the Great Revolution of 1925–7.

'Many of the students disliked the False Foreign Devil because of his inhuman queue, but I liked hearing him talk about Japan. He taught music and English. One of his songs was Japanese and was called "The Battle on the Yellow Sea". I still remember some charming words from it :

> The sparrow sings,
> The nightingale dances,
> And the green fields are lovely in the spring.
> The pomegranate flowers crimson,
> The willows are green-leaved,
> And there is a new picture.

At that time I knew and felt the beauty of Japan, and felt something of her pride and might, in this song of her victory over Russia.† I did not think there was also a barbarous Japan – the Japan we know today.

'This is all I learned from the False Foreign Devil.

'I recall also that at about this time I first heard that the Emperor and Tzu Hsi, the Empress Dowager, were both dead, although the new Emperor, Hsuan T'ung [P'u Yi], had already been ruling for two years. I was not yet an antimonarchist; indeed, I considered

*Liang Ch'i-ch'ao, a talented essayist at the end of the Manchu Dynasty, was the leader of a reform movement which resulted in his exile. K'ang Yu-wei and he were the 'intellectual godfathers' of the first revolution, in 1911.

†The poem evidently referred to the spring festival and tremendous rejoicing in Japan following the Treaty of Portsmouth and the end of the Russo-Japanese War.

the Emperor as well as most officials to be honest, good, and clever men. They only needed the help of K'ang Yu-wei's reforms. I was fascinated by accounts of the rulers of ancient China: Yao, Shun, Ch'in Shih Huang Ti, and Han Wu Ti, and read many books about them.* I also learned something of foreign history at this time, and of geography. I had first heard of America in an article which told of the American Revolution and contained a sentence like this: "After eight years of difficult war, Washington won victory and built up his nation." In a book called *Great Heroes of the World*, I read also of Napoleon, Catherine of Russia, Peter the Great, Wellington, Gladstone, Rousseau, Montesquieu, and Lincoln.'

---

*Yao and Shun were semilegendary first emperors (3,000–2,205 BC?), credited with forming Chinese society in the Wei and Yellow River valleys, and taming the floods (with dikes, canals); Ch'in Shih Huang Ti (259–221 BC) unified the empire and completed the Great Wall; Han Wu Ti solidified the foundations of the Han Dynasty, which followed Ch'in and lasted (including the later Han) 426 years.

2

Days in Changsha

MAO TSE-TUNG continued:

'I began to long to go to Changsha, the great city, the capital of the province, which was 120 *li* from my home. It was said that this city was very big, contained many, many people, numerous schools, and the yamen of the governor. It was a magnificent place altogether. I wanted very much to go there at this time, and enter the middle school for Hsiang Hsiang people. That winter I asked one of my teachers in the higher primary school to introduce me there. The teacher agreed, and I walked to Changsha, exceedingly excited, half fearing that I would be refused entrance, hardly daring to hope that I could actually become a student in this great school. To my astonishment, I was admitted without difficulty. But political events were moving rapidly and I was to remain there only half a year.

'In Changsha I read my first newspaper, *Min-li-pao* [*People's Strength*], a nationalist revolutionary journal which told of the Canton Uprising against the Manchu Dynasty and the death of the Seventy-two Heroes, under the leadership of a Hunanese named Huang Hsing. I was most impressed with this story and found the *Min-li-pao* full of stimulating material. It was edited by Yu Yu-jen, who later became a famous leader of the Kuomintang. I learned also of Sun Yat-sen at this time, and of the programme of the T'ung Meng Hui.* The country was on the eve of the First Revolution. I was so agitated that I wrote an article, which I posted on the school wall. It was my first expression of a political opinion, and it was somewhat muddled. I had not yet given up my admiration of K'ang Yu-wei and Liang Ch'i-ch'ao. I did not clearly understand the

---

*The T'ung Meng Hui, a revolutionary secret society, was founded by Dr Sun Yat-sen and was the forerunner of the Kuomintang. Most of its members were exiles in Japan, where they carried on a vigorous 'brush-war' (war by writing brushes, or pens) against Liang Ch'i-ch'ao and K'ang Yu-wei, leaders of the 'reformed monarchist' party.

differences between them. Therefore in my article I advocated that Sun Yat-sen must be called back from Japan to become president of the new government, that K'ang Yu-wei be made premier, and Liang Ch'i-ch'ao minister of foreign affairs !*

'The anti-foreign-capital movement began in connection with the building of the Szechuan-Hankow railway, and a popular demand for a parliament became widespread. In reply to it the Emperor decreed merely that an advisory council be created. The students in my school became more and more agitated. They demonstrated their anti-Manchu sentiments by a rebellion against the pigtail.† One friend and I clipped off our pigtails, but others, who had promised to do so, afterwards failed to keep their word. My friend and I therefore assaulted them in secret and forcibly removed their queues, a total of more than ten falling victim to our shears. Thus in a short space of time I had progressed from ridiculing the False Foreign Devil's imitation queue to demanding the general abolition of queues. How a political idea can change a point of view !

'I got into a dispute with a friend in a law school over the pigtail episode, and we each advanced opposing theories on the subject. The law student held that the body, skin, hair, and nails are heritages from one's parents and must not be destroyed, quoting the Classics to clinch his argument. But I myself and the antipigtailers developed a counter-theory, on an anti-Manchu political basis, and thoroughly silenced him.

'After the Wuhan Uprising occurred,‡ led by Li Yuan-hung, martial law was declared in Hunan. The political scene rapidly altered. One day a revolutionary appeared in the middle school and made a stirring speech, with the permission of the principal. Seven or eight students arose in the assembly and supported him with vigorous denunciation of the Manchus, and calls for action to establish the Republic. Everyone listened with complete attention.

---

*An absurd coalition, since K'ang and Liang were monarchists at that time, and Sun Yat-sen was antimonarchist.

† An act perhaps more anti-Confucian than anti-Manchu. Some orthodox Confucianists held that man should not interfere with nature, including growth of hair and fingernails.

‡ In 1911, the start of the revolution that overthrew the Manchu Dynasty.

Not a sound was heard as the orator of the revolution, one of the officials of Li Yuan-hung, spoke before the excited students.

'Four or five days after hearing this speech I determined to join the revolutionary army of Li Yuan-hung. I decided to go to Han-kow with several other friends, and we collected some money from our classmates. Having heard that the streets of Hankow were very wet, and that it was necessary to wear rain shoes, I went to borrow some from a friend in the army, who was quartered outside the city. I was stopped by the garrison guards. The place had become very active, the soldiers had for the first time been furnished with bullets, and they were pouring into the streets.

'Rebels were approaching the city along the Canton-Hankow railway, and fighting had begun. A big battle occurred outside the city walls of Changsha. There was at the same time an insurrection within the city, and the gates were stormed and taken by Chinese labourers. Through one of the gates I re-entered the city. Then I stood on a high place and watched the battle, until at last I saw the *Han** flag raised over the yamen. It was a white banner with the character *Han* in it. I returned to my school, to find it under military guard.

'On the following day, a *tutu* † government was organized. Two prominent members of the Ke Lao Hui [Elder Brother Society] were made *tutu* and vice-*tutu*. These were Chiao Ta-feng and Chen Tso-hsing, respectively. The new government was established in the former buildings of the provincial advisory council, whose chief had been T'an Yen-k'ai, who was dismissed. The council itself was abolished. Among the Manchu documents found by the revolutionaries were some copies of a petition begging for the opening of parliament. The original had been written in blood by Hsu T'eh-li who is now commissioner of education in the Soviet Govern-

Han-jen means the ethnical descendants of 'men of Han', referring to the long-lived Han Dynasty (206 BC–AD 220). Europeans derived the name 'China' and 'Chinese' from the Ch'in Dynasty which immediately preceded the Han. China was known to *Han-jen* as Chung-kuo, the 'Central Realm', also translated as 'Middle Kingdom'. In official terminology all its inhabitants, including non-Han peoples, were called *Chung-kuo-jen*, or 'Central-Realm People'. Thus the Manchu (*Man-chou-jen*) were also *Chung-kuo-jen* (China-men) but not *Han-jen*.

† A *tutu* was a military governor.

ment. Hsu had cut off the end of his finger, as a demonstration of sincerity and determination, and his petition began, "Begging that parliament be opened, I bid farewell [to the provincial delegates to Peking] by cutting my finger."

'The new *tutu* and vice-*tutu* did not last long. They were not bad men, and had some revolutionary intentions, but they were poor and represented the interests of the oppressed. The landlords and merchants were dissatisfied with them. Not many days later, when I went to call on a friend, I saw their corpses lying in the street. T'an Yen-k'ai had organized a revolt against them, as representative of the Hunan landlords and militarists.

'Many students were now joining the army. A student army had been organized and among these students was T'ang Sheng-chih.* I did not like the student army; I considered the basis of it too confused. I decided to join the regular army instead, and help complete the revolution. The Ch'ing Emperor had not yet abdicated, and there was a period of struggle.

'My salary was seven yuan a month – which is more than I get in the Red Army now, however – and of this I spent two yuan a month on food. I also had to buy water. The soldiers had to carry water in from outside the city, but I, being a student, could not condescend to carrying, and bought it from the water peddlers. The rest of my wages were spent on newspapers, of which I became an avid reader. Among journals then dealing with the revolution was the *Hsiang Chiang Jih-pao* [*Hsiang River Daily News*]. Socialism was discussed in it, and in these columns I first learned the term. I also discussed socialism, really social-reformism, with other students and soldiers. I read some pamphlets written by Kiang K'ang-hu about socialism and its principles. I wrote enthusiastically to several of my classmates on this subject, but only one of them responded in agreement.

'There was a Hunan miner in my squad, and an ironsmith, whom I liked very much. The rest were mediocre, and one was a rascal. I persuaded two more students to join the army, and came to be on friendly terms with the platoon commander and most of the

---

*T'ang Sheng-chih later became commander of the Nationalist armies of the Wuhan Government of Wang Ching-wei (see BN) in 1927. He betrayed both Wang and the Reds and began the 'peasant massacre' of Hunan.

soldiers. I could write, I knew something about books, and they respected my "great learning". I could help by writing letters for them or in other such ways.

'The outcome of the revolution was not yet decided. The Ch'ing had not wholly given up power, and there was a struggle within the Kuomintang concerning the leadership. It was said in Hunan that further war was inevitable. Several armies were organized against the Manchus and against Yuan Shih-k'ai.* Among these was the Hunan army. But just as the Hunanese were preparing to move into action, Sun Yat-sen and Yuan Shih-k'ai came to an agreement, the scheduled war was called off, North and South were "unified", and the Nanking Government was dissolved. Thinking the revolution was over, I resigned from the army and decided to return to my books. I had been a soldier for half a year.

'I began to read advertisements in the papers. Many schools were then being opened and used this medium to attract new students. I had no special standard for judging schools; I did not know exactly what I wanted to do. An advertisement for a police school caught my eye and I registered for entrance to it. Before I was examined, however, I read an advertisement of a soap-making "school". No tuition was required, board was furnished and a small salary was promised. It was an attractive and inspiring advertisement. It told of the great social benefits of soap making, how it would enrich the country and enrich the people. I changed my mind about the police school and decided to become a soap maker. I paid my dollar registration fee here also.

'Meanwhile a friend of mine had become a law student and he

---

* Yuan Shih-k'ai, army chief of staff to the Manchu rulers, forced their abdication in 1911. Sun Yat-sen, regarded as 'father of the Republic', returned to China and was elected president by his followers in a ceremony at Nanking. Yuan held military control throughout most of the country, however. To avoid a conflict, Sun resigned when Yuan Shih-k'ai agreed to a constitutional convention and formation of a parliament. Yuan continued to rule as a military dictator, and in 1915 proclaimed himself emperor, whereupon his warlord supporters deserted him. The proclamation was rescinded after a few months. Yuan died, and the Republic (if not constitutional government) survived, to enter a period of provincial warlordism and national division.

urged me to enter his school. I also read an alluring advertisement of this law school, which promised many wonderful things. It promised to teach students all about law in three years and guaranteed that at the end of this period they would instantly become mandarins. My friend kept praising the school to me, until finally I wrote to my family, repeated all the promises of the advertisement, and asked them to send me tuition money. I painted a bright picture for them of my future as a jurist and mandarin. Then I paid a dollar to register in the law school and waited to hear from my parents.

'Fate again intervened in the form of an advertisement for a commercial school. Another friend counselled me that the country was in economic war, and that what was most needed were economists who could build up the nation's economy. His argument prevailed and I spent another dollar to register in this commercial middle school. I actually enrolled there and was accepted. Meanwhile, however, I continued to read advertisements, and one day I read one describing the charms of a higher commercial public school. It was operated by the government, it offered a wide curriculum, and I heard that its instructors were very able men. I decided it would be better to become a commercial expert there, paid my dollar and registered, then wrote my father of my decision. He was pleased. My father readily appreciated the advantages of commercial cleverness. I entered this school and remained – for one month.

'The trouble with my new school, I discovered, was that most of the courses were taught in English, and, in common with other students, I knew little English; indeed, scarcely more than the alphabet. An additional handicap was that the school provided no English teacher. Disgusted with this situation, I withdrew from the institution at the end of the month and continued my perusal of the advertisements.

'My next scholastic adventure was in the First Provincial Middle School. I registered for a dollar, took the entrance examination, and passed at the head of the list of candidates. It was a big school, with many students, and its graduates were numerous. A Chinese teacher there helped me very much; he was attracted to me because of my literary tendency. This teacher lent me a book called the *Yu-p'i T'ung-chien* [*Chronicles with Imperial Commentaries*], which contained imperial edicts and critiques by Ch'ien Lung.*

'About this time a government magazine exploded in Changsha. There was a huge fire, and we students found it very interesting. Tons of bullets and shells exploded, and gunpowder made an intense blaze. It was better than firecrackers. About a month later T'an Yen-k'ai was driven out by Yuan Shih-k'ai, who now had control of the political machinery of the Republic. T'ang Hsiang-ming replaced T'an Yen-k'ai and he set about making arrangements for Yuan's enthronement [in an attempted restoration of the monarchy, which speedily failed].

'I did not like the First Middle School. Its curriculum was limited and its regulations were objectionable. After reading *Yu-p'i T'ung-chien* I had also come to the conclusion that it would be better for me to read and study alone. After six months I left the school and arranged a schedule of education of my own, which consisted of reading every day in the Hunan Provincial Library. I was very regular and conscientious about it, and the half-year I spent in this way I consider to have been extremely valuable to me. I went to the library in the morning when it opened. At noon I paused only long enough to buy and eat two rice cakes, which were my daily lunch. I stayed in the library every day reading until it closed.

'During this period of self-education I read many books, studied world geography and world history. There for the first time I saw and studied with great interest a map of the world. I read Adam Smith's *The Wealth of Nations*, and Darwin's *Origin of Species*, and a book on ethics by John Stuart Mill. I read the works of Rousseau, Spencer's *Logic*, and a book on law written by Montesquieu. I mixed poetry and romances, and the tales of ancient Greece, with serious study of history and geography of Russia, America, England, France, and other countries.

'I was then living in a guild house for natives of Hsiang Hsiang district. Many soldiers were there also – "retired" or disbanded men from the district, who had no work to do and little money. Students and soldiers were always quarrelling in the guild house, and one night this hostility between them broke out in physical violence.

*The gifted fourth emperor of the Manchu, or Ch'ing, Dynasty, who took the throne in 1736.

The soldiers attacked and tried to kill the students. I escaped by fleeing to the toilet, where I hid until the fight was over.

'I had no money then, my family refusing to support me unless I entered school, and since I could no longer live in the guild house I began looking for a new place to lodge. Meanwhile, I had been thinking seriously of my "career" and had about decided that I was best suited for teaching. I had begun reading advertisements again. An attractive announcement of the Hunan Normal School now came to my attention, and I read with interest of its advantages: no tuition required, and cheap board and cheap lodging. Two of my friends were also urging me to enter. They wanted my help in preparing entrance essays. I wrote of my intention to my family and I received their consent. I composed essays for my two friends, and wrote one of my own. All were accepted – in reality, therefore, I was accepted three times. I did not then think my act of substituting for my friends an immoral one; it was merely a matter of friendship.

'I was a student in the normal school for five years, and managed to resist the appeals of all future advertising.[1] Finally I actually got my degree. Incidents in my life here, in the Hunan Provincial First Normal [Teachers' Training] School, were many, and during this period my political ideas began to take shape. Here also I acquired my first experiences in social action.

'There were many regulations in the new school and I agreed with very few of them. For one thing, I was opposed to the required courses in natural science. I wanted to specialize in social sciences. Natural sciences did not especially interest me, and I did not study them, so I got poor marks in most of these courses. Most of all I hated a compulsory course in still-life drawing. I thought it extremely stupid. I used to think of the simplest subjects possible to draw, finish up quickly and leave the class. I remember once, drawing a picture of the 'half-sun, half-rock',* which I represented by a straight line with a semicircle over it. Another time during an examination in drawing I contented myself with making an oval. I called it an egg. I got 40 in drawing, and failed. Fortunately my marks in social sciences were all excellent, and they balanced my poor grades in these other classes.

*The reference is to a line in a poem by Li T'ai-po.

'A Chinese teacher here, whom the students nicknamed "Yuan the Big Beard", ridiculed my writing and called it the work of a journalist. He despised Liang Ch'i-ch'ao, who had been my model, and considered him half-literate. I was obliged to alter my style. I studied the writings of Han Yu, and mastered the old Classical phraseology. Thanks to Yuan the Big Beard, therefore, I can today still turn out a passable Classical essay if required.

'The teacher who made the strongest impression on me was Yang Ch'ang-chi,[2] a returned student from England, with whose life I was later to become intimately related. He taught ethics, he was an idealist and a man of high moral character. He believed in his ethics very strongly and tried to imbue his students with the desire to become just, moral, virtuous men, useful in society. Under his influence I read a book on ethics translated by Ts'ai Yuan-p'ei and was inspired to write an essay which I entitled "The Energy of the Mind". I was then an idealist and my essay was highly praised by Professor Yang Ch'ang-chi, from his idealist viewpoint. He gave me a mark of 100 for it.

'A teacher named T'ang used to give me old copies of *Min Pao* [*People's Journal*], and I read them with keen interest. I learned from them about the activities and programme of the T'ung Meng Hui. One day I read a copy of the *Min Pao* containing a story about two Chinese students who were travelling across China and had reached Tatsienlu, on the edge of Tibet. This inspired me very much. I wanted to follow their example; but I had no money, and thought I should first try out travelling in Hunan.

'The next summer I set out across the province by foot, and journeyed through five counties. I was accompanied by a student named Hsiao Yu.[3] We walked through these five counties without using a single copper. The peasants fed us and gave us a place to sleep; wherever we went we were kindly treated and welcomed. This fellow, Hsiao Yu, with whom I travelled, later became a Kuomintang official in Nanking, under Yi Pei-ch'i,[4] who was then president of Hunan Normal School. Yi Pei-ch'i became a high official at Nanking and had Hsiao Yu appointed to the office of custodian of the Peking Palace Museum. Hsiao sold some of the most valuable treasures in the museum and absconded with the funds in 1934.[5]

'Feeling expansive and the need for a few intimate companions, I one day inserted an advertisement in a Changsha paper inviting young men interested in patriotic work to make a contact with me. I specified youths who were hardened and determined, and ready to make sacrifices for their country. To this advertisement I received three and one half replies. One was from Lu Chiang-lung, who later was to join the Communist Party and afterwards to betray it. Two others were from young men who later were to become ultra-reactionaries. The "half" reply came from a noncommittal youth named Li Li-san. Li listened to all I had to say, and then went away without making any definite proposals himself, and our friendship never developed.*

'But gradually I did build up a group of students around myself, and the nucleus was formed of what later was to become a society † that was to have a widespread influence on the affairs and destiny of China. It was a serious-minded little group of men and they had no time to discuss trivialities. Everything they did or said must have a purpose. They had no time for love or "romance" and considered the times too critical and the need for knowledge too urgent to discuss women or personal matters. I was not interested in women. My parents had married me when I was fourteen to a girl of twenty, but I had never lived with her – and never subsequently did. I did not consider her my wife and at this time gave little thought to her. Quite aside from the discussions of feminine charm, which usually play an important role in the lives of young men of this age, my companions even rejected talk of ordinary matters of daily life. I remember once being in the house of a youth who began to talk to me about buying some meat, and in my presence called in his servant and discussed the matter with him, then ordered him to buy a piece. I was annoyed and did not see that fellow again. My friends and I preferred to talk only of large matters – the nature of men, of human society, of China, the world, and the universe !

'We also became ardent physical culturists. In the winter holi-

---

*Li Li-san later became responsible for the CCP 'Li Li-san line', which Mao Tse-tung bitterly opposed. Further on Mao tells of Li's struggle with the Red Army, and of its results. See also BN.
† The Hsin-min Hsueh-hui, New People's Study Society.

days we tramped through the fields, up and down mountains, along city walls, and across the streams and rivers. If it rained we took off our shirts and called it a rain bath. When the sun was hot we also doffed shirts and called it a sun bath. In the spring winds we shouted that this was a new sport called "wind bathing". We slept in the open when frost was already falling and even in November swam in the cold rivers. All this went on under the title of "body training". Perhaps it helped much to build the physique which I was to need so badly later on in my many marches back and forth across South China, and on the Long March from Kiangsi to the North-West.[6]

'I built up a wide correspondence with many students and friends in other towns and cities. Gradually I began to realize the necessity for a more closely knit organization. In 1917, with some other friends, I helped to found the Hsin-min Hsueh-hui. It had from seventy to eighty members, and of these many were later to become famous names in Chinese communism and in the history of the Chinese Revolution. Among the better-known Communists who were in the Hsin-min Hsueh-hui were Lo Man (Li Wei-han), now secretary of the Party Organization Committee; Hsia Hsi,[*] now in the Second Front Red Army; Ho Shu-heng, who became high judge of the Supreme Court in the Central Soviet regions and was later killed by Chiang Kai-shek (1935); Kuo Liang, a famous labour organizer, killed by General Ho Chien in 1930; Hsiao Chu-chang,[†] a writer now in Soviet Russia; Ts'ai Ho-sen, a member of the Central Committee of the Communist Party, killed by Chiang Kai-shek in 1927; Yeh Li-yun, who became a member of the Central Committee, and later "betrayed" to the Kuomintang and became a capitalist trade-union organizer; and Hsiao Chen, a prominent Party leader, one of the six signers of the original agreement for the formation of the Party, who died not long ago from illness. The majority of the members of the Hsin-min Hsueh-hui were killed in the counter-revolution of 1927.[‡]

[*] See BN.

[†] Hsiao San (Emi Siao), brother of Hsiao Yu (Saio Yu). See Bibliography.

[‡] Other members included Liu Shao-ch'i, Jen Pi-shih, Li Fu-ch'un, Wang Jo-fei, T'eng Tai-yuan, Li Wei-han, Hsiao Ching-kuang, and at least one

'Another society that was formed about that time, and resembled the Hsin-min Hsueh-hui, was the "Social Welfare Society" of Hupeh. Many of its members also later became Communists. Among them was Yun Tai-ying, who was killed during the counter-revolution by Chiang Kai-shek. Lin Piao, now president of the Red Army University, was a member. So was Chang Hao, now in charge of work among White troops [those taken prisoner by the Reds]. In Peking there was a society called Hu Sheh, some of whose members later became Reds. Elsewhere in China, notably in Shanghai, Hangchow, Hankow, and Tientsin,* radical societies were organized by the militant youth then beginning to assert an influence on Chinese politics.

'Most of these societies were organized more or less under the influences of *Hsin Ch'ing-nien* [*New Youth*], the famous magazine of the literary renaissance, edited by Ch'en Tu-hsiu.[7] I began to read this magazine while I was a student in the normal school and admired the articles of Hu Shih and Ch'en Tu-hsiu very much. They became for a while my models, replacing Liang Ch'i-ch'ao and Kang Yu-wei, whom I had already discarded.

'At this time my mind was a curious mixture of ideas of liberalism, democratic reformism, and utopian socialism. I had somewhat vague passions about "nineteenth-century democracy", utopianism, and old-fashioned liberalism, and I was definitely antimilitarist and anti-imperialist.

'I had entered the normal school in 1912. I was graduated in 1918.'

---

woman, Ts'ai Chang, the sister of Ts'ai Ho-sen. All of these achieved high rank in the CCP. Mao's favourite professor and future father-in-law, Yang Ch'ang-chi, and Hsu T'eh-li, Mao's teacher at the First Normal School, were patrons.

*In Tientsin it was the Chueh-wu Shih, or 'Awakening Society', which led an organization of radical youth. Chou En-lai was one of the founders. Others included Teng Ying-ch'ao (Mme Chou En-lai); Ma Chun, who was executed in Peking in 1927; and Sun Hsiao-ch'ing, who later became secretary of the Canton Committee of the Kuomintang.

3

Prelude to Revolution

DURING Mao's recollections of his past I noticed that an auditor at least as interested as I was Ho Tzu-ch'en, his wife. Many of the facts he told about himself and the Communist movement she had evidently never heard before, and this was true of most of Mao's comrades in Pao An. Later on, when I gathered biographical notes from other Red leaders, their colleagues often crowded around interestedly to listen to the stories for the first time. Although they had all fought together for years, very often they knew nothing of each other's pre-Communist days, which they had tended to regard as a kind of Dark Ages period, one's real life beginning only when one became a Communist.

It was another night, and Mao sat cross-legged, leaning against his dispatch boxes. He lit a cigarette from a candle and took up the thread of the story where he had left off the evening before:

'During my years in normal school in Changsha I had spent, altogether, only $160 – including my numerous registration fees! Of this amount I must have used a third for newspapers, because regular subscriptions cost me about a dollar a month, and I often bought books and journals on the news-stands. My father cursed me for this extravagance. He called it wasted money on wasted paper. But I had acquired the newspaper-reading habit, and from 1911 to 1927, when I climbed up Chingkangshan, I never stopped reading the daily papers of Peking, Shanghai, and Hunan.

'In my last year in school my mother died, and more than ever I lost interest in returning home. I decided, that summer, to go to Peking. Many students from Hunan were planning trips to France, to study under the "work and learn" scheme, which France used to recruit young Chinese in her cause during the World War. Before leaving China these students planned to study French in Peking. I helped to organize the movement, and in the groups who went abroad were many students from the Hunan Normal School, most of whom were later to become famous radicals. Hsu T'eh-li was influenced by the movement also, and when he was over forty he left his professorship at Hunan Normal School and went to France. He did not become a Communist, however, till 1927.

'I accompanied some of the Hunanese students to Peking. However, although I had helped organize the movement, and it had the support of the Hsin-min Hsueh-hui, I did not want to go to Europe. I felt that I did not know enough about my own country, and that my time could be more profitably spent in China. Those students who had decided to go to France studied French then from Li Shih-tseng, who is now president of the Chung-fa [Sino-French] University, but I did not. I had other plans.

'Peking seemed very expensive to me. I had reached the capital by borrowing from friends, and when I arrived I had to look for work at once. Yang Ch'ang-chi, my former ethics teacher at the normal school, had become a professor at Peking National University. I appealed to him for help in finding a job, and he introduced me to the university librarian. He was Li Ta-chao, who later became a founder of the Communist Party of China, and was afterwards executed by Chang Tso-lin.* Li Ta-chao gave me work as assistant librarian, for which I was paid the generous sum of $8 a month.

'My office was so low that people avoided me. One of my tasks was to register the names of people who came to read newspapers, but to most of them I didn't exist as a human being. Among those who came to read I recognized the names of famous leaders of the renaissance movement, men like Fu Ssu-nien, Lo Chia-lun, and others, in whom I was intensely interested. I tried to begin conversations with them on political and cultural subjects, but they were very busy men. They had no time to listen to an assistant librarian speaking southern dialect.

'But I wasn't discouraged. I joined the Society of Philosophy,

---

*The ex-bandit who became military dictator of Manchuria. Marshal Chang held power in Peking before the arrival of the Nationalists there. He was killed by the Japanese in 1928. His son, Chang Hsueh-liang, known as the 'Young Marshal', succeeded him.

and the Journalism Society, in order to be able to attend classes in the university. In the Journalism Society I met fellow students like Ch'en Kung-po, who is now a high official at Nanking; [1] T'an P'ing-shan, who later became a Communist and still later a member of the so-called "Third Party"; and Shao P'iao-p'ing. Shao, especially, helped me very much. He was a lecturer in the Journalism Society, a liberal, and a man of fervent idealism and fine character. He was killed by Chang Tso-lin in 1926.

'While I was working in the library I also met Chang Kuo-t'ao,* now vice-chairman of the Soviet Government; K'ang P'ei-ch'en, who later joined the Ku Klux Klan in California [! ! ! – E.S.]; and Tuan Hsi-p'eng, now Vice-Minister of Education in Nanking. And here also I met and fell in love with Yang K'ai-hui. She was the daughter of my former ethics teacher, Yang Ch'ang-chi, who had made a great impression on me in my youth, and who afterwards was a genuine friend in Peking.

'My interest in politics continued to increase, and my mind turned more and more radical. I have told you of the background for this. But just now I was still confused, looking for a road, as we say. I read some pamphlets on anarchy, and was much influenced by them. With a student named Chu Hsun-pei, who used to visit me, I often discussed anarchism and its possibilities in China. At that time I favoured many of its proposals.

'My own living conditions in Peking were quite miserable, and in contrast the beauty of the old capital was a vivid and living compensation. I stayed in a place called San Yen-ching ["Three-Eyes Well"], in a little room which held seven other people. When we were all packed fast on the *k'ang* there was scarcely room enough for any of us to breathe. I used to have to warn people on each side of me when I wanted to turn over. But in the parks and the old palace grounds I saw the early northern spring, I saw the white plum blossoms flower while the ice still held solid over Pei Hai ["the North Sea"].† I saw the willows over Pei Hai with the ice crystals hanging from them and remembered the description of the scene by the T'ang poet Chen Chang, who wrote about

* See B N.

† Pei Hai and the other 'seas' were artificial lakes in the former Forbidden City.

Pei Hai's winter-jewelled trees looking "like ten thousand peach trees blossoming". The innumerable trees of Peking aroused my wonder and admiration.

'Early in 1919 I went to Shanghai with the students bound for France. I had a ticket only to Tientsin, and I did not know how I was to get any further. But, as the Chinese proverb says, "Heaven will not delay a traveller", and a fortunate loan of ten yuan from a fellow student, who had got some money from the Auguste Comte School in Peking, enabled me to buy a ticket as far as P'u-k'ou. On the way to Nanking I stopped at Ch'u Fu and visited Confucius' grave. I saw the small stream where Confucius' disciples bathed their feet and the little town where the sage lived as a child. He is supposed to have planted a famous tree near the historic temple dedicated to him, and I saw that. I also stopped by the river where Yen Hui, one of Confucius' famous disciples, had once lived, and I saw the birthplace of Mencius. On this trip I climbed T'ai Shan, the sacred mountain of Shantung, where General Feng Yu-hsiang retired and wrote his patriotic scrolls.

'But when I reached P'u-k'ou I was again without a copper, and without a ticket. Nobody had any money to lend me; I did not know how I was to get out of town. But the worst of the tragedy happened when a thief stole my only pair of shoes! Ai-ya! What was I to do? But again, "Heaven will not delay a traveller", and I had a very good piece of luck. Outside the railway station I met an old friend from Hunan, and he proved to be my "good angel". He lent me money for a pair of shoes, and enough to buy a ticket to Shanghai. Thus I safely completed my journey – keeping an eye on my new shoes. At Shanghai I found that a good sum had been raised to help send the students to France, and an allowance had been provided to help me return to Hunan. I saw my friends off on the steamer and then set out for Changsha.

'During my first trip to the North, as I remember it, I made these excursions:

'I walked around the lake of T'ung T'ing, and I circled the wall of Paotingfu. I walked on the ice of the Gulf of Pei Hai. I walked around the wall of Hsuchou, famous in the *San Kuo* [*Three Kingdoms*], and around Nanking's wall, also famous in history. Finally

I climbed T'ai Shan and visited Confucius' grave. These seemed to me then achievements worth adding to my adventures and walking tours in Hunan.

'When I returned to Changsha I took a more direct role in politics. After the May Fourth Movement * I had devoted most of my time to student political activities, and I was editor of the *Hsiang River Review*, the Hunan students' paper, which had a great influence on the student movement in South China. In Changsha I helped found the Wen-hua Shu-hui [Cultural Book Society], an association for study of modern cultural and political tendencies. This society, and more especially the Hsin-min Hsueh-hui, were violently opposed to Chang Ching-yao, then *tuchun* of Hunan, and a vicious character. We led a general student strike against Chang, demanding his removal, and sent delegations to Peking and the South-West, where Sun Yat-sen was then active, to agitate against him. In retaliation for the students' opposition, Chang Ching-yao suppressed the *Hsiang River Review*.

'After this I went to Peking, to represent the New People's Study Society and organize an antimilitarist movement there. The society broadened its fight against Chang Ching-yao into a general anti-militarist agitation, and I became head of a news agency to promote this work. In Hunan the movement was rewarded with some success. Chang Ching-yao was overthrown by T'an Yen-k'ai, and a new regime was established in Changsha. About this time the society began to divide into two groups, a right and left wing – the left wing insisting on a programme of far-reaching social and economic and political changes.

'I went to Shanghai for the second time in 1919. There once more I saw Ch'en Tu-hsiu.† I had first met him in Peking, when I was at Peking National University, and he had influenced me

*Considered the beginning of the 'Second Revolution', and of modern Chinese nationalism.

†Ch'en Tu-hsiu was born in Anhui in 1879, became a noted scholar and essayist, and for years headed the department of literature at Peking National University – 'cradle of the literary renaissance'. His *New Youth* magazine began the movement for adoption of the *pai-hua*, or vernacular Chinese, as the national language to replace the 'dead' *wen-yen*, or Classical language. With Li Ta-chao, he was a chief promoter of Marxist study in China and a pioneer organizer of the Chinese Communist Party. See BN.

perhaps more than anyone else. I also met Hu Shih at that time, having called on him to try to win his support for the Hunanese students' struggle. In Shanghai I discussed with Ch'en Tu-hsiu our plans for a League for Reconstruction of Hunan. Then I returned to Changsha and began to organize it. I took a place as a teacher there, meanwhile continuing my activity in the New People's Study Society. The society had a programme then for the "independence" of Hunan, meaning, really, autonomy. Disgusted with the Northern Government, and believing that Hunan could modernize more rapidly if freed from connections with Peking, our group agitated for separation. I was then a strong supporter of America's Monroe Doctrine and the Open Door.

'T'an Yen-k'ai was driven out of Hunan by a militarist called Chao Heng-t'i, who utilized the "Hunan independence" movement for his own ends. He pretended to support it, advocating the idea of a United Autonomous State of China, but as soon as he got power he suppressed the democratic movement with great energy. Our group had demanded equal rights for men and women, and representative government, and in general approval of a platform for a bourgeois democracy. We openly advocated these reforms in our paper, the New Hunan. We led an attack on the provincial parliament, the majority of whose members were landlords and gentry appointed by the militarists. This struggle ended in our pulling down the scrolls and banners, which were full of nonsensical and extravagant phrases.

'The attack on the parliament was considered a big incident in Hunan, and frightened the rulers. However, when Chao Heng-t'i seized control he betrayed all the ideas he had supported, and especially he violently suppressed all demands for democracy. Our society therefore turned the struggle against him. I remember an episode in 1920, when the Hsin-min Hsueh-hui organized a demonstration to celebrate the third anniversary of the Russian October Revolution. It was suppressed by the police. Some of the demonstrators had attempted to raise the Red flag at that meeting, but were prohibited from doing so by the police. The demonstrators pointed out that, according to Article 12 of the Constitution, the people had the right to assemble, organize, and speak, but the police were not impressed. They replied that they were not there to be taught the Constitution, but to carry out the orders of the governor, Chao Heng-t'i. From this time on I became more and more convinced that only mass political power, secured through mass action, could guarantee the realization of dynamic reforms.*

'In the winter of 1920 I organized workers politically for the first time, and began to be guided in this by the influence of Marxist theory and the history of the Russian Revolution. During my second visit to Peking I had read much about the events in Russia, and had eagerly sought out what little Communist literature was then available in Chinese. Three books especially deeply carved my mind, and built up in me a faith in Marxism, from which, once I had accepted it as the correct interpretation of history, I did not afterwards waver. These books were the *Communist Manifesto*, translated by Ch'en Wang-tao and the first Marxist book ever published in Chinese; *Class Struggle*, by Kautsky; and a *History of Socialism*, by Kirkup. By the summer of 1920 I had become, in theory and to some extent in action, a Marxist, and from this time on I considered myself a Marxist. In the same year I married Yang K'ai-hui.'†

---

*In October 1920, Mao organized a Socialist Youth Corps branch in Changsha, in which he worked with Lin Tsu-han to set up craft unions in Hunan.

†Mao made no further reference to his life with Yang K'ai-hui, except to mention her execution. She was a student at Peking National University and later became a youth leader during the Great Revolution, and one of the most active women Communists. Their marriage had been celebrated as an 'ideal romance' among radical youths in Hunan.

4

The Nationalist Period

MAO was now a Marxist but not a Communist, because as yet there did not exist in China an organized Communist Party. As early as 1919 Ch'en Tu-hsiu had established contact with the Comintern through Russians living in Peking, as had Li Ta-chao. It was not until the spring of 1920 that Gregori Voitinsky, an authorized representative of the Communist International, reached Peking, in the company of Yang Ming-chai, a member of the Russian Communist Party who acted as his interpreter. They conferred with Li Ta-chao and probably also met members of Li's Society for the Study of Marxist Theory. In the same year the energetic and persuasive Jahn Henricus Sneevliet,[1] a Dutch agent of the Third International – Ti-san Kuo-chi, in Chinese – came to Shanghai for talks with Ch'en Tu-hsiu, who was conferring with serious Chinese Marxists there. It was Ch'en who, in May 1920, summoned a conference that organized a nuclear Communist group. Some members of it became (with Li Ta-chao's group in Peking, another group set up in Canton by Ch'en, groups in Shantung and Hupeh, and Mao's group in Hunan) conveners of a Shanghai conference the following year that (with the help of Voitinsky) summoned the first Chinese Communist Party congress.

When one remembered, in 1937, that the Chinese Communist Party was still an adolescent in years, its achievements could be regarded as not inconsiderable. It was the strongest Communist Party in the world, outside of Russia, and the only one, with the same exception, that could boast an army of its own.

Another night, and Mao carried on his narrative:

'In May of 1921 I went to Shanghai to attend the founding meeting of the Communist Party. In its organization the leading roles were played by Ch'en Tu-hsiu and Li Ta-chao, both of whom were among the most brilliant intellectual leaders of China. Under Li Ta-chao, as assistant librarian at Peking National University, I had rapidly developed towards Marxism, and Ch'en Tu-hsiu had been instrumental in my interests in that direction too. I had discussed with Ch'en, on my second visit to Shanghai, the Marxist books that I had read, and Ch'en's own assertions of belief had deeply impressed me at what was probably a critical period of my life.

'There was only one other Hunanese * at that historic meeting [the First National Congress of the Party] in Shanghai. Others present were Chang Kuo-t'ao, now vice-chairman of the Red Army military council; Pao Hui-sheng; and Chou Fu-hai.[2] Altogether there were twelve of us. In Shanghai [those elected to] the Central Committee of the Party included Ch'en Tu-hsiu, Chang Kuo-t'ao, Ch'en Kung-po, Shih Tseng-tung (now a Nanking official), Sun Yuan-lu, Li Han-chun (killed † in Wuhan in 1927), Li Ta,‡ and Li Sun (later executed). The following October the first provincial branch of the Party was organized in Hunan and I became a member of it. Organizations were also established in other provinces and cities. Members in Hupeh included Tung Pi-wu ‡ (now chairman of the Communist Party School in Pao An), Hsu Pai-hao, and Shih Yang (executed in 1923). In the Shensi Party were Kao Chung-yu (Kao Kang‡) and some famous student leaders. In [the Party branch of] Peking were Li Ta-chao (executed, with nineteen other Peking Communists, in 1927), Teng Chung-hsia (executed by Chiang Kai-shek in 1934), Lo Chung-lun, Liu Jen-ching (now a Trotskyite), and others. In Canton were Lin Po-chu (Lin Tsu-han), now Commissioner of Finance in the Soviet Government, and P'eng P'ai ‡ (executed in 1929). Wang Chun-mei and Teng En-ming were among the founders of the Shantung branch.

'Meanwhile, in France, a Chinese Communist Party § had been organized by many of the worker-students there, and its founding was almost simultaneous with the beginning of the organization

---

*Ho Shu-heng, Mao's old friend and co-founder of the New People's Study Society; he was executed in 1935 by the Kuomintang.

†Those here noted as 'killed' or 'executed' were liquidated by warlord regimes if before 1927, and by Nationalist generals if after March 1927.

‡See BN.

§ Meaning the Communist Youth League, which began as the Socialist Youth Corps (Society, League). Other members included Teng Ying-ch'ao and Li Fu-ch'un and his wife, Ts'ai Ch'ang. See BN.

in China. Among the founders of the Party [CYL] there were Chou En-lai, Li Li-san, and Hsiang Ching-wu, the wife of Ts'ai Ho-sen. Lo Man (Li Wei-han) and Ts'ai Ho-sen were also founders of the French branch. A Chinese Party was organized in Germany, but this was somewhat later; among its members were Kao Yu-han, Chu Teh (now commander-in-chief of the Red Army), and Chang Sheng-fu (now a professor at Tsinghua University). In Moscow the founders of the branch were Ch'u Ch'iu-pai * and others, and in Japan there was Chou Fu-hai.

'In May 1922, the Hunan Party, of which I was then secretary,† had already organized more than twenty trade unions among miners, railway workers, municipal employees, printers, and workers in the government mint. A vigorous labour movement began that winter. The work of the Communist Party was then concentrated mainly on students and workers, and very little was done among the peasants. Most of the big mines were organized, and virtually all the students. There were numerous struggles on both the students' and workers' fronts. In the winter of 1922, Chao Heng-t'i, civil governor of Hunan, ordered the execution of two Hunanese workers, Huang Ai and Pang Yuan-ch'ing, and as a result a widespread agitation began against him. Huang Ai, one of the two workers killed, was a leader of the right-wing labour movement, which had its base in the industrial-school students and was opposed to us, but we supported them in this case, and in many other struggles. Anarchists were also influential in the trade unions, which were then organized into an All-Hunan Labour Syndicate. But we compromised and through negotiation prevented many hasty and useless actions by them.

'I was sent to Shanghai to help organize the movement against Chao Heng-t'i. The Second Congress of the Party was convened in Shanghai that winter [1922], and I intended to attend. How-

---

* See BN.

† Mao was also a leading member of the provincial KMT. Following his agreement with Adolf Joffe for a two-party alliance, Sun Yat-sen had begun a secret purge of anti-Communist elements in the KMT. In Hunan, Sun authorized his old colleague Lin Tsu-han, together with Mao Tse-tung and Hsia Hsi, to reorganize the Party. By January 1923 they had turned the Hunan KMT into a radical tool of the left.

ever, I forgot the name of the place where it was to be held, could not find any comrades, and missed it. I returned to Hunan and vigorously pushed the work among the labour unions. That spring there were many strikes for better wages and better treatment and recognition of the labour unions. Most of these were successful. On 1 May, a general strike was called in Hunan, and this marked the achievement of unprecedented strength in the labour movement of China.

'The Third Congress of the Communist Party was held in Canton in [May] 1923 and the historic decision was reached to enter the Kuomintang, cooperate with it, and create a united front against the northern militarists.[3] I went to Shanghai and worked in the Central Committee of the Party. Next spring [1924] I went to Canton and attended the First National Congress of the Kuomintang. In March, I returned to Shanghai and combined my work in the executive bureau [Central Committee] of the Communist Party with membership in the executive bureau [Central Executive Committee] of the Kuomintang of Shanghai. The other members of this bureau then were Wang Ching-wei * (later premier at Nanking) and Hu Han-min, with whom I worked in coordinating the measures of the Communist Party and the Kuomintang. That summer the Whampoa Military Academy was set up. Galin became its adviser, other Soviet advisers arrived from Russia, and the Kuomintang–Communist Party entente began to assume the proportions of a nationwide revolutionary movement. The following winter I returned to Hunan for a rest [4] – I had become ill in Shanghai – but while in Hunan I organized the nucleus of the great peasant movement of that province.

'Formerly I had not fully realized the degree of class struggle among the peasantry, but after the 30 May Incident [1925],† and during the great wave of political activity which followed it, the

* See BN.

† Communist and Nationalist cadres in 1925 organized the first Shanghai Federation of Trade Unions, which led to the 30 May demonstration, with demands for an end to extraterritoriality and a return of the Shanghai International Settlement to Chinese sovereignty. British Settlement police fired on the demonstrators and killed several, which provoked a boycott of British goods. Leading organizers were Liu Shao-ch'i and Ch'en Yun. See BN.

Hunanese peasantry became very militant. I left my home where I had been resting, and began a rural organizational campaign. In a few months we had formed more than twenty peasant unions, and had aroused the wrath of the landlords, who demanded my arrest. Chao Heng-t'i sent troops after me, and I fled to Canton. I reached there just at the time the Whampoa students had defeated Yang Hsi-ming, the Yunnan militarist, and Lu Tsung-wai, the Kwangsi militarist, and an air of great optimism pervaded the city and the Kuomintang. Chiang Kai-shek had been made commander of the First Army and Wang Ching-wei chairman of the government, following the death of Sun Yat-sen in Peking.

'I became editor of the *Political Weekly*, a publication of the propaganda department of the Kuomintang [headed by Wang Ching-wei]. It later played a very active role in attacking and discrediting the right wing of the Kuomintang, led by Tai Chi-t'ao. I was also put in charge of training organizers for the peasant movement [the Peasant Movement Training Institute *], and established a course for this purpose which was attended by representatives from twenty-one different provinces, and included students from Inner Mongolia. Not long after my arrival in Canton I became chief of the agit-prop department of the Kuomintang, and candidate for the Central Committee. Lin Tsu-han was then chief of the peasant department of the Kuomintang, and T'an P'ing-shan, another Communist, was chief of the workers' department.

'I was writing more and more, and assuming special responsibilities in peasant work in the Communist Party. On the basis of my study and of my work in organizing the Hunan peasants, I wrote two pamphlets, one called *Analysis of Classes in Chinese Society* and the other called *The Class Basis of Chao Heng-t'i, and the Tasks Before Us.*[5] Ch'en Tu-hsiu opposed the opinions expressed in the first one, which advocated a radical land policy and vigorous

---

*In 1925 Mao was director of the Peasant Movement Training Institute, succeeding P'eng P'ai (see BN), who had set it up in Canton in 1924. Chou En-lai also lectured there. Mao's brother, Mao Tse-min (see BN), was one of his students, who included a large percentage of Hunanese, probably recruited by Mao's provincial Party committee. Their publication was *Chungkuo Nung-min (The Chinese Peasant)*.

organization of the peasantry, under the Communist Party, and he refused it publication in the Communist central organs. It was later published in Chung-kuo Nung-min [*The Chinese Peasant*], of Canton, and in the magazine Chung-kuo Ch'ing-nien [*Chinese Youth*]. The second thesis was published as a pamphlet in Hunan. I began to disagree with Ch'en's Right-opportunist policy about this time, and we gradually drew further apart, although the struggle between us did not come to a climax until 1927.

'I continued to work in the Kuomintang in Canton until about the time Chiang Kai-shek attempted his first *coup d'état* there in March 1926. After the reconciliation of left- and right-wing Kuomintang and the reaffirmation of Kuomintang–Communist solidarity, I went to Shanghai, in the spring of 1926. The Second Congress of the Kuomintang was held in May of that year, under the leadership of Chiang Kai-shek.* In Shanghai I directed the Peasant Department of the Communist Party, and from there was sent to Hunan, as inspector of the peasant movement [for both the Kuomintang and the Communist Party].† Meanwhile, under the united front of the Kuomintang and the Communist Party, the historic Northern Expedition began in the autumn of 1926.

In Hunan I inspected peasant organization and political conditions in five *hsien* – Changsha, Li Ling, Hsiang T'an, Hung Shan and Hsiang Hsiang – and made my report [*Report on an Investigation into the Peasant Movement in Hunan* 6] to the Central Committee, urging the adoption of a new line in the peasant movement. Early next spring, when I reached Wuhan, an interprovincial meeting of peasants was held, and I attended it and discussed the proposals of my thesis, which carried recommendations for a widespread redistribution of land. At this meeting were P'eng P'ai, Fang Chih-min,‡ and two Russian Communists, Jolk [York?] and Volen, among others. A resolution was passed adopting my pro-

*Mao attended the Second KMT Congress and was re-elected an alternate to the CEC. Communist membership in the Kuomintang CEC at that time was still about one third of the total.

†Since its inception, the Peasant Department of the Kuomintang had been headed by Communists, of whom Mao was the last of five. Mao was first chief of the CCP Peasant Department (May–October 1926), formed at this time.

‡See BN.

posal for submission to the Fifth Congress of the Communist Party. The Central Committee, however, rejected it.

'When the Fifth Congress of the Party was convened in Wuhan in May 1927, the Party was still under the domination of Ch'en Tu-hsiu. Although Chiang Kai-shek had already led the counter-revolution and begun his attacks on the Communist Party in Shanghai and Nanking, Ch'en was still for moderation and concessions to the Wuhan Kuomintang. Overriding all opposition, he followed a Right-opportunist petty-bourgeois policy. I was very dissatisfied with the Party policy then, especially towards the peasant movement. I think today that if the peasant movement had been more thoroughly organized and armed for a class struggle against the landlords, the soviets would have had an earlier and far more powerful development throughout the whole country.

'But Ch'en Tu-hsiu violently disagreed.* He did not understand the role of the peasantry in the revolution and greatly underestimated its possibilities at this time. Consequently the Fifth Congress, held on the eve of the crisis of the Great Revolution, failed to pass an adequate land programme. My opinions, which called for rapid intensification of the agrarian struggle, were not even discussed, for the Central Committee, also dominated by Ch'en Tu-hsiu, refused to bring them up for consideration. The Congress dismissed the land problem by defining a landlord as 'a peasant who owns over 500 *mou* of land' † – a wholly inadequate and unpractical basis on which to develop the class struggle, and quite without consideration of the special character of land economy in China. Following the Congress, however, an All-China Peasants' Union was organized and I became first president of it.

'By the spring of 1927 the peasant movement in Hupeh, Kiangsi, and Fukien, and especially in Hunan, had developed a startling militancy, despite the lukewarm attitude of the Communist Party

---

*So did Stalin. Mao was not present during the terminal sessions of the Fifth Congress, when a resolution was passed to limit land confiscation only to great landlords who were also 'enemies of the people', in line with Stalin's directives.

† About thirty-three hectares, or nearly a hundred times the available cultivable land per farmer.

to it, and the definite alarm of the Kuomintang. High officials and army commanders began to demand its suppression, describing the Peasants' Union as a "vagabond union", and its actions and demands as excessive. Ch'en Tu-hsiu had withdrawn from Hunan, holding me responsible for certain happenings there, and violently opposing my ideas.*

'In April, the counter-revolutionary movement had begun in Nanking and Shanghai, and a general massacre of organized workers had taken place under Chiang Kai-shek. The same measures were carried out in Canton. On 21 May, the Hsu K'o-hsiang Uprising occurred in Hunan. Scores of peasants and workers were killed by the reactionaries. Shortly afterwards the Left Kuomintang at Wuhan annulled its agreement with the Communists and "expelled" them from the Kuomintang and from a government which quickly ceased to exist.

'Many Communist leaders were now ordered by the Party to leave the country, go to Russia or Shanghai or places of safety. I was ordered to go to Szechuan. I persuaded Ch'en Tu-hsiu to send me to Hunan instead, as secretary of the Provincial Committee, but after ten days he ordered me to return at once, accusing me of organizing an uprising against T'ang Sheng-chih, then in command at Wuhan. The affairs of the Party were now in a chaotic state. Nearly everyone was opposed to Ch'en Tu-hsiu's leadership and his opportunist line. The collapse of the entente at Wuhan soon afterwards brought about his downfall.'

*Mao supported (and probably initiated) the Hunan Peasants' Union resolutions demanding confiscation of all large land holdings.

5

The Soviet Movement

A CONVERSATION I had with Mao Tse-tung concerning the much-disputed events of the spring of 1927 seemed to me of sufficient interest to mention here. It was not part of his autobiography, as he told it to me, but it was important to note as a personal reflection on what was a turning-point experience in the life of every Chinese Communist.

I asked Mao whom he considered most responsible for the failure of the Communist Party in 1927, the defeat of the Wuhan coalition government, and the whole triumph of the Nanking dictatorship. Mao placed the greatest blame on Ch'en Tu-hsiu, whose 'wavering opportunism deprived the Party of decisive leadership and a direct line of its own at a moment when further compromise clearly meant catastrophe'.

After Ch'en, the man he held responsible for the defeat was Mikhail Markovich Borodin, chief Russian political adviser, who was answerable directly to the Soviet Politburo. Mao explained that Borodin had completely reversed his position, favouring a radical land redistribution in 1926, but strongly opposing it in 1927, without any logical support for his vacillations. 'Borodin stood just a little to the right of Ch'en Tu-hsiu,' Mao said, 'and was ready to do everything to please the bourgeoisie, even to the disarming of the workers, which he finally ordered.' M. N. Roy, the Indian delegate to the Comintern, 'stood a little to the left of both Ch'en and Borodin, but he only stood'. He 'could talk', according to Mao, 'and he talked too much, without offering any method of realization.' Mao thought that, objectively, Roy had been a fool, Borodin a blunderer, and Ch'en an unconscious traitor.

'Ch'en was really frightened of the workers and especially of the armed peasants. Confronted at last with the reality of armed insurrection, he completely lost his senses. He could no longer see clearly what was happening, and his petty-bourgeois instincts betrayed him into panic and defeat.'

Mao asserted that Ch'en was at that time complete dictator of the Chinese Party, and took vital decisions without even consulting the Central Committee. 'He did not show other Party leaders the orders of the Comintern,' according to Mao, 'or even discuss them with us.' [1] But in the end it was Roy who forced the break with the Kuomintang. The Comintern sent a message to Borodin ordering the Party to begin a limited confiscation of the landlords' land. Roy got hold of a copy of it and promptly showed it to Wang Ching-wei, then chairman of the Left Kuomintang Government at Wuhan. The result of this caprice [2] is well known. The Communists were expelled from the Kuomintang by the Wuhan regime, which soon afterwards collapsed, having lost the support of regional warlords, who now sought safety in compromises with Chiang Kai-shek. Borodin and other Comintern agents fled to Russia, and arrived there in time to see the Opposition crushed and Trotsky's 'permanent revolution' discredited, while Stalin set out in earnest to 'build socialism [Stalinism?] in one country'.

Mao did not think that the counter-revolution would have been defeated in 1927 even if the Communist Party had carried out a more aggressive policy of land confiscation and created Communist armies from among the workers and peasants before the split with the Kuomintang. 'But the soviets could have got an immense start in the South, and a base in which, afterwards, they would never have been destroyed.'

In his narrative of himself Mao had now reached the beginning of the soviets, which arose from the wreckage of the revolution and struggled to build a victory out of defeat. He continued:

'On 1 August 1927, the Twentieth Army, under Ho Lung and Yeh T'ing, and in cooperation with Chu Teh, led the historic Nanchang Uprising,[3] and the beginning of what was to become the Red Army was organized. A week later, on 7 August, an extraordinary meeting [Emergency Conference] of the Central Committee of the Party deposed Ch'en Tu-hsiu as secretary. I had been a member of the political bureau of the Party since the

Third Conference at Canton in 1924, and was active in this decision, and among the ten other members present at the meeting
were: Ts'ai Ho-sen, P'eng P'ai, Chang Kuo-t'ao and Ch'u Ch'iu-
pai.* A new line was adopted by the Party, and all hope of cooperation with the Kuomintang was given up for the present,
as it had already become hopelessly the tool of imperialism and
could not carry out the responsibilities of a democratic revolution.
The long, open struggle for power now began.

'I was sent to Changsha to organize the movement which later
became known as the Autumn Harvest Uprising. My programme
there called for the realization of five points: (1) complete severance of the provincial Party from the Kuomintang, (2) organization of a peasant-worker revolutionary army, (3) confiscation of
the property of small and middle, as well as great, landlords, (4)
setting up the power of the Communist Party in Hunan, independent of the Kuomintang, and (5) organization of soviets. The
fifth point at that time was opposed by the Comintern, and not
till later did it advance it as a slogan.

'In September we had already succeeded in organizing a widespread uprising, through the peasant unions of Hunan, and the
first units of a peasant-worker army were formed. Recruits were
drawn from three principal sources – the peasantry itself, the Hanyang miners, and the insurrectionist troops of the Kuomintang.
This early military force of the revolution was called the "First
Division of the First Peasants' and Workers' Army". The first
regiment was formed from the Hanyang [P'ing Shan] miners.† A
second was created among the peasant guards in P'ing Kiang, Liu
Yang, Li Ling and two other *hsien* of Hunan, and a third from

---

*Ch'u Ch'iu-pai was here chosen general secretary of the Politburo,
replacing Ch'en Tu-hsiu, who was accused of 'rightism' and dropped from
the Politburo.

† Miners who had been organized by Mao, Liu Shao-ch'i and Ch'en Yun.
In forming a peasants' and workers' army, and soldiers' soviets and people's
councils, Mao acted independently of the Central Committee and was
reprimanded. By the time he had set up his first soldiers' soviets the CMT
line had changed again. In November of 1927 the Central Committee expelled Mao from the Politburo for 'rightism'. All the basic work he did in
Chingkangshan that winter was 'illegal', although Mao was not aware of
it for some months. He was reinstated in June 1928.

part of the garrison forces of Wuhan, which had revolted against Wang Ching-wei. This army was organized with the sanction of the Hunan Provincial Committee, but the general programme of the Hunan Committee and of our army was opposed by the Central Committee of the Party, which seemed, however, to have adopted a policy of wait-and-see rather than of active opposition.

'While I was organizing the army and travelling between the Hanyang miners and the peasant guards, I was captured by some *min-t'uan*, working with the Kuomintang. The Kuomintang terror was then at its height and hundreds of suspected Reds were being shot. I was ordered to be taken to the *min-t'uan* headquarters, where I was to be killed. Borrowing several tens of dollars from a comrade, however, I attempted to bribe the escort to free me. The ordinary soldiers were mercenaries, with no special interest in seeing me killed, and they agreed to release me, but the subaltern in charge refused to permit it. I therefore decided to attempt to escape, but had no opportunity to do so until I was within about two hundred yards of the *min-t'uan* headquarters. At that point I broke loose and ran into the fields.

'I reached a high place, above a pond, with some tall grass surrounding it, and there I hid until sunset. The soldiers pursued me, and forced some peasants to help them search. Many times they came very near, once or twice so close that I could almost have touched them, but somehow I escaped discovery, although half a dozen times I gave up hope, feeling certain I would be recaptured. At last, when it was dusk, they abandoned the search. At once I set off across the mountains, travelling all night. I had no shoes and my feet were badly bruised. On the road I met a peasant who befriended me, gave me shelter and later guided me to the next district. I had seven dollars with me, and used this to buy some shoes, an umbrella, and food. When at last I reached the peasant guards safely, I had only two coppers in my pocket.

'With the establishment of the new division, I became chairman of its Party Front Committee, and Yu Sha-t'ou, a commander of the garrison troops at Wuhan, became commander of the First Army. Yu, however, had been more or less forced to take the position by the attitude of his men; soon afterwards he deserted and joined the Kuomintang. He is now working for Chiang Kai-shek at Nanking.

'The little army, leading the peasant uprising, moved southward through Hunan. It had to break its way through thousands of Kuomintang troops and fought many battles, with many reverses. Discipline was poor, political training was at a low level, and many wavering elements were among the men and officers. There were many desertions. After Yu Sha-t'ou fled, the army was reorganized when it reached Ningtu. Ch'en Hao was made commander of the remaining troops, about one regiment; he, too, later on betrayed. But many in that first group remained loyal to the end, and are today still in the Red Army – men such as Lo Jung-huan,* political commissar of the First Army Corps, and Yang Li-san, now an army commander. When the little band finally climbed up Chingkangshan they numbered in all only about one thousand.⁴

'Because the programme of the Autumn Harvest Uprising had not been sanctioned by the Central Committee, because also the First Army had suffered some severe losses, and from the angle of the cities the movement appeared doomed to failure, the Central Committee now definitely repudiated me.† I was dismissed from the Politburo, and also from the Party [General] Front Committee. The Hunan Provincial Committee also attacked us, calling us "the rifle movement". We nevertheless held our army together at Chingkangshan, feeling certain that we were following the correct line, and subsequent events were to vindicate us fully. New recruits were added and the division filled out again. I became its commander.

'From the winter of 1927 to the autumn of 1928, the First Division held its base at Chingkangshan. In November 1927, the first soviet was set up in Tsalin [Ch'aling] on the Hunan border, and the first soviet government was elected.‡ Iits chairman was Tu Chung-pin. In this soviet, and subsequently, we promoted a

* See BN.

† Mao was reprimanded three times by the Central Committee and three times expelled by it. See Chang Kuo-t'ao, BN.

‡ In the same month a 'soviet' was established by P'eng P'ai in Hailufeng, but it was quickly destroyed.

democratic programme, with a moderate policy, based on slow but regular development. This earned Chingkangshan the recriminations of putschists in the Party, who were demanding a terrorist policy of raiding, and burning and killing of landlords, in order to destroy their morale. The First **Army** Front Committee refused to adopt such tactics, and were therefore branded by the hotheads as "reformists". I was bitterly attacked by them for not carrying out a more "radical" policy.

'Two former bandit leaders near Chingkangshan, named Wang Tso and Yuan Wen-t'sai, joined the Red Army in the winter of 1927. This increased the strength to about three regiments. Wang and Yuan were both made regimental commanders and I was an army commander. These two men, although former bandits, had thrown in their forces with the Nationalist Revolution, and were now ready to fight against the reaction. While I remained on Chingkangshan they were faithful Communists, and carried out the orders of the Party. Later on, when they were left alone at Chingkangshan, they returned to their bandit habits. Subsequently they were killed by the peasants, by then organized and sovietized and able to defend themselves.

'In May of 1928, Chu Teh arrived at Chingkangshan and our forces were combined. Together we drew up a plan [at the first Maoping Conference *] to establish a six-*hsien* soviet area, to stabilize and consolidate gradually the Communist power in the Hunan–Kiangsi–Kwangtung border districts, and, with that as a base, to expand over greater areas. This strategy was in opposition to recommendations of the Party, which had grandiose ideas of rapid expansion. In the army itself Chu Teh and I had to fight against two tendencies: first, a desire to advance on Changsha [the capital of Hunan] at once, which we considered adventurism; second, a desire to withdraw to the south of the Kwangtung border, which we regarded as "retreatism" [capitulationism]. Our main tasks, as we saw them then, were two: to divide the land,

---

*Here Mao Tse-tung and Chu Teh formed an alliance with Lin Piao, Ch'en Yi, Hsiao K'e, Ho Chang-kung, T'an Chen-lin, Chang Wen-ping, Hsia Hsi, and others, which held together against all pressure from Comintern-backed Politburo leader Li Li-san and, later on, the Moscow-educated returned students called the 'Twenty-eight Bolsheviks'. See Chapter 6 and BN.

and to establish soviets. We wanted to arm the masses to hasten those processes. Our policy called for free trade [with the White areas], generous treatment of captured enemy troops, and, in general, democratic moderation.

'A representative meeting [the second Maoping Conference] was called at Chingkangshan in the autumn of 1928, and was attended by delegates from soviet districts north of Chingkang-shan. Some division of opinion still existed among Party men in the soviet districts concerning the points mentioned above, and at this meeting differences were thoroughly aired. A minority argued that our future on this basis was narrowly limited, but the majority had faith in the policy, and when a resolution was proposed declaring that the soviet movement would be victorious, it was easily passed. The Party Central Committee, however, had not yet given the movement its sanction. This was not received till the winter of 1928, when the report of proceedings at the Sixth Congress of the Chinese Communist Party, held in Moscow, reached Chingkangshan.

'With the new line adopted at that Congress, Chu Teh and I were in complete agreement.[5] From that time on, the differences between the leaders of the Party and the leaders of the soviet movement in the agrarian districts disappeared. Party harmony was re-established.

'Resolutions of the Sixth Congress summarized the experience of the 1925–7 revolution and the Nanchang, Canton, and Autumn Harvest uprisings. It concluded with approval of the emphasis on the agrarian movement. About this time Red armies began to appear elsewhere in China. Uprisings had occurred in western and eastern Hupeh, in the winter of 1927, and these furnished the basis for new soviet districts. Ho Lung in the west and Hsu Hai-tung * in the east began to form their own worker–peasant armies. The latter's area of operations became the nucleus of the Oyuwan Soviet,† to which later on went Hsu Hsiang-ch'ien * and Chang Kuo-t'ao. Fang Chih-min and Hsiao Shih-ping had also begun a movement along the north-eastern frontier of Kiangsi, adjacent to Fukien, in the winter of 1927, and out of this later developed a

* See BN.
† See Part Nine, Chapter 1.

powerful soviet base. After the failure of the Canton Uprising, P'eng P'ai had led part of the loyal troops to Hailufeng, and there formed a soviet, which, following a policy of putschism, was soon destroyed. Part of the army, however, emerged from the district under the command of Ku Ta-chen,* and made connections with Chu Teh and myself, later on becoming the nucleus of the Eleventh Red Army.

'In the spring of 1928, partisans became active in Hsingkuo and Tungku in Kiangsi, led by Li Wen-lung and Li Shao-tsu. This movement had its base around Kian, and these partisans later became the core of the Third Army, while the district itself became the base of the Central Soviet Government. In western Fukien soviets were established by Chang Ting-ch'eng,† Teng Tzu-hui,* and Hu Pei-teh, who afterwards became a Social Democrat.

'During the "struggle v. adventurism" period at Chingkangshan, the First Army had defeated two attempts by White troops to retake the mountain. Chingkangshan proved to be an excellent base for a mobile army such as we were building. It had good natural defences, and grew enough crops to supply a small army. It had a circuit of 500 *li* and was about 80 *li* in diameter. Locally it was known otherwise, as Ta Hsiao Wu Chin [Big-Little Five Wells], the real Chingkangshan being a nearby mountain, long deserted, and got its name from five main wells on its sides – *ta, hsiao, shang, hsia,* and *chung,* or big, small, upper, lower, and middle wells. The five villages on the mountain were named after these wells.

'After the forces of our army combined at Chingkangshan there was a reorganization, the famous Fourth Red Army was created, and Chu Teh was made commander, while I became political commissar. More troops arrived at Chingkangshan after uprisings and mutinies in Ho Chien's army, in the winter of 1928, and out of these emerged the Fifth Red Army, commanded by P'eng Teh-huai.* In addition to P'eng there were Teng P'ing, killed at Tsunyi, Kweichow, during the Long March, Huang Kuo-nu, killed in Kwangsi in 1931, and T'ien Teh-yuan.

*See BN.

† One of Chang's recruits was Yang Ch'eng-wu, whom the author met in north Shensi in 1936. For both, see BN.

'Conditions on the mountain, with the arrival of so many troops, were becoming very bad. The troops had no winter uniforms, and food was extremely scarce. For months we lived practically on squash. The soldiers shouted a slogan of their own: "Down with capitalism, and eat squash!" – for to them capitalism meant landlords and the landlords' squash. Leaving P'eng Teh-huai at Chingkangshan, Chu Teh broke through the blockade established by the White troops, and in January 1929 our first sojourn on the embattled mountain ended.

'The Fourth Army now began a campaign through the south of Kiangsi which rapidly developed successfully. We established a soviet in Tungku, and there met and united with local Red troops. Dividing forces, we continued into Yungting, Shangheng, and Lung Yen, and established soviets in all those counties. The existence of militant mass movements prior to the arrival of the Red Army assured our success, and helped to consolidate soviet power on a stable basis very quickly. The influence of the Red Army now extended, through the agrarian mass movement and partisans, to several other *hsien*, but the Communists did not fully take power there until later on.

'Conditions in the Red Army began to improve, both materially and politically, but there were still many bad tendencies. "Partisanism", for example, was a weakness reflected in lack of discipline, exaggerated ideas of democracy, and looseness of organization. Another tendency that had to be fought was "vagabondage" – a disinclination to settle down to the serious tasks of government, a love of movement, change, new experience and incident. There were also remnants of militarism, with some of the commanders maltreating or even beating the men, and discriminating against those they disliked personally, while showing favouritism to others.

'Many of the weaknesses were overcome after the convening of the Ninth Party Conference of the Fourth Red Army, held in west Fukien [at Ku-t'ien] [6] in December 1929. Ideas for improvements were discussed, many misunderstandings levelled out, and new plans were adopted, which laid the foundations for a high type of ideological leadership in the Red Army. Prior to this the tendencies already described were very serious, and were utilized by a Trotskyist faction in the Party and military leadership to undermine the strength of the movement. A vigorous struggle was now begun against them, and several were deprived of their Party positions and army command. Of these Liu En-k'ang, an army commander, was typical. It was found that they intended to destroy the Red Army by leading it into difficult positions in battles with the enemy, and after several unsuccessful encounters their plans became quite evident. They bitterly attacked our programme and everything we advocated. Experience having shown their errors, they were eliminated from responsible positions and after the Fukien Conference lost their influence.

'This conference prepared the way for the establishment of the soviet power in Kiangsi. The following year was marked with some brilliant successes. Nearly the whole of southern Kiangsi fell to the Red Army. The base of the central soviet regions had been established.

'On 7 February 1930, an important local Party conference was called in south Kiangsi to discuss the future programme of the soviets. It was attended by local representatives from the Party, the army, and the government. Here the question of the land policy was argued at great length, and the struggle against "opportunism", led by those opposed to redistribution, was overcome. It was resolved to carry out land redistribution and quicken the formation of soviets. Until then the Red Army had formed only local and district soviets. At this conference it was decided to establish the Kiangsi Provincial Soviet Government. To the new programme the peasants responded with a warm, enthusiastic support which helped, in the months ahead, to defeat the extermination campaigns of the Kuomintang armies.'

6

Growth of the Red Army

MAO TSE-TUNG'S account had begun to pass out of the category of 'personal history', and to sublimate itself somehow intangibly in the career of a great movement in which, though he retained a dominant role, you could not see him clearly as a personality. It was no longer 'I' but 'we'; no longer Mao Tse-tung, but the Red Army; no longer a subjective impression of the experiences of a single life, but an objective record by a bystander concerned with the mutations of collective human destiny as the material of history.

As his story drew to a close it became more and more necessary for me to interrogate him about himself. What was *he* doing at that time? What office did *he* hold then? What was *his* attitude in this or that situation? And my questioning, generally, evoked such references as there are to himself in this last chapter of the narrative:

'Gradually the Red Army's work with the masses improved, discipline strengthened, and a new technique in organization developed. The peasantry everywhere began to volunteer to help the revolution. As early as Chingkangshan the Red Army had imposed three simple rules of discipline upon its fighters, and these were: prompt obedience to orders; no confiscations whatever from the poor peasantry; and prompt delivery directly to the government, for its disposal, of all goods confiscated from the landlords. After the 1928 Conference [second Maoping Conference] emphatic efforts to enlist the support of the peasantry were made, and eight rules were added to the three listed above. These were as follows:

1. Replace all doors when you leave a house;*
2. Return and roll up the straw matting on which you sleep;

*This order is not so enigmatic as it sounds. The wooden doors of a Chinese house are easily detachable, and are often taken down at night, put across wooden blocks, and used for an improvised bed.

3. Be courteous and polite to the people and help them when you can;

4. Return all borrowed articles;

5. Replace all damaged articles;

6. Be honest in all transactions with the peasants;

7. Pay for all articles purchased;

8. Be sanitary, and, especially, establish latrines a safe distance from people's houses.

'The last two rules were added by Lin Piao. These eight points were enforced with better and better success, and today are still the code of the Red soldier, memorized and frequently repeated by him.* Three other duties were taught to the Red Army, as its primary purpose: first, to struggle to the death against the enemy; second, to arm the masses; third, to raise money to support the struggle.

'Early in 1929 several groups of partisans under Li Wen-lung and Li Shao-tsu were reorganized into the Third Red Army, commanded by Wang Kung-lu, and with Ch'en Yi as political commissar. During the same period, part of Chu Pei-teh's *min-t'uan* mutinied and joined the Red Army. They were led to the Communist camp by a Kuomintang commander, Lo P'ing-hui,† who was disillusioned about the Kuomintang and wanted to join the Red Army. He is now commander of the Thirty-second Red Army of the Second Front Army. From the Fukien partisans and nucleus of regular Red troops the Twelfth Red Army was created under the command of Wu Chung-hao, with T'an Chen-lin as political commissar. Wu was later killed in battle and replaced by Lo P'ing-hui.

'It was at this time that the First Army Corps was organized, with Chu Teh as commander and myself as political commissar. It was composed of the Third Army, the Fourth Army commanded by Lin Piao, and the Twelfth Army, under Lo P'ing-hui. Party leadership was vested in a Front Committee, of which I was chairman. There were already more than 10,000 men in the First Army Corps then, organized into ten divisions. Besides this main force, there were many local and independent regiments, Red Guards and partisans.

*They were also sung daily in a Red Army song.
† See BN.

'Red tactics, apart from the political basis of the movement, explained much of the successful military development. At Ching-kangshan four slogans had been adopted, and these give the clue to the methods of partisan warfare used, out of which the Red Army grew. The slogans were:

1. When the enemy advances, we retreat!
2. When the enemy halts and encamps, we trouble them!
3. When the enemy seeks to avoid a battle, we attack!
4. When the enemy retreats, we pursue!

'These slogans [of four characters each in Chinese] were at first opposed by many experienced military men, who did not agree with the type of tactics advocated. But much experience proved that the tactics were correct. Whenever the Red Army departed from them, in general, it did not succeed. Our forces were small, exceeded from ten to twenty times by the enemy; our resources and fighting materials were limited, and only by skilfully combining the tactics of manoeuvring and guerrilla warfare could we hope to succeed in our struggle against the Kuomintang, fighting from vastly richer and superior bases.

'The most important single tactic of the Red Army was, and remains, its ability to concentrate its main forces in the attack, and swiftly divide and separate them afterwards. This implied that positional warfare was to be avoided, and every effort made to meet the living forces of the enemy while in movement, and destroy them. On the basis of these tactics the mobility and the swift, powerful "short attack" of the Red Army was developed.*

'In expanding soviet areas in general the programme of the Red Army favoured a wavelike or tidal development, rather than an uneven advance, gained by "leaps" or "jumps", and without deep consolidation in the territories gained. The policy was pragmatic, just as were the tactics already described, and grew out of many years of collective military and political experience. These tactics were severely criticized by Li Li-san, who advocated the concentration of all weapons in the hands of the Red Army, and the absorption of all partisan groups. He wanted attacks rather than consolidation; advances without securing the rear; sensational

*For details see Lin Piao, BN.

assaults on big cities, accompanied by uprisings and extremism. The Li Li-san line dominated the Party then – outside soviet areas – and was sufficiently influential to force acceptance, to some extent, in the Red Army, against the judgement of its field command. One result of it was the attack on Changsha and another was the advance on Nanchang. But the Red Army refused to immobilize its partisan groups and open up its rear to the enemy during these adventures.

'In the autumn of 1929 the Red Army moved into northern Kiangsi, attacking and occupying many cities, and inflicting numerous defeats on Kuomintang armies. When within striking distance of Nanchang the First Army Corps turned sharply west and moved on Changsha. In this drive it met and joined forces with P'eng Teh-huai, who had already occupied Changsha once, but had been forced to withdraw to avoid being surrounded by vastly superior enemy troops. P'eng had been obliged to leave Chingkang-shan in April 1929, and had carried out operations in southern Kiangsi, resulting in greatly increasing his troops. He rejoined Chu Teh and the main forces of the Red Army at Juichin in April 1930, and after a conference it was decided that P'eng's Third Army should operate on the Kiangsi-Hunan border, while Chu Teh and I moved into Fukien. It was in June 1930 that the Third Army and the First Army corps re-established a junction and began the second attack on Changsha. The First and Third Army corps were combined into the First Front Army, with Chu Teh as commander-in-chief and myself as political commissar. Under this leadership we arrived outside the walls of Changsha.

'The Chinese Workers' and Peasants' Revolutionary Committee was organized about this time, and I was elected chairman. The Red Army's influence in Hunan was widespread, almost as much so as in Kiangsi. My name was known among the Hunanese peasants, for big rewards were offered for my capture, dead or alive, as well as for Chu Teh and other Reds. My land* in Hsiang T'an was confiscated by the Kuomintang. My wife and my sister, as well as the wives of my two brothers, Mao Tse-min and Mao Tse-t'an,† and

---

*The rent from which Mao had used earlier for the peasant movement in Hunan.

† See BN.

my own sons were all arrested by Ho Chien [the warlord governor]. My wife (K'ai-hui) and my sister (Tse-hung) were executed.[1] The others were later released. The prestige of the Red Army even extended to my own village, in Hsiang T'an, for I heard the tale that the local peasants believed that I would be soon returning to my native home. When one day an airplane passed overhead, they decided it was I. They warned the man who was then tilling my land that I had come back to look over my old farm, to see whether or not any trees had been cut. If so, I would surely demand compensation from Chiang Kai-shek, they said.

'But the second attack on Changsha proved to be a failure. Great reinforcements had been sent to the city and it was heavily garrisoned; besides, new troops were pouring into Hunan in September to attack the Red Army. Only one important battle occurred during the siege, and in it the Red Army eliminated two brigades of enemy troops. It could not, however, take the city of Changsha, and after a few weeks withdrew to Kiangsi.[2]

'This failure helped to destroy the Li Li-san line and saved the Red Army from what would probably have been a catastrophic attack on Wuhan, which Li was demanding. The main tasks of the Red Army then were the recruiting of new troops, the sovietization of new rural areas, and, above all, the consolidation under thorough soviet power of such areas as already had fallen to the Red Army. For such a programme the attacks on Changsha were not necessary and had an element of adventure in them. Had the first occupation been undertaken as a temporary action, however, and not with the idea of attempting to hold the city and set up a state power there, its effects might have been considered beneficial, for the reaction produced on the national revolutionary movement was very great. The error was a strategic and tactical one, in attempting to make a base of Changsha while the soviet power was still not consolidated behind it.'

To interrupt Mao's narrative for a moment: Li Li-san was a Hunanese and a returned student from France. He divided time in Shanghai and Hankow, where the Communist Party had 'underground' headquarters – only after 1930 was the Central Committee transferred to the soviet districts. Li dominated the Chinese

Party from 1929 to 1930, when he was removed from the Polit-buro and sent to Moscow. Like Ch'en Tu-hsiu, Li Li-san lacked faith in the rural soviets, and urged that strong aggressive tactics be adopted against strategic big capitals like Changsha, Wuhan, and Nanchang. He wanted a 'terror' in the villages to demoralize the gentry, a 'mighty offensive' by the workers, risings and strikes to paralyse the enemy in his bases, and 'flank attacks' in the North, from Outer Mongolia and Manchuria, backed by the USSR.*

To continue:

'But Li Li-san overestimated both the military strength of the Red Army at that time and the revolutionary factors in the national political scene. He believed that the revolution was nearing success and would shortly have power over the entire country. This belief was encouraged by the long and exhausting civil war then pro-ceeding between Feng Yu-hsiang and Chiang Kai-shek, which made the outlook seem highly favourable to Li Li-san. But in the opinion of the Red Army the enemy was making preparations for a great drive against the soviets as soon as the civil war was con-cluded, and it was no time for possibly disastrous putschism and adventures. This estimate proved to be entirely correct.

'With the events in Hunan, the Red Army's return to Kiangsi, and especially after the capture of Kian, "Lilisanism" was over-come in the army; and Li himself, proved to have been in error, soon lost his influence in the Party. There was, however, a critical period in the army before "Lilisanism" was definitely buried. Part of the Third Corps favoured following out Li's line, and demanded the separation of the Third Corps from the rest of the army. P'eng Teh-huai fought vigorously against this tendency, however, and succeeded in maintaining the unity of the forces under his com-mand and their loyalty to the high command. But the Twentieth Army, led by Liu Teh-ch'ao, rose in open revolt, arrested the chair-man of the Kiangsi Soviet, arrested many officers and officials, and attacked us politically on the basis of the Li Li-san line.[3] This oc-curred at Fu T'ien and is known as the Fu T'ien Incident. Fu T'ien being near Kian, then the heart of the soviet districts, the events

*Briefly to supplement this quite inadequate account of Li, see note 3 to this chapter and Li Li-san, BN.

produced a sensation, and to many it must have seemed that the fate of the revolution depended on the outcome of this struggle. However, the revolt was quickly suppressed, due to the loyalty of the Third Army, to the general solidarity of the Party and the Red troops, and to the support of the peasantry. Liu Teh-ch'ao was arrested, and other rebels disarmed and liquidated. Our line was reaffirmed, "Lilisanism" was definitely suppressed, and as a result the soviet movement subsequently scored great gains.

'But Nanking was now thoroughly aroused to the revolutionary potentialities of the soviets in Kiangsi, and at the end of 1930 began its First Extermination Campaign* against the Red Army. Enemy forces totalling over 100,000 men began an encirclement of the Red areas, penetrating by five routes, under the chief command of Lu Ti-p'ing. Against these troops the Red Army was then able to mobilize a total of about 40,000 men. By skilful use of manoeuvring warfare we met and overcame this First Campaign, with great victories. Following out the tactics of swift concentration and swift dispersal, we attacked each unit separately, using our main forces. Admitting the enemy troops deeply into soviet territory, we staged sudden concentrated attacks, in superior numbers, on isolated units of the Kuomintang troops, achieving positions of manoeuvre in which, momentarily, we could encircle them, thus reversing the general strategic advantage enjoyed by a numerically greatly superior enemy.

'By January 1931 this First Campaign had been completely defeated. I believe that this would not have been possible except for three conditions achieved by the Red Army just before its commencement. First, the consolidation of the First and Third Army corps under a centralized command; second, the liquidation of the Li Li-san line; and third, the triumph of the Party over the anti-Bolshevik (Liu Teh-ch'ao) faction and other active counter-revolutionaries within the Red Army and in the soviet districts.

'After a respite of only four months, Nanking launched its Second Campaign, under the supreme command of Ho Ying-ch'in, now Minister of War. His forces exceeded 200,000 men, who moved into the Red areas by seven routes. The situation for the Red Army

*This campaign is described in interesting detail by Yang Chien in *The Communist Situation in China* (Nanking, 1931).

was then thought to be very critical. The area of soviet power was very small, resources were limited, equipment scanty, and enemy material strength vastly exceeded that of the Red Army in every respect. To meet this offensive, however, the Red Army still clung to the same tactics that had thus far won success. Admitting the enemy columns well into Red territory, our main forces suddenly concentrated against the Second Route of the enemy, defeated several regiments, and destroyed their offensive power. Immediately afterwards we attacked in quick succession the Third Route, the Sixth, and the Seventh, defeating each of them in turn. The Fourth Route retreated without giving battle, and the Fifth Route was partly destroyed. Within fourteen days the Red Army had fought six battles, and marched eight days, ending with a decisive victory. With the break-up or retreat of the other six routes the First Route Army, commanded by Chiang Kuang-nai and Ts'ai T'ing-k'ai, withdrew without any serious fighting.

'One month later, Chiang Kai-shek took command of an army of 300,000 men "for the final extermination of the 'Red bandits' ". He was assisted by his ablest commanders: Ch'en Ming-shu, Ho Ying-ch'in, and Chu Shao-liang, each of whom had charge of a main route of advance. Chiang hoped to take the Red areas by storm – a rapid "wiping-up" of the "Red bandits". He began by moving his armies 80 *li* a day into the heart of soviet territory. This supplied the very conditions under which the Red Army fights best, and it soon proved the serious mistake of Chiang's tactics. With a main force of only 30,000 men, by a series of brilliant manoeuvres, our army attacked five different columns in five days. In the first battle the Red Army captured many enemy troops and large amounts of ammunition, guns and equipment. By September the Third Campaign had been admitted to be a failure, and Chiang Kai-shek in October withdrew his troops.

'The Red Army now entered a period of comparative peace and growth. Expansion was very rapid. The First Soviet Congress was called on 11 December 1931, and the Central Soviet Government was established, with myself as chairman. Chu Teh was elected commander-in-chief of the Red Army. In the same month there occurred the great Ningtu Uprising, when more than 20,000 troops of the Twenty-eighth Route Army of the Kuomintang revolted and joined the Red Army. They were led by Tung Chen-t'ang and Chao Po-sheng. Chao was later killed in battle in Kiangsi, but Tung is today still commander of the Fifth Red Army – the Fifth Army Corps having been created out of the troops taken in from the Ningtu Uprising.

'The Red Army now began offensives of its own. In 1932 it fought a great battle at Changchow, in Fukien, and captured the city. In the South it attacked Ch'en Chi-t'ang at Nan Hsiang, and on Chiang Kai-shek's front it stormed Lo An, Li Chuan, Chien Ning and T'ai Ning. It attacked but did not occupy Kanchow. From October 1932 onwards, and until the beginning of the Long March to the North-West, I myself devoted my time almost exclusively to work with the Soviet Government, leaving the military command to Chu Teh and others.

'In April 1933 began the fourth and, for Nanking, perhaps the most disastrous of its "extermination campaigns".* In the first battle of this period two divisions were disarmed and two divisional commanders were captured. The Fifty-ninth Division was partly destroyed and the Fifty-second was completely destroyed. Thirteen thousand men were captured in this one battle at Ta Lung P'ing and Chiao Hui in Lo An Hsien. The Kuomintang's Eleventh Division, then Chiang Kai-shek's best, was next eliminated, being almost totally disarmed; its commander was seriously wounded. These engagements proved decisive turning points and the Fourth

---

*There was considerable confusion, in many accounts written of the anti-Red wars, concerning the number of major expeditions sent against the soviet districts. Some writers totalled up as many as eight 'extermination' or 'annihilation' drives, but several of these big mobilizations by Nanking were purely defensive. Red Army commanders spoke of only five main anti-Red campaigns. These were, with the approximate number of Nanking troops directly involved in each, as follows: First, December 1930 to January 1931, 100,000; Second, May to June 1931, 200,000; Third, July to October 1931, 300,000; Fourth, April to October 1933, 250,000; Fifth, October 1933 to October 1934, 400,000 (over 900,000 troops were *mobilized* against the three main soviet districts). No major expedition was launched by Nanking during 1932, when Chiang Kai-shek was using approximately 500,000 troops in defensive positions around the Red districts. It was, on the contrary, a year of big Red offensives. Evidently Nanking's defensive operations in 1932, which were, of course, propagandized as 'anti-Red campaigns', were misunderstood by many writers as major expeditions.

Campaign soon afterwards ended. Chiang Kai-shek at this time wrote to Ch'en Ch'eng, his field commander, that he considered this defeat "the greatest humiliation" in his life. Ch'en Ch'eng did not favour pushing the campaign. He told people then that in his opinion fighting the Reds was a "lifetime job" and a "life sentence". Reports of this coming to Chiang Kai-shek, he removed Ch'en Ch'eng from the high command.

'For his fifth and last campaign, Chiang Kai-shek mobilized nearly one million men and adopted new tactics and strategy. Already, in the Fourth Campaign, Chiang had, on the recommendation of his German advisers, begun the use of the blockhouse and fortifications system. In the Fifth Campaign he placed his entire reliance upon it.

'In this period we made two important errors. The first was the failure to unite with Ts'ai T'ing-k'ai's army in 1933 during the Fukien Rebellion. The second was the adoption of the erroneous strategy of simple defence, abandoning our former tactics of maneouvre. It was a serious mistake to meet the vastly superior Nanking forces in positional warfare, at which the Red Army was neither technically nor spiritually at its best.[4]

'As a result of these mistakes, and the new tactics and strategy of Chiang's campaign, combined with the overwhelming numerical and technical superiority of the Kuomintang forces, the Red Army was obliged, in 1934, to seek to change the conditions of its existence in Kiangsi, which were rapidly becoming more unfavourable. Second, the national political situation influenced the decision to move the scene of main operations to the North-West.[5] Following Japan's invasion of Manchuria and Shanghai, the Soviet Government had, as early as February 1932, formally declared war on Japan. This declaration, which could not, of course, be made effective owing to the blockade and encirclement of Soviet China by the Kuomintang troops, had been followed by the issuance of a manifesto calling for a united front of all armed forces in China to resist Japanese imperialism. Early in 1933 the Soviet Government announced that it would cooperate with any White army on the basis of cessation of civil war and attacks on the soviets and the Red Army, guarantee of civil liberties and democratic rights to the masses, and arming of the people for an anti-Japanese war.[6]

'The Fifth Extermination Campaign began in October 1933. In January 1934, the Second All-China Congress of Soviets was convened in Juichin, the soviet capital, and a survey of the achievements of the revolution took place. Here I gave a long report, and here the Central Soviet Government, as its personnel exists today, was elected. Preparations soon afterwards were made for the Long March. It was begun in October 1934, just a year after Chiang Kai-shek launched his last campaign – a year of almost constant fighting, struggle and enormous losses on both sides.

'By January 1935 the main forces of the Red Army reached Tsunyi,* in Kweichow. For the next four months the army was almost constantly moving and the most energetic combat and fighting took place. Through many, many difficulties, across the longest and deepest and most dangerous rivers of China, across some of its highest and most hazardous mountain passes, through the country of fierce aborigines, through the empty grasslands, through cold and through intense heat, through wind and snow and rainstorm, pursued by half the White armies of China, through all these natural barriers, and fighting its way past the local troops of Kwangtung, Hunan, Kwangsi, Kweichow, Yunnan, Sikang, Szechuan, Kansu, and Shensi, the Red Army at last reached northern Shensi in October 1935, and enlarged its base in China's great North-West.

'The victorious march of the Red Army, and its triumphant arrival in Kansu and Shensi with its living forces still intact, was due first to the correct leadership of the Communist Party, and second to the great skill, courage, determination, and almost superhuman endurance and revolutionary ardour of the basic cadres of our soviet people. The Communist Party of China was, is, and will ever be faithful to Marxism-Leninism, and it will continue its struggles against every opportunist tendency. In this determination lies one explanation of its invincibility and the certainty of its final victory.'[7]

---

*In this account Mao made no reference to the important meeting of the Central Committee held at Tsunyi, which elected him to the leadership. For further comment on the Fifth Campaign and Tsunyi, see note 3 to this chapter and Li Teh in BN.

Part Five

THE LONG MARCH[1]

I

The Fifth Campaign

HERE I could not even outline the absorbing and then only fragmentarily written history of the six years of the soviets of South China – a period that was destined to be a prelude to the epic of the Long March. Mao Tse-tung had told briefly of the organic development of the soviets and of the birth of the Red Army. He had told how the Communists built up, from a few hundred ragged and half-starved but young and determined revolutionaries, an army of several tens of thousands of workers and peasants, until by 1930 they had become such serious contenders for power that Nanking had to hurl its first large-scale offensive against them. The initial 'annihilation drive', and then a second, a third, and a fourth were net failures. In each of those campaigns the Reds destroyed many brigades and whole divisions of Kuomintang troops, replenished their supplies of arms and ammunition, enlisted new warriors, and expanded their territory.

Meanwhile, what sort of life went on beyond the impenetrable lines of the Red irregulars? It seemed to me one of the amazing facts of our age that during the entire history of the soviets in South China not a single 'outside' foreign observer had entered Red territory – the only Communist-ruled nation in the world besides the USSR. Everything written about the southern soviets by foreigners was therefore secondary material. But a few salient points seemed now confirmable from accounts both friendly and inimical, and these clearly indicated the basis of the Red Army's support. Land was redistributed and taxes were lightened. Collective enterprise was established on a wide scale; by 1933 there were more than 1,000 soviet cooperatives in Kiangsi alone. Unemployment, opium, prostitution, child slavery, and compulsory marriage were reported to be eliminated, and the living conditions of the workers and poor peasants in the peaceful areas greatly improved. Mass education made much progress in the stabilized soviets. In some counties the

Reds attained a higher degree of literacy among the populace in three or four years than had been achieved anywhere else in rural China after centuries. In Hsing Ko, the Communists' model *hsien*, the populace was said to be nearly 80 per cent literate.

'Revolution,' observed Mao Tse-tung, 'is not a tea party.' That 'Red' terror methods were widely used against landlords and other class enemies – who were arrested, deprived of land, condemned in 'mass trials', and often executed – was undoubtedly true, as indeed the Communists' own reports confirmed.[2] Were such activities to be regarded as atrocities or as 'mass justice' executed by the armed poor in punishment of 'White' terror crimes by the rich when they held the guns? Never having seen Soviet Kiangsi, I could add little, with my testimony, to an evaluation of second-hand materials about it, or to the usefulness of this book, which is largely limited to the range of an eye-witness. For that reason I decided to omit from this volume some interview material concerning Soviet Kiangsi which the reader would be entitled to regard as self-serving, in the absence of independent corroboration.[3] Speculation on the southern soviets in any case was now a matter chiefly of academic interest. For late in October 1933, Nanking mobilized for the fifth and greatest of its anti-Red wars, and one year later the Reds were finally forced to carry out a general retreat. Nearly everyone then supposed it was the end, the Red Army's funeral march. How badly mistaken they were was not to become manifest for almost two years, when a remarkable comeback, seldom equalled in history, was to reach a climax with events that put into the hands of the Communists the life of the Generalissimo, who for a while really had believed his own boast – that he had 'exterminated the menace of communism'.

It was not until the seventh year of the fighting against the Reds that any notable success crowned the attempts to destroy them. The Reds then had actual administrative control over a great part of Kiangsi, and large areas of Fukien and Hunan. There were other soviet districts, not physically connected with the Kiangsi territory, located in the provinces of Hunan, Hupeh, Honan, Anhui, Szechuan, and Shensi.

Against the Reds, in the Fifth Campaign, Chiang Kai-shek mobilized about 900,000 troops, of whom perhaps 400,000 – some

360 regiments – actively took part in the warfare in the Kiangsi-Fukien area, and against the Red Army in the Anhui-Honan-Hupeh (Oyuwan) area. But Kiangsi was the pivot of the whole campaign. Here the regular Red Army was able to mobilize a combined strength of 180,000 men, including all reserve divisions, and it had perhaps 200,000 partisans and Red Guards, but altogether could muster a firing power of somewhat less than 100,000 rifles, no heavy artillery, and a very limited supply of grenades, shells, and ammunition, all of which were being made in the Red arsenal at Juichin.

Chiang adopted a new strategy to make the fullest use of his greatest assets – superior resources, technical equipment, access to supplies from the outside world (to which the Reds had no outlet), and some mechanized equipment, including an air force that had come to comprise nearly 400 navigable war planes. The Reds had captured a few of Chiang's airplanes, and they had three or four pilots, but they lacked gasoline, bombs, and mechanics. Instead of an invasion of the Red districts and an attempt to take them by storm of superior force, which had in the past proved disastrous, Chiang now used the majority of his troops to surround the 'bandits' and impose on them a strict economic blockade.

And it was very costly. Chiang Kai-shek built hundreds of miles of military roads and thousands of small fortifications, which were made connectable by machine-gun or artillery fire. His defensive-offensive strategy and tactics tended to diminish the Reds' superiority in manoeuvring, and emphasized the disadvantages of their smaller numbers and lack of resources.

Chiang wisely avoided exposing any large body of troops beyond the fringes of his network of roads and fortifications. They advanced only when very well covered by artillery and airplanes and rarely moved more than a few hundred yards ahead of the noose of forts, which stretched through the provinces of Kiangsi, Fukien, Hunan, Kwantung, and Kwangsi. Deprived of opportunities to decoy, ambush, or outmanoeuvre their enemy in open battle, the Reds began to place their main reliance on positional warfare – and the error of this decision, and the reasons for it, will be alluded to further on.

The Fifth Campaign was said to have been planned largely by

Chiang Kai-shek's German advisers, notably General von Falken-hausen of the German Army, who was then the Generalissimo's chief adviser. The new tactics were thorough, but they were also very slow and expensive. Operations dragged on for months and still Nanking had not struck a decisive blow at the main forces of its enemy. The effect of the blockade, however, was seriously felt in the Red districts, and especially the total absence of salt. The little Red base was becoming inadequate to repel the combined military and economic pressure being applied against it. Consider-able exploitation of the peasantry must have been necessary to maintain the astonishing year of resistance which was put up dur-ing this campaign. At the same time, it must be remembered that their fighters were peasants, owners of newly acquired land. For land alone most peasants in China would fight to the death. The Kiangsi people knew that return of the Kuomintang meant return to the landlords.

Nanking believed that its efforts at annihilation were about to succeed. The enemy was caged and could not escape. Thousands supposedly had been killed in the daily bombing and machine-gunning from the air, as well as by 'purgations' in districts re-occupied by the Kuomintang. The Red Army itself, according to Chou En-lai, suffered over 60,000 casualties in this one siege. Whole areas were depopulated, sometimes by forced mass migrations, sometimes by the simpler expedient of mass executions. Kuomin-tang press releases estimated that about 1,000,000 people were killed or starved to death in the process of recovering Soviet Kiangsi.

Nevertheless, the Fifth Campaign proved inconclusive. It failed to destroy the 'living forces'* of the Red Army. A Red military conference was called at Juichin, and it was decided to withdraw, transferring the main Red strength to a new base.

The retreat from Kiangsi evidently was so swiftly and secretly managed that the main forces of the Red troops, estimated at about 90,000 men, had already been marching for several days before the enemy headquarters became aware of what was taking place. They had mobilized in southern Kiangsi, withdrawing most of their regular troops from the northern front and replacing them

* An expression used by the Reds, meaning main combat forces.

with partisans. Those movements occurred always at night. When practically the whole Red Army was concentrated near Yutu, in southern Kiangsi, the order was given for the Great March, which began on 16 October 1934.

For three nights the Reds pressed in two columns to the west and to the south. On the fourth they advanced, totally unexpectedly, almost simultaneously attacking the Hunan and Kwangtung lines of fortifications. They took these by assault, put their astonished enemy on the run, and never stopped until they had occupied the ribbon of blockading forts and entrenchments on the southern front. This gave them roads to the south and to the west, along which their vanguard began its sensational trek.

Besides the main strength of the army, thousands of Red peasants began this march – old and young, men, women, children, Communists and non-Communists. The arsenal was stripped, the factories were dismantled, machinery was loaded onto mules and donkeys – everything that was portable and of value went with this strange cavalcade. As the march lengthened out, much of this burden had to be discarded, and the Reds told me that thousands of rifles and machine guns, much machinery, much ammunition, even much silver, lay buried on their long trail from the South. Some day in the future, they said, Red peasants, now surrounded by thousands of policing troops, would dig it up again. They awaited only the signal – and the war with Japan might prove to be that beacon.

After the main forces of the Red Army evacuated Kiangsi, it was still many weeks before Nanking troops succeeded in occupying the chief Red bases. Thousands of peasant Red Guards continued guerrilla fighting. To lead them, the Red Army left behind some of its ablest commanders: Ch'en Yi, Su Yu,* T'an Chen-lin, Hsiang Ying, Fang Chih-min, Liu Hsiao,* Teng Tzu-hui, Ch'u Ch'iu-pai, Ho Shu-heng, and Chang Ting-ch'eng. They had only 6,000 able-bodied regular troops, however – and 20,000 wounded, sheltered among the peasants.[4] Many thousands of them were captured and executed, but they managed to fight a rear-guard action which enabled the main forces to get well under way before Chiang Kai-shek could mobilize new forces to pursue and attempt to annihilate

*See BN.

them on the march. Even in 1937 there were regions in Kiangsi,
Fukien, and Kweichow held by these fragments of the Red Army,
and that spring the government announced the beginning of
another anti-Red campaign for a 'final clean-up' in Fukien.[5]

2

A Nation Emigrates

HAVING successfully broken through the first line of fortifications, the Red Army set out on its epochal year-long trek to the west and to the north, a varicoloured and many-storied expedition describable here only in briefest outline. The Communists told me that they were writing a collective account of the Long March, with contributions from dozens who made it, which already totalled about 300,000 words.[1] Adventure, exploration, discovery, human courage and cowardice, ecstasy and triumph, suffering, sacrifice, and loyalty, and then through it all, like a flame, an undimmed ardour and undying hope and amazing revolutionary optimism of those thousands of youths who would not admit defeat by man or nature or God or death – all this and more seemed embodied in the history of an odyssey unequalled in modern times.

The Reds themselves generally spoke of it as the '25,000-li March', and with all its twists, turns and countermarches, from the farthest point in Fukien to the end of the road in far north-west Shensi, some sections of the marchers undoubtedly did that much or more. An accurate stage-by-stage itinerary prepared by the First Army Corps* showed that its route covered a total of 18,088 li, or 6,000 miles – about twice the width of the American continent – and this figure was perhaps the average march of the main forces. The journey took them across some of the world's most difficult trails, unfit for wheeled traffic, and across the high snow mountains and the great rivers of Asia. It was one long battle from beginning to end.

Four main lines of defence works, supported by strings of concrete machine-gun nests and blockhouses, surrounded the soviet districts in South-West China, and the Reds had to shatter those before they could reach the unblocked areas to the west. The

*An Account of the Long March, First Army Corps (Yu Wang Pao, August 1936).

first line, in Kiangsi, was broken on 21 October 1934; the second, in Hunan, was occupied on 3 November; and a week later the third, also in Hunan, fell to the Reds after bloody fighting. The Kwangsi and Hunan troops gave up the fourth and last line on 29 November, and the Reds swung northward into Hunan, to begin trekking in a straight line for Szechuan, where they planned to enter the soviet districts and combine with the Fourth Front Army there, under Hsu Hsiang-ch'ien. Between the dates mentioned above, nine battles were fought. In all, a combination of 110 regiments had been mobilized in their path by Nanking and by the provincial warlords Ch'en Ch'i-tang, Ho Chien, and Pai Chung-hsi.

During the march through Kiangsi, Kwangtung, Kwangsi, and Hunan, the Reds suffered very heavy losses. Their numbers were reduced by about one third by the time they reached the border of Kweichow province. This was due, first, to the impediment of a vast amount of transport, 5,000 men being engaged in that task alone. The vanguard was very much retarded, and in many cases the enemy was given time to prepare elaborate obstructions in the line of march. Second, from Kiangsi an undeviating north-westerly route was maintained, which enabled Nanking to anticipate most of the Red Army's movements.

Serious losses as a result of these errors caused the Reds to adopt new tactics in Kweichow. Instead of an arrow-like advance, they began a series of distracting manoeuvres, so that it became more and more difficult for Nanking planes to identify the day-by-day objective of the main forces. Two columns, and sometimes as many as four columns, engaged in a baffling series of manoeuvres on the flanks of the central column, and the vanguard developed a pincer-like front. Only the barest and lightest essentials of equipment were retained, and night marches for the greatly reduced transport corps –a daily target for the air bombing – became routine.

Anticipating an attempt to cross the Yangtze River into Szechuan, Chiang Kai-shek withdrew thousands of troops from Hupeh, Anhui, and Kiangsi and shipped them hurriedly westward, to cut off (from the north) the Red Army's route of advance. All crossings were heavily fortified; all ferries were drawn to the north bank of the river; all roads were blocked; great areas were denuded of grain. Other thousands of Nanking troops poured into Kwei-

chow to reinforce the opium-soaked provincials of warlord Wang
Chia-lieh, whose army in the end was practically immobilized by
the Reds. Still others were dispatched to the Yunnan border, to set
up obstacles there. In Kweichow, therefore, the Reds found a reception committee of a couple of hundred thousand troops, and
obstructions thrown up everywhere in their path. This necessitated
two great counter-marches across the province, and a wide circular
movement around the capital.

Manoeuvres in Kweichow occupied the Reds for four months,
during which they destroyed five enemy divisions, captured the
headquarters of Governor Wang and occupied his foreign-style
palace in Tsunyi, recruited about 20,000 men, and visited most of
the villages and towns of the province, calling mass meetings and
organizing Communist cadres among the youth. Their losses were
negligible, but they still faced the problem of crossing the Yangtze.
By his swift concentration on the Kweichow-Szechuan border,
Chiang Kai-shek had skilfully blocked the short, direct roads that
led to the great river. He now placed his main hope of exterminat-
ing the Reds on the prevention of this crossing at any point, hoping
to push them far to the south-west, or into the wastelands of Tibet.
To his various commanders and the provincial warlords he telegraphed : 'The fate of the nation and the party depends on bottling
up the Reds south of the Yangtze.'

Suddenly, early in May 1935, the Reds turned southward and
entered Yunnan, where China's frontier meets Burma and Indochina. A spectacular march in four days brought them within ten
miles of the capital, Yunnanfu, and warlord Lung Yun (Dragon
Cloud) frantically mobilized all available troops for defence.
Chiang's reinforcements meanwhile moved in from Kweichow in
hot pursuit. Chiang himself and Mme Chiang, who had been staying in Yunnanfu, hastily repaired down the French railway towards
Indochina. A big squadron of Nanking bombers kept up their
daily egg-laying over the Reds but on they came. Presently the
panic ended. It was discovered that their drive on Yunnanfu had
been only a diversion carried out by a few troops. The main Red
forces were moving westward, obviously with the intention of
crossing the river at Lengkai, one of the few navigable points of
the Upper Yangtze.

Through the wild mountainous country of Yunnan, the Yangtze River flows deeply and swiftly between immense gorges, great peaks in places rising in defiles of a mile or more, with steep walls of rock lifting almost perpendicularly on either side. The few crossings had all been occupied long ago by government troops. Chiang was well pleased. He now ordered all boats drawn to the north bank of the river and burned. Then he started his own troops, and Lung Yun's, in an enveloping movement around the Red Army, hoping to finish it off forever on the banks of this historic and treacherous stream.

Seemingly unaware of their fate, the Reds continued to march rapidly westward in three columns toward Lengkai. The boats had been burned there, and Nanking pilots reported that a Red vanguard had begun building a bamboo bridge. Chiang became more confident; this bridge-building would take weeks. But one evening, quite unobtrusively, a Red battalion suddenly reversed its direction. On a phenomenal forced march it covered eighty-five miles in one night and day, and in late afternoon descended upon the only other possible ferry crossing in the vicinity, at Chou P'ing Fort. Dressed in captured Nanking uniforms, the battalion entered the town at dusk without arousing comment, and quietly disarmed the garrison.

Boats had been withdrawn to the north bank – but they had not been destroyed. (Why spoil boats, when the Reds were hundreds of *li* distant, and not coming there anyway? So the government troops may have reasoned.) But how to get one over to the south bank? After dark the Reds escorted a village official to the river and forced him to call out to the guards on the opposite side that some government troops had arrived and wanted a boat. Unsuspectingly one was sent across. Into it piled a detachment of these 'Nanking' soldiers, who soon disembarked on the north shore – in Szechuan at last. Calmly entering the garrison, they surprised guards who were peacefully playing mah-jong and whose stacked weapons the Reds took over without any struggle.

Meanwhile the main forces of the Red Army had executed a wide countermarch, and by noon of the next day the vanguard reached the fort. Crossing was now a simple matter. Six big boats worked constantly for nine days. The entire army was transported into Szechuan without a life lost. Having concluded the operation, the Reds promptly destroyed the vessels and lay down to sleep. When Chiang's forces reached the river, two days later, the rear guard of their enemy called cheerily to them from the north bank to come on over, the swimming was fine. The government troops were obliged to make a detour of over 200 li to the nearest crossing, and the Reds thus shook them from their trail. Infuriated, the Generalissimo now flew to Szechuan, where he mobilized new forces in the path of the oncoming horde, hoping to cut them off at one more strategic river – the great Tatu.

3

The Heroes of Tatu

THE crossing of the Tatu River was the most critical single incident of the Long March. Had the Red Army failed there, quite possibly it would have been exterminated. The historic precedent for such a fate already existed. On the banks of the remote Tatu the heroes of the *Three Kingdoms* and many warriors since then had met defeat, and in these same gorges the last of the T'ai-p'ing rebels, an army of 100,000 led by Prince Shih Ta-k'ai, was in the nineteenth century surrounded and completely destroyed by the Manchu forces under the famous Tseng Kuo-fan. To warlords Liu Hsiang and Liu Wen-hui, his allies in Szechuan, and to his own generals in command of the government pursuit, Generalissimo Chiang now wired an exhortation to repeat the history of the T'ai-p'ing.

But the Reds also knew about Shih Ta-k'ai, and that the main cause of his defeat had been a costly delay. Arriving at the banks of the Tatu, Prince Shih had paused for three days to honour the birth of his son – an imperial prince. Those days of rest had given his enemy the chance to concentrate against him, and to make the swift marches in his rear that blocked his line of retreat. Realizing his mistake too late, Prince Shih had tried to break the enemy encirclement, but it was impossible to manoeuvre in the narrow terrain of the defiles, and he was erased from the map.

The Reds determined not to repeat his error. Moving rapidly northward from the Gold Sand River (as the Yangtze there is known) into Szechuan, they soon entered the tribal country of warlike aborigines, the 'White' and 'Black' Lolos of Independent Lololand. Never conquered, never absorbed by the Chinese who dwelt all around them, the turbulent Lolos had for centuries occupied that densely forested and mountainous spur of Szechuan whose borders are marked by the great southward arc described by the Yangtze just east of Tibet. Chiang Kai-shek could well have confidently counted on a long delay and weakening of the Reds here which would enable him to concentrate north of the Tatu. The Lolos' hatred of the Chinese was traditional, and rarely had any Chinese army crossed their borders without heavy losses or extermination.

But the Reds had already safely passed through the tribal districts of the Miao and the Shan peoples, aborigines of Kweichow and Yunnan, and had won their friendship and even enlisted some tribesmen in their army. Now they sent envoys ahead to parley with the Lolos. On the way they captured several towns on the borders of independent Lololand, where they found a number of Lolo chieftains who had been imprisoned as hostages by provincial Chinese warlords. Freed and sent back to their people, these men naturally praised the Reds.

In the vanguard of the Red Army was Commander Liu Po-ch'eng,* who had once been an officer in a warlord army of Szechuan. Liu knew the tribal people, and their inner feuds and discontent. Especially he knew their hatred of Chinese, and he could speak something of the Lolo tongue. Assigned the task of negotiating a friendly alliance, he entered their territory and went into conference with the chieftains. The Lolos, he said, opposed warlords Liu Hsiang and Liu Wen-hui and the Kuomintang; so did the Reds. The Lolos wanted to preserve their independence; Red policies favoured autonomy for all the national minorities of China. The Lolos hated the Chinese because they had been oppressed by them; but there were 'White' Chinese and 'Red' Chinese, just as there were 'White' Lolos and 'Black' Lolos, and it was the White Chinese who had always slain and oppressed the Lolos. Should not the Red Chinese and the Black Lolos unite against their common enemies, the White Chinese? The Lolos listened interestedly. Slyly they asked for arms and bullets to guard their independence and help Red Chinese fight the Whites. To their astonishment, the Reds gave them both.

And so it happened that not only a speedy but a politically useful passage was accomplished. Hundreds of Lolos enlisted with the 'Red' Chinese to march to the Tatu River to fight the common enemy. Some of those Lolos were to trek clear to the North-West. Liu Po-ch'eng drank the blood of a newly killed chicken before the high chieftain of the Lolos, who drank also, and they swore blood

* See BN.

brotherhood in the tribal manner. By this vow the Reds declared that whosoever should violate the terms of their alliance would be even as weak and cowardly as the fowl.

Thus a vanguard division of the First Army Corps, led by Lin Piao, reached the Tatu Ho. On the last day of the march they emerged from the forests of Lololand (in the thick foliage of which Nanking pilots had completely lost track of them), to descend suddenly on the river town of An Jen Ch'ang, just as unheralded as they had come into Chou P'ing Fort. Guided over narrow mountain trails by the Lolos, the vanguard crept quietly up to the little town and from the heights looked down to the river bank, and saw with amazement and delight one of the three ferryboats made fast on the *south* bank of the river ! Once more an act of fate had befriended them.

How had it happened? On the opposite shore there was only one regiment of the troops of General Liu Wen-hui, the co-dictator of Szechuan province. Other Szechuan troops, as well as reinforcements from Nanking, were leisurely proceeding towards the Tatu, but the single regiment meanwhile must have seemed enough. A squad should have been ample, with all boats moored to the north. But the commander of that regiment was a native of the district; he knew the country the Reds must pass through, and how long it would take them to penetrate to the river. They would be many days yet, he could have told his men. And his wife, one learned, had been a native of An Jen Ch'ang, so he must cross to the south bank to visit his relatives and his friends and to feast with them. Thus it happened that the Reds, taking the town by surprise, captured the commander, his boat, and their passage to the north.

Sixteen men from each of five companies volunteered to cross in the first boat and bring back the others, while on the south bank the Reds set up machine guns on the mountainsides and over the river spread a screen of protective fire concentrated on the enemy's exposed positions. It was May. Floods poured down the mountains, and the river was swift and even wider than the Yangtze. Starting far upstream, the ferry took two hours to cross and land just opposite the town. From the south bank the villagers of An Jen Ch'ang watched breathlessly. They would be wiped out ! But wait. They saw the voyagers land almost beneath the guns of the enemy.

Now, surely, they would be finished. And yet ... from the south bank the Red machine guns barked on. The onlookers saw the little party climb ashore, hurriedly take cover, then slowly work their way up a steep cliff overhanging the enemy's positions. There they set up their own light machine guns and sent a downpour of lead and hand grenades into the enemy redoubts along the river.

Suddenly the White troops ceased firing, broke from their redoubts, and fled to a second and then a third line of defence. A great murmur went up from the south bank and shouts of 'Hao!' drifted across the river to the little band who had captured the ferry landing. Meanwhile the first boat returned, towing two others, and on the second trip each carried eighty men. The enemy had fled. That day and night, and the next, and the next, those three ferries of An Jen Ch'ang worked back and forth, until at last nearly a division had been transferred to the northern bank.

But the river flowed faster and faster. The crossing became more and more difficult. On the third day it took four hours to shift a boatload of men from shore to shore. At this rate it would be weeks before the whole army and its animals and supplies could be moved. Long before the operation was completed they would be encircled. The First Army Corps had now crowded into An Jen Ch'ang, and behind were the flanking columns, and the transport and rear guard. Chiang Kai-shek's airplanes had found the spot, and heavily bombed it. Enemy troops were racing up from the south-east; others approached from the north. A hurried military conference was summoned by Lin Piao. Chu Teh, Mao Tse-tung, Chou En-lai, and P'eng Teh-huai had by now reached the river. They took a decision and began to carry it out at once.

Some 400 *li* to the west of An Jen Ch'ang, where the gorges rise very high and the river flows narrow, deep, and swift, there was an iron-chain suspension bridge called the Liu Ting Chiao – the Bridge Fixed by Liu.* It was the last possible crossing of the Tatu east of Tibet. Towards this the barefoot Reds now set out along a trail that wound through the gorges, at times climbing several thousand feet, again dropping low to the level of the swollen stream itself and wallowing through waist-deep mud. If they captured the Liu Ting Chiao the whole army could enter central Szechuan. If they

*Literally the bridge 'made fast' by Liu.

failed they would have to retrace their steps through Lololand, re-enter Yunnan, and fight their way westward towards Likiang, on the Tibetan border – a detour of more than a thousand *li*, which few might hope to survive.

As their main forces pushed westward along the southern bank, the Red division already on the northern bank moved also. Sometimes the gorges between them closed so narrowly that the two lines of Reds could shout to each other across the stream; sometimes that gulf between them measured their fear that the Tatu might separate them forever, and they stepped more swiftly. As they wound in long dragon files along the cliffs at night their 10,000 torches sent arrows of light slanting down the dark face of the imprisoning river. Day and night these vanguards moved at double-quick, pausing only for brief ten-minute rests and meals, when the soldiers listened to lectures by their weary political workers, who over and over again explained the importance of this one action, exhorting each to give his last breath, his last urgent strength, for victory in the test ahead of them. There could be no slackening of pace, no halfheartedness, no fatigue. 'Victory was life,' said P'eng Teh-huai; 'defeat was certain death.'

On the second day the vanguard on the right bank fell behind. Szechuan troops had set up positions in the road, and skirmishes took place. Those on the southern bank pressed on more grimly. Presently new troops appeared on the opposite bank, and through their field glasses the Reds saw that they were White reinforcements, hurrying to the Bridge Fixed by Liu. For a whole day these troops raced each other along the stream, but gradually the Red vanguard, the pick of all the Red Army, pulled away from the enemy's tired soldiers, whose rests were longer and more frequent, whose energy seemed more spent, and who were perhaps none too anxious to die for a bridge.

The Bridge Fixed by Liu was built centuries ago, and in the manner of all bridges of the deep rivers of western China. Sixteen heavy iron chains, with a span of some 100 yards or more, were stretched across the river, their ends imbedded on each side under great piles of cemented rock, beneath the stone bridgeheads. Thick boards lashed over the chains made the road of the bridge, but upon their arrival the Reds found that half this wooden flooring had been removed, and before them only the bare iron chains swung to a point midway in the stream. At the northern bridgehead an enemy machine-gun nest faced them, and behind it were positions held by a regiment of White troops. The bridge should, of course, have been destroyed, but the Szechuanese were sentimental about their few bridges; it was not easy to rebuild them, and they were costly. Of Liu Ting it was said that 'the wealth of the eighteen provinces contributed to build it'. And who would have thought the Reds would insanely try to cross on the chains alone? But that was what they did.

No time was to be lost. The bridge must be captured before enemy reinforcements arrived. Once more volunteers were called for. One by one Red soldiers stepped forward to risk their lives, and, of those who offered themselves, thirty were chosen. Hand grenades and Mausers were strapped to their backs, and soon they were swinging out above the boiling river, moving hand over hand, clinging to the iron chains. Red machine guns barked at enemy redoubts and spattered the bridgehead with bullets. The enemy replied with machine-gunning of his own, and snipers shot at the Reds tossing high above the water, working slowly towards them. The first warrior was hit, and dropped into the current below; a second fell, and then a third. But as others drew nearer the centre, the bridge flooring somewhat protected these dare-to-dies, and most of the enemy bullets glanced off, or ended in the cliffs on the opposite bank.

Probably never before had the Szechuanese seen fighters like these – men for whom soldiering was not just a rice bowl, and youths ready to commit suicide to win. Were they human beings or madmen or gods? Was their own morale affected? Did they perhaps not shoot to kill? Did some of them secretly pray that these men would succeed in their attempt? At last one Red crawled up over the bridge flooring, uncapped a grenade, and tossed it with perfect aim into the enemy redoubt. Nationalist officers ordered the rest of the planking torn up. It was already too late. More Reds were crawling into sight. Paraffin was thrown on the planking, and it began to burn. By then about twenty Reds were moving forward on their hands and knees, tossing grenade after grenade into the enemy machine-gun nest.

Suddenly, on the south shore, their comrades began to shout with joy: 'Long live the Red Army! Long live the Revolution! Long live the heroes of Tatu Ho!' For the enemy was withdrawing in pell-mell flight. Running full speed over the remaining planks of the bridge, through the flames licking towards them, the assailants nimbly hopped into the enemy's redoubt and turned the abandoned machine guns against the shore.

More Reds now swarmed over the chains, and arrived to help put out the fire and replace the boards. And soon afterwards the Red division that had crossed at An Jen Ch'ang came into sight, opening a flank attack on the remaining enemy positions, so that in a little while the White troops were wholly in flight – either in flight, that is, or with the Reds, for about a hundred Szechuan soldiers here threw down their rifles and turned to join their pursuers. In an hour or two the whole army was joyously tramping and singing its way across the River Tatu into Szechuan. Far overhead angrily and impotently roared the planes of Chiang Kaishek, and the Reds cried out in delirious challenge to them.

For their distinguished bravery the heroes of An Jen Ch'ang and Liu Ting Chiao were awarded the Gold Star, highest decoration in the Red Army of China.

4

Across the Great Grasslands

SAFELY across the Tatu, the Reds struck off into the comparative freedom of western Szechuan, where the blockhouse system had not been completed, and where the initiative rested largely in their own hands. But hardships between battles were not over. Another 2,000 miles of marching, studded by seven great mountain ranges, still lay ahead of them.

North of the Tatu River the Reds climbed 16,000 feet over the Great Snowy Mountain, and in the rarefied air of its crest looked to the west and saw a sea of snow peaks – Tibet. It was already June, and in the lowlands very warm, but as they crossed the Ta Hsueh Shan many of those poorly clad, thin-blooded southerners, unused to the high altitudes, perished from exposure. Harder yet to ascend was the desolate Paotung Kang Mountain, up which they literally built their own road, felling long bamboos and laying them down for a track through a tortuous treacle of waist-deep mud. 'On this peak,' Mao Tse-tung told me, 'one army corps lost two thirds of its transport animals. Hundreds fell down and never got up.'

They climbed on. The Chung Lai range next, and more lost men and animals. Then they straddled the lovely Dream Pen Mountain, and after it the Big Drum, and these also took their toll of life. Finally, on 20 July 1935, they entered the rich Moukung area, in north-west Szechuan, and connected with the Fourth Front Army and the soviet regions of the Sungpan. Here they paused for a long rest, took assessment of their losses, and re-formed their ranks.

The First, Third, Fifth, Eighth, and Ninth Army corps, which had begun the journey in Kiangsi nine months earlier with about 90,000 armed men, could now muster beneath their hammer-and-sickle banners about 45,000. Not all had been lost, strayed, or captured. Behind the line of march in Hunan, Kweichow, and Yunnan the Red Army had, as part of its tactics of defence, left small cadres of regular troops to organize partisan groups among the peasantry, and create disturbances and diversionist activity on the enemy's flanks. Hundreds of captured rifles had been distributed along the route, and stretching clear from Kiangsi to Szechuan were new zones of trouble for the Kuomintang forces. Ho Lung still held his little soviet area, in northern Hunan, and had been joined there by the army of Hsiao K'eh. The numerous newly created partisan detachments began working slowly towards that region. Nanking was not to dislodge Ho Lung for a whole year, and then only after he had been ordered by Red Army headquarters to move into Szechuan, an operation which he would complete – via Tibet – against amazing obstacles.

The journey of the Kiangsi Reds thus far had provided them with much food for reflection. They had won many new friends and made many bitter enemies. Along their route they had provisioned themselves by 'confiscating' the supplies of the rich – the landlords, officials, bureaucrats, and big gentry. Finance Commissioner Lin Tsu-han told me that such seizures were systematically carried out according to soviet laws, and that only the confiscation department of the finance commission was empowered to distribute the goods that were taken. It husbanded the army's resources, was informed by radio of all confiscations made, and assigned quantities of provisions for each section of the marchers, who often made a solid serpentine·of fifty miles or more curling over the hills.

There were big 'surpluses' – more than the Reds could carry – and these were distributed among the local poor. In Yunnan the Reds seized thousands of hams from rich packers there, and peasants came from miles around to receive their free portions – a new incident in the history of the ham industry, said Mao Tse-tung. Tons of salt were likewise distributed. In Kweichow many duck farms were seized from the landlords and officials and the Reds ate duck until, in the words of Wu Liang-p'ing, they were 'simply disgusted with duck'. From Kiangsi they had carried Nanking notes, and silver dollars and bullion from their state bank, and in poor districts in their path they used this money to pay for their needs. Land deeds were destroyed, taxes abolished, and the poor peasantry armed.

Except for their experiences in western Szechuan, the Reds told me they were welcomed everywhere by the mass of the peasantry. Their Robin Hood policies were noised ahead of them, and often the 'oppressed peasantry' sent groups to urge them to detour and 'liberate' their districts. They had little conception of the Red Army's political programme, of course; they only knew that it was 'a poor man's army', said Wu Liang-p'ing. That was enough. Mao Tse-tung told me laughingly of one such delegation which arrived to welcome 'Su Wei-ai Hsien-sheng' – Mr Soviet! * These rustics were no more ignorant, however, than the Fukien militarist Lu Hsing-pang, who once posted a notice throughout his fiefdom offering a reward for the 'capture, dead or alive, of Su Wei-ai'. Lu announced that this fellow had been doing a lot of damage everywhere, and must be exterminated.

In Maoerhkai and Moukung the southern armies rested for three weeks, while the revolutionary military council, and representatives of the Party and the Soviet Government, discussed plans for the future. It may be recalled that the Fourth Front Red Army, which had made its base in Szechuan as early as 1933, had originally been formed in the Honan–Hupeh–Anhui soviet districts. Its march across Honan to Szechuan had been led by Hsu Hsiang-ch'ien and Chang Kuo-t'ao, two veteran Reds, of whom something more is said later on. Remarkable successes – and tragic excesses – had marked their campaigns in Szechuan, the whole northern half of which had once been under their sway. At the time of its junction in Moukung with the southern Bolsheviks, Hsu Hsiang-ch'ien's army numbered about 50,000 men, so that the combined Red force concentrated in western Szechuan in July 1935 was nearly 100,000.

Here the two armies divided, part of the southerners continuing northward while the rest remained with the Fourth Front Army in Szechuan. There was disagreement about the correct course to pursue. Chang Kuo-t'ao and Hsu Hsiang-ch'ien favoured remain-

* *Su*, the first Chinese character used in transliterating the word 'soviet', is a common family name, and *wei-ai*, suffixed to it, might easily seem like a given name.

ing in Szechuan and attempting to reassert Communist influence south of the Yangtze. Mao Tse-tung, Chu Teh, and the majority of the Politburo were determined to continue into the North-West. The period of indecision was ended by two factors. First was an enveloping movement by Chiang Kai-shek's troops, moving into Szechuan from the east and from the north, which succeeded in driving a wedge between two sections of the Red Army. Second was the rapid rise of one of the hurried rivers of Szechuan, which then physically divided the forces, and which suddenly became impassable. There were other factors of intraparty struggle involved which need not be discussed here.[1]

In August, with the First Army Corps as vanguard, the main forces from Kiangsi continued the northward march, leaving Chu Teh and Li Hsien-nien * with Hsu Hsiang-ch'ien and Chang Kuo-t'ao. The Fourth Front Army was to remain here and in Tibet for another year, and be joined by Ho Lung's Second Front Army,† before making a sensational march into Kansu. Leading the Red cavalcade that in August 1935 moved towards the Great Grasslands, on the border of Szechuan and Tibet, were Commanders Lin Piao, P'eng Teh-huai, Tso Ch'uan,* Ch'en Keng,* Chou En-lai, and Mao Tse-tung, most of the officials from the Kiangsi Central Government, and a majority of the members of the Central Committee of the Party. They began this last phase of the march with about 30,000 men.

The most dangerous and exciting travel lay before them, for the route they chose led through wild country inhabited by the independent Mantzu tribesmen and the nomadic Hsifan, a warring people of eastern Tibet. Passing into the Mantzu and Tibetan territories, the Reds for the first time faced a populace united in its hostility to them, and their sufferings on this part of the trek exceeded anything of the past. They had money but could buy no food. They had guns but their enemies were invisible. As they marched into the thick forests and jungles and across the headwaters of a dozen great rivers, the tribesmen withdrew from the vicinity of the march. They stripped their houses bare, carried off

* See BN.
† Jen Pi-shih was Ho Lung's political commissar. See BN.

all edibles, drove their cattle and fowl to the plateaus, and simply disinhabited the whole area.

A few hundred yards on either side of the road, however, it was quite unsafe. Many a Red who ventured to forage for a sheep never returned. The mountaineers hid in the thick bush and sniped at the marching 'invaders'. They climbed the mountains, and when the Reds filed through the deep, narrow, rock passes, where sometimes only one or two could move abreast, the Mantzu rolled huge boulders down to crush them and their animals. Here were no chances to explain 'Red policy towards national minorities', no opportunities for friendly alliance. The Mantzu Queen had an implacable traditional hatred for Chinese of any variety, and recognized no distinctions between Red and White. She threatened to boil alive anyone who helped the travellers.

Unable to get food except by capturing it, the Reds were obliged to make war for a few cattle. Mao told me that they had a saying then, 'To buy one sheep costs the life of one man.' From the Mantzu fields they harvested green Tibetan wheat, and vegetables such as beets and turnips – the latter of an enormous size that would 'feed fifteen men', according to Mao Tse-tung.* On such meagre supplies they equipped themselves to cross the Great Grasslands. 'This is our only foreign debt,' Mao said to me humorously, 'and some day we must pay the Mantzu and the Tibetans for the provisions we were obliged to take from them.' Only by capturing tribesmen could they find guides through the country. But of these guides they made friends, and after the Mantzu frontier was crossed many continued the journey. Some of them were now students in the Communist Party school in Shensi, and might one day return to their land to tell the people the difference between 'Red' and 'White' Chinese.

In the Grasslands there was no human habitation for ten days. Almost perpetual rain falls over this swampland, and it was possible to cross its centre only by a maze of narrow footholds known to the native mountaineers who led the Reds. More animals were lost, and more men. Many foundered in the weird sea of wet grass and dropped from sight into the depth of the swamp, beyond reach

* Vegetable crops in the rarefied air of the Tibetan highlands attain five to ten times 'normal' size during the brief growing season.

of their comrades. There was no firewood; they were obliged to eat their wheat green and vegetables raw. There were no trees for shelter, and the lightly equipped Reds carried no tents. At night they huddled under bushes tied together, which gave but scant protection against the rain. But from this trial, too, they emerged triumphant – more so, at least, than the White troops, who pursued them, lost their way, and turned back with only a fraction of their number intact.

The Red Army now reached the Kansu border. Several battles still lay ahead, the loss of any one of which might have meant decisive defeat. More Nanking, Tungpei, and Moslem troops had been mobilized in southern Kansu to stop their march, but they managed to break through all these blockades, and in the process annexed hundreds of horses from the Moslem cavalry which people had confidently predicted would finish them once and for all. Footsore, weary, and at the limit of human endurance, they finally entered northern Shensi, just below the Great Wall. On 20 October 1935, a year after its departure from Kiangsi, the vanguard of the First Front Army connected with the Twenty-fifth, Twenty-sixth, and Twenty-seventh Red armies, which had already established a small base of soviet power in Shensi in 1933. Numbering fewer than 20,000 survivors now, they sat down to realize the significance of their achievement.[2]

The statistical recapitulation * of the Long March is impressive. It shows that there was an average of almost a skirmish a day, somewhere on the line, while altogether fifteen whole days were devoted to major pitched battles. Out of a total of 368 days en route, 235 were consumed in marches by day, and 18 in marches by night. Of the 100 days of halts – many of which were devoted to skirmishes – 56 days were spent in north-western Szechuan, leaving only 44 days of rest over a distance of about 5,000 miles, or an average of one halt for every 114 miles of marching. The mean daily stage covered was 71 *li*, or nearly 24 miles – a phenomenal pace for a great army and its transport to *average* over some of the most hazardous terrain on earth.

According to data furnished to me by Commander Tso Ch'uan,

*An Account of the Long March, First Army Corps (Yu Wang Pao, August 1936).

the Reds crossed eighteen mountain ranges, five of which were perennially snow-capped, and they crossed twenty-four rivers. They passed through twelve different provinces, occupied sixty-two cities and towns, and broke through enveloping armies of ten different provincial warlords, besides defeating, eluding, or out-manoeuvring the various forces of Central Government troops sent against them. They crossed six different aboriginal districts, and penetrated areas through which no Chinese army had gone for scores of years.

However one might feel about the Reds and what they represented politically (and there was plenty of room for argument), it was impossible to deny recognition of their Long March – the Ch'ang Cheng, as they called it – as one of the great exploits of military history. In Asia only the Mongols had surpassed it, and in the past three centuries there had been no similar armed *migration of a nation* with the exception, perhaps, of the amazing Flight of the Torgut, of which Sven Hedin told in his *Jehol, City of Emperors*. Hannibal's march over the Alps looked like a holiday excursion beside it. A more interesting comparison was Napoleon's retreat from Moscow, when the Grand Army was utterly broken and demoralized.

While the Red Army's March to the North-West was unquestionably a strategic retreat, forced upon it by regionally decisive defeats, the army finally reached its objective with its nucleus still intact, and its morale and political will evidently as strong as ever. The Communists rationalized, and apparently believed, that they were advancing towards an anti-Japanese front, and this was a psychological factor of great importance. It helped them turn what might have been a demoralized retreat into a spirited march of victory. History has subsequently shown that they were right in emphasizing what was undoubtedly the second fundamental reason for their migration: an advance to a region which they correctly foresaw was to play a determining role in the immediate destinies of China, Japan, and Soviet Russia. This skilful propagandive manoeuvre must be noted as a piece of brilliant political strategy. It was to a large extent responsible for the successful conclusion of the heroic trek.

In one sense this mass migration was the biggest armed propa-

ganda tour in history. The Reds passed through provinces populated by more than 200,000,000 people. Between battles and
skirmishes, in every town occupied, they called mass meetings,
gave theatrical performances, heavily 'taxed' the rich, freed many
'slaves' (some of whom joined the Red Army), preached 'liberty,
equality, democracy', confiscated the property of the 'traitors'
(officials, big landlords, and tax collectors) and distributed their
goods among the poor. Millions of the poor had now seen the Red
Army and heard it speak, and were no longer afraid of it. The
Reds explained the aims of agrarian revolution and their anti-
Japanese policy. They armed thousands of peasants and left cadres
behind to train Red partisans who kept Nanking's troops busy.
Many thousands dropped out on the long and heartbreaking
march, but thousands of others – farmers, apprentices, slaves, deserters from the Kuomintang ranks, workers, all the disinherited
– joined in and filled the ranks.

Some day someone will write the full epic of this exciting expedition. Meanwhile, as epilogue, I offer a free translation of a
classical poem about this 6,000-mile excursion written by Chairman Mao Tse-tung – a rebel who could write verse as well as lead
a crusade :

> The Red Army, never fearing the challenging Long March,
> Looked lightly on the many peaks and rivers.
> Wu Liang's Range rose, lowered, rippled,
> And green-tiered were the rounded steps of Wu Meng.
> Warm-beating the Gold Sand River's waves against the rocks,
> And cold the iron-chain spans of Tatu's bridge.
> A thousand joyous li of freshening snow on Min Shan,
> And then, the last pass vanquished, Three Armies smiled.[3]

Part Six

RED STAR IN THE NORTH-WEST

I

The Shensi Soviets: Beginnings[1]

WHILE the Communists in Kiangsi, Fukien, and Hunan from 1927 onwards gradually built bases for their opposition to Nanking, Red armies appeared in other widely scattered parts of China. Of these the biggest single area was the Honan–Anhui–Hupeh Soviet, which covered a good part of those three rich provinces of the Central Yangtze Valley, and embraced a population of more than 2,000,000 people. The Red Army there began under the command of Hsu Hai-tung and, later on, to lead it came Hsu Hsiang-ch'ien, a graduate of the first class of Whampoa Academy, a former colonel in the Kuomintang Army, and a veteran of the Canton Commune.

Far in the mountains to the north-west of them, another Whampoa cadet, Liu Chih-tan, was laying the foundations for the soviet areas in Shensi, Kansu, and Ninghsia. Liu was a modern Robin Hood, with the mountaineer's hatred of rich men; among the poor he was becoming a name of promise, and among landlords and moneylenders the scourge of the gods.

This chaotic warrior was born in the hill-cradled town of Pao An, north Shensi, the son of a landlord family. He went to high school in Yulin, which stood under the shadow of the Great Wall and was the seat of Shensi's prosperous trade with the caravans of Mongolia. Leaving Yulin, Liu Chih-tan secured an appointment to the Whampoa Academy in Canton, completed his course there in 1926, and became a Communist and a young officer in the Kuomintang. With the Nationalist Expedition as far as Hankow, he was there when the split occurred in the Kuomintang–Communist alliance.

In 1927, following the Nanking *coup d'état*, he fled from the 'purgation' and worked secretly for the Communist Party in Shanghai. Returning to his native province in 1928, he re-established connections with some of his former comrades, then in the

Kuominchun, the 'People's Army', of General Feng Yu-hsiang. Next year he led a peasant uprising in south Shensi. Although Liu's uprising was sanguinarily suppressed, out of it grew the nucleus of the first guerrilla bands of Shensi.

Liu Chih-tan's career from 1929 to 1932 was a kaleidoscope of defeats, failures, discouragements, escapades, adventure, and remarkable escapes from death, interspersed with periods of respectability as a reinstated officer. Several small armies under him were completely destroyed. Once he was made head of the *min-t'uan* at Pao An, and he used his office to arrest and execute several landlords and moneylenders – strange behaviour for a *min-t'uan* leader. The magistrate of Pao An was dismissed, and Liu fled, with but three followers, to a neighbouring *hsien*. There one of General Feng Yu-hsiang's officers invited them to a banquet, in the midst of which Liu and his friends disarmed their hosts, seized twenty guns, and made off to the hills, where they soon collected a following of about 300 men.

This little army was surrounded, however, and Liu sued for peace. His offer was accepted, and he became a colonel in the Kuomintang Army, with a garrison post in west Shensi. Again he began an anti-landlord movement and again he was outlawed, this time arrested. Owing chiefly to his influence in the Shensi Ke Lao Hui, he was pardoned once more, but his troops were reorganized into a transportation brigade, of which he was made commander. And then for the third time Liu Chih-tan repeated the error of his ways. Some landlords in his district, long accustomed to tax exemption (a more or less 'hereditary right' of landlords in Shensi), refused to pay taxes. Liu promptly arrested a number of them, with the result that the gentry rose up in arms and demanded that Sian remove and punish him. His troops were surrounded and disarmed.

Finally he was driven back to Pao An with a price on his head – but followed by many young Communist officers and men from his own brigade. Here at last he set about organizing an independent army under a Red flag in 1931, took possession of Pao An and Chung Yang counties, and rapidly pushed operations in north Shensi. Government troops sent against him very often turned over to the Reds in battle; deserters even drifted across the Yellow

River from Shansi to join this outlaw whose daredeviltry, courage, and impetuousness soon won him fame throughout the North-West and created the usual legend that he was 'invulnerable to bullets'.

Killings of officials, tax collectors, and landlords became widespread. Unleashing long-hushed fury, the armed peasants raided, plundered, carried off captives, whom they held for ransom in their fortified areas, and conducted themselves much like ordinary bandits. By 1932 Liu Chih-tan's followers had occupied eleven counties in the loess hills of northern Shensi, and the Communist Party had organized a political department at Yulin to direct Liu's troops. Early in 1933 the first Shensi Soviet and a regular administration were established, and a programme was attempted similar to that in Kiangsi.

In 1934 and 1935 these Shensi Reds expanded considerably, improved their armies, and somewhat stabilized conditions in their districts. A Shensi Provincial Soviet Government was set up, a Party training school established, and military headquarters were located at An Ting. The soviets opened their own bank and post office and began to issue crude money and stamps. In the completely sovietized areas a soviet economy was begun, landlords' land was confiscated and redistributed, all surtaxes were abolished, cooperatives were opened, and a call was sent out by the Party to enlist members to volunteer as teachers for primary schools.

Meanwhile Liu Chih-tan moved well south of the Red base towards the capital. He occupied Lintung, just outside Sianfu, and besieged the city for some days, without success. A column of Reds pushed down to southern Shensi and established soviets in several counties there. They had some bad defeats and reverses in battles with General Yang Hu-ch'eng (later to become the Reds' ally), and they won some victories. As discipline increased in the army, and bandit elements were eliminated, support for the Reds deepened among the peasantry. By the middle of 1935 the soviets controlled twenty-two counties in Shensi and Kansu. The Twenty-sixth and Twenty-seventh Red armies, with a total of over 5,000 men, were now under Liu Chih-tan's command, and could establish contact by radio with the main forces of the Red Army in the South and in the West. As the southern Reds began to withdraw from their

Kiangsi–Fukien base, these hill men of Shensi greatly strengthened themselves, until in 1935 Chiang Kai-shek was forced to send his vice-commander-in-chief, Marshal Chang Hsueh-liang, to lead a big army against them.

Late in 1934 the Twenty-fifth Red Army, under Hsu Hai-tung, left Honan with some 8,000 men. By October it had reached south Shensi and connected with about 1,000 Red partisans in that area who had been armed by Liu Chih-tan. Hsu encamped for the winter there, helped the partisans to build a regular army, fought several successful battles against General Yang Hu-ch'eng's troops, and armed peasants in five counties of south Shensi. A provisional soviet government was established, with Cheng Wei-shan, a twenty-three-year-old member of the Central Committee of Shensi province, as chairman, and Li Lung-kuei and Cheng Shan-jui as commanders of two independent Red brigades. Leaving them to defend this area, Hsu Hai-tung then moved into Kansu with his Twenty-fifth Army, and fought his way into the soviet districts through thousands of government troops, capturing five county seats en route and disarming two regiments of Mohammedan troops under General Ma Hung-ping.

On 25 July 1935, the Twenty-fifth, Twenty-sixth, and Twenty-seventh armies united near Yung Ch'ang, north Shensi. Their troops were reorganized into the Fifteenth Red Army Corps, with Hsu Hai-tung as commander and Liu Chih-tan as vice-commander and chairman of the Shensi–Kansu–Shansi Revolutionary Military Committee.* In August 1935, this army corps met and defeated two divisions of Tungpei (Manchurian) troops, under General Wang Yi-che. New recruits were added and much-needed guns and ammunition.

And now a curious thing occurred.[2] In August there came to north Shensi a delegate of the Central Committee of the Communist Party, a stout young gentleman named Chang Ching-fu (Chang Mu-t'ao?). According to my informant, who was then a staff officer under Liu Chih-tan, this Mr Chang (nicknamed Chang the Corpulent) was empowered to 'reorganize' the Party and the army. He was a kind of superinspector.

Chang the Corpulent proceeded to collect evidence to prove

*Of which Li Hsueh-feng was a member. See BN.

that Liu Chih-tan had not followed the 'Party line'. He 'tried' Liu, and demanded his resignation from all posts. Liu Chih-tan did not put Mr Chang against a wall as an interloper for presuming to criticize him, but retired from all active command and went, Achilles-like, to sulk in his cave in Pao An. Mr Chang also ordered the arrest and imprisonment of more than a hundred other 're-actionaries' in the Party and the army and quietly sat back, well satisfied with himself.

It was into this queer scene that the vanguard of the southern Reds, the First Army Corps, headed by Lin Piao, Chou En-lai, P'eng Teh-huai, and Mao Tse-tung, entered in October 1935. According to my local informants in Pao An, Mao and his Politburo called for a re-examination of evidence, found most of it baseless, dis-covered that Chang Ching-fu had exceeded his orders and been misled by 'reactionaries' himself. They reinstated Liu and all his confederates. Chang the Corpulent was himself arrested, tried, imprisoned for a term, and later given menial tasks to perform.

Thus it happened that when, early in 1936, the combined Red armies attempted their famous 'anti-Japanese' expedition, crossed the river, and invaded neighbouring Shansi, Liu Chih-tan was again in command. He distinguished himself in that remarkable campaign during which the Reds occupied over eighteen counties of the so-called 'model province' in two months. He was fatally wounded in March 1936, when he led a raiding party against an enemy fortification, the capture of which enabled the Red Army to cross the Yellow River. Liu Chih-tan was carried back to Shensi and died gazing upon the hills he had roamed and loved as a boy, and among the mountain people he had led along the road he be-lieved in, the road of revolutionary struggle. He was buried at Wa Ya Pao, and the soviets renamed a county of their Red China after him – Chih-tan *hsien*.

In Pao An I met his widow and his child, a beautiful little girl of six. The Reds had tailored her a special uniform; she wore an officer's belt, and a red star on her cap. She was the idol of every-body there. Young Liu carried herself like a field marshal and she was mightily proud of her 'bandit' father.

But although Liu Chih-tan was the personality around which these soviets of the North-West grew up, it was not Liu, but the conditions of life itself, which produced this convulsive movement of his people. And to understand whatever success they had had it was necessary not so much just now to look at what these men fought for, as to examine what they fought against.

Death and Taxes

DURING the great North-West famine, which lasted roughly for three years and affected four huge provinces, I visited some of the drought-stricken areas in Suiyuan, on the edge of Mongolia, in June 1929. How many people starved to death in those years I do not accurately know, and probably no one will ever know; it is forgotten now. A conservative semi-official figure of 3,000,000 is often accepted, but I am not inclined to doubt other estimates ranging as high as 6,000,000.

This catastrophe passed hardly noticed in the Western world, and even in the coastal cities of China, but a few courageous Chinese and foreigners attached to the American-financed China International Famine Relief Commission – including its secretary, Dwight Edwards; O. J. Todd, the American engineer; and a wonderful American missionary doctor, Robert Ingram * – risked their lives in those typhus-infested areas, trying to salvage some of the human wreckage. I spent some days with them, passing through cities of death, across a once-fertile countryside turned into desert wasteland, through a land of naked horror.

I was twenty-three. I had come to the East looking for the 'glamour of the Orient', searching for adventure. This excursion to Suiyuan had begun as something like that. But here for the first time in my life I came abruptly upon men who were dying because they had nothing to eat. In those hours of nightmare I spent in Suiyuan I saw thousands of men, women, and children starving to death before my eyes.

Have you ever seen a man – a good honest man who has worked hard, a 'law-abiding citizen', doing no serious harm to anyone – when he has had no food for more than a month? It is a most agonizing sight. His dying flesh hangs from him in wrinkled

---

*Dr Ingram was killed a few years later by Chinese bandits, but *not* Red bandits.

folds; you can clearly see every bone in his body; his eyes stare out unseeing; and even if he is a youth of twenty he moves like an ancient crone, dragging himself from spot to spot. If he has been lucky he has long ago sold his wife and daughters. He has sold everything he owns – the timber of his house itself, and most of his clothes. Sometimes he has, indeed, even sold the last rag of decency, and he sways there in the scorching sun, his testicles dangling from him like withered olive seeds – the last grim jest to remind you that this was once a man.

Children are even more pitiable, with their little skeletons bent over and misshapen, their crooked bones, their little arms like twigs, and their purpling bellies, filled with bark and sawdust, protruding like tumors. Women lie slumped in corners, waiting for death, their black blade-like buttocks protruding, their breasts hanging like collapsed sacks. But there are, after all, not many women and girls. Most of them have died or been sold.

Those were things I myself had seen and would never forget. Millions of people died that way in famine, and thousands more still died in China like that. I had seen fresh corpses on the streets of Saratsi, and in the villages I had seen shallow graves where victims of famine and disease were laid by the dozens. But these were not the most shocking things after all. The shocking thing was that in many of those towns there were still rich men, rice hoarders, wheat hoarders, moneylenders, and landlords, with armed guards to defend them, while they profiteered enormously. The shocking thing was that in the cities – where officials danced or played with sing-song girls – there were grain and food, and had been for months; that in Peking and Tientsin and elsewhere were thousands of tons of wheat and millet, collected (mostly by contributions from abroad) by the Famine Commission, but which could not be shipped to the starving. Why not? Because in the North-West there were some militarists who wanted to hold all of their railroad rolling stock and would release none of it towards the east, while in the east there were other Kuomintang generals who would send no rolling stock westward – even to starving people – because they feared it would be seized by their rivals.

While famine raged the Commission decided to build a big canal (with American funds) to help flood some of the lands baked by drought. The officials gave them every cooperation – and promptly began to buy for a few cents an acre all the lands to be irrigated. A flock of vultures descended upon this benighted country and purchased from the starving farmers thousands of acres for the taxes in arrears, or for a few coppers, and held it to await tenants and rainy days.

Yet the great majority of those people who died did so without any act of protest.

'Why don't they revolt?' I asked myself. 'Why don't they march in a great army and attack the scoundrels who can tax them but cannot feed them, who can seize their lands but cannot repair an irrigation canal? Or why don't they sweep into the great cities and plunder the wealth of the rascals who buy their daughters and wives, the men who continue to gorge on thirty-six-course banquets while honest men starve? Why not?'

I was profoundly puzzled by their passivity. For a while I thought nothing would make a Chinese fight.

I was mistaken. The Chinese peasant was not passive; he was not a coward. He would fight when given a method, an organization, leadership, a workable programme, hope – *and arms*. The development of 'communism' in China had proved that. Against the above background, therefore, it should not surprise us to learn that Communists were popular in the North-West, for conditions there had been no better for the mass of the peasantry than elsewhere in China.

Evidence to that effect had been vividly documented by Dr A. Stampar,* the distinguished health expert sent by the League of Nations as adviser to the Nanking Government. It was the best thing available on the subject. Dr Stampar had toured the Kuomintang areas of Shensi and Kansu, and his reports were based on his own observations as well as official data opened for him.

He pointed out that 'in the year 240 B.C. an engineer called Cheng Kuo is said to have constructed a system for irrigating nearly a million acres' in the historic Wei Valley of Shensi, cradle of the Chinese race, but that 'this system was neglected; the dams

*Dr A. Stampar, *The North-western Provinces and Their Possibilities of Development*, published privately by the National Economic Council (Nanking, July 1934).

collapsed, and, though new works were from time to time carried out, the amount of territory irrigated at the end of the Manchu Dynasty (1912) was less than 20,000 *mou'* – about 3,300 acres. Figures he obtained showed that during the great famine 62 per cent of the population died outright in one county of Shensi; in another, 75 per cent; and so on. Official estimates revealed that 2,000,000 people starved in Kansu alone – about 20 per cent of the population.

To quote from this Geneva investigator on conditions in the North-West before the Reds arrived:

In the famine of 1930 twenty acres of land could be purchased for three days' food supply. Making use of this opportunity, the wealthy classes of the province [Shensi] built up large estates, and the number of owner-cultivators diminished. The following extract from the report for 1930 of Mr Findlay Andrew of the China International Famine Relief Commission conveys a good impression of the situation in that year:

'... The external appearances of the Province have much improved on those of last year. Why? Because in this particular section of Kansu with which our work deals, death from starvation, pestilence, and sword have doomed during the past two years such large numbers of the population that the very demand for food has considerably lessened.'

Much land had become waste, much had been concentrated in the hands of landlords and officials. Kansu especially had 'surprisingly large' areas of cultivable but uncultivated land. 'Land during the famine of 1928–30 was bought at extremely cheap rates by landowners who, since that period, have realized fortunes by the execution of the Wei Pei Irrigation project' (a famine-relief measure financed by the Commission).

In Shensi it is considered a mark of honour to pay no land tax, and wealthy landowners are therefore as a rule exempted. . . . A practice which is particularly undesirable is to claim arrears of taxes, for the period during which they were absent, from the farmers who abandoned their land during famines, the farmers being forbidden to resume possession until their arrears are paid.

Dr Stampar found that Shensi farmers (evidently excluding the landlords, who were 'as a rule exempted') had to pay land taxes and surtaxes amounting to about 45 per cent of their income, while other taxes 'represent a further 20 per cent'; and 'not only is taxation thus fantastically heavy, but its assessment appears to be haphazard and its manner of collection wasteful, brutal, and in many cases corrupt.'

As for Kansu, Dr Stampar said :

The revenues of Kansu have during the last five years averaged over eight millions . . . heavier taxation than in Chekiang, one of the richest and most heavily taxed provinces in China. It will be seen also that this revenue, especially in Kansu, is not drawn from one or two major sources, but from a multitude of taxes each yielding a small sum, scarcely any commodity or productive or commercial activity going untaxed. The amount which the population pays is even higher than is shown by the published figures. In the first place, the tax collectors are able to retain a share – in some cases a very large share – of the amounts collected. In the second place, to the taxes levied by the provincial or *hsien* governments must be added those imposed by military leaders, which in Kansu province are officially estimated at more than ten millions.*

A further cause of expense to the population is the local militia [*min-t'uan*], which, formed originally for defence against the bandits, has in many instances degenerated into a gang living at the cost of the countryside.

Dr Stampar quoted figures showing that the cost of supporting the *min-t'uan* ranged from 30 to 40 per cent of the total local government budget – this quite in addition, of course, to the burden of maintaining the big regular armies. These latter, according to Dr Stampar, had absorbed over 60 per cent of the provincial revenues in both Kansu and Shensi.

A foreign missionary I met in Shensi told me that he had once personally followed a pig from owner to consumer, and in the process saw six different taxes being paid. Another missionary, of Kansu, described seeing peasants knock down the wooden walls of their houses (wood being expensive in the North-West) and cart it to market to sell in order to pay tax collectors. He said that the

*This was a conservative estimate, since it included no mention of the chief illegal military taxation in both Kansu and Shensi, for many years the opium revenue.

attitude of even some of the 'rich' peasants, while not friendly when the Reds first arrived, was one of indifference, and a belief that 'no government could be worse than the old'.

And yet the North-West was by no means a hopeless country economically. It was not overpopulated; much of its land was very rich; it could easily produce far more than it could consume; and with an improved irrigation system parts of it might become a 'Chinese Ukraine'. Shensi and Kansu had abundant coal deposits. Shensi had oil. Dr Stampar prophesied that 'Shensi, especially the plain in the neighbourhood of Sian, may itself become an industrial centre of an importance second only to the Yangtze Valley, and needing for its service its own coal fields.' Mineral deposits of Kansu, Chinghai, and Sinkiang, said to be very rich, were scarcely touched. In gold alone, said Stampar, 'the region may turn out to be a second Klondike.'

Here, surely, were conditions which seemed overripe for change. Here, surely, were things for men to fight against, even if they had nothing to fight for. And no wonder, when the Red Star appeared in the North-West, thousands of men arose to welcome it as a symbol of hope and freedom.

But did the Reds, after all, prove any better?

3

Soviet Society

WHATEVER it may have been in the South, Chinese communism as I found it in the North-West might more accurately be called rural equalitarianism than anything Marx would have found acceptable as a model child of his own. This was manifestly true economically, and although in the social, political, and cultural life of the organized soviets there was a crude Marxist guidance, limitations of material conditions were everywhere obvious.

There was no machine industry of any importance in the North-West. It was farming and grazing country primarily, the culture of which had been for centuries in stagnation, though many of the economic abuses prevalent no doubt reflected the changing economy in the semi-industrialized cities. Yet the Red Army itself was an outstanding product of the impact of 'industrialization' on China, and the shock of the ideas it had brought into the fossilized culture here was in a true sense revolutionary.

Objective conditions, however, denied the Reds the possibility of organizing much more than the political framework for the beginnings of a modern economy, of which naturally they could think only in terms of a future which might give them power in the great cities, where they could take over the industrial bases from the foreign concessions and thus lay the foundations for a socialist society. Meanwhile, in the rural areas their activity centred chiefly on the solution of the immediate problems of the peasants – land and taxes. But Chinese Communists never regarded land distribution as anything more than a phase in the building of a mass base, a stage enabling them to develop the revolutionary struggle towards the conquest of power and the ultimate realization of thoroughgoing socialist changes. In *Fundamental Laws of the Chinese Soviet Republic,** the First All-China Soviet Congress

* Mao Tse-tung et al.

in 1931 had set forth in detail the 'maximum programme' of the Communist Party of China – and reference to it showed clearly that the ultimate aim of Chinese Communists was a socialist state of the Marxist–Leninist conception. Meanwhile, however, the social, political, and economic organization of the Red districts had all along been a very provisional affair. Even in Kiangsi it was little more than that. Because the soviets had to fight for an existence from their beginning, their main task was always to build a military and political base for the extension of the revolution on a wider and deeper scale, rather than to 'try out communism in China', which is what some people thought the Reds were attempting in their little blockaded areas.

The immediate basis of support for the Reds in the North-West was obviously not so much the idea of 'from each according to his ability, to each according to his needs' as it was something like the promise of Dr Sun Yat-sen : 'Land to those who till it.'

While theoretically the soviets were a 'workers' and peasants'' government, in actual practice the whole constituency was over-whelmingly peasant in character and occupation, and the regime had to shape itself accordingly. An attempt was made to balance peasant influence, and offset it, by classifying the rural population into these categories: great landlords, middle and small land-lords, rich peasants, middle peasants, poor peasants, tenant peas-ants, rural workers, handicraft workers, *lumpen* proletariat, and a division called *tzu-yu chih-yeh chieh*, or professional workers – which included teachers, doctors, and technicians, the 'rural in-telligentsia'.[1] These divisions were political as well as economic, and in the soviet elections the tenant peasants, rural workers, handicraft workers, and so on were given a very much greater representation than the other categories – the aim apparently being to create some kind of democratic dictatorship of the 'rural proletariat'.

Within these limitations the soviets seemed to work very well in areas where the regime was stabilized. The structure of repre-sentative government was built up from the village soviet, as the smallest unit: above it were the district soviet, the county soviet, and the provincial and central soviets. Each village elected its delegates to the higher soviets clear up to the delegates elected for the Soviet Congress. Suffrage was universal over the age of sixteen, but it was not equal, for reasons mentioned above.

Various committees were established under each of the district soviets. An all-powerful committee, usually elected in a mass meeting shortly after the occupation of a district by the Red Army, and preceded by an intensified propaganda campaign, was the revolutionary committee. It called for elections or re-elections, and closely cooperated with the Communist Party. Under the district soviet, and appointed by it, were committees for education, cooperatives, military training, political training, land, public health, partisan training, revolutionary defence, enlargement of the Red Army, agrarian mutual aid, Red Army land tilling, and others. Such committees were found in every branch organ of the soviets, right up to the Central Government, where policies were coordinated and state decisions made.

Organization did not stop with the government itself. The Communist Party had an extensive membership among farmers and workers, in the towns and in the villages. In addition there were the Young Communists, and under them two organizations which embraced in their membership most of the youth. These were called the Shao-Nien Hsien-Feng Tui and the Erh-T'ung T'uan – the Young Vanguards and the Children's Brigades. The Communist Party organized the women also into Communist Youth leagues, anti-Japanese societies, nursing schools, weaving schools, and tilling brigades. Adult farmers were organized into the P'in-Min Hui, or Poor People's Society, and into anti-Japanese societies. Even the Elder Brother Society was brought into soviet life and given open and legal work to do. The Nung-min Tui, or Peasant Guards, and the Yu Chi Tui, or Partisan (Roving) Brigades, were also part of the intensely organized rural political and social structure.

The work of all these organizations and their various committees was coordinated by the Central Soviet Government, the Communist Party, and the Red Army. Here we need not enter into statistical detail to explain the organic connections of these groups, but it can be said in general that they were all skilfully interwoven, and each directly under the guidance of some Communist, though decisions of organization, membership, and work seemed to be carried out in a democratic way by the peasants themselves. The aim of soviet organization obviously was to make every man, woman, and child a member of something, with definite work assigned to him to perform.

Rather typical of the intensity of soviet efforts were the methods used to increase production and utilize great areas of wasteland. I procured copies of many orders, quite astonishing in their scope and common-sense practicality, issued by the land commission to its various branches to guide them in organizing and propagandizing the peasants in the tasks of cultivation. To illustrate: in one of these orders that I picked up in a branch land office, instructions were given concerning spring cultivation, the commission urging its workers to 'make widespread propaganda to induce the masses to participate voluntarily, without involving any form of compulsory command'. Detailed advice was offered on how to achieve the four main demands of this planting period, which the previous winter had been recognized by the soviets to be: more extensive utilization of wasteland, and expansion of Red Army land; increased crop yields; greater diversity of crops, with special emphasis on new varieties of melons and vegetables; and expansion of cotton acreage.

Among the devices recommended by this order * to expand labour power, and especially to bring women directly into agricultural production (particularly in districts where the male population had declined as a result of enlistments in the Red Army), the following ingenious instruction suggested the efficiency with which the Reds went about utilizing their available materials:

To mobilize women, boys, and old men to participate in spring planting and cultivation, each according to his ability to carry on either a principal or an auxiliary task in the labour processes of production. For example, 'large feet' [natural feet] and young women should be mobilized to organize production-teaching corps, with tasks varying from land clearance up to the main tasks of agricultural production itself. 'Small feet' [bound feet], young boys, and old men must be mobilized to help in weed-pulling, collecting dung, and for other auxiliary tasks.

But how did the peasants feel about this? The Chinese peasant

*Order of Instruction, Land Commission (Wayapao, Shensi), 28 January 1936.

was supposed to hate organization, discipline, and any social activity beyond his own family. The Reds laughed when that was mentioned. They said that no Chinese peasant disliked organization or social activity if he was working for himself and not the *min-t'uan* – the landlord or the tax collector. And I had to admit that most of the peasants to whom I talked seemed to support soviets and the Red Army. Many of them were very free in their criticisms and complaints, but when asked whether they preferred it to the old days, the answer was nearly always an emphatic yes. I noticed also that most of them talked about the soviets as *womenti chengfu* – 'our government' – and this struck me as something new in rural China.

One thing which suggested that the Reds had their 'base' in the mass of the population was that in all the older soviet districts the policing and guarding was done almost entirely by the peasant organizations alone. There were few actual Red Army garrisons in the soviet districts, all the fighting strength of the army being kept at the front. Local defence was shared by the village revolutionary defence corps, peasant guards, and partisans. This fact could explain some of the apparent popularity of the Red Army with the (poor) peasantry, for it was rarely planted down on them as an instrument of oppression and exploitation, like other armies, but was generally at the front, fighting for its food there, and engaged in meeting enemy attacks. On the other hand, the intensive organization of the peasantry created a rear guard and base which freed the Red Army to operate with the extreme mobility for which it was noted.

To understand peasant support for the Communist movement it was necessary to keep in mind the burden borne by the peasantry in the North-West under the former regime. Now, wherever the Reds went there was no doubt that they radically changed the situation for the tenant farmer, the poor farmer, the middle farmer, and all the 'have-not' elements. All forms of taxation were abolished in the new districts for the first year, to give the farmers a breathing space, and in the old districts only a progressive single tax on land was collected, and a small single tax (from 5 to 10 per cent) on business. Second, the Reds gave land to the land-hungry peasants, and began the reclamation of great areas of 'wasteland' –

mostly the land of absentee or fleeing landlords. Third, they took land and livestock from the wealthy classes and redistributed them among the poor.

Redistribution of land was a fundamental of Red policy. How was it carried out? Later on, for reasons of national political manoeuvre, there was to be a drastic retreat in the soviet land policy, but when I travelled in the North-West the land laws in force (promulgated by the North-West Soviet Government in December 1935) provided for the confiscation of all landlords' land and the confiscation of all land of rich peasants that was not cultivated by the owners themselves. However, both the landlord and the rich peasant were allowed as much land as they could till with their own labour. In districts where there was no land scarcity – and there were many such districts in the North-West – the lands of resident landlords and rich peasants were in practice not confiscated at all, but the wasteland and land of absentee owners was distributed, and sometimes there was a redivision of best-quality land, poor peasants being given better soil, and landlords being allotted the same amount of poorer land.

What was a landlord? According to the Communists' definition (greatly simplified), any farmer who collected the greater part of his income from land rented out to others, and not from his own labour, was a landlord. By this definition the usurers and *t'u-hao** were put in about the same category as landlords, and similarly treated. Usury rates, according to Dr Stampar, had formerly ranged as high as 60 per cent in the North-West, or very much higher in times of stress. Although land was very cheap in many parts of Kansu, Shensi, and Ninghsia, cash was unbelievably scarce. In practice it was nearly impossible for a farm worker or tenant with no capital to accumulate enough to buy sufficient land for his family. I met farmers in the Red districts who formerly had never been able to own any land, although rates in some places were as low as two or three dollars (in silver) an acre.†

---

* *T'u-hao*, which actually means 'local rascals', was the Reds' term for landowners who also derived a large part of their income from lending money and buying and selling mortgages.

† Domestic animals were far more costly than land. See Part Seven, Chapter 2.

Classes other than those mentioned above were not subject to confiscatory action, so a big percentage of the farmers stood to benefit immediately by the redistribution. The poorest farmers, tenants, and farm labourers were all provided with land enough for a livelihood. There did not seem to be an attempt to 'equalize' land ownership. The primary purpose of the soviet land laws, as explained to me by Wang Kuan-lan (the twenty-nine-year-old Russian-returned student who was land commissioner for the three Red provinces of the North-West), was to provide for every person sufficient land to guarantee him and his family a decent livelihood – which was claimed to be the most 'urgent demand' of the peasantry.

The land problem – confiscation and redistribution – was greatly simplified in the North-West by the fact that big estates were formerly owned by officials, tax collectors, and absentee landlords. With the confiscation of these, in many cases the immediate demands of the poor peasantry were satisfied, without much interference with either the resident small landlords or the rich peasants. Thus the Reds not only created the economic base for support in the poor and landless peasantry by giving them farms, but in some cases won the gratitude of middle peasants by abolishing tax exploitation, and in a few instances enlisted the aid of small landlords on the same basis or through the patriotic appeals of the anti-Japanese movement. Several prominent Shensi Communists came from landlord families.

Additional help was given to the poor farmers in the form of loans at very low rates of interest or no interest at all. Usury was entirely abolished, but private lending, at rates fixed at a maximum of 10 per cent annually, was permitted. The ordinary government lending rate was 5 per cent. Several thousand simple agricultural implements made in the Red arsenals, and thousands of pounds of seed grain, were supplied to landless peasants breaking wasteland. A primitive agricultural school had been established, and I was told it was planned to open an animal-husbandry school as soon as an expert in this field, expected from Shanghai, had arrived.

A cooperative movement was being vigorously pushed. These activities extended beyond production and distribution cooperatives, branching out to include cooperation in such novel (for China) forms as the collective use of farm animals and implements – especially in tilling public lands and Red Army lands – and in the organization of labour mutual-aid societies. By the latter device great areas could be quickly planted and harvested collectively, and periods of idleness by individual farmers eliminated. The Reds saw to it that a man earned his new land! In busy periods the system of 'Saturday Brigades' was used, when not only all the children's organizations but every soviet official, Red partisan, Red Guard, women's organization member, and any Red Army detachment that happened to be nearby, were mobilized to work at least one day a week at farming tasks. Even Mao Tse-tung took part in this work.

Here the Reds were introducing the germs of the drastically revolutionary idea of collective effort – and doing primary education work for some future period when collectivization might become practicable. At the same time, into the dark recesses of peasant mentality there was slowly penetrating the concept of a broader realm of social life. For the organizations created among the peasantry were what the Reds called three-in-one: economic, political, and cultural in their utility.

What cultural progress the Reds had made among these people was by advanced Western standards negligible indeed. But certain outstanding evils common in most parts of China had definitely been eliminated in the score of long-sovietized counties in north Shensi, and a crusade of propaganda was being conducted among inhabitants of newer areas to spread the same elementary reforms there. As an outstanding achievement, opium had been completely eliminated in north Shensi, and in fact I did not see any sign of poppies after I entered the soviet districts. Official corruption was almost unheard of. Beggary and unemployment did seem to have been, as the Reds claimed, 'liquidated'. I did not see a beggar during all my travels in the Red areas. Foot binding and infanticide were criminal offences, child slavery and prostitution had disappeared, and polyandry and polygamy were prohibited.

The myths of 'communized wives' and 'nationalization of women' are too patently absurd to be denied, but changes in marriage, divorce, and inheritance were in themselves radical against the background of semifeudal law and practice elsewhere in China. Marriage regulations * included interesting provisions against mother-in-law tyranny, the buying and selling of women as wives and concubines, and the custom of 'arranged matches'. Marriage was by mutual consent, the legal age had been moved up sharply to twenty for men and eighteen for women, dowries were prohibited, and any couple registering as man and wife before a county, municipal, or village soviet was given a marriage certificate without cost. Men and women actually cohabiting were considered legally married, whether registered or not – which seemed to rule out 'free love'. All children were legitimate under soviet law.

Divorce could also be secured from the registration bureau of the soviet, free of charge, on the 'insistent demand' of either party to the marriage contract, but wives of Red Army men were required to have their husbands' consent before a divorce was granted. Property was divided equally between the divorcees, and both were legally obliged to care for their children, but responsibility for debts was shouldered by the male alone (!), who was also obliged to supply two thirds of the children's living expenses.

Education, in theory, was 'free and universal', but parents were obliged to supply their children with food and clothing. In practice, nothing like 'free and universal' education had yet been achieved, although old Hsu T'eh-li, the commissioner of education, boasted to me that if they were given a few years of peace in the North-West they would astound the rest of China with the educational progress they would make. Further on I was to learn in more detail what the Communists had done and hoped to do to liquidate the appalling illiteracy of this region, but first it was interesting to know how the government was financing not only the educational programme, such as it was, but this whole seemingly simple and yet in its way vastly complex organism which I have called soviet society.

The Marriage Law of the Chinese Soviet Republic (reprinted in Pao An, July 1936).

4

Anatomy of Money

IT was imperative for soviet economy to fulfil at least two elementary functions: to feed and equip the Red Army, and to bring immediate relief to the poor peasantry. Failing in either, the soviet base would soon collapse. To guarantee success at these tasks it was necessary for the Reds, even from the earliest days, to begin some kind of economic construction.

Soviet economy in the North-West was a curious mixture of private capitalism, state capitalism, and primitive socialism. Private enterprise and industry were permitted and encouraged, and private transaction in the land and its products was allowed, with restrictions. At the same time the state owned and exploited enterprises such as oil wells, salt wells, and coal mines, and it traded in cattle, hides, salt, wool, cotton, paper, and other raw materials. But it did not establish a monopoly in these articles, and in all of them private enterprises could, and to some extent did, compete.

A third kind of economy was created by the establishment of cooperatives, in which the government and the masses participated as partners, competing not only with private capitalism, but also with state capitalism! But it was all conducted on a very small and primitive scale. Thus although the fundamental antagonisms in such an arrangement were obvious, and in an economically more highly developed area would have been ruinous, here in the Red regions they somehow supplemented each other.

The Reds defined the cooperative as 'an instrument to resist private capitalism and develop a new economic system', and they listed its five main functions as follows: 'to combat the exploitation of the masses by the merchants; to combat the enemy's blockade; to develop the national economy of the soviet districts; to raise the economic-political level of the masses; and to prepare the conditions for socialist construction' – a period in which 'the democratic revolution of the Chinese bourgeoisie, under the leadership of the proletariat, may create energetic conditions enabling the transition of this revolution into socialism.'*

The first two of those high-sounding functions in practice meant simply that the cooperative could help the masses organize their own blockade-running corps, as auxiliaries to the blockade-running activity of the government. Trade between Red and White districts was prohibited by Nanking, but by using small mountain roads, and by oiling the palms of border guards, the Reds at times managed to carry on a fairly lively export business. Taking out raw materials from the soviet districts, the transport corps in the service of the state trade bureau or the cooperatives exchanged them for Kuomintang money and needed manufactures.

Consumption, sales, production, and credit cooperatives were organized in the village, district, county, and province. Above them was a central bureau of cooperatives, under the finance commissioner and a department of national economy. These cooperatives were really constructed to encourage the participation of the lowest strata of society. Shares entitling the purchaser to membership were priced as low as fifty cents, or even twenty cents, and organizational duties were so extensive as to bring nearly every shareholder into the economic or political life of the cooperative. While there was no restriction on the number of shares an individual member could buy, each member was entitled to but one vote, regardless of how many shares he held. Cooperatives elected their own managing committees and supervisory committees, with the assistance of the central bureau, which also furnished trained workers and organizers. Each cooperative had departments for business, propaganda, organization, survey, and statistics.

Various prizes were offered for efficient management, and widespread propaganda stimulated and educated the peasants concerning the usefulness of the movement. Financial as well as technical help was furnished by the government, which participated in the enterprises on a profit-sharing basis, like the members. Some $70,000 in non-interest-bearing loans had been invested by the government in the cooperatives of Shensi and Kansu.

Only soviet paper was in use, except in the border counties,

*Outline for Cooperative Development, Department of National Economy (Wayapao, Shensi, November 1935), p. 4.

where White paper was also accepted. In their soviets in Kiangsi, Anhui, and Szechuan the Reds minted silver dollars, and subsidiary coins in copper, and some also in silver, and much of this metal was transported to the North-West. But after the decree of November 1935, when Nanking began the confiscation of all silver in China, and its price soared, the Reds withdrew their silver and held it as reserve for their note issue.

Paper currency in the South, bearing the signature of the 'Chinese Workers' and Peasants' Soviet Government State Bank', was excellently printed, on good bank paper. In the North-West, technical deficiencies resulted in a much cruder issue on poor paper, and sometimes on cloth. Their slogans appeared on all money. Notes issued in Shensi bore such exhortations as: 'Stop civil war!' 'Unite to resist Japan!' 'Long live the Chinese revolution!'

But how could merchants sell articles imported from the White regions for currency which had no exchange value outside the soviet districts? This difficulty was met by the state treasury, which had fixed an exchange rate of soviet $1.21 to Kuomintang $1. Regulations provided that

all goods imported from the White districts, and sold directly to the State Trade Bureau, will be paid for in foreign [Kuomintang] currency; imports of necessities, when not sold directly to the State Trade Bureau, but through cooperatives or by private merchants, shall first be registered with the State Trade Bureau, and proceeds of their sale for soviet currency may be exchanged for White paper; other exchange will be given when its necessity is established.*

In practice this of course meant that all 'foreign' imports had to be paid for in 'foreign' exchange. But as the value of imported manufactures (meagre enough) greatly exceeded the value of soviet exports (which were chiefly raw materials, and were all sold in a depressed market as smuggled goods), there was always a tendency towards a heavy unfavourable balance of payments. In other words, bankruptcy. How was it overcome?

It was not, entirely. As far as I could discover, the problem was met principally by the ingenuity of Lin Tsu-han, the dignified white-haired Commissioner of Finance, whose task was to make

---

* 'Concerning Soviet Monetary Policy', *Tangti Kungtso* [*Party Work*], No. 12 (Pao An, 1936).

Red ends meet. This interesting old custodian of the exchequer had once been treasurer of the Kuomintang, and behind him lay an amazing story.

Son of a Hunanese schoolteacher, Lin Tsu-han was born in 1882, educated in the Classics, attended normal college at Changtehfu, and later studied in Tokyo. While in Japan he met Sun Yat-sen, then exiled from China by the Manchus, and joined his secret revolutionary society, the T'ung Meng Hui. When Sun merged his T'ung Meng Hui with other revolutionary groups to found the Kuomintang, Lin became a charter member. Later on he met Ch'en Tu-hsiu, was much influenced by him, and in 1922 joined the Communist Party. He continued to work closely with Dr Sun Yat-sen, however, who admitted Communists to his party, and Lin was in turn treasurer and chairman of the General Affairs Department of the Kuomintang. He was with Sun Yat-sen when he died.

At the beginning of the Nationalist Revolution, Lin was one of the several elders in the Central Executive Committee of the Kuomintang who held seniority over Chiang Kai-shek. In Canton he was chairman of the Peasant Department and during the Northern Expedition he became political commissar of the Sixth Army, commanded by General Ch'eng Ch'ien – the late chief of staff at Nanking. When Chiang Kai-shek began the extermination of the Communists in 1927, Lin denounced him, fled to Hongkong, and then to Soviet Russia, where he studied for four years in the Communist academy. On his return to China he took passage on the 'underground railway' and safely reached Kiangsi. Now a widower, Lin had not seen his grown-up daughter and son since 1927. At the age of forty-five he had abandoned the comfortable assets of his position and staked his destiny with the young Communists.

Into my room in the Foreign Office one morning came this fifty-five-year-old veteran of the Long March, wearing a cheerful smile, a faded uniform, a red-starred cap with a broken peak, and in front of his kindly eyes a pair of spectacles one side of which was trussed up over his ear with a piece of string. The Commissioner of Finance! He sat down on the edge of the *k'ang* and we began to talk about sources of revenue. The government, I understood, collected practically no taxes; its industrial income must be negligible; then where, I wanted to know, did it get its money?

Lin began to explain: 'We say we do not tax the masses, and this is true. But we do heavily tax the exploiting classes, confiscating their surplus cash and goods. Thus all our taxation is direct. This is just the opposite of the Kuomintang practice, under which ultimately the workers and the poor peasants have to carry most of the tax burden. Here we tax less than 10 per cent of the population – the landlords and usurers. We also levy a small tax on a few big merchants, but none on small merchants. Later on we may impose a small progressive tax on the peasantry, but at the present moment all mass taxes have been completely abolished.

'Another source of income is from voluntary contributions of the people. Revolutionary patriotic feeling runs very high where war is on and the people realize that they may lose their soviets. They make big voluntary contributions of food, money, and clothing to the Red Army. We derive some income also from state trade, from Red Army lands, from our own industries, from the cooperatives, and from bank loans. But of course our biggest revenue is from confiscations.'

'By confiscation,' I interrupted, 'you mean what is commonly described as loot?'

Lin laughed shortly. 'The Kuomintang calls it loot. Well, if taxation of the exploiters of the masses is loot, so is the Kuomintang's taxation of the masses. But the Red Army does no looting in the sense that White armies loot. Confiscations are made only by authorized persons, under the direction of the Finance Commission. Every item must be reported by inventory to the government, and is utilized only for the general benefit of society. Private looting is heavily punished. Just ask the people if Red soldiers take anything without paying for it.'

'Well, you are quite right. The answer to that naturally would depend on whether you asked a landlord or a peasant.'

'If we did not have to conduct incessant war,' Lin continued, 'we could easily build a self-supporting economy here. Our budget is carefully made, and every possible economy is practised. Because every soviet official is also a patriot and a revolutionary, we demand no wages, and we can exist on but little food. It will probably surprise you to know how small our budget is. For this whole area*

*Then about the size of Austria.

our present expenditure is only about $320,000 per month. This represents goods value as well as money value. Of this sum, from 40 to 50 per cent comes from confiscations, and 15 or 20 per cent comes from voluntary contributions, including cash raised by the Party among our supporters in the White districts.* The rest of our revenue is derived from trade, economic construction, Red Army lands, and bank loans to the government.'

The Reds claimed to have devised a squeeze-proof machinery of budgeting, of receipts and disbursements. I read part of Lin Tsuhan's *Outline for Budget Compilation*, which gave a detailed description of the system and all its safeguards. Its integrity seemed to be based primarily on collective control of receipts and disbursements. From the highest organ down to the village, the treasurer was accountable, for both payments and collections, to a supervising committee, so that juggling of figures for individual profit was extremely difficult. Commissioner Lin was very proud of his system, and asserted that under it any kind of squeeze was effectively impossible. It may have been true. Anyway, it was obvious that in the Red districts the real problem as yet was not one of squeeze, in the traditional sense, but of squeezing through. Despite Lin's cheerful optimism, this was what I wrote in my diary after that interview:

Whatever Lin's figures may mean exactly, it is simply a Chinese miracle, when one remembers that partisans have been fighting back and forth across this territory for five years, that the economy maintains itself at all, that there is no famine, and that the peasants on the whole seem to accept soviet currency, with faith in it. In fact this cannot be explained in terms of finance alone, but is only understandable on a social and political basis.

Nevertheless it is perfectly clear that the situation is extremely grave, even for an organization that exists on such shoestrings as the Reds feed upon, and one of three changes must shortly occur in soviet economy: (1) some form of machine industrialization, to supply the market with needed manufactures; (2) the establishment of a good connection with some modern economic base in the outside world, or the capture of some economic base on a higher level than the present one (Sian or Lanchow, for example); or (3) the actual coalescence of such a base, now under White control, with the Red districts.

* At that time this soviet area was probably receiving little or no financial aid from Russia, with which it had no direct geographical connection.

The Reds did not share my pessimism. 'A way out is sure to be found.' And in a few months it was. The 'way out' appeared in the form of an 'actual coalescence'.

Lin didn't seem to be 'getting ahead' financially very fast himself, by the way. His 'allowance' as Commissioner of Finance was five dollars a month – Red money.

5

Life Begins at Fifty!

I CALLED him 'Old Hsu' because that was what everyone in the soviet districts called him – Lao Hsu, the Educator – for, although sixty-one was only just an average age for most high government officials elsewhere in the Orient, in Red China he seemed a sort of hoary grandfather by contrast with others. Yet he was no specimen of decrepitude. Like his sexagenarian crony, Hsieh Chu-tsai (and you could often see this pair of white-haired bandits walking along arm-in-arm like middle-school lads), he had an erect and vigorous step, bright and merry eyes, and a pair of muscular legs that had carried him across the greatest rivers and mountain ranges of China on the Long March.

Hsu T'eh-li had been a highly respected professor until at the age of fifty he amazingly gave up his home, four children, and the presidency of a normal school in Changsha to stake his future with the Communists. Born in 1877 near Changsha, not far from P'eng Teh-huai's birthplace, he was the fourth son in a poor peasant family. By various sacrifices his parents gave him six years of schooling, at the end of which he became a schoolteacher under the Manchu regime. There he remained till he was twenty-nine, when he entered the Changsha Normal College, graduated, and became an instructor in mathematics – a discipline in which he was self-taught.

Mao Tse-tung was one of his students in the normal school (Hsu said he was terrible in maths), and so were many youths who later became Reds. Hsu himself had a role in politics long before Mao knew a republican from a monarchist. He still bore that mark of combat from feudal politics in days of the empire, when he cut off the tip of his little finger to demonstrate his sincerity in begging by petition that a parliament be granted the people. After the first revolution, when for a while Hunan had a provincial parliament, Old Hsu was a member of it.

He accompanied the Hunanese delegation of 'worker-students' to France after the war, and he studied a year at Lyons, where he paid his way by odd-time work in a metal factory. Later he was a student for three years at the University of Paris, earning his tuition then by tutoring Chinese students in mathematics. Returning to Hunan in 1923, he helped establish two modern normal schools in the capital, and for four years enjoyed some prosperity. Not till 1927 did he become a Communist and an outcast from bourgeois society.

During the Nationalist Revolution, Hsu T'eh-li was active in the provincial Kuomintang, but he sympathized with the Communists. He openly preached Marxism to his students. When the 'purgation' period began he was a marked man; he had to do the disappearing act, and, having no connection with the Communist Party, he had to find a haven on his own. 'I had wanted to be a Communist,' he told me rather wistfully, 'but nobody ever asked me to join. I was already fifty, and I concluded that the Communists considered me too old.' But one day a Communist sought out Hsu in his hiding place and asked him to enter the Party. He told me he wept then to think that he was still of some use in building a new world.

The Party sent him to Russia, where he studied for two years. On his return he ran the blockade to Kiangsi; soon afterwards he became assistant commissioner of education, under Ch'u Ch'iu-pai, and after Ch'u was killed, the Executive Committee appointed Hsu in his place. Since then he had been Lao Hsu, the Educator. And surely his varied experience – life and teaching under monarchist, capitalist, and Communist forms of society – seemed to qualify him for the tasks that faced him. He certainly needed all that experience – and more, for those tasks were so great that any Western educator would have despaired. But Old Hsu was too young to be discouraged.

One day when we were talking he began humorously to enumerate some of his difficulties. 'As nearly as we can estimate,' he asserted, 'virtually nobody but a few landlords, officials, and merchants could read in the North-West before we arrived. The illiteracy seemed to be about 95 per cent. This is culturally one of the darkest places on earth. Do you know the people in north Shensi and Kansu believe that water is harmful to them? The average man here has a bath all over only twice in his life – once when he is born, the second time when he is married. They hate to wash their feet, hands, or faces, or cut their nails or their hair. There are more pigtails left in this part of China than anywhere else.

'But all this and many other prejudices are due to ignorance, and it's my job to change their mentality. Such a population, compared with Kiangsi, is very backward indeed. There the illiteracy was about 90 per cent, but the cultural level was very much higher, we had better material conditions to work in, and many more trained teachers. In our model *hsien*, Hsing Ko, we had over 300 primary schools and about 800 schoolteachers – which is as many as we have of both in all the Red districts here. When we withdrew from Hsing Ko, illiteracy had been reduced to less than 20 per cent of the population.

'Here the work is very much slower. We have to start everything from the beginning. Our material resources are very limited. Even our printing machinery has been destroyed, and now we have to print everything by mimeograph and stone-block lithograph. The blockade prevents us from importing enough paper. We have begun to make paper of our own, but the quality is terrible. But never mind these difficulties. We have already been able to accomplish something. If we are given time we can do things here that will astonish the rest of China. We are training scores of teachers from the masses now, and the Party is training others. Many of them will become voluntary teachers for the mass-education schools. Our results show that the peasants here are eager to learn when given the chance.

'And they are not stupid. They learn very quickly, and they change their habits when they are given good reasons for doing so. In the older soviet districts here you won't see any girl children with bound feet and you will see many young women with bobbed hair. The men are gradually cutting off their queues now and a lot of them are learning to read and write from the Young Communists and the Vanguards.'

Hsu explained that under the emergency soviet educational system there were three sections: institutional, military, and social. The first was run more or less by the soviets, the second by the Red Army, the third by Communist organizations. Emphasis in all of them was primarily political – even the smallest children learned their first characters in the shape of simple revolutionary slogans, and then worked forward into stories of conflict between the Reds and the Kuomintang, landlords and peasants, capitalists and workers, and so on, with plenty of heroics about the Young Communists and the Red Army, and promises of an earthly paradise in the soviet future.

Under institutional education the Reds already claimed to have established about 200 primary schools, and they had one normal school for primary teachers, one agricultural school, a textile school, a trade-union school of five grades, and a Party school with some 400 students. Courses in all the technical schools lasted only about six months.

Great emphasis naturally was on military education, and here much had been achieved in two years, despite all the handicaps of the beleaguered little state. There were the Red Army University, the cavalry and infantry schools, and two Party training schools, already described. There was a radio school, and a medical school, which was really for training nurses. There was an engineering school, where students received the rudimentary training of apprentices. Like the whole soviet organization itself, everything was very provisional and designed primarily as a kind of rear-line activity to strengthen the Red Army and provide it with new cadres. Many of the teachers were not even middle-school graduates. What was interesting was the collective use of whatever knowledge they had. These schools were really Communist, not only in ideology but in the utilization of every scrap of technical experience they could mobilize, to 'raise the cultural level'.

Even in social education the soviet aims were primarily political. There was no time or occasion to be teaching farmers literature or flower arrangement. The Reds were practical people. To the Lenin clubs, the Communist Youth leagues, the Partisans, and the village soviets they sent simple, crudely illustrated *Shih-tzu* ('Know Characters') texts, and helped mass organizations form self-study groups of their own, with some Communist or literate among them as a leader. When the youths, or sometimes even aged peasants, began droning off the short sentences, they found themselves absorbing ideas along with their ideographs. Thus, entering one of these little 'social education centres' in the mountains, you might hear these people catechizing themselves aloud :

'What is this?'

'This is the Red Flag.'

'What is this?'

'This is a poor man.'

'What is the Red Flag?'

'The Red Flag is the flag of the Red Army.'

'What is the Red Army?'

'The Red Army is the army of the poor men !'

And so on, right up to the point where, if he knew the whole five or six hundred characters before anyone else, the youth could collect the red tassel or pencil or whatever was promised. When farmers and farmers' sons and daughters finished the book they could not only read for the first time in their lives, but they knew who had taught them, and why. They had grasped the basic fighting ideas of Chinese communism.

In an effort to find a quicker medium for bringing literacy to the masses, the Communists had begun a limited use of Latinized Chinese. They had worked out an alphabet of twenty-eight letters by which they claimed to be able to reproduce nearly all Chinese phonetics, and had written and published a little pocket dictionary with the commonest phrases of Chinese rendered into polysyllabic, easily readable words. Part of the paper *Hung Ssu Chung Hua* (*Red China*) was published in *Latin-hua*, and Old Hsu was experimenting with it on a class of youngsters he had picked up in Pao An. He believed that the complicated Chinese characters would eventually have to be abandoned in education on a mass scale, and he had many arguments in favour of his system, on which he had been working for years.

Thus far he wasn't boasting about results, either with his *Latin-hua* or his other educational efforts. 'The cultural level was so low here it couldn't be made worse, so naturally we've made some progress,' he said. As for the future, he only wanted time. Meanwhile he urged me to concentrate on studying educational methods in the Red Army, where he claimed real revolutionary teaching could be seen.

Part Seven

EN ROUTE TO THE FRONT

I

Conversation with Red Peasants

As I travelled beyond Pao An, towards the Kansu border and the front, I stayed in the rude huts of peasants, slept on their mud *k'ang* (when the luxury of wooden doors was not available), ate their food, and enjoyed their talk. They were all poor people, kind and hospitable. Some of them refused any money from me when they heard I was a 'foreign guest'. I remember one old bound-footed peasant woman, with five or six youngsters to feed, who insisted upon killing one of her half-dozen chickens for me.

'We can't have a foreign devil telling people in the outer world that we Reds don't know etiquette,' I overheard her say to one of my companions. I am sure she did not mean to be impolite. She simply knew no other words but 'foreign devil' to describe the situation.

I was travelling then with Fu Chin-kuei, a young Communist who had been delegated by the Red Foreign Office to accompany me to the front. Like all the Reds in the rear, Fu was delighted at the prospect of a chance to be with the army, and he looked upon me as a godsend. At the same time he regarded me frankly as an imperialist, and viewed my whole trip with open scepticism. He was unfailingly helpful in every way, however, and before the trip was over we were to become very good friends.

One night at Chou Chia, a village of north Shensi near the Kansu border, Fu and I found quarters in a compound where five or six peasant families lived. A farmer of about forty-five, responsible for six of the fifteen little children who scampered back and forth incessantly, agreed to accommodate us, with ready courtesy. He gave us a clean room with new felt on the *k'ang*, and provided our animals with corn and straw. He sold us a chicken for twenty cents, and some eggs, but for the room would take nothing. He had been to Yenan and he had seen foreigners before, but none of the other men, women, or children had seen one, and they all now came round diffidently to have a peek. One of the young children burst into frightened tears at the astonishing sight.

After dinner a number of the peasants came into our room, offered me tobacco, and began to talk. They wanted to know what we grew in my country, whether we had corn and millet, horses and cows, and whether we used goat dung for fertilizer. (One peasant asked whether we had chickens, and at this our host sniffed contemptuously. 'Where there are men, there must be chickens,' he observed.) Were there rich and poor in my country? Was there a Communist Party and a Red Army?

In return for answering their numerous questions, I asked a few of my own. What did they think of the Red Army? They promptly began to complain about the excessive eating habits of the cavalry's horses. It seemed that when the Red Army University recently moved its cavalry school it had paused in this village for several days, with the result that a big depression had been made in the corn and straw reserves.

'Didn't they pay you for what they bought?' demanded Fu Chin-kuei.

'Yes, yes, they paid all right; that isn't the question. We haven't a great amount, you know, only so many *tan* of corn and millet and straw. We have only enough for ourselves and maybe a little more, and we have the winter ahead of us. Will the cooperatives sell us grain next January? That's what we wonder. What can we buy with soviet money? We can't even buy opium!'

This came from a ragged old man who still wore a queue and looked sourly down his wrinkled nose and along the two-foot stem of his bamboo pipe. The younger men grinned when he spoke. Fu admitted they couldn't buy opium, but he said they could buy in the cooperatives anything else they needed.

'Can we now?' demanded our host. 'Can we buy a bowl like this one, eh?' And he picked up the cheap red celluloid bowl (Japanese-made, I suspect) which I had brought with me from Sian. Fu confessed that the cooperatives had no red bowls, but said they had plenty of grain, cloth, paraffin, candles, needles, matches, salt – what did they want?

'I hear you can't get more than six feet of cloth per man; now, isn't it so?' demanded one farmer.

Fu wasn't sure; he thought there was plenty of cloth. He resorted to the anti-Japanese argument. 'Life is as bitter for us as for you,' he said. 'The Red Army is fighting for you, the farmers and workers, to protect you from the Japanese and the Kuomintang. Suppose you can't always buy all the cloth you want, and you can't get opium, it's a fact you don't pay taxes, isn't it? You don't go in debt to the landlords and lose your house and land, do you? Well, old brother, do you like the White Army better than us, or not? – just answer that question. What does the White Army give you for your crops, eh?'

At this, all complaints appeared to melt away, and opinion was unanimous. 'Certainly not, Old Fu, certainly not!' Our host nodded. 'If we have to choose, we take the Red Army. A son of mine is in the Red Army, and I sent him there. Does anyone deny that?'

I asked why they preferred the Red Army.

In answer the old man who had sneered at the cooperatives for having no opium gave a heated discourse.

'What happens when the Whites come?' he asked. 'They demand such and such amounts of food, and never a word about payment. If we refuse, we are arrested as Communists. If we give it to them we cannot pay the taxes. *In any case* we cannot pay the taxes! What happens then? They take our animals to sell. Last year, when the Red Army was not here and the Whites returned, they took my two mules and my four pigs. These mules were worth $30 each, and the pigs were full grown, worth $2 each. What did they give me?

'Ai-ya, ai-ya! They said I owed $80 in taxes and rent, and they allowed me $40 for my stock. They demanded $40 more. Could I get it? I had nothing else for them to steal. They wanted me to sell my daughter; it's a fact! Some of us here had to do that. Those who had no cattle and no daughters went to jail in Pao An, and plenty died from the cold . . .'

I asked this old man how much land he had.

'Land?' he croaked. 'There is my land,' and he pointed to a hilltop patched with corn and millet and vegetables. It lay just across the stream from our courtyard.

'How much is it worth?'

'Land here isn't worth anything unless it's valley land,' he said. 'We can buy a mountain like that for $25. What costs money are mules, goats, pigs, chickens, houses, and tools.'

'Well, how much is your farm worth, for example?'

He still refused to count his land worth anything at all. 'You can have the house, my animals and tools for $100 – with the mountain thrown in,' he finally estimated.

'And on that you had to pay how much in taxes and rent?'

'Forty dollars a year!'

'That was before the Red Army came?'

'Yes. Now we pay no taxes. But who knows about next year? When the Reds leave, the Whites come back. One year Red, the next White. When the Whites come they call us Red bandits. When the Reds come they look for counter-revolutionaries.'

'But there is this difference,' a young farmer interposed. 'If our neighbours say we have not helped the Whites that satisfies the Reds. But if we have a hundred names of honest men, but no land-lord's name, we are still Red bandits to the Whites! Isn't that a fact?'

The old man nodded. He said the last time the White Army was here it had killed a whole family of poor farmers in a village just over the hill. Why? Because the Whites had asked where the Reds were hiding, and this family refused to tell them. 'After that we all fled from here, and took our cattle with us. We came back with the Reds.'

'Will you leave next time, if the Whites return?'

'Ai-ya!' exclaimed an elder with long hair and fine teeth. 'This time we will leave, certainly! They will kill us!'

He began to tell of the villagers' crimes. They had joined the Poor People's League, they had voted for the district soviets, they had given information to the Red Army about the White Army's movements, two had sons in the Red Army, and another had two daughters in a nursing school. Were these crimes or not? They could be shot for any one of them, I was assured.

But now a barefoot youth in his teens stepped up, engrossed in the discussion and forgetful of the foreign devil. 'You call these things crimes, grandfather? These are patriotic acts! Why do we do them? Isn't it because our Red Army is a poor people's army and fights for our rights?'

He continued enthusiastically: 'Did we have a free school in Chou Chia before? Did we ever get news of the world before the Reds brought us wireless electricity? Who told us what the world is like? You say the cooperative has no cloth, but did we ever even have a cooperative before? And how about your farm, wasn't there a big mortgage on it to landlord Wang? My sister starved to death three years ago, but haven't we had plenty to eat since the Reds came? You say it's bitter, but it isn't bitter for us young people if we can learn to read! It isn't bitter for us Young Vanguards when we learn to use a rifle and fight the traitors and Japan!'

This constant reference to Japan and the 'traitors' may sound improbable to people who know the ignorance (not indifference) of the mass of the ordinary Chinese peasants concerning Japanese invasions or any other national problems. But I found it constantly recurring, not only in the speech of the Communists but among peasants like these. Red propaganda had made such a wide impression that many of these backward mountaineers believed themselves in imminent danger of being enslaved by the 'Japanese dwarfs' – a specimen of which most of them had yet to see outside Red posters and cartoons.

The youth subsided, out of breath. I looked at Fu Chin-kuei and saw a pleased smirk on his face. Several others present called out in approval, and most of them smiled.

The dialogue went on until nearly nine o'clock, long past bedtime. It interested me chiefly because it took place before Fu Chin-kuei, whom the farmers appeared to hold in no awe as a Red 'official'. They seemed to look upon him as one of themselves – and indeed, as a peasant's son, he was.

The last one to leave us was the old man with the queue and most of the complaints. As he went out the door he leaned over and whispered once more to Fu. 'Old comrade,' he implored, 'is there any opium at Pao An; now, is there any?'

When he had left, Fu turned to me in disgust. 'Would you believe it?' he demanded. 'That old defile-mother * is chairman of the Poor People's Society here, and still he wants opium. This village needs more educational work.'

---

*T'a ma-ti is a shortened version of one of the commonest oaths in China. It means, 'I have raped your (or his or her or their) mother (mothers).' Lu Hsun wrote a delightful satirical essay on this subject. See Edgar Snow, *Living China* (New York, 1935).

2

Soviet Industries

A FEW days north-west of Pao An, on my way to the front, I stopped to visit Wu Ch'i Chen, a soviet 'industrial centre' of Shensi. Wu Ch'i Chen was remarkable, not for any achievements in industrial science of which Detroit or Manchester need take note, but because it was there at all.

For hundreds of miles around there was only semipastoral country, the people lived in cave houses exactly as their ancestors did millenniums ago, many of the farmers still wore queues braided around their heads, and the horse, the ass, and the camel were the latest thing in communications. Rape oil was used for lighting here, candles were a luxury, electricity was unknown, and foreigners were as rare as Eskimoes in Africa.

In this medieval world it was astonishing suddenly to come upon soviet factories, and find machines turning, and a colony of workers busily producing the goods and tools of a Red China.

In Kiangsi the Communists had, despite the lack of a seaport and the handicap of an enemy blockade which cut them off from contact with any big modern industrial base, built up several prosperous industries. They operated China's richest tungsten mines, for example, annually turning out over one million pounds of this precious ore – secretly selling it to General Ch'en Chi-t'ang's Kwangtung tungsten monopoly. In the central soviet printing plant at Kian with its 800 workers, many books, magazines, and a 'national' paper – the *Red China Daily News* – were published.

In Kiangsi also were weaving plants, textile mills, and machine shops. Small industries produced sufficient manufactured goods to supply their simple needs. The Reds claimed to have had a 'foreign export trade' of over $12,000,000 in 1933, most of which was carried on through adventurous southern merchants, who made extraordinary profits by running the Kuomintang blockade. The bulk of manufacturing, however, was by handicraft and home industry, the products of which were sold through production cooperatives.

According to Mao Tse-tung, in September 1933 the soviets had 1,423 'production and distribution' cooperatives in Kiangsi, all owned and run by the people.* Testimony by League of Nations investigators left little doubt that the Reds were succeeding with this type of collective enterprise – even while they were still fighting for their existence. The Kuomintang was attempting to copy the Red system in parts of the South, but results thus far suggested that it was extremely difficult, if not impossible, to operate such cooperatives under a strictly *laissez-faire* capitalism.

But in the North-West I had not expected to find any industry at all. Much greater handicaps faced the Reds here than in the South, for even a small machine industry was almost entirely absent before the soviets were set up. In the whole North-West, in Shensi, Kansu, Chinghai, Ninghsia and Suiyuan, provinces in area nearly the size of all Europe excluding Russia, the combined machine-industry investment certainly must have been far less than the plant of one big assembly branch of, for instance, the Ford Motor Company.

Sian and Lanchow had a few factories, but for the most part were dependent upon industrial centres further east. Any major development of the tremendous industrial possibilities of the North-West could take place only by borrowing technique and machinery from the outside. And if this were true in Sian and Lanchow, the two great cities of the region, the difficulties which confronted the Reds, occupying the even more backward areas of Kansu, Shensi, and Ninghsia, were manifest.

The blockade cut off the Soviet Government from imports of machinery, and from 'imports' of technicians. Of the latter, however, the Reds said their supply was ample. Machinery and raw materials were more serious problems. Battles were fought by the Red Army just to get a few lathes, weaving machines, engines, or a little scrap iron. Nearly everything they had in the category of machinery while I was there had been 'captured'. During their

*Mao Tse-tung, *Red China* . . . , p. 26. (See Bibliography.)

expedition to Shansi province in 1936, for example, they had seized machines, tools, and raw materials, which were carried by mule all the way across the mountains of Shensi, to their fantastic cliff-dwelling factories.

Soviet industries, when I visited Red China, were all handicraft; there was no electric power. They included clothing, uniform, shoe, and paper factories at Pao An and Holienwan (Kansu), rug factories at Tingpien (on the Great Wall), mines at Yung P'ing which produced the cheapest coal* in China, and woollen and cotton-spinning factories in seven *hsien* – all of which had plans to produce enough goods to stock the 400 cooperatives in Red Shensi and Kansu. The aim of this 'industrial programme', according to Mao Tse-min, brother of Mao Tse-tung and Commissioner of People's Economy, was to make Red China 'economically self-sufficient' – strong enough to survive despite the Kuomintang blockade if Nanking refused to accept the Communists' offers for a united front and a cessation of civil war.

The most important soviet state enterprises were the salt-refining plants at Yen Ch'ih, the salt lakes on the Ninghsia border, along the Great Wall, and the oil wells at Yung P'ing and Yen Ch'ang, which produced gasoline, paraffin, and vaseline, wax, candles, and other by-products on a very small scale. Salt deposits at Yen Ch'ih were the finest in China and yielded beautiful rock-crystal salt in large quantities. Consequently salt was cheaper and more plentiful in the soviet districts than in Kuomintang China, where it was a principal source of government income. After the capture of Yen Ch'ih the Reds won the sympathy of the Mongols north of the Wall by agreeing to turn over part of the production to them, revoking the Kuomintang's practice of monopolizing the entire output.

North Shensi's oil wells were the only ones in China, and their output had formerly been sold to an American company which had leases on other reserves in the district. After they had seized Yung P'ing the Reds sank two new wells, and claimed increased produc-

*The price quoted in the Red districts was 800 catties – about half a ton – for $1 silver. See Mao Tse-min, 'Economic Construction in the Kansu and Shensi Soviet Districts', *Tou Tsung [Struggle]* (Pao An, Shensi), 24 April 1936.

tion, by about 40 per cent over any previous period, when Yung P'ing and Yen Ch'ang were in 'non-bandit' hands. This included increases of '2,000 catties of petrol, 25,000 catties of first-class oil, and 13,500 catties of second-class oil' during a three-month period reported upon. (A few barrels at best.) *

Efforts were being made to develop cotton growing in areas cleared of poppies, and the Reds had established a spinning school at An Ting, with 100 women students. The workers were given three hours' general education daily and five hours' instruction in spinning and weaving. Upon completion of their course, after three months, students were sent to various districts to open handicraft textile factories. 'It is expected that in two years north Shensi will be able to produce its entire supply of cloth.' †

But Wu Ch'i Chen had the largest 'concentration' of factory workers in the Red districts, and was important also as the location of the Reds' main arsenal. It commanded an important trade route leading to Kansu, and the ruins of two ancient forts nearby testified to its former strategic importance. The town was built high up on the steep clay banks of a rapid stream, and was made up half of *yang-fang*, or 'foreign houses' – as the Shensi natives still called anything with four sides and a roof – and half of *yao-fang*, or cave dwellings.

I arrived late at night and I was very tired. The head of the supply commissariat for the front armies had received word of my coming, and he rode out to meet me. He 'put me up' at a workers' Lenin Club – an earthen-floored *yao-fang* with clean whitewashed walls strung with festoons of coloured paper chains encircling a portrait of the immortal Ilyitch.

Hot water, clean towels – stamped with slogans of Chiang Kai-shek's New Life movement! – and soap soon appeared. They were followed by an ample dinner, with good *baked* bread. I began to feel better. I unrolled my bedding on the table-tennis court and lighted a cigarette. But man is a difficult animal to satisfy. All this luxury and attention only made me yearn for my favourite beverage.

And then, of all things, this commissar suddenly produced, from

*Mao Tse-min, op. cit.
† ibid.

heaven knows where, some rich brown coffee and sugar ! Wu Ch'i Chen had won my heart.

'Products of our five-year plan !' the commissar laughed.

'Products of your confiscation department, you mean,' I amended.

3

'They Sing Too Much'

I STAYED three days at Wu Ch'i Chen, visiting workers in the factories, 'inspecting' their working conditions, attending their theatre and their political meetings, reading their wall newspapers and their character books, talking – and getting athletic. I took part in a basketball game on one of Wu Ch'i's three courts. We made up a scratch team composed of the Foreign Office emissary, Fu Chinkuei; a young English-speaking college student working in the political department; a Red doctor; a soldier; and myself. The arsenal basketball team accepted our challenge and beat us to a pulp.

The arsenal, like the Red University, was housed in a big series of vaulted rooms built into a mountain-side. They were cool, well ventilated, and lighted by a series of shafts sunk at angles in the walls, and had the major advantage of being completely bombproof. Here I found over a hundred workers making hand grenades, trench mortars, gunpowder, pistols, small shells and bullets, and a few farming tools. A repair department was engaged in rehabilitating stacks of broken rifles, machine guns, automatic rifles and submachine guns. But the arsenal's output was crude work, and most of its products equipped the Red partisans, the regular Red forces being supplied almost entirely with guns and munitions captured from enemy troops.

Ho Hsi-yang, director of the arsenal, took me through its various chambers, introduced his workers, and told me something about them and himself. He was thirty-six, unmarried, and had formerly been a technician in the famous Mukden arsenal, before the Japanese invasion. After 18 September 1931, he went to Shanghai, and there he joined the Communist Party, later on making his way to the North-West, and into Red areas. Most of the machinists here were also 'outside' men. Many had been employed at Hanyang, China's greatest iron works (Japanese-owned), and a few had worked in Kuomintang arsenals. I met two young Shanghai master mechanics, and an expert fitter, who showed me excellent letters of recommendation from the noted British and American firms of Jardine, Matheson & Co., Anderson Meyer & Co., and the Shanghai Power Company. Another had been foreman in a Shanghai machine shop. There were also machinists from Tientsin, Canton, and Peking, and some had made the Long March with the Red Army.

I learned that of the arsenal's 114 machinists and apprentices only 20 were married. These had their wives with them in Wu Ch'i Chen, either as factory workers or as party functionaries. In the arsenal trade union, which represented the most highly skilled labour in the Red districts, more than 80 per cent of the members belonged to the Communist Party or to the Communist Youth League.

Besides the arsenal, in Wu Ch'i Chen there were cloth and uniform factories, a shoe factory, a stocking factory, and a pharmacy and drug dispensary, with a doctor in attendance. He was a youth just out of medical training school in Shansi and his young and pretty wife was with him working as a nurse. Both of them had joined the Reds during the Shansi expedition the winter before. Nearby was a hospital, with three army doctors in attendance and filled mostly with wounded soldiers, and there was a radio station, a crude laboratory, a cooperative, and the army supply base.

Except in the arsenal and the uniform factory, most of the workers were young women from age eighteen to twenty-five or thirty. Some of them were married to Red soldiers then at the front; nearly all were Kansu, Shensi, or Shansi women; and all had bobbed hair. 'Equal pay for equal labour' was a slogan of the Chinese soviets, and there was supposed to be no wage discrimination against women. Workers appeared to get preferential financial treatment over everybody else in the soviet districts. This included Red commanders, who received no regular salary, but only a small living allowance, which varied according to the weight of the treasury.

Wu Ch'i Chen was headquarters for Miss Liu Ch'un-hsien, aged twenty-nine. A former mill worker from Wusih and Shanghai, she was a student in Moscow's Sun Yat-sen University when she met and married Po Ku (Ch'in Pang-hsien).* From her Moscow days she warmly remembered Rhena Prohm, the improbable red-haired American rebel goddess enshrined in Vincent Sheean's *Personal History*. Now Miss Liu was director of the women's department of the Red trade unions. She said that factory workers were paid $10 to $15 monthly, with board and room furnished by the state. Workers were guaranteed free medical attention (such as it was) and compensation for injuries. Women were given four months of rest with pay during and after pregnancy, and there was a crude 'nursery' for workers' children – but most of them seemed to run wild as soon as they could walk. Mothers could collect part of their 'social insurance', which was provided from a fund created by deducting 10 per cent of the workers' salaries, to which the government added an equal amount. The government also contributed the equivalent of 2 per cent of the wage output for workers' education and recreation, funds managed jointly by the trade unions and the workers' factory committees. There was an eight-hour day and a six-day week. When I visited them the factories were running twenty-four hours a day, with three shifts working.

All this seemed progressive, though perhaps far from a Communistic utopia. That such conditions were actually being realized in the midst of the soviets' impoverishment was really interesting. How *primitively* they were being realized was quite another matter. They had clubs, schools, ample dormitories – all these, certainly – but in cave houses with earthen floors, no shower baths, no movies, no electricity. They were furnished food; but meals consisted of millet, vegetables, and sometimes mutton, with no delicacies whatever. They collected their wages and social insurance all right in soviet currency, but the articles they could buy were strictly limited to necessities – and none too much of those.

'Unbearable,' the average American or English worker would say. But I remembered Shanghai factories where little boy and girl slave workers sat or stood at their tasks twelve or thirteen hours a day, and then dropped, in exhausted sleep, to the dirty cotton quilt, their bed, directly beneath their machines. I remembered little girls in silk filatures, and the pale young women in cotton factories sold into jobs as virtual slaves for four or five years, un-

*See BN.

able to leave the heavily guarded, high-walled premises day or night without special permission. And I remembered that during 1935 more than 29,000 bodies were picked up from the streets and rivers and canals of Shanghai – bodies of the destitute poor, of the starved or drowned babies or children they could not feed.

For these workers in Wu Ch'i Chen, however primitive it might be, here seemed to be a life at least of good health, exercise, clean mountain air, freedom, dignity, and hope, in which there was room for growth. They knew that nobody was making money out of them, I think they felt they were working for themselves and for China, and they said they were *revolutionaries*! They took very seriously their two hours of daily reading and writing, their political lectures, and their dramatic groups, and they keenly contested for the miserable prizes offered in competitions between groups and individuals in sport, literacy, public health, wall newspapers, and 'factory efficiency'. All these things were *real* to them, things they had never known before, could never possibly know in any other factory of China, and they seemed grateful for the doors of life opened up for them.

It was hard for an old China hand like me to believe, and I was confused about its ultimate significance, but I could not deny the evidence I saw. To present that evidence in detail I would have had to tell a dozen stories of workers to whom I talked; quote from their essays and criticisms in the wall newspapers – written in the childish scrawl of the newly literate – many of which I translated, with the aid of the college student; tell of the political meetings I attended; and of the plays created and dramatized by these workers; and of the many little things that go to make up an 'impression'.

As one example, I met an electrical engineer in Wu Ch'i Chen, a man named Chu Tso-chih. He knew English and German very well, he was a power expert, and he had written an engineering textbook widely used in China. He had once been with the Shanghai Power Company, and later with Anderson Meyer & Co. Until recently he had had a practice of $10,000 a year in South China, where he was a consulting engineer and efficiency man, and had given it up and left his family to come up to these wild dark hills of Shensi and offer his services to the Reds for nothing. Incredible! The background of this phenomenon traced to a beloved grandfather, a famous philanthropist of Ningpo, whose deathbed injunction to young Chu had been to 'devote his life to raising the cultural standard of the masses'. And Chu had decided the quickest method was the Communist one.

Chu had come into the thing somewhat melodramatically, in the spirit of the martyr and zealot. It was a solemn thing for him; he thought it meant an early death, and he expected everyone else to feel that way. I believe he was a little shocked when he found so much that he considered horseplay going on, and everybody apparently happy. When I asked him how he liked it, he replied gravely that he had but one serious criticism. 'These people spend entirely too much time *singing*!' he complained. 'This is no time to be singing!'

Part Eight
WITH THE RED ARMY

I

The 'Real' Red Army

AFTER two weeks of hacking and walking over the hills and plains of Kansu and Ninghsia I came to Yu Wang Pao, a walled town in southern Ninghsia, which was then the headquarters of the First Front Red Army * – and of its commander-in-chief, P'eng Teh-huai.

Although in a strict military sense all Red warriors might be called 'irregulars' (and some people would say 'highly irregulars'), the Reds themselves made a sharp distinction between their front armies, independent armies, partisans, and peasant guards. During my first brief travels in Shensi I had not seen any of the 'regular' Red Army, for its main forces were then moving in the west, nearly two hundred miles from Pao An. I had planned a trip to the front, but news that Chiang Kai-shek was preparing to launch another major offensive from the south had inclined me towards the better part of valour and an early departure while I could still get past the lines to write my story.

One day I had expressed these doubts to Wu Liang-p'ing, the young soviet official who had acted as interpreter in my long official interviews with Mao Tse-tung. He had been dumbfounded. 'You have a chance to go to the front, and you wonder whether you should take it? Don't make such a mistake! Chiang Kai-shek has been trying to destroy us for ten years, and he is not going to succeed now. You can't go back without seeing the *real* Red Army!' He had produced evidence to show why I shouldn't, and it was well that I took his advice.

Perhaps the best way to approach an understanding of these so-called bandits was – statistical. The facts assembled below were furnished from his files by Yang Shang-k'un,† the Russian-speak-

---

*Of which Nieh Ho-t'ing was chief of staff and Hsiao Hua was deputy political commissar of the army's Second Division. See BN.

† See BN.

ing, twenty-nine-year-old chairman of the political department of the First Front Red Army. With a few exceptions, this statistical report is confined to matters which I had some opportunity to verify by observation.

First of all, many people supposed the Reds to be a hardbitten lot of outlaws and malcontents. I vaguely had some such notion myself. I soon discovered that the great mass of the Red soldiery was made up of young peasants and workers who believed themselves to be fighting for their homes, their land, and their country.

According to Yang, the average age of the rank and file was nineteen. Although many men with the Reds had fought for seven or eight or even ten years, they were balanced by a vast number of youths still in their middle teens. And even most of the 'old Bolsheviks', veterans of many battles, were only now in their early twenties. The majority had joined the Reds as Young Vanguards, or enlisted at the age of fifteen or sixteen.

In the First Front Army a total of 38 per cent of the men came from either the agrarian working class (including craftsmen, muleteers, apprentices, farm labourers, etc.) or from the industrial working class, while 58 per cent came from the peasantry. Only 4 per cent were from the petty bourgeoisie – sons of merchants, intellectuals, small landlords, and such. In this army over 50 per cent of the troops, including commanders, were members of the Communist Party or the Communist Youth League.

Between 60 and 70 per cent of the soldiers were literate – that is, they could write simple letters and texts, posters, handbills, etc. This was much higher than the average among ordinary troops in the White districts, and it was very much higher than the average in the peasantry of the North-West. Red soldiers began to study characters in Red texts specially prepared for them, from the day of their enlistment. Prizes were offered (cheap notebooks, pencils, tassels, etc., much valued by the soldiers) for rapid progress and a great effort was made to stimulate the spirit of ambition and competition.

Red soldiers, like their commanders, received no regular salaries. But every enlisted man was entitled to his portion of land, and some income from it. This was tilled in his absence either by his family or by his local soviet. If he was not a native of the soviet

districts, however, his remuneration came from a share in the proceeds of crops from 'public lands' (confiscated from the 'great'
landlords), which also helped provision the Red Army. Public lands
were tilled by villagers in the local soviets. Such free labour was
obligatory, but the majority of the peasants, having benefited in
the land redistribution, may have cooperated willingly enough to
defend a system that had bettered their livelihood.

The average age of the officers in the Red Army was twenty-
four. This included squad leaders and all officers up to army commanders, but despite their youth these men had behind them
an average of eight years' fighting experience. All company commanders or higher were literate, though I met several who had not
learned to read and write till after they had entered the Red Army.
About a third of the Red Commanders were former Kuomintang
soldiers. Among Red commanders were many graduates of Whampoa Academy, graduates of the Red Army Academy in Moscow,
former officers of Chang Hsueh-liang's 'North-Eastern Army',
cadets of the Paoting Military Academy, former Kuominchun
('Christian General' Feng Yu-hsiang's army) men, and a number
of returned students from France, Soviet Russia, Germany, and
England. I met only one returned student from America. The Reds
did not call themselves *ping*, or 'soldiers' – a word to which much
odium was attached in China – but *chan-shih*, which means
'fighters' or 'warriors'.

The majority of the soldiers as well as officers of the Red Army
were unmarried. Many of them were 'divorced' – that is, they had
left their wives and families behind them. In several cases I had
serious suspicions that the desire for this kind of divorce, in fact,
might have had something to do with their joining the army, but
this may be a cynical opinion.

My impression, from scores of conversations on the road and at
the front, was that most of these 'Red fighters' were still virgins.
There were few Communist women at the front with the army,
and they were nearly all soviet functionaries in their own right or
married to soviet officials.

As far as I could see or learn, the Reds treated the peasant women
and girls with respect, and the peasantry seemed to have a good
opinion of Red Army morality. I heard of no cases of rape or abuse

of the peasant women, though I learned from some of the southern soldiers of 'sweethearts' left behind them. There was no law against fornication, but any Red Army man who got into difficulties with a girl was expected to marry her. As men far outnumbered women here, the opportunities were few. I saw nothing going on that looked like promiscuity. The Red Army was puritanical in its views on sexual licence, and a vigorous daily routine kept the young troops occupied. Very few of the Reds smoked or drank; abstention was one of the 'eight disciplines' of the Red Army, and although no special punishment was provided for either vice, I read in the 'black column' of wall newspapers several grave criticisms of habitual smokers. Drinking was not forbidden, but drunkenness was unheard of.

Commander P'eng Teh-huai, who had been a Kuomintang general, told me that the extreme youth of the Red Army explained much of its capacity to withstand hardship, and that was quite believable. It also made the problem of feminine companionship less poignant. P'eng himself had not seen his own wife since 1928, when he led an uprising of Kuomintang troops and joined the Reds.

Casualties among Red Army commanders were very high. They customarily went into battle side by side with their men, from regimental commanders down. Joseph Stilwell[1] once said to me that one thing alone might explain the fighting power of the Reds against an enemy with vastly superior resources. That was the Red officers' habit of saying, 'Come on, boys !' instead of, 'Go on boys !' During Nanking's first and second 'final annihilation' campaigns, casualties among Red officers were often as high as 50 per cent. But the Red Army could not stand these sacrifices, and later adopted tactics tending somewhat to reduce the risk of life by experienced commanders. Nevertheless, in the Fifth Kiangsi Campaign, Red commanders' casualties averaged about 23 per cent of the total officer personnel. One could see plenty of evidence of this in the Red districts. Common sights were youths still in their early twenties with an arm or a leg missing, or fingers shot away, or with ugly wounds on the head or anatomy – but still cheerful optimists about their revolution.

Nearly every province in China was represented in the various armies. In this sense the Red Army was probably the only *national* army in China. It was also the 'most widely travelled'. Veteran cadres had crossed parts of eighteen provinces. They probably knew more about Chinese geography than any other army. On their Long March they had found most of the old Chinese maps quite useless, and Red cartographers remapped many hundreds of miles of territory, especially in aboriginal country and on the western frontiers.

In the First Front Army, consisting of about 30,000 men, there was a high percentage of southerners, about one third coming from Kiangsi, Fukien, Hunan, or Kweichow. Nearly 40 per cent were from the western provinces of Szechuan, Shensi, and Kansu. The First Front Army included some aborigines – Miaos and Lolos – and also attached to it was a newly organized Mohammedan Red Army. In the independent armies the percentage of natives was much higher, averaging three fourths of the total.

From the highest commander down to the rank and file these men ate and dressed alike. Battalion commanders and higher, however, were entitled to the use of a horse or a mule. I noticed there was even an equal sharing of the delicacies available – expressed, while I was with the Red Army, chiefly in terms of watermelons and plums. There was very little difference in living quarters of commanders and men, and they passed freely back and forth without any formality.

One thing had puzzled me. How did the Reds manage to feed, clothe, and equip their armies? Like many others, I had assumed that they must live entirely on loot. This I discovered to be wrong, as I have already shown, for I saw that they started to construct a self-supplying economy of their own as soon as they occupied a district, and this single fact made it possible for them to hold a base despite enemy blockade. I had also failed to realize on what almost unbelievably modest sums it was possible for a Chinese proletarian army to exist.

The Reds had a very limited output of armaments; their enemy was really their main source of supply. For years the Reds had called the Kuomintang troops their 'ammunition carriers', and they claimed to capture more than 80 per cent of their guns and more than 70 per cent of their ammunition from enemy troops.

The regular troops (as distinct from local partisans) I saw were equipped mainly with British, Czechoslovakian, German, and American machine guns, rifles, automatic rifles, Mausers, and mountain cannon, such as had been sold in large quantities to the Nanking Government.*

The only Russian-made rifles I saw with the Reds were the vintage of 1917. These had been captured from the troops of General Ma Hung-kuei, as I heard directly from some of Ma's ex-soldiers themselves. General Ma, governor of what remained of Kuomintang Ninghsia, had inherited those rifles from General Feng Yu-hsiang, who ruled this region in 1924 and got some arms from Outer Mongolia. Red regulars disdained to use these ancient weapons, which I saw only in the hands of the partisans.

While I was in the soviet districts any contact with a Russian source of arms was physically impossible. The Reds were surrounded by various enemy troops totalling nearly 400,000 men, and the enemy controlled every road to Outer Mongolia, Sinkiang, or the USSR. I gathered that they would be glad to get some of the manna they were frequently accused of receiving by some miracle from Russia. But it was quite obvious from a glance at the map that, until the Chinese Reds possessed much more territory to the north and to the west, Moscow would be unable to fill any orders, assuming Moscow to be so inclined, which was open to serious doubts.

Second, it was a fact that the Reds had no highly paid and squeezing officials and generals, who in other Chinese armies absorbed most of the military funds. Great frugality was practised in both the army and the soviets. In effect, about the only burden of the army upon the people was the necessity of feeding and clothing it.

Actually, as I have already said, the entire budget of the North-West soviets was then only $320,000 a month. Nearly 60 per cent went to the maintenance of the armed forces. Old Lin Tsu-han, the finance commissioner, was apologetic about that, but said that it

* 'Questioned as to the source of the Reds' munitions, Generalissimo Chiang admitted that most of them had been taken from defeated government troops' (in an interview with the *North China Daily News*, 9 October 1934).

was 'inevitable until the revolution has been consolidated'. The armed forces then numbered (not including peasant auxiliaries) about 40,000 men. This was before the arrival in Kansu of the Second and Fourth Front armies, after which Red territory greatly expanded, and the main Red forces in the North-West soon approached a total of 90,000 men.

So much for statistics. But to understand why the Chinese Reds had survived all these years it was necessary to get a glimpse of their inner spirit, their morale and fighting will, and their methods of training. And, perhaps still more important, their political and military leadership.

For example, what sort of man was P'eng Teh-huai, for whose head Nanking once offered a reward sufficient to maintain his whole army (if Finance Commissioner Lin's figures were correct) for more than a month?

2

Impression of P'eng Teh-huai

THE consolidation of command of the First, Second, and Fourth
Front Red armies had not yet occurred when I visited the front
in August and September. Eight 'divisions' of the First Front Red
Army were then holding a line from the Great Wall in Ninghsia
down to Kuyuan and Pingliang in Kansu. A vanguard of the
First Army Corps was moving southward and westward, to clear
a road for Chu Teh, who was leading the Second and Fourth Front
armies up from Sikang and Szechuan, breaking through a deep
cordon of Nanking troops in southern Kansu. Yu Wang Pao, an
ancient Mohammedan walled city in south-east Ninghsia, was
headquarters of the First Front Army, and here I found its staff
and Commander P'eng Teh-huai.*

P'eng's career as a 'Red bandit' had begun almost a decade before, when he led an uprising in the Kuomintang army of the
polygamous warlord-governor, General Ho Chien. P'eng had risen
from the ranks and won admission to a military school in Hunan
and later on to another school at Nanchang. After graduation he
had quickly distinguished himself and secured rapid promotions.
By 1927, when he was twenty-eight years old, he was already
a brigade commander, and noted throughout the Hunanese army
as the 'liberal' officer who actually consulted his soldiers' committee.

P'eng's influence in the then left-wing Kuomintang, in the
army, and in the Hunan military school were serious problems
for Ho Chien. In the winter of 1927 General Ho began a drastic
purgation of leftists in his troops and launched the notorious
Hunan 'Peasant Massacre', in which thousands of radical farmers
and workers were killed as 'Communists'. He hesitated to act

* At this point in my travels I was joined by Huang Hua (Wang Ju-mei),
a Yenching University student whom I had asked to come to assist me. See
BN.

against P'eng, however, because of his widespread popularity. It was a costly delay. In July 1928, with his own famous First Regiment as nucleus, and joined by parts of the Second and Third regiments and the cadets of the military school, P'eng Teh-huai directed the P'ing Kiang Insurrection, which united with a peasant uprising and established the first Hunan Soviet Government.

Two years later P'eng had accumulated an 'iron brotherhood' of about 8,000 followers, and this was the Fifth Red Army Corps. With this force he attacked and captured the great walled city of Changsha, capital of Hunan, and put to rout Ho Chien's army of 60,000 men – then mostly opium smokers. The Red Army held this city for ten days against counter-attacks by combined Nanking–Hunan troops, but was finally forced to evacuate by greatly superior forces, including bombardment by foreign gunboats.

It was shortly afterwards that Chiang Kai-shek began his first 'grand annihilation campaign' against the Red bandits. On the Long March of the southern Reds, P'eng Teh-huai was commander of the vanguard First Army Corps. He broke through lines of tens of thousands of enemy troops, captured vital points on the route of advance, and secured communications for the main forces, at last winning his way to Shensi and a refuge in the base of the North-West soviets. Men in his army told me that he walked most of the 6,000 miles of the Long March, frequently giving his horse to a tired or wounded comrade.

I found P'eng a gay, laughter-loving man, in excellent health except for a delicate stomach – the result of a week's forced diet of uncooked wheat grains and grass during the Long March, and of semi-poisonous food, and of a few days of no food at all. A veteran of scores of battles, he had been wounded but once, and then only superficially.

I stayed in the compound where P'eng had his headquarters in Yu Wang Pao, and so I saw a great deal of him at the front. This headquarters, by the way – then in command of over 30,000 troops – was a simple room furnished with a table and wooden bench, two iron dispatch boxes, maps made by the Red Army, a field telephone, a towel and washbasin, and the *k'ang* on which his blankets were spread. He had only a couple of uniforms, like the rest of his men, and they bore no insignia of rank. One personal article of attire, of which he was childishly proud, was a vest made from a parachute captured from an enemy airplane shot down during the Long March.

We shared many meals together. He ate sparingly and simply, of the same food his men were given – consisting usually of cabbage, noodles, beans, mutton, and sometimes bread. Ninghsia grew beautiful melons of all kinds, and P'eng was very fond of these. Your pampered investigator, however, found P'eng poor competition in the business of melon eating, but had to bow before the greater talents of one of the doctors on P'eng's staff, whose capacity had won him the nickname of Han Ch'ih-kua-ti (Han the Melon Eater).

Open, forthright, and undeviating in his manner and speech, quick in his movements, full of laughter and wit, P'eng was physically very active, an excellent rider, and a man of endurance. Perhaps this was partly because he was a nonsmoker and a teetotaller. I was with him one day during manoeuvres of the Red Second Division when we had to climb a very steep hill. 'Run to the top!' P'eng suddenly called out to his panting staff and me. He bounded off like a rabbit, and beat us all to the summit. Another time, when we were riding, he yelled out a similar challenge. In this way and others he gave the impression of great unspent energy.

P'eng retired late and arose early, unlike Mao Tse-tung, who retired late and also got up late. As far as I could learn, P'eng slept an average of only four or five hours a night. He never seemed rushed, but he was always busy. I remember the morning of the day the First Army Corps received orders to advance 200 li to Haiyuan, in enemy territory: P'eng issued all the commands necessary before breakfast and came down to eat with me; immediately afterwards he started off on the road, as if for an excursion to the countryside, walking along the main street of Yu Wang Pao with his staff, stopping to speak to the Moslem priests who had assembled to bid him good-bye. The big army seemed to run itself.

Government airplanes frequently dropped leaflets over Red lines offering from $50,000 to $100,000 for P'eng, dead or alive, but he had only one sentry on duty before his headquarters, and he sauntered down the streets of the city without any bodyguard. While I was there, when thousands of handbills had been dropped offering rewards for himself, Hsu Hai-tung, and Mao Tse-tung, P'eng Teh-huai ordered that they be preserved. They were printed on only one side, and there was a paper shortage in the Red Army. The blank side of these handbills was used later for printing Red Army propaganda.

P'eng was very fond of children, I noticed, and he was often followed by a group of them. Many youngsters, who acted as mess boys, buglers, orderlies, and grooms, were organized as regular units of the Red Army, in the groups called Shao-nien Hsien-feng-tui, or Young Vanguards. I often saw P'eng seated with two or three 'little Red devils', talking seriously to them about politics or their personal troubles. He treated them with great dignity.

One day I went with P'eng and part of his staff to visit a small arsenal near the front, and to inspect the workers' recreation room, their own Lieh-ning T'ang, or Lenin Club. There was a big cartoon, drawn by the workers, on one side of the room. It showed a kimonoed Japanese with his feet on Manchuria, Jehol, and Hopei, and an upraised sword, dripping with blood, poised over the rest of China. The caricatured Japanese had an enormous nose.

'Who is *that*?' P'eng asked a Young Vanguard whose duty it was to look after the Lenin Club.

'That,' replied the lad, 'is a Japanese imperialist!'

'How do you know?' P'eng demanded.

'Just look at his big nose!' was the response.

P'eng laughed and looked at me. 'Well,' he said, indicating me, 'here is a *yang kuei-tzu* [foreign devil], is he an imperialist?'

'He is a foreign devil all right,' the Vanguard replied, 'but not a Japanese imperialist. He has a big nose, but it isn't big enough for a Japanese imperialist!'

I pointed out to P'eng that such cartoons might result in serious disillusionment when the Reds actually came into contact with the Japanese and found Japanese noses quite as reasonable as their own. They might not recognize the enemy and might refuse to fight.

'Don't worry!' said the commander. 'We will know a Japanese, whether he has a nose or not.'

Once I went to a performance of the First Army Corps' Anti-Japanese Theatre with P'eng, and we sat down with the other soldiers on the turf below the improvised stage. He seemed to enjoy the plays immensely, and he led a demand for a favourite song. It grew quite chilly, after dark, although it was still late August. I wrapped my padded coat closer to me. In the middle of the performance I suddenly noticed with surprise that P'eng had removed his own coat. Then I saw that he had put it around a little bugler sitting next to him.

I understood P'eng's affection for these 'little devils' later on, when he yielded to persuasion one night and told me something of his childhood. The trials of his own youth might amaze an Occidental ear, but they were typical enough of background events which explained many of the young Chinese who, like him, 'saw Red'.

3

Why Is a Red?

P'ENG TEH-HUAI was born in a village of Hsiang T'an *hsien*, near the native place of Mao Tse-tung. It was a wealthy farming community beside the blue-flowing Hsiang River, about 90 *li* from Changsha. Hsiang T'an was one of the prettiest parts of Hunan – a green countryside quilted with deep rice lands and thickets of tall bamboo. More than a million people lived in this one county. Though the soil of Hsiang T'an was rich, the majority of the peasants were miserably poor, illiterate, and 'little better than serfs', according to P'eng. Landlords were all-powerful there, owned the finest lands, and charged exorbitant rents and taxes, for they were in many cases also the officials – the gentry.

Several great landlords in Hsiang T'an had incomes of from forty to fifty thousand *tan* * of rice annually, and some of the wealthiest grain merchants in the province lived there.

P'eng's own family were rich peasants. His mother died when he was six, his father remarried, and this second wife hated P'eng because he was a constant reminder of her predecessor. She sent him to an old-style Chinese school, where the teacher frequently beat him. P'eng was apparently quite capable of looking after his own interests: in the midst of one of these beatings he picked up a stool, scored a hit, and fled. The teacher brought a lawsuit against him in the local courts, and his stepmother denounced him.

His father was rather indifferent in this quarrel, but to keep peace with his wife he sent the young stool tosser off to live with an aunt, whom he liked. She put the boy into a so-called modern school. There he met a 'radical' teacher, who did not believe in filial worship. One day, when Teh-huai was playing in the park, this teacher came along and sat down to talk with him. P'eng asked whether he worshipped his parents, and whether he thought P'eng should worship his. As for himself, said the teacher, he did

* About 2,600 to 3,300 tons.

not believe in such nonsense. Children were brought into the world while their parents were playing, just as Teh-huai had been playing in this park.

'I liked this notion,' said P'eng, 'and I mentioned it to my aunt when I went home. She was horrified, and the very next day had me withdrawn from the evil "foreign influence".' Hearing something of the young man's objection to filial worship, his grandmother began to pray regularly 'on the first and fifteenth of each month, and at festivals, or when it stormed', for heaven to strike this unfilial child and destroy him.

In P'eng's own words:

'My grandmother regarded us all as her slaves. She was a heavy smoker of opium. I hated the smell of it, and one night, when I could stand it no longer, I got up and kicked a pan of her opium from the stove. She was furious. She called a meeting of the whole clan and formally demanded my death by drowning, because I was an unfilial child. She made a long list of charges against me.

'The clan was about ready to carry out her demand. My stepmother agreed that I should die, and my father said that since it was the family will, he would not object. Then an uncle, my own mother's brother, stepped forward and bitterly attacked my parents for their failure to educate me properly. He said that it was their fault and that in this case no child could be held responsible.

'My life was spared, but I had to leave home. I was nine years old, it was cold October, and I owned nothing but my coat and trousers. My stepmother tried to take those from me, but I proved that they did not belong to her, but had been given to me by my own mother.'

Such was the beginning of P'eng Teh-huai's life in the great world. He got a job first as a cowherd, and next as a coal miner, where he pulled a bellows for fourteen hours a day. Weary of these long hours, he fled from the mine to become a shoemaker's apprentice, working only twelve hours a day. He received no salary, and after eight months he ran away again, this time to work in a sodium mine. The mine closed; he was forced to seek work once more. Still owning nothing but the rags on his back, he became a dike-builder. Here he had a 'good job', actually received wages, and in two years had saved 1,500 *cash* – about $12 !

But he 'lost everything' when a change of warlords rendered the currency worthless. Very depressed, he decided to return to his native district.

Now sixteen, P'eng went to call on a rich uncle, the uncle who had saved his life. This man's own son had just died; he had always liked Teh-huai, and he welcomed him and offered him a home. Here P'eng fell in love with his own cousin, and the uncle was favourably disposed to a betrothal. They studied under a Chinese tutor, played together, and planned their future.

These plans were interrupted by P'eng's irrepressible impetuosity. Next year there was a big rice famine in Hunan, and thousands of peasants were destitute. P'eng's uncle helped many, but the biggest stores of rice were held by a great landlord-merchant who profiteered fabulously. One day a crowd of over two hundred peasants gathered at his house, demanding that the merchant sell them rice without profit – traditionally expected of a virtuous man in time of famine. The rich man refused to discuss it, had the people driven away, and barred his gates.

P'eng went on : 'I was passing his place, and paused to watch the demonstration. I saw that many of the men were half starved, and I knew this man had over 10,000 *tan* of rice in his bins, and that he had refused to help the starving at all. I became infuriated, and led the peasants to attack and invade his house. They carted off most of his stores. Thinking of it afterwards, I did not know exactly why I had done that. I only knew that he should have sold rice to the poor, and that it was right for them to take it from him if he did not.'

P'eng had to flee once more for his life, and this time he was old enough to join the army. His career as a soldier began. Not long afterwards he was to become a revolutionary.

At eighteen he was made a platoon commander and was involved in a plot to overthrow the ruling governor – *Tuchun* Hu. P'eng had been deeply influenced by a student leader in his army, whom the *tuchun* had killed. Entrusted with the task of assassinating Hu, he entered Changsha, waited for him to pass down the street one day, and threw a bomb at him. The bomb failed to explode. P'eng escaped.

Not long afterwards Dr Sun Yat-sen became Generalissimo of

the allied armies of the South-West, and succeeded in defeating *Tuchun* Hu, but was subsequently driven out of Hunan again by the northern militarists. P'eng fled with Sun's army. Sent upon a mission of espionage by Ch'eng Ch'ien, one of Sun's commanders, P'eng returned to Changsha, was betrayed and arrested. Chang Ching-yao was then in power in Hunan. P'eng described his experiences:

'I was tortured every day for about an hour in many different ways. One night my feet were bound and my hands were tied behind my back. I was hung from the roof with a rope around my wrists. Then big stones were piled on my back, while the jailers stood around kicking me and demanding that I confess – for they still had no evidence against me. Many times I fainted.

'This torture went on for about a month. I used to think after every torture that next time I would confess, as I could not stand it. But each time I decided that I would not give up till the next day. In the end they got nothing from me, and to my surprise I was finally released. One of the deep satisfactions of my life came some years later when we [the Red Army] captured Changsha and destroyed that old torture chamber. We released several hundred political prisoners there – many of them half-dead from beatings, fiendish treatment, and starvation.'

When P'eng regained his freedom he went back to his uncle's home to visit his cousin. He intended to marry her, as he still considered himself betrothed. He found that she had died. Re-enlisting in the army, he soon afterwards received his first commission and was sent to the Hunan military school. Following his graduation he became a battalion commander in the Second Division, under Lu Ti-p'ing, and was assigned to duty in his native district.

'My uncle died and, hearing of it, I arranged to return and attend the funeral. On the way there I had to pass my childhood home. My old grandmother was alive, now past eighty, and still very active. Learning that I was returning, she walked down the road ten *li* to meet me, and begged my forgiveness for the past. She was very humble and very respectful. I was quite surprised by this change. What could be the cause of it? Then I reflected that it was not due to any change in her personal feeling, but to my rise in the world from a social outcast to an army officer with a salary of $200 a month. I gave the old lady a little money, and she sang my praises in the family as a model "filial son"!'

I asked P'eng what reading had influenced him. He said that when as a youth he read Ssu-ma Kuang's * *Sze Chih Chien (History of Governing)*, he began for the first time to have some serious thoughts concerning the responsibility of a soldier to society. 'The battles described by Ssu-ma Kuang were completely pointless, and only caused suffering to the people – very much like those that were being fought between the militarists in China in my own time. What could we do to give purpose to our struggles, and bring about a permanent change?'

P'eng read Liang Ch'i-ch'ao and K'ang Yu-wei and many of the writers who had influenced Mao Tse-tung. For a time he had some interest in anarchism. In Ch'en Tu-hsiu's *New Youth* he learned of socialism, and from that point he began to study Marxism. The Nationalist Revolution was forming, he was a regimental commander, and he felt the necessity of a political doctrine to give morale to his troops. Sun Yat-sen's *San Min Chu I (Three Principles of the People)* 'was an improvement over Liang Ch'i-ch'ao', but P'eng felt that it was 'too vague and confused', although he was by then a member of the Kuomintang. Bukharin's *ABC of Communism* seemed to him 'for the first time a book that presented a practicable and reasonable form of society and government'.

By 1926 P'eng had read the *Communist Manifesto*, an outline of *Capital*, *A New Conception of Society* (by a leading Chinese Communist), Kautsky's *Class Struggle*, and many articles and pamphlets giving a materialist interpretation of the Chinese Revolution. 'Formerly,' said P'eng, 'I had been merely dissatisfied with society, but saw little chance of making any fundamental improvement. After reading the *Communist Manifesto* I dropped my pessimism and began working with a new conviction that society could be changed.'

Although P'eng did not join the Communist Party until 1927, he enlisted Communist youths in his troops, began Marxist courses of political training, and organized soldiers' committees. In 1926 he married a middle-school girl who was a member of the Socialist

*Ssu-ma Kuang was an outstanding historian (1019–86).

Youth, but during the revolution they became separated. P'eng had not seen her since 1928. It was in July of that year that P'eng revolted, seized P'ing Kiang, and began his long career as a rebel, or bandit – as you prefer.

He had been pacing back and forth, grinning and joking as he told me these incidents of his youth and struggle, carrying in his hand a Mongolian horsehair fly swatter, which he brandished absent-mindedly for emphasis. A messenger now brought in a sheaf of radiograms, and he suddenly looked the serious commander again as he turned to read them.

'Well, that's about all, anyway,' he concluded. 'That explains something about how a man becomes a "Red bandit" !'

ao Tse-tung at Pao An, 1936.

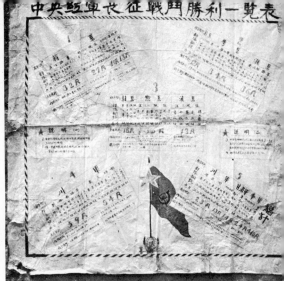

Wall posters and mural cartoons covered much of the available space in the soviet districts. The poster at right lists victories on the Long March; below, 'The Struggle of America and Japan for Hegemony of the Pacific'; right, below, France is the little man, Germany the big one (with a stomach full of marks) demanding revision of the Versailles Treaty; at bottom of page, the Chinese version of 'The Internationale'.

A Red Army mass meeting in Ninghsia. The soldiers (and some local Moslems) gathered at sundown to hear their weekly lecture on the political situation by P'eng Teh-huai. The grass hats at their feet are for camouflage against air raids.

Pao An, its *yao-fang* (cave houses) sheltered in the loess hills.

A closer view of the town, as seen from the cliffs above.

American, British, Czechoslovakian, and other foreign arms makers equipped the main forces of the Red Army with arms originally sold to the Kuomintang and captured from them by the Communists.

A Red combat team that captured the Moslem fort in the background. Kansu, 1936.

'Even the poorest shall read' was the slogan of the Communist Government Educational Commission in north Shensi. These children began early – reading the *ABC of Communism*.

...ti-Japanese People's Red Army Dramatic Society of the Fifteenth Army Corps, ...otographed at Hsuan Chih during the Red Army's Eastern Expedition to Shansi in ...arch 1936, which was part of the anti-Japanese campaign launched among the Shansi ...ople. (Photograph taken in Shansi; reproduction by the author.)

Chou En-lai welcomes the author to the Red districts.

'Saturday Brigades', organized by the Communist Youth League, moved through the countryside to help farmers with sons in the Red Army. They also cultivated the Red Army's own farms, reclaimed wasteland in the North-West.

Photograph taken at the Eleventh Plenum of the Sixth CCP Congress, 1931. Left, Fang Chih-min; next left, Chu Teh, Teng Fa, Hsiao K'e, Mao Tse-tung, and Wang Chia-hsiang. (Photograph reproduction by the author.)

Army athletics in Pao An.

Teenage Red Army nurses in Kansu; the corps was open to boys and girls aged fourteen and up.

Manchurian volunteers, once White, now Red. Most of these men and also most of their arms were formerly in the army of Marshal Chang Hsueh-liang.

glers of the Fifteenth Army Corps, Ninghsia.

A Red theatre in Pao An – a converted Taoist temple.

A Lenin Club room in the arsenal in north Shensi. Above the portraits hung a pennant for first prize in a workers' literacy competition, and below them the 'airplane banner' given to the workers' group ranking highest for one month in all competitions.

Red cooperatives were established in towns under soviet control. Here villagers examine the materials offered in Holienwan, Kansu.

The Soviet Government operated post offices throughout its territory.

Workers, soldiers, students, and the people found magazines, newspapers, and books available in soviet centres.

Flood refuges in the sandstone bluffs of north Shensi. These caves also made excellent shelter against air bombardment, and good sniping positions.

Lin Piao, a Whampoa graduate who became president of the Red Army University in Pao An. At twenty-eight he was considered the outstanding tactical genius of all military officers in China.

Teng Fa, chief of the Revolutionary Defence Corps, the Reds' security police. (Photograph reproduction by the author.)

Hsu Hai-tung, commander of the Fifteenth Red Army Corps. (Photograph reproduction by the author.)

Chu Teh, commander-in-chief of the Red Army. (Photograph reproduction by the author.)

Mao Tse-tung with his second wife, Ho Tzu-ch'en.

Chingkangshan veterans, Pao An, 1936. Seated, far left, Lu Ting-yi, Chang Wen-ping; far right, Lin Piao. Standing, third from right, Mao Tse-tung.

'ittle Red Devils' was the pet name given to these boy soldiers of the Red Army. rganized in disciplined units by the CYL, they received compulsory education in ading, writing, athletics – and politics.

ung actors in costume for a tableau presented at a mass meeting of the First Army rps in Ninghsia.

Left to right: Hsieh Chu-tsai, education minister in the Shensi Soviet; Huang Hua, then a Yenching University student, who accompanied the author during part of his journey; Wang Lin, a courier between Peking and Pao An; and the author, interviewing Hsieh in his cave.

4

Tactics of Partisan Warfare

WE SAT in the house of a former magistrate, in Yu Wang Pao, in a two-story edifice with a balustraded porch – a porch from which you could look out towards Mongolia, across the plains of Ninghsia.

On the high, stout walls of Yu Wang Pao a squad of Red buglers was practising, and from a corner of the fortlike city flew a big scarlet flag, its yellow hammer and sickle cracking out in the breeze now and then as though a fist were behind it. We could look down on one side to a clean courtyard, where Mohammedan women were hulling rice and baking. Washing hung from a line on another side. In a distant square some Red soldiers were practising wall scaling, broad jumping, and grenade throwing.

Although P'eng Teh-huai and Mao Tse-tung were *t'ung-hsien-ti*, or natives of the same county, they had not met until the Red Army was formed. P'eng spoke with a pronounced southern accent, and machine-gun rapidity. I could understand him clearly only when he spoke slowly and simply, which he was generally too impatient to do. For this interview Huang Hua, whose English was excellent, acted as my interpreter.

'The main reason for partisan warfare in China,' P'eng began, 'is economic bankruptcy, and especially rural bankruptcy. Imperialism, landlordism, and militaristic wars have combined to destroy the basis of rural economy, and it cannot be restored without eliminating its chief enemies. Enormous taxes, together with Japanese invasion, both military and economic, have accelerated the rate of this peasant bankruptcy, aided by the landlords. The gentry's exploitation of power in the villages makes life difficult for the majority of the peasants. There is widespread unemployment in the villages. There is a readiness among the poor classes to fight for a change.

'Second, partisan warfare has developed because of the backwardness of the hinterland. Lack of communications, roads, railways, and bridges makes it possible for the people to arm and organize.

'Third, although the strategic centres of China are all more or less dominated by the imperialists, this control is uneven and not unified. Between the imperialist spheres of influence there are wide gaps, and in these partisan warfare can quickly develop.

'Fourth, the Great Revolution of 1925–7 fixed the revolutionary idea in the minds of many, and even after the counter-revolution in 1927 and the killings in the cities, many revolutionaries refused to submit, and sought a method of opposition. Owing to the special system of joint imperialist-comprador* control in the big cities, and the lack of an armed force in the beginning, it was impossible to find a base in urban areas, so many revolutionary workers, intellectuals, and peasants returned to the rural districts to lead the peasant insurrections. Intolerable social and economic conditions had created the demand for revolution: it was only necessary to give leadership, form, and objectives to this rural mass movement.

'All these factors contributed to the growth and success of revolutionary partisan warfare. They are, of course, quite simply stated, and do not go into the deeper problems behind them.

'Besides these reasons, partisan warfare has succeeded and partisan detachments have developed their invincibility because of the identity of the masses with the fighting forces. Red partisans are not only warriors; they are at the same time political propagandists and organizers. Wherever they go they carry the message of the revolution, patiently explain to the mass of the peasantry the real missions of the Red Army, and make them understand that only through revolution can their needs be realized, and why the Communist Party is the only party which can lead them.

'But as regards the specific tasks of partisan warfare, you have asked why in some places it developed very rapidly and became a strong political power, while in others it was easily and quickly suppressed. This is an interesting question.

'First of all, partisan warfare in China can only succeed under the revolutionary leadership of the Communist Party, because

* Compradors were Chinese who served as middlemen between Western and native businessmen.

only the Communist Party wants to and can satisfy the demands of the peasantry, understands the necessity for deep, broad, constant political and organizational work among the peasantry, and can fulfil its promises.

'Second, the active field leadership of partisan units must be determined, fearless, and courageous. Without these qualities in the leadership, partisan warfare not only cannot grow, but it must wither and die under the reactionary offensive.

'Because the masses are interested only in the practical solution of their problems of livelihood, it is possible to develop partisan warfare only by the *immediate* satisfaction of their most urgent demands. This means that the exploiting class must be promptly disarmed.

'Partisans can never remain stationary; to do so is to invite destruction. They must constantly expand, building around themselves ever new peripheral and protective groups. Political training must accompany every phase of the struggle, and local leaders must be developed from every new group added to the revolution. Leaders from the outside can be introduced to a limited extent, but no lasting success can be achieved if the movement fails to inspire, awaken, and constantly create new leaders from the local mass.'

One of the chief reasons why Marshal Chang Hsueh-liang began to respect the Reds (the enemy he had been sent to destroy) was that he had been impressed with their skill at this type of combat, and had come to believe they could be utilized in fighting Japan. After he had reached a kind of truce with them he invited Red instructors to teach in the new officers' training school opened for his Manchurian army in Shensi, and there the Communist influence rapidly developed. Marshal Chang and most of his officers, bitterly anti-Japanese, had become convinced that it was superior mobility and manoeuvring ability on which China would ultimately have to depend in a war with Japan. They were anxious to know all that the Reds had learned about the tactics and strategy of manoeuvring warfare during ten years of fighting experience.

Was it possible, I had asked P'eng Teh-huai, to summarize the 'principles of Red partisan warfare'? He had promised to do so and had written down a few notes from which he now read. For a fuller discussion of the subject he referred me to a small book written by Mao Tse-tung and published in the soviet districts; but this I was unable to get.*

'There are certain rules of tactics which must be followed,' P'eng explained, 'if the newly developing partisan army is to be successful. These we have learned from our long experience, and though they are variable according to conditions, I believe that departures from them generally lead to extinction. The main principles can be summarized under ten points, like this:

'First, partisans must not fight any losing battles. Unless there are strong indications of success, they should refuse any engagement.

'Second, surprise is the main offensive tactic of the well-led partisan group. Static warfare must be avoided. The partisan brigade has no auxiliary force, no rear, no line of supplies and communications except that of the enemy. In a lengthy positional war the enemy has every advantage, and in general the chances of partisan success diminish in proportion to the duration of the battle.

'Third, a careful and detailed plan of attack, and especially of retreat, must be worked out before any engagement is offered or accepted. Any attack undertaken without full knowledge of the particular situation opens the partisans to outmanoeuvre by the enemy. Superior manoeuvring ability is a great advantage of the partisans, and errors in its manipulation mean extinction.

'Fourth, in the development of partisan warfare the greatest attention must be paid to the *min-tu'an*,† the first, last, and most determined line of resistance of the landlords and gentry. The *min-t'uan* must be destroyed militarily, but must, if at all possible, be won over politically on the side of the masses. Unless the *min-t'uan* in a district is disarmed it is impossible to mobilize the masses.

'Fifth, in a regular engagement with enemy troops the partisans must exceed the enemy in numbers. But if the enemy's regular troops are moving, resting, or poorly guarded, a swift, determined,

---

* Mao's *Yu-chi Chan-cheng* (*Guerrilla Warfare*), published in Wayapao, Shensi, in 1935, was out of print.

† P'eng Teh-huai estimated that the *min-t'uan* numbered at least 3,000,000 men (in addition to China's huge regular army of 2,000,000 men).

surprise flank attack on an organically vital spot of the enemy's line can be made by a much smaller group. Many a Red "short attack" has been carried out with only a few hundred men against an enemy of thousands. Surprise, speed, courage, unwavering decision, flawlessly planned manoeuvre, and the selection of the most vulnerable and vital spot in the enemy's "anatomy" are absolutely essential to the complete victory of this kind of attack. Only a highly experienced partisan army can succeed at it.

'Sixth, in actual combat the partisan line must have the greatest elasticity. Once it becomes obvious that their calculation of enemy strength or preparedness or fighting power is in error, the partisans should be able to disengage and withdraw with the same speed as they began the attack. Reliable cadres must be developed in every unit, fully capable of replacing any commander eliminated in battle. Resourcefulness of subalterns must be greatly relied upon in partisan warfare.

'Seventh, the tactics of distraction, decoy, diversion, ambush, feint, and irritation must be mastered. In Chinese these tactics are called "the principle of pretending to attack the east while attacking the west".

'Eighth, partisans must avoid engagements with the main force of the enemy, concentrating on the weakest link, or the most vital.

'Ninth, every precaution must be taken to prevent the enemy from locating the partisans' main forces. For this reason, partisans should avoid concentrating in one place when the enemy is advancing, and should change their position frequently – two or three times in one day or night, just before an attack. Secrecy in the movements of the partisans is absolutely essential to success. Well-worked-out plans for dispersal after an attack are as important as plans for the actual concentration to meet an enemy advance.

'Tenth, besides superior mobility, the partisans, being inseparable from the local masses, have the advantage of superior intelligence, and the greatest use must be made of this. Ideally, every peasant should be on the partisans' intelligence staff, so that it is impossible for the enemy to take a step without the partisans knowing of it. Great care should be taken to protect the channels of information about the enemy, and several auxiliary lines of intelligence should always be established.'

These were the main principles, according to Commander P'eng, on which the Red Army had built up its strength, and it was necessary to employ them in every enlargement of Red territory. He finished up:

'So you see that successful partisan warfare demands these fundamentals: fearlessness, swiftness, intelligent planning, mobility, secrecy, and suddenness and determination in action. Lacking any of these, it is difficult for partisans to win victories. If in the beginning of a battle they lack quick decision, the battle will lengthen. They must be swift, otherwise the enemy will be reinforced. They must be mobile and elastic, otherwise they will lose their advantages of manoeuvre.

'Finally, it is absolutely necessary for the partisans to win the support and participation of the peasant masses. If there is no movement of the armed peasantry, there is in fact no partisan base, and the army cannot exist. Only by implanting itself deeply in the hearts of the people, only by fulfilling the demands of the masses, only by consolidating a base in the peasant soviets, and only by sheltering in the shadow of the masses, can partisan warfare bring revolutionary victory.'

P'eng had been pacing up and down the balcony, delivering one of his points each time he returned to the table where I sat writing. Now he suddenly stopped and stood thoughtfully reflecting.

'But nothing, absolutely nothing,' he said, 'is more important than this – that the Red Army is a people's army, and has grown because the people helped us.

'I remember the winter of 1928, when my forces in Hunan had dwindled to a little over 2,000 men, and we were encircled. The Kuomintang troops burned down all the houses in a surrounding area of about 300 *li*, seized all the food there, and then blockaded us. We had no cloth, we used bark to make short tunics, and we cut up the legs of our trousers to make shoes. Our hair grew long, we had no quarters, no lights, no salt. We were sick and half-starved. The peasants were no better off, and we would not touch what little they had.

'But the peasants encouraged us. They dug up from the ground the grain which they had hidden from the White troops and gave it to us, and they ate potatoes and wild roots. They hated the Whites for burning their homes and stealing their food. Even before we arrived they had fought the landlords and tax collectors, so they welcomed us. Many joined us, and nearly all helped us in some way. They wanted us to win! And because of that we fought on and broke through the blockade.'

He turned to me and ended simply. 'Tactics are important, but we could not exist if the majority of the people did not support us. We are nothing but the fist of the people beating their oppressors!'

5

Life of the Red Warrior

THE Chinese soldier had had a poor reputation abroad. Many people thought his gun was chiefly ornamental, that he did his only fighting with an opium pipe, that any rifle shots exchanged were by mutual agreement and in the air, that battles were fought with silver and the soldier was paid in opium. Some of that had been true enough of most armies in the past, but the well-equipped first-class Chinese soldier (White as well as Red) was now no longer a vaudeville joke.

There were still plenty of comic-opera armies in China, but in recent years there had arisen a new type of Chinese warrior, who would soon supplant the old. Civil war, especially the class war between Reds and Whites, had been very costly, and often heavily and brutally fought, with no quarter or umbrella truces given by either side. Those ten years of strife in China had, if nothing else, created the nucleus of a fighting force and military brains experienced in the use of modern technique and tactics, which would before long build a powerful army that could no longer be dismissed as a tin-soldier affair.

The trouble had never been with the human material itself. The Chinese could fight as well as any people, as I had learned during the Shanghai War in 1932. Technical limitations disregarded, the trouble had been the inability of the command to train that human material at its disposal and give to it military discipline, political morale, and the will to victory. Therein lay the superiority of the Red Army – it was so often the only side in a battle that believed it was fighting for something. It was the Reds' greater success at the educative tasks in the building of an army that enabled them to withstand the tremendous technical and numerical superiority of their enemy.

For sheer dogged endurance, and ability to stand hardship without complaint, the Chinese peasants, who composed the greater part of the Red Army, were unbeatable. This was shown by the Long March, in which the Reds took a terrific pummelling from all sides, slept in the open and lived on unhulled wheat for many days, but still held together and emerged as a potent military force. It was also demonstrated by the rigours and impositions of daily life in the Red Army.

The Red troops I saw in Ninghsia and Kansu were quartered in caves, former stables of wealthy landlords, hastily erected barracks of clay and wood, and in compounds and houses abandoned by former officials or garrison troops. They slept on hard k'ang, without mattresses and with only a cotton blanket each – yet these rooms were fairly neat, clean and orderly, although their floors, walls and ceilings were of whitewashed clay. They seldom had tables or desks, and piles of bricks or rocks served as chairs, most of the furniture having been destroyed or carted off by the enemy before his retreat.

Every company had its own cook and commissariat. The Reds' diet was extremely simple: millet and cabbage, with a little mutton and sometimes pork, were an average meal, but they seemed to thrive on it. Coffee, tea, cake, sweets of any kind, or fresh vegetables were almost unknown, but also unmissed. Coffee tins were more valuable than their contents; nobody liked coffee, it tasted like medicine, but a good tin could be made into a serviceable canteen. Hot water was almost the only beverage consumed, and the drinking of cold water (very often contaminated) was specifically forbidden.

The Red soldier, when not fighting, had a full and busy day. In the North-West, as in the South, he had long periods of military inactivity, for when a new district was occupied, the Red Army settled down for a month or two to establish soviets and otherwise 'consolidate', and only put a small force on outpost duty. The enemy was nearly always on the defensive, except when one of the periodic big annihilation drives was launched.

When not in the trenches or on outpost duty, the Red soldier observed a six-day week. He arose at five and retired to a 'Taps' sounded at nine. The schedule of the day included: an hour's exercise immediately after rising; breakfast; two hours of military drill; two hours of political lectures and discussion; lunch; an hour of rest; two hours of character study; two hours of games and sports; dinner; songs and group meetings; and 'Taps'.

Keen competition was encouraged in broad jumping, high jumping, running, wall scaling, rope climbing, rope skipping, grenade throwing, and marksmanship. Watching the leaps of the Reds over walls, bars, and ropes, you could easily understand why the Chinese press had nicknamed them 'human monkeys', for their swift movement and agile feats of mountain climbing. Pennants were given in group competitions, from the squad up to the regiment, in sports, military drill, political knowledge, literacy, and public health. I saw these banners displayed in the Lenin clubs of units that had won such distinctions.

There was a Lenin Club for every company and for every regiment, and here all social and 'cultural' life had its centre. The regimental Lenin rooms were the best in the unit's quarters, but that said little; such as I saw were always crude, makeshift affairs, and what interest they aroused derived from the human activity in them rather than from their furnishings. They all had pictures of Marx and Lenin, drawn by company or regimental talent. Like some of the Chinese pictures of Christ, they generally bore a distinctly Oriental appearance, with eyes like stitches, and either a bulbous forehead like an image of Confucius, or no forehead at all. Marx, whose Chinese moniker is Ma K'e-ssu, was nicknamed by the Red soldiers Ma Ta Hu-tzu, or Ma the Big Beard. They seemed to have an affectionate awe for him. That was especially true of the Mohammedans, who appeared to be the only people in China capable of growing luxuriant beards as well as appreciating them.

Another feature of the Lenin Club was a corner devoted to the study of military tactics, in models of clay. Miniature towns, mountains, forts, rivers, lakes, and bridges were constructed in these corners, and toy armies battled back and forth, while the class studied some tactical problem. Thus in some places you saw the Sino–Japanese battles of Shanghai refought, in another the battles on the Great Wall, but most of the models were devoted to past battles between the Reds and the Kuomintang. They were also used to explain the geographical features of the district in which the army was stationed, to dramatize the tactics of a hypothetical campaign, or merely to animate the geography and political lessons which Red soldiers got as part of their military training. In a hospital company's Lenin room I saw displays of clay models of various parts of the anatomy, showing the effects of certain diseases, illustrating body hygiene, and so on.

Another corner of the club was devoted to character study, and here one saw the notebook of each warrior hanging on its appointed peg on the wall. There were three character-study groups: those who knew fewer than 100 characters; those who knew from 100 to 300; and those who could read and write more than 300 characters. The Reds had printed their own textbooks (using political propaganda as materials of study) for each of these groups. The political department of each company, battalion, regiment, and army was responsible for mass education, as well as political training. Only about 20 per cent of the First Army Corps, I was told, was still *hsia-tzu*, or 'blind men', as the Chinese call total illiterates.

'The principles of the Lenin Club,' it was explained to me by Hsiao Hua,* the twenty-two-year-old political director of the Second Division, 'are quite simple. All the life and activity in them must be connected with the daily work and development of the men. It must be done by the men themselves. It must be simple and easy to understand. It must combine recreational value with practical education about the immediate tasks of the army.'

The 'library' of the average Lenin Club consisted chiefly of standard Chinese Red Army textbooks and lectures, a history of the Russian Revolution, miscellaneous magazines which might have been smuggled in or captured from the White areas, and files of Chinese soviet publications like the *Red China Daily News*, *Party Work*, *Struggle*, and others.

There was also a wall newspaper in every club, and a committee of soldiers was responsible for keeping it up to date. The wall newspaper gave considerable insight into the soldier's problems and a measure of his development. I took down full notes, in translation, of many of these papers. A typical one was in the Lenin Club, Second Company, Third Regiment, Second Division, in Yu Wang Pao, for 1 September. Its contents included daily and weekly notices

*See BN.

of the Communist Party and the Communist Youth League; a couple of columns of crude contributions by the newly literate, mostly revolutionary exhortations and slogans; radio bulletins of Red Army victories in south Kansu; new songs to be learned; political news from the White areas; and, perhaps most interesting of all, two sections called the red and black columns, devoted respectively to praise and criticism.

'Praise' consisted of tributes to the courage, bravery, unselfishness, diligence, or other virtues of individuals or groups. In the black column comrades lashed into each other and their officers (by name) for such things as failure to keep a rifle clean, slackness in study, losing a hand grenade or bayonet, smoking on duty, 'political backwardness', 'individualism', 'reactionary habits', etc. On one black column I saw a cook criticized for his 'half-done' millet; in another a cook denounced a man for 'always complaining' about his productions.

Many people had been amused to hear about the Reds' passion for the English game of table tennis. It was bizarre, somehow, but every Lenin Club had in its centre a big ping-pong table, usually serving double duty as dining table. The Lenin clubs were turned into mess halls at chow time, but there were always four or five 'bandits', armed with bats, balls, and the net, urging the comrades to hurry it up; they wanted to get on with their game. Each company boasted a ping-pong champion, and I was no match for them.

Some of the Lenin clubs had record players confiscated from the homes of former officials or White officers. One night I was entertained with a concert on a captured American Victrola, described as a 'gift' from General Kao Kuei-tzu, who was then in command of a Kuomintang army fighting the Reds on the Shensi–Suiyuan border. General Kao's records were all Chinese, with two exceptions, both French. One had on it 'The Marseillaise' and 'Tipperary'. The other was a French comic song. Both brought on storms of laughter from the astonished listeners, who understood not a word.

The Reds had many games of their own, and were constantly inventing new ones. One, called *Shih-tzu P'ai*, or 'Know Characters Cards', was a contest that helped illiterates learn their basic hieroglyphics. Another game was somewhat like poker, but the high cards were marked 'Down with Japanese Imperialism', 'Down with the Landlords', 'Long Live the Revolution', and 'Long Live the Soviets'. Minor cards carried slogans that changed according to the political and military objectives. There were many group games. The Communist Youth League members were responsible for the programmes of the Lenin clubs, and likewise led mass singing every day. Many of the songs were sung to Christian hymn tunes.

All these activities kept the mass of the soldiers fairly busy and fairly healthy. There were no camp followers or prostitutes with the Red troops I saw. Opium smoking was prohibited. I saw no opium or opium pipes with the Reds on the road, nor in any barracks I visited. Cigarette smoking was not forbidden except while on duty, but there was propaganda against it, and few Red soldiers seemed to smoke.

Such was the organized life of the regular Red soldiers behind the front. Not so very exciting, perhaps, but rather different from the propagandists' tales, from which one might have gathered that the Reds' life consisted of wild orgies, entertainment by naked dancers, and rapine before and after meals. The truth seemed to be that a revolutionary army anywhere was always in danger of becoming too puritanical, rather than the contrary.

Some of the Reds' ideas had now been copied – with much better facilities for realizing them – by Chiang Kai-shek's crack 'new army' and his New Life movement. But one thing the White armies could not copy, the Reds claimed, was their 'revolutionary consciousness'. What this was like could best be seen at a political session of Red troops – where one could hear the firmly implanted credos that these youths fought and died for.

6

Session in Politics

FINDING myself with an idle afternoon, I went around to call on Liu Hsiao, a member of the Red Army political department, with offices in a guardhouse on the city wall of Yu Wang Pao.

By now it was obvious that the Red commanders were loyal Marxists, and were effectively under the guidance of the Communist Party, through its representatives in the political department of every unit of the army. Of course, Mr Trotsky might have disputed whether they were good Marxists or bad Marxists, but the point was that they were conscious fighters for socialism, in their fashion; they knew what they wanted, and believed themselves to be part of a world movement.

Liu Hsiao was one of the most serious-minded young men I had met among the Reds, and one of the hardest-working. An intensely earnest youth of twenty-five, with an aesthetic, intellectual face, he was extremely courteous, gentle, and inoffensive. I sensed an immense inner spiritual pride in him about his connection with the Red Army. He had a pure feeling of religious absolutism about communism, and I believed he would not have hesitated, on command, to shoot any number of 'counter-revolutionaries' or 'traitors'.

I had no right to break in on his day, but I knew he had orders to assist me in any way possible – he had several times acted as my interpreter – so I made the most of it. I think also that he disliked foreigners, and when later on he gave me a brief biography of himself, I could not blame him. He had been twice arrested and imprisoned by foreign police in his own country.

Liu was an ex-student of Eastview Academy, an American missionary school in Shengchoufu, Hunan. He had been a devout Christian, a fundamentalist, and a good YMCA man until 1926 and the Great Revolution. One day he led a student strike, was expelled, and was disowned by his family. Awakened to the 'imperialistic basis of missionary institutions' in China, he went to

Shanghai, became active in the student movement there, joined the Communist Party, and was imprisoned by police in the French Concession. Released in 1929, he rejoined his comrades, worked under the provincial committee of the Communist Party, was arrested by British police, put in the notorious Ward Road Jail, tortured by electricity to extort a confession, handed over to the Chinese authorities, jailed again, and did not get his freedom till 1931. He was then just twenty years old. Shortly afterwards he was sent by the Reds' 'underground railway' to the Fukien Soviet district, and had ever since been with the Red Army.

Liu agreed to accompany me, and together we found our way to a Lenin Club where there was a political class in session. It was a meeting of a company in the Second Regiment of the Second Division, First Army Corps, and sixty-two were present. This was the 'advanced section' of the company; there was also a 'second section'. Political education in the Red Army is conducted through three main groups, each of which is divided into the two sections mentioned. Each elects its soldiers' committee, to consult with its superior officers and send delegates to the soviets. The three groups are for company commanders and higher; squad commanders and the rank and file; and the service corps – cooks, grooms, muleteers, carriers, sweepers, and Young Vanguards.

Green boughs decorated the room, and a big red paper star was fixed over the doorway. Inside were the usual pictures of Marx and Lenin, and on another wall were photographs of Generals Ts'ai T'ing-k'ai and Chiang Kuang-nai, heroes of the Shanghai War.* There was a big picture of the Russian Red Army massed in Red Square in an October anniversary demonstration – a photograph torn from a Shanghai magazine. Finally, there was a large lithograph of General Feng Yu-hsiang, with a slogan under it, 'Huan Wo Shan Ho' – 'Give back our mountains and rivers !' – an old Classical phrase, now revived by the anti-Japanese movement.

The men sat on brick seats, which they had brought with them (one often saw soldier students going to school with notebooks in one hand and a brick in the other), and the class was led by the

---

*The Shanghai War, or 'Incident', occurred in January 1932. Display of photographs of these non-Communist but anti-Japanese generals reflected the united-front policy of the CCP adopted in 1935.

company commander and the political commissar, both members of the Communist Party. The subject, I gathered, was 'Progress in the Anti-Japanese Movement'. A lanky, gaunt-faced youth was speaking. He seemed to be summarizing five years of Sino–Japanese 'undeclared war', and he was shouting at the top of his lungs. He told of the Japanese invasion of Manchuria, and his own experiences there, as a former soldier in the army of Marshal Chang Hsueh-liang. He condemned Nanking for ordering 'non-resistance'. Then he described the Japanese invasion of Shanghai, Jehol, Hopei, Chahar, and Suiyuan. In each case, he maintained, the 'Kuomintang dog-party' had retreated without fighting. They had 'given the Japanese bandits a fourth of our country'.

'Why?' he demanded, intensely excited, his voice breaking a little. 'Why don't our Chinese armies fight to save China? Because they don't want to? No! We Tungpei men asked our officers nearly every day to lead us to the front, to fight back to our homeland. Every Chinese hates to become a Japanese slave! But China's armies cannot fight because of our *mai-kuo cheng-fu*' (literally, 'sell-country government').

'But the people will fight if our Red Army leads ...' He ended up with a summary of the growth of the anti-Japanese movement in the North-West, under the Communists.

Another arose, stood at rigid attention, his hands pressed closely to his sides. Liu Hsiao whispered to me that he was a squad leader – a corporal – who had made the Long March. 'It is only the traitors who do not want to fight Japan. It is only the rich men, the militarists, the tax collectors, the landlords and the bankers, who start the 'cooperate-with-Japan' movement, and the 'joint-war-against-communism' slogan. They are only a handful, they are not Chinese.

'Our peasants and workers, every one, want to fight to save the country. They only need to be shown a road.... Why do I know this? In our Kiangsi soviets we had a population of only 3,000,000, yet we recruited volunteer partisan armies of 500,000 men! Our loyal soviets enthusiastically supported us in the war against the traitorous White troops. When the Red Army is victorious over the whole country our partisans will number over ten million. Let Japan dare to try to rob us then!'

And much more of it. One after another they stood up to utter their hatred against Japan, sometimes emphasizing, sometimes disagreeing with a previous speaker's remark, sometimes giving their answers to questions from the discussion leaders, making suggestions for 'broadening the anti-Japanese movement', and so on.

One youth told of the response of the people to the Red Army's anti-Japanese Shansi expedition last year. 'The *lao-pai-hsing* [the people] welcomed us,' he shouted. 'They came by the hundreds to join us. They brought us tea and cakes on the road as we marched. Many left their fields to come to join us, or cheer us. . . . They understood quite clearly who were the traitors and who the patriots – who want to fight Japan, and who want to sell China to Japan. Our problem is to awaken the whole country as we awakened the people of Shansi. . .'

One talked about the anti-Japanese student movement in the White districts, another about the anti-Japanese movement in the South-West, and a Tungpei man told of the reasons why Marshal Chang Hsueh-liang's Manchurian soldiers refused to fight the Reds any more. 'Chinese must not fight Chinese, we must all unite to oppose Japanese imperialism, we must win back our lost homeland !' he concluded with terse eloquence. A fourth spoke of the Manchurian anti-Japanese volunteers, and another of the strikes of Chinese workers in the Japanese mills of China.

The discussion continued for more than an hour. Occasionally the commander or political commissar interrupted to sum up what had been said, to elaborate a point, or to add new information, occasionally to correct something that had been said. The men took brief laborious notes in their little notebooks, and the serious task of thought furrowed their honest peasant faces. The whole session was crudely propagandist, and exaggeration of fact did not bother them in the least. It was self-proselytizing in a way, with materials selected to prove a single thesis. But that it was potent in its effects was manifest. Simple but powerful convictions, logical in shape, were forming in these young, little-tutored minds – credos such as every great crusading army has found necessary in order to stiffen itself with that spiritual unity, that courage, and that readiness to die in a cause, which we call morale.

I interrupted to ask some questions. They were answered by a show of hands. I discovered that of the sixty-two present, nine were from urban working-class families, while the rest were straight from the land. Twenty-one were former White soldiers and six were from the old Manchurian Army. Only eight of this group were married, and twenty-one were from Red families – that is, from families of poor peasants who had shared in the land redistribution under some soviet. Thirty-four of the group were under twenty years of age, twenty-four were between twenty and twenty-five, four were over thirty.

'In what way,' I asked, 'is the Red Army better than other armies of China?' This brought half a dozen men to their feet at once.

'The Red Army is a revolutionary army.'

'The Red Army is anti-Japanese.'

'The Red Army helps the peasants.'

'Living conditions in the Red Army are entirely different from the White Army life. Here we are all equals; in the White Army the soldier masses are oppressed. Here we fight for ourselves and the masses. The White Army fights for the gentry and the land-lords. Officers and men live the same in the Red Army. In the White Army the soldiers are treated like slaves.'

'Officers of the Red Army come from our own ranks, and win their appointments by merit alone. White officers buy their jobs, or use political influence.'

'Red soldiers are volunteers; White soldiers are conscripted.'

'Capitalist armies are for preserving the capitalist class. The Red Army fights for the proletariat.'

'The militarists' armies' work is to collect taxes and squeeze the blood of the people. The Red Army fights to free the people.'

'The masses hate the White Army; they love the Red Army.'

'But how,' I interrupted once more, 'do you know the peasants really like the Red Army?' Again several jumped up to answer. The political commissar recognized one.

'When we go into a new district,' he said, 'the peasants always volunteer to help our hospital service. They carry our wounded back to our hospitals from the front.'

Another: 'On our Long March through Szechuan the peasants brought us grass shoes, made by themselves, and they brought us tea and hot water along the road.'

A third: 'When I fought in Liu Chih-tan's Twenty-sixth Army, in Tingpien, we were a small detachment defending a lonely out-post against the Kuomintang general, Kao Kuei-tzu. The peasants brought us food and water. We did not have to use our men to bring supplies, the people helped us. Kao Kuei-tzu's men were defeated. We captured some and they told us they had had no water for almost two days. The peasants had poisoned the wells and run away.'

A Kansu peasant soldier: 'The people help us in many ways. During battles they often disarm small parties of the enemy, cut their telephone and telegraph wires, and send us news about the movements of the White troops. But they never cut our telephone lines; they help us put them up!'

Another: 'When an enemy airplane crashed against a moun-tain in Shensi recently, nobody saw it but a few farmers. They were armed only with spears and spades, but they attacked the airplane, disarmed the two aviators, arrested them, and brought them to us in Wa Ya Pao!'

Still another: 'Last April, in Yen Ch'ang, five villages formed soviets, where I was stationed. Afterwards we were attacked by T'ang En-p'o, and had to retreat. The *min-t'uan* returned, arrested eighteen villagers, and cut off their heads. Then we counter-attacked. The villagers led us by a secret mountain path to attack the *min-t'uan*. We took them by surprise, and we attacked and disarmed three platoons.'

One youth with a long scar on his cheek got up and told of some experiences on the Long March. 'When the Red Army was passing through Kweichow,' he said, 'I was wounded with some other comrades, near Tsunyi. The army had to move on; it could not take us along. The doctors bandaged us and left us with some peasants, asking them to look after us. They fed us and treated us well, and when the White troops came to that village they hid us. In a few weeks we recovered. Later on the Red Army returned to that district and captured Tsunyi a second time. We rejoined the army, and some of the young men of the villages went with us.'

Another: 'Once we were staying in a village of An Ting [north Shensi] and we were only a dozen men and rifles. The peasants there made bean curd for us, and gave us a sheep. We had a feast and we ate too much and went to sleep, leaving only one sentry on guard. He went to sleep too. But in the middle of the night a peasant boy arrived and woke us up. He had run ten *li* from [some mountain] to warn us that *min-t'uan* were there and intended to surround us. The *min-t'uan* did attack us about an hour later, but we were ready for them and drove them off.'

A bright-eyed lad without a shadow of whisker on his face arose and declared: 'I have only this to say. When the White Army comes to a village in Kansu, nobody helps it, nobody gives it any food, and nobody wants to join. When the Red Army comes, the peasants organize, and form committees to help us, and young men volunteer to join. Our Red Army is the people, and this is what I have to say!'

Every youth there seemed to have a personal experience to relate to prove that 'the peasants like us'. I wrote down seventeen different answers to that question. It proved so popular that another hour had passed before I realized that these warriors had been delayed long past their dinner call. I apologized and prepared to leave, but one 'small devil' attached to the company stood up and said: 'Don't worry about ceremony. We Reds don't care about going without food when we are fighting, and we don't care about missing our food when we can tell a foreign friend about our Red Army.'

Part Nine

WITH THE RED ARMY

(continued)

I

Hsu Hai-tung, the Red Potter

ONE morning I went to P'eng Teh-huai's headquarters and found several members of his staff there, just finishing up a conference. They invited me in and opened a watermelon. As we sat around tables, spitting out seeds on the k'ang, I noticed a young commander I had not seen before.

P'eng Teh-huai saw me looking at him, and he said banteringly, 'That's a famous Red bandit over there. Do you recognize him?' The new arrival promptly grinned, blushed crimson, and in a most disarming way exposed a big cavern where two front teeth should have been. It gave him a childish and impish appearance, and everybody smiled.

'He is the man you have been eager to meet,' supplied P'eng. 'He wants you to visit his army. His name is Hsu Hai-tung.'

Of all the Red military leaders of China, probably none was more 'notorious', and certainly none was more of a mystery than Hsu Hai-tung. Scarcely anything was known of him to the outside world except that he had once worked in a Hupeh pottery and that Chiang Kai-shek had branded him a scourge of civilization. Recently Nanking airplanes had visited the Red lines to drop leaflets containing, among other inducements to deserters (including $100 to every Red soldier who brought his rifle with him to the Kuomintang), the following promise:

'Kill P'eng Teh-huai or Hsu Hai-tung and we will give you $100,000 when you join our army. Kill any other bandit leader and we will reward you accordingly.'

And here, poised shyly over a pair of square boyish shoulders, sat that head which Nanking apparently valued no less than P'eng Teh-huai's.

I acknowledged the pleasure, wondering what it felt like to have a life worth that much to any one of your subordinates, and asked

Hsu whether he was really serious about the invitation to visit his army. He was commander of the Fifteenth Red Army Corps, with headquarters then located about 80 *li* to the north-west, in Yu Wang *hsien*.

'I already have a room arranged for you in the bell tower,' he responded. 'Just let me know when you want to come, and I'll send an escort for you.'

We made it a bargain on the spot.

And so a few days later, carrying a borrowed automatic (a 'confiscation' of my own from a Red officer), I set out for Yu Wang, accompanied by ten Red troopers armed with rifles and Mausers – for in places our road skirted Red positions only a short distance behind the front lines. In contrast with the eternal hills and valleys of Shensi and Kansu, the road we followed – a road that led to the Great Wall and the lonely, beautiful grasslands of Inner Mongolia – crossed high tablelands, striped with long green meadows and dotted with tall bunch grass and softly rounded hills, on which great herds of sheep and goats grazed. Eagles and buzzards sometimes flew overhead. Once a herd of wild gazelles came near us, sniffed the air, and then swooped off with incredible speed and grace around a protecting mountainside.

In five hours we reached the centre of Yu Wang, an ancient Mohammedan city of four or five hundred families, with a magnificent wall of stone and brick. Outside the city was a Mohammedan temple, with its own walls of beautiful glazed brick unscarred. But other buildings showed signs of the siege this city had undergone before it was taken by the Reds. A two-storey building that had been the magistrate's headquarters was partly ruined, and its façade was pitted with bullet holes. I was told that this and other buildings on the outskirts had been destroyed by the defending troops of General Ma Hung-kuei when the Red siege had first begun. The enemy had withdrawn from all extramural buildings, after setting fire to them, to prevent the Reds' occupying them as positions of attack against the city walls.

'When the city fell,' Hsu Hai-tung told me, 'there was only a very minor battle. We surrounded and blockaded Yu Wang for ten days. Inside there was one brigade of Ma Hung-kuei's cavalry and about 1,000 *min-t'uan*. We made no attack at all until the tenth night. It was very dark. We put a ladder on the wall, a company scaled it before the enemy guards discovered it, and then they defended the ladder with a machine gun, while a regiment of our troops mounted the wall.

'There was little fighting. Before dawn we had disarmed all the *min-t'uan* and surrounded the brigade of cavalry. Only one of our men was killed, and only seven wounded. We gave the *min-t'uan* a dollar apiece and sent them back to their farms, and we gave Ma's men two dollars each. Several hundred of them stayed and enlisted with us. The magistrate and the brigade commander escaped over the east wall while their troops were being disarmed.'

I spent five days with the Fifteenth Army Corps, and found every waking hour intensely interesting.* And of it all nothing was better material, for an 'investigator of the soviet regions', as I was labelled in Yu Wang, than the story of Hsu Hai-tung himself. I talked with him every night when his duties were finished. I rode with him to the front lines of the Seventy-third Division, and I went to the Red theatre with him. He told me for the first time the history of the Honan-Anhui-Hupeh Soviet Republic, which had never been fully known. As organizer of the first partisan army of that great Red area, which was second in size only to the Central Soviets of Kiangsi, Hsu Hai-tung knew nearly every detail of its development.

Hsu struck me as the most strongly 'class-conscious' man – in manner, appearance, conversation, and background – of all the Red leaders I met. While the majority of the subordinate officers were from the poor peasantry, many of the higher commanders were from middle-class or middle-peasant families or from the intelligentsia. Hsu was a very obvious exception. He was proud of his proletarian origin, and he often referred to himself, with a grin, as a 'coolie'. One could tell he sincerely believed that the poor of China, the peasants and the workers, were the good people – kind, brave, unselfish, honest – while the rich had a monopoly of all the vices. It was as simple as that for him, I thought: he was fighting to get rid of the vices. The absolutism of faith kept his cocky comments about his own daredeviltry and his army's superi-

*Here Wang Shuo-tao, chief of the political department of the Fifteenth Army Corps, told me something of his personal history. See BN.

ority from sounding like vanity and conceit. When he said, 'One Red is worth five Whites,' it was to him a statement of irrefutable fact.

He was immensely proud of his army – the men as individuals, their skill as soldiers, as horsemen, and as revolutionaries. He was proud of their Lenin clubs and their artistically made posters – which were really very good. And he was proud of his division commanders, two of whom were 'coolies like myself' and one of whom – a Red for six years – was only twenty-one years old.

Hsu valued very highly any act of physical prowess, and it was his regret that eight wounds he had collected in ten years of fighting now slightly handicapped him. He did not smoke or drink, and he still had a slender, straight-limbed body, every inch of which seemed to be hard muscle. He had been wounded in each leg, in each arm, in the chest, a shoulder, and a hip. One bullet had entered his head just below the eye and emerged behind his ear. And yet he still gave the impression of a peasant youth who had but recently stepped out of the rice fields, rolled down his trouser legs, and joined a passing 'free company' of warriors.

I found out also about the missing teeth. They had been lost during a riding accident. Galloping along the road one day, his horse's hoof struck a soldier, and Hsu turned in the saddle to see whether he had been hurt. The horse shied and knocked Hsu into a tree. When he regained consciousness two weeks later, it was to discover that his upper incisors had been left with the tree.

'Aren't you afraid you'll be hurt some day?' I asked him.

'Not much,' he laughed. 'I've been taking beatings since I was a child, and I'm used to it by now.'

Like most other combat Reds, he spoke mainly about battles, but his few references to his childhood seemed to me significant.

Hsu Hai-tung was born in 1900 in Huangpi *hsien* – Yellow Slope county – near Hankow. His family had for generations been potters, and in his grandfather's day had owned land, but since then, through drought, flood, and taxation, had been proletarianized. His father and five brothers had worked in a kiln at Huangpi and made enough to live. They were all illiterate, but ambitious for Hai-tung, a bright child and the youngest son, and they scraped together the money necessary to send him to school.

'My fellow students,' Hsu told me, 'were nearly all the sons of landlords or merchants, as few poor boys ever got to school. I studied at the same desks with them, but many hated me because I seldom had any shoes and my clothes were poor and ragged. I could not avoid fighting with them when they cursed me. If I ran to the teacher for help, I was invariably beaten by him. But if the landlords' sons got the worst of it and went to the teacher, I was also beaten.

'In my fourth year in school, when I was eleven, I got involved in a 'rich-against-poor' quarrel and was driven to a corner by a crowd of 'rich sons'. We were throwing sticks and stones, and one I threw cut the head of a child named Huang, son of a wealthy landlord. This boy went off crying, and in a short time returned with his family. The elder Huang said that I had 'forgotten my birth', and he kicked and beat me. The teacher then gave me a second beating. After that I ran away from school and refused to return. The incident made a deep impression on me. I believed from then on that it was impossible for a poor boy to get justice.'

Hsu became an apprentice in a pottery, where he received no wages during his 'thanking-the-master years'. At sixteen he was a full journeyman, and the highest-paid potter among 300 workers. 'I can turn out a good piece of pottery as fast as anyone in China,' Hsu smilingly boasted, 'so when the revolution is over I'll still be a useful citizen !'

He recalled an incident that did not increase his love for the gentry : 'A travelling theatrical troupe came to our neighbourhood, and the workers went to see it. Wives of the gentry and officials were also there. Naturally the workers were curious to see what these closely guarded wives of the great ones looked like, and they kept staring into the boxes. At this the gentry ordered the *min-t'uan* to drive them out of the theatre, and there was a fight. Later on our factory master had to give a banquet for the offended 'nobility', and shoot off some firecrackers, to compensate for the 'spoiled purity' of those women who had been gazed upon by the people. The master tried to take the money for this banquet from our wages, but we threatened to strike and he changed his mind. This was my first experience of the power of organization as a weapon of defence for the poor.'

When he was twenty-one, angered by a domestic quarrel, Hsu left home. He walked to Hankow, then made his way to Kiangsi, where he worked for a year as a potter, saved his money, and planned to return to Huangpi. But he caught cholera and exhausted his savings while recovering. Ashamed to return empty-handed, he joined the army, where he was promised $10 a month. He received 'only beatings'. Meanwhile the Nationalist Revolution was beginning in the South, and Communists were propagandizing in Hsu's army. Several of them were beheaded. Disgusted with the warlord army, he deserted with one of the officers, fled to Canton, and joined the Fourth Kuomintang Army under Chang Fa-kuei. There he remained until 1927. He had become a platoon commander.

In the spring of 1927 the Nationalist forces were breaking into left-wing and right-wing groups, and this conflict was especially sharp in Chang Fa-kuei's army, which had reached the Yangtze River. Siding with the radicals, Hsu was forced to flee, and secretly he returned to Yellow Slope. By now he had become a Communist, having been much influenced by some student propagandists, and in Huangpi he at once began building up a local branch of the Party.

The Right *coup d'état* occurred in April 1927, and communism was driven underground. But not Hsu Hai-tung. He organized most of the workers in the potteries, and some local peasants. From these he now recruited the first 'workers' and peasants' army' of Hupeh. They numbered in the beginning only seventeen men, and they had one revolver and eight bullets – Hsu's own.

This was the nucleus of what later became the Fourth Front Red Army of 60,000 men, which in 1932 had under its control a sovietized territory the size of Ireland. It had its own post office, credit system, mints, cooperatives, textile factories, and in general a fairly well-organized rural economy. Hsu Hsiang-ch'ien, a Whampoa graduate and former Kuomintang officer, became commander-in-chief of the Fourth Army. His political leader was Chang Kuo-t'ao (a founder of the Communist Party who was later to challenge Mao for control of the Central Committee). Together they set up a Chinese type of soviet government in the border areas of three provinces: Hupeh, Anhui, and Honan. The ancient names of those provinces were O, Yu, and Wan. Combining them, the Reds named their interprovincial regime the Oyuwan Soviet and affiliated it with the All-China Soviet Government headed by Mao Tsetung south of the Yangtze.

Oyuwan withstood several 'surroundings' and expanded its territory until October 1932. By then the Nationalists had succeeded in penetrating far into the richest base area. To avoid encirclement, Chang Kuo-t'ao and Hsu Hsiang-ch'ien withdrew their main forces westward. Hsu Hai-tung was ordered to remain behind, with his Twenty-fifth Army, to regroup scattered partisan units and make a new stand, while the main Nationalist forces pursued the Hsu Hsiang-ch'ien command. Unexpectedly Hsu Hai-tung's guerrillas won important victories and once more the Nationalists were forced out of Oyuwan. In 1933 they returned to the offensive and in 1934, coincident with his Fifth Annihilation Campaign in the South, the Generalissimo strangled the little republic to death. At the end of 1934 Hsu Hai-tung led a band of no more than 2,000 men in a breakthrough to the west, finally uniting with Mao Tsetung's forces in northern Shensi in 1935.

Besides the economic blockade, daily air bombing, and the construction of a network of thousands of small forts around the Oyuwan area, the Nanking generals evidently pursued a policy of systematic removal or annihilation of the civilian population. During the Fifth Campaign the anti-Red forces in Hupeh and Anhui, then numbering about 300,000, were stiffened with officers whom Chiang Kai-shek had spent a year indoctrinating with anti-Red propaganda in his Nanchang and Nanking military academies. The result was civil war with the intensity of religious wars.

2

Class War in China

FOR three days, several hours every afternoon and evening, I had been asking Hsu Hai-tung and his staff questions about their personal histories, about their troops, about the fate of the Oyuwan Soviet Republic, and about their present situation in the North-West. Then, in answer to my question, 'Where is your family now?' Hsu Hai-tung replied matter-of-factly, 'All of my clan have been killed except one brother, who is with the Fourth Front Army.'

'You mean killed in fighting?'

'Oh, no; only three of my brothers were Reds. The rest of the clan were executed by Generals T'ang En-p'o and Hsia Tou-yin. Altogether the Kuomintang officers killed sixty-six members of the Hsu clan.'

'Sixty-six!'

'Yes, twenty-seven of my near relatives were executed and thirty-nine distant relatives – everyone in Huangpi *hsien* named Hsu. Old and young men, women, children, and even babies were killed. The Hsu clan was wiped out, except my wife and three brothers in the Red Army, and myself. Two of my brothers were killed in battle later on.'

'And your wife?'

'I don't know what happened to her. She was captured when the White troops occupied Huangpi in 1931. Afterwards I heard that she had been sold as a concubine to a merchant near Hankow. My brothers who escaped told me about that, and about the other killings. During the Fifth Campaign, thirteen of the Hsu clan escaped from Huangpi and fled to Lihsiang *hsien*, but were all arrested there. The men were beheaded; the women and children were shot.'

Hsu noticed the shocked look on my face and grinned mirthlessly. 'That was nothing unusual,' he said. 'That happened to the clans of many Red officers, though mine had the biggest losses. Chiang Kai-shek had given an order that when my district was captured no one named Hsu should be left alive.'

I wrote many pages of notes of conversations with Hsu and his comrades, notes of dates, places, and detailed accounts of outrages allegedly inflicted on civilians by Nationalist troops in Oyuwan. It would be pointless to repeat the details of the more horrendous crimes reported; like the tragic events in Spain of the same period, they would seem incredible to sceptics who read of them from afar. For the person who has not actually witnessed atrocities, all remains hearsay and suspect; to accept the degradation of any man by man injures our self-esteem. And even if the stories were true, were not the Reds themselves engaged in violence differing only in the choice of class victims? The Kuomintang press, however, had for years been telling only their side of the class-war story. To help fill in the picture for history it should not be unedifying to know what the leaders of this fundamentally 'peasant revolution' (as Mao Tse-tung insisted it was) said of their fellow man and saw themselves as fighting against.

During the Fifth Anti-Red Campaign, as already noted, Nationalist officers gave orders in many areas to exterminate the civilian population. This was held to be militarily necessary because, as the Generalissimo remarked in one of his speeches, where the soviets had been long established 'it was impossible to tell a Red bandit from a good citizen'. The method appears to have been applied with singular savagery in the Oyuwan Republic, chiefly because some of the leading Kuomintang generals in charge of anti-Red operations were natives of that region, sons of landlords who had lost their land to the Reds, and hence had an insatiable desire for revenge. The population in the soviets had decreased by about 600,000 at the end of the Fifth Campaign.

Red tactics in Oyuwan had depended upon mobility over a wide territory, and at the beginning of every annihilation drive their main forces had moved out of the Red districts, to engage the enemy on its own ground. They had no important strategic bases to defend, and readily moved from place to place, to decoy, divert, distract, and otherwise gain manoeuvring advantages. This left the periphery of their 'human base' very much exposed, but in the past

Kuomintang troops had not killed the farmers and townsmen whom they found peacefully pursuing their tasks in soviet areas they occupied.

In the Fifth Campaign, as in Kiangsi, new tactics were adopted. Instead of engaging the Red Army in the open field, the Nanking troops advanced in heavily concentrated units, behind extensive fortifications, bit by bit penetrating into Red territory, systematically either annihilating or transporting the entire population in wide areas inside and outside the Red borders. They sought to make of such districts a desolate, uninhabited wasteland, incapable of supporting the Red troops if they should later recapture it.

Thousands of children were taken prisoner and driven to Hankow and other cities, where they were sold into 'apprenticeships'. Thousands of young girls and women were transported and sold into the factories as slave girls and as prostitutes. In the cities they were palmed off as 'famine refugees', or 'orphans of people killed by the Reds'. I remembered that hundreds of them reportedly reached the big industrial centres in 1934. A considerable trade grew up, with middlemen buying the boys and women from Kuomintang officers. It became a very profitable business for a while, but threatened to corrupt the ranks of the army. Missionaries began talking about it, and Chiang Kai-shek was obliged to issue a stern order forbidding this 'bribetaking' and ordering strict punishment for officers engaged in the traffic.

'By December 1933,' said Hsu Hai-tung, 'about half of Oyuwan had become a vast wasteland. Over a once rich country there were very few houses left standing, cattle had all been driven away, the fields were unkept, and there were piles of bodies in nearly every village that had been occupied by the White troops. Four counties in Hupeh, five in Anhui, and three in Honan were almost completely ruined. In an area some 400 *li* from east to west and about 300 *li* from north to south the whole population was being killed or removed.

'During the year's fighting we recaptured some of these districts from the White troops, but when we returned we found fertile lands had become semideserts. Only a few old men and women remained, and they would tell tales that horrified us. We could not believe such crimes had been committed by Chinese against Chinese.

'In November 1933, we retreated from T'ien Tai Shan and Lao Chun Shan, soviet districts where there were then about 60,000 people. When we returned, two months later, we found that these peasants had been driven from their land, their houses had been burned or destroyed by bombing, and there were not more than 300 old men and a few sickly children in all that region. From them we learned what had happened.

'As soon as the White troops arrived the officers had begun dividing the women and girls. Those with bobbed hair or natural feet had been shot as Communists. Higher officers had looked over the others and picked out pretty ones for their own, and then the lower officers had been given their choice. The rest had been turned over to the soldiers to use as prostitutes. They had been told that these women were 'bandit wives', and therefore they could do what they liked with them.

'Many of the young men in those districts had joined the Red Army, but many of those who remained behind, and even some of the old men, tried to kill the White officers for these crimes. Those who protested were all shot as Communists. The survivors told us that many fights had occurred among the Whites, who had quarrelled among themselves about the distribution of women. After they had been despoiled, these women and girls were sent to the towns and cities, where they were sold, only the officers keeping a few pretty ones for concubines.'

'Do you mean to say these were the troops of the National Government?' I asked.

'Yes, they were the Thirteenth Army Corps of General T'ang En-p'o, and the Third Army Corps of General Wang Chun. Generals Hsia Tou-yin, Liang Kuan-yin, and Sung T'ien-tsai were also responsible.'

Hsu told of another district, Huangan *hsien*, in Hupeh, which the Reds recovered from General Wang Chun in July 1933: 'In the town of Tsu Yun Chai, where there was a once a street of flourishing soviet cooperatives and a happy people, everything was in ruins and only a few old men were alive. They led us out to a valley and showed us the scattered bodies of seventeen young women lying half-naked in the sun. They had all been raped and killed. The White troops had evidently been in a great hurry; they had taken the time to pull off only one leg of a girl's trousers. That day we called a meeting, the army held a memorial service there, and we all wept.

'Not long afterwards, in Ma Cheng, we came to one of our former athletic fields. There in a shallow grave we found the bodies of twelve comrades who had been killed. Their skin had been stripped from them, their eyes gouged out, and their ears and noses cut off. We all broke into tears of rage at this barbaric sight.

'In the same month, also in Huangan, our Twenty-fifth Red Army reached Ao Kung Chai. This had once been a lively place, but it was now deserted. We walked outside the town and saw a peasant's hut with smoke coming from it, on a hillside, and some of us climbed up to it, but the only occupant was an old man who had apparently gone insane. We walked down into the valley again until we came upon a long pile of dead men and women. There were more than 400 bodies lying there, and they had evidently been killed only a short time before. In some places the blood was several inches deep. Some women were lying with their children still clutched to them. Many bodies were lying one on top of another.

'Suddenly I noticed one of the bodies move, and, going over to it, found that it was a man still alive. We found several more alive after that, altogether more than ten. We carried them back with us and treated their wounds, and they told us what had happened. These people had fled from the town to hide in this valley, and had encamped in the open. Afterwards the White officers had led their troops to the spot, ordered them to put up their machine guns on the mountainsides, and had then opened fire on the people below. They had kept firing for several hours until they thought everybody was dead. Then they had marched away again without even coming down to look at them.'

Hsu said that the next day he led his whole army out to that valley and showed them the dead, among whom some of the soldiers recognized peasants they had known, men and women who must have given them shelter at one time, or sold them melons, or traded at the co-operatives. They were deeply moved. Hsu said that this experience steeled his troops with a stubborn morale and a determination to die fighting, and that throughout the entire twelve months of the last great annihilation drive not a single man had deserted from the Twenty-fifth Army.

'Towards the end of the Fifth Campaign,' he continued, 'nearly every house had dead in it. We used to enter a village that seemed empty until we looked into the ruined houses. Then we would find corpses in the doorways, on the floor, or on the *k'ang*, or hidden away somewhere. Even the dogs had fled from many villages. In those days we did not need spies to watch the enemy's movements. We could follow them quite easily by the skies filled with smoke from burning towns and hamlets.'

This was a very small part of what I heard from Hsu Hai-tung and others who fought through the terrible year, and finally trekked westward, not their army but its human 'base' destroyed, its hills and valleys stained with the blood of its youth, the living heart of it torn out. Later on I talked to many warriors from Oyuwan, and they told tales more pitiful still. They did not like to talk of what they had seen; they did so only under questioning, and it was clear their experiences had permanently marked the matrix of their minds with a class hatred ineradicable for life.

Again one asked whether that meant that the Reds were innocent of atrocity and class revenge themselves. I thought not. It was true that during my four months with them, as far as I could learn from unrestricted but limited inquiry, they had executed but two civilians. It was also true that I did not see a single village or town burned by them, or hear, from the many farmers I questioned, that the Reds were addicted to arson. But my personal experience started and ended with the few months spent with them in the North-West: what 'killing and burning' might have been done elsewhere I could not confirm or deny.

One of the two ill-fated 'counter-revolutionaries' mentioned above was not killed by the Reds, but by some Ninghsia Moslems with a strong distaste for tax collectors. Further on it will be told in what manner he met his demise, but first let us see how these Moslems had been ruled.

3

Four Great Horses

ONE might say that Chinghai, Ninghsia, and northern Kansu were the prototype of that fantasia of Swift's, the land of the Houyhnhnms, for they were ruled as the satrapy of Four Great Horses whose fame was widespread in China. Over the areas mentioned power was divided (before the Reds began edging the Houyhnhnms out of considerable portions of their domain) by a family of Mohammedan generals named Ma – the Messrs Ma Hung-kuei, Ma Hung-ping, Ma Pu-fang, and Ma Pu-ch'ing. And this particular *Ma* means *horse*.*

Ma Hung-kuei was governor of Ninghsia, and his cousin, Ma Hung-ping, former governor of the same province, was now ruler of a shifting fiefdom in northern Kansu. They were distantly related to Ma Pu-fang, many-wived son of the famous Mohammedan leader Ma Keh-chin. Ma Pu-fang inherited his father's toga and in 1937 became the Nanking-appointed Pacification Commissioner of that province, while his brother, Ma Pu-ch'ing, helped out in Chinghai and in addition ruled the great Kansu panhandle which in the west separated Chinghai from Ninghsia. For a decade this distant country had been run like a medieval sultanate by the Ma family, with some assistance from an Allah of their own.

Two of the Great Horses claimed to be nobles, descendants of a Mohammedan aristocracy which sometimes played a decisive role in the history of China's North-West. The brothers Ma, like many Moslems in China, had Turkish blood in them. As early as the sixth century a race which we now know as the Turks had become powerful enough on China's north-west frontier to make important demands on the monarchs of the plains. In a couple

*It is an interesting character, written 馬, and deriving from an ancient form 馬, in which one clearly sees its evolution from the original ideograph.

of centuries they had built up an empire extending from eastern Siberia across part of Mongolia and into Central Asia. Gradually they filtered southward, and by the seventh century their Great Khan was received almost as an equal at the court of Yang Ti, last Emperor of the Sui Dynasty. It was this same Turkish Khan who helped the half-Turkish General Li Yuan overthrow the Emperor Yang Ti and establish the celebrated T'ang Dynasty, which for three centuries reigned over Eastern Asia from Ch'ang An (now Sianfu) – then perhaps the most cultured capital on earth.

Mohammedan mosques had already been built in Canton by seafaring Arab traders before the middle of the seventh century. With the advent of the tolerant T'ang power the religion rapidly penetrated by land routes through the Turks of the North-West. Mullahs, traders, embassies, and warriors brought it from Persia, Arabia, and Turkestan, and the T'ang emperors formed close ties with the caliphates to the west. Especially in the ninth century, when vast hordes of Ouigour Turks (whose great leader Seljuk had not yet been born) were summoned to the aid of the T'ang court to suppress rebellion, Islamism entrenched itself in China. Following their success, many of the Ouigours were rewarded with titles and great estates and settled in the North-West and in Szechuan and Yunnan.

Over a period of centuries the Mohammedans stoutly resisted Chinese absorption, but gradually lost their Turkish culture, adopted much that was Chinese, and became more or less submissive to Chinese law. Yet in the nineteenth century they were still powerful enough to make two great bids for power: one when Tu Wei-hsiu for a time set up a kingdom in Yunnan and proclaimed himself Sultan Suleiman; and the last, in 1864, when Mohammedans seized control of all the North-West and even invaded Hupeh. The latter rebellion was put down after a campaign lasting eleven years. At that time of waning Manchu power the able Chinese General Tso Tsung-t'ang astounded the world by recapturing Hupeh, Shensi, Kansu, and eastern Tibet, finally leading his victorious army across the desert roads of Turkestan, where he re-established Chinese power on that far frontier in Central Asia.

Since then no single leader had been able to unite the Moslems of China in a successful struggle for independence, but there had been sporadic uprisings against Chinese rule, with savage and bloody massacres on both sides. The most serious recent rebellion occurred in 1928, when General Feng Yu-hsiang was warlord of the North-West. It was under Feng that the Wu-Ma, or 'Five Ma',* combination acquired much of its influence and secured the nucleus of its present wealth and power.

Although theoretically the Chinese considered the Hui or Moslem people one of the five great races of China,† most Chinese seemed to deny Moslem racial separateness, claiming that they had been Sinicized. In practice, the Kuomintang decidedly followed a policy of absorption, even more direct (though perhaps less successful) than that pursued towards the Mongols. The Chinese official attitude towards the Mohammedans seemed to be that they were a 'religious minority' but not a 'national minority'. However, it was quite evident to anyone who saw them in their own domain in the North-West that their claims to racial unity and the right to nationhood as a people were not without substantial basis in fact and history.

The Mohammedans of China were said to number about 20,000,000, and of these at least half were concentrated in the provinces of Shensi, Kansu, Ninghsia, Szechuan, Chinghai, and Sinkiang. In many districts – particularly in Kansu and Chinghai – they were a majority, and in some large areas outnumbered Chinese as much as ten to one. Generally their religious orthodoxy seemed to vary according to their strength of numbers in a given spot, but in the dominantly Mohammedan region of northern Kansu and southern Ninghsia the atmosphere was distinctly that of an Islamic country.

It could be said that the Mohammedans were the largest community left in China among whom religious leaders were the real arbiters of temporal as well as spiritual life, with religion a decid-

---

* Ma Chung-ying was the fifth Ma, but had now been eliminated from an active role by tribal politics and international intrigue. Sven Hedin gives an interesting account of him in *The Flight of 'Big Horse'* (New York, 1936).

† These are the Han (Chinese), Man (Manchu), Meng (Mongol), Hui (Mohammedan), and Tsang (Tibetan).

ing factor in their culture, politics, and economy. Mohammedan society revolved round the *men-huang* and the *ahun* (ameer and mullah), and their knowledge of the Koran and of Turkish or Arabic (scant as it usually was) provided the sources of authority. Mohammedans in the North-West prayed daily in the hundreds of well-kept mosques, observed Mohammedan feast days, fast days, and marriage and funeral ceremonies, rejected pork, and were offended by the presence of pigs and dogs. The pilgrimage to Mecca was an ambition frequently realized by rich men and *ahuns*, who thereby strengthened their political and economic power. To many of them pan-Islamism rather than pan-Hanism was an ideal.

Chinese cultural influence was nevertheless very marked. Moslems dressed like Chinese (except for round white caps or ceremonial fezzes worn by the men and white turbans by the women) and all spoke Chinese as the language of daily life (although many knew a few words from the Koran). While markedly Turkish features were common among them, the physiognomy of the majority was hardly distinguishable from that of the Chinese, with whom they had for centuries intermarried. Because of their law that any Chinese who married a Mohammedan must not only adopt the faith but also be adopted into a Mohammedan family, cutting away from his or her own kinsmen, the children of mixed marriages tended to grow up regarding themselves as a species different from their Chinese relatives.

The struggle of three sects among the Chinese Moslems somewhat weakened their unity, and created a convenient alignment for the Chinese Communists to work among them. The three sects were simply the Old, New, and Modern * schools. Old and New had formed a kind of 'united front' of their own to oppose the heretical Modern school. The latter nominally advocated giving up many of the ceremonies and customs of Mohammedanism and embracing 'science', but its real objectives were evidently to destroy the temporal power of the mullahs, which the Four Mas found inconvenient. Since it was supported by the Kuomintang, many Mohammedans believed the Modern school aimed at a so-called 'pan-Hanism' – absorption of the national minorities by the Chinese. In the North-West the Four Mas were leaders of the

* *Hsin-hsin chiao*, literally, 'new-new faith'.

Modern school. Around them they grouped their own satellites, bureaucrats, and wealthy landowners and cattle barons upon whom their regime depended. And yet the Great Horses were not precisely the men one would expect to lead a reform movement in religion.

Take Ma Hung-kuei, probably the richest and strongest of the quartet. He had numerous wives, was said to own about 60 per cent of the property of Ninghsia city, and had made a fortune in millions from opium, salt, furs, taxes, and his own paper currency. Still, he proved himself modern enough in one sense when he chose his famous 'picture bride'. Importing a secretary from Shanghai, he had him gather photographs of eligible educated beauties and made his choice. The price was fixed at $50,000. Old Ma hired an airplane, flew out of the northern dust clouds to Soochow, where he swooped up the latest addition to his harem – a graduate of Soochow Christian University – and then swept back again to Ninghsia like an Aladdin on his carpet, amid a blaze of publicity. That news was well reported by the Kuomintang press at the time, as were some of the 'death and taxes' data mentioned below.

A government bulletin published in Ninghsia listed the following taxes collected in that province by General Ma : sales, domestic animals, camels, salt carrying, salt consumption, opium lamps, sheep, merchants, porters, pigeons, land, middlemen, food, special food, additional land, wood, coal, skins, slaughter, boats, irrigation, millstones, houses, wood, milling, scales, ceremonies, tobacco, wine, stamp, marriage, and vegetables.* While this did not exhaust the inventory of petty taxes collected, it was enough to suggest that people had relatively little to fear from the Reds.

Ma Hung-kuei's method of salt distribution was unique. Salt was not only a monopoly, every person was required to buy half a pound per month, whether he could use it or not. He was not allowed to resell; private trade in salt was punishable by whipping or (according to Mohammedan Reds) even death. Other measures against which the inhabitants protested were the collection of a 30-per-cent tax on the sale of a sheep, cow, or mule, a 25-cent tax on the ownership of a sheep, a dollar tax for the slaughter of a pig, and a 40-cent tax on the sale of a bushel of wheat.

*Ninghsia Kung Pao (Ninghsia city, December 1934).

Excessive taxation and indebtedness had forced many farmers to sell all their cattle and abandon their lands. Great areas had been bought up by officials, tax collectors, and lenders at very cheap rates, but much of it remained wasteland because no tenants could be found to work under the tax burden and rents imposed. The concentration of land, cattle, and capital was accelerating and there was a big increase in hired farm labourers. In one district investigated it was found that over 70 per cent of the farmers were in debt, and about 60 per cent were living on food bought on credit.* In the same district 5 per cent of the people reportedly owned from 100 to 200 *mou* of land, twenty to fifty camels, twenty to forty cows, five to ten horses, five to ten carts, and had from $1,000 to $2,000 in trading capital, while at the same time about 60 per cent of the population had less than 15 *mou* of land, no livestock other than one or two donkeys, and an average indebtedness of $35 and 366 pounds of grain – much more than the average value of their land.

According to the Communist press, Ma Hung-kuei was suspected of intriguing for Japanese support against the Reds. A Japanese military mission had been established in Ninghsia city, and General Ma had given them permission to build an airfield north of the city, in the Alashan Mongol territory.† Some of the Moslems and Mongols feared an actual armed Japanese invasion.

Such was the picture, as the Reds saw it, which encouraged them to believe that they could 'stir up a great wind' that could bring the Ma brothers' empire toppling in ruins. Ma's troops might have had little interest in fighting, but it still remained for the Communists to overcome the Moslems' aversion to cooperating with Chinese, and to offer them a suitable programme. This the Reds were trying hard to do, for the strategic significance of the Mohammedan areas was manifest. They occupied a wide belt in the North-West which dominated the roads to Sinkiang and Outer

*Liu Hsiao, 'A Survey of Yu Wang Hsien', *Tang-ti Kung-Tso* (Pao An), 3 August 1936. This was a Communist and certainly not disinterested source, but the picture in general was supported by studies included in the Stampar report for the League of Nations, to which earlier reference was made.

†The Japanese were later forced to abandon both their mission and their airfield. In 1937 the Mas pledged their loyalty to the Central Government.

Mongolia – and direct contact with Soviet Russia. As the Communists themselves saw it:

There are more than ten million Mohammedans in the North-West occupying an extremely important position. Our present mission and responsibility is to defend the North-West and to create an anti-Japanese base in these five provinces, so that we can more powerfully lead the anti-Japanese movement of the whole country and work for an immediate war against Japan. At the same time, in the development of our situation we can get into connection with the Soviet Union and Outer Mongolia. However, it would be impossible to carry out our mission if we failed to win over the Mohammedans to our sphere and to the anti-Japanese front.*

Communist work among the Mohammedans had begun several years before in the North-West. Early in 1936, when the Red Army moved across Ninghsia and Kansu towards the Yellow River, vanguards of young Moslems were already propagandizing among the Ninghsia troops, urging the overthrow of the 'Kuomintang running-dog' and 'traitor to Mohammedanism', Ma Hung-kuei – and some had lost their heads for it. These were the main promises the Reds made to them:

To abolish all surtaxes.

To help form an autonomous Mohammedan government.

To prohibit conscription.

To cancel old debts and loans.

To protect Mohammedan culture.

To guarantee religious freedom of all sects.

To help create and arm an anti-Japanese Mohammedan army.

To help unite the Mohammedans of China, Outer Mongolia, Sinkiang, and Soviet Russia.

Here, presumably, was something to appeal to nearly every Moslem. Even some of the *ahuns* reportedly saw in it an opportunity to get rid of Ma Hung-kuei (punishing him for burning the mosques of the Old and New schools), and also a chance to realize an old aspiration – to re-establish direct contact with Turkey

*Company Discussion Materials: 'The Mohammedan Problem', p. 2, First Army Corps, Pol. Dept, 2 June 1936.

through Central Asia. By May, the Communists were claiming that they had achieved what sceptics had said was impossible. They boasted that they had created the nucleus of a Chinese Moslem Red Army.

Moslem and Marxist

ONE morning I went with an English-speaking member of Hsu Hai-tung's staff to visit the Moslem training regiment attached to the Fifteenth Army Corps. It was quartered in the compound of a Moslem merchant and official – a thick-walled edifice with Moorish windows looking down on a cobbled street through which filed donkeys, horses, camels, and men.

Inside, the place was cool and neatly kept. Every room had in the centre of its brick floor a place for a cistern, connected to a subterranean drain, to be used for bathing. Properly orthodox Moslems showered themselves five times daily, but although these soldiers were still loyal to their faith and obviously made use of the cistern occasionally, I gathered that they did not believe in carrying a good thing to extremes. Still, they easily had the cleanest habits of any soldiers I had seen in China, and carefully refrained from the national gesture of spitting on the floor.

The Reds had organized two training regiments of Mohammedans at the front, both recruited largely from former troops of Ma Hung-kuei and Ma Hung-ping. They were taller and more strongly built than the Chinese, heavier of beard, and darker-skinned, with large black almond-shaped eyes and strong, sharp Caucasian features. They all carried the big sword of the North-West, and gave a skilful demonstration of various strokes by which you can remove your enemy's head at one swift blow.

Cartoons, posters, maps, and slogans covered the walls of their barracks. 'Down with Ma Hung-kuei!' 'Abolish Ma Hung-kuei's Kuomintang Government!' 'Oppose Japan's building of airfields, map making, and invasion of Ninghsia!' 'Realize the Independent Government of the Mohammedan people!' 'Build your own anti-Japanese Mohammedan Red Army!'

From this it may be gathered that there was some dissatisfaction with General Ma Hung-kuei among his soldiers, and this seemed to be shared by the Ninghsia peasants. I stopped on the road one morning to buy a melon from a Moslem farmer who had a whole hillside covered with them. He was an engaging old rustic with a jolly face, a humorous manner, and a truly beautiful daughter – so rare an apparition in those parts that I stayed and bought three melons. I asked him if Ma Hung-kuei's officials were really as bad as the Reds claimed. He threw up his hands comically in indignation, spluttering watermelon seeds between his gums. 'Ai-ya! Ai-ya! Ai-ya!' he cried. 'Ma Hung-kuei, Ma Hung-kuei! Taxing us to death, stealing our sons, burning and killing! *Ma-ti Ma Hung-kuei!*' By which last expression he meant you could defile Ma's mother and it would be too good for him. Everyone in the court-yard laughed. On the other hand, the occasion was hardly appropriate for the old gentleman to offer testimony to Allah in praise of Ma Hung-kuei – if he had been so inclined.

The Moslem soldiers with the Reds ostensibly had been won over by subversive propaganda conducted among Ma's troops, and by political lectures when they reached the Red camp. I asked one commander why he had joined.

'To fight Ma Hung-kuei,' he said. 'Life is too bitter for us *Hui-min* under Ma Hung-kuei. No family is secure. If a family has two sons, one of them must join his army. If it has three sons, two must join. There is no escape – unless you are rich and can pay the tax for a substitute. What poor man can afford it? Not only that, but every man must bring his own clothes, and his family must pay for his food, fires, and lighting. This costs several tens of dollars a year.'

Although these Red Moslem regiments had been organized less than half a year, they had already achieved considerable 'class consciousness', it seemed. They had read, or heard read, the *Communist Manifesto*, brief lessons from *Class Struggle*, and daily political lectures, à la Marxism, on the immediate problems of the Mohammedan people. This instruction was given to them, not by Chinese, but by Mohammedan members of the Communist Party – men who had been through the Reds' Party school. I was told that more than 90 per cent of Ma Hung-kuei's troops were illiterate, and that most of the Moslem recruits to the Red Army had been unable to read at all when they joined. Now they were said to know a few hundred characters each, and to be able to study the simple lessons given to them. Out of their two training regiments the Communists hoped to develop cadres for a big Moslem Red Army, to defend the autonomous Moslem republic they dreamed of seeing established in the North-West. Already nearly 25 per cent of these Moslems had joined the Communist Party.[1]

With the autonomy slogan the Moslem population could be expected to agree; that had been their demand for many years. Whether the majority of them believed the Reds were sincere in their promises was quite another matter. I doubted it. Years of maltreatment by the Chinese militarists, and racial hatreds between Han and Hui (Chinese and Moslem), had left among them a deep and justified distrust of the motives of all Chinese, and it was unbelievable that the Communists had been able to break down this Moslem scepticism in so short a time.

Such Moslems as cooperated with the Reds probably had reasons of their own. If Chinese offered to help them drive out the Kuomintang, help them create and equip an army of their own, help them get self-government, and help them despoil the rich (they no doubt said to themselves), they were prepared to take the opportunity – and later on turn that army to uses of their own, if the Reds failed to keep their bargain. But it seemed, from the friendliness of the farmers, and their readiness to organize under the Reds, that their programme had some attraction, and that their careful policy of respecting Moslem institutions had made an impression.

Among the soldiers themselves it appeared that some of the historic racial animosity was being overcome, or gradually metamorphosed into class antagonism. Thus when I asked some Moslem soldiers whether they thought the Hui and Han peoples could cooperate under a soviet form of government, one replied:

'The Chinese and the Moslems are brothers; we Moslems also have Chinese blood in us; we all belong to Ta Chung Kuo [China], and therefore why should we fight each other? Our common enemies are the landlords, the capitalists, the moneylenders, our oppressive rulers, and the Japanese. Our common aim is revolution.'

'But what if the revolution interferes with your religion?'

'There is no interference. The Red Army does not interfere with Mohammedan worship.'

'Well, I mean something like this. Some of the *ahuns* are wealthy landlords and moneylenders, are they not? What if they oppose the Red Army? How would you treat them?'

'We would persuade them to join the revolution. But most *ahuns* are not rich men. They sympathize with us. One of our company commanders was an *ahun*.'

'Still, suppose some *ahuns* can't be persuaded, but join with the Kuomintang to oppose you?'

'We would punish them. They would be bad *ahuns*, and the people would demand their punishment.'

Meanwhile intensive instruction was going on throughout the First and Fifteenth Army corps to educate the soldiers to an understanding of the Communist policy towards Moslems and their effort to create a 'Hui-Han United Front'. I attended several political sessions in which soldiers were discussing the 'Mohammedan revolution', and they were quite interesting. At one session there were long debates, especially about the land question. Some argued that the Red Army should confiscate the land of great Mohammedan landlords; others opposed it. The political commissar then gave a concise statement of the Party's position, explaining why it was necessary for the Mohammedans themselves to carry on their own land revolution, led by a strong revolutionary organization of their own, with a base in the Moslem masses.

Another company reviewed a brief history of relationships between the Moslems and Chinese, and another discussed the necessity for strict observance of the rules of conduct which had been issued to all soldiers stationed in Mohammedan districts. These latter decreed that Red soldiers must not: enter the home of a Moslem without his consent; molest a mosque or a priest in any way; say 'pig' or 'dog' before Moslems, or ask them why they don't eat pork; or call the Moslems 'small faith' and the Chinese 'big faith'.

Besides these efforts to unite the whole army intelligently behind the Moslem policy of the Reds, there was incessant work with the peasantry. The two Moslem training regiments led in this propaganda, but companies in the Red Army also sent their propaganda corps from house to house, explaining Communist policies and urging the farmers to organize; army dramatic clubs toured the villages, giving Mohammedan plays, based on local situations and incidents of history, and designed to 'agitate' the population; leaflets, newspapers, and posters were distributed, written in Chinese and Arabic; and mass meetings were frequently called to form revolutionary committees and village soviets. The peasant, Chinese or Moslem, had a hard squeeze of it to avoid indoctrination to at least some degree. By July several dozen Mohammedan communities in Ninghsia had elected village soviets, and were sending delegates to Yu Wang Pao to confer with Moslem Communists there.

Four months later the Fourth Front Red Army was to cross the Yellow River, move over 200 miles further west, and reach Hsuchow, in Ma Pu-fang's territory, astride the main road to Sinkiang. Early in September enough progress had been made in Ninghsia to convene a meeting of over 300 Moslem delegates from soviet committees elected by the villages then under the Red Army. A number of *ahuns*, teachers, merchants, and two or three small landlords were among them, but mostly they were poor farmers, members of the wealthier class having fled with the arrival of the 'Han bandits'. The meeting of delegates elected a chairman and a provisional Moslem Soviet Government Committee. They passed resolutions to cooperate with the Red Army and accept its offer to help create an anti-Japanese Mohammedan army, and to begin at once the organization of a Chinese-Moslem unity league, a poor people's league, and a mass anti-Japanese society.

The last item of business attended to by this historic little convention – and I suspect the most important to the peasants there – was the disposal of a Kuomintang tax collector. This man had evidently earned himself considerable enmity before the Reds arrived, and after that he had fled into the neighbouring hill villages, to a place called Changchia Cha, and there continued to collect his taxes. It was alleged that he had doubled his levies – and had announced that this was due to the regulations of the new Red government which he claimed to represent! But the Mohammedan farmers learned that the Reds appointed no tax collectors, and half a dozen of them captured this miscreant and brought him into Yu Wang Pao for a mass trial. My personal reaction to the story was that any man who had sufficient nerve to act as an imposter in such a role at such a time had talents that should be preserved. The Moslems thought otherwise. There was no dissenting vote when the delegates took the decision to execute him.

As far as I could learn, he was the only civilian shot during the two weeks I spent in Yu Wang Pao.

Part Ten

WAR AND PEACE

I

More About Horses

ON 29 August I rode out to Hung Ch'eng Shui (Red City Waters), a pretty little town in Weichow county, famous for its beautiful fruit gardens of pears, apples, and grapes, irrigated by crystal springs that bubbled through the canals. Here part of the Seventy-third Division was encamped. Not far away was a fortified pass, and a temporary line with no trenches but with a series of small mole-like machine-gun nests and round hilltop forts – low-walled earth-work defences – from which the Reds faced an enemy that had generally withdrawn from five to ten miles to the walled towns. There had been no movement on this front for several weeks, while the Reds rested and 'consolidated' the new territory.

Back in Yu Wang again, I found the troops celebrating with a melon feast the radio news from south Kansu that a whole division of Ma Hung-kuei's Chinese troops had turned over to Chu Teh's Fourth Front Red Army. Li Tsung-yi, the commander of this Kuomintang division, had been sent to impede Chu Teh's march to the North. His younger officers, among whom were secret Communists, led an uprising and took some 3,000 troops, including a battalion of cavalry, to join the Reds near Lung Hsi. It was a big blow to the Generalissimo's defences in the South, and hastened the northward advance of the two southern armies.

Two days later two of the three divisions of Hsu Hai-tung's Fifteenth Army Corps were prepared to move again, one column towards the South, to break open a path for Chu Teh, and the other to the West, and the valley of the Yellow River. Bugles began sounding at about three in the morning, and by six o'clock the troops were already marching. I was myself returning to Yu Wang Pao that morning with two Red officers who were reporting to P'eng Teh-huai, and I left the city by the south gate with Hsu Hai-tung and his staff, marching towards the end of the long column of troops and animals that wound like a grey dragon across the interminable grasslands, as far as you could see.

The big army left the city quietly, except for the bark of bugles that never ceased, and gave an impression of efficient command. Plans for the march had been completed days earlier, I was told; every detail of the road had been examined, the enemy's concentrations were all carefully charted on maps prepared by the Reds themselves, and guards had stopped all travellers from moving across the lines (which the Reds permitted, to encourage trade, except during battles or troop movements), and now they went ahead unknown to the Kuomintang troops, as later surprise captures of enemy outposts were to prove.

With this army I saw no camp followers except thirty or more wild Kansu greyhounds who ran in a closed pack, ranging back and forth across the plain in chase of an occasional distant gazelle or a prairie hog. They barked joyously and scrapped in excellent humour and evidently liked going to war. Many of the soldiers carried their pets along with them. Several had little monks on leashes of string; one had a slate-coloured pet pigeon perched on his shoulder; some had little white mice; and some had rabbits. Was this an army? From the youth of the warriors, and the bursts of song that rang down the long line, it seemed more like a prep school on a holiday excursion.

A few *li* beyond the city an order was suddenly given for a practice air-raid defence. Squads of soldiers left the road and melted into the tall grass, donning their big wide camouflage hats made of grass, and their grass shoulder capes. Machine guns (they had no anti-aircraft) were pitched at angles on grassy knolls beside the road in hopeful anticipation of a low-flying target. In a few moments that whole dragon had simply been swallowed up in the landscape, and you could not distinguish men from the numerous clumps of bunch grass. Only the mules, camels, and horses remained visible on the road, and aviators might have taken these for ordinary commercial caravans. The cavalry (which was then in the vanguard, out of sight) had to take it in the neck, however, their only possible precautionary measure being to seek cover if it was available, otherwise merely to scatter as widely as possible, but always remaining mounted. Unmounted during an air raid, these Mongolian ponies were impossible to manage, and a whole regiment could be thrown into complete disorder. The first command to a cavalry unit at the drone of airplanes was '*Shang ma!*' ('Mount horse!')

The manoeuvre having been pronounced satisfactory, we marched on.

Li Chiang-lin had been right. The Reds' good horses were all at the front. Their cavalry division was the pride of the army, and every man aspired to promotion to it. They were physically the pick of the army, mounted on about 3,000 beautiful Ninghsia ponies, fine fleet animals taller and stronger than the Mongolian ponies of North China, with sleek flanks and well-filled buttocks. Most of them had been captured from Ma Kung-kuei and Ma Hung-ping, but three whole battalions of horses had been taken in a battle nearly a year before with General Ho Chu-kuo, commander of Nanking's First Cavalry Army, including one battalion of all-white animals and one of all-black. They were the nucleus of the First Red Cavalry.

I rode with the Red cavalry several days in Kansu – or more precisely, I walked with it. They lent me a fine horse with a captured Western saddle, but at the end of each day I felt that I had been giving the horse a good time instead of the contrary. This was because our battalion commander was so anxious not to tire his four-legged charges that we two-legged ones had to lead horse three or four *li* for every one we rode. I concluded that anyone who qualified for this man's cavalry had to be a nurse, not a *mafoo*, and an even better walker than rider. I paid them due respect for kindness to animals – no common phenomenon in China – but I was glad to disengage myself and get back to freelance movement of my own, in which occasionally I could actually ride a horse.

I had been grumbling mildly about this to Hsu Hai-tung, and I suspect he decided to play a joke on me. To return to Yu Wang Pao he lent me a splendid Ninghsia pony, strong as a bull, that gave me one of the wildest rides of my life. My road parted with the Fifteenth Army Corps near a big fort in the grassland. There I bade Hsu and his staff good-bye. Shortly afterwards I got on my borrowed steed, and from then on it was touch and go to see which of us reached Yu Wang Pao alive.

The trouble with that ride was the wooden Chinese saddle, so narrow that I could not sit in the seat, but had to ride on my inner thighs the whole distance, while the short, heavy iron stirrups cramped my legs.

The road lay level across the plain for over fifty li. In that whole distance we got down to a walk just once. We raced at a steady gallop for the last five miles, and at the finish swept up the main street of Yu Wang Pao with my companions trailing far behind. Before P'eng's headquarters I slithered off and examined my mount, expecting him to topple over in a faint. He was puffing very slightly and had a few beads of sweat on him, but was otherwise quite unruffled, the beast.

2

'Little Red Devils'

ONE morning I climbed the wide, thick, yellow wall of Yu Wang Pao, from the top of which you could look down thirty feet and see at a glance a score of different and somehow incongruously prosaic and intimate tasks being pursued below. It was as if you had prized off the lid of the city. A big section of the wall was being demolished. Walls were impediments to guerrilla warriors like the Reds, who endeavoured to come to battle with an enemy in open country and, if they failed there, not to waste men in an exhausting defence of a walled city, where they could be endangered by blockade or annihilation, but to withdraw and let the enemy put himself in that position. The broken wall simplified their work if and when they were strong enough to attempt a reoccupation of the city.

Halfway around the crenellated battlement I came upon a squad of buglers – at rest for once, I was glad to observe, for their plangent calls had been ringing incessantly for days. They were all Young Vanguards, mere children, and I assumed a somewhat fatherly air towards one to whom I stopped and talked. He wore tennis shoes, grey shorts, and a faded grey cap with a dim red star on it. But there was nothing faded about the bugler under the cap: he was rosy-faced and had bright shining eyes. How homesick he must be, I thought. I was soon disillusioned. He was no mama's boy, but already a veteran Red. He told me that he was fifteen, and had joined the Reds in the South four years ago.

'Four years!' I exclaimed incredulously. 'Then you must have been only eleven when you became a Red? And you made the Long March?'

'Right,' he responded with comical swagger. 'I have been a *hung-chun* for four years.'

'Why did you join?' I asked.

'My family lived near Changchow, in Fukien. I used to cut

wood in the mountains, and in the winter I went there to collect bark. I often heard the villagers talk about the Red Army. They said it helped the poor people, and I liked that. Our house was very poor. We were six people, my parents and three brothers, older than I. We owned no land. Rent ate more than half our crop, so we never had enough. In the winter we cooked bark for soup and saved our grain for planting in the spring. I was always hungry.

'One year the Reds came very close to Changchow. I climbed over the mountains and went to ask them to help our house because we were very poor. They were good to me. They sent me to school for a while, and I had plenty to eat. After a few months the Red Army captured Changchow, and went to my village. All the landlords and moneylenders and officials were driven out. My family was given land and did not have to pay the tax collectors and landlords any more. They were happy and they were proud of me. Two of my brothers joined the Red Army.'

'Where are they now?'

'Now? I don't know. When we left Kiangsi they were with the Red Army in Fukien; they were with Fang Chih-min. Now I don't know.'

'Did the peasants like the Red Army?'

'Like the Red Army, eh? Of course they liked it. The Red Army gave them land and drove away the landlords, the tax collectors, and the exploiters.' (These 'little devils' all had their Marxist vocabulary.)

'But really, how do you *know* they liked the Reds?'

'They made us a thousand, ten thousands, of shoes, with their own hands. The women made uniforms for us, and the men spied on the enemy. Every home sent sons to our Red Army. That is how the *lao-pai-hsing* treated us.'

Scores of youngsters like him were with the Reds. The Young Vanguards were organized by the Communist Youth League, and altogether, according to the claims of Fang Wen-p'ing, secretary of the CYL, there were then some 40,000 in the North-West soviet districts. There must have been several hundred with the Red Army alone: a 'model company' of them was in every Red encampment. They were youths between twelve and seventeen (really eleven to sixteen by foreign count*), and they came from all over China. Many of them, like this little bugler, had survived the hardships of the march from the South. Many had joined the Red Army during its expedition to Shansi.

The Young Vanguards worked as orderlies, messboys, buglers, spies, radio operators, water carriers, propagandists, actors, mafoos, nurses, secretaries, and even teachers. I once saw such a youngster, before a big map, lecturing a class of new recruits on world geography. Two of the most graceful child dancers I had ever seen were Young Vanguards in the dramatic society of the First Army Corps, and had marched from Kiangsi.

One might wonder how they stood such a life. Hundreds must have died or been killed. In the filthy jail in Sianfu there were over 200 of them, captured doing espionage or propaganda, or as stragglers unable to keep up with the army on its march. But their fortitude was amazing, and their loyalty to the Red Army was the intense and unquestioning loyalty of the very young.

Most of them wore uniforms too big for them, with sleeves dangling to their knees and coats dragging nearly to the ground. They washed their hands and faces three times a day, they claimed, but they were always dirty, their noses were usually running, and they were often wiping them with a sleeve, and grinning. The world nevertheless was theirs: they had enough to eat, they had a blanket each, the leaders even had pistols, and they wore red bars, and broken-peaked caps a size or more too large, but with the red star. They were often of uncertain origin: many could not remember their parents, many were escaped apprentices, some had been slaves,† most of them were runaways from huts with too many mouths to feed, and all of them had made their own decisions to join. Sometimes a whole group of youngsters had run off to the Reds together.

Many stories of courage were told of them. They gave and asked

---

*Traditionally, Chinese age count begins at conception, and everyone becomes one year older on New Year's Day.

† Child slavery had been abolished by Kuomintang law, but the mandate was seldom enforced even in areas where the law was known; elsewhere child slavery was still common.

no quarter as children, and many had actually participated in battles. It was said that in Kiangsi, after the main Red Army left, hundreds of Young Vanguards and Young Communists fought beside adult partisans, and even made bayonet charges – so that the White soldiers laughingly said they could grab their bayonets and pull them into their trenches, they were so small and light. Many of the captured 'Reds' in Chiang's reform schools for bandits in Kiangsi were youths from ten to fifteen years old.

Perhaps the Vanguards liked the Reds because among them they were treated like human beings probably for the first time. They ate and lived like men; they seemed to take part in everything; they considered themselves any man's equal. I never saw one of them struck or bullied. They were certainly 'exploited' as orderlies and messboys (and it was surprising how many orders starting at the top were eventually passed on to some Young Vanguard), but they had their own freedom of activity, too, and their own organization to protect them. They learned games and sports, they were given a crude schooling, and they acquired a faith in simple Marxist slogans – which in most cases meant to them simply helping to shoot a gun against the landlords and masters of apprentices. Obviously it was better than working fourteen hours a day at the master's bench, and feeding him, and emptying his 'defile-mother's' night-bowl.

I remember one such escaped apprentice I met in Kansu who was nicknamed the Shansi Wa-wa – the Shansi Baby. He had been sold to a shop in a town near Hung T'ung, in Shansi, and when the Red Army came he had stolen over the city wall, with three other apprentices, to join it. How he had decided that he belonged with the Reds I did not know, but evidently all of Yen Hsi-shan's anti-Communist propaganda, all the warnings of his elders, had produced exactly the opposite effect from that intended. He was a fat rolypoly lad with the face of a baby, and only twelve, but he was quite able to take care of himself, as he had proved during the march across Shansi and Shensi and into Kansu. When I asked him why he had become a Red he said: 'The Red Army fights for the poor. The Red Army is anti-Japanese. Why should any man not want to become a Red soldier?'

Another time I met a bony youngster of fifteen, who was head of the Young Vanguards and Young Communists working in the hospital near Holienwan, Kansu. His home had been in Hsing Ko, the Reds' model *hsien* in Kiangsi, and he said that one of his brothers was still in a partisan army there, and that his sister had been a nurse. He did not know what had become of his family. Yes, they all liked the Reds. Why? Because they 'all understood that the Red Army was our army – fighting for the *wu-ch'an chieh-chi*' – the proletariat. I wondered what impressions the great trek to the North-West had left upon his young mind, but I was not to find out. The whole thing was a minor event to this serious-minded boy, this little matter of a hike over a distance twice the width of America.

'It was pretty bitter going, eh?' I ventured.

'Not bitter, not bitter. No march is bitter if your comrades are with you. We revolutionary youths can't think about whether a thing is hard or bitter; we can only think of the task before us. If it is to walk 10,000 *li*, we walk it, or if it is to walk 20,000 *li*, we walk it!'

'How do you like Kansu, then? Is it better or worse than Kiangsi? Was life better in the South?'

'Kiangsi was good. Kansu is also good. Wherever the revolution is, that place is good. What we eat and where we sleep is not important. What is important is the revolution.'[1]

Copybook replies, I thought. Here was one lad who had learned his answers well from some Red propagandist. Next day I was quite surprised when at a mass meeting of Red soldiers I saw that he was one of the principal speakers, and a 'propagandist' in his own right. He was one of the best speakers in the army, I was told, and in that meeting he gave a simple but competent explanation of the present political situation, and the reasons why the Red Army wanted to stop civil war and form a 'united front' with all anti-Japanese armies.

I met a youth of fourteen who had been an apprentice in a Shanghai machine shop, and with three companions had found his way, through various adventures, to the North-West. He was a student in the radio school in Pao An when I saw him. I asked whether he missed Shanghai, but he said no, he had left nothing in Shanghai, and that the only fun he had ever had there was looking into the shop windows at good things to eat – which he could not buy.

One 'little devil' in Pao An served as orderly to Li K'e-nung, chief of the communications department of the Foreign Office. He was a Shansi lad of about thirteen or fourteen, and he had joined the Reds I knew not how. The Beau Brummell of the Vanguards, he took his role with utmost gravity. He had inherited a Sam Browne belt from somebody, he had a neat little uniform tailored to a good fit, and a cap whose peak he regularly refilled with new cardboard whenever it broke. Underneath the collar of his well-brushed coat he always managed to have a strip of white linen showing. He was easily the snappiest-looking soldier in town. Beside him Mao Tse-tung looked a tramp.

This *wa-wa*'s name happened by some thoughtlessness of his parents to be Shang Chi-pang. There is nothing wrong with that, except that Chi-pang sounds very much like *chi-pa*, and so, to his unending mortification, he was always called *chi-pa*, which simply means 'penis'. One day Chi-pang came into my little room in the Foreign Office with his usual quota of dignity, clicked his heels together, gave me the most Prussian-like salute I had seen in the Red districts, and addressed me as 'Comrade Snow'. He then proceeded to unburden his small heart of certain apprehensions. What he wanted to do was to make it perfectly clear to me that his name was not Chi-pa, but Chi-pang, and that between these two there was all the difference in the world. He had his name carefully scrawled down on a scrap of paper, and this he deposited before me.

Astonished, I responded in all seriousness that I had never called him anything but Chi-pang, and had no thought of doing otherwise. He thanked me, made a grave bow, and once more gave that preposterous salute. 'I wanted to be sure,' he said, 'that when you write about me for the foreign papers you won't make a mistake in my name. It would give a bad impression to the foreign comrades if they thought a Red soldier was named Chi-pa!' Until then I had had no intention of introducing Chi-pang into this strange book, but with that remark I had no choice in the matter, and he walked into it right beside the Generalissimo.

One of the duties of the Young Vanguards in the soviets was

to examine travellers on roads behind the front, and see that they had their road passes. They executed this duty quite determinedly, and marched anyone without his papers to the local soviet for examination. P'eng Teh-huai told me of being stopped once and being asked for his *lu-t'iao* by some Young Vanguards, who threatened to arrest him.

'But I am P'eng Teh-huai,' he said. 'I write those passes myself.'

'We don't care if you are Commander Chu Teh,' said the young sceptics: 'you must have a road pass.' They signalled for assistance, and several boys came running from the fields to reinforce them.

P'eng had to write out his *lu-t'iao* and sign it himself before they allowed him to proceed.

Altogether, the 'little devils' were one thing in Red China with which it was hard to find anything seriously wrong. Their spirit was superb. I suspected that more than once an older man, looking at them, forgot his pessimism and was heartened to think that he was fighting for the future of lads like those. They were invariably cheerful and optimistic, and they had a ready *'hao!'* for every how-are-you, regardless of the weariness of the day's march. They were patient, hard-working, bright, and eager to learn, and seeing them made you feel that China was not hopeless, that no nation was more hopeless than its youth. Here in the Vanguards was the future of China, if only this youth could be freed, shaped, made aware, and given a role to perform in the building of a new world. It sounds somewhat evangelical, I suppose, but nobody could see these heroic young lives without feeling that man in China is not born rotten, but with infinite possibilities of personality.

3

United Front in Action

IN the beginning of September 1936, while I was at the front in Ninghsia and Kansu, the army under P'eng Teh-huai commenced moving westward towards the Yellow River, and southward towards the Sian-Lanchow highway, to establish connections with Chu Teh's troops coming up from the South – a manoeuvre which was to be brilliantly concluded at the end of October, when the combined Red Armies occupied nearly all north Kansu above the Sian-Lanchow highway.

But having now decided to seek a compromise with the Kuomintang in an attempt to 'coerce' the latter into resistance against Japan, the Reds were becoming every day more of a force of political propagandists and less of an army intent on seizing power by conquest. New instructions from the Party ordered the troops to observe 'united-front tactics' in their future movements. And what were 'united-front tactics'? Perhaps a day-by-day diary account of the manoeuvres of the army at this time could best answer that question :

Pao Tou Shui, 1 September. Leaving Yu Wang Pao, the headquarters of the First Front Army, walked for about forty *li*, Commander P'eng Teh-huai joking with the muleteers and generally having a lark. Most of the region travelled was hilly and mountainous. P'eng made his headquarters for the night in a Mohammedan peasant's home in this little village.

Maps immediately were put up on the wall and the radio began functioning. Messages came in. While P'eng was resting, he called in the Mohammedan peasants and explained the Red Army's policies to them. An old lady sat and talked with him for nearly two hours, pointing out her troubles. Meanwhile a Red Army harvesting brigade passed by, on its way to reap the crop of a runaway landlord. Since he was a 'traitor' his land was subject to confiscation. Another squad of men has been appointed to guard and keep clean the premises of the local mosque. Relations with the peasants seem good. A week ago the peasants in this *hsien*, who have now lived under the Reds for several months without paying taxes, came in a delegation to present P'eng with six cartloads of grain and provisions as an expression of gratitude for the relief. Yesterday some peasants presented P'eng with a handsome wooden bed – which amused him very much. He turned it over to the local *ahun*.

Li Chou K'ou, 2 September. On the road at four a.m. P'eng up long before. Met ten peasants, who had come with the army from Yu Wang Pao to help carry the wounded back to the hospital. They voluntarily asked to do this in order to fight Ma Hung-kuei, hated because he'd forced their sons to join the army. A Nanking bomber flew overhead, spotted us, and we scattered for cover. The whole army melted into the landscape. The plane circled twice and dropped one bomb – 'laid an iron egg', or 'dropped some bird dung', as the Reds say – then strafed the horses and flew on to bomb our vanguard. One soldier, slow in taking cover, was wounded in the leg – a slight injury – and after it was dressed he walked without assistance.

From this village, where we are spending the night, very little can be seen. One regiment of the enemy is holding a fort near here, a Fifteenth Army Corps detachment attacking.

From Yu Wang Pao comes a radio message reporting the visit of enemy bombers, which attacked the city and dropped ten bombs this morning. Some peasants were killed and wounded; no soldiers hit.

Tiao Pao Tzu, 3 September. Left Li Chou K'ou, and on the way many peasants came out and brought the soldiers *pai ch'a* (white tea) – i.e., hot water, the favourite beverage in these parts. Mohammedan schoolteachers came over to bid P'eng good-bye and thank him for protecting the school. As we neared Tiao Pao Tzu (now over 100 *li* west of Yu Wang Pao) some of Ma Hung-kuei's cavalry, withdrawing from an isolated position, ran into our rear. They were only a few hundred yards from us. Nieh Jung-chen,* chief of staff of the First Army Corps, sent a detachment of headquarters cavalry to chase them, and they galloped off in a whirl

*Teng Hsiao-p'ing was his deputy political commissar. For both, see BN.

of dust. A Red pack train was attacked, and another detachment of soldiers was sent to recover the mules and loads. The caravan returned intact.

Tonight some interesting items of news were posted on the bulletin board. Li Wang Pao is now surrounded, and in a fort near there a trench-mortar shell fell almost directly on Hsu Hai-tung's headquarters. One Young Vanguard was killed and three soldiers were wounded. In another place nearby, a White platoon commander, reconnoitring the Reds' position, was captured by a surprise attack party. The Reds slightly wounded him and sent him back to headquarters. P'eng raised hell over the radio because he was wounded. 'Not good united-front tactics,' he commented. 'One slogan is worth ten bullets.' He lectured the staff on the united front and how to work it out in practice.

Peasants sold fruit and melons on the road, the Reds paying for everything they bought. One young soldier traded his pet rabbit for three melons in a long transaction with a peasant. After he'd eaten the melons he was very dour, wanting his rabbit back.

Today's news was celebrated by P'eng Teh-huai with a large watermelon feast: the melons here are cheap and excellent.

Tiao Pao Tzu, 4–5 September. Liu Hsiao (of the political department) is now working among the Mohammedans near Li Wang Pao. Today he sent a report of some recent developments there. One of Ma's regiments asked to have a Mohammedan sent from the Red Moslem regiment to talk to them. Ma's regimental commander refused to meet the Red delegate, but permitted him to talk to his men.

Wang (this Red Moslem delegate) returned and reported that he had seen the Red handbills all over the troops' quarters. He said that after he had talked to the troops for a few hours they became more and more interested, and finally the commander listened in too but, getting worried, decided to have him arrested. The men protested, and he was safely escorted back to the Red lines. The regiment sent a letter in reply to the one which Wang had carried to them from Liu Hsiao. They said they would not retreat because they had been ordered to hold this district, and must do so; that they were ready to make an agreement to fight Japan, but the Reds should negotiate with their division commander; that if the Reds would not fight them, they would not fight the Reds; and that letters and pamphlets sent by the Reds had been distributed among the men.

Two planes bombed a Red cavalry detachment near here today. No men nor horses were hit, but one bomb struck a corner of a village mosque and three old Moslem attendants were killed. This doesn't increase local affection for Nanking.

Tiao Pao Tzu, 6 September. A day of rest and recreation. All commanders of the First Army Corps met at P'eng's headquarters for a melon feast, while the soldiers rested and had sports and a melon feast of their own. P'eng called a meeting of all company commanders and higher, and there was a political session. They permitted me to attend. A summary of P'eng's speech follows:

'Reasons for our movement to these districts are first to enlarge and develop our soviet districts; second, to cooperate with movement and advance of the Second and Fourth Front armies (in south Kansu); third, to liquidate the influence of Ma Hung-kuei and Ma Hung-ping in these regions and form a united front directly with their troops.

'We must enlarge the basis of the united front here. We must decisively influence those White commanders who are now sympathetic and win them over definitely to our side. We have good contacts with many of them now; we must continue our work, by letter, in our press, through delegates, through the secret societies, etc.

'We must intensify our educational work among our own troops. In several recent instances our men have violated the united-front policy by firing on troops that we had agreed to permit to withdraw. In other instances men were reluctant to return captured rifles and had to be ordered several times to do so. This is not a breach of discipline, but a lack of confidence in their commanders' orders, showing that the men do not fully understand the reasons for such actions, some men actually accusing their leaders of "counter-revolutionary orders". One company commander received a letter from a White commander and did not even read it, but tore it up, saying, "They are all the same, these Whites." This shows that we must more deeply instruct the rank and file; our first lectures have not made their position clear to them. We must ask for their criticism and make such modifications in our policy as they think necessary after thorough discussion and explanation. We must impress upon them that the united-front policy is no trick to fool the Whites, but that it is a basic policy and in line with the decisions of our Party.

'After the East Attack [into Shansi] many of our comrades, coming here to Kansu and Ninghsia, felt discouraged because the contrast was so great compared with the response we received there. They felt depressed because of the poverty of the country here and the low level of political enthusiasm among the people. Don't be discouraged! Work harder! These people are also brothers, and will respond to the same treatment as other human beings. We must not miss a single opportunity to convince a White soldier or a Mohammedan peasant. We are not working hard enough.

'As for the masses, we must urge them to take the lead in every revolutionary action. We must not touch any Mohammedan landlord ourselves, but we must show the people clearly that they have the freedom to do so, that we will protect their mass organizations that do so, that this is their revolutionary right, that it is the produce of their labour and belongs to them. We must intensify our efforts to raise the political consciousness of the masses. Remember that they have heretofore had no political consciousness except racial hatred. We must awaken a patriotic consciousness in them. We must deepen our work in the Ke Lao Hui and other secret societies and make them active, not merely passive, allies on the anti-Japanese front. We must consolidate our good relations with the *ahuns* and urge them to take places of leadership in the anti-Japanese movement. We must strengthen the basis of revolutionary power by organizing every Mohammedan youth.'

P'eng's statement was followed by long critical comments from the political commissars of the First and Fifteenth Army corps. Both of them reviewed their efforts in 'united-front educational work' and suggested improvements. All commanders took copious notes, and afterwards there was a session of long debate and argument which lasted till dinner. P'eng moved that the two army corps be enlarged by 500 new enlistments each, and this was seconded and passed unanimously.

After dinner there was a new play by the dramatic club of the

First Army Corps, based on experiences of the past week. It portrayed in an amusing way the mistakes of the commanders and men in carrying out the new policy. One scene showed an argument between a commander and a warrior; another between two commanders; a third showed a company commander tearing up a letter he had received from the Whites.

In the second act most of these mistakes were shown corrected and the Red Army and anti-Japanese Moslem Army were marching together, and singing and fighting side by side against the Japanese and the Kuomintang. Seemed magically quick work by the education-through-entertainment department.

During the next month the attention of every Red in China was to be focused anxiously upon the series of manoeuvres by which, for the first time in the history of the soviets, all the main forces of the Red Army were eventually united and concentrated in a single great area. And here some illumination should be shed upon the leadership of this second great trek from the South – upon Chu Teh, commander-in-chief of the 'All China' Red Army, who, after a heartbreaking winter spent on the frozen marches of Tibet, was now pouring the Second and Fourth Front armies into the North-West.[1]

4

Concerning Chu Teh[1]

LI CHIANG-LIN told me:

As a youth Chu Teh was reckless, adventurous, and courageous, moved by the legends of his people, by the tales of 'free companions' of the *Shui Hu Chuan*, and by the exploits of the heroes of the *Romance of Three Kingdoms*, who had fought over the fields and mountains of his native Szechuan. He gravitated naturally towards military life. Helped by his family's political influence, he was accepted in the new Yunnan Military Academy, and he was among the first cadets in China to be given modern military training. Upon graduation from the Yunnan Academy he was commissioned a lieutenant, and entered what the Chinese referred to as the 'foreign army' – 'foreign' because it used Western methods of drill and tactics, because it did not go into battle accompanied by Chinese musicians, and because for arms it used 'foreign spears' – rifles with fixed bayonets on them.

In the overthrow of the Manchu Dynasty in 1912 this modern army of Yunnan played a prominent role, and Chu Teh, leading a battalion of braves, soon distinguished himself as a warrior of the republic. By 1916, when Yuan Shih-k'ai attempted to restore the monarchy, he was a brigadier general, and his Yunnanese troops under the celebrated Ts'ai O were the first to raise the banner of revolt, which doomed Yuan's imperial ambitions to defeat. At this time Chu Teh first became known throughout the southern provinces as one of the 'four fierce generals' of Ts'ai O.

With his prestige thus established, Chu Teh's political fortunes pyramided rapidly. He became director of the Bureau of Public Safety in Yunnanfu, and then Provincial Commissioner of Finance. People of Yunnan and Szechuan agreed that there were two things certain about officials: one was that they were corrupt, the other that they were opium smokers. Reared in a region where opium was as commonly smoked as tea was drunk, and where parents customarily spread the drug on sugarcane to soothe their bellowing infants, Chu Teh had inevitably become a smoker. And given office by a bureaucracy which looked upon plunder of public funds as not so much a right but a duty to one's family, he followed the example of superiors and manipulated the privileges of office to enrich himself and his heirs.

He went in for a harem, too. He was said to have acquired several wives and concubines, and he built for them and his progeny a palatial home in the capital of Yunnan. One might have thought he had everything he desired: wealth, power, love, descendants, poppy dreams, eminent respectability, and a comfortable future in which to preach the proprieties of Confucianism. He had, in fact, only one really bad habit, but it was to prove his downfall. He liked to read books.

Pure realist though he had been till now, there must have been a strain of idealism and genuine revolutionary ardour latent in his character. Influenced by reading, influenced also by a few returned students who occasionally drifted into the backwash of Yunnan, Chu Teh gradually understood that the revolution of 1911 had been for the mass of the people a complete cipher; that it had merely replaced one despotic bureaucracy of exploitation with another. What was more, he seemed to have worried about it – as anyone of feeling, living in Yunnanfu, a city of 40,000 slave girls and boys, might well have done. He was apparently possessed by a sense of shame and simultaneously with an ambition to emulate the popular heroes of the West, and a desire to 'modernize' China. The more books he read the more he realized his own ignorance and China's backwardness. He wanted to study and he wanted to travel.

By 1922 Chu Teh had unburdened himself of his wives and concubines, pensioning them off in Yunnanfu. To one who knew the conservatism of China, and especially the feudal taboos of Yunnan, this act of repudiation of tradition was hardly believable, and indicated in itself a personality of unusual independence and resolution. Leaving Yunnan, he went to Shanghai, where he met many young revolutionaries of the Kuomintang, which he had joined. Here also he came into contact with left-wing radicals, who tended to look upon him condescendingly as an old-fashioned militarist. A corrupt official from feudal Yunnan, a many-wived general, an opium addict – could this also be a revolutionary?

Before this trip Chu Teh had determined to break himself of the drug habit. It was not easy: he had been using opium for a long time. But this man had more steel in his will than his acquaintances supposed. For days he lay almost unconscious as he fought his noxious craving; then, taking a medicine cure along, he boarded a British steamer on the Yangtze and took passage for Shanghai. No opium could be bought or sold on board, and for weeks he sailed down the river, pacing the deck, never going ashore, fighting this hardest battle of his life. But after a month on board he left the ship with clear eyes, a ruddy glow on his cheeks, and a new confidence in his step. After a final hospital cure in Shanghai, he began a new life in earnest. So said his aide, Li Chiang-lin.

Chu Teh was then nearing forty, but he was in excellent health and his mind was eagerly reaching out for new knowledge. Accompanying some Chinese students, he went to Germany, where he lived for a while near Hannover. There he met many Communists, and at this time seems to have seriously taken up the study of Marxism and become enamoured of new perspectives opened up by the theory of social revolution. In this study he was chiefly tutored by Chinese students young enough to be his own sons – for he never learned French, he knew only a smattering of German, and he was a poor linguist. One of his student teachers in Germany told me how deadly in earnest he had been; how patiently, ploddingly, stubbornly, he struggled amid the confusion of an impact of a new world of ideas to integrate the basic truths and meanings, how great had been the intellectual effort with which he divested himself of all the prejudices and limitations of his traditional Chinese training.

In this way he read some histories of the Great War, and familiarized himself with the politics of Europe. One day a student friend of his* came to see him, talking excitedly about a book called *State and Revolution*. Chu Teh asked him to help him read it, and thus he became interested in Marxism and the Russian Revolution. He read Bukharin's *ABC of Communism*, and his works on dialectical materialism, and then he read more of Lenin. The

* Chou En-lai.

powerful revolutionary movement then active in Germany swept him, with hundreds of Chinese students, into the struggle for world revolution. He joined the Chinese branch of the Communist Party founded in Germany.

'Chu Teh had an experienced, disciplined, practical mind,' a comrade who knew him in Germany told me. 'He was an extremely simple man, modest and unassuming. He always invited criticism; he had an insatiable appetite for criticism. In Germany he lived the simple life of a soldier. Chu Teh's original interest in communism sprang from his sympathy for the poor, which had also brought him into the Kuomintang. He believed strongly in Sun Yat-sen for a while, because of Sun's principles advocating land for the tillers, and the limitation of private capital. But not until he began to understand Marxism did he realize the inadequacy of Sun Yat-sen's programme.'

Chu Teh also lived for some time in Paris, where he entered a school for Chinese students which had been established by Wu Tze-hui, a veteran national revolutionary of the Kuomintang. In France and in Germany he sat at the feet of his young German, French, and Chinese instructors, and he humbly listened, quietly interrogated, debated, sought clarity and understanding. 'To be modern, to understand the meaning of the revolution,' his youthful tutors kept repeating, 'you must go to Russia. There you can see the future.' And again Chu Teh followed their advice. In Moscow he entered the Eastern Toilers' University, where he studied Marxism under Chinese teachers. Late in 1925 he returned to Shanghai, and from that time on he worked under the direction of the Communist Party, to which he soon gave his fortune.

Chu Teh rejoined his former superior and fellow Yunnanese, General Chu Pei-teh, whose power in the Kuomintang Army was second only to that of Chiang Kai-shek. In 1927, when General Chu Pei-teh's forces occupied several provinces south of the Yangtze, he made Chu Teh chief of the Bureau of Public Safety in Nanchang, capital of Kiangsi. There also he took command of a training regiment of cadets, and there he made contact with the Ninth Kuomintang Army, stationed further south in Kiangsi. In the Ninth Army were detachments that had formerly been under his personal command in Yunnan. Thus the stage was prepared for the August Uprising in Nanchang, in which Communist troops first began the long open struggle for power against the Kuomintang.

The first of August 1927 was a day of great decision for Chu Teh. Ordered by his commander-in-chief, Chu Pei-teh, to suppress the insurrection, Chu Teh (who had helped organize it) instead joined with the rebels, renouncing the remaining connections with his past. When, after the defeat of Ho Lung, he headed his police and his training regiment southward with the rebels, the city gates which closed behind him were symbolic of the final break with the security and success of his youth. Ahead of him lay years of unceasing struggle.

Part of the Ninth Army went with Chu Teh also, as the straggling band of revolutionaries swept down to Swatow, captured it, were driven out, and then withdrew again to Kiangsi and Hunan. Among Chu Teh's chief lieutenants at that time were three Whampoa cadets: Wang Erh-tso (later killed in battle); Ch'en Yi; and Lin Piao, who became president of the Red University.* They did not call themselves a Red Army, but renamed themselves only the National Revolutionary Army. After the retreat from Fukien, Chu Teh's forces were reduced, by desertions and casualties, to 900 men, with a fire power of only 500 rifles, one machine gun, and a few rounds of ammunition each.

In this situation Chu Teh accepted an offer to connect with General Fan Shih-sheng, another Yunnan commander, whose big army was then stationed in southern Hunan, and who, though not a Communist, tolerated Communists in his army, hoping to use them politically against Chiang Kai-shek.[2] As a Yunnanese he was also inclined to give haven to his fellow provincials. Here Chu Teh's troops were incorporated as the 140th Regiment, and he became chief political adviser to the Sixteenth Army. And here he had the narrowest escape of his life.

Communist influence in Fan Shih-sheng's army rapidly increased, and soon an anti-Bolshevik faction, secretly connected with Chiang Kai-shek, planned a coup against Chu Teh. One night he was staying in an inn with only forty of his followers, when he was attacked by a force under Hu Chi-lung, leader of the coup. Shooting began

*Li Hsien-nien was then also with Chu Teh.

at once, but it was dark and the assassins could not see clearly. When several of them aimed revolvers at Chu Teh's head he cried out excitedly, 'Don't shoot me, I'm only the cook. Don't shoot a man who can cook for you!' The soldiers, touched to the stomach, hesitated, and Chu Teh was led outside for closer inspection. There he was recognized by a cousin of Hu Chi-lung, who shouted, 'Here is Chu Teh! Kill him!' But Chu Teh pulled out a concealed weapon of his own, shot the man, overcame his guard, and fled. Only five of his men escaped with him.

This incident explained the nickname by which Chu Teh had ever since been known in the Red Army – 'Chief of the Cooks'.

Rejoining his regiment, Chu Teh notified Fan Shih-sheng that he was withdrawing, whereupon Fan was said to have presented him with a gift of $50,000 to keep his good will, for the issue against Chiang Kai-shek was still not clearly decided, and freelance allies like the young Communists, who had considerable influence on many of Fan's officers and men, were not to be lightly spurned. But in the months ahead the money was to prove inadequate. The little army was now held together almost solely by loyalty to Chu Teh and a few of his commanders. Party affairs were in great confusion, no definite 'line' had been established, and military strategy was undecided. Chu's troops still wore Kuomintang uniforms, but they were in rags; many of them had no shoes; and poor food, or often no food at all, caused steady desertions. But some encouragement had been provided by the news of the Canton Commune, which had suggested a clear line of action. Chu Teh re-formed his army into three sections, calling it the 'Peasant Column Army', and moved to the Hunan-Kiangsi-Kwangtung border, where he united with some bandits led by a radical student, and began a programme of tax abolition, redistribution of land, and confiscation of the property of the rich. Yih Chang *hsien* was occupied as a base, after a bloody struggle, and the young army eked out the winter on squash and political debates.

Meanwhile Mao Tse-tung's peasant army had marched ingloriously through Hunan, to come at last to sanctuary at Chingkangshan, on the southern Kiangsi-Hunan border, where, with the help of the bandit leaders Wang Tso and Yuan Wen-t'sai, they had occupied two surrounding counties and built up in the mountains a nearly impregnable base. To Chu Teh, not far away, the 'Peasants' and Workers' Red Army' of Mao Tse-tung sent as delegate his brother, Mao Tse-min. He brought instructions from the Party to unite forces, and news of a definite programme of partisan warfare, agrarian revolution, and the building of soviets. When, in May 1928, the two armies combined at Chingkangshan, they were in control of five counties, and had some 50,000 followers. Of these about 4,000 were armed with rifles, some 10,000 being equipped only with spears, swords, and hoes, while the rest were unarmed Party workers, propagandists, or families of the warriors, including a large number of children.

Thus began the famous Chu-Mao combination which was to make history in South China for the next six years. Chu Teh's ascension as a formidable military leader followed the same curve of growth as the soviets.

At the First Soviet Congress, in 1931, Chu Teh was unanimously elected commander-in-chief of the Red Army. Within two years four army corps had been built up, with a firing power of some 50,000 rifles and hundreds of machine guns, mostly captured from enemy troops, and the soviets controlled vast areas of southern Kiangsi and parts of Hunan and Fukien. Intensified political training had begun, an arsenal had been erected, elementary social-revolutionary economic and political reforms were being realized throughout the soviets, Red Army uniforms were being turned out day and night to equip new partisans, and revolutionary morale was strengthening. In two years more the Red forces had been doubled.

During these years in the South, Chu Teh was in overall military command of combined Red Armies in hundreds of skirmishes, through scores of major battles, and through the brunt of five great annihilation campaigns, in the last of which he faced an enemy with technical offensive power (including heavy artillery, aviation, and mechanized units) estimated at from eight to nine times greater than his own, and resources many, many times exceeding anything at his disposal. However his degree of success or failure is to be measured, it must be admitted that for tactical ingenuity, spectacular mobility, and richness of versatility in manoeuvre, he established beyond any doubt the formidable fighting power of revolutionized Chinese troops in partisan warfare. The great mistakes of the Red Army in the South were strategic, and for those the political leadership must be held chiefly responsible.

Chu Teh's devotion to his men was proverbial. Since assuming command of the army he had lived and dressed like the rank and file, had shared all their hardships, often going without shoes in the early days, living one whole winter on squash, another on yak meat, never complaining, rarely sick. He liked to wander through the camp, they said, sitting with the men and telling stories, or playing games with them. He played a good game of table tennis, and a 'wistful' game of basketball. Any soldier in the army could bring his complaints directly to the commander-in-chief. Chu Teh took off his hat when he addressed his men. On the Long March he lent his horse to tired comrades, walking much of the way, seemingly tireless.

Popular myths about Chu Teh were said to credit him with miraculous powers: the power to see 100 *li* on all sides, the power to fly, and the mastery of Taoist magic, such as creating dust clouds before an enemy, or stirring a wind against them. Superstitious folk believed him invulnerable, for had not thousands of bullets and shells failed to destroy him? Others said he had the power of resurrection, for had not the Kuomintang repeatedly declared him dead, often giving minute details of the manner in which he expired? Millions knew the name Chu Teh in China, and to each it was a menace or a bright star of hope, according to his status in life, but to all it was a name imprinted on the pages of a decade of history.

Part Eleven

BACK TO PAO AN

I

Casuals of the Road

FROM Ninghsia I turned southward again into Kansu. In four or five days I was back in Holienwan, where I again saw Ts'ai Ch'ang and her husband, Li Fu-ch'un, and had another meal of French cooking with them, and met the young and pretty wife of Nieh Jung-chen, political commissar of the First Army Corps. She had but recently slipped into the soviet districts from the White world, and had now just returned from a visit to her husband, whom she had not seen for five years.

I stayed three days in Holienwan with the supply commissariat, which was quartered in a big compound formerly owned by a Mohammedan grain merchant. Architecturally it was an interesting group of buildings of a generally Central Asian appearance, with flat heavy roofs, and deep Arabic windows set into walls at least four feet thick. As I led my horse into its spacious stables a tall white-bearded man, wearing a faded grey uniform, with a long leather apron that reached to the ground, stepped up and saluted his red-starred cap, while his sunburned face wreathed a toothless smile. He took charge of Ma Hung-kuei, my horse.

How, I wondered, had this grandfather wandered into our boy-scout encampment? I stopped to ask, and forced a story from him. He was from Shansi, and had joined the Red Army during its expedition there. His name was Li, he was sixty-four, and he claimed the distinction of being the oldest Red warrior. Rather apologetically he explained that he was not at the front just then 'because Commander Yang thinks I am more useful here at this horse work, and so I stay'.

Li had been a pork seller in the town of Hung T'ung, Shansi, before he became a Red, and he roundly cursed 'Model Governor' Yen Hsi-shan and the local officials and their ruinous taxes. 'You can't do business in Hung T'ung,' he said; 'they tax a man's excrement.' When old Li heard the Reds were coming he had decided to join them. His wife was dead, and his two daughters were both married; he had no sons; he had no ties at all in Hung T'ung except his overtaxed pork business; and Hung T'ung was a 'dead-man' sort of place, anyway. He wanted something livelier, and so the adventurer had crept out of the city to offer himself to the Reds.

'When I wanted to enlist they said to me, "You are old. In the Red Army life is hard." And what did I say? I said, "Yes, this body is sixty-four years old, it's true, but I can walk like a boy of twenty, I can shoot a gun, I can do the work of any man. If it's men you need, I can also serve." So they told me to come along, and I marched through Shansi with the Red Army, and I crossed the Yellow River with the Red Army, and here I am in Kansu.'

I smiled and asked him whether it was any better than pork selling. Did he like it?

'Oh-ho! Pork selling is a turtle man's sort of business! Here is work worth doing. A poor man's army fighting for the oppressed, isn't it? Certainly I like it.' The old man fumbled in his breast pocket and brought forth a soiled cloth, which he carefully unwrapped to reveal a worn little notebook. 'See here,' he said. 'I already recognize over 200 characters. Every day the Red Army teaches me four more. In Shansi I lived for sixty-four years and nobody ever taught me to write my name. Is the Red Army good or isn't it?' He pointed with intense pride to the crude scrawl of his characters that resembled the blobs of muddy hen's feet on clean matting, and falteringly he read off some newly inscribed phrases. And then, as a sort of climax, he produced a stub of pencil and with an elaborate flourish he wrote his name for me.

'I suppose you're thinking of marrying again,' I joked with him. He shook his head gravely and said no, what with one defile-mother horse after another he had no time to think about the woman problem, and with that he ambled away to look after his beasts.

Next evening, as I was walking through an orchard behind the courtyard, I met another Shansi man, twenty years Li's junior, but just as interesting. I heard a *hsiao-kuei* calling out, 'Li Pai T'ang! Li Pai T'ang!' and looked in curiosity to see whom he was addressing as the 'House-of-Christian-Worship'.* There upon a little hill I found a barber shaving a youth's head clean as an egg. Upon

*Literally, 'Sunday Temple'.

inquiry I discovered that his real name was Chia Ho-chung, and that he had formerly worked in the pharmacy of an American missionary hospital in P'ing Yang, Shansi. The 'little devils' had given him this nickname because he was a Christian, and still said his prayers daily.

Chia pulled up his trousers and showed me a bad wound on his leg, from which he still limped, and he yanked up his coat to display a wound on his belly, where he had also been hit. These, he explained, were souvenirs of battles, and that was why he was not at the front. This hair cutting wasn't his real job at all: he was either a pharmacist or a Red warrior.

Chia said that two other attendants in that Christian hospital had joined the Reds with him. Before leaving, they had discussed their intention with the American doctor in the hospital, whose Chinese name was Li Jen. Dr Li Jen was 'a good man, who healed the poor without charge and never oppressed people', and when Chia and his companions asked his advice he had said, 'Go ahead. I have heard that the Reds are good and honest men and not like the other armies, and you should be glad to fight with them.' So off they had gone to become red, red Robin Hoods.

'Maybe Dr Li Jen just wanted to get rid of you,' I suggested.

The barber indignantly denied it. He said he had always got along very well with Li Jen, who was an excellent man. He asked me to tell this Li Jen, if I ever saw him, that he was still alive, well, and happy, and that as soon as the revolution was over he was coming back to take his old job in the pharmacy. I left House-of-Worship with much reluctance. He was a fine Red, a good barber, and a real Christian.

Incidentally, I met several Christians and ex-Christians among the Reds. Many Communists had once been active Christians. Dr Nelson Fu, head of the Red Army Medical Corps, was formerly a doctor in a Methodist hospital in Kiangsi. Although he volunteered to work with the Reds, and enthusiastically supported them, he still adhered to his faith, and hence had not joined the Communist Party.

In Kiangsi the soviets carried on extensive 'anti-God' propaganda. All temples, churches, and church estates were converted into state property, and monks, nuns, priests, preachers, and foreign missionaries were deprived of the rights of citizenship; but in the

North-West a policy of religious toleration was practised. Freedom of worship was a primary guarantee, in fact. All foreign mission property was protected, and refugee missionaries were invited to return to their flocks.[1] The Communists reserved the right to preach antireligious propaganda of their own, holding the 'freedom to oppose worship' to be a corollary of the democratic privilege of the freedom to worship.

The only foreigners who took advantage of the new Communist policy towards religious institutions were some Belgian missionaries who were among the great landlords of Suiyuan. They owned one vast estate of 20,000 *mou*, and another of some 5,000 *mou* of land near Tingpien, on the Great Wall. After the Red Army occupied Tingpien, one side of the Belgians' property lay adjacent to soviet territory and the other side was held by White troops. The Reds did not attempt to expropriate the Belgians' land, but made a 'treaty' in which they guaranteed to protect the church property, provided the priests permitted them to organize anti-Japanese societies among the tenants who tilled the land of this big Catholic missionary fiefdom. Another stipulation of the curious agreement provided that the Belgians would dispatch a message from the Chinese Soviet Government to Premier Blum of France, congratulating him on the triumph of the People's Front.

There had been a series of raids by *min-t'uan* near Holienwan, and one village only a short distance away had been sacked two nights before I arrived. A band had crept up to the place just before dawn, overpowered and killed the lone sentry, and had then brought up bunches of dry brushwood and set fire to the huts in which about a dozen Red soldiers were sleeping. As the Reds ran out, blinded by the smoke, the *min-t'uan* had shot them down and seized their guns. Then they had joined with a gang of some 400, most of them armed by the Kuomintang general, Kao Kuei-tzu, who were raiding down from the North and burning farms and villages. The Twenty-eighth Army had sent a battalion out to attempt to round them up, and the day I left Holienwan these young warriors came back after a successful chase.

The battle had occurred only a few *li* from Holienwan, which the White bandits were said to be preparing to attack. Some peasants had discovered the *min-t'uan* lair in the inner mountains and, acting on this information, the Reds had divided into three columns, the centre one meeting the bandits in a frontal clash. The issue was decided when the two flanking columns of Reds closed in and surrounded the enemy. Some forty *min-t'uan* were killed, and sixteen Reds, while many on both sides were wounded. The *min-t'uan* were entirely disarmed, and their two chieftains taken captive.

We passed the battalion returning with their captives as we rode back towards Shensi. A big welcome had been organized in the villages, and the peasants lined the road to cheer the victorious troops. Peasant Guards stood holding their long red-tasselled spears in salute, and the Young Vanguards sang Red songs to them, while girls and women brought refreshments, tea and fruit and hot water – all they had, but it creased the faces of the weary soldiers with smiles. They were very young, much younger than the frontline regulars, and it seemed to me that many who wore bloodstained bandages were no more than fourteen or fifteen. I saw one youth on a horse, half-conscious and held up by a comrade on each side, who had a white bandage around his forehead, in the exact centre of which was a round red stain.

There in the midst of this column of youngsters, who carried rifles almost as big as themselves, marched the two bandit chieftains. One of them was a grizzled middle-aged peasant, and one wondered whether he felt ashamed, being led by these warriors all young enough to be his sons. Yet there was something rather splendid about his fearless bearing, and I thought that he was, after all, possibly a poor peasant like the rest, perhaps one who had also believed in something when he fought them, and it was regrettable that he was to be killed. Fu Chin-kuei shook his head when I asked him.

'We don't kill captured *min-t'uan*. We educate them and give them a chance to repent, and many of them later become good Red partisans.'

It was fortunate that the Reds had erased this group of bandits, for it cleared our road back to Pao An. We made the trip from the Kansu border in five days, doing more than 100 *li* on the fifth, but though there was plenty of incident there was no event, and I returned with no trophies except cantaloupes and melons I had bought along the road.

2

Life in Pao An

BACK in Pao An again, I settled down once more in the Waichiaopu – the Foreign Office – where I stayed through late September and half of October. I collected enough biographies to fill
a *Who's Who in Red China*, and every morning turned up a new
commander or soviet official to be interviewed. But I was becoming
increasingly uneasy about departure: Nanking troops were pouring into Kansu and Shensi, and were gradually replacing the
Tungpei troops everywhere they held a front with the Reds, as
Chiang Kai-shek made all preparations for a new annhiliation
drive from the South and the West. Someone else could write
that story. I wished to publish the one I already had. But I wouldn't
be able to do that unless I got out alive, and it took time for my
hosts to guarantee a secure passage back over the lines. Unless I
got out soon it might prove impossible: the last fissure in the
blockade might be closed.

Meanwhile life in Pao An went on tranquilly enough and you
would not have supposed that these people were aware of their
imminent 'annihilation'. Not far from me a training regiment of
new recruits was quartered. They spent their time marching and
countermarching all day, playing games and singing songs. Some
nights there were dramatics, and every night the whole town rang
with song, as different groups gathered in barracks or in cave
grottoes, yodelling down the valley. In the Red Army University
the cadets were hard at work on a ten-hour day of study. A new
mass-education drive was beginning in the town, even the 'little
devils' in the Waichiaopu being subjected to daily lessons in reading, politics, and geography.

As for myself, I lived a holiday life, riding, bathing, and playing
tennis. There were two courts, one set up on the grassy meadow,
clipped close by the goats and sheep, near the Red University, the
other a clay court next door to the cottage of Po Ku, the gangling

former Party general secretary, now chairman of the North-West Branch Soviet Government. Here, every morning, as soon as the sun rose above the hills, I played tennis with three faculty members of the Red University: the German Li Teh, Commissar Ts'ai Shu-fan,* and Commissar Wu Hsiu-ch'uan.* The court was full of stones, it was fatal to run after a fast ball, but the games were nevertheless hotly contested. Ts'ai and Wu both spoke Russian to Li Teh, while I talked to Li Teh in English and to Ts'ai and Wu in Chinese, so that we thus had a trilingual game.

A more corrupting influence I had on the community was my gambling club. I had a pack of cards, unused since my arrival, and one day I got these out and taught Commissar Ts'ai to play rummy. Ts'ai had lost an arm in battle, but it handicapped him very little at either tennis or cards. After he had learned rummy he easily beat me with one hand. For a while rummy was the rage. Even the women began sneaking up to the Waichiaopu gambling club. My mud *k'ang* became the rendezvous of Pao An's élite, and you could look around at the candle-lit faces there at night and recognize Mrs Chou En-lai (Teng Ying-ch'ao), Mrs Po Ku (Liu Ch'un-hsien), Mrs K'ai Feng, Mrs Teng Fa, and even Mrs Mao (Ho Tzu-ch'en). It set tongues wagging.

But the real menace to soviet morals didn't appear till Pao An took up poker. Our tennis quartet started this, alternating nights at Li Teh's hut and my own base of iniquity in the Foreign Office. Into this sinful mire we dragged such respectable citizens as Po Ku, Li K'e-nung, K'ai Feng, Lo Fu, and others. Stakes rose higher and higher. One-armed Ts'ai Shu-fan finally cleaned up $120,000 from Chairman Po Ku in a single evening, and it looked as if Po Ku's only way out was embezzlement of state funds. We settled the matter by ruling that Po Ku would be allowed to draw $120,000 on the treasury to pay Ts'ai, provided Ts'ai would use the money to buy airplanes for the nonexistent soviet air force. It was all in matches, anyway – and, unfortunately, so were the airplanes Ts'ai bought.

One-armed Ts'ai was quick-witted, excitable, full of repartee and badinage. He had been a Red for a decade, having joined while he was a railway worker in Hunan. Later on he had gone to Mos-

*See BN.

cow and studied there for two or three years, and found time to
fall in love with, and marry, a Russian. Sometimes he looked ruefully at his empty sleeve and wondered whether his wife wouldn't
divorce him when she saw his missing arm. 'Don't worry about a
little thing like that,' Professor Wu, who was also a returned Russian student, would comfort him. 'If you haven't had your posterity
shot off when you see her again you'll be lucky.' Nevertheless, Ts'ai
kept urging me to send him an artificial arm when I got back to the
White world.

This was only one of the impossible requests I had for things
to be sent in. Lu Ting-yi * wanted me to buy, equip, and man an
air fleet for them from the proceeds of the sale of my pictures of
the Reds. Hsu Hai-tung wanted a couple of false teeth to fill in
the gap in his gums: he had fallen in love. Everybody had something wrong with his teeth; they hadn't seen a dentist for years.
Most of the older leaders suffered from some kind of ailment,
especially from ulcers and other stomach trouble, as a result of
years on a dubious diet. But I never heard anybody complaining.

Personally I thrived on the food and put on weight, and my
disgust at facing the unvaried menu every day did not prevent
me from swallowing embarrassing quantities of it. They made me
the concession of steamed bread made from whole-wheat flour,
which when toasted was not bad, and occasionally I had pork or
mutton shaslik. Besides that I lived on millet – boiled millet, fried
millet, baked millet, and vice versa. Cabbage was plentiful, and
peppers, onions, and beans. I missed coffee, butter, sugar, milk,
eggs, and a lot of things, but I went right on eating millet.

A batch of copies of the *North China Daily News* arrived for the
library one day and I read a recipe for what seemed to be a very
simple chocolate sponge cake. I knew Po Ku was hoarding a tin
of cocoa in his hut, and I schemed that with some of this, and by
substituting pig's fat for butter, I could make that cake. Accordingly I got Li K'e-nung to write out a formal application to the
Chairman of the North-West Branch Soviet Government of the
Chinese Soviet Republic to supply me with two ounces of chocolate. After several days of delay, and hemming and hawing, and
doubts and aspersions cast upon my ability to bake a cake anyway,

* See BN.

and a lot of unravelling of red tape, and conflicts with the bureaucracy in general, we finally forced those two ounces of cocoa out
of Po Ku, and got other materials from the food cooperative. Before I could mix up the batter my bodyguard came in to investigate, and the wretch knocked the cocoa on the ground. Followed
more red tape, but finally I got the order refilled and began the
great experiment. Why labour the result? Any intelligent *hausfrau*
can foresee what happened. My improvised oven failed to function
properly, the cake did not rise, and when I took it off the fire it
was a two-inch layer of charcoal on the bottom, and a top still in
a state of slimy fluidity. However, it was eaten by the interested
onlookers in the Waichiaopu with great relish: there were too
many good materials in it to be wasted. I lost immense face and
thereafter docilely consumed my millet.

Li Teh compensated by asking me to a 'foreign meal' with him.
He had a way of getting rice and eggs sometimes, and, being
German, he made his own sausages. You could see them swinging
in strings, drying outside his door near the main street of Pao An.
He was getting ready his winter's supply. He had also built himself a fireplace and taught his Chinese wife,[1] a girl who had come
with him from Kiangsi, how to bake. He showed me that the
materials were there for tolerable cooking. It was only that the
food cooperative (where our meals were cooked in common) didn't
know how it should be done. Mrs Lo P'ing-hui, wife of a Red Army
commander (and the only lily-footed woman who made the Long
March), was chief chef of the cooperative, and I think Li Teh's
wife had a pull with her, and that is how he garnered his eggs and
sugar.

But Li Teh was more than a good cook and a good poker player.
Who was this mystery man of the Chinese soviet district? Had his
importance been exaggerated by the Kuomintang General Lo Chou-
ying, who, after reading some of Li Teh's writings found in Kiangsi,
described him as the 'brain trust' of the Reds? What was his connection with Soviet Russia? How much influence, in fact, did
Russia exercise over the affairs of Red China?

3

The Russian Influence[1]

THIS volume does not have as one of its primary purposes an examination of relations between the Communist Party of China and the Communist Party of Russia, or the Comintern, or the Soviet Union as a whole. No adequate background has been provided here for such a task. But the book would be incomplete without some discussion of these organic connections and their more significant effects on the revolutionary history of China.

Certainly and obviously Russia had for the past dozen or more years been a dominating influence – and particularly among educated youth it had been *the* dominating external influence – on Chinese thought about the social, political, economic, and cultural problems of the country. This had been almost as true, though unacknowledged, in the Kuomintang areas as it had been an openly glorified fact in the soviet districts. Everywhere in China that youth had any fervent revolutionary beliefs the impact of Marxist ideology was apparent, both as a philosophy and as a kind of substitute for religion. Among such young Chinese, Lenin was almost worshipped, Stalin was the most popular foreign leader, socialism was taken for granted as the future form of Chinese society, and Russian literature had the largest following – Maxim Gorky's works, for example, outselling all native writers except Lu Hsun, who was himself a great social revolutionary although not a Communist.

And all that was quite remarkable for one reason especially. America, England, France, Germany, Japan, Italy, and other capitalist or imperialist powers had sent thousands of political, cultural, economic, or missionary workers into China, actively to propagandize the Chinese masses with credos of their own states. Yet for many years the Russians had not had a single school, church, or even a debating society in China where Marxist-Leninist doctrines could legally be preached. Their influence, except in the soviet districts, had been largely indirect. Moreover, it had been aggressively opposed everywhere by the Kuomintang. Yet few who had been in China during that decade, and conscious of the society in which they lived, would dispute the contention that Marxism, the Russian Revolution, and the new society of the Soviet Union had probably made more profound impressions on the Chinese people than all Christian missionary influences combined.

One had to remember that the Chinese Communists' adherence to the Comintern, and unity with the USSR, were voluntary, and could have been liquidated at any time by the Chinese from within. The role of the Soviet Union for them had been most potent as a living example that bred hope and faith. The Chinese Reds stoutly believed that the Chinese revolution was not isolated, and that hundreds of millions of workers, not only in Russia but throughout the world, were anxiously watching them, and when the time came would emulate them, even as they themselves had emulated the comrades in Russia. In the day of Marx and Engels it might have been correct to say that 'the workers have no country', but the Chinese Communists believed that, besides their own little bases of power, they had a mighty fatherland in the Soviet Union.

'The Soviet Government in China,' read the Constitution adopted at the first All-China Soviet Congress, 'declares its readiness to form a revolutionary united front with the world proletariat and all oppressed nations, and *proclaims the Soviet Union, the land of proletarian dictatorship, to be its loyal ally.*' How much the words italicized meant to the Chinese soviets, which in truth most of the time were completely isolated geographically, economically, and politically, was hard to understand for any Westerner who had never known a Chinese Communist.

This idea of having behind them a great ally – even though it was less and less validated by demonstrations of positive support from the Soviet Union – was of primary importance to the morale of the Chinese Reds. It imparted to their struggle the universality of a religious cause, and they deeply cherished it. When they shouted, 'Long Live the World Revolution!' and 'Proletarians of All Lands, Unite!' it was an idea that permeated all their teaching and faith, and in it they reaffirmed their allegiance to the dream of a socialist world brotherhood.

It seemed to me that these concepts had already shown that they could change Chinese behaviour. I never suffered from any 'antiforeignism' in the Reds' attitude towards me. They were certainly anti-imperialist, but racial prejudice seemed to have been sublimated in class antagonism that knew no national boundaries. Even their anti-Japanese agitation was not directed against the Japanese on a racial basis. In their propaganda the Reds constantly emphasized that they opposed only the Japanese militarists, capitalists, and other 'Fascist oppressors', and that the Japanese masses were their potential allies. Indeed, they derived great encouragement from that conviction. This changing of national prejudice from racism to class antagonism was no doubt traceable to the education in Russia of scores of the Chinese Red leaders, who had attended Sun Yat-sen University, or the Red Academy, or some other school for international cadres of communism, and had returned as teachers to their own people.

One example of their internationalism was the intense interest with which the Reds followed the events of the Spanish Civil War. Bulletins were issued in the press, were pasted up in the meeting rooms of village soviets, were announced to the armies at the front. Special lectures were given by the political department on the cause and significance of the Spanish war, and the 'people's front' in Spain was contrasted with the 'united front' in China. Mass meetings of the populace were summoned, demonstrations were held, and public discussions were encouraged. It was quite surprising sometimes to find, even far back in the mountains, Red farmers who knew a few rudimentary facts about such things as the Italian conquest of Abyssinia and the German-Italian 'invasion' of Spain, and spoke of these powers as the 'Fascist allies' of their enemy, Japan. Despite their geographical isolation, these rustics now knew much more about that aspect of world politics, thanks to radio news and wall newspapers and Communist lecturers and propagandists, than the rural population anywhere else in China.

The strict discipline of Communist method and organization had seemingly produced among Chinese Marxists a type of cooperation and a suppression of individualism which the average 'Old China Hand', or treaty-port merchant, or missionary who 'knew Chinese psychology' would have found impossible to believe without witnessing for himself. In their political life the existence of the individual was an atomic pulse in the social whole, the mass, and must bend to its will, either consciously in the role of leadership, or unconsciously as part of the material demiurge. There had been disputes and internecine struggles among the Communists, but none severe enough to deal a fatal injury to either the army or the Party.

Had Nanking been able at any time to split their military and political strength into contradictory and permanently warring factions, as it did with all other Opposition groups – as Chiang Kai-shek did with his own rivals for power within the Kuomintang – the task of Communist suppression might have been rewarded with final success. But its attempts were failures. For example, a few years before, Nanking had hoped to utilize the worldwide Stalin-Trotsky controversy to divide the Chinese Communists, but although so-called Chinese 'Trotskyites' did appear, they never developed any important mass influence or following.

The Reds had generally discarded much of the ceremony of traditional Chinese etiquette, and their psychology and character were quite different from our old conceptions of Chinese. They were direct, frank, simple, undevious, and scientific-minded. They were also implacable enemies of the old Chinese familism.*

With their zealous adoration of the Soviet Union there had naturally been a lot of copying and imitating of foreign ideas, institutions, methods, and organizations. The Chinese Red Army was constructed on Russian military lines, and much of its tactical knowledge derived from Russian experience. Social organizations in general followed the pattern laid down by Russian Bolshevism. Many Red songs were put to Russian music and widely sung in the soviet districts. *Su wei-ai* – Chinese for 'soviet' – was only one example of many words transliterated directly from Russian into Chinese.

*Here I do not speak of the peasant masses as a whole, but of a Communist vanguard. But even among the sovietized peasantry, attitudes were in striking contrast with those described, for example, in Arthur H. Smith's *Chinese Characteristics* (NY, 1894).

But in their borrowing there was much adaptation; few Russian ideas or institutions survived without drastic changes to suit the milieu in which they operated. The empirical process of a decade eliminated indiscriminate wholesale importations, and also resulted in the introduction of peculiarly Chinese features. A process of imitation and adaptation of the West had, of course, been going on in the bourgeois world of China, too – for there was very little left even of poetry of the ancient feudal heritage, that 'scrap material of a great history' as Spengler calls it, which the Chinese were able to use in building either a modern bourgeois or a socialist society capable of grappling with the vast new demands of the country. While the Reds leaned heavily on Russia for organizational methods with youth, Generalissimo Chiang Kai-shek not only used Italian bombing planes to destroy them, but also borrowed from the YMCA in building his anti-Communist New Life movement.

And finally, of course, the political ideology, tactical line, and theoretical leadership of the Chinese Communists had been under the close guidance, if not positive direction, of the Communist International. Great benefits undoubtedly accrued to the Chinese Reds from sharing the collective experience of the Russian Revolution, and from the leadership of the Comintern. But it was also true that the Comintern could be held responsible for serious reverses suffered by the Chinese Communists in the anguish of their growth.

4

Chinese Communism and the Comintern[1]

IT is possible to divide the history of Sino-Russian relations from 1923 to 1937 roughly into three periods. The first, from 1923 to 1927, was a period of triple alliance between the Soviet Union and the Nationalist revolutionaries, consisting of strange bedfellows aligned under the banners of the Kuomintang and the Communist Parties, and aiming at the overthrow by revolution of the then extant government of China, and the restoration of China's complete sovereignty. That enterprise ended with the triumph of the right-wing Kuomintang, the founding of the National Government at Nanking, the latter's compromise with the colonial power, and the severance of Sino-Russian relations.

From 1927 to 1933 there was a period of isolation of Russia from (Nationalist) China, and its complete insulation against Russian influence. This era closed when Moscow resumed diplomatic relations with Nanking late in 1933. The third period began with a lukewarm Nanking-Moscow *rapprochement*, embarrassed considerably by the continued heavy civil war between Nanking and the Chinese Communists. It was to end dramatically early in 1937, when a partial reconciliation was effected between the Communists and the Kuomintang, with new possibilities opened up for Sino-Russian cooperation.

The three periods of Sino-Russian relationship mentioned here accurately reflected also the changes in the character of the Comintern and its stages of transition. It is impossible here to enter into the complex causes, domestic and international, which brought about those changes, both in the Soviet Union and in the Comintern, but it is pertinent to see how in the main they had affected, and were affected by, the Chinese Revolution.

The 1927 crisis of the Chinese Revolution coincided with a crisis in Russia, and in the Comintern, expressed in the struggle between

Trotskyism and Stalinism for theoretical and practical control of Russia. Had Stalin been able to advance his slogan, 'socialism in one country', much earlier than 1924, had the issue been fought out and had he been able to dominate the Comintern before then, quite possibly the 'intervention' in China might never have begun. Such a speculation in any case was idle now. When Stalin did develop his fight, the line in China had already been cast. The active military, political, financial, and intellectual collaboration given to the Chinese Nationalist Revolution was until 1926 under the direction chiefly of Zinoviev, who was chairman of the Communist International. Then from early 1926 onward Stalin became chiefly responsible for the affairs and policies of the Comintern as well as the Communist Party of the Soviet Union, and it was nowhere disputed that he had tightened his grasp on both organizations ever since.

Thus it was Stalin who led the Comintern that gave the Chinese Communists their tactical line and 'directives' in 1926 and during the catastrophe of the spring of 1927. During those fateful months, in which disaster gathered above the heads of the Chinese Communists, Stalin's line was subjected to continuous bombardment from the Opposition, dominated by Trotsky, Zinoviev, and Kamenav. While he was Comintern chairman, Zinoviev had fully supported the line of Communist cooperation with the Kuomintang, but he violently attacked this same line as carried out by Stalin. Particularly after Chiang Kai-shek's first 'treachery' – the abortive attempt at a *coup d'état* in Canton in 1926 – Zinoviev predicted an inevitable counter-revolution in which the national bourgeoisie would compromise with imperialism and 'betray the masses'.

At least a year before Chiang Kai-shek's second and successful *coup d'état*, Zinoviev began demanding the separation of the Communists from the Kuomintang, 'the party of the national bourgeoisie', which he now considered incapable of carrying out the two main tasks of the revolution – anti-imperialism, i.e. the overthrow of foreign domination of China, and 'antifeudalism', or the destruction of the landlord-gentry rule in rural China. Just as early, Trotsky began urging the formation of soviets and an independent Chinese Red Army. The Opposition in general foretold the failure of the 'bourgeois-democratic' revolution – all they hoped for in this period – if Stalin's line was continued.

Stalin defended himself, after the débâcle, by ridiculing as non-Marxist the Trotskyist contentions that the tactical line of the Comintern had been the main cause of the failure:

Comrade Kamenev [declared Stalin] said that the policy of the Communist International was responsible for the defeat of the Chinese Revolution, and that we 'bred Cavaignacs in China.' ... How can it be asserted that the tactics of a party can abolish or reverse the relation of class forces? What are we to say of people who forget the relation of class forces in time of revolution, and who try to explain everything by the tactics of a party? Only one thing can be said of such people – that they have abandoned Marxism.

Trotsky required no help from me in framing appropriate replies to Stalin's self-exculpations, but as his wit had not prevented the earlier destruction of Communist regimes in Hungary and Bavaria, nor the general defeat of the Comintern's hopes throughout the East, so it did not save the Chinese Communists from a catastrophe which all but destroyed the Party. Only Stalin won – that is, he drove Trotsky from the temple – and consequently Stalin dominated future activities of the Comintern in China – which for a time were practically nil. Russian organs in China were closed, Russian Communists were killed or driven from the country, the flow of financial, military, and political help from Russia dwindled. The Chinese Communist Party was thrown into great confusion, and for a time its interior leadership lost contact with the Comintern. The rural soviet movement and (Mao's) Chinese Red Army began spontaneously, and they did not, in fact, get much applause from Russia till after the Sixth Congress, when the Communist International gave its postnatal sanction.[2]

After 1927 it became impossible for Russia to have any direct physical connection with the Chinese Red areas, which had no seaport and were entirely surrounded by a ring of hostile troops. Whereas in the past there had been scores of Comintern workers in China, there were now two or three, often almost isolated from society as a whole, seldom able to risk a stay of more than a few months. Whereas a large flow of Russian gold and arms had formerly gone to Chiang Kai-shek's Nationalists, now a trickle reached the Reds. And whereas the whole Soviet Union had backed the Great Revolution of 1925–7, the Chinese Communist movement was now aided only by a Comintern which could no longer command the vast resources of the 'base of the world revolution', but had to limp along as a kind of poor stepchild which might be officially disinherited whenever it did anything malaprop.

Actual financial help given to the Chinese Reds by Moscow or the Comintern during this decade seemed to have been amazingly small. When Mr and Mrs Hilaire Noulens were arrested in Shanghai in 1932 and convicted in Nanking as chief Far Eastern agents of the Comintern, police evidence showed that total outpayments for the whole Orient (not just China) had not at most exceeded the equivalent of about US $15,000 per month. That was a trifle compared with the vast sums poured into China to support Japanese and Nazi-Fascist propaganda. It was rather pitiful also in contrast, for example, with America's $50,000,000 Wheat Loan to Nanking in 1933 – the proceeds of which were of decisive value to Chiang Kai-shek's civil war against the Reds, according to reports of foreign military observers.

America, England, Germany, and Italy sold Nanking great quantities of airplanes, tanks, guns, and munitions, but of course sold none to the Reds. The American Army released officers to train the Chinese air force, which demolished towns in Red China, and Italian and German instructors actually led some of the most destructive bombing expeditions themselves – as happened on a larger scale in Spain. To Chiang Kai-shek's aid Germany sent Von Seeckt, and after him Von Falkenhausen, with a staff of Prussian officers who improved Nanking's technique of annihilation. It seemed that Chiang Kai-shek was propped up for nearly ten years by more important aid than any foreign power gave to the Reds.

Probably the Chinese Reds fought with less material foreign help than any army in modern Chinese history.

That Foreign Brain Trust

THERE had not been a single foreign adviser with China's Red Army during the first five years of its existence. Not until 1933 did Li Teh appear in the Kiangsi soviet districts as a German representative of the Comintern, to take a high position both politically and militarily. Yet despite the numerical insignificance of this 'foreign influence', several responsible Communists in the North-West apparently felt that Li Teh's advice had been to a great extent responsible for two costly mistakes in the Kiangsi Red republic. The first, as Mao Tse-tung pointed out, was the failure of the Red Army to unite with the Nineteenth Route Army, when the latter arose in revolt against Nanking in the autumn of 1933.

The Nineteenth Route Army, commanded by Generals Chen Ming-hsiu, Ts'ai T'ing-k'ai, and Chiang Kuang-nai, made an impressive defence of Shanghai against the Japanese attack in 1932, and had demonstrated its strong national-revolutionary character. Transferred to Fukien after the Shanghai Truce, it gradually became a centre of political opposition to Nanking's 'nonresistance' policy. Following Nanking's negotiation of the humiliating Tangku Truce with Japan, the Nineteenth Route Army leaders set up an independent government in Fukien province and started a movement for a democratic republic and the destruction of Chiang Kai-shek's regime.

The Nineteenth Route Army was one of the few Kuomintang military units never defeated by the Reds, and they had great respect for its fighting ability. Composed mostly of Cantonese, it really reflected in its political character a loosely organized left-wing opposition movement. It was the main military support of several factions on the periphery of the Kuomintang, led by the She-hui Min-chu T'ang, the Chinese Social Democrats.

Sent to Fukien to participate in Communist suppression late in 1932, the Nineteenth Route Army leaders instead quickly built up a base of their own from which to oppose Chiang Kai-shek. They entered into a nonaggression agreement with the Reds and proposed an anti-Nanking, anti-Japanese alliance along much the same lines that were later on evolved in the North-West between the Manchurian, the North-Western, and the Communist armies. But instead of cooperating with the Nineteenth Route Army the Reds withdrew their main forces from the Fukien border to western Kiangsi. That left Chiang Kai-shek free to descend from Chekiang into neighbouring Fukien with little impediment. The Generalissimo struck before the Nineteenth Route Army was prepared militarily or politically, and quickly quashed the insurgents. The Reds consequently lost their strongest potential allies. There is no doubt that elimination of the Nineteenth Route Army very much facilitated the task of destroying the southern soviets, to which Chiang Kai-shek at once turned with a new confidence early in 1934.

The Reds' second serious mistake was made in the planning of strategy and tactics to meet Chiang's new offensive – the Fifth Campaign. In previous campaigns the Reds had relied on superiority in manoeuvring warfare, and their ability to take the initiative from Chiang Kai-shek in strong swift concentrations and surprise attacks. Positional warfare and regular fighting had always played minor roles in their operations. But in the Fifth Campaign, according to Red commanders to whom I talked, Li Teh insisted upon a strategy of positional warfare, relegating partisan and guerrilla tactics to auxiliary tasks, and somehow won acceptance for his scheme against (so I was told) 'unanimous' opposition of the Red military council.[1]

But whatever errors of judgement Li Teh may have made, there was little question that his long experience with Chinese fighting methods, and on Chinese terrain, made him one of the best qualified Occidental military authorities on China. And the personal courage of a man who had endured the severe hardships of the Long March commanded admiration and remained a challenge to armchair revolutionaries all over the world. For Li Teh, an outsize foreigner, the Long March had presented some special hardships. He had stomach complaints, and was badly in need of a dentist, but his first problem was to keep supplied with shoes large enough for his enormous number elevens. There did not seem to be any shoes that big in China. For three years he had lived without any contact with Europeans, most of the time without books to read. When I was in Pao An he was delighted to have got hold of a copy of the huge *China Year Book*, which he carefully digested from cover to cover, including its innumerable tables of statistics – a feat constituting one of the few things he could boast in common with the *Year Book* editor, H. G. W. Woodhead, CBE. This blue-eyed, fair-haired Aryan had not spoken a word of Chinese when he first immersed himself alone with his Oriental comrades, and he still had to conduct all his serious conversations through inter-preters or in German, Russian, or French.

It was almost impossible to believe that under any genius of command the Reds could have emerged victorious against the odds that faced them throughout the year of the Fifth Campaign. It was not the phenomenon of foreign support on the side of the Reds, but its presence in a major degree on the side of the Kuomintang, that characterized the last struggle of the Kiangsi Soviet Republic. Quite clearly the Chinese Red Army was not 'officered by Russian Bolsheviks', 'mercenaries of Moscow roubles', or 'puppet troops of Stalin'. Chinese and foreign newspapers during the anti-Red wars used regularly to report how many 'corpses of Russian officers' were found on the battlefield after a Kuomintang attack on the Reds. No foreign corpses were ever produced, yet so effective was this propaganda that many non-Communist Chinese really thought of the Red Army as some kind of foreign invasion.

So much for Kiangsi. During the next two years of the Long March the Reds were almost entirely cut off from contact even with their own Party members in the coastal cities of China, and the Comintern only infrequently got in direct communication with the Red Army. Wang Ming (Ch'en Shao-yu),* the Chinese Party's chief delegate in Moscow, must have found it very difficult at times to get accurate information even on the location of the main forces of the Red Army for his reports to the Comintern, and some of his articles in *Inprecorr* † seemed to reflect that. I happened

---

*See BN.

† 'International Press Correspondence', organ of the Third, or Communist, International (Comintern), published in Moscow.

to be in Pao An one day when some copies of *Inprecorr* arrived, and I saw Lo Fu, the American-educated secretary of the Central Committee of the Party, eagerly devouring them. He mentioned casually that he had not seen an *Inprecorr* for nearly three years.

And not until September 1936, while I was still with the Reds, did the detailed account of the proceedings of the Seventh Congress of the Communist International, held just a year previously, finally reach the Red capital of China. It was these reports which brought to the Chinese Communists for the first time the fully developed thesis of the international anti-Fascist united-front tactics which were to guide them in their policy during the months ahead, when revolt was to spread throughout the North-West, and to shake the entire Orient. And once more the Comintern and Stalin were to assert their will in the affairs of China, in a manner that would sharply affect the development of the revolution.

I was to view that episode from the sidelines again in Peking.

6

Farewell to Red China

Two interesting things happened before I left Pao An. On 9
October radio messages from Kansu reached us telling of the
successful junction at Huining of the vanguard of the Fourth Red
Army with Ch'en Keng's First Division of the First Army Corps.[1]
All the regular Red Army forces were now concentrated in North-
West China with good lines of communications established. Orders
for winter uniforms poured into the factories of Pao An and Wu
Ch'i Chen. The combined forces of the three armies reportedly
numbered between 80,000 and 90,000 seasoned, well-equipped warriors. Celebrations and rejoicing were held in Pao An and throughout the soviet districts. The long period of suspense during the
fighting in south Kansu was ended. Everyone now felt a new confidence in the future. With the whole of the best Red troops in
China concentrated in a large new territory, and near-by another
100,000 sympathetic troops of the Tungpei Army, whom they had
come to think of as allies, the Reds now believed that their proposals for a united front would be heard with keener interest at
Nanking.

The second important event was an interview I had with Mao
Tse-tung just before I left, in which, for the first time, he indicated
concrete terms on the basis of which the Communists would
welcome peace with the Kuomintang and cooperation to resist
Japan. Some of these terms had already been announced in a
manifesto issued by the Communist Party in August. In my conversation with Mao I asked him to explain the reasons for his new
policy.[2]

'First of all,' he began, 'the seriousness of Japanese aggression:
it is becoming more intensified every day, and is so formidable a
menace that before it all the forces of China must unite. Besides
the Communist Party there are other parties and forces in China,
and the strongest of these is the Kuomintang. Without its co-

operation our strength at present is insufficient to resist Japan in war. Nanking must participate. The Kuomintang and the Communist Party are the two main political forces in China, and if they continue to fight now in civil war the effect will be unfavourable for the anti-Japanese movement.

'Second, since August 1935 the Communist Party has been urging, by manifesto, a union of all parties in China for the purpose of resisting Japan, and to this programme the entire populace has responded with sympathy, notwithstanding the fact that the Kuomintang has continued its attacks upon us.

'The third point is that many patriotic elements even in the Kuomintang now favour a reunion with the Communist Party. Anti-Japanese elements even in the Nanking Government, and Nanking's own armies, are today ready to unite because of the peril to our national existence.

'These are the main characteristics of the present situation in China, and because of them we are obliged to reconsider in detail the concrete formula under which such cooperation in the national liberation movement can become possible. The fundamental point of unity which we insist upon is the national-liberation anti-Japanese principle. In order to realize it we believe there must be established a national defence democratic government. Its main tasks must be to resist the foreign invader, to grant popular rights to the masses of the people, and to intensify the development of the country's economy.

'We will therefore support a parliamentary form of representative government, an anti-Japanese salvation government, a government which protects and supports all popular patriotic groups. If such a republic is established, the Chinese soviets will become a part of it. We will realize in our areas measures for a democratic parliamentary form of government.'

'Does that mean,' I asked, 'that the laws of such a [democratic] government would also apply in soviet districts?'

Mao replied in the affirmative. He said that such a government should restore and once more realize Sun Yat-sen's final will, and his three 'basic principles' during the Great Revolution, which were: alliance with the USSR and those countries which treat China as an equal; union with the Chinese Communist Party; and fundamental protection of the interests of the Chinese working class.

'If such a movement develops in the Kuomintang,' he continued, 'we are prepared to cooperate with and support it, and to form a united front against imperialism such as existed in 1925–7. We are convinced that this is the only way left to save our nation.'

'Is there any *immediate* cause for the new proposals?' I inquired. 'They must certainly be regarded as the most important decision in your Party's history in a decade.'

'The immediate causes,' Mao explained, 'are the severe new demands of Japan,* capitulation to which must enormously handi- cap any attempts at resistance in the future, and the popular response to this deepening threat of Japanese invasion in the form of a great people's patriotic movement. These conditions have in turn produced a change in attitude among certain elements in Nanking. Under the circumstances it is now possible to hope for the realization of such a policy as we propose. Had it been offered in this form a year ago, or earlier, neither the country nor the Kuo- mintang would have been prepared for it.

'At present, negotiations are being conducted. While the Com- munist Party has no great positive hopes of persuading Nanking to resist Japan, it is nevertheless possible. As long as it is, the Com- munist Party will be ready to cooperate in all necessary measures. If Chiang Kai-shek prefers to continue the civil war, the Red Army will also receive him.'

In effect, Mao made a formal declaration of the readiness of the Communist Party, the Soviet Government, and the Red Army to cease civil war and further attempts to overthrow Nanking by force, and to submit to the high command of a representative cen- tral government, provided there was created the political frame- work in which the cooperation of other parties besides the Kuo- mintang would be possible. At this time also, though not as part of the formal interview, Mao indicated that the Communists would be prepared to make such changes in nomenclature as would facili- tate 'cooperation', without fundamentally affecting the inde- pendent role of the Red Army and the Communist Party. Thus, if it

* Foreign Minister Hirota's 'Three-Point' demands, served on the Nanking Government.

were necessary, the Red Army would change its name to National Revolutionary Army, the name 'soviets' would be abandoned, and the agrarian policy would be modified during the period of preparation for war against Japan. During the turbulent weeks that lay ahead, Mao's statement was to have an important influence on events.*

In the middle of October 1936, after I had been with the Reds nearly four months, arrangements were finally completed for my return to the White world. It had not been easy. Chang Hsuehliang's friendly Tungpei troops had been withdrawn from nearly every front and replaced by Nanking or other hostile forces. There was only one outlet, then, through a Tungpei division which still had a front with the Reds near Lochuan, a walled city a day's motor trip north of Sian.

I walked down the main street of Defended Peace for the last time, and the farther I got towards the gate, the more reluctantly I moved. People popped their heads out of offices to shout last remarks. My poker club turned out *en masse* to bid the *maestro* good-bye, and some 'little devils' trudged with me to the walls of Pao An. I stopped to take a picture of Old Hsu and Old Hsieh, their arms thrown around each other's shoulders. Only Mao Tse-tung failed to appear; he was still asleep.

'Don't forget my artificial arm!' called Ts'ai.

'Don't forget my films!' urged Lu Ting-yi.[3]

'We'll be waiting for the air fleet!' laughed Yang Shang-k'un.

'Send me a wife!' demanded Li K'e-nung.

'And send back those four ounces of cocoa,' chided Po Ku.

The whole Red University was seated out in the open, under a great tree, listening to a lecture by Lo Fu, when I went past. They all came over, and we shook hands, and I mumbled a few words. Then I turned and forded the stream, waved them a farewell, and rode up quickly with my little caravan. I might be the last foreigner to see any of them alive, I thought. It was very depressing. I felt that I was not going home, but leaving it.

In five days we reached the southern frontier, and I waited there for three days, staying in a tiny village and eating black beans

---

*The full text of this interview appeared in *The China Weekly Review* (Shanghai), 14 and 21 November 1936.

and wild pig. It was a beautiful wooded country, alive with game, and I spent the days in the hills with some farmers and Red soldiers, hunting pig and deer. The bush was crowded with huge pheasants, and one day we even saw, far out of range, two tigers streaking across a clearing in a valley drenched with the purple-gold of autumn. The front was absolutely peaceful, and the Reds had only one battalion stationed here.

On the 20th I got through no man's land safely and behind the Tungpei lines, and on a borrowed horse next day I rode into Lochuan, where a truck was waiting for me. A day later I was in Sianfu. At the Drum Tower I jumped down from beside the driver and asked one of the Reds (who were wearing Tungpei uniforms) to toss me my bag. A long search, and then a longer search, while my fears increased. Finally there was no doubt about it. My bag was not there. In that bag were a dozen diaries and notebooks, thirty rolls of film – the first still and moving pictures ever taken of the Chinese Red Army – and several pounds of Red magazines, newspapers, and documents. It had to be found.

Excitement under the Drum Tower, while traffic policemen curiously gazed from a short distance away. Whispered consultations. Finally it was realized what had happened. The truck had been loaded with gunnysacks full of broken Tungpei rifles and guns being sent for repairs, and my bag, in case of any search, had been stuffed into such a sack also. Back at Hsienyang, on the opposite shore of the Wei River, twenty miles behind us, the missing object had been thrown off with the other loads. The driver stared ruefully at the truck. 'T'*a ma'ti*,' he offered in consolation.

It was already dusk, and the driver suggested that he wait till morning to go back and hunt for it. Morning! Something warned me that morning would be too late. I insisted, and I finally won the argument. The truck reversed and returned, and I stayed awake all night in a friend's house in Sianfu wondering whether I would ever see that priceless bag again. If it were opened at Hsienyang, not only would all my things be lost forever, but that 'Tungpei' truck and all its occupants would be *huai-la* – finished. There were Nationalist gendarmes at Hsienyang.

The bag was found. But my hunch about the urgency of the search had been absolutely correct, for early next morning all traffic was completely swept from the streets, and all roads leading into the city were lined with gendarmes and troops. Peasants were cleared out of their homes along the road. Some of the more unsightly huts were simply demolished, so that there would be nothing offensive to the eye. Generalissimo Chiang Kai-shek was paying a sudden call on Sianfu. It would have been impossible then for our truck to return over that road to the Wei River, for it skirted the heavily guarded airfield.

This arrival of the Generalissimo made an unforgettable contrast with the scenes still fresh in my mind – of Mao Tse-tung, or Hsu Hai-tung, or Lin Piao, or P'eng Teh-huai nonchalantly strolling down a street in Red China. And the Generalissimo did not have a price on his head. But the precautions taken to protect him in Sian were to prove inadequate. He had too many enemies among the very troops who were guarding him.

Part Twelve

WHITE WORLD AGAIN

I

A Preface to Mutiny

I EMERGED from Red China to find a sharpening tension between the Tungpei troops of Young Marshal Chang Hsueh-liang and Generalissimo Chiang Kai-shek, who was now not only commander in-chief of China's armed forces, but also chairman of the Executive Yuan – a position comparable to that of premier.

I have described* how the Tungpei troops were gradually being transformed, militarily and politically, from mercenaries who had been shipped to half a dozen different provinces to fight the Reds into an army infected by the national patriotic anti-Japanese slogans of its enemy, convinced of the futility of continued civil war, stirred by only one exhortation, loyal to but one central idea – the hope of 'fighting back to the old homeland', of recovering Manchuria from the Japanese who had driven them from their homes and abused and murdered their families. These notions being directly opposed to the maxims then held by Nanking, the Tungpei troops had found themselves with a growing fellow-feeling for the anti-Japanese Red Army.

The estrangement had been widened by important occurrences during the four months of my travels. In the South-West a revolt against Nanking had been led by Generals Pai Chung-hsi and Li Tsung-jen, whose chief political demands were based on opposition to the Nationalist Government's nonresistance policies. After weeks of near-war, a compromise settlement had finally been reached, but the interim had provided a tremendous stimulus to the anti-Japanese movement throughout China. Three or four Japanese had been killed by angry mobs in various parts of the interior, and Japan had presented to Nanking strong demands for apologies, compensations, and new political concessions. Another Sino-Japanese 'incident', followed by a Japanese invasion, seemed a possibility.

*See especially Part One, Chapter 3.

Meanwhile the anti-Japanese movement, led by the left-wing National Salvation Association, was, despite stern measures of suppression, rising in strength everywhere, and considerable mass pressure was being indirectly exerted on Nanking to stiffen its attitude. Such pressure multiplied when, in October, Japanese-led Mongol and Chinese puppet troops, equipped and trained in Japan's conquered Jehol and Chahar, began an invasion of northern Suiyuan (Inner Mongolia). But the widespread popular demand that this be considered 'the last extremity', and the signal for a 'war of resistance' on a national scale, was ignored. No mobilization orders were forthcoming. Nanking's standing reply remained. 'Internal unification' – i.e., extermination of the Reds – must come first. Many patriotic quarters began to urge that the Communists' proposals for an end to civil war, and the creation of a national front on the basis of 'voluntary unification', be accepted by Nanking, in order to concentrate the entire energies of the people to oppose the common peril of Japan. Proponents of such opinions were arrested as 'traitors'.

The highest degree of emotional excitement centred in the North-West. Few people realized then how closely the anti-Japanese sentiment of the Tungpei Army was connected with the determination to stop the war against the Reds. Sian seemed a long way off to most Chinese as well as to foreigners in the big treaty ports of China, and it was little visited by journalists. An exception was Miss Nym Wales, an American writer, who in October journeyed to Sian and interviewed the Young Marshal. Miss Wales reported:

The serious anti-Japanese movement in China is formulating itself not in the various 'incidents' ranging from North to South, but here in Sianfu among the Northeastern exiles from Manchuria – as one might expect that it logically should. While the movement is being suppressed in other parts of China, in Sianfu it is under the open and enthusiastic leadership of Young Marshal Chang Hsueh-liang – ardently supported by his troops, if not compelled by them to act in this direction.*

Reflecting on the significance of her interview with the Young Marshal, Miss Wales wrote:

In effect, and read in relation to its background, this interview may be interpreted as an attempt to influence Chiang Kai-shek to lead active

* Written for the *New York Sun, circa* 25 October 1936.

resistance ... implying a threat (in his statement) that 'only by resistance to foreign aggression [i.e., not by civil war] can the *real* unification of China be manifested,' and that 'if the Government does not obey the will of the people it cannot stand.' Most significant, this Deputy Commander-in-Chief (second only to Chiang Kai-shek) said that 'if the Communists can sincerely cooperate to resist the common foreign invader, perhaps it is possible that this problem can be settled peacefully.' ...

But Chiang Kai-shek plainly underestimated the seriousness of the warning. In October he sent the First Army – his best – to attack the Reds in Kansu, and when he arrived in Sianfu it was for the purpose of completing preliminary plans for his sixth general offensive against the Reds. In Sian and Lanchow arrangements were made to accommodate more than 100 bombers. Tons of bombs arrived. It was reported that poison gas was to be used. This was seemingly the only explanation of Chiang's queer boast that he would 'destroy the remnant Red bandits in a couple of weeks, or at most a month'.*

One thing Chiang must have understood after his October visit to Sian. That was that the Tungpei troops were becoming useless in the war against the Communists. In interviews with Tungpei commanders the Generalissimo could now discern a profound lack of interest in his new offensive. One of Chang Hsueh-liang's staff told me later that at this time the Young Marshal formally presented to the Generalissimo the programme for a national front, cessation of civil war, alliance with Russia, and resistance to Japan. Chiang Kai-shek replied, 'I will never talk about this until every Red soldier in China is exterminated, and every Communist is in prison. Only then would it be possible to cooperate with Russia.' A little before this the Generalissimo had rejected a Russian offer of a mutual-defence pact through his then foreign minister, Wang Ching-wei.[1]

Now the Generalissimo went back to his headquarters in Loyang and supervised preparations for his new campaign. Twenty divisions of troops were to be brought into the North-West if necessary. By late November over ten full war-strength divisions had already been concentrated near Tungkuan, outside the historic pass at the gateway to Shensi. Trainloads of shells and supplies

*See Chiang's diary.

poured into Sian. Tanks, armoured cars, motor transports were prepared to move after them.

A flame of strong nationalist feeling swept through the country, and the Japanese demanded the suppression of the National Salvation movement, which they held responsible for the anti-Japanese agitation. Nanking obliged. Seven of the most prominent leaders of the organization, all respectable citizens, including a prominent banker, a lawyer, educators, and writers, were arrested. At the same time the government suppressed fourteen nationally popular magazines. Strikes in the Japanese mills of Shanghai, partly in patriotic protest against the Japanese invasion of Suiyuan, were also broken up with considerable violence by the Japanese, in co-operation with the Kuomintang. When other patriotic strikes occurred in Tsingtao, the Japanese landed their own marines, arrested the strikers, occupied the city. The marines were withdrawn only after Chiang had agreed virtually to prohibit all strikes in Japanese mills of Tsingtao in the future.

All those happenings had further repercussions in the North-West. In November, under pressure from his own officers, Chang Hsueh-liang dispatched his famous appeal to be sent to the Suiyuan front. 'In order to control our troops,' this missive concluded,

we should keep our promise to them that whenever the chance comes they will be allowed to carry out their desire of fighting the enemy. Otherwise they will regard not only myself, but also Your Excellency, as a cheat, and thus will no longer obey us. Please give us the order to mobilize at least a part, if not the whole, of the Tungpei Army, to march immediately to Suiyuan as reinforcements to those who are fulfilling their sacred mission of fighting Japanese imperialism there. If so, I, as well as my troops, of more than 100,000, shall follow Your Excellency's leadership to the end.

The earnest tone of this whole letter,* the hope of restoring an army's lost prestige, were overwhelmingly evident. But Chiang rejected the suggestion. He still wanted the Tungpei Army to fight the Reds.

Not long afterwards, importunate, the Marshal flew his plane to Loyang to repeat the request in person. At this time also he

---

*Published in Sianfu, 2 January 1937, by the North-West Military Council.

interceded for the arrested leaders of the National Salvation Association. Later on, after the arrest of the Generalissimo, Chang Hsueh-liang recounted that conversation : *

'Recently Generalissimo Chiang arrested and imprisoned seven of our National Salvation leaders in Shanghai. I asked him to release those leaders. Now, none of the National Salvation leaders are my friends or relatives, and I do not even know most of them. But I protested at their arrest because their principles are the same as mine. My request that they be released was rejected. To Chiang I then said : "Your cruelty in dealing with the patriotic movement of the people is exactly the same as that of Yuan Shih-k'ai or Chang Tsung-chang." †

'Generalissimo Chiang replied : "That is merely your viewpoint. I am the Government. My action is that of a revolutionary."

'Fellow countrymen, do you believe this?'

The question was answered by an angry roar from the assembled thousands.

But Chang Hsueh-liang's flight to Loyang at that time had one positive result. The Generalissimo agreed that when he next came to Sian he would explain his plans and strategy to the Tungpei division generals in detail. The Young Marshal returned to await impatiently his superior's second visit. Before Chiang arrived, however, two occurrences intervened which further antagonized the North-West.

The first of these was the signing of the German-Japanese anti-Communist agreement, and Italy's unofficial adherence thereto. Italy had already tacitly recognized Japan's conquest of Manchuria, in return for which Japan had acknowledged Italy's control of Abyssinia. The opening of Italian relations with Manchukuo had infuriated the Young Marshal, who had once been pals with Count Ciano. With receipt of this news he denounced both Ciano and Mussolini, and swore to destroy Italian influence in his country. 'This is absolutely the end of the Fascist movement in China !' he exclaimed in a speech before his cadets.

Then, in November also, came news of the disaster to Hu Tsung-nan's famed First Army, which on the 21st suffered a severe defeat from the Reds. General Hu, ablest of Nanking's tacticians, had for

---

* A speech reported by the *Hsiking Min Pao* (Sianfu), 17 December 1936.
† Warlords who had capitulated to Japanese demands two decades earlier.

weeks been moving almost unimpeded into northern Kansu. The Reds had slowly withdrawn, refusing battle except in minor skirmishes. But in various ways they propagandized the Nanking troops about the 'united front', trying to persuade them to halt, issuing declarations that the Red Army would attack no anti-Japanese troops, urging the enemy to join them in resisting Japan. 'Chinese must not fight Chinese!' The propaganda was to prove highly effective.

General Hu pushed on. The Reds continued to withdraw until they had almost reached Holienwan. Then they decided to retreat no farther; the enemy needed a lesson.* It needed to be shown that the united front also had teeth in it. Slowly turning, they skilfully manoeuvred General Hu's troops into a valley of loessland, surrounded them at dusk, when the air bombardment had ceased, and at night staged a surprise frontal attack supported by bayonet charges from both flanks. It was zero weather, and the Reds' bare hands were so cold they could not pull the caps from their hand grenades. Hundreds of them went into the enemy lines using their potato-masher grenades for clubs. The fierce onslaught, led by the First Army Corps, resulted in the complete destruction and disarming of two infantry brigades and a regiment of cavalry, while thousands of rifles and machine guns were captured, and one government regiment turned over intact to join the Reds. General Hu beat a hasty retreat, giving up in a few days all the territory which he had 'recovered' over a period of weeks.

The Tungpei generals must have been amused. Was it not just as they had said? Did not the Reds have more punch in them than ever? Did not this inauspicious beginning of the new campaign show how difficult the process of annihilation was going to be? A year, two years, three, and where would they be? Still fighting the Reds. And Japan? In occupation of new and greater areas of Chinese territory. But the obstinate Generalissimo, angered by the humiliation of his best army, censured General Hu and only became more determined to destroy his ten-year enemy.

Into this main theatre of events Chiang Kai-shek stepped from his airplane onto the flying field of Sian on 7 December 1936.

---

*According to a letter reporting details of the battle written to me by Dr Ma Hai-teh. He was then with the Red Army. See BN.

Meanwhile, important things had happened on both the right and left wings of the stage. Among the Tungpei commanders an agreement had been reached to present a common request for cancellation of civil war, and resistance to Japan. Into this agreement had come the officers of the army of General Yang Hu-ch'eng, the pacification commissioner of Shensi. General Yang's army, of about 40,000 men, had even less interest in continuing the war against the Reds than the Tungpei troops. To them it was Nanking's war, and they saw no good reason for wrecking themselves against the Reds, many of whom were Shensi people like themselves. It was to them also a disgraceful war, when Japan was invading the neighbouring province of Suiyuan. General Yang's troops, known as the Hsipei Chun, or North-West Army, had some months previously formed a close solidarity with the Tungpei troops, and secretly joined in the truce with the Reds.

The substance of all that surely must have been known to the Premier-Generalissimo. Although he had no regular troops in Sian, a few months earlier some 1,500 of the Third Gendarmes, a so-called 'special service' regiment of the Blueshirts, commanded by his nephew, General Chiang Hsiao-hsien, who was credited with the abduction, imprisonment, and killing of hundreds of radicals, had arrived in the city. They had established espionage headquarters throughout the province, and had begun to arrest and kidnap alleged Communist students, political workers, and soldiers. Shao Li-tzu, the Nanking-appointed governor of Shensi, was in control of the police force of the capital. As neither the Young Marshal nor Yang Hu-ch'eng had any troops but bodyguards in the city, the Generalissimo had practical command there.

This situation helped to provoke a further incident. On the 9th, two days after Chiang's arrival, several thousand students held an anti-Japanese demonstration and started to march to Lintung, to present a petition to the Generalissimo. Governor Shao ordered it to be dispersed. The police, assisted by some of Chiang Kai-shek's gendarmes, handled the students roughly, and at one stage opened fire on them. Two students were wounded, and as they happened to be children of a Tungpei officer the shooting was especially inflammatory. Chang Hsueh-liang intervened, stopped the fight, persuaded the students to return to the city, and agreed to present their petition to the Generalissimo. Infuriated, Chiang Kai-shek reprimanded Chang for his 'disloyalty' in trying 'to represent *both sides*'. Chiang Kai-shek himself wrote that he considered this incident between them the immediate cause of the revolt.

So, despite all the objections and warnings, the Generalissimo summoned a General Staff Congress on the 10th, when final plans were formally adopted to push ahead with the Sixth Campaign. A general mobilization order was prepared for the Hsipei, Tungpei, and Nanking troops already in Kansu and Shensi, together with the Nanking troops waiting at Tungkuan. It was announced that the order would be published on the 12th. It was openly stated that if Marshal Chang refused these orders his troops would be disarmed by Nanking forces, and he himself would be dismissed from his command. General Chiang Ting-wen had already been appointed to replace Chang Hsueh-liang as head of the Bandit Suppression Commission. At the same time reports reached both Chang and Yang that the Blueshirts, together with the police, had prepared a 'black list' of Communist sympathizers in their armies, who were to be arrested immediately after publication of the mobilization order.

Thus it was as the culmination of this completed chain of events that Chang Hsueh-liang called a joint meeting of the division commanders of the Tungpei and Hsipei armies at ten o'clock on the night of 11 December. Orders had been secretly given on the previous day for a division of Tungpei troops and a regiment of Yang Hu-ch'eng's army to move into the environs of Sianfu. The decision was now taken to use these forces to 'arrest' the Generalissimo and his staff. The mutiny of 170,000 troops had become a fact.

2

The Generalissimo Is Arrested

WHATEVER we may say against its motives, or the political energies behind them, it must be admitted that the *coup de théâtre* enacted at Sian was brilliantly timed and executed. No word of the rebels' plans reached their enemies until too late. By six o'clock on the morning of 12 December the whole affair was over. Tungpei and Hsipei troops were in control at Sian. The Blueshirts, surprised in their sleep, had been disarmed and arrested; practically the whole General Staff had been surrounded in its quarters at the Sian Guest House, and was imprisoned; Governor Shao Li-tzu and the chief of police were also prisoners; the city police force had surrendered to the mutineers; and fifty Nanking bombers and their pilots had been seized at the airfield.

But the arrest of the Generalissimo was a bloodier affair. Chiang Kai-shek was staying ten miles from the city, at Lintung, a famous hot-springs resort, which had been cleared of all other guests. To Lintung, at midnight, went twenty-six-year-old Captain Sun Ming-chiu,* commander of the Young Marshal's bodyguard. Halfway there he picked up 200 Tungpei troops, and at 3 a.m. drove to the outskirts of Lintung. There they waited till five o'clock, when the first truck, with about fifteen men, roared up to the hotel, was challenged by sentries, and opened fire.

Reinforcements soon arrived for the Tungpei vanguard, and Captain Sun led an assault on the Generalissimo's residence. Taken by complete surprise, the bodyguards put up a short fight – long enough, however, to permit the astounded Generalissimo to escape. When Captain Sun reached Chiang's bedroom he had already fled. Sun took a search party up the side of the rocky, snow-covered hill behind the resort. Presently they found the Generalissimo's personal servant, and not long afterwards came upon the man himself. Clad only in a loose robe thrown over his nightshirt, his bare

*See BN.

feet and hands cut in his nimble flight up the mountain, shaking in the bitter cold, and minus his false teeth, he was crouching in a cave beside a great rock:

Sun Ming-chiu hailed him, and the Generalissimo's first words were, 'If you are my comrade, shoot me and finish it all.' To which Sun replied, 'We will not shoot. We only ask you to lead our country against Japan.'

Chiang remained seated on his rock, and said with difficulty, 'Call Marshal Chang here, and I will come down.'

'Marshal Chang isn't here. The troops are rising in the city; we came to protect you.'

At this the Generalissimo seemed much relieved, and called for a horse to take him down the mountain. 'There is no horse here,' said Sun, 'but I will carry you down the mountain on my back.' And he knelt at Chiang's feet. After some hesitation, Chiang accepted, and climbed painfully onto the broad back of the young officer. They proceeded solemnly down the slope in this fashion, escorted by troops, until a servant arrived with Chiang's shoes. The little group got into a car at the foot of the hill and set off for Sian.

'The past is the past,' Sun said to him. 'From now on there must be a new policy for China. What are you going to do? ... The one urgent task for China is to fight Japan. This is the special demand of the men of the North-East. Why do you not fight Japan, but instead give the order to fight the Red Army?'

'I am the leader of the Chinese people,' Chiang shouted. 'I represent the nation. I think my policy is correct.' *

In this way, a little bloody but unbowed, the Generalissimo arrived in the city, where he became the involuntary guest of General Yang Hu-ch'eng and the Young Marshal.

On the day of the coup all division commanders of the Tung-pei and Hsipei armies signed and issued a circular telegram addressed to the Central Government, to various provincial leaders, and to the people at large. The brief missive explained that 'in order to stimulate his awakening' the Generalissimo had been 'requested to remain for the time being in Sianfu'. Meanwhile his personal safety was guaranteed. The demands of 'national salvation' submitted to the Generalissimo were broadcast to the nation

---

* Part of an interview with Sun Ming-chiu by James Bertram, who was acting for me as correspondent in Sianfu for the London *Daily Herald.*

– but everywhere suppressed in the Kuomintang-censored newspapers. Here are the rebels' eight points:

(1) Reorganize the Nanking Government and admit all parties to share the joint responsibility of national salvation.

(2) End all civil war immediately *and adopt the policy of armed resistance against Japan.*

(3) Release the [seven] leaders of the patriotic movement in Shanghai.

(4) Pardon all political prisoners.

(5) Guarantee the people liberty of assembly.

(6) Safeguard the people's rights of patriotic organization and political liberty.

(7) Put into effect the will of Dr Sun Yat-sen.

(8) Immediately convene a National Salvation conference.

To this programme the Chinese Red Army, the Chinese Soviet Government, and the Communist Party of China immediately offered their support.* A few days later Chang Hsueh-liang sent to Pao An his personal plane, which returned to Sian with three Red delegates: Chou En-lai, vice-chairman of the military council; Yeh Chien-ying, chief of staff of the East Front Army; and Po Ku, chairman of the North-West Branch Soviet Government. A joint meeting was called between the Tungpei, Hsipei, and Red Army delegates, and the three groups became open allies. On the 14th an announcement was issued of the formation of a United Anti-Japanese Army, consisting of about 130,000 Tungpei troops, 40,000 Hsipei troops, and approximately 90,000 troops of the Red Army.

Chang Hsueh-liang was elected chairman of a United Anti-Japanese Military Council, and Yang Hu-ch'eng vice-chairman. Tungpei troops under General Yu Hsueh-chung had on the 12th carried out a coup of their own against the Central Government officials and troops in Lanchow, capital of Kansu province, and had disarmed the Nanking garrison there. In the rest of Kansu the Reds and the Manchurian troops together held control of all

---

*Seven of the above eight points corresponded exactly to the programme of 'national salvation' advocated in a circular telegram issued by the Communist Party and the Soviet Government on 1 December 1936.

main communications, surrounding about 50,000 Nanking troops in that province, so that the rebels had effective power in all Shensi and Kansu.

Immediately after the incident, Tungpei and Hsipei troops moved eastward to the Shensi–Shansi and Shensi–Honan borders, on instructions from the new Council. From the same Council the Red Army took orders to push southward. Within a week the Reds had moved their 'capital' to Yenan city and occupied virtually the whole of north Shensi above the Wei River. A Red vanguard under P'eng Teh-huai was located at San Yuan, a city only thirty miles from Sianfu. Another contingent of 10,000 Reds under Hsu Hai-tung was preparing to move over to the Shensi–Honan border. The Red, North-Eastern, and North-Western troops stood shoulder to shoulder along the Shensi border. While these defensive arrangements proceeded, all three armies issued clear-cut statements declaring their opposition to a new internal war.

Steps were taken at once to carry out the eight points. All orders for war against the Reds were cancelled. More than 400 political prisoners in Sianfu were released. Censorship of the press was removed, and all suppression of patriotic (anti-Japanese) organizations was lifted. Hundreds of students were freed to work among the populace, building united-front organizations in every class. They toured into the villages also, where they began to train and arm the farmers, politically and militarily. In the army the political workers conducted an unprecedented anti-Japanese campaign. Mass meetings were summoned almost daily.

But news of those happenings was suppressed outside the provinces of the North-West. Editors who dared publish anything emanating from Sian, as even the highly respectable *Ta Kung Pao* pointed out, were threatened with instant arrest. Meanwhile Nanking's propaganda machine threw out a smokescreen that further confused an already befuddled public. Dumbfounded by the news, the government at Nanking first called a meeting of the Standing Committee (of the Central Executive Committee and the Central Political Council) of the Kuomintang, which promptly pronounced Chang Hsueh-liang a rebel, dismissed him from his posts, and demanded the release of the Generalissimo, failing which punitive operations would begin.

For three days few people knew whether Chiang Kai-shek was dead or alive – except the Associated Press, which flatly announced that Chang Hsueh-liang had described over the radio how and why he had killed him. Few people knew exactly what the rebels planned to do. Nanking cut all communications with the North-West, and its papers and manifestoes were burned by the censors.

Hundreds of words were deleted from my own dispatches. I made several attempts to send out the eight demands of the North-West – which might have helped a little to clarify the enigma for Western readers – but the censors let out not a word. Many of the foreign correspondents were themselves completely ignorant of recent happenings in the North-West. While real news and facts were rigorously suppressed, the Kuomintang and its adherents released to the world some puerile lies which made China appear much more of a madhouse than it really was: the rebels had nailed the chief of police to the city gates; the Reds had occupied Sian, were looting the city and flying Red banners on the walls; Chang Hsueh-liang had been assassinated by his own men. Almost daily it was stated by Nanking that riots were taking place in Sian. The Reds were abducting young boys and girls. Women were being 'communized'. The entire Tungpei and Hsipei armies had turned bandit. There was looting everywhere. Chang Hsueh-liang was demanding $80,000,000 ransom for the Generalissimo.*

Many of the wildest rumours circulated had their origin also with the Japanese press in China, and even with high Japanese officials. The Japanese were especially fertile with imaginary 'eye-witness' reports of the 'Red menace' in Sian. The Japanese also discovered Soviet Russian intrigue behind the coup. But they met their masters in propaganda in Moscow's press. *Izvestia* and *Pravda* went so far in their official disclaimers of responsibility, denunciations of Chang Hsueh-liang, and hosannas to Chiang Kai-shek that they invented a story showing that the Sian affair was jointly inspired by the former Chinese premier, Wang Ching-wei, and 'the Japanese imperialists' – a libel so antipodal to the facts that even the most reactionary press in China had not dared to suggest

---

* Mme Chiang Kai-shek, deploring such rumours, wrote that 'no question of money or increased power or position was at any time brought up'.

it, out of fear of ridicule. 'Prevarication is permissible, gentlemen,' it was Lenin who once exclaimed, 'but within limits!'

After the first week of Chiang's captivity Nanking's efforts to cork up the facts proved inadequate. Leaks occurred, and then big gaps. The eight-point programme was widely published in the surreptitious press, and the public began to realize that the North-West did not mean to make civil war, but to stop it. Sentiment slowly began to change from fear for the safety of an individual militarist into fear for the safety of the state. Civil war now could not save Chiang, but it might ruin China.

Intrigue for seizure of power had begun in Nanking with the news of Chiang's capture. Ambitious War Minister Ho Ying-ch'in, closely affiliated with the pro-Japanese 'political-science clique' of the Kuomintang, then in high office at Nanking – and against whom the eight-point programme was primarily directed – was hot for a 'punitive expedition'. In this General Ho was fully supported by the pro-Fascist Whampoa clique, the Blue-shirts, the Wang Ching-wei (out-of-office) faction, the Western Hills group, the 'CC' faction,* and Nanking's German and Italian advisers. Their enemies said that they all saw in the situation an opportunity to seize power, relegating the liberal, pro-American, pro-British, pro-Russian, and united-front groups in the Kuomin-tang to political nonentity. General Ho mobilized twenty Nanking divisions and moved them towards the Honan–Shensi border. He sent squadrons of airplanes roaring over Sianfu, and made tenta-tive thrusts at the rebels' lines with his infantry. Some of the Nanking planes (anti-Japanese 'fiftieth-birthday gifts' to the Gen-eralissimo) experimentally bombed Weinan and Huahsien, inside the Shensi border, and reportedly killed a number of factory workers.

The big question now became this: whether Chiang Kai-shek could, even from his seat of captivity in Sian, still muster enough support in Nanking to prevent the outbreak of an exhausting war which was likely to mean his own political, if not physical, demise. In Nanking and Shanghai his brothers-in-law – T. V. Soong, chairman of the Central Bank of China, and H. H. Kung,

---

* The two 'Cs' were Ch'en Li-fu and Ch'en Kuo-fu, brothers who controlled the Kuomintang Party apparatus.

acting premier – and Mme Chiang rallied Chiang's personal followers and worked frantically to prevent the more reactionary elements in Nanking from initiating an offensive in the name of an 'anti-Communist punitive expedition'.

Meanwhile, swift changes of heart were taking place in Sian. Soon after his capture the Generalissimo had begun to realize that perhaps his worst 'betrayers' were not in Sian but in Nanking. Contemplating this situation, Chiang Kai-shek must have decided that he did not choose to be the martyr over whose dead body General Ho Ying-ch'in or anybody else would climb to dictatorial power.

Chiang, Chang, and the Reds

CHINA was no parliamentary democracy, but was ruled by party or individual dictators. Very often in politics it reverted to feudal practice. With the press completely stifled, and the populace disfranchised, there was but one effective way to censure Nanking, or alter its policies. That was by armed insurrection or armed demonstration, or what the Chinese call *ping chien* – 'military persuasion' – a recognized tactic in Chinese political manoeuvre. Chang Hsueh-liang probably chose the most humane and direct method conceivable by which to achieve his purpose when he used direct action upon the head of the dictatorship. It cost a minimum loss of life, and a minimum of bloodshed. It was a feudal method, but the Marshal was dealing with a personality whose role in semi-feudal politics he intuitively understood. Because the objective result of Chang's action was to unite China to confront a national peril, most Chinese I knew came to regard Chang as a patriot.

Was Chiang Kai-shek's life ever really in serious danger?

It appears that it was. Not from the Young Marshal, and not from the Reds. From Yang Hu-ch'eng, possibly. But most certainly from the radical younger officers of the North-Eastern and North-Western armies, from the discontented and mutinous soldiery, and from the organized and arming masses, all of whom demanded a voice in the disposal of the Premier. Resolutions passed by the young officers called for a mass trial of 'Traitor' Chiang and all his staff. The mood of the army decidedly favoured the Generalissimo's immolation. Curiously enough, it fell to the lot of the Communists to persuade them that his life should be saved.

Communist policy throughout the Sian Incident was never clearly explained. Many people assumed that the Communists, in triumphant revenge for the decade of relentless war which Chiang Kai-shek had waged against them, would now demand his death. Many believed that they would use this opportunity to coalesce with the Tungpei and Hsipei armies, greatly enlarge their base, and challenge Nanking in a great new struggle for power. Instead, they not only urged a peaceful settlement, and the release of Chiang Kai-shek, but also his return to leadership in Nanking. Even Mme Chiang wrote that, 'quite contrary to outside beliefs, they [the Reds] were not interested in detaining the Generalissimo.' But why not? Economically, politically, militarily, in every way, they really needed internal peace.[1]

'The victory of the Chinese national liberation movement,' said Mao Tse-tung, 'will be part of the victory of world socialism, because to defeat imperialism in China means the destruction of one of its most powerful bases. If China wins its independence, the world revolution will progress very rapidly. If our country is subjugated by the enemy, we shall lose everything. *For a people being deprived of its national freedom, the revolutionary task is not immediate socialism, but the struggle for independence. We cannot even discuss communism if we are robbed of a country in which to practise it.*' *

Thus it was fundamentally on this thesis that the Communists based their united-front proposals to the Kuomintang, even before the capture of the Generalissimo. In that crisis they recognized an opportunity to demonstrate the sincerity of their offer. If they had nothing to do with the arrest of Chiang Kai-shek, they had much to do with its dénouement.[2]

Immediately after hearing of the event, the Soviet Government and the Communist Party called a joint meeting, at which it was decided to support the eight-point programme and to participate in the United Anti-Japanese Council. Soon afterwards they issued a circular telegram † expressing the belief that 'the Sian leaders acted with patriotic sincerity and zeal, wishing speedily to formulate a national policy of immediate resistance to Japan.' The telegram strongly condemned Ho Ying-ch'in's punitive expedition, declaring that 'if civil war is launched, the whole nation will be plunged into complete chaos, the Japanese robbers, taking advantage of this, will invade our nation, and enslavement will be

*In his interview with me at Pao An. Italics mine.
† 'Proposal for the Convention of a Peace Conference', Pao An, 19 December 1936.

our fate.' To secure a peaceful settlement, the Reds urged that negotiations be opened on the basis of no war, and the summoning of a peace conference of all parties, at which would be discussed the programme of united national resistance to Japan. This telegram clearly indicated the policy followed out by the Red delegates whom Marshal Chang summoned to Sian.

Shortly after his arrival, the head of the Communist delegation, Chou En-lai, went to see Chiang Kai-shek.* One could easily imagine the effect of this meeting on the Generalissimo. Still physically weak and psychologically deeply shaken by his experiences, Chiang was said to have turned pale with apprehension when Chou En-lai – his former political attaché for whose head he had once offered $80,000 – entered the room and gave him a friendly greeting. He must have at once concluded that the Red Army had entered Sian, and that he was to be turned over to it as captive. Such a fear also troubled the comely head of Mme Chiang Kai-shek, who said that she 'felt the objective [if Chiang were removed from Sian] would be somewhere behind the Red lines'.

But the Generalissimo was relieved of this apprehension by Chou and the Marshal, both of whom acknowledged him as commander-in-chief and sat down to explain the attitude of the Communists towards the national crisis. At first frigidly silent, Chiang gradually thawed as he listened, for the first time during his decade of war against the Communists, to their proposals for ending civil war.[3]

By 20 December general agreement 'in principle' seemed to have already been reached. The following excerpts from the statement issued to the foreign press by Marshal Chang Hsueh-liang on the 19th indicated that he, at least, regarded the settlement as virtually complete:

The Generalissimo's prolonged stay here is not of our doing. As soon as Mr Donald † arrived last Monday, and the Generalissimo had some-

---

*In his own account Chiang does not mention having talked to Chou En-lai.

† An Australian confidant of both Chiang Kai-shek and Chang Hsueh-liang, W. H. Donald was Nanking's first envoy to Sian (sent at Mme Chiang's insistence).

what recovered from his natural indignation, and his reluctance to talk, he calmly enough discussed the problem confronting us all, and by Tuesday had agreed in principle with the points we had in view ... and in accordance with the will of the late Dr Sun Yat-sen.

I therefore telegraphed, welcoming anyone to come from Nanking to hear the Generalissimo's views, and arrange with him for the necessary safeguards to prevent the development of civil warfare. The Generalissimo naturally vigorously demanded that he be released to proceed to Nanking, but while I personally had full confidence that the Generalissimo would carry out his promises, it was impossible to risk his being persuaded after his arrival at Nanking to continue with the warfare. ... He acquiesced in the view, however, and ever since then he has been waiting in vain, as have we, for someone to arrive from Nanking competent to deal with the matter [i.e., to offer adequate guarantees], so that the Generalissimo can return to the capital.

That is all. It is a strange thing that there has been this delay. Had someone come, he could have returned some days ago...

CHANG HSUEH-LIANG.*

But serious trouble was developing in the ranks of the radical younger officers of the Tungpei Army. They had acquired strong direct voice in the affairs of Chang's military council, and their views were important. Infected by the temper of the strong mass movement now spreading throughout the North-West, they were at first fiercely opposed to the release of Chiang Kai-shek before Nanking began to carry out the eight-point programme. The majority, in fact, insisted upon giving Chiang a 'popular trial' for his life, before an enormous mass meeting which they planned to call.

The possibility of this public humiliation had also occurred to Chiang. No one knew any better than he the potentialities of the movement that had been set afoot in the North-West, for a similar rising had almost overwhelmed him in 1927. Chiang's whole career had been a struggle against the intervention in his well-ordered chain of events of that disturbing imperative which he called 'the mob'. Talk of the 'popular trial' was even on the lips of the sentries

*This telegram was sent from Sianfu on 19 December, addressed to Frazer, London *Times* correspondent in Shanghai, with the request that it be given to other correspondents. Nanking censors suppressed it. A copy was also given to Mr Donald, who is the source of this quotation.

around him; Chiang wrote of listening through the doorway to the conversation of his jailers, in which his fate was discussed: 'When I heard [the words] "the people's verdict", I realized that it was a malicious plot to kill me by using the mob as their excuse.'

Chiang Kai-shek may have been saved from further humiliation only by the Communists' opposition to any such plan. Even before Chou's talk with Chiang, the Communists had begun to state that they had received enough assurances from him (aside from assurances to be inferred from the objective situation) to believe that if released he would be obliged to stop civil war, and in general to carry out the whole 'united-front' programme. But to do so Chiang's position had to be preserved and he must return to Nanking with his prestige intact. If he were submitted to the indignity of a 'people's trial', civil war would inevitably develop, the decade of stalemate in the Red-Kuomintang war would be very much prolonged, and hopes of achieving an anti-Japanese national front would become remote indeed. From such a prospect no party could hope to benefit, only China could suffer, and only Japan gain. So, at least, the Reds explained their policy to me.[4]

By 22 December several envoys and negotiators from the Central Government had arrived in Sian, including T. V. Soong, chairman of the National Economic Council (and Chiang's brother-in-law), the Minister of Interior, the Vice-Minister of War, the president of the Military Advisory Council, the chief aide-de-camp of the Generalissimo – as well as assorted members of the General Staff, who had been 'detained' with Chiang Kai-shek. Most of them took some part in the parleys with Chang Hsueh-liang, Yang Hu-ch'eng, Chou En-lai, and high commanders of the Tungpei Army.

The substantial meaning of the eight demands to those who supported them was, in correct order of importance, as follows: (1) cessation of civil war and cooperation between the Kuomintang and the Communists in (2) a definite policy of armed resistance against any further Japanese aggression; (3) dismissal of certain 'pro-Japanese' officials in 'Nanking, and the adoption of an active diplomacy for creating closer relations (alliances, if possible) with Great Britain, America, and Soviet Russia; (4) reorganization of the Tungpei and Hsipei armies on an equal footing (politically and militarily) with Nanking's forces; (5) greater political freedom for the people; and (6) the creation of some sort of democratic political structure at Nanking.

Those seemed to be the main points of agreement between Chiang Kai-shek and Chang Hsueh-liang before they left Sian. Chiang also made a personal guarantee that there would be no more civil war. It is certain that Chiang Kai-shek was quite honest in saying that he signed no document, and there is no evidence to support any claims that he did. But although Nanking and the Generalissimo still had their 'face', subsequent events were to show that the Young Marshal had not lost his entirely in vain.

The arrival of Mme Chiang on the 22nd no doubt hastened the termination of the interviews, and (as in her lively account of her three days in Sian she made abundantly clear) her own importunity and scolding of Chang Hsueh-liang speeded up the Generalissimo's release. Just as her husband compared himself with Jesus Christ on the Cross, so also Mme Chiang recognized herelf in a Biblical role, quoting: 'Jehovah will now do a new thing, and that is, he will make a woman protect a man.' On the 25th, when Mme Chiang was wistfully wondering if 'Santa Claus would pass by Sian', old St Nick appeared in the person of Chang Hsueh-liang, who announced that he had won all the arguments with his officers. He would that day fly them back to Nanking. And he did.

Finally, there was that last and flabbergasting gesture of face-saving. Marshal Chang Hsueh-liang, flying in his own plane, went with the Generalissimo to the capital to await punishment !

4

'Point Counter Point'

DURING the next three months most of the political involutions created at Sian were completely unravelled, and in the end the scene was radically altered. Great conquests were made and victories won. Great losses and retreats were recorded too. But the duels fought were like those in a Chinese theatre between two warriors of old. They fling out blood-curdling yells, viciously slashing the air but never actually touching each other. In the end, after the loser has acknowledged his demise by languidly draping himself on the floor for a moment, he pulls himself together and stalks from the stage under his own locomotion, a dignified walking corpse.

Such was the fascinating shadowboxing that went on at Nanking. Everybody 'won', and only history was cheated – of a victim.

'Blushing with shame, I have followed you to the capital for the appropriate punishment I deserve, so as to vindicate discipline,' said Chang Hsueh-liang to the Generalissimo, immediately after reaching Nanking.

'Due to my lack of virtue and defects in my training of subordinates,' gallantly responds Chiang, 'an unprecedented revolt broke out. . . . Now that you have expressed repentance, I will request the central authorities to adopt suitable measures for rehabilitation of the situation.'

And what were the rehabilitation measures? How superbly all acts of severity were commuted by acts of conciliation, how fine the adjustment of punishment and compensation. Here was the work of a master in the strategy of compromise, of perfect knowledge of how to split the difference between what the Chinese call *yu shih wu ming*, the 'reality without the name', and *yu ming wu shih*, the 'name without the reality'.

As Chiang's first move on returning to Nanking he issued a long statement confessing his inability to prevent the revolt, and his failure as Premier. He immediately ordered the withdrawal of all government troops from Shensi – thus fulfilling his promise to prevent civil war – and offered his resignation (he was to repeat it the traditional three times). In reality he took his resignation no more seriously than did his government, for on 29 December he called an emergency meeting of the standing committee of the Central Executive Committee and 'requested' this highest organ of the Kuomintang to do four important things: to hand over to the Military Affairs Commission (of which he was chairman) the punishment of Chang Hsueh-liang; to delegate to the Military Affairs Commission the settlement of the North-West problem; to terminate military operations against the rebels; and to abolish 'punitive expedition' headquarters which had been set up, during Chiang's absence, to attack Sian. His 'recommendations' were 'obeyed'.

On 31 December Chang Hsueh-liang was sentenced by tribunal (at which Chiang was not present) to ten years' imprisonment and deprivation of civil rights for five years. On the following day he was pardoned.[1] And all the time he was the personal guest of Chiang Kai-shek's brother-in-law and recent envoy to Sian, T. V. Soong. On 6 January the Generalissimo's Sian headquarters for Bandit Suppression (Anti-Communist Campaign) was abolished. Two days later it was already known that the skids were under Japanese-speaking, Japanese-educated Foreign Minister Chang Chun, important leader of the 'political-science clique' in the Kuomintang. Chang Chun had been the principal target of the North-West in its charges of 'pro-Japanese' officials at Nanking. He was replaced by Dr Wang Chung-hui, British-educated barrister, and a leader of the Ou-Mei P'ai, the anti-Japanese 'European-American clique' of Kuomintang politicians, whom the North-West junta regarded with favour.

Again at Chiang's request, a plenary session of the Kuomintang Central Executive Committee was summoned for 15 February. In the past its functions had been easily predictable, and confined to legalizing important changes in Party policy decided in advance by the ruling cliques, which in coalition were the Chiang Kai-shek dictatorship. What were the important changes of policy now to be introduced? Hundreds of resolutions were prepared for presentation to that august body. The great majority dealt with 'national salvation'.

During January and early February, Chiang Kai-shek took 'sick leave'. He retired, with Chang Hsueh-liang, to rest in the Generalissimo's country home near Fenghua, his native place in Chekiang. His first resignation rejected, Chiang repeated it. Meanwhile, ostensibly freed from official duties, he had complete command of the settlement of the North-West issue, complete control of the conversations going on with the Tungpei, Hsipei, and Red Army commanders. Chang Hsueh-liang, 'in disgrace', was at his side, still a virtual prisoner.

On 10 February the Central Executive Committee of the Communist Party addressed to the National Government at Nanking, and to the Third Plenary Session, a historic telegram.* It congratulated the government on the peaceful settlement of the Sian affair, and on the 'impending peaceful unification' of the country. To the Plenary Session it proposed four important changes in policies: to end civil war; to guarantee freedom of speech, press, and assembly, and to release political prisoners; to invoke a national plan of resistance to Japanese aggression; and to return to the 'three principles' of Dr Sun Yat-sen's will.

If these proposals were adopted, in form or in substance, the Communists stated they were prepared, for the purpose of 'hastening national unification and resistance to Japan', to suspend all attempts to overthrow the government and to adopt the following policies: (1) change the name of the Red Army to the 'National Revolutionary Army', and place it under the command of Chiang Kai-shek's Military Affairs Commission; (2) change the name of the Soviet Government to the 'Special Area Government of the Republic of China'; (3) realize a 'completely democratic' (representative) form of government within the soviet districts; and (4) suspend the policy of land confiscation and concentrate the efforts of the people on the tasks of national salvation – that is, anti-Nipponism.

But the Plenary Session, when it convened on 15 February, took no formal notice of the bandits' telegram. There was much more important business to be accomplished. Chiang Kai-shek in his

*See *New China*, a Communist publication (Yenan), 15 March 1937.

first speech to the Session once more recounted, in complete and (for him) impassioned utterance, the whole story of his captivity in Sian. Dramatically he described how he refused to sign any pledge to carry out the rebels' demands. He told also how the rebels were converted to his own point of view, and were moved to tears by the revelations of patriotism in his confiscated diary. And not until he had said all this did he at last, in a very offhand and contemptuous manner, submit the rebels' eight demands to the Session. Reiterating its complete confidence in the Generalissimo, the Session rejected his third resignation, condemned Chang Hsueh-liang, and just as casually and contemptuously rejected the impertinent demands.

Meanwhile, however, in its well-trained way, the Central Executive Committee was accomplishing things on its own initiative. Significant above everything else, perhaps, was the opening statement of Wang Ching-wei, second only to Chiang Kai-shek in party leadership. For the first time since the beginning of the anti-Red wars, Comrade Wang made a speech in which he did not say that 'internal pacification' (eradication of communism) was the most important problem before the country, in which he did not repeat his famous phrase, 'resistance *after* unification'. The 'foremost question' before the country now, he said, was 'recovery of the lost territories'. Moreover, the Session actually adopted resolutions to begin by recovering east Hopei and northern Chahar, and abolishing the Japan-made 'autonomous' Hopei-Chahar Council. Of course that did not mean that Nanking was to launch a war against Japan. Its significance was simply that further Japanese military aggression in China would meet with armed resistance from Nanking. But that was a real leap forward.

Second, the CEC, again on the Premier's recommendation, decided to convene on 12 November the long-delayed 'People's Congress', which was supposed to inaugurate 'democracy' in China. More important, the standing committee was authorized to revise the organic laws of the Congress to increase representation of 'all groups'. The Generalissimo – through Wang Ching-wei again – announced that the second great problem before the nation was the speedy realization of democracy.

Finally, on the last day of the Session, Chiang Kai-shek made a statement in which he promised greater liberty of speech to all but traitors – and he said nothing about the 'intellectual bandits'. He also promised 'release of political prisoners who repent'. Very quietly an order went out to the press that no longer were the epithets 'Red bandit' and 'Communist bandit' to be used. A few prisons began to pour out a trickle of their less important victims.

Then, as if in afterthought, on 21 February, last day of the historic Session, a long manifesto was issued, ostensibly to denounce the Communists. The history of ten years of crime and vandalism was recapitulated. Was it not obvious that any talk of 'reconciliation' with brigands, thieves, and murderers was out of the question? But all that explosion of wind, it turned out, was actual preparation for the terms of peace which, to the extreme distaste of Tories who still opposed peace at any price, concluded the manifesto.

What were these proposals? The Session offered the Communists a chance 'to make a new start in life', on four conditions: (1) abolition of the Red Army and its incorporation into the national army; (2) dissolution of the 'Soviet Republic'; (3) cessation of Communist propaganda that was diametrically opposed to Dr Sun Yat-sen's 'three principles'; and (4) abandonment of the class struggle. Thus, though phrased in terms of 'surrender' instead of 'co-operation', the Kuomintang had accepted the Reds' basis for negotiation of a 'reconciliation'.* Note that those terms still left the Reds in possession of their little autonomous state, their own army, their organizations, their Party, and their 'maximum programme' for the future. Or so, at least, the Reds could hope. And so, indeed, they did. For on 15 March the Communist Party, the Soviet Government, and the Red Army issued a long manifesto requesting the opening of negotiations with Nanking.

What was the purpose of all these complex manoeuvres by Chiang? Obviously they were skilfully interwoven in such a manner as to conciliate the Opposition without weakening the prestige either of himself or of Nanking. Read in their proper sequence, his orders and statements, and the resolutions of the Plenary Session, showed that he *partly* satisfied the political de-

* For full text of these important resolutions see *The China Year Book* (Shanghai, 1938).

mands of all groups of the Opposition – just enough to shatter their solidarity and resolution in defying him, but not enough to cause a revolt in the Kuomintang. Civil war had been stopped, and it was clear that Nanking had at last shouldered the task of armed resistance to Japan. Promises of greater political freedom had been made, and a definite date had been set for the realization of 'democracy'. Finally, a formula had been proposed by which the Kuomintang and the Communists might at least live together in armed truce, if not 'cooperation'. At the same time the government had nominally rejected the rebels' demands and the Communists' proposals for 'cooperation'. It was all very wonderful.

One should not fail to note that these conciliatory gestures were forced through by Chiang Kai-shek in the face of considerable antagonism to them in Nanking, and at the conclusion of a terrific personal shock which might have embittered and unbalanced a man less gifted with foresight, and hastened him into precipitate actions of revenge – which, in fact, Chiang's outraged followers in Nanking demanded. But Chiang was shrewder than they. It was real genius of political strategy that he did not ignore the promises made in Sian, that he took no immediate overt revenge against his captors, that he tactfully employed a policy combining just the right weight of threat with the necessary softening of concession. In that way he eventually succeeded in breaking up the North-West bloc (his first objective), and peacefully transferred the Tungpei Army from Shensi into Anhui and Honan, while the Hsipei Army of General Yang Hu-ch'eng was reorganized under the central command. In February, Nanking troops were able to occupy Sian and its environs without disturbance or opposition, and in the following month – with his guns at their frontiers – Chiang opened negotiations with the Communists.[2]

Auld Lang Syne?

DURING the Sian Incident the Red Army had occupied large new areas. In Shensi it now held the greater part of the province, including nearly everything north of the Wei River. In their some fifty counties – an area between 60,000 and 70,000 square miles, or, roughly, twice the size of Austria – the Reds controlled the biggest single realm they had ever ruled. But it was economically poor, very limited in its possibilities of development, and thinly populated, with perhaps less than 2,000,000 inhabitants.

Strategically the area was extremely important. From it the Reds could, if they chose, block the trade ways to Central Asia, or perhaps later themselves make direct connections with Chinese Turkestan (Sinkiang) or Outer Mongolia. It was one of only two Chinese frontiers, and sources of supply, which Japan could not blockade. More than half of Chinese Turkestan, roughly 550,000 square miles in area, was ruled by a warlord seemingly sympathetic to the Chinese Reds and the USSR. North-east of it, Outer Mongolia, another 900,000 square miles of former dependency of China – Chinese suzerainty over which was still nominally recognized, even by Russia – was now definitely under the Red banner, as a result of the military alliance (Mutual Defence Pact) concluded with the USSR in 1936.

These three regions of Communist control in what could still be called 'Greater China' were altogether about a third the size of the former Chinese Empire. Separating them from physical contact with each other were only politically ambiguous buffer districts inhabited by Mongols, Moslems, and frontiersmen whose ties with Nanking were fragile, and against whom the threat of Japanese conquest was a deepening reality. Those areas might later on be brought into the orbit of the 'Anti-Japanese United Front', and under soviet influence. That would close in an immense future Red base extending from Central Asia and Mongolia into the heart of North-West China. But all that realm was backward, some of it barren steppe and desert, with poor communications, and sparsely populated. It could become a decisive factor in Eastern politics only in close alliance with the advanced industrial and military bases of either the USSR or Central China, or both.

Immediate gains of the Chinese Reds were confined to these categories: the cessation of civil war, a certain degree of liberalization and tolerance in Nanking's internal policies, a stiffening towards Japan, and a partial release of the soviet districts from their long isolation. As a result of negotiations conducted between General Chang Chung, the Generalissimo's envoy in Sian, and Chou En-lai, the Reds' delegate there, a number of important changes took place during April, May, and June. The economic blockade was lifted. Trade relations were established between the Red districts and the outside world. More important, communications between the two areas were quietly restored. On the frontiers the Red Star and the Kuomintang White Sun were crossed in symbolic union.

Mail and telegraph services were partly reopened. The Reds purchased a fleet of American trucks in Sian and operated a bus service connecting the principal points in their region. Needed technical materials of all sorts began to pour in. Most precious to the Communists were books. A new Lu Hsun Memorial Library was established in Yenan, and to fill it Communist comrades throughout the country sent in tons of new literature. Hundreds of young Chinese Communists migrated from the great cities to Yenan, the new Red capital in north Shensi. By May over 2,000 students had been accepted for enrolment in the Red University (renamed the 'Anti-Japanese University'), and some 500 were in the Communist Party school. Among them were Mongols, Moslems, Tibetans, Formosans, and Miao and Lolo tribesmen. Scores were also studying in a number of technical training institutes.

Enthusiastic young radicals as well as veteran Party workers rolled in from all parts of China, some walking over great distances. By July, despite the rigours of student life, there were so many applicants that no more could be accommodated. Scores were turned back to wait for another term, when the Reds prepared to receive 5,000. Many trained technicians also arrived, and were given work as teachers, or in the 'construction plan' which was now begun. In this, perhaps, lay the biggest immediate benefit of peace: a base in which freely to train, equip, and discipline new cadres for the ranks of the revolution and the anti-Japanese war.

Of course, the Kuomintang continued strictly to supervise the Reds' connections with the outer world. There was less restriction on the movement of Communists now, but there was as yet no open acknowledgement of the fact. Many parties of non-Communist intellectuals also arrived in Red China to investigate conditions there – and many of them stayed on, to work. In June, the Kuomintang itself secretly sent a semi-official group of delegates, headed by Hsiao Hua, to visit the Red capital. They toured the soviet districts and made appropriate rufescent anti-Japanese speeches before huge mass meetings. They acclaimed the return to the anti-imperialist united front between Communists and the Kuomintang. Nothing of this was allowed to appear in the Kuomintang press, however.

Conditions in the Kuomintang areas also improved for the followers of Lenin. The Communist Party was still nominally illegal, but it became possible to extend its influence and widen its organization, for the oppression somewhat diminished. A small but steady stream of political prisoners was released from the jails. The special gendarmes, the Blueshirts, continued their espionage on Communists, but kidnappings and torture ceased. Word was sent out that Blueshirt activities henceforth should centre primarily on 'pro-Japanese traitors'. A number of the latter were arrested, and several Chinese agents in Japan's pay were reported to have been executed.

By May, in an exchange of concessions, the soviets had prepared to adopt the name Special Area Government, and the Red Army had petitioned to be included in the national defence forces as the National Revolutionary Army. Great 'all-China' meetings of Party and Red Army delegates were called in May and June. Decisions were made on measures by which the new policies, calling for co-operation with the Kuomintang, could be realized. At these meetings the portraits of Lenin, Marx, Stalin, Mao Tse-tung, Chu Teh, and other Red leaders appeared beside those of Chiang Kai-shek and Sun Yat-sen.

The most important changes in Red policy were the cessation of the practice of confiscation of the landlords' land, the cessation of anti-Nanking, anti-Kuomintang propaganda, and the promise of equal rights and the voting franchise to all citizens, regardless of their class origin. Cessation of land confiscation did not mean the return of land to the landlords in areas where redistribution had already been realized, but was an agreement to abandon the practice in districts newly brought under Communist control.*

On his side, Generalissimo Chiang agreed to consider the soviet districts part of the 'national defence area', and pay accordingly. The first payment to the Reds ($500,000) was delivered shortly after Chiang Kai-shek's return to Nanking. Some of the Kuomintang money was used to convert soviet currency, to buy manufactures for their cooperatives, and to purchase needed equipment. The exact monthly allowance from Nanking was still under negotiation – as, indeed, was the whole definitive working agreement for future cooperation – while the storm of Japanese invasion was gathering in the North.

In June the Generalissimo sent his private plane to Sian for Chou En-lai, the Reds' chief delegate, who flew to Kuling, China's summer capital. There Chou held further conversations with Chiang Kai-shek and members of the cabinet. Among points discussed was the Communists' demand for representation in the People's Congress – the Congress scheduled to adopt a 'democratic' constitution – in November. It was reported that an agreement was reached whereby the 'Special Area' would be permitted to elect nine delegates on a regional basis.

However, these delegates in all probability would not be known as 'Communists'. Nanking had not openly acknowledged the so-called remarriage. It preferred to regard the relationship rather as the annexation of a concubine whose continence had yet to be proved, and one about which, for diplomatic reasons, the less said

---

*New land-rent policies were, however, to penalize the landlords, and in practice the bias in 'democratic' political organizations favoured the poor peasants. At no time, not even in the early months of the brief-lived two-party cooperation, did the Communists cease propagandizing for their cause or repudiate their ultimate Marxist programme.

outside family circles the better. But even this furtive *mésalliance* was an astounding and open defiance of Japan, unthinkable a few months previously. Meanwhile Japan's own offer (through Match-maker Hirota) of a respectable 'anti-Red' marriage* with Nanking was finally spurned. In this was perhaps a last and definite indica-tion that Nanking's foreign policy had undergone a fundamental change.

All that seemed an utterly incomprehensible dénouement to many an observer, and serious errors were made in its analysis. After a decade of the fiercest kind of civil war, Red and White suddenly burst into 'Auld Lang Syne'. What was the meaning of it? Had the Reds turned White, and the Whites turned Red? Neither one. But surely someone must have won, and someone lost? Yes, China had won, Japan had lost. For it seemed that a final decision in the profoundly complicated internal struggle had been postponed once more, by the intervention of a third ingredient – Japanese imperialism.

*The essence of Japan's proposals was to make of China a kind of satellite partner in the Rome-Berlin-Tokyo alliance.

6

Red Horizons

THERE was an accomplished social scientist named Lenin. 'History generally,' he wrote, 'and the history of revolutions in particular, is always richer in content, more varied, more many-sided, more lively and "subtle", than the best parties and the most class-conscious vanguards of the most advanced class imagine. This is understandable, because the best vanguards express the class consciousness, the will, the passion, the fantasy of tens of thousands, while the revolution is made, at the moment of its climax and exertion of all human capabilities, by the class consciousness, the will, the passion, and the fantasy of tens of millions who are urged on by the very acutest class struggle.'*

In what ways had Chinese history proved 'richer in content, more varied, more many-sided, more lively and "subtle",' than the Communist theoreticians had foreseen a decade or so ago? To be specific, why had the Red Army failed to win power in China? In attempting to answer one had to recall again, and keep clearly in mind, the Communist conception of the Chinese revolution, and of its main objectives.

The Communists said that the Chinese capitalist class was not a true bourgeoisie, but a 'colonial bourgeoisie'. It was a 'comprador class', an excrescence of the foreign finance and monopoly capitalism which it primarily served. It was too weak to lead the revolution. It could achieve the conditions of its own freedom only through the fulfilment of the anti-imperialist movement, the elimination of foreign domination. But only the workers and peasants could lead such a revolution to its final victory. And the Communists intended that the workers and peasants should not turn over the fruits of that victory to the neo-capitalists whom they were thus to release, as had happened in France, Germany,

*V. I. Lenin, 'Left-Wing' Communism: An Infantile Disorder (London, 1934).

Italy – everywhere, in fact, except in Russia. Instead, they should retain power throughout a kind of 'NEP' period, a brief epoch of 'controlled capitalism', and then a period of state capitalism, followed at last by a speedy transition into socialist construction, with the help of the USSR. All that was indicated quite clearly in *Fundamental Laws of the Chinese Soviet Republic.**

'The aim of the driving out of imperialism, and destroying the Kuomintang,' repeated Mao Tse-tung in 1934,† 'is to unify China, to bring the *bourgeois democratic revolution* to fruition, and to make it possible to turn this revolution into a higher stage of socialist revolution. This is the task of the soviet.'

At the apex of the Great Revolution (1925–7) there was present the necessary revolutionary mood among both the peasant masses and the proletariat. But there were many differences from the situation which had produced the Russian Revolution. One of these was very great. Survivals of feudalism were even more pronounced in Russia than in China, but China was a semicolonial country, an 'oppressed nation', while Russia was an imperialist country, an 'oppressor nation'. In the Russian Revolution the proletariat had to conquer only a single class, its own native bourgeois-imperialist class, while the Chinese revolution had to contend with an indigenous enemy of dual personality – both its own nascent bourgeoisie and the entrenched interests of foreign imperialism. Theoretically, in the beginning, the Chinese Communists expected this dual nature of their enemy to be offset by the dual nature of their own assault, which would be aided by their 'proletarian allies' of the world, and the 'toilers of the USSR'.

Nearly half of all the industrial workers of China huddled in Shanghai, under the gunboats of the world's great powers. In Tientsin, Tsingtao, Shanghai, Hankow, Hongkong, Kowloon, and other spheres of imperialism were probably three quarters of all the industrial workers of China. Shanghai provided the classic prototype. Here were British, American, French, Japanese, Italian, *and Chinese* soldiers, sailors, and police, all the forces of world imperialism combined with native gangsterism and the comprador

* Mao Tse-tung *et al.*

† *Red China: President Mao Tse-tung Reports* ... (See Bibliography.)

bourgeoisie, the most degenerate elements in Chinese society, 'co-operating' in wielding the truncheon over the unarmed workers.

Rights of freedom of speech, assembly, or organization were denied these workers. Mobilization of the industrial proletariat in China for political action was hardly conceivable *as long as the dual system of native and foreign policing power was maintained.* Only once in history had it been broken – in 1927 – when for a few days Chiang Kai-shek made use of the workers to secure his victory over the northern warlords. But immediately afterwards they were suppressed in one of the demoralizing bloodbaths of history, with the sanctification of the foreign powers and the financial help of foreign capitalists.

The Nanking regime could and did count upon the security of the industrial bases held by the foreign powers in the treaty ports – and on their troops, their guns, their cruisers, and their inland police, the river gunboats – and on their wealth, their press, their propaganda, and their spies. It did not matter that instances of direct participation of these powers in actual warfare against the Red Army were few. They occurred on the occasions when such action was necessary. But their chief services were rendered by policing the industrial workers, by furnishing Nanking with munitions and airplanes, and by entering into a conspiracy which complacently denied the very existence of civil war by the simple device of calling the Communists 'bandits', so that the embarrassing question of 'nonintervention committees' (as in the case of Spain) was never even allowed to rise.

Communist leaders were obliged to fall back on the rural districts, where the soviet movement, while retaining the aims and ideology of proletarian class consciousness, in practice assumed a peasant-based national social revolution. In the rural areas the Reds hoped eventually to build up sufficient strength to be able to attack urban bases where foreign influence was less firmly established and later – with the help, they hoped, of the world proletariat – to invest the citadels of foreign power in the treaty ports.

But while the imperialist powers were the objective allies of the Chinese bourgeoisie against communism, the assistance that Communists expected from the world proletariat failed to materialize.

Although in the *Communist International Programme** it was clearly recognized that successful proletarian movements in semi-colonial countries such as China 'will be possible only if direct support is obtained from the countries in which the proletarian dictatorship is established' (i.e., in the USSR), the Soviet Union in fact did not extend to the Chinese comrades the promised 'assistance and support of the proletarian dictatorship' in any degree commensurate with the need. On the contrary, the great help, amounting to intervention, which the Soviet Union gave to Chiang Kai-shek until 1927 had the objective effect of assisting him into power – although, at the same time, it helped create the revolutionary opposition in the Red Army movement that arose later on. Of course, the rendering of direct aid to the Chinese Communists after 1927 became quite incompatible with the position adopted by the USSR – for that would have been to jeopardize by the danger of international war the whole programme of socialist construction in one country. Nevertheless, it must be noted that the influence of this factor on the Chinese revolution was very great.

Deprived of material help from an outside ally, the Chinese Communists continued to struggle alone for the 'hegemony of the bourgeois revolution', believing that deep changes in internal and international politics would release new forces in their favour. They were quite mistaken.

The Kuomintang's power remained relatively secure in the great urban centres, for the reasons mentioned, but in the villages it developed only very slowly. Paradoxically – and dialectically – the rural anaemia of the bourgeoisie was traceable to the same source as Nanking's strength in the cities – to foreign imperialism. For while imperialism was eager enough to 'cooperate' in preventing or suppressing urban insurrection, or possibilities of it, at the same time it was objectively engaged – chiefly through Japan, the focus of the system's point of greatest stress in the Far East – in collecting heavy fees for this service, in the form of new annexations of territory (Manchuria, Jehol, Chahar, and East Hopei), new concessions, and new wealth belonging to China. The great burdens placed upon the Nanking Government by this newest phase of

*London, 1929.

imperialist aggression made it impossible for the Kuomintang to introduce in the rural areas the necessary capitalist 'reforms' – commercial banking, improved communications, centralized taxing and policing power, etc. – fast enough to suppress the spread of rural discontent and peasant rebellion. By carrying out a land revolution the Reds were able to satisfy the demands of a substantial peasant following, take the leadership of part of rural China, and even build several powerful bases on an almost purely agrarian economy. But meanwhile they could grow no stronger in the cities, on which their enemies continued to be based.

In this situation, the Communists argued that the Kuomintang's attacks on the soviets prevented the Chinese people from fufilling their mission of 'national liberation' in driving out the Japanese, and that the Kuomintang's own unwillingness to defend the country proved the bankruptcy of its leadership. But the enraged Nationalists retorted that the Communists' attempts to overthrow the government prevented them from resisting Japan, while the continued practice of 'Red banditry' in the interior, despite the grave national crisis, retarded the realization of internal reforms. And here in essence was the peculiar stalemate, the fundamental impotence of this period of the Chinese revolution.

Over this decade the imperialist pressure gradually became so severe, the Japanese price for the protection of the interests of the Chinese compradors in the cities became so excessive, that it tended to neutralize the class antagonisms between the Kuomintang, the party of the bourgeoisie and the landlords, and the Kungch'antang, the party of the workers and peasants. It was precisely because of this – and because of the immediate events described in the foregoing chapters – that the Kuomintang and the Communist Party were thus able, after a decade of ceaseless warfare, to reunite in a synthesis expressed in terms of their essential unity on the higher plane of a common antagonism against Japanese imperialism. This unity was not stable; it was not permanent; it might break up again whenever the internal denials outweighed the external ones. But it began a new era.

At the end of a decade of class war the Communists had been forced to abandon temporarily their thesis that 'only under the hegemony of the proletariat' could the bourgeois democratic movement develop. Instead it was acknowledged that *only* 'a union of all classes' could achieve those purposes. Its practical significance was the clear recognition of the *present* leadership – which was here synonymous with power – of the Kuomintang in the national revolution. For the Reds it had certainly to be considered 'a great retreat', as Mao Tse-tung had frankly admitted, from the days in Kiangsi, when they fought 'to consolidate the workers' and peasants' dictatorship, to extend this dictatorship to the whole country, and to mobilize, organize, and arm the soviets and the masses to fight in this revolutionary war'.* The armed struggle for immediate power had ceased. Communist slogans became these: to support the Central Government, to hasten peaceful unification under Nanking, to realize bourgeois democracy, and to organize the whole nation to oppose Japan.

Practical gains resulting from these concessions have already been discussed. But what guarantees had the Communists that these gains could be held? What guarantees were there that the internal peace would be maintained, that the promised democracy would be realized, that a policy of resistance to Japan would last?

In such periods 'it is necessary', wrote Lenin, 'to combine the strictest loyalty to the ideas of communism with the ability to make all necessary compromises, to "tack", to make agreements, zigzags, retreats, and so on.' And thus, although among the Chinese Communists there was this great shift in strategy, still they believed it was now possible to conduct the contest in a much more favourable atmosphere than in the past. There had been an 'exchange of concessions', as Mao Tse-tung said, and an exchange to which 'there are definite limits'.

He continued:

> The Communist Party retains the leadership on problems in the soviet districts and the Red Army, and retains its independence and freedom of criticism in its relations with the Kuomintang. On these points no concessions can be made. . . . The Communist Party will never abandon its aims of socialism and communism, it will still pass through the stage of democratic revolution of the bourgeoisie to attain the stages of socialism and communism. The Communist Party retains its own programme and its own policies.[1]

*Red China: President Mao Tse-tung Reports . . . , p. 11. (See Bibliography.)

Quite clearly the Kuomintang would utilize to the fullest extent the benefits of the new Communist policy towards itself. With Nanking's authority recognized by the only political party in China capable of challenging it, Chiang Kai-shek would continue to extend his military and economic power in peripheral areas where warlord influence was still strong, areas such as Kwangsi, Yunnan, Kweichow, and Szechuan. Improving his military position all around the Reds, he would meanwhile extract political concessions from them in return for his temporary toleration. Eventually, by skilful combination of political and economic tactics, he hoped so to weaken them politically that, when the moment was right for the final demand of their complete surrender (which he undoubtedly still aspired to secure), he might isolate the Red Army, fragmentize it on the basis of internal political dissensions, and deal with the recalcitrant remnant as a purely regional military problem.

The Reds were under no delusions about that. Likewise they were under no delusions that the promise of 'democracy' could be fulfilled without a continued active opposition of their own. No party of dictatorship in history ever yielded up its power except under the heaviest pressure, and the Kuomintang would prove no exception. The achievement of even the measure of 'democracy' now in prospect would have been impossible without the ten-year presence of an armed Opposition. Indeed, without that Opposition no 'democracy' would have been necessary, and no state power with the degree of centralization which we now began to witness in China would have been conceivable. For the growth of popular government was, like the maturing of the modern state itself, a manifestation of the need for a power and mechanism in which to attempt to reconcile contradictions inherent in capitalist society – the basic class antagonisms.

These contradictions were not diminishing in China, but rapidly increasing, and, to the extent that they sharpened, the state had to take recognition of them. The achievement of internal peace itself made it inevitable, if that internal peace were to last, that Nanking reflect a wider representation of social stratifications. That did not mean that there was any likelihood of the Kuomintang quietly signing its own death warrant by genuinely realizing bourgeois democracy, and by permitting the Communist Party to compete with it in open election campaigning (for it was quite possible that the vote of the peasantry alone would have given the Communists an overwhelming majority), although that is what the Communists and other parties demanded, and would continue to agitate for. But it did mean that some recognition of peasant demands would have to be made by the tiny minority which monopolized the state economy and policing power. The tentative concession of representation of the soviet areas in the National Congress was an indication of that.

The centripetal spread of economic, political, and social interests, the process of so-called 'unification' – the very measures which created the system – at the same time required, for their own preservation, that ever widening groups be focused in the centre in an attempt to resolve the insoluble – the deepening conflict of class interests. And the more Nanking tended to represent different and wider class interests throughout the country – the nearer it came to achieving democracy – the more it was forced to seek a solution of self-survival by resistance to the increasingly greedy demands of Japan.

The guarantees of increased Communist influence, the guarantee against future annihilation campaigns, therefore, were seen by the Communists to be inherent in the organic economic, social, and political relationships of the country – precisely those formations which had resulted in the present situation. These were, first of all, a wide popular demand among both the armed and unarmed masses for continued internal unity, for improved livelihood, for popular government, and for resistance to Japan in a common struggle for national freedom. Second, the Communist Party's 'guarantees' lay in the leadership it could continue to give to the movement for those demands throughout the country, and in the actual military and political fighting strength of the Communist Party.

In the spring of 1937 the temporary diminution in Japanese pressure on China, a pause in the invasion of Inner Mongolia, the opening of Anglo-Japanese conversations for 'cooperation in China', and the hopes of the British Government to mediate a Sino-Japanese agreement and a 'fundamental peace' in the Far East caused some people to wonder whether the Communist estimate of the political scene was not in error. Was it not reckless gambling to pivot a strategy on the central inevitability of an early Sino-Japanese war? Now that internal peace was established in China, now that the Reds had ceased their attempts to overthrow the Kuomintang, Japan was really turning a conciliatory face to Nanking, it was argued. Japan's imperialists realized that they had pushed the Chinese bourgeoisie too far and too fast along the road of surrender, with the result that China's class war was cancelled in the universal hatred of Japan. They now saw the wisdom of enforcing a new and friendly policy towards the Chinese bourgeoisie, in order to renew its freedom to engage in internal conflict. And such a Tokyo-Nanking *rapprochement* would destroy the Communists' political influence, which was too heavily based on *k'ang jih* – the 'resist Japan' movement.

But history in flood must seek its outlets according to the laws of dynamics. It cannot be forced back into its preflood channels. Japan could not revert to a static policy in China even though Japan's ablest leaders realized the imperative necessity for a halt. And this Red prescience seemed fully vindicated on 8 July by the Liukochiao Incident. Japanese troops, holding 'midnight manoeuvres' (quite illegally) on Chinese territory at the town of Wanping, about ten miles west of Peking, claimed to have been fired on by Chinese railway guards. The incident gave the Japanese Army the pretext. By the middle of July the Japanese had rushed some 10,000 troops into the Peking–Tientsin area and had made new imperialist demands, capitulation to which would have meant virtually the acceptance of a Japanese protectorate in North China.

The Communists' conception of that situation, and of the kindling events which it must set in motion, was that the growing pressure of the whole nation for resistance, not only here but everywhere that new acts of aggression occurred, would oblige Chiang Kai-shek's regime to take a position in which, if Japan did not reverse her policies and make amends for the past, there was no way out but war. Which meant that there was no way out but war. And the Communists continued to interpret such a war not only as a struggle for national independence, but as a revolutionary movement, 'because to defeat imperialism in China means the destruction of one of its most powerful bases' and because *the victory of the Chinese revolution itself 'will correspond with the victory of the Chinese people against Japanese aggression'* (Mao Tse-tung). According to Mao Tse-tung's analysis of the breaking-point politico-economic tension in Japan, China, and throughout the world, this settlement in human destinies could not be delayed for any important length of time.

The Reds foresaw that in this war it would become necessary to arm, equip, train, and mobilize tens of millions of people in a struggle which could serve the dual surgical function of removing the external tumour of imperialism and the internal cancer of class oppression. Such a war, as they conceived it, could be conducted only by the broadest mobilization of the masses, by the development of a highly politicized army. And such a war could be *won* only under the most advanced revolutionary leadership. It could be initiated by the bourgeoisie. It would be completed only by the revolutionary workers and peasants. Once the people were really armed and organized on an immense scale, the Communists would do everything possible to establish a decisive victory over Japan. They would march with the Kuomintang as long as it led the resistance. But they would be prepared to take over this leadership whenever the government faltered, turned 'defeatist', and exhibited a willingness to submit to Japan – a tendency which they anticipated would appear soon after the first great losses of the war.

Probably the Nanking regime fully understood those objectives of the Communists, and hence they would seek out every possible road of compromise; they would, if they could avoid the internal consequences, make further concessions to Japan, at least until the odds seemed very greatly in favour of the regime's ability not only to enter a war with power, but to emerge from it with that power still intact, and with the internal revolution still in abeyance. But the Communists were sufficiently content with their own analysis of the course of history behind them to be satisfied with the chart of direction which they had chosen for the voyage ahead, through events which would *compel* Nanking to make a stand for its own survival. They foresaw that Nanking might continue to vacillate, that Japan might continue to feint and manoeuvre in myriad ways, until the utmost agony of antagonism was reached between the interests of Japanese imperialism and the national interests of China externally, and between the Chinese and Japanese masses and their landlord-gentry rulers internally, until the moment when all the physical restraints and oppressions became utterly intolerable, the barriers of history broke down, the mighty catastrophe bred by imperialism was set loose, Frankenstein-like, to destroy imperialism, and *le déluge* swept forward.

Thus 'capitalism digs its own grave', thus imperialism would destroy imperialism, in that only a great imperialist war would release the forces that could bring to the Asian masses the arms, the training, the political experience, the freedom of organization, and the mortal weakening of the internal policing power which were the necessary accessories for any conceivably successful revolutionary ascent to power in the relatively near future. Whether or not, even then, the 'armed masses' were likely to follow Communist leadership with final success depended upon many variable and unpredictable factors – internal factors first of all, but such factors also as the policies in the East of America, Great Britain, France, Germany, and Italy, and to the very greatest extent the policies of the USSR.

And that, I believed, was the contour of the Communist picture of the future as China waited for Japan to strike. One might not follow all of it, but this at least seemed certain – that what Lenin had written more than twenty years before was still true : 'Whatever may be the fate of the great Chinese revolution, against which various "civilized" hyenas are now sharpening their teeth, no forces in the world will restore the old serfdom in Asia, nor erase from the face of the earth the heroic democracy of the popular masses in the Asiatic and semi-Asiatic countries.'

And another thing seemed equally certain. Neither could the democratic socialist ideas for which tens of thousands of youths had already died in China, nor the energies behind them, be destroyed. The movement for social revolution in China might suffer defeats, might temporarily retreat, might for a time seem to languish, might make wide changes in tactics to fit immediate necessities and aims, might even for a period be submerged, be forced underground, but it would not only continue to mature;

in one mutation or another it would eventually win, simply because (as this book proves, if it proves anything) the basic conditions which had given it birth carried within themselves the dynamic necessity for its triumph.

Epilogue
1944*

WHAT had happened to the Chinese of this book in seven years since the Liukochiao Incident, when Japan began her attempt to conquer China in July 1937? For one thing, the passage of time had vindicated the judgement of Mao Tse-tung and other Communist leaders that the achievement of national unity for the struggle against Japan was more important than any other immediate objective of the revolutionary movement.

In this perspective the Sian Incident now loomed as a happening of decisive importance in contemporary Chinese history. Few remembered how close China came to adherence to the Anti-Comintern pact, just before the Sian affair, but it was now quite clear that after it there came the final parting of the ways between Tokyo and Nanking. Sian made certain that China would be on the anti-Fascist side of the coming world struggle.

In other respects time had confirmed the validity of the ideas for which the revolutionaries whose stories were told in these pages had fought and died. It had brought immense prestige to the survivors, and to their greatly increased following, during the long ordeal now drawing to a close. A revolutionary movement demands of its leader the ability to know a little ahead of anyone else what is going to happen; and in this respect Mao Tse-tung had been so successful that millions of Chinese now reposed as much confidence in his judgement as in that of Chiang Kai-shek.

However they might feel about the Communists and what they now represented, most Chinese would admit that Mao Tse-tung accurately analyzed the internal and international forces involved, and correctly depicted the general shape of events to come. Civil war did end and the Communist Party and the Red Army not only survived but were strengthened. Mao's suggestion that

*Condensed from RSOC (Modern Library edition, 1944).

at a certain stage in the war part of the Kuomintang would betray China and turn puppet for the Japanese was long resented; but after the defection of Wang Ching-wei, deputy leader of the KMT and second only to the Generalissimo, it could not be denied that Mao had intimately understood the contradictory elements in the Central Government.

Again, Mao predicted that the war would be long and difficult, and this must be one of the few instances in history in which an advocate of armed struggle did not promise his adherents a speedy triumph. His candour disarmed in advance the kind of defeatism that preys upon shattered illusions. On the other hand Mao helped to build up a more durable self-confidence in the nation by correctly estimating the enormous staying power guaranteed by China's own human and material resources, when mobilized in a revolutionary way. And he indicated the kind of strategy and tactics which China would have to adopt to hold on until the national war merged with the world war, including Japanese attacks on the British, the French, the Dutch, and the Americans, which he warned were inevitable in a period when many Europeans and Americans thought otherwise.

By 1944 the Chinese Communists provided the leadership in North China for what was much the largest guerrilla organization in the world. Stretching from the Yangtze Valley to the Mongolian steppe, and to the mountains and rivers of southern Manchuria, thousands of villages behind the Japanese lines made up the pattern of this 'people's war'. Its organizers were youths chiefly inspired and trained by the Eighteenth Group Army – the combined Eighth Route and New Fourth armies. These forces were led by Chu Teh, P'eng Teh-huai, and other veterans of the former Red Army of China, who now had behind them an amazing record of survival and growth through seventeen years of difficult civil and national war.

Foreign observers who visited the guerrilla districts in 1943 estimated that behind the Japanese lines the Eighteenth Group Army had organized and given crude training to militia numbering about 7,000,000 people. These were the reserves of the main fighting units. In addition, there were said to be some 12,000,000 members of various anti-Japanese associations which helped to clothe, feed, house, equip, and transport the regular troops, and were their eyes and ears. Official data showed partisan penetration in 455 *hsien*, or counties, of North China and in 52,800 villages, with a population of more than 60,000,000. From three fifths to two thirds of the so-called conquered territory was in guerrilla hands most of the time.

For nearly seven years the Japanese had been trying to exterminate these tireless enemies. Eighth Route regulars numbered hardly 50,000 men in 1937, and diverted only a few divisions of Japanese troops. But that vanguard multiplied in every direction. In 1944 more than half of Japan's 350,000 troops in China proper (excluding Manchuria) and some 200,000 puppet troops were occupied in defending fortified areas against the Eighteenth Group Army and in fighting punitive actions against it. Japanese military reports put its strength at from 500,000 to 600,000.

In every one of the provinces occupied by the Japanese, which covered an area three times the size of France, partisans had set up village and county councils. They had established four 'border' governments in bases held throughout the war, except for brief intervals; and each of these regional governments represented liberated areas of several neighbouring provinces. These behind-the-lines regimes performed nearly all the functions of normal administration. They had their own postal system and radio communications. They published their own newspapers, magazines, and books. They maintained an extensive system of schools and enforced a reformed legal code recognizing sex equality and adult suffrage. They regulated rents, collected taxes, controlled trade and issued currency, operated industries, maintained a number of experimental farms, extended agricultural credit, had a grain-rationing system, and in several places had undertaken fairly large afforestation projects.

The defence perimeter held by Japanese troops in China in 1944 was already stabilized before the end of 1939. When the enemy originally moved into the conquered provinces most of the old officials of the Kuomintang Government, as well as its troops, withdrew to the West and South. Behind them the administrative bureaucracy collapsed. In the cities it was replaced by Japanese and their Chinese puppets, but a kind of political vacuum existed in the hinterland towns and villages, the interstices between enemy garrisons. Into that temporary vacuum moved the former Red Army of China – with arms, with teachers, and with faith in the people's strength.

This movement began with the Generalissimo's acquiescence. It was made possible first of all, as we have seen, by Marshal Chang Hsueh-liang's earlier 'detention' of the Generalissimo at Sian, in order to persuade him to stop fighting the Reds and unite with them against Japan. After the Japanese invaded North China, an agreement was reached which ended a decade of civil war. This provided that the Red Army should be incorporated into the national forces, that the soviets should be abolished in favour of a government in which all classes would be represented, and that the Communists would abandon the slogans of class warfare and cease confiscating and redistributing the land. The northern Red forces dropped the Red flag and the Red star and accepted the designation 'Eighth Route Army'. South-east of Shanghai other Red elements under Generals Yeh T'ing and Han Ying were regrouped in 1938 as the 'New Fourth Army'.*

Both the Kuomintang and the Kungch'antang now claimed to be the legitimate heirs of Dr Sun Yat-sen, founder of the Chinese Republic. Both supported him in the early days of the revolution. Even after 1937, however, there was no agreement over the practical application of Sun Yat-sen's Three Principles of 'nationalism, livelihood and democracy'. The Communists still regarded Sun as a social revolutionary and demanded a radical interpretation of his principles. Briefly, they wanted a 'thoroughgoing democratic revolution', with equalization of land ownership, universal suffrage, and constitutional government establishing the people's power, by which they meant the Communist Party and, ultimately, a 'proletarian dictatorship'. Since the Kuomintang still drew its chief internal support from the landlord class, it was naturally opposed to radical land reform. In general it wanted to keep economic and political relationships intact and to superimpose its dictatorship on the old Chinese semifeudal structure. If it acknowledged the

* See Edgar Snow, *The Battle for Asia* (New York, 1941), for an account of the reorganization of the Red Army and growth of partisan warfare from 1937 to 1941.

legality of other parties and their conflicting interpretations, especially if it conceded adult suffrage, that structure would almost certainly be overthrown.

While questions of class power and of the ultimate form of the state and society remained in momentary abeyance, the Communists and Nationalists at least agreed upon the principle of 'nationalism' when Japan invaded the country. The Reds then took their military orders from the Generalissimo. In 1937 he sent them into the battle line in North China, where many Kuomintang leaders confidently expected them to be swallowed up in the Japanese drive. They did not disintegrate in that way, however, as some of the northern warlord armies did. They met the attack and were defeated in the cities, but instead of retreating or surrendering they withdrew to the villages and hills and continued fighting.

Infiltrating all the northern provinces with experienced partisan leaders and political organizers, they soon enlisted valuable reinforcements from a thickening stream of refugees fleeing from the cities: students, workers, and various professional men and women, including some intellectuals belonging to the non-Communist liberal political parties, long suppressed by both the Chinese and Japanese regimes. Cut off from the rear, whole divisions of defeated Chinese troops came under Red leadership. In North China the *min-t'uan* lost its central direction and cohesion when Nationalist regulars were driven out by Japan. Their landlord-gentry paymasters fled, or stayed to make deals with the Japanese, and the militia had to become puppet troops for the Japanese, or flee to Chiang Kai-shek's territory, or join the Communist-led partisans. *Japan served the Communists by destroying or demoralizing the whole rural police-power system with which the old rural landlord-gentry alliance with the urban property owners had been maintained.* At the outset it was the disintegration of that police system, rather than victories over the Japanese, that made possible the rapid expansion of the Eighth Route Army. Their rifle power, however, steadily increased. By 1939 their strongholds had become so formidable that the Japanese were compelled to launch a full-dress offensive against them. They went on doing so semi-annually from then on.

The first partisan regime entirely inside occupied territory was set up in the mountains of north-eastern Shansi, east of the Yellow River, and included areas as far north as Jehol, or Inner Mongolia. Another regime, with its capital in south-east Shansi, directed operations in recovered territory which stretched for over 300 miles across southern Hopei and Shantung eastward to the Yellow Sea. There was a third border region centring in northern Kiangsu, north of Shanghai, which was controlled by the New Fourth Army, with nearly 100,000 troops. A fourth regional government was established in the mountainous country north of the Yangtze River above Hankow, where the borders of Anhui and Hupeh enclose the southern extremity of Honan.

Political and military methods used to organize the people borrowed heavily from the pattern developed in the old soviet districts of north Shensi. After the Soviet Government was abolished in 1937, a 'Shensi-Kansu-Ninghsia Border Area Government' took its place and the town of Yenan, the so-called 'mother of the Chinese partisans', became its capital. I revisited Yenan in 1939, after the new government was established. It remained until 1944 the last trip made there by any foreign newspaper correspondent, for soon afterwards the region was cut off by the Kuomintang's military blockade.

On the other side of the Yellow River, behind Japanese lines, the organization of the social, political, and economic life was naturally more difficult than in Yenan, but in general the goals, if not always the degree of success achieved, were comparable. Although newspaper correspondents in Free China were not able to investigate the Shansi and Hopei areas, the various foreigners who escaped from the Japanese in Peking and made their way southward across the guerrilla territory gave fairly complete pictures of the system which prevailed. Among these observers was Professor William Band, of the famous American missionary institution, Yenching University, whom I knew when I lectured there in 1934–5. Another was Professor Michael Lindsay, also of Yenching, whose report of conditions there was published in *Amerasia* magazine in 1944.* The most comprehensive account of the partisan areas to reach the outside world for some time, it was

* New York, 31 March and 14 April 1944.

released for publication by the author's father, A. D. Lindsay, Master of Balliol College, Oxford.

According to Professor Lindsay, the partisan governments were elected from candidates nominated directly by the people and their organizations. The Chinese partisans aimed to establish a united front of all groups and hence the Communist Party limited its own members to one third of the total of any elected body. This peculiar policy was vigorously enforced, according to Lindsay. The purpose was to give representation in the government to both landowners (except absentee landlords) and merchants, but above all to develop political leaders among the poor peasants and workers. It was 'education in democracy by practising democracy', according to the partisan leaders.

In the mass organizations there were no limitations on Communist leadership, however; and these organizations were the guerrillas' sinew and life. They included separate unions or associations for farmers, workers, youth, children, and women, and membership in each ran into the millions. Most important of all such organizations were the self-defence corps, the militia, and the Young Vanguards. These were crude but basic military organizations which locally supported the Eighteenth Group Army's main forces.

G. Martel Hall, former manager of the National City Bank in Peking, who was the last American to escape from the Japanese across the partisan areas, told me that there was simply no other way he could explain the success of the partisan leaders with the peasants, 'except through their own incorruptibility and honesty, their energetic patriotism, their devotion to practical democracy, their faith in the common people, and the continuous effort they made to arouse them to action and responsibility'.

Mutual hatred of the Japanese provided the atmosphere in which these zealots exploited the people's patriotism, but side by side with political reforms went economic and social changes. In the case of women the enforcement of laws like monogamy, freedom of marriage at the age of consent, free education, and suffrage at the age of eighteen won a surprising response. Professor Lindsay said there were over 3,000,000 members of the women's organizations in the partisan areas. Many women had been elected to village and town councils and large numbers of young girls carried serious political and military responsibilities.

The primary school system operated widely in all the 'permanent' guerrilla bases and education was free and compulsory in theory if, because of poverty, seldom attainable in fact. Yet in a few places as high as 80 per cent of the younger children of school age were literate. The basic reform was a drastic reduction in land rent. Land of absentee landlords was tilled in common; the aim was to cultivate all cultivable land. Taxes were collected mainly in grain, and were kept at about 10 per cent of those demanded by the Japanese. Consumer, marketing and industrial cooperatives were widespread. Lindsay stated that there were over 4,000 cooperatives in Shansi and 5,000 in central Hopei alone.

Unimaginable hardships accompanied partisan organization at every step.* While it is true the Japanese failed to destroy the partisan forces, or to stop their increase, they carried out literally thousands of large- and small-scale punitive expeditions against them. They looted and burned thousands of villages, raped the womenfolk and slaughtered countless civilians, in a terror aimed to wipe out all thought of resistance. The guerrillas always found ways to overcome the demoralizing effects of these tactics, but not without sacrifices as bitter as any endured in Russia. It was true that the Japanese were still unable to control any village much beyond the range of their garrisons along North China's railways and roads, but it was also true that their fortified points had greatly increased and could now be seized only at heavy cost.

So much for the background. How did all this affect American plans to defeat Japan through China?

'After all, you saved the Kuomintang,' a Chinese intellectual in Chungking said to me when I returned to China (1942–3) as a war correspondent for the *Saturday Evening Post*. 'It is your baby now and you cannot avoid responsibility for its actions.'

He meant simply that American money, arms, and economic aid were given to the Kuomintang authorities, without any conditions concerning policies pursued inside China. American govern-

---

*For a vivid and almost painfully realistic eye-witness account of these sufferings of growth in the midst of war, see Agnes Smedley's powerful book, *Battle Hymn of China*.

ment representatives had several times made it clear to Chungking that we would disapprove of a renewal of civil strife during the joint war against Japan, but Americans had not gone beyond that nor sought to have the blockade lifted against the partisan areas.

Chungking established its blockade against the Eighteenth Group Army when Kuomintang party leaders became increasingly alarmed by the Communists' success in recovering control of areas behind the Japanese lines. The Generalissimo described their activity as 'illegal occupation of the national territory'. The Kuomintang's War Areas Political and Party Affairs Commission took the position that all the guerrilla administrations were 'illegal' and should be abolished to await the re-establishment of the Kuomintang system.

In 1940 some Kuomintang troops engaged the rear echelon of the New Fourth Army while it was moving from its base south of the Yangtze River, near Shanghai, to an area entirely behind the Japanese lines to which it was assigned by the Generalissimo. It was apparently a surprise attack and the partisans were reportedly outnumbered eight to one. The little detachment of about 4,000 was not a combat unit and it was easily encircled and destroyed. General Yeh T'ing, the commander of the New Fourth Army (who was himself not a Communist), was wounded and taken prisoner, and General Han Ying, the field commander, was killed together with many of his staff, some doctors and nurses of the medical battalions, a number of convalescent wounded soldiers, some cadets, men and women students, and some Industrial Cooperative workers attached to the army.

The incident failed to liquidate the New Fourth Army, whose main forces were already north of the Yangtze River, engaging Japanese troops there, but it was the effective end of Nationalist-Communist collaboration in the field and the beginning of an open struggle for leadership in the joint war against Japan. The Generalissimo ruled that the incident was caused by the New Fourth's 'insubordination' and henceforth withdrew all aid not only from that army but also from the Eighth Route.

For some months previous to the tragedy no part of the Eighteenth Group Army had been paid. From this time on they not

only received no pay or ammunition but were blockaded by a ring
of strong government forces from access to supplies in Free China,
which they might have purchased or received as gifts from the
people. Ironically enough, the Kuomintang troops enforcing this
blockade were largely supplied by Soviet Russia. There were two
group armies (the Thirty-seventh and Thirty-eighth) engaged exclusively in the blockading enterprise. American officers in 1942
suggested that they were needed in the campaign to recover Burma,
but Chungking considered their 'policing role' in the North-West
of greater importance and there they remained.

All such facts were known to Americans in China, but probably
few at home realized that our lend-lease aid went exclusively to
the Kuomintang authorities. We maintained no consular representation in Yenan and no military liaison with the partisans.*
All our supplies flown over the Hump into China – modern
bombers and fighters, artillery, transport, and ammunition – supported only the one party, of course. Financial aid sent to China
by the CIO, AFL, and Railway Brotherhoods also went exclusively to Kuomintang groups,

What could be done about this 'internal affair' of China? Our
new treaty with China (1943) renounced extraterritoriality rights
and restored full sovereignty to the Chinese Government. Could
we now tell the present government how to run its business without being branded neo-imperialists? But inevitably the war had
already caused us to intervene in support of the Kuomintang, in
terms of economic and military aid. Was it not merely playing
ostrich to pretend that our future economic help to China did not
carry implicit political responsibilities of the gravest kind?

Once Japan was defeated, would Chiang Kai-shek then destroy
the Communists and their partisan allies? The Kuomintang spent
ten fruitless years in the attempt before 1937. Even with the use
of American bombers and fighters on his side, the Generalissimo
was not likely to secure greater success than the Japanese had had
against these experienced guerrilla warriors. It had become a
physical impossibility for the Chungking Government to destroy

---

*Not until late in 1944 did Chiang Kai-shek grant permission for an
American observer team to be stationed in Yenan, where they were welcomed, although they brought no military or economic assistance.

this opposition in anything short of a long and bloody war, fully backed by Allied troops.

By the summer of 1944 it had thus become manifest that the tiny band of youths who raised the Red flag on the lonely mountain of Chingkangshan far back in 1928 had launched a demonstration which evolved into a crusade which finally rose to the stature of a national movement of such scope that no arbiters of China's destiny could much longer deny its claims to speak for vast multitudes of people.

Notes to the Revised Edition

PART ONE : In Search of Red China

Chapter 1: Some Unanswered Questions

1. Written in invisible ink, the letter was given to me by Hsu Ping, then a professor at Tungpei University. In 1966, as for some years earlier, Hsu Ping was deputy secretary of the United Front Department of the CCP CC. In 1960, K'e Cheng-shih, then mayor of Shanghai, told me he had written the letter, which was authorized by Liu Shao-ch'i. (K'e died in 1965.) Liu Shao-ch'i was chief of the underground North China Bureau of the CC, and his first deputy was P'eng Chen. Others in his branch CC included Hsu Ping, Po I-po, Ch'en Po-ta, Hsiang Ching, Huang Hua, and Yao I-lin. See Biographical Notes – hereafter BN – pages 512–587. Abbreviations are given on page 503.

Chapter 2: Slow Train to 'Western Peace'

1. Tai Chi-tao and Shao Li-tzu were Marxist-oriented members of the Kuomintang who formed a Communist study-group nucleus in Shanghai with Ch'en Tu-hsiu in 1920. Neither man joined the organization of the first CC in July 1921. During the Second Civil War (1946–9), Shao Li-tzu supported the Communists against Chiang Kai-shek, and helped form the People's Republic of China. See BN.

Chapter 3: Some Han Bronzes

1. A genuine pastor, he was Wang Hua-jen, a member of the national executive committee of the Chinese Red Cross.

PART TWO : The Road to the Red Capital

Chapter 2: The Insurrectionist

1. This account, based on an interview with Chou En-lai and his comrades, was quite incomplete, but in 1936 it was fresh news to the outside world. Kyo Gizors, hero of La Condition Humaine (Man's Fate), by André Malraux, was said to have been based on Chou En-lai's role in this period. 'Things happened quite otherwise,' according to Chou. See BN.

2. Concerning such 'old and patriotic gentlemen', see Benjamin Schwartz's

penetrating study, *In Search of Wealth and Power: Yen Fu and the West* (Cambridge, 1964).

3. Other sources give lower estimates. For example, Harold Isaacs mentions 400 to 500 killed. (Mao Tse-tung told me in 1960 that Chiang Kai-shek's sudden 'purge' in Shanghai and other centres, which caught the Party un-prepared, killed about 40,000 members.) Isaacs holds Stalin and the CMT largely responsible for the Shanghai deaths, since they refused to break with the KMT even after Chiang's men had begun killing Communists prior to the 'Shanghai Massacre'. See Isaacs, *The Tragedy of the Chinese Revolution*, pp. 165–85. See Bibliography for further comment.

Chapter 3: Something About Ho Lung

1. Inaccuracies in this colourful version of Ho Lung's life notwithstanding, it does parallel the main facts, and seems worth preserving as a contemporary first-hand impression by a comrade-in-arms. See BN.

PART THREE : In 'Defended Peace'

Chapter 1: Soviet Strong Man

1. More properly Li T'eh, or Li T'e, according to Wade, but throughout the text Otto Braun's Chinese *nom de guerre* is transliterated as Braun himself wrote it. See BN.

2. The remarkable Ma Hai-teh. See BN.

3. Not including a family-arranged betrothal, which Mao ignored. In 1937 Ho Tzu-ch'en and Mao were divorced and in 1939 Mao married Chiang Ch'ing (Lan P'ing). See BN.

Chapter 2: Basic Communist Policies

1. From *Democracy*, Peking, 15 May 1937, a brief-lived English-language anti-imperialist and anti-Nazi publication, edited by John Leaning. Among its associate editors (besides myself) were J. Leighton Stuart, president of Yenching University and later US Ambassador to Nationalist China, and Soong Ch'ing-ling.

2. See *The Agrarian Reform Law of the People's Republic of China* (Peking, 1952), and Ch'en Po-ta, *A Study of Land Rent in Pre-Liberation China*. Com-munist figures on tenancy have been questioned by J. Lossing Buck and other foreign agriculturists. See Bibliography. For Ch'en Po-ta, see also BN.

3. Part of this paragraph has been revised from my original text in order to include facts not fully known to me in 1937. The CCP until 1935 aimed at a complete overthrow of Kuomintang leadership and held that a 'united front from below' could succeed only under its leadership of the masses against both the Kuomintang and the imperialists. The CC changed its policy at the Tsunyi Conference in January 1935, when Mao Tse-tung proposed a united front to include all anti-Japanese elements (with Chiang Kai-shek and the right-wing KMT still excluded, however) and sought

approval of that line from the CMT. In August 1935, the CEC of the CMT adopted an anti-Fascist international-united-front line reconcilable with the Tsunyi decisions and going beyond them to include the national bourgeoisie. On that line the CCP built its united-front proposals of 1936. See Part Four, Chapter 6, note 3, and Wang Ming, BN.

Chapter 3: On War with Japan

1. Mao's strategic views set forth here paraphrased his report to Party activists at Wayapao, in north Shensi, immediately following an important Politburo meeting held there, December 1935, and formed the embryo of his later works, 'Problems of Strategy in the Guerrilla War Against Japan', 'Problems of War and Strategy', and 'On Protracted War'. See *Selected Military Writings of Mao Tse-tung*. These concepts, followed throughout the war against Japan, outline a general strategy of 'people's war' which Mao later held valid against American armed expansion in Asia.

2. Since Dr Sun Yat-sen and the Kuomintang had always placed Taiwan among 'lost territories' to be brought back under China's sovereignty, it seems hardly likely that Mao intended to concede future 'independence' there. The CCP had never officially done so.

Chapter 5: Red Theatre

1. The 'decadent' and 'meaningless' Chinese opera died hard. Thirty years later the GPCR drafted opera stars wholesale to produce modern plays in forms which would 'serve the people' by dramatizing revolution and the Thought of Mao Tse-tung, and which were not susceptible to undesirable historical analogies. *The Red Lantern*, a play of the 1960s popularized during the GPCR, was in content basically the same play as *Invasion*, of 1936 – lacking only the comic relief of the marauding goats. (See Chiang Ch'ing, BN.)

2. In his speech at the inception of the CPR (October 1949) Mao Tse-tung declared, 'China has at last stood up.'

PART FOUR: *Genesis of a Communist*

Chapter 1: Childhood

1. Mao did not mention the day of his birth, later reported as 26 December. In 1949 Mao called upon the CC to ban the naming of provinces, streets, and enterprises after leaders and to forbid the celebration of their birthdays. See *Selected Works of Mao Tse-tung* (Peking, 1961), IV, 38.

Chapter 2: Days in Changsha

1. Mao was nineteen when he entered First Teachers' Training School, which was for scholarship students only, who were expected to become primary-school teachers. 'Humanism was the guiding principle, with emphasis on moral conduct, physical culture, and social activities. The First

Teachers' Training School was the only Western-style building in Chang-sha. . . . "I have never been to a university," Mao recalled, "nor have I studied abroad. The groundwork of my knowledge and scholarship was laid at the First Teachers' Training School, which was a good school" ' (Jerome Ch'en, *Mao and the Chinese Revolution*, p. 32).

2. Yang had an even greater influence on Mao's early interest in philo-sophical idealism than is acknowledged here. He was familiar with both Oriental and Western cultures, to a degree then rare among Chinese savants. His family were wealthy landowners of Hunan who could afford to give him a good education in the Chinese Classics and then send him to study for six years in Japan. At the age of thirty he went to Europe for another four years of study in Britain and Germany. That he chose to accept a post in a secondary institution indicated the high standing of the First Teachers' Training School. He went on to a professorship at Peking National University, where he continued to befriend Mao. Versed in Kant, Rousseau, and Spencer, Yang was also a follower of the Hunanese hero-patriot, Wang Fu-chih, a pragmatist philosopher as well as a warrior. Wang's seventeenth-century writings strongly appealed to Mao and other students of Yang who later became Communists, including Ts'ai Ho-sen (see BN). Yang is credited with having introduced Mao to Friedrich Paulsen's *A System of Ethics*. A copy of Ts'ai Yuan-p'ei's translation of that book still exists, with 12,000 words of marginal notes in Mao's handwriting which reveal his admiration of Paulsen's emphasis on discipline, self-control, and will power (Ch'en, op. cit., p. 44).

3. Hsiao Yu (Siao Yu) wrote *Mao Tse-tung and I Were Beggars*. See Biblio-graphy.

4. Yi gave Mao, his former student, a job as principal of his 'model' pri-mary school, a satellite of the Hunan Normal School. Mao taught Chinese literature there until 1922. In 1965 Mao told me that at that time he really had had no ambition in life other than to be a teacher. In 1969 Mao told me that he would reject the 'titles' bestowed on him during the GPCR except that of 'Teacher'.

5. Yi Pei-ch'i was himself 'responsible' for the theft. He was director of the museum at the time the treasures disappeared, and Hsiao was his assis-tant. The treasures were later sold in Europe.

6. In 1966-7, Mao encouraged the Red Guards of the GPCR to emulate such boyhood experiences, and to sally forth on 'little Long Marches' of their own.

7. Mao Tse-tung published an article in *New Youth*, April 1917, under the pseudomyn *Erh-Shih-Pa Hua Sheng* or 'Twenty-eight-Stroke Student'. (The three characters of Mao's full name are written with twenty-eight brush strokes.) His article, 'A Study of Physical Education', offers interesting in-sights into Mao's character at the age of twenty-four. Since the body itself 'contains knowledge and houses virtue', Mao saw perfect physical fitness as the foundation of mental perfection and, above all, will power. His article

also glorified 'military heroism'. See Stuart Schram's translation, *Une étude de l'éducation physique.*

Chapter 3: Prelude to Revolution

1. Ch'en supported Wang Ching-wei's puppet government under the Japanese, became its premier after Wang's death, and was executed as a traitor by Chiang Kai-shek in 1946.

Chapter 4: The Nationalist Period

1. Sneevliet had a long Indonesian background, and was a veteran member of the Second International. He supported Lenin's break with the older European Socialist International, to form the Third International. He was active in prewar revolutionary agitation in Indonesia and helped found a Social Democratic Party there. For further information about Sneevliet and his role in the Comintern and the Chinese Revolution see Harold Isaacs, 'Documents on the Comintern and the Chinese Revolution', *China Quarterly*, Jan.–Mar. 1971. Sneevliet perished during the Nazi occupation of Holland.

2. Chou Fu-hai ended by collaborating with the Japanese under the puppet premier, Wang Ching-wei (see BN).

3. The Third CCP Congress confirmed the Sun-Joffe agreement, whereby Communists were to join the KMT, but the demand of Sneevliet, the CMT representative, that control of the labour movement should be shared with the KMT, was opposed by Chang Kuo-t'ao, then chief of the Orgburo and the Trade-Union Secretariat. Mao at first supported Chang Kuo-t'ao, but after the resolution was passed, by one vote, Mao adopted the Comintern view. Chang lost his post in the Orgburo, Mao succeeded him, and antagonism between the two increased (Rue, *Mao Tse-tung in Opposition*, p. 38).

4. In fact Mao's 'coordinating' activities were so successful that he was attacked for 'rightism' and expelled (for the first time) from the CC. His return to Hunan, 'for a rest', coincided with a reversal in CMT policy, now favouring separate CCP organization of labour. Mao was re-elected to the CC but Chang also recovered Party face (Rue, ibid.).

5. Official English translations of both works (FLP, Peking) show a few differences from the originals in Chinese, especially marked in the analysis of Chao Heng-t'i.

6. Mao's *Report*, now a scriptural classic, stressed that 'without the poor peasant there can be no revolution'. *Analysis of Classes in Chinese Society* opens Mao's *Selected Works*, and is followed by the above *Report* (*SW*, Vol. I).

Chapter 5: The Soviet Movement

1. Several important research studies of this period in recent years (see Bibliography) have assessed, in varying degrees, Stalin's responsibility for the '1927 débâcle', but Chinese historiography has yet to produce a documented analysis even from the official CCP point of view. Ch'en, Roy, and

Borodin certainly followed directives from Stalin, who had taken control of the Executive Committee of the Comintern from Zinoviev in 1926. Thus it was *Stalin's* line which Mao here criticized by implication. Was Ch'en merely a scapegoat for Stalin's mistakes? In his own defence before the Emergency Party CC meeting of 7 August 1927, Ch'en asserted that he had opposed the CMT line in the spring of 1927, but that his protests were rejected; after that he had followed CMT discipline to enforce Stalin's directives despite his better judgement. (He had distrusted both Chiang Kai-shek and Wang Ching-wei.) After he was dropped from the PB, Ch'en circulated a letter to the CC in which he objected to its adoption of 'defence of the USSR' as a duty taking primacy over all other revolutionary considerations.

In 1929 the issue had become critical when Chang Hsueh-liang seized the Russian-administered sections of the jointly owned Chinese Eastern Railway in Chinese Manchuria and declared them 'nationalized'. In retaliation, Moscow moved Red Army troops into Manchuria to restore Russian rights, while the Comintern demanded that the CCP (and all Communist parties) support Russian policy against the Chinese Nationalists. Ch'en was expelled from the Party in November 1929, and later organized a 'left opposition' party with Trotsky's support. That did not save him from arrest (and five years of imprisonment) by the Kuomintang authorities. Released in 1937, he died in 1942.

Borodin was recalled to Moscow in 1927 and for some years edited the English-language *Moscow Daily News*, with Anna Louise Strong as a co-editor. After the Second World War, Stalin had Borodin incarcerated and he died in Siberia. Stalin's police also imprisoned Anna Louise Strong, then deported her as an 'American spy'. Khrushchev ordered Borodin posthumously rehabilitated. He also ordered the rehabilitation of Miss Strong, who soon went to live in Peking, which became anti-Khrushchev headquarters. Roy remained in Stalin's good graces until 1929, when he suddenly left Moscow under an assumed name, and shortly afterwards was officially expelled from the Comintern. (During the Second World War he led a pro-British faction in India.) Besso Lominadze and Heinz Neumann succeeded Roy and Borodin as Stalin's agents in China. Following Stalin's ambivalent orders, Neumann called for the Canton Commune (December 1927), a failure for which Stalin held him personally responsible. He returned to Russia and was last seen there in 1931. In 1930 Lominadze joined the Opposition and tried to remove Stalin from CMT leadership. Stalin had him exiled to Magnitogorsk, where he soon committed suicide. Adolf A. Joffe, a veteran of the October Revolution who had served Lenin in arranging the Brest-Litovsk treaty before he negotiated the Sino-Soviet pact with Sun Yat-sen, committed suicide (1927) in protest against Stalin's expulsion of Trotsky from the Bolshevik Party.

Lominadze had been Li Li-san's strongest supporter in the Comintern. His attacks on Stalin were only partly connected with Chinese affairs but they coincided with a crisis in the 'Li Li-san line' in China and helped influence Stalin to discredit Li and back a new leadership for the Chinese Politburo. Among Stalin's Comintern functionaries in China during this fateful period was Earl Browder, who was recalled from China by Pavel Mif. Browder was not expelled from the Comintern, however, which Stalin himself abolished with a stroke of his pen, in 1943.

2. An interesting account of this incident, and the whole period, from the Left Kuomintang point of view, is given by T'ang Leang-li in *The Inner History of the Chinese Revolution* (London, 1930).

3. Mao was not present during the Uprising but General Chu Teh credited Mao with having helped to plan it (Smedley, *The Great Road*, p. 200). A poster commonly sold throughout the PRC showed Mao speaking at a meeting (18 July 1927) held near Nanchang, where decisions were made for the Uprising. Leading participants in the Nanchang Uprising included Chu Teh, Ho Lung, Chang Kuo-t'ao, Chou En-lai, Fang Chih-min, Li Li-san, Lin Tsu-han, Lin Piao, Liu Po-ch'eng, P'eng P'ai, Su Yu, Ch'en Keng, Ch'en Yi, Su Chao-cheng, Nieh Ho-t'ing, Nieh Jung-chen, T'an Chen-lin, T'an Ping-shan, Yeh Chien-ying, Hsu T'eh-li, and Teng Ying-ch'ao (Mme Chou En-lai). The 1 August (Nanchang) Uprising came to be celebrated as the birthday of the PLA.

4. Chingkangshan was a nearly impregnable mountain stronghold, formerly held by bandits, on the Hunan–Kiangsi border. For an account of the Communists' seizure of this mountain and their subsequent experiences there, see Smedley, *The Great Road*, pp. 225ff.

5. Mao may have meant that he agreed with the 'line' of the CCP Sixth Congress, while reserving for himself the thought that he did not agree with the Politburo's interpretation of it. In any case his statement to me was directly contradicted by his 1945 'Report on Some Questions in the History of Our Party', made at the Seventh Congress of the CCP. In that long critique he identified three main mistakes of the Sixth Congress. The fundamental one was its failure to recognize that the '*Chinese bourgeois democratic revolution is in essence a peasant revolution . . .*' (SW, IV, 177).

6. The Ku-t'ien Conference, called by Mao when he was convalescing from a severe illness (he was at the time reported dead by the CMT), resulted in agreements which gave Mao's 'Front Committee' political command over the entire Fourth Army. Mao's basic theses of revolutionary strategy and aims were : principal reliance on the support of the poor peasantry; the establishment of rural soviet bases; and the development of political and military organization and tactics learned from experiences on Chingkangshan which Mao had formulated at the two conferences held at Maoping. From this time on the Politburo opposition to Mao never quite succeeded in separating Mao from army and peasant support in the rural soviets.

Chapter 6: Growth of the Red Army

1. Mao's sons were united with him at a later date. Yang K'ai-hui reportedly was offered the choice of repudiating the Party or death; she refused to recant. See Mao An-ch'ing, Mao An-ying, BN.

2. As head of the General Front Committee, backed by army commanders Chu Teh and P'eng Teh-huai, Mao opposed the orders of the PB, headed by Li Li-san, to lead the second attack on Changsha. Mao was overruled by the Revolutionary Military Committee, and the September attack began. After a week of heavy reverses, Mao, Chu Teh, and P'eng 'repudiated the Li Li-san . . . policy of the CC' and ordered a general retreat. See Smedley, *The Great Road*, pp. 278–9.

3. In Mao's published writings one finds only a few references to the Li Li-san period – which was really only one phase of a struggle for power between the urban-based CC and the rural-based soviets where Mao won a dominant position. Mao's laconic comment may now be supplemented, however, by much material uncovered concerning the whole series of differences (1927–35) within the Chinese leadership and between its various personalities and the Comintern under Stalin.

Generally, Mao's disputes with Moscow-oriented PB leaders revolved around his conviction that the land-hungry poor peasants were the 'main force' of the revolution and that rural bases had to be built before the metropolitan areas could be encompassed and held. Those opposed to him tended to share Stalin's view of the peasants as primarily auxiliaries to be manipulated by the urban proletariat, the true 'main force' of the revolution.

Fragments of the story may be found in the Biographical Notes about Ch'en Tu-hsiu, Ch'u Ch'iu-pai, Hsiang Chung-fa, Yang Shan-k'un, Li Li-san, Wang Ming, Po Ku, Lo Fu, Liu Shao-ch'i, Chou En-lai, Chang Kuo-t'ao, and Li Teh (Otto Braun). See also Ch'en Po-ta, to help fill out this brief summary.

From its inception the CCP accepted the discipline of a 'democratic centralism' principle (acknowledged in the Party constitution) which required obedience to CMT directives on matters of overall strategy or 'line'. Within that concept the Chinese rural soviet and Red Army 'combat Communists' under Mao's influence increasingly differed with the 'dogmatists' and 'theorists' trained in Moscow. It was not until January 1935 that Mao finally won PB leadership from them when he delivered his Tsunyi critique of Po Ku, general secretary of the PB, and of Lo Fu, then chairman of a 'council of commissars' of the Soviet Government. Po Ku and Otto Braun (CMT delegate) were downgraded by the revolutionary military affairs council, and the PB (under 'Chairman' Mao) called for an anti-Japanese 'united front', with patriotic elements of all classes, seven months before the CMT did so. In 1936, however, Mao glossed over bitter intraparty quarrels when, in his interviews with me, he spoke of the 'extraordinary ability and courage and loyalty' of such 'revolutionary cadres' as Po Ku,

Lo Fu, Teng Fa, Wang Ming, P'eng Teh-huai, and even Chang Kuo-t'ao. (See Appendices, Further Interviews with Mao Tse-tung, pp. 510–11).

In 1927 Ch'en Tu-hsiu (see note 1, Chapter 5, above) had been found culpable for mistakes made by him under CMT directives. After the defeat of the Nanchang Uprising an *ad hoc* session (Emergency Conference) of the CC was called 7 August. Held under the domination of a twenty-nine-year-old Georgian Russian CMT agent, Lominadze, the conference replaced Ch'en as general secretary with Ch'u Ch'iu-pai. New disasters then occurred at Swatow and in the December uprising in Canton. The latter was called by Stalin's CMT 'expert' on uprisings, the German agent Heinz Neumann, aged twenty-six. Meanwhile, Mao Tse-tung had been expelled from the Central Committee and the Hunan Front Committee for 'deviations' during and after the August uprising in Hunan.

In July 1928, the CCP Sixth Congress was called in Moscow, under the wing of the CMT, also then holding its own Sixth Congress. Now Ch'u Ch'iu-pai was denounced and replaced by Hsiang Chung-fa, another choice of Lominadze's. Hsiang was a poorly educated Shanghai worker whom Lominadze used as a 'proletarian' front man for Li Li-san, the 'intellectual' who became chief of labour organization. With the backing of the CMT, Li Li-san returned to Shanghai, to find that Mao and Chu Teh were entrenched with their own peasant armed forces in rural soviets.

'The Sixth Congress recognized,' Li wrote to Mao (who had been restored to the Front Committee), 'that there is a danger that the base of our Party may shift from the working class to the peasantry and that we must make every effort to restore the Party's working-class base.'

Li's directives obliged Mao and Chu to try to use the infant Red Army to seize large urban areas, including an attack on Nanchang and two costly attempts to take and hold Changsha (1930). Mao and Chu Teh disobeyed Li's second order to attack Changsha. An anti-Mao clique in the Kiangsi provincial committee engaged in manoeuvres to overthrow Mao. One eventual result was the Fu T'ien Incident (December 1930), which Mao alleged was traceable to the 'Li Li-san line'. A brief and bloody localized intraparty war followed, coinciding with Mao's suppression of an 'Anti-Bolshevik Corps'. A number of Communists were killed and many alleged anti-Maoists reportedly were imprisoned. Most of them were 'thought-remoulded' – an early Maoist technique – and released.

Meanwhile, in Moscow, the CMT had prepared a younger generation of cadres to take over the leadership of Eastern revolutions. In 1925 the CMT had set up the Sun Yat-sen University. Among hundreds who studied there, only twenty-eight Chinese consistently supported Stalin during his struggles with Trotsky, Zinoviev, and Bukharin. These were protégés of Pavel Mif, who was twenty-seven years old when Stalin made him director of the university and chief of the CMT Far Eastern Section, after 1927. By 1930 Mif had built them into a hard-core 'professional Bolshevik' élite schooled to take over China. Once called 'Stalin's China Section' by their opponents, they later came to be known as the 'Twenty-eight Bolsheviks'. In 1930 their leader was a youth of twenty-four named Wang Ming (Ch'en Shao-yu), and his closest comrade was Po Ku (Ch'in Pang-hsien), aged twenty-three. Others of importance were Lo Fu (Chang Wen-t'ien), Shen Tse-min, Yang Shan-k'un, Ch'en Chang-hao, Chu Jui, Tso Ch'uan, and Teng Fa. Through the influence of the CMT they eventually exercised discipline over most of the 'returned students' from Russia.

In mid-1930 Pavel Mif secretly returned to the sanctuary of the foreign-ruled International Settlement of Shanghai with Wang Ming, Po Ku, Lo Fu, Teng Fa, and other Stalinist disciples, who were introduced into the CCP CC. When they opposed Li Li-san, however, Li resisted Mif's manoeuvre and he and Hsiang Chung-fa dismissed Wang Ming and others from the PB, with the support of Chou En-lai. Mif secured Li's recall to Moscow, where Li confidently expected support from Lominadze. Unknown to him, Lominadze had become involved in a move to oust Stalin from the leadership of the CPSU and CMT. Li therefore found himself arbitrarily classified with the opposition and was silenced with it, by Stalin. He remained in disgrace and was not to return to China for some years. Although Hsiang Chung-fa remained nominal general secretary, Ch'u Ch'iu-pai was expelled from the PB and Chou En-lai retained his position only after a confession of error in supporting Li Li-san.

In July 1936, at Pao An, Po Ku told me of Li Li-san: 'His mistake was *putchism*. He favoured armed uprisings in the cities, attempts to seize factories through armed struggle of the workers, collectivization in the soviet districts, capture of big cities by armed attack. . . . Basically he denied the practicability of rural soviets; he considered that the Red Army should mobilize for storming of cities. . . . He wanted Outer Mongolian forces to join in and support uprisings and civil war in Manchuria and North China. . . . His mistake was that he insisted that China was, in 1930, . . . the "centre of the world revolution", denying the Soviet Union as that centre.' Po Ku said that only he, Wang Chia-hsiang, and Ho Meng-hsiung originally supported Wang Ming in his attempts to capture the PB leadership from Li Li-san (RNORC, p. 16).

In January 1931, Mif had (with Stalin's support) summoned a Fourth Plenum of the CC, of which he made himself chairman. There he succeeded in establishing Wang Ming in practical leadership of a CCP PB dominated by Mif's disciples. In June 1931, Hsiang Chung-fa's address was betrayed to KMT police by Ku Shun-chang, a Li Li-san sympathizer. Hsiang was executed in Shanghai. According to KMT police, the PB had Ku Shun-chang's entire family assassinated. Wang Ming then replaced Hsiang as general secretary in a PB which included Po Ku, Chou En-lai, Lo Fu, Han Ying, Liu Shao-ch'i, Lo Man, Meng Ch'ing-shu (Mme Wang Ming), and Jen Pi-shih. (Mao was now a member of a CC branch or 'Central Bureau' in Kiangsi.) Mif returned to Moscow, to remain in charge of the Chinese section of the CMT. Again the CMT line tended to harness the rural soviets to schemes of seizure of power by the urban proletariat. After the Japanese invasion of Manchuria (September 1931), Wang Ming and his wife were recalled to help Mif in Moscow and Po Ku became PB general secretary. The PB now sent Chou En-lai, Chang Kuo-t'ao, Jen Pi-shih, and other members into various rural soviets north and south of the Yangtze, to enforce its directives. In the sanctuary of the foreign-ruled International Settlement of Shanghai, Po Ku maintained underground PB headquarters and sent directives to the 1931 All-Soviet Congress in Kiangsi, which he was unable to attend.

Hunted by the Shanghai police, who cut off sources of funds from Russia, Po Ku and Lo Fu finally moved the PB headquarters to Soviet Kiangsi late in 1932. They were reinforced by the arrival of a new CMT delegate, Otto Braun, known in China as Li Teh, a German with some military experience. Serious differences which had long divided the 'Twenty-eight Bolsheviks' from Mao Tse-tung, chairman of the All-Soviet Government, chief commissar of the Red Army, and also a member of the PB, now erupted in a definitive struggle.

Chou En-lai became commissar general of the Red Army, but as Party general secretary it was Po Ku who matched forces with Mao for overall political leadership. Po Ku, junior to Mao by sixteen years, had never been in battle before he entered Soviet Kiangsi late in 1932, he told me, but he was armed with years of study of theory, dogma, and training in the use of Party control machinery. He also had solid CMT backing, with Li Teh at his side and Wang Ming, in Moscow, sitting in the shadow of Stalin. Strong in practical experience and popular support in the soviets and the armed forces, Mao lacked Po Ku's fluency in the scripture and techniques of CMT in-fighting, and had to tread warily to avoid open defiance of Moscow.

Invoking the prestige of the CMT and the 'expert' military knowledge of Li Teh (who spoke no Chinese and voiced his views through Po Ku, as interpreter), Po Ku undermined the authority of both Chu Teh and Mao Tse-tung. By late 1933 Mao Tse-tung was excluded from PB policy making. In the defeated opposition, Mao was assigned the task of organizing the economy to meet Nationalist offensives (see SW, I, 129–37). While Chiang Kai-shek was diverted by provincial warlord rebellions, the Red Army expanded and the new PB strategy seemed successful. A debate over whether the Red Army should implement an alliance with the Nationalist Nineteenth Route Army during the Fukien Rebellion was closed out when the PB ruled against active collaboration even with anti-Japanese 'bourgeois' armies and continued an uncompromising do-it-alone line, later denounced as left-deviationist.

Partly for his opposition to the latter policy, Mao was in 1934 also dropped from the all-powerful revolutionary military council, which included Chou En-lai, Po Ku, Li Teh, Lo Fu, Yeh Chien-ying, and Chu Teh. But Chu Teh was now subordinate to Chou En-lai as general commissar of the Red Army.

Mao was suspended from the PB and may have been put under surveillance by the newly organized security police (modelled after Stalin's) headed by Teng Fa.

In those circumstances Chiang Kai-shek launched his well-prepared Fifth Extermination Campaign which ended in the defeat of the Red Army and the dissolution of Soviet Kiangsi. Mao blamed the catastrophe on the Party's failure to support the Fukien rebels (1933) and its reliance on positional warfare against Chiang, instead of following his tried and tested guerrilla strategy (as laid down at the Maoping Conferences) of 'luring the enemy in deep' and declining major battles except with overwhelming superiority. Pro-Maoist commanders, resentful and distrustful of the seizure of power by the 'Twenty-eight Bolsheviks', and 'obedient in word, disobedient in action', may well have sabotaged the fine German battle plans of Li Teh, as he implied in remarks made to me in Pao An in 1936.

By October 1934, the Red Army was hemmed into an area confined to six Kiangsi counties and was forced to evacuate its capital, Juichin. Li Teh, Chou En-lai, and Yeh Chien-ying drew up a plan of retreat; their first objective was to join Ho Lung's forces in Hunan. That plan was thwarted, with heavy losses, and the Reds then turned their columns into weakly defended Kweichow province, where they won a two months' breathing spell. After they captured Tsunyi, the summer capital, an emergency meeting was demanded by Mao Tse-tung, backed by a majority of the political and military officers of regimental units or higher. At an enlarged conference of officers and PB and CC members, Mao Tse-tung delivered a critique of the leadership which won him majority support. Mao was elected chairman of a new Party revolutionary military council (also termed military affairs committee), with Chou En-lai and Yeh Chien-ying retained. Chu Teh was confirmed field commander of the Red Army. Po Ku remained in the CC PB but was replaced by Lo Fu as general secretary. The office no longer carried the leadership, however; both military and political supreme command were now conceded to the *Chu-hsi* – 'Chairman' Mao. At Tsunyi the historic decisions were taken for the Long March to the North-West.

Li Teh made the Long March as a guest adviser, but no longer invoked his CMT authority. In 1936, in Pao An, he told me that 'the Chinese after all understand their revolution better than any foreigner could'. Ch'en Yun was sent from Tsunyi to report decisions taken there to the Party in East China (headed by Liu Shao-ch'i?) and to Moscow. After Ch'en Yun's arrival in Moscow a meeting of the CMT elected Mao Tse-tung to the Central Executive Committee for the first time. Wang Ming continued as a resident delegate there in the CMT but Ch'en Yun was Mao's spokesman. Mao had won vindication and Stalin's practical recognition.

Moscow made no further attempts to intervene directly in Chinese Party affairs – with one exception. That was in December 1936, during the Sian Incident, when Stalin cabled a threat, via Shanghai, to cut off all connections with the CCP unless it insisted upon Chiang Kai-shek's release, unharmed, from his captivity by Chang Hsueh-liang in Sian. (See *RNORC*, pp. 1–5.)

Except for details based on the author's personal knowledge, the foregoing condensation of extremely complicated history may be filled out and documented by consulting basic research works listed in the Bibliography, especially Benjamin Schwartz's brilliant pioneer study, *Chinese Communism and the Rise of Mao*, and John E. Rue's recent and remarkably thorough interpretation, *Mao Tse-tung in Opposition: 1927–35*. Additional light on Mao's role during the Kiangsi period may be found in an article by Dieter Heinzig, 'The Otto Braun Memoirs and Mao's Rise to Power', *China Quarterly*, Apr.–June 1971. See Bibliography. The role of Li Li-san and the 'Twenty-eight Bolsheviks', the extent of Comintern responsibility for revolutionary reverses in China before 1935, and the means whereby Mao Tse-tung took command of the Party from Moscow-trained leaders at Tsunyi, are questions for continued research, as indicated by new titles in the 1971 Bibliography. The CCP's official version of the period is largely contained in Mao's 1945 report to the Seventh Congress entitled 'Resolution on Some Questions in the History of Our Party' (*SW*, IV, 171) and a few other references (*SW*, I, pp. 114 and 153); and in Hu Chiao-mu's *Thirty Years of the Chinese Communist Party*. Wang Ming's *The Two Lines* (Moscow, 1932, and Yenan, 1940) contains the main theses of the revolution as advocated and practised by the 'Twenty-eight Bolsheviks'.

4. Here, if not before, see note 3, above.

5. The possibility of a move to the North-West was undoubtedly debated at this time, but it was not until the Tsunyi Conference that decisions were taken to move there. See note 3, above.

6. Such an offer was made and yet it was not implicated in the case of the Nineteenth Route Army, for reasons mentioned in note 3, above.

7. Mao subsequently published his own close analysis of the tactical and strategic problems of all the Kiangsi campaigns. See *SW*, Vol. I, and *Selected Military Writings of Mao Tse-tung*. Communist analyses offered for both victories and defeats during the Kiangsi campaigns never adequately conceded the general strategic handicaps imposed on Chiang Kai-shek by preoccupation with his national defence responsibilities during Japan's invasion of Manchuria (1931), attack on Shanghai (1932), and military attrition in North China (1933), as well as with the warlords' war of 1930. For Chiang's estimate of the importance of such factors, see his *Soviet Russia in China*, pp. 62–4.

PART FIVE : *The Long March*

1. This was the first detailed account of the Long March to be published, and was based largely on eye-witness testimony of many participants (reflecting their heroic view of the retreat), as gathered in direct personal interviews. Official and nonofficial versions of the epic have since become available (see Bibliography). The Long March became ever more glorified in

Communist propaganda, so that it may be years before fact can entirely be separated from fiction. It is now evident that the plan of retreat was largely improvised until the armies reached Tsunyi, where Mao apparently won approval for his 'destination Shensi' concept which became the Long March. By the 1960s Peking's new Museum of the Revolution devoted a whole floor to historical relics, montages, and recapitulations of the Long March. The display included a very large electrically illuminated and animated map showing the route of the heroes. Every fifteen minutes a young girl, her hair in a pony tail, picked up a pointer and began to recite a stage-by-stage account of the adventure to ever waiting crowds, wide-eyed and open-mouthed, gathered below her. One of the features of the museum was a motion film made by the author of some of the survivors after their arrival in Kansu and Shensi, at the end of the March.

Chapter 1: The Fifth Campaign

1. See especially Yang Chien's *The Communist Situation in China*, published in Nanking under the auspices of the Kuomintang-sponsored Academy of Sciences. Yang's report concedes the Communist reforms mentioned, as part of an analysis of Red successes among the poor peasants. For a recapitulation of 'Red terror' charges see Chiang Kai-shek's *Soviet Russia in China*. Mao Tse-tung's *Report on an Investigation into the Peasant Movement in Hunan* describes activities carried out by Communist-led peasants against 'local bullies', 'bad gentry', and 'corrupt officials' for whom the 'only effective' suppression was 'to execute . . . at least some of those whose crimes and wrongdoings are most serious'. (SW, I, 38.)

2. See note 1, above.

3. Some very extensive interview material elicited in response to my questions to Wu Liang-p'ing, Hsu T'eh-li, Lo Fu, Chou Hsing, and others concerning matters of life, death, and taxes in Soviet Kiangsi was omitted from this book, for the reason stated – that I had no experience there on which to base a judgement – but was later published in *RNORC*.

4. Smedley, *The Great Road*, p. 309.

5. These Red remnants, after a rebirth as the New Fourth Army, developed into the very large force that crushed Chiang Kai-shek's Nationalists in Central China a decade later. See Ch'en Yi, BN.

Chapter 2: A Nation Emigrates

1. As far as I know, that 'collective account' was never published. For books on the Long March see Bibliography.

Chapter 4: Across the Great Grasslands

1. The dramatic duel between Mao Tse-tung and Chang Kuo-t'ao, to which brief reference was made here, was the last major challenge to Mao's Party leadership for about three decades. In 1936 I had but fragmentary informa-

tion concerning the nature of the split. Chang Kuo-t'ao later denied that Chu Teh stayed with him involuntarily. Among others who remained with Chang in Sikang was Li Ching-ch'uan (see BN). In 1960, when I asked Mao Tse-tung what was 'the darkest moment of his life', he said it was the struggle with Chang Kuo-t'ao, when the break-up of the Party and even civil war 'hung in the balance'. See Chang Kuo-t'ao, Li Hsien-nien, T'ao Chu, BN. For details of the Mao-Chang struggle and Chang's flight to KMT China, see RNORC and Bibliography.

2. The following is partly based on a conversation with Chou En-lai at Pao An; diary record dated 26 September 1936:

Chou says that the greater part of the Red Army losses took place in Szechuan, Kweichow, and Sikang. Losses due to actual fighting with the Kuomintang forces were less than those from fatigue, sickness, starvation, and attacks from tribesmen.

About 90,000 armed men left Kiangsi with the main forces. Of these 45,000 had been 'lost' by the time the Red Army crossed the Chin-sha River into Szechuan. Meanwhile Hsu Hsiang-ch'ien left the Oyuwan area in 1934, with between 50,000 and 60,000 troops. When he had been in Szechuan six months he increased his forces to more than 100,000. Late in 1935 Ho Lung left Hunan with about 40,000 troops. He reached Sikang with not more than 20,000, more likely 15,000.

On the arrival of the three armies in Szechuan, therefore, the figures were roughly as follows.

	LEFT OLD BASE WITH	STRENGTH IN SZECHUAN:	LOSSES:
First Front Army: Chu Teh – Mao – Chou	(1934) 90,000	45,000 ·	45,000
Fourth Front Army: Hsu Hsiang-ch'ien – Chang	(1933) 50,000	100,000 (+50,000)	?
Second Front Army: Ho Lung – Hsiao K'e	(1935) 40,000	15,000	25,000

A total of 160,000 men, of whom more than half were (1935) under Hsu Hsiang-ch'ien and Chang Kuo-t'ao, while the Kiangsi-Hunan forces had lost 70,000 men en route (1934 and 1935).

In 1935 the First Army Corps (First Front Army) arrived in Shen-pei with about 7,000 men. There it joined Liu Chih-tan's force of about 10,000. Hsu Hai-tung also came up from Honan in 1935 with 3,000 troops left out of a starting force of 8,000. New enlistments in Shen-pei (north Shensi), Shansi, Kansu and Ninghsia resulted in approximately the following:

First Army Corps (arrived from Szechuan with):		7,000
Shen-pei troops under Liu Chih-tan (later used as replacements):		10,000
Hsu Hai-tung forces from Oyuwan:		3,000
Shansi enlistments on 1935 expedition:		8,000
New enlistments in Shen-pei, and deserters from Manchurian and Mohammedan armies:		7,000
Approximate strength of regular forces in North-West now:		35,000
Partisans and Red Guards in all Shen-Kan-Ning:		30,000 (estimate)

Chou En-lai estimates the present strength of the Second Front and Fourth Front armies now en route to north Kansu, all the survivors from the winter in Sikang, as between 40,000 and 50,000.* What, then, has happened to the rest of the troops?

	LEFT BASE WITH:	1935:	REACHED NORTH-WEST IN 1936 WITH:	UNACCOUNTED FOR:
1. Hsu Hsiang-ch'ien and Chang Kuo-t'ao	50,000	100,000 ⎫	40,000	
2. Chu Teh	90,000	45,000 ⎬	to	
3. Ho Lung	40,000	15,000 ⎭	50,000?	
* Their combined forces arriving at the North-West were at most 50,000, according to Chou. If the peak strength of each command is combined we get a figure of 230,000 men. Subtracting from that the 7,000 men who reached Shensi with Mao-P'eng leaves a total of 223,000 and				173,000
4. Mao Tse-tung and P'eng	?	First Army Corps	7,000	?
5. Hsu Hai-tung	8,000		3,000	5,000
			60,000	178,000

FORCES ADDED IN NORTH-WEST:

Shen-pei troops under Liu Chih-tan	10,000
New enlistments in Shansi	8,000
Enlistments in Shen-pei and Kansu-Ninghsia	7,000
	25,000

The above figures would suggest a total combined loss in all Red armies over a period of a little less than two years of about 180,000 men. . . . My guess would be that the present* Red strength may not exceed 30,000 to 50,000 regulars, with no more than 30,000 rifles.

Comment added in 1967:

The peak strength (1934–5) of the three main armies was 230,000, consisting of the First Front Army, commanded by Chu Teh and Mao Tse-tung (90,000), the Second Front Army, commanded by Ho Lung and Hsiao K'e (40,000), and the Fourth Front Army, commanded by Chang Kuo-t'ao and Hsu Hsiang-ch'ien (100,000). Chu Teh's army was divided at Moukung during the Mao-Chang dispute, after which Mao, P'eng Teh-huai, Chou En-lai and Lin Piao proceeded to Shensi, where they arrived with only 7,000 men. A year later Ho Lung and Hsiao K'e reached Szechuan and met Chang Kuo-t'ao's surviving forces. The two Front armies proceeded northward but not as a coordinated operation. Chu Teh, Ho Lung, and Hsiao K'e arrived at Kansu and were met by P'eng Teh-huai, when their combined regular forces probably were no more than 40,000. Meanwhile, Hsu Hsiang-ch'ien, obeying Chang Kuo-t'ao's orders, followed a different route with the intention of occupying north-western Kansu and seizing the road to Sinkiang. Hsu's army was trapped by KMT troops west of Sian, badly mauled, and split in half. The northern column, led by Li Hsien-nien and renamed the West Front Army, proceeded towards Sinkiang. Heavily attacked by Chinese Moslem troops with greatly superior numbers and arms, Li reached Urumchi with only 2,000 survivors. Hsu Hsiang-ch'ien and Chang Kuo-t'ao were cut off from their own remnant forces and arrived in Yenan sick and accompanied only by their personal bodyguards. Rupture of communications and coordination between Chang and Yenan, and then the split between Chang and Chu Teh and Ho Lung – and even some armed skirmishes between the two Party factions – had left the Fourth Front Army isolated and an easy prey. In brief, after my conversation with Chou En-lai, in September 1936, Chang Kuo-t'ao's once formidable army of '100,000' virtually disintegrated before his part of the Long March ended early in 1937.

3. The 'three armies' were the First, Second, and Fourth Front (see note 2, above). Mao later rewrote the poem, of which several translations now exist.

* 'Present' in this diary note meant 1936, when these notes were compiled for but not used in RSOC. It may be of academic interest to add that my guess of '30,000 to 50,000' regulars, with no more than 30,000 rifles, was close to the 40,000 Communist 'effectives' recognized and paid by the National Government of Nanking, as the Eighth Route Army, when the old Red Army was incorporated into the National Army of China after the KMT-CP agreement, reached after the Sian Incident.

PART SIX : Red Star in the North-West

Chapter 1: The Shensi Soviets: Beginnings

1. Thirty years later Mark Selden published a detailed and absorbing study of the origins of the revolution in Shensi, based on extensive and newly unearthed research data, entitled, 'The Guerrilla Movement in Northwest China', *China Quarterly*, Nos. 28-9 (Oct.-Dec. 1966, Jan.-March 1967).

2. Mao Tse-tung gives a different version of this incident in his SW, Vol. I.

Chapter 3: Soviet Society

1. See Mao Tse-tung, 'How to Differentiate the Classes in the Rural Areas', SW, I, 137-9.

PART EIGHT : With the Red Army

Chapter 1: The 'Real' Red Army

1. Joseph W. Stilwell was in 1937 US military attaché in China. He became commander-in-chief of US forces in the China-Burma-India theatre during the Second World War. See *The Stilwell Papers* (New York, 1948).

PART NINE : With the Red Army (continued)

Chapter 4: Moslem and Marxist

1. 'Feudal' and 'backward' the ruling Ma family indeed was, as this report of three decades ago attests, but to conclude that the Communists easily convinced the *Hui-min* that they had nothing to fear in a future socialist state would be greatly to minimize the troubles which lay ahead. Schisms among the Red troops themselves proved as serious as the quarrels then rife among the 'three faiths' and the four Mas and their subjects. Such divisions led to serious Red defeats (see Chang Kuo-t'ao, Hsu Hsiang-ch'ien and Li Hsien-nien, BN). Not until the Liberation War were the Ma brothers finally driven from the North-West.

The Communists did keep their promises to create autonomous Mohammedan states in Ninghsia and Sinkiang, but religious leaders continued to resist communization. Behind their smouldering discontent, which broke out in sporadic revolts after formation of the CPR, was the *Hui-min's* fear of loss of their grazing lands to Chinese farmers, and absorption such as overtook the Mongols of Inner Mongolia. The CCP policy towards minority nationalities was in many respects far more enlightened than anything pursued under the Kuomintang, but ancient quarrels between the Chinese and their frontier peoples were not to be settled in a generation or two. On their part, the Russians exploited signs of instability behind such Chinese frontiers after the breakdown in Sino-Soviet relations from 1960 onwards.

PART TEN : *War and Peace*

Chapter 2: 'Little Red Devils'

1. On my return to China in 1960, 1964–5 and 1970–1 I met several former 'little devils' holding positions of major responsibility. One was Tai Ch'un-ch'i, vice-director of the Institute of Venereology and Skin Diseases, whom I first knew in 1936. In the same institute I renewed old acquaintance with Dr George Hatem (Ma Hai-teh), an American, and the only foreign doctor with the Communist forces since 1936. See BN.

Chapter 3: United Front in Action

1. See Part Eleven, Chapter 6, note 1.

Chapter 4: Concerning Chu Teh

1. Retained to preserve the form and spirit of the original text, this sketch is based chiefly on biographical notes given to me by Commander Li Chiang-lin (who was on Chu Teh's staff from the earliest days in Kiangsi), supplemented by brief data from Mao Tse-tung, P'eng Teh-huai, and others. It contains many inaccuracies but, as in the case of the story of Ho Lung, may be regarded as part of the Red Army legend at a time when no documentation was available. See BN.

2. More accurate versions of Chu Teh's relations with Fan Shih-sheng later appeared in Smedley, *The Great Road*, and Rue, *Mao Tse-tung in Opposition*. See Bibliography.

PART ELEVEN : *Back to Pao An*

Chapter 1: Casuals of the Road

1. Communists continued to observe a tolerant policy towards foreign missionaries throughout most of the Resistance War, but foreign missionary activity was ended soon after the CPR was established. See *TOSOTR* for some details.

Chapter 2: Life in Pao An

1. The wife here referred to arrived with Li Teh from Kiangsi. Later he divorced her and married an actress from Shanghai. Li Teh left his second Chinese wife behind when he climbed aboard the one and only Soviet Russian plane that landed in Yenan during the Resistance War.

Chapter 3: The Russian Influence

1. Consult Part Four, Chapter 6, note 3 in connection with this chapter and the two chapters following.

Chapter 4: Chinese Communism and the Comintern

1. This chapter is retained to preserve the form of the original book. Its inadequacy reflects the poverty of information available thirty years ago, and should be read in contrast with annotations such as Part Four, Chapter 6, note 3.

2. In a general sense this assessment still has validity in retrospect, but it reflects a limited knowledge of complex Sino-Russian Party relationships at that time. Direct contact with Moscow was indeed often lost for months, but conformance with the Comintern's general line and directives was the expressed intention and constant preoccupation of the Chinese PB. Not until after the Tsunyi Conference of January 1935 did Mao's national leadership prevail over Russian-trained and Russian-oriented Chinese Communists. Mao never openly denied the supreme wisdom of Stalin until twenty years later, when he agreed with the Party evaluation of Stalin contained in the articles 'On the Historical Experience of the The Dictatorship of the Proletariat'. For details see *TOSOTR*.

Chapter 5: That Foreign Brain Trust

1. The 'Red military council', as constituted in 1934 and headed by Chou En-lai, was not 'unanimously' opposed to Li Teh's plans. The 'so I was told' above referred chiefly to a statement made in Kansu (12 August 1936) by Hsiao Ching-kuang, who blamed the 'Kiangsi disaster' on attempts to fight positional warfare during the Fifth Campaign. 'This was largely due to Li Teh's advice,' he told me. 'He was very confident and very authoritative. He pounded his fist on the table. He told Mao and others that they knew nothing about military matters; they should heed him.' How was he able to do that? 'He had the prestige of the world Communist supporters behind him.' See *RNORC*. For further discussion see Li Teh, BN, Otto Braun and Dieter Heinzig, Bibliography.

Chapter 6: Farewell to Red China

1. The Red reports of victory given to me proved premature. The 'joyous reunion', while doubtless genuine enough between the rank and file, opened a new chapter of reckoning for differences which had divided the camps of Chang Kuo-t'ao and Mao Tse-tung in the Party leadership. For comment on Red losses reported later, see Hsu Hsiang-ch'ien, Chang Kuo-t'ao, and Li Hsien-nien, BN.

2. In Mao's earlier interview with me (16 July 1936) he had proposed a 'united front' with 'all anti-Japanese forces,' but not specifically a coalition with the Kuomintang Government itself. The 'immediate' cause of the change was doubtless the decision of the Central Committee based on newly received interpretations of the proceedings of the Seventh Congress of the Comintern.

3. When I left the Red areas I sent back my camera and some film to Lu

Ting-yi, as promised – by hand of the courier, Wang Lin – on condition that Lu would supply me with newsworthy photographs from time to time. The only picture he ever got to me was an enlargement of what he considered his masterpiece, some Shensi apple blossoms.

PART TWELVE : White World Again

Chapter 1: A Preface to Mutiny

1. Wang later headed a Japanese puppet government. See BN.

Chapter 3: Chiang, Chang, and the Reds

1. The limitations and purposes of this kind of coalition regime were set forth by Mao Tse-tung in *The New Democracy* (Yenan, 1938).

2. Although the Communists had 'nothing to do' with the actual physical seizure of Chiang, personnel in their liaison group in Sian at the time probably had prior (though perhaps very brief) knowledge of the plan. Captain Sun Ming-chiu, the young Tungpei officer whose troops 'arrested' Chiang, was under strong Communist influence. As noted earlier, Chang Hsueh-liang had CCP CC members in his own headquarters and Wang Ping-nan (see BN) was personal secretary to General Yang Hu-ch'eng, whose troops participated in the 'arrest.'

The Communist delegation sent from Pao An to Sian to negotiate immediately after the incident included, besides Chou En-lai (then vice-chairman of the Revolutionary Military Committee): Yeh Chien-ying, chief of staff of the 'Anti-Japanese Red Army', and Po Ku, 'Minister of Foreign Affairs' of the Communist provisional government. After this book was published I was told by Po Ku (in 1938) that Chou En-lai was the only one of their delegation who saw the Generalissimo in Sian. Po Ku said that in Chou's single brief interview no agreement was signed and Chiang merely expressed sentiments in favour of ending the civil war which Chou interpreted as a moral commitment. Shortly afterwards, to their disappointment, the Young Marshal released the Generalissimo without informing Chou or the other Communists. According to Po Ku they had hoped that the Generalissimo would remain in Sian long enough at least to reach concrete terms of a truce agreement on the basis of which to restore a united front of national resistance. Further evidence concerning the incident (referred to in RNORC, pp. 1–15) indicates that the Communists in Yenan debated a public trial for Chiang Kai-shek. Any such intention was certainly abandoned after a message reached the Communists directly from Stalin, in which he threatened publicly to disown the CCP unless they demanded Chiang's release unharmed, a message which was said to have greatly annoyed Mao. I know of nothing, however, to support the view that Mao Tse-tung ever demanded the 'execution' of the Generalissimo, a view attributed to me without foundation by Stuart Schram in *Mao Tse-tung*, p. 199.

3. See RNORC.

4. While this account seemed plausible to me on the basis of information available at the time, I now believe that the idea of a 'popular trial' may have been debated by the Communists, who repudiated it for reasons mentioned in note 2 above.

Chapter 4: 'Point Counter Point'

1. Chiang Kai-shek never forgave Chang Hsueh-liang and never freed him. Thirty years later Chang was still Chiang Kai-shek's personal prisoner on Taiwan.

2. For documentation of the official Communist position throughout the Sian affair, see *SW*, Vol. I, pp. 255ff.

Chapter 6: Red Horizons

1. Report to the Communist Party (Yenan, 10 April 1937). See *SW*, Vol. I. Mao's frank declaration should have destroyed all notions that he sought to establish anything less than all-out proletarian (Communist-led) power. Not many months later, in an interview with me, Mao even more categorically derided any deviation from that 100-per-cent Communist aim. (See Appendices. Further Interviews with Mao Tse-tung, p. 508.)

APPENDICES

Abbreviations

Further Interviews with Mao Tse-tung

OWING to space limitations the text of my interviews with Mao Tse-tung in 1936 was not included in its entirety in the original edition of *Red Star Over China*, although most of it was published in the *Shanghai Evening Post & Mercury*, 3, 4, 5 February 1937. The following extracts may be of contemporary interest. (Italics added.)

On the Comintern, China, and Outer Mongolia   *Pao An, 23 July 1936*

SNOW : In actual practice, if the Chinese revolution were victorious, would the economic and political relationship between Soviet China and Soviet Russia be maintained within the Third International or a similar organization, or would there probably be some kind of actual merger of governments? Would the Chinese Soviet Government be comparable in its relation to Moscow to the present government of Outer Mongolia?

MAO TSE-TUNG : I assume this is a purely hypothetical question. As I have told you, the Red Army is not now seeking the hegemony of power, but a united China against Japanese imperialism.

The Third International is an organization in which the vanguard of the world proletariat brings together its collective experience for the benefit of all revolutionary peoples throughout the world. It is not an administrative organization nor has it any political power beyond that of an advisory capacity. Structurally it is not very different from the Second International, though in content it is vastly different. But just as no one would say that in a country where the cabinet is organized by the Social Democrats the Second International is dictator, so it is ridiculous to say that the Third International is dictator in countries where there are Communist parties.

In the USSR the Communist Party is in power, yet even there the Third International does not rule nor does it have any direct political power over the people at all. Similarly, it can be said that although the Communist Party of China is a member of the Comintern, still this in no sense means that Soviet China is ruled by Moscow or by the Comintern. We are certainly not fighting for an emancipated China in order to turn the country over to Moscow!

The Chinese Communist Party is only one party in China, and in its victory it will have to speak for the whole nation. It cannot speak for the Russian people or rule for the Third International, but only in the interests of the Chinese masses. Only where the interests of the Chinese masses coincide with the interests of the Russian masses can it be said to be 'obeying the will' of Moscow. But of course this basis of common benefit will be tremendously broadened, once the masses of China are in democratic power and socially and economically emancipated, like their brothers in Russia.

When soviet governments have been established in many countries, the problem of an international union of soviets may arise, and it will be interesting to see how it will be solved. But today I cannot suggest the formula; it is a problem which has not been and cannot be solved in advance. In the world today, with increasingly close economic and cultural intimacies between different states and peoples, such a union would seem to be highly desirable, *if achieved on a voluntary basis.*

Clearly, however, the last point is of utmost importance; such a world union could be successful only if every nation had the right to enter or leave the union according to the will of its people, and with its sovereignty intact, and certainly never at the 'command' of Moscow. No Communist ever thought otherwise, and the myth of 'world domination from Moscow' is an invention of the Fascists and counter-revolutionaries.

The relationship between Outer Mongolia and the Soviet Union, now and in the past, has always been based on the principle of complete equality. When the People's Revolution has been victorious in China, the Outer Mongolian republic will automatically become a part of the Chinese federation, at its own will. The Mohammedan and Tibetan peoples, likewise, will form autonomous republics attached to the China federation. The unequal treatment of national minorities, as practised by the Kuomintang, can have no part in the Chinese programme, nor can it be part of the programme of any democratic republic.

On China as the 'Key'

SNOW: With the achievement of victory of a Red movement in China, do you think that revolution would occur quickly in other Asiatic or semicolonial countries, such as Korea, Indochina, the Philippines, and India? Is China at present the 'key' to world revolution?

MAO: The Chinese revolution is a key factor in the world situation. . . . When the Chinese revolution comes into full power the masses of many colonial countries will follow the example of China and win a similar victory of their own. But I emphasize again that the seizure of power is not our (immediate) aim. We want to stop civil war, create a people's democratic government with the Kuomintang and other parties, and fight for our independence against Japan.

On Land Distribution   *Pao An, 19 July 1936*

SNOW : What is the foremost internal task of the revolution, after the struggle against Japanese imperialism?

MAO : The Chinese revolution, being of bourgeois-democratic character, has as its primary task the readjustment of the land problem – the realization of agrarian reform. Some idea of the urgency of rural reform may be secured by referring to figures on the distribution of land in China today. During the Nationalist Revolution I was secretary of the Peasant Committee [department] of the Kuomintang and had charge of collecting statistics for areas throughout twenty-one provinces.

Our investigation showed astonishing inequalities. About 70 per cent of the whole rural population was made up of poor peasants, tenants or part-tenants, and of agricultural workers. About 20 per cent was made up of middle peasants tilling their own land. Usurers and landlords were about 10 per cent of the population. Included in the 10 per cent also were rich peasants, exploiters like the militarists, tax collectors, and so forth.

The 10 per cent of the rich peasants, landlords, and usurers together owned about 70 per cent of the cultivated land. From 12 to 15 per cent was in the hands of the middle peasants. The 70 per cent of the poor peasants, tenants and part-tenants, and agricultural workers, owned only from 10 to 15 per cent of the total cultivated land.... The revolution is caused chiefly by two oppressions – the imperialists and that 10 per cent of landlords and Chinese exploiters. So we may say that in our new demands for democracy, land reform, and war against imperialism we *are opposed by less than 10 per cent of the population*. And really not 10 per cent, but probably only about 5 per cent, for not more than that many Chinese will turn traitor to join with Japan in subjugating their own people under the device of the joint 'Anti-Red Pact'.

SNOW: Other things in the soviet programme having been postponed in the interest of the united front, is it not possible to delay land redistribution also?

MAO : Without confiscating the estates of the landlords, without meeting the main democratic demand of the peasantry, it is impossible to lay the broad mass basis for a successful revolutionary struggle for national liberation. *In order to win the support of the peasants for the national cause it is necessary to satisfy their demand for land ...*

On Education and Latinized Chinese

SNOW : Could you give me a brief statement of policy concerning ... illiteracy?

MAO : ... As for the problem of illiteracy, this is not a difficult task for a people's government which really wants to raise the economic and cultural standard of the masses ...

In Kiangsi our Society for the Liquidation of Illiteracy, under the leadership of the Commissioner of Education, has had astonishing successes. It built up in every village groups led by young students, Young Communists and Young Vangards, to teach people how to read and write. These mass-education schools, hundreds of them, were created by the organized peasantry themselves, and instructed by the enthusiastic Red youths, who freely gave their time and energy to this task, without pay. After three or four years the majority of the peasants in our soviet districts in Kiangsi knew several hundred Chinese characters and could read simple texts, lectures, and our newspapers and other publications.

Our statistics were lost during the Long March, but my report before the Second All-Soviet Congress * contained a full account of the progress made in education, both through the people's mass-education movement, and through the regular school system maintained by the soviets ...

In Shensi and Kansu there has also been established a Society for the Liquidation of Illiteracy. The cultural level here was formerly much lower than in Kiangsi, and great tasks of education still face us today. ... In order to hasten the liquidation of illiteracy here we have begun experimenting with *Hsin-Wen-Tzu* – Latinized Chinese. *It is now used in our Party school, in the Red Academy, in the Red Army, and in a special section of the* Red China Daily News. We believe Latinization is a good instrument with which to overcome illiteracy. Chinese characters are so difficult to learn that even the best system of rudimentary characters, or simplified teaching, does not equip the people with a really efficient and rich vocabulary. *Sooner or later, we believe, we will have to abandon the Chinese character altogether if we are to create a new*

---

*The Second All-China Soviet Congress was held in Juichin, Kiangsi, in January 1934. See Mao Tse-tung, *Red China: President Mao Tse-tung Reports* ... (See Bibliography.)

social culture in which the masses fully participate. We are now widely using Latinization, and if we stay here for three years the problem of illiteracy will have been largely overcome ...

Following are excerpts from 1939 interviews never fully published outside China, where they appeared in the *China Weekly Review*, Shanghai, 13 and 20 January 1940. (Italics added.)

'We Are Never Reformists'   *Yenan, 25 September 1939*

SNOW : Because the Communist Party of China has abandoned propaganda emphasizing class struggle, abolished its soviets, submitted to leadership of the Kuomintang and the Kuomintang Government, adopted the *San Min Chu I* [Dr Sun Yat-sen's *Three Principles of the People*], ceased confiscating the property of landlords and capitalists, and stopped (overt) organizational work and propaganda in Kuomintang areas, many people now assert that Chinese Communists are in fact no longer social revolutionaries but mere reformists – bourgeois in methods and in aims. How do you answer such claims?

MAO : *We are always social revolutionaries; we are never reformists.* There are two main objectives in the thesis of the Chinese revolution. The first consists of the realization of the tasks of a national democratic revolution. The other is social revolution. The latter must be achieved, and completely achieved. For the present the revolution is national and democratic in the character of its aims, *but after a certain stage it will be transformed into social revolution.* The present 'becoming' of the social revolutionary part in the thesis of the Chinese revolution will turn into its 'being' – unless our work in the present phase is a failure, in which case there is no early possibility of social revolution.

Preparation for Counterattack

SNOW : In what stage, according to your theory of the 'Protracted War', is Chinese resistance at the present time? Has the stage of 'stalemate' been reached?

MAO : Yes, the war is in a stage of stalemate, but with certain qualifications. Under the condition of a new international system, and under the condition that Japan's position is becoming more difficult, while China will not seek a reconciliation, the war is in a stage of stalemate ... the meaning of which (for us) is preparation for a counterattack.

On the Nazi-Soviet Pact

SNOW : I read your comment on the signature of the Soviet–German pact. You seem to think it unlikely that the Soviet Union can be drawn into the European War.... Do you think the USSR would remain neutral, as long as it is not attacked, even if Nazi Germany appears to be near victory?

MAO : The Soviet Union will not participate in this war, because both sides are imperialists, and it is simply robber war with justice on neither side. Both sides are struggling for the balance of power and rule over the peoples of the world. Both are wrong, and the Soviet Union will not become involved in this kind of war, but will remain neutral. . . . As for the outcome of the present European war, the Soviet Union cannot be frightened by the threat of the victorious power to herself, whether it is England or Germany. Whenever the Soviet Union is attacked it will have the support of the peoples of various countries, and of the national minorities in colonial and semicolonial countries ...

On Soviet Economic Cooperation with Hitler

I had submitted a long list of written questions for perusal by Mao in advance. At this point I interpolated a question outside that list, asking why, if Germany was imperialist and no different from Britain and France, the Soviet Union should participate in Germany's imperialist adventure to the extent of making available to Germany Russia's great reserves of wheat, oil, and other war materials. Why, incidentally, did Russia continue to lease oil lands to Japan in Sakhalin, or to give Japan fishing rights? The latter were of great value in enabling Japan to export large quantities of fish, and thus establish foreign credits with which to buy munitions and carry on a 'robber imperialist' war against the 'national liberation movement' of 'semicolonial China'.

Mao replied that it was an extremely complicated question, and could not be answered until one saw the end of the policy. The conditions under which the Soviet Union was selling oil to Japan were not clear to him. In any case, the Soviet Union was supplying neither Germany nor Japan with any war instruments, and to maintain ordinary trade did not make her a participant in the war.

I asked whether there was any difference, in modern war, between supplying a belligerent with fuel for tanks or airplanes and supplying the tanks and planes themselves. Why was the United States a participant in Japan's imperialist invasion of China because she sold Japan the raw materials of war, but the Soviet Union not a participant in Germany's imperialist war in Europe, nor Japan's war in Asia, when she supplied the same kind of materials to the two combatants?

Mao conceded that the distinction between trade in war materials and trade in war instruments was not great. What mattered, he said, was whether the country in question was really supporting revolutionary wars of liberation. In that judgement there was no question where the USSR stood. She had given positive support to revolutionary wars in China, in 1925–7, in Spain, and in China at present. *The Soviet Union would always be on the side of just revolutionary wars* but would not take sides in imperialist war, though she might maintain ordinary trade with all belligerents.

On the Question of Poland

MAO : The Nazi invasion of Poland presented the Soviet Union with this problem: whether to permit the whole Polish population to fall victim to Nazi persecution, or whether to liberate the national minorities of Eastern Poland. The Soviet Union chose to follow the second course of action.

In Eastern Poland there is a vast stretch of territory inhabited by 8,000,000 Byelo-Russians and 3,000,000 Ukrainians. This territory was forcibly seized from the young Soviet Socialist Republics as the price of the Brest–Litovsk Treaty, and fell under the dominion of the reactionary Polish Government. Today the Soviet Union, no longer weak and young, takes back its own, and liberates them ...

Mao Praises Fellow Leaders   *Pao An, 25 July 1936*

As a kind of postscript to the end of his account of the Long March, Mao attributed its successful conclusion to the 'correct leadership' of the Party and then singled out eighteen comrades by name. As the remarks seemed somewhat anticlimactic to the main account I did not use them, but today these sentences may be of some historical interest. Attention need hardly be called to the order in which Mao listed the names, to the fact that they included the men with whom Mao had but recently struggled and against whom he would struggle again, and to the names omitted.

MAO : Another reason for its [the Party's] invincibility lies in the extraordinary ability and courage and loyalty of the human material, the revolutionary cadres. Comrades Chu Teh, Wang Ming, Lo Fu, Chou En-lai, Po Ku, Wang Chia-hsiang, P'eng Teh-huai, Lo Man, Teng Fa,

Hsiang Ying, Hsu Hai-tung, Ch'en Yun, Lin Piao, Chang Kuo-t'ao, Hsu Hsiang-ch'ien, Ch'en Chang-hao, Ho Lung, Hsiao K'eh – and many, many excellent comrades who gave their lives for the revolution – all these, working together for a single purpose, have made the Red Army and the soviet movement. And these and others yet to come will lead us to ultimate victory.

Biographical Notes

In 1960 Mao Tse-tung told the author that there had been about 50,000 Communists at the start of Chiang Kai-shek's counter-revolution. 'After the killings' only about 10,000 were left. By 1960 there were about 800 survivors of all the years between. By and large, Mao said, China was being run and for some years would be run by those 800. About one-fourth of the 800 were members or alternate members of the Central Committee.* At the summit several dozen made up the Politburo and the Secretariat of the Party Central Committee until the GPCR (1966–9), at the climax of which the Ninth Party Congress in 1969 elected a CC and PB with sixteen new members, including many drawn from outside 'the 800'.

The data given below is not intended to indicate by its length or inclusion the relative Party rank of the individual listed so much as to help readers trace the subsequent careers of persons introduced in *Red Star*. Those best known under their Party names are here alphabetized accordingly. The figures in parentheses following each name refer to the book page on which the person is first mentioned. Abbreviations used are given on page 503. In some instances additional biographical details supplied to the author at first hand, but not included in the original edition of this book, are taken from *Random Notes on Red China*. Sketches of many of the persons listed have now been published in several biographical dictionaries, notably *Biographical Dictionary of Republican China* (BDRC) (Columbia University, NY, 1967).

Bluecher, General Vasili (p. 89), alias Galin, chief Soviet military adviser to the KMT 1925–7. He returned to Russia and was later either executed or died a prisoner in Siberia.

Borodin, Mikhail Markovich (p. 89), after returning to Russia in 1927, edited the *Moscow Daily News*. In Stalin's last days of paranoia, Borodin was exiled and died in prison camp. He was posthumously 're-habilitated' under Khrushchev. (See Part Four, Chapter 5, note 1.)

*See Red China Today: The Other Side of the River.

Braun, Otto. See Li Teh.

Chang Hsueh-liang (p. 54) was born in Liaoning, Manchuria, in 1898. Despite an official sentence, followed by an official 'pardon', General-issimo Chiang Kai-shek held Marshal Chang his personal prisoner from 1936 onward. When Chiang fled to Taiwan he took Chang with him. In 1963, Chang was reportedly permitted some very limited 'freedom to move' outside his home. To date (1971) Marshal Chang has never been able to tell his version of the Sian Incident. In Taiwan he was reported to have become a leading authority, as a research scholar, on the Ming Dynasty.

Chang Kuo-t'ao (p. 177) was Mao Tse-tung's most important rival for Party leadership in 1934–6. He was born in Chishui, Kiangsi, in 1897, in a rich landlord family. A student leader while at Peking University (Peiching Ta Hsueh), 1916–20, Chang met Ch'en Tu-hsiu and Li Ta-chao (*qq.v.*) there during the period when Mao Tse-tung was also influenced by them towards Marxism. One of the twelve founders of the CCP (July 1921), Chang at once entered the Party CC as secretary of the Orgburo. He helped set up the railway workers' union of North China and a 1923 strike in which eighty members were executed. After the Party reorganization at the Fifth Congress of the CCP, Chang was elected to the Party PB, again heading the Orgburo.

Chang participated in the Nanchang Uprising (1 August 1927) and the Canton Commune. In 1928 he attended the Sixth CCP Congress in Moscow and remained in the USSR three years. Again in the PB in Shanghai, in 1931, he was sent to lead Communist partisan groups north of the Yangtze River and was elected one of two vice-chairmen of the All-China Soviet Government of which Mao Tse-tung was chair-man. Chang's sphere of operational influence lay in partisan bases formed in the Honan-Hupeh-Anhui (Oyuwan) border areas, where he became chief commissar of the Red Army. His top military commander was Hsu Hsiang-ch'ien, and an important subordinate was Hsu Hai-tung (*qq.v.*). Forced to abandon Central China (1932) he moved to the Shensi-Szechuan border areas. In 1934 he was driven by KMT troops into western Szechuan.

Two main columns of Red forces met in June 1935, in the middle of the Long March. Mao led the southern group, Chang Kuo-t'ao those in retreat from north of the Yangtze. A decisive duel arose between them. Chang and his supporters in the CC refused to recognize Mao's supreme authority as 'chairman', as decided by an enlarged PB-CC meeting at Tsunyi, 1935. Chang opposed Mao's strategic plans to move to Shensi and wished to seek a compromise peace with the KMT. He also insisted that Mao was violating the CMT 'line', that the Tsunyi Conference was illegal, and that a new CC plenum must be called to unseat Mao. According to Chang Kuo-t'ao, Mao had already been thrice reprimanded by the CC and thrice expelled by it (John E. Rue, *Mao Tse-tung in Opposition*, Stanford, 1966, pp. 8–9). Following events described in RSOC, Chang divided the Red Army, keeping his troops (Fourth Front Army) in west Szechuan, and detaining (?) Chu Teh, while Mao led the First Front Army to Shensi. A year later, badly pressed, he was obliged to move north. While crossing the Yellow River his columns were nearly annihilated. Chang and Hsu Hsiang-ch'ien barely managed to reach Yenan, leaving their scattered forces under the command of Li Hsien-nien (q.v.).

In 1937 Chang was 'censured' by the CC, meeting in Yenan. He left the Red areas in 1938 and joined the KMT at Hankow. In an 'Appeal to My Countrymen' he described the KMT as 'the most revolutionary party' and Chiang Kai-shek as 'the only leader'. He was then expelled from the Party.

After 1949, Chang became an exile in Hongkong, where Mao Tse-tung sent his family to join him. For more detailed accounts of the Mao-Chang struggle see RNORC and Agnes Smedley's *The Great Road*. Chang Kuo-t'ao's autobiography was scheduled for publication in English at this writing.

Chang Ting-ch'eng (p. 196), an important Fukien CP leader, was born in 1897, in Chinsha, Yungting county, Fukien, of a poor peasant family. Re-elected to the CC secretariat in August 1966, he was Fukien Party secretary when Red Guards reportedly reorganized the Fukien provincial government, to combine an 'alliance of Red Guards, PLA and dependable cadres', and remove those Party leaders 'taking the capitalist road', but Chang was re-elected to the CC in 1969.

A primary-school teacher, Chang joined the CP in 1926, while attending the Peasant Movement Training Institute at Canton under Mao Tse-tung. He organized a peasant movement in his home area and in 1928 led an uprising in Chinsha. He then became chairman of a west Fukien soviet, entered the CC in 1930, and supported Mao Tse-tung in disputes with Li Li-san. He stayed behind in Fukien during the Long March and joined forces with Ch'en Yi and Su Yu, who later formed the New Fourth Army. From 1940 to 1944 he taught at the Central Party School, Yenan. Deputy commander, East China PLA and Third Field Army, 1948–9, under Ch'en Yi, he became Party secretary, Fukien, 1949; chairman, Land Reform Committee, Fukien, 1951; chairman, Fukien government, 1949–54; and concurrently a member of the

East China Party Bureau, 1953, deputy to the National People's Congress, 1954, chief procurator of the Supreme People's Procuracy, 1954, and member of the Control Committee of the CC, 1956.

Chang Wen-t'ien. See Lo Fu.

Ch'en Keng (p. 234) was born in Hsianghsiang, Hunan, in 1904, and died in 1961. A Whampoa graduate (1925), he studied in Russia in 1926 and participated in the Nanchang Uprising in 1927. He had an adventurous career, ending as a full general (1955), and was deputy defence minister at the time of his death. A long account of his life, as told to the author in 1936, throws interesting light on Chiang Kai-shek's efforts to win over former Whampoa cadets among the Red Army commanders. For Ch'en Keng's own story, see R N O R C.

Ch'en Po-ta (p. 478) achieved international notice when he jumped from No. 23 spot in the PB, as constituted in 1962, to No. 5 in accordance with ranking announced after the CC eleventh plenary session, Eighth Congress, August 1966. He was also a vice-premier of the government in charge of ideological training of the Red Guards, and editor of *Red Flag (Hung Ch'i)*, theoretical organ of the CCP. His rise dated only from his arrival in Yenan, in 1937, when he met Mao Tse-tung and became his 'political secretary' and literary amanuensis.

Born in Huian county, Fukien, 1904, Ch'en attended primary and middle school in Amoy, Kwangtung, then became secretary to warlord Chang Chen. He was said to have secretly joined the CCP in 1925. He was a student at the CMT's Sun Yat-sen University in 1926, and he remained in Russia until 1930, but he seemed to play no significant role in intense intraparty struggles of the period. In 1930 he joined the faculty of China University (Chung-Kuo Ta Hsueh), Peking, where he taught under an assumed name (Ch'en Chih-mei) and wrote exhortative patriotic articles under his real name. Although Ch'en later stated that he had revealed his identity at China University, he somehow went unmolested there. *The Roar of the Nation* (Peking, 1963) asserts that 'Ch'en Po-ta, one of the leaders of the North China Bureau of the CCP CC, also taught in China University. . . . His lessons on the philosophy of the Later Chou Dynasty were based on Marxism-Leninism.' Its author adds that 'reactionaries' made unsuccessful 'attempts on his life' and later tried to have him dismissed from the university because of his Fukien accent (*sic*), but that they failed. No detail is furnished concerning his role during the student demonstrations of 1935, when the Party underground was led by Liu Shao-ch'i. Of Ch'en's Party activity during the first seven years after his return from Russia, in fact, very little is revealed.

Following the Japanese occupation of Peking (July 1937) Ch'en made his way to Yenan. He taught at the Party school, and did research work for the propaganda department of the CC under Lu Ting-yi (q.v.). Primarily a polemicist, he had no combat experience, but his writings interested Mao and so did his familiarity with Russian Party history.

In 1942 Ch'en went to Chungking briefly as an editor of the Communist wartime newspaper, *New China Daily* (*Hsin-hua Jih-pao*), but in 1943 he resumed work in the Yenan propaganda department, which brought him in close touch with Mao. During that period (1937-47), Mao Tse-tung produced his principal theoretical, historical, and military works. Ch'en's counsel was available at an interesting time when Mao's leadership and theses on the united-front period of 1937 were attacked by Wang Ming (q.v.), which led to Mao's 'rectification' movement of 1942. The Party's definitive rejection of Wang Ming was written by Ch'en.

In 1945, when he was consulted during Mao's composition of the important 'Resolutions on Some Questions in the History of Our Party', Ch'en was elected to the CC at the CCP Eighth Congress. In 1946 he appeared for the first time as an alternate member in the PB. By 1949 he was senior deputy director of the propaganda department under Lu Ting-yi and in 1955-6 was deputy director of the rural-work department of the CC – spectacular advances for a man with virtually no known history in the pre-1937 Party.

Ch'en accompanied Mao to Moscow on his first visit there in 1949-50, and may have interpreted Mao's talks with Stalin. He was with Mao again in Moscow when Mao attended the fortieth-anniversary celebrations of the October Revolution in 1957, and made his 'East-Wind-prevailing' speech.

Ch'en was one of the few Chinese students educated in Moscow during the 1920s who avoided overt involvement in the manoeuvres of Pavel Mif or any of the several factions of Soviet-oriented Chinese Party leaders (the 'Twenty-eight Bolsheviks') who clashed with Mao before 1935 (see Po Ku, Wang Ming, etc.). Mao may have had less reason to distrust him as a loyal disciple and political Boswell, which he aspired to be and to an important degree became, than other 'returned students', who perhaps erred by excluding Ch'en from their counsels in the thirties.

Ch'en Po-ta probably published more philosophical, political, and Party historical books than any prominent Chinese Communist except Mao himself. In 1937-8 he wrote about means of mobilizing intellectuals for resistance and united-front work. In the 1940s he produced *Notes on Ten Years of Civil War, 1927–36*, and *Notes on Mao Tse-tung's Report on an Investigation of the Peasant Movement in Hunan*, both in close consultation with Mao. In 1949 and 1952 he produced short books eulogizing Stalin's contributions to the Chinese revolution – tactically required in periods of the CCP's maximum dependence on Stalin. But his status-making works in China were his essay 'Mao Tse-tung's Theory of the Chinese Revolution Is the Combination of Marxism-Leninism with the Chinese Revolution', and his book *Mao Tse-tung on the Chinese Revolution* (both 1951). He was also the editor of *The Thought of Mao Tse-tung (Mao Tse-tung Ssuhsiang)*. In 1958 he became chief editor of *Red Flag*. As vice-president of the Chinese Academy of Sciences he was a dominating force in Party historiography.

Ch'en was instrumental in the removal of Lu Ting-yi, whom he replaced (after the fall of T'ao Chu in 1966) as chief of the CCP propaganda department. As such, he was also boss of the Ministry of Culture. At a PB level just below Mao, Lin Piao, and Chou En-lai, and as Mao's writing arm during the GPCR, he was responsible for the official press campaigns against chosen purgees. Probably Ch'en was the main source of supply, to unsophisticated teenage Red Guards, of highly recondite materials of inner-Party history that appeared on many of the 'large character' wall posters used during the accompanying purge, including attacks on his former superiors, Lu Ting-yi, Liu Shao-ch'i, and Teng Hsiao-p'ing. Ch'en was also said to be chiefly responsible for compiling *Quotations from Chairman Mao Tse-tung*, the 'little red book' that became a universal best-seller, and for a long series of polemical articles called 'The Great Proletarian Cultural Revolution', circulated (1966–7) in many languages in pamphlet form.

In 1966 Ch'en was described by the official Hsin Hua news agency as 'the leader of the cultural relations group under the CC'. One of his closest collaborators was his first deputy, Chiang Ch'ing (Mme Mao Tse-tung), who also served as cultural adviser to the PLA.

By 1968 Ch'en was seemingly heir to fractions of administrative authority formerly exercised by PB members with whom Mao had ruptured relations. Apart from the propaganda apparatus he did not, however, seem to have any secure 'base' in either the Party or the army and was known to be unpopular with the leadership of the latter. As the pendulum swung from left back towards centre in the post-GPCR period Ch'en's influence waned. After June 1970, he made no public appearances, being absent at the October anniversary celebrations in 1970, at the 1 May manifestation, and the July anniversary of the observation of the fiftieth birthday of the CCP.

Ch'en Shao-yu. See Wang Ming.

Ch'en Tu-hsiu (p. 87), the first general secretary (1921–7) of the CCP, influenced radical youths during 1919–27 more than any other Chinese cultural and political leader except Li Ta-chao (*q.v.*), with whom he laid the foundations of Chinese Marxism upon which rose the edifice of Maoism. Ch'en was born in 1879 in Huaining, Kiangsu, of a wealthy official family, studied the Classics, led a great revolution, and died (1942) a writer of essays and studies in the ancient Chinese language.

Dean of the College of Letters of Peking University (1915), he became best known as the founder and editor of *New Youth* (*Hsin Ch'ing-nien*), which in 1917 initiated a language and cultural reform of profound impact, and was also the voice of the May Fourth Movement (1919). After three months in jail for participating in the May Fourth Movement, Ch'en resigned from Peking University's faculty, went to Shanghai (1920), organized Communist study groups throughout China, and was, with Li Ta-chao, one of the two leading founders of the CCP. For comment on his difference with the CMT and CCP after July 1927, see Part Four, Chapter 5, note 1, and Chapter 6, note 3. Discussion of Ch'en Tu-hsiu may now be supplemented from many other sources, including his own works. See also Bibliography, especially Chow Tse-tung, *The May Fourth Movement*, Isaacs, Schwartz, and the BDRC.

Ch'en Yi (p. 195n.), an authentic military hero and China's Foreign Minister from 1958, was one of the ten marshals of the PLA. Born in Lochih, Szechuan, in 1901, Ch'en was the son of a district magistrate. He received his middle-school education in Chengtu, where he also learned to play basketball at a local American-operated YMCA. After winning a scholarship to a French-language preparatory school in Peking for a year, he went to France, where (1919–21) he combined labour (barge-loading, washing dishes, and work at the Michelin and Creusot plants) with study in a vocational school and at the Institut Polytechnique in Grenoble. In 1921 he joined the Chinese Socialist Youth Corps, which evolved into the CYL (see Chou En-lai). In the same year he and some other members were deported from France for staging a sit-down strike at the Institut Franco-Chinois in Lyons. Returning to Szechuan, he joined the staff of warlord Yang Sen. In Peking, in 1923, he joined the KMT. As a member of the CYL he was admitted to the CCP in 1923. After two years (1923–5) at Sino-French University, in Peking, he next worked at Whampoa Academy, Canton, as political instructor under Chou En-lai.

Assigned to Yeh T'ing's (*q.v.*) staff during the Northern Expedition (1926), he took part in the Nanchang Uprising. Retreating with Ho Lung and Yeh T'ing to Swatow, he fell in with Chu Teh's retreat to southern Kiangsi. In early 1928 he accompanied Chu Teh to Chingkangshan. Ch'en headed the political department of the Fourth Red Army until 1929, when he took command of the Thirteenth Division. In 1930 he sided with Mao in a dispute with the CC under Li Li-san and, with P'eng Teh-huai, suppressed the anti-Maoist forces of the Party involved in the Fu-t'ien Incident. During the Long March, Ch'en stayed behind with Hsiang Ying (Han Ying) to command a Red rear guard in Kiangsi, and from 1934 until 1937 fought bitter battles for survival. With the outbreak of major Sino-Japanese war the remnant Reds in the South were permitted by Chiang Kai-shek to regroup under the command of Yeh T'ing and Hsiang Ying as the New Fourth Army. It grew very rapidly. Alarmed, the Generalissimo sought to drive it entirely into Japanese-occupied territory. In January 1941, part of the New Fourth was ambushed by Nationalists. Hsiang Ying was killed and Yeh T'ing wounded and taken prisoner. Supported by units under Su Yu, T'an Chen-lin, and Chang Ting-ch'eng (*qq.v.*), Ch'en Yi held his detachments together and was named acting commander by Mao Tse-tung. Liu Shao-ch'i soon joined him as political commissar.

By 1945 the New Fourth Army had carved an immense territory from the Japanese conquest and built up the largest Red force in Central China. At the CCP Seventh Congress Ch'en was elected to the CC. Following Japan's surrender and the death of Yeh T'ing, in 1946, Ch'en became full field commander of the New Fourth – renamed the East China PLA. With renewal of civil war in 1947, Ch'en Yi's army played a decisive role; in June 1948, it captured Kaifeng, capital of Honan province. Soon afterwards Ch'en assumed a new 'general front command' which included Liu Po-ch'eng, Su Yu, T'an Chen-lin and, as chief political commissar, Teng Hsiao-p'ing. In the 'Hwai-Hai' campaign, in November, Ch'en defeated the main forces of Chiang Kai-shek so decisively that the KMT lost East Central China. As the Third Field Army, Ch'en Yi's troops pushed on to Nanking, Shanghai, and the provinces of Fukien and Chekiang, south of the Yangtze River.

Following victory, Ch'en Yi was successively or concurrently commander of the East China military area; second secretary of the East

China Bureau of the CP; mayor of Shanghai; secretary of the Shanghai CP committee, and a member of the Party revolutionary military council. With adoption of the constitution and formation of the NPC, in 1954, he became a vice-premier of the CPR State Council and vice-chairman of the National Defence Council. In 1956 he was elected to the PB for the first time. From 1949 onwards Chou En-lai had been concurrently premier and minister of foreign affairs; in 1958, Ch'en Yi took over the latter post. At the same time Ch'en relinquished the mayoralty of Shanghai.

Ch'en led the Chinese delegation to Indonesia which signed a treaty of friendship in 1961; accompanied Liu Shao-ch'i on visits to Indonesia, Burma and Cambodia in 1963; represented China on Kenya's independence day; joined Chou En-lai on a 1963–4 tour of ten African countries; and represented China at the tenth-anniversay celebration of the Algerian Republic. In 1965 he visited Jakarta for the tenth anniversary of the Bandung Conference.

At the eleventh session of the Eighth Party Congress (August 1966) Ch'en retained his rank in the PB and his government posts, but he was not immune from attacks by the Red Guards of the GPCR. Wall posters appeared that accused him of barring the gates of the Waichiaopu (Ministry of Foreign Affairs) to Red Guards who wished to search the premises for persons or indications of reactionary or revisionist thoughts or things. Many attacks were levelled at the Ministry, and Ch'en's diplomatic agents abroad were accused of having taken on decadent bourgeois habits of dress, eating, and culture, including attendance at nude pictures and excessive indulgence in alcohol. Many were recalled for interrogation in Peking. At the October 1967 anniversary celebration, however, Ch'en Yi's name stood high on the PB list. Ch'en was re-elected to the CC at the Ninth Party Congress (1969) but not to the PB. By 1971 some of the leaders of the coup which replaced Ch'en in the Foreign Ministry in 1967 were accused as counter-revolutionary elements of the 5–16 (16 May) clique held responsible for burning the British Office in Peking in 1967 and inciting riots in Hongkong.

In 1965 Marshal Ch'en Yi told the author that if the United States continued to escalate the war in Vietnam, China would sooner or later become involved, and that when that happened the war would 'know no boundaries'.

Ch'en's first wife died in Kiangsi in 1934. Chang Chien, his second wife, was formerly a schoolteacher.

Ch'en Yun (Liao Ch'eng-yun) (p. 185n.), a vice-chairman of the CCP CC from 1934, was re-elected to the PB in 1966, and despite his long-time association with Liu Shao-ch'i (*q.v.*) and many Red Guard verbal attacks, was still favourably mentioned in the official press in 1967.

Born in 1900 in a Shanghai working-class family, Ch'en Yun was a typesetter when he joined the CCP in 1924. He specialized in labour unions and in Soviet Kiangsi (1931–4) organized the handicraft workers. At Tsunyi, in 1935, after supporting Mao Tse-tung against the former PB leadership, he became a member of the Party military affairs committee, and was sent to Moscow as a delegate to the Seventh CMT Congress (July–August). His report on the Tsunyi conference probably explained why Mao was there elected (for the first time) to the CEC of the CMT. Ch'en returned to China with Wang Ming and K'ang Sheng (*qq.v.*) in 1937 and quickly took pro-Mao positions in Yenan. His book, *How To Be a Good Communist Party Member* (1939), together with Liu Shao-ch'i's *How To Be a Good Communist* (1939), became an essential tool in the *cheng-feng* (rectification) programme (1942) to establish the prevalence of Maoist-Marxist orthodoxy over imported dogma. (By 1967 Liu Shao-ch'i's book was denounced in Peking as a 'poison weed'.)

Ch'en specialized in economic and financial affairs (1940–45) and in 1945 was a top CC leader sent to North-East China with Lin Piao (*q.v.*) to prepare for a capture of power there, following Japan's surrender. From 1949 onward he held senior responsibilities in heavy industry, finance, state planning, and labour organization. In 1954 he became a vice-premier.

Ch'en was, like Liu Shao-ch'i, one of very few Chinese Communists with a long practical experience in urban working-class organization. His fall from fifth place in the PB hierarchy to eleventh place in 1966, after the Eleventh Plenum of the Eighth Congress, suggested that de-emphasis on centralized economic and industrial planning and management might be part of the drive to break up some of the power accumulated by Party technocrats accused by the Red Guards of practising 'economism' – meaning the use of material incentives along lines of the 'capitalist road' – specifically, 'Liebermanism'.

Ch'en was not re-elected to the Ninth Party Congress or its CC and reportedly was living in a 7 May school and commune for re-education of cadres.

Chiang Ch'ing (Green River) (p. 479), Mao Tse-tung's third wife (excluding an unconsummated childhood marriage), was suddenly given great power as a cultural arbiter during the GPCR from 1966 onward. Her real name was Li Chung-chin (Yun-ho), and she was born in 1912, in Taian, Shantung, in the shadow of Tai Shan, one of China's five 'sacred mountains'.

Chiang Ch'ing's parents, of middle-class origin and with scant assets, separated when she was a young child, but her mother managed to put her through primary school, in Tsinan. She then entered a provincial theatrical training institute, at government expense. The principal of the school, Chao T'ai-mou, later became chancellor of Tsingtao National University, where Chiang Ch'ing worked as an assistant librarian. While there she met Yu Ch'i-wei (Huang Ching, *q.v.*), who became perhaps the most important leader of the North China student 'rebellions' of 1935–7. His sister, Yu San, was already a well-known opera singer and actress when she married Chao T'ai-mou, through whom Chiang Ch'ing met both Yu San and Yu Ch'i-wei. Their uncle, Yu Ta-wei, was minister of defence in the Nationalist Government at Nanking, while another uncle, Tseng Chao-lin, was a former vice-minister of education. At the time Chiang Ch'ing met Yu Ch'i-wei he was propaganda chief of the Communist underground apparatus in Tsingtao.

Chiang Ch'ing may have joined the CYL in 1933. In the same year Yu Ch'i-wei was arrested and sentenced to death by the KMT authorities, but his influential uncle, Yu Ta-wei, secured his release in 1934. That account was given to the author when he first met Yu Ch'i-wei in Peking (1935) as David Yu. He was then propaganda secretary of the underground Peking Party CC, under the name Huang Ching, and chief Communist adviser to students who participated in and partly led the 9 December student movement.

Chiang Ch'ing returned to Tsinan in 1934 and married an actor with the stage name T'ang Na. They worked in the infant Shanghai film industry, Chiang Ch'ing taking the name Lan P'ing (Blue Apple) for the parts given to her. They were divorced in 1937. Chiang Ch'ing joined a patriotic propaganda theatrical troupe which took her from Shanghai first to Wuhan, then Chunking. She did some drama and film work and moved on to Sian and thence to Yenan, where she arrived in 1938. There she enrolled in the Lu Hsun art institute, which trained theatrical troupes for service at the front. She also entered the Party school, attended lectures given by Mao Tse-tung, and became one of his most assiduous students.

It is not true, as sometimes reported, that Mao Tse-tung was still married to Ho Tzu-ch'en (*q.v.*) at the time he met Chiang Ch'ing. They had been divorced in 1937, at Mao's demand, by a special tribunal set up by the CCP CC, which heard the complaints of both spouses concerning their incompatibility. Mao and Chiang Ch'ing were married late in 1938 or early in 1939. The author met Chiang Ch'ing in Mao's cave in Yenan when he visited them in September 1939. She was slender, vivacious, and rather tall for a Chinese. We played bridge once or twice and she cooked a simple excellent meal for us, done to Mao's taste for hot foods. At that time she was a Party member of junior standing. During the war she bore Mao two daughters, both of whom were by 1970 reportedly married.

Chiang Ch'ing took little overt part in political activity before 1964 aside from her appearances as Mme Mao. Her important new independent role became manifest after the meeting of the CC (August 1966) which launched the GPCR. She was unexpectedly declared 'first deputy leader' under Ch'en Po-ta, officially 'the leader of the Cultural Group within the Central Committee'. In the motor cavalcade and parade following the August meeting, Chiang Ch'ing stood in the first car beside Premier Chou En-lai.

All that was clarified in 1967 when the Party's theoretical organ, *Red Flag* (edited by Ch'en Po-ta), published Chiang Ch'ing's speech made before cultural workers in July 1964, which *Red Flag* now declared was the 'great beginning' of the GPCR. Subsequent revelations credited her with having issued 'directives' for the rewriting of operas, plays, ballets, and symphonies to introduce proletarian heroes and bourgeois villains to correspond to Mao Tse-tung's cultural guidelines in his 1942 *Talks at the Yenan Forum on Art and Literature*.

Mme Mao, it was also disclosed, had initiated the 'clarion call' for the GPCR when (late 1965) she led 'exposures' of *Hai Jui Dismissed from Office*, a play by Wu Han (*q.v.*), as a bourgeois-reactionary and thinly veiled allegorical attack on Mao Tse-tung.

Chiang Ch'ing had worked in Shanghai for several years developing Mao's 'proletarian line' in art, literature, drama and ballet, when she was a formidable opponent of P'eng Chen's deputy in cultural matters, Chou Yang. One of her closest collaborators in the fight against bourgeois-oriented culture was Yao Wen-yuan, who wrote the definitive critique of *Hai Jui Dismissed from Office*, a document reportedly rewritten eleven times, with help from both Chiang Ch'ing and Mao himself. That critique, which really launched the GPCR, as the first distant shot in a major offensive, led on to Mao's order of the day (August 1966), 'Bombard the Headquarters' of Liu Shao-ch'i. Counter-attempts allegedly were made by P'eng Chen, Liu Shao-ch'i (*qq.v.*), and other 're-visionists' to take over the burgeoning GPCR, before they themselves were purged along with Wu Han. *Red Flag* reported that they were partly frustrated by Chiang Ch'ing's address delivered in February 1966, before a meeting of army cultural workers, sponsored by Marshal Lin Piao. Their rout was completed by a pronouncement written by Mao and issued in the name of the CCP CC in May 1966, which turned the GPCR into the purge of 'anti-Maoists' that followed.

As Mao's deputy, Chiang Ch'ing became cultural adviser to the armed forces. Among writers and artists in opera, drama, films, and the musical world, she became the No. 1 authority on acceptable proletarian art. Many were required to undergo thought remoulding, while others – including whole opera troupes – were drafted into service with the army. Traditional and historical operatic and dramatic themes and forms virtually disappeared from the stage during that period when Chiang Ch'ing and the Red Guards determinedly sought to replace 'old habits, old ideas, old culture', and all that was bourgeois, feudal, and foreign, with new folk heroes glorifying the proletariat. With curbing of the Red Guards following army intervention to end factional fighting, in 1967, Chiang Ch'ing's leadership role of the youthful left was considerably reduced. Her contribution in the GPCR was doubtless great, and her ability was recognized by her election by the Ninth Congress CC to the PB. So was that of her protégé Yao Wen-yuan, aged forty-one, and the youngest member of the PB today.

Chiang Ching-kuo (p. 55), Chiang Kai-shek's son by his first wife, whom Chiang divorced when he married Soong Mei-ling, was in effective control of the political and security forces in Taiwan in 1968 and was considered most likely successor to Chiang Kai-shek to head the American-protected regime there. Born in 1909 in Fenghua, Chekiang, he was educated by private tutors before 1925, when he went to Russia. He graduated from the CMT's Sun Yat-sen University in 1927, having joined the CYL. After the 1927 split in China, Chiang Ching-kuo remained in Russia, studying military and political science. He opposed Wang Ming (*q.v.*) and was punished with various forms of exile, then given work as a plant director. In 1937 Stalin personally permitted him to return to China, where he effected a reconciliation with his father and joined the KMT. During the war his father gave him a job in Kiangsi; his chief task was to suppress the Reds. He joined the Methodist Church, together with his wife, a Russian. In 1949 he fled to Taiwan with his father. He was Chiang's only son by birth; his foster brother, Chiang Wei-kuo, was adopted, the son of right-wing KMT leader Tai Chi-tao and a Japanese mother.

By 1971 Chiang Ching-kuo was, as deputy defence chief to the Generalissimo, head of the secret police, and boss of the Nationalist Party, heir apparent to succeed his father as ruler of Taiwan and the remnant Nationalist Government. His task of negotiating a way out with the PRC, as the US moved towards dissolution of its protectorate in

Taiwan and full recognition of Peking, would decide what, if anything, he could salvage from a dwindling legacy.

Ch'in Pang-hsien. See Po Ku.

Chou En-lai (p. 63) was also known by his Party name, Shao Shan (Small Mountain). In his laconic account of himself, as given to me in 1936, Chou understated his prominence in the Party and drama-charged moments when his life and political fate had stood in peril. That is suggested in Part Four, Chapter 6, note 3, which discusses intraparty and CMT disputes in the 1927–35 period. After he visited Russia in 1928, when he was re-elected to the CC and the PB of the CCP Sixth Congress, he stayed on for special indoctrination at Sun Yat-sen University, and received some military instruction as well, Chou was already a candidate for supreme leadership. That seemed often within grasp thereafter, but Chou never quite made the reach for it.

On his return to Shanghai in 1929 he supported General Secretary Hsiang Chung-fa and Li Li-san, who dominated Hsiang (*qq.v.*). In Moscow in 1930 as CCP chief delegate to the CMT, Chou might have led an attack on Li, but it was Wang Ming (*q.v.*) who took the offensive. Back in Shanghai, in the sanctuary of the foreign-ruled International Settlement, Chou continued to work with Li until the latter, summoned to Moscow in November 1930, was held responsible for his (and the CMT's) failures at urban insurrection. In January 1931, Pavel Mif (Stalin's CMT agent) manoeuvred Chou aside and put Wang Ming in PB control. Only then did Chou abandon Li Li-san, recant, and call upon the Party to 'condemn my mistakes'. Chou was retained in the Shanghai PB and held his position as chief of the military affairs committee. In that year he was sent by the new leadership to Kiangsi, where he succeeded Hsiang Yin as chief of the 'Central Bureau'. In that role he took on the significant task of reconciling the remote control exercised by Po Ku, the new PB general secretary, from Shanghai, backed by Wang Ming (in Moscow), with Mao Tse-tung's *de facto* dominance among the rural combat Communists. (Mao was 'chairman' of the Soviet Government but only a member of the PB and its Branch Central Bureau.)

When Chou became political commissar to Chu Teh's command, in 1932, his prestige in Kiangsi began to overshadow that of Mao. As political chief at Whampoa Academy he had early won the confidence of cadets and instructors such as Lin Piao, Tso Chuan, Nieh Jung-chen, Li Ta, Yeh Chieng-ying, Hsiao Ching-kuang, Hsu Hsiang-ch'ien and Ch'en Keng. As organizer of the Shanghai and Nanchang uprisings he was already a combat hero. His sojourns in Moscow had brought him into contact with Stalin and among the 'Twenty-eight Bolsheviks' of the

Wang Ming-Po Ku group. His pioneer CYL activity in organizing young intellectuals in France had won respect among important Hunanese in Mao's own camp. Now his control of Party indoctrination in Kiangsi expanded his influence among the newest army cadres. Perhaps it was the unequalled breadth of Chou's viable connections with all factions that committed him to the role of chief reconciler and balancer of forces rather than to bitter-end struggle for personal leadership attainable only by violent repression of one or the other element in a core dispute.

Even in 1934, when Po Ku and Lo Fu (*qq.v.*) ousted Mao from the PB, and Chou became general commissar of the entire army, he managed to avoid a final break with either Chu Teh or Mao Tse-tung. When, in January 1935, the turning-point conference at Tsunyi repudiated the Party leadership of Po Ku and Lo Fu, Chou En-lai made a smooth transition into the new supreme Party revolutionary military council chaired by Mao Tse-tung. (See Jerome Ch'en, 'Resolutions of the Tsunyi Conference', Bibliography, and note 3, Chapter 6, Part Four.) From that time Chou never wavered in his loyalty to Mao's leadership.

After the arrival of the Red Army in the North-West, Chou increasingly took on the role of chief diplomatist. He negotiated the truce agreement with Marshal Chang Hsueh-liang. That soon led to the Sian Incident, which Chou eventually utilized to extract from Chiang Kai-shek an agreement to end civil war. During the war against Japan, Chou headed Communist delegations accredited to Chiang Kai-shek's government, which moved from Nanking to Hankow and then to Chungking. In 1939 Chou spent six months in Moscow, with Chiang's consent. He returned to Yenan and then went to Chungking to head the Eighth Route (Communist) Army mission there and sit on the Supreme National Defence Council. His urbane contacts with non-Communist intellectuals and frequent talks with Western diplomats greatly enhanced his own and Yenan's prestige. At the same time Chou also headed the South China Bureau of the Party, which still lacked a legal status.

As KMT-CP relations greatly worsened, Chou returned to Yenan, in 1943, but again was sent to Chungking, in 1944, to negotiate terms of a coalition government. The effort failed, as did peace talks sponsored by General Patrick Hurley, American ambassador, which Chou and Mao attended in Chungking in 1945. At the CCP Seventh Congress in Yenan (1945), where Chou made a lengthy report, he was elected to the PB's five-man secretariat, to a vice-chairmanship, and to the supreme revolutionary military council. He then led the CP's delegation in peace negotiations with the KMT held under General George Marshall's auspices, until all-out civil war was resumed in 1946. Back in Yenan, he worked side by side with Mao, in supreme command. After the fall of Peking, in 1949, Chou set up the apparatus of a new provisional government and became its premier and foreign minister. In 1950 he joined Mao and Stalin in Moscow, to negotiate the thirty-year Sino-Soviet alliance; in 1952 he negotiated the return of Russian concessions in China; and in 1953 he initiated truce talks in Korea.

With the formation of constitutional government under the Chinese People's Republic, Chou became concurrently premier (from 1954) and foreign minister (1954–8). At the Geneva Conference of 1954, Chou won recognition for China's international position. He drew up the Five Principles of Coexistence which, with Indian and Burmese adherence, became the platform of the brief-lived Afro-Asian unity proclaimed at the Bandung Conference of 1955. In the same year he opened up Sino-American ambassadorial talks, which then gave hope of a peaceful settlement of differences. His visits to many Asian countries in 1955 and 1956 further improved China's visage among the ex-colonial peoples. In Europe, Chou's personal intervention (1957) in grave disputes between Moscow and Poland, Hungary, and Czechoslovakia, was credited with having restored 'solidarity in the Socialist camp led by the Soviet Union' – after Khrushchev's denunciation of Stalin had introduced a 'thaw' in Soviet policies.

Chou relinquished his post of foreign minister to Marshal Ch'en Yi in 1958, but it was Chou who broke the brinkmanship crisis over Taiwan, when he announced China's readiness to resume the suspended Sino-American ambassadorial talks. During the next two years Chou made more moves towards peaceful coexistence by signing treaties of friendship with several neighbouring states. Significantly, he failed to settle a boundary dispute with India, over which (1962) a brief war ensued – not unconnected with the breakdown of Sino-Soviet cooperation which became manifest in 1960, and the Kennedy-Khrushchev-Castro confrontation crisis of 1962. Now the pattern of China's diplomacy hardened. As old blocs crumbled, China made strident demands that Communist parties choose between her and the USSR. Chou carried out the CC line of independent support of revolutionary wars in many countries, downgrading competitive coexistence and vociferously rejecting all compromise with both American imperialism and Soviet revisionism.

At this writing there is no available evidence that Chou En-lai ever joined an opposition to Mao's increasingly bitter ideological war with Khrushchev and his heirs in the CPSU. For China, one consequence of the feud was diplomatic immobility, as more and more states and parties opted out of Mao's total irreconcilability with both the USA and the USSR. Chou En-lai's two tours of remaining friendly states in Asia and new states in Africa, in 1964 and 1965, climaxed by French recognition of the CPR, marked one apex of China's diplomatic achievement. With intensification of the American-Vietnamese war, coinciding with the GPCR, in 1966, Peking's abrasive Red Guard demonstrations against governments of socialist as well as non-socialist states all but ended China's diplomacy for that period – and alienated some of China's most patient friends in the so-called Third World.

After he was confirmed in his position in the Party hierarchy at the eleventh plenary session of the Eighth Congress CC, in August 1966, Premier Chou's responsibilities, as the centre of stable continuity in the CPR, enormously increased. At Red Guard demonstrations he took the salute, standing just below Mao's 'closest comrade-in-arms', Lin Piao. Beyond that, his preoccupation plainly was to hold the administrative machinery together and try to prevent cracks in the Party bureaucratic apparatus from causing disaster. That the trains, planes, engines, workers, farmers, and intellectuals on the whole continued to function, that general civil war had not, at this writing, returned China to its former disunity and quasi-anarchy, redounded to the credit of tireless efforts by Chou. Limitations of GPCR control over the Party apparatus were indicated by the questionable results of the attempts politically to destroy its principal targets, 'China's Khrushchev' – meaning President Liu Shao-ch'i, constitutional chief of state – and his CC supporters. It may have been indicative of a coming change in the climate of opinion in China that it was Chou En-lai (often called 'the man in the middle') who in August 1967, after a mob sacked and burned the British Embassy and assaulted its chargé, reportedly ordered the Red Guards to 'go home and stay there'.

Chou skilfully manoeuvred between left and right elements during the GPCR and became the indispensable man in the middle. Following the crash of the superstructure built by Liu Shao-ch'i, a new edifice had to be erected by combining elements of the 'reliable Party cadres', responsible army leaders, and 'new blood' pumped into the deflated Party body. At the Ninth Party Congress Chou again took second place to Lin Piao, designated Mao's 'close comrade-in-arms and successor', while in fact he assumed the main tasks of reorganizing a badly shattered central government administrative apparatus. Beginning in 1970 he moved with utmost speed, once government underpinnings were considered stable, to restore and expand China's diplomatic and trade contacts with the world.

Chou En-lai, Mme. See Teng Ying-ch'ao.

Chu Teh (p. 47) was born in Ilung, Szechuan, on 18 December 1886, in a family which had emigrated from Kwantung. He was one of thirteen children. He became the commander-in-chief of the Red Army at its inception in Chingkangshan in 1927, and remained so until after establishment of the PRC (1949).

Chu Teh's extraordinarily adventurous and vigorous life, as told by him to Agnes Smedley (see *The Great Road: The Life and Times of Chu Teh*, NY, 1956), is a document of rich sociological and historical importance. In 1936, however, practically no accurate information had been published about Chu Teh. The author's notes were gathered from comrades who had fought side by side with Chu Teh for years. It was characteristic of Communist relationships that their knowledge of his personal life was vague or hearsay. For example, the author was told that Chu Teh came from a 'family of rich landlords'. In reality his father was an impoverished peasant; at the age of nine Chu Teh was adopted by a prosperous uncle, who helped educate him.

Chu Teh joined the CCP in 1922, in Berlin, through the influence of Chou En-lai. From 1927 onward he was always found beside Mao Tse-tung, as Mao's 'third arm', except for one year when Chu Teh was detained – 'by force', Chu Teh told Miss Smedley – by Chang Kuo-t'ao in western China. It is difficult to imagine Mao's rise and success in the special pattern of peasant-based revolution which he developed without the unvarying loyalty and self-effacing support of Chu Teh.

From 1950 to 1956 Chu Teh was vice-chairman of the CPG of the CPR. In 1956 he became chairman of the NPC. He was for many years the top-ranking marshal in the Communist armed forces. Until 1966 he was a member of the PB standing committee, which consisted of the vice-chairmen and Mao.

Chu Teh was a plain-living man of astonishing physical endurance; at eighty he still played basketball, his favourite sport, which he learned at a YMCA in Szechuan and popularized in the army. At the eleventh session of the Eighth Congress CC, Chu Teh was dropped from the PB standing committee although he remained in the PB. During the GPCR he was attacked by schoolboy Red Guards, together with Marshal Ho Lung, his lifelong comrade-in-arms. However, in the October 1967 anniversary celebrations, Chu Teh appeared beside Mao on the rostrum and was officially listed as a PB member only one step below the level of the standing committee. In 1969 the ageing warrior was re-elected to the CC and also to the PB. See Smedley, *The Great Road*, and BDRC.

Ch'u Ch'iu-pai (p. 184), second general secretary of the CCP, was born in a bankrupt Kiangsu gentry family in 1889 and was executed on Chiang Kai-shek's order in 1935. His brief political leadership seemed, according to his own 'final testament', a comic error, a 'historical mis-understanding'; he considered himself pre-eminently a literary figure, by temperament unsuited to politics.

Ch'u's father abandoned his wife and six children. Ch'u's mother was educated: she taught Ch'iu-pai to write poetry. As a primary school teacher he helped keep the family from starving. When he was seventeen his mother committed suicide. In 1916 Ch'u tried to enrol in Peking National University but could not pay the tuition. He then entered a tuition-free Russian-language school (1916–19) and there also began to learn the politics of revolution. In 1920 he reached Russia as a correspondent for the Peking *Ch'en Pao*. His reports of life in Soviet Russia were collected and became widely read books. In 1922 he joined the CCP branch in Moscow, and entered the CMT's Sun Yat-sen (Eastern Toilers') University as a student and teacher. When Ch'en Tu-hsiu attended the Fourth Congress of the CMT he 'discovered' Ch'u and made him his secretary-interpreter. Ch'en brought Ch'u back to China, where he became, at Canton, a member of both the CC of the CCP (1923) and the CEC of the KMT (1924). In 1925 he taught at the Communist-sponsored Shanghai University and participated in the 30 May Incident.

In 1927 Ch'u joined the opposition group which held Ch'en Tu-hsiu responsible for the collapse of the CP-KMT united front. In accordance with new directives from Moscow, surviving CCP leaders in the central China area called an emergency conference (7 August 1927) after the Nanchang Uprising, which denounced Ch'en Tu-hsiu and elected Ch'u Ch'iu-pai general secretary. Dominated by Lominadze (Stalin's repre-sentative), the new leadership called for the Canton Uprising, which swiftly ended in disaster.

In the summer of 1928 Ch'u reappeared in Moscow, and made his report before the Sixth Congress, CCP. Held responsible for 'left opportunism', he was replaced as general secretary by Hsiang Chung-fa (q.v.). He remained in Moscow, wrote polemical articles, and briefly visited CP meetings in Paris and Berlin. He also devised a system of transliterating Chinese into Cyrillic script, which was later adopted by the Russians.

Pavel Mif is said to have secured Ch'u's removal from membership in the CEC of the CMT and the CC after Ch'u joined Chang Kuo-t'ao in a 'united front' against Mif's domination. He returned to China late in 1930. For several years Ch'u was an effective leader of the underground League of Left Writers. He wrote extensively, using pseudonyms, and was a protégé of Lu Hsun, who was able to give him some sanctuary in the Shanghai French Concession. He translated numerous Russian works and advocated writing which 'served the people'. In 1931 Ch'u was rehabilitated in the Party and was elected commissioner of education at the first All-China Soviet Congress, but he was unable to leave Shanghai. (His post was meanwhile filled by Hsu T'eh-li.) In January 1934, he entered the Kiangsi soviet areas, and there became minister (commissar) of education and art in the Soviet Government of which Mao Tse-tung was chairman.

When the Long March began, Ch'u was ill and remained behind. While attempting to reach Shanghai he was intercepted by Nationalist forces, early in 1935. He was executed in June. Twenty years later his remains were buried in the Peking Cemetery of Revolutionary Heroes. He was regarded as a martyr-hero of the Party. A four-volume collection of his literary works was published in Peking, but not his political writings or his *To-yu-teh Hua* (*Superfluous Words*) which he wrote as a 'last testament' while in prison. For a detailed commentary, see T. A. Hsia, 'Ch'u Ch'iu-pai's Autobiographical Writings', *China Quarterly* (London, January–March 1966). In 1967 Red Guard attacks classified Ch'u as a 'renegade' and in 1968 the official press vilified him as a bourgeois influence. By 1971 such attacks ceased and the Party press referred to him with some respect.

Fang Chih-min (p. 187) was a leader of the Kiangsi provincial CP and organizer of peasant partisan warfare before his capture and execution in 1935. In 1927 he was Kiangsi secretary of both the KMT and the CP. He supported Mao's 'peasant line' (rejected by Ch'en Tu-hsiu and the CC in 1927) and led the first peasant detachments in the Kiangsi Autumn Harvest Uprisings. He joined Mao and Chu Teh at Chingkangshan and later he supported Mao's programme at the important Ku-t'ien Conference (1930), where Mao laid down basic laws for the development of the Red Army, including great emphasis on local Red Guards. He continued to adhere closely to Mao's views throughout the pre-Long March period. Left behind with the rear guard (see Ch'en Yi, Su Yu, etc.), he was captured by KMT troops. After being paraded through the countryside in a bamboo cage, he was beheaded in 1935.

Hatem, Dr George. See Ma Hai-teh.

Ho Lung (p. 93) led an even more remarkable life than the largely hearsay account of him in this text may suggest. Born in 1896 (during the Ch'ing Dynasty), in Sangchi county, Hunan province, the son of a military officer, he organized armed peasant insurrections at least a decade before Mao Tse-tung tried it. His reputation as a 'bandit' was well earned. A youth of sixteen, with little schooling and an empty belly, he tried to kill a government officer, then gathered a band of outlaws in the mountains. By the time he was twenty-one his 19,000 followers held eight counties. Rebels in three provinces united around him, calling themselves a Peasant Army. They became so formidable that government forces were obliged to grant them amnesty and monetary rewards to disband. Ho Lung went down to Changsha, a free man, to ally himself with Dr Sun Yat-sen.

In 1920 Ho raised a brigade for the Nationalist Army. In 1926 he joined the CCP, while he was in command of the Twentieth KMT Army. At Nanchang he joined Yeh T'ing and Chu Teh in the armed uprising of 1 August 1927. Defeated, he escaped to Shanghai but then re-entered the Kiangsi-Hunan area and recruited new forces for Chu Teh and Mao. From 1927 onwards he was a top army leader, but he was not admitted to the CC until 1945.

Ho Lung's refusal to give the support of his Second Front Army to Chang Kuo-t'ao during the Mao-Chang dispute of 1935-6 was decisive in Chang's final defeat. Throughout the war against Japan and the Second Civil War he held major field commands; in 1955 he was commissioned a marshal of the PLA. A member of the cabinet (minister of physical culture) and a vice-premier, he held his rank in the Party PB at the eleventh plenary session, 1966, but in 1967 was reported under mild attack by wall posters for alleged sympathies with Lo Jui-ch'ing (q.v.). Criticisms of Ho Lung continued in 1967 and 1968 as he was blamed for developing a personality cult of his own, particularly in glorifying his role in the museum of the Nanchang Uprising. He was not re-elected to the CC at the Ninth Party Congress.

Ho Tzu-ch'en (p. 107), Mao's second wife (excluding his unconsummated childhood marriage), was the daughter of a Kiangsi landlord. A teacher before she joined the Communists, she married Mao in 1930. In 1937 Ho Tzu-ch'en formally charged Wu Kuang-wei ('Lily Wu'), an interpreter in Yenan, with having alienated Mao's affections. Mao denied the charges in the same year and then sought a divorce, which was granted by a special court set up by the CCP CC. Both Miss Wu and Ho Tzu-ch'en were exiled from Yenan. Ho Tzu-ch'en and Mao had two children in Kiangsi, left behind in the care of Red peasants when the Long March began. The children were never found after the war. In Shensi, Ho Tzu-ch'en bore Mao a daughter. In Yenan, in 1939, I was told that Ho Tzu-ch'en had gone, with her child, to live in Russia. In 1970 a mutual friend of myself and Ho Tzu-ch'en said that she had returned to China and was living obscurely in a Kiangsi commune.

Hsia Hsi (p. 173) was a member of the New People's Study Society organized by Mao in 1918. He joined the first CCP cell organized (by Mao) in Hunan. He was in 1967 a high-ranking member of the CC.

Hsiang Chung-fa (p. 485) was, while general secretary of the CCP CC (1928–31), largely a puppet of Li Li-san (*q.v.*) and Li's backer, Lominadze, Stalin's agent in the CMT. Hsiang replaced Ch'u Ch'iu-pai at the Sixth Congress of the CCP held in Moscow (July 1928), a meeting which coincided with the CMT Sixth Congress.

Of Shanghai working-class origin, semiliterate in Chinese, Hsiang was trained in the CMT's Sun Yat-sen University in Russia. He was the CMT choice to break a deadlock between left and right Chinese 'intellectuals' in the PB. As a 'proletarian', Hsiang provided a front behind which Lominadze supported Li Li-san and the CMT line of the period. Under Stalin's control, the CMT had just decided that the capitalist world was disintegrating, and compromise even with Social Democrats was ruled out; the Party was to lead imminent great upsurges.

When Li Li-san's line – uprisings in the cities supported by Red Army attacks – failed, Li was discredited at a Party plenum in January 1931. Hsiang Chung-fa was retained in the PB only after his abject confession of error. The CMT's Pavel Mif had become the new power behind the CC PB. When Li Li-san led a revolt against Mif's domination, Mif had Li recalled to Moscow. Meanwhile Hsiang Chung-fa's address was betrayed to KMT police by a Li Li-san adherent, Ku Shun-chang. After Hsiang's arrest and execution in June, Wang Ming (*q.v.*) became general secretary. Ku Shun-chang's entire family was assassinated, the KMT police reporting that the CCP PB had ordered the deaths in reprisal. True or not, the report shattered CP influence in the Shanghai labour unions, where Ku had had a following. See Part Four, Chapter 6, note 3.

Hsiao Ching-kuang (p. 175), born in Changsha, Hunan, in 1902, was in 1967 one of a dozen powerful military leaders in China. The son of a middle-class family, Hsiao attended Hunan Normal School (Mao's alma mater). He joined the Socialist Youth Corps in Shanghai in 1920 and in that year reached Russia and entered the Comintern's Sun Yat-sen University, where he joined the branch CCP. Returning to China in 1924, he became an instructor and student cadet at Whampoa Academy. He took part in the Northern Expedition (1926). After the 1927 débâcle he studied in Russia (Red Army College) until 1930.

Back in China, he entered Soviet Kiangsi, where he commanded the Seventh Army Corps.

Hsiao never became part of the 'returned students' ('Twenty-eight Bolsheviks') group. In 1933 he supported the so-called 'Lo-Ming' line, a pro-Mao position in intraparty struggle which was also favoured by T'an Chen-lin, Teng Hsiao-p'ing, Teng Tzu-hui, and Mao's brother, Tse-t'an. He was, with them, disciplined for acting contrary to the PB's directives. In 1936 Hsiao Ching-kuang told the author that Li Teh, the German CMT adviser, had overruled Mao and Chu Teh to decide the strategy followed during 1934 which ended in success for Chiang Kai-shek's fifth anti-Communist campaign.

After the Long March, Hsiao took part in the 1935 Shansi expedition and was credited with recruiting 8,000 volunteers there. A deputy commander under Lin Piao, he distinguished himself in the Second World War and the second KMT–CP civil war. In 1955 he was made a marshal of the army. A member of the CC from 1945 and of the NPC from 1954, Hsiao Ching-kuang became (with Lin Piao's rise to No. 2 position in the PB in 1966) a member of the all-powerful Party military affairs committee and an alternate in the PB. In 1969 Hsiao was re-elected to the CCP CC. His wife was Russian. Hsiao's autobiography (to 1936) appears in *RNORC*.

Hsiao Hua (p. 295n.), born in 1914, was chairman of the general political department of the PLA in 1967, and was responsible for indoctrination of PLA Red Guards in the Thought of Mao Tse-tung.

He was born in Hsing-ko county, Kiangsi, in 1914, in a poor peasant family. In 1936 he told the author that he had been 'educated entirely by the Red Army and the CCP'. He was a youth organizational leader in the army (beginning at Chingkangshan) from the age of fifteen. Only twenty at the start of the Long March, he was political commissar of the Second Division, First Army Corps, two years later. Commander of the Hopei-Chahar-Liaoning Military Region in 1946, he was a group army leader in 1948. In the CCP CC from 1945, he was director of the General Cadres Department, PLA, from 1956, deputy secretary general, Party military commission, from 1961, deputy chief of the CC Control Committee and a member of the CC secretariat from 1963. A loyal Maoist for nearly four decades, he was, during the GPCR, still 'one of the youngest' veteran combat Communists. In 1967 he was deputy chief of the 'all-army cultural affairs group', a member of the supreme military affairs committee, and an alternate member of the PB. Hsiao Hua fell from grace during the 'period of near-anarchy' (as Mao described it), when so-called counter-revolutionary elements momentarily took power in Peking in 1967. His current status is obscure.

Hsieh Fu-chih (p. 136n.) in 1966 was elected to the PB (as an alternate member) and succeeded to Lo Jui-ch'ing (*q.v.*) as Minister of Public Security. He became an important figure in the purge activities as one of those 'leading the cultural revolution under the CC'.

Born in Hunan in 1899, Hsieh joined the partisans in the Oyuwan Soviet in the early thirties and was said to have received most of his education in the army. In 1938 he was a deputy brigade commander under Ch'en Keng. He took part in the '100 Regiments Battle' (1940) and continued to distinguish himself as Ch'en Keng's forces grew to group army size. From 1949 onwards Hsieh held leading roles in the South-West Military Region, including secretaryship of the Yunnan provincial Party when Ch'en Keng was military commander (1950–53) of the area. Briefly Minister of Interior (1949), Hsieh was first elected to the CC in 1956. After 1953 he specialized in security, legal, and political organizational affairs. Hsieh's ascendancy in security affairs continued throughout the GPCR. He became acting chief of the Peking Party committee, a position confirmed by election in 1971. He was re-elected to the CC and PB at the 1969 Ninth Party Congress. Hsieh was a key person in the rebuilding of the Party and worked in close liaison with both Chou En-lai and Lin Piao in blending military and leading Party cadres into a new administration. His wife, Wang Ting-kuo, was a member of the People's Supreme Court.

Hsu Hai-tung (p. 196) became, with the outbreak of the Sino-Japanese war, a brigade commander in the Eighth Route Army. In 1939 he organized guerrilla forces in Shantung which by 1944 had spread into his old stamping grounds in Honan and Hupeh. Invalided by wounds, he was given rear-area assignments from 1945 onwards. In 1956 he was elected to the Eighth CCP CC. By 1957 he appeared in public only occasionally, in a wheel chair. Hsu was re-elected to the CC in 1969; at his death in 1970 he received full honours in a state funeral.

Hsu Hsiang-ch'ien (p. 196) commanded a division of the Eighth Route Army from 1937 and in 1939 led troops across Japanese lines to form a guerrilla base in Shantung. During the Liberation War (1946–9) he captured Taiyuan, capital of Shansi. He was elected to the CC in 1945 and became one of the ten marshals of the army named in 1955. In 1966 he was elected to the PB for the first time, and became a vice-chairman of the supreme CC military affairs committee. In January 1967, he was made chairman of the subcommittee of the GPCR in the PLA, under the new chief of staff, Yang Ch'eng-wu. He thus seemed to have completely overcome the political handicap of his past with Chang Kuo-t'ao.

Born in Wu T'ai county, Shansi, in 1902, in a landlord family, Hsu was educated at a normal school; in 1924 he entered Whampoa Academy. He joined the CP in 1927, took part in the Canton Uprising, worked with P'eng P'ai in the Hailufeng Soviet, and then went underground in Shanghai. In 1930 he organized Anhui guerrilla forces and rose to the rank of army commander. Hsu won a major victory over one of Chiang Kai-shek's best commanders in 1931, and his skill helped build up the Fourth Red Army, north of the Yangtze River, under his political chief, Chang Kuo-t'ao. In 1933 defeats forced them to move westward and set up the Szechuan Soviet, where the Fourth Army grew rapidly until 1935, when the southern Reds met the Chang-Hsu forces (100,000?) at Moukung. Owing to the Chang-Mao dispute and failure to agree at Maoerhkai, the two main armies divided, Hsu remaining in Sikang with Chang, Chu Teh and others, while Mao moved on to Shensi (1935). A year later (December 1936) Hsu's army moved north and followed Mao but was ambushed while attempting to cross the Yellow River. The Red forces were badly defeated and Hsu and Chang arrived in Pao An in a parlous state. The northern column was badly cut up by attacks and reduced, under the command of Li Hsien-nien, to 2,000 men. At a CC meeting in Shensi in 1937 Hsu Hsiang-ch'ien was exonerated of political responsibility for Political Commissar Chang's 'anti-Party' decisions during the Szechuan schism. See RNORC. Hsu was re-elected to the CC and membership in the PB at the Ninth Party Congress in 1969.

Hsu Ping (p. 478) was deputy director of the United-Front Department of the CCP CC until he came under attack during the GPCR.

Hsu was born in Honan, in 1902, in a family able to send him to Germany to study economics. In Berlin he joined the CYL (1920), which merged with the CCP. After studying at the CMT's Sun Yat-sen University (1925–7), in Moscow, he returned to do underground work in China. A university professor in Peking when the author met him in 1935, he provided important liaison between the Manchurian exiled armies in China, and the Red Army, which led to a united front. Deputy mayor of Peking in 1949, he was also deputy director of the United-Front Department of the CCP CC from that time onwards. In 1967 he was denounced by Red Guard publications for having authorized Communists held in KMT jails in Peking in 1936 (!) to sign repudiations of communism (in order to secure their release on the eve of war against Japan). Hsu was also charged with 'sheltering renegades' in the Party – when Liu Shao-ch'i was his chief in the North China Bureau of the Party. His wife, Chang Hsiao-mei, was a veteran Communist and vice-chairman of the All-China Federation of Democratic Women. By 1971 both Hsu and his wife had lost all positions but had not been expelled from the Party. Rehabilitation seemed possible.

Hsu T'eh-li (p. 101) was hailed by Mao as his 'most respected and beloved teacher'. Born in 1877 in Changsha, Hunan, in a poor family, he had primary school education, entered a teachers' school, then taught school, tutoring himself in maths. After taking part in the 1911 overthrow of the imperial government, he taught at Hunan First Normal, where he helped Yang Chang-ch'i prevent Mao Tse-tung's expulsion as a student. At the age of forty-three he joined a Work-Study group, went to France, and worked part time as a cook while studying at Paris and Lyons universities. He was in the band of students (including Ch'en Yi, Li Li-san and Ts'ai Ho-sen, qq.v.) who 'occupied' the Institut Franco-Chinois, and was deported with them. Returning to Hunan, he taught at the Changsha Girls' Normal School, finally being admitted to the CCP in 1927. A participant in the Nanchang Uprising, he retreated to Swatow and escaped to Shanghai. For two years (1928–30) he studied at the CMT's Sun Yat-sen University in Moscow, then returned to China, to become director (commissar) of education in the All-Central Soviet Government, except for the period that office was held by Ch'u Ch'iu-pai. At fifty-seven he was the oldest man to make the Long March. A deputy to the NPC from 1954, he remained active in a wide range of political and cultural tasks, and ranked fifteenth in the CCP CC.

Huang Ching (Yu Ch'i-wei, or David Yu) (p. 51n.), who became the first Communist mayor of Tientsin, in 1949, won national fame in the CCP as a hero of the 1935–7 student movement of North China. Its leaders helped to restore Party influence among youth in the great cities after a decade of bloody suppression.

A native of Chekiang, born in 1911, Huang Ching came from a prominent bourgeois family; one uncle, Yu Ta-wei, served as KMT minister of defence; another had been a vice-minister of education in Peking. While a student at Shantung University (Tsingtao) Huang Ching was chief of the underground CCP CC propaganda department. There he met Chiang Ch'ing, and was influential in her turn towards communism. In 1933 Huang Ching was arrested and sentenced to death. Yu Ta-wei saved Huang's life; after his release Huang went to Peking, where he again joined the CC propaganda department. He was, however, in deep hiding – in the North China Bureau, under Liu Shao-ch'i – before the 9 December student demonstration.

At that time all patriotic (not to mention radical) organizations were strictly suppressed by Kuomintang gendarmes. Hundreds of students had been jailed for anti-Japanese activity; campuses were infested with spies. Police even protected Japan-paid puppets who marched in support of Japanese attempts to install a puppet regime in Peking by force and bribery. An exception was the oasis of relative freedom on the campus of the American-financed and missionary-founded Yenching University. Yenching's immunity from KMT gendarmes traced to foreign extraterritoriality rights enjoyed by some of its teachers. Those happened to include the writer, and Yenching's president and chief founder, Dr J. Leighton Stuart, who was to be the last US ambassador to the Kuomintang Nationalist government at Nanking.

In 1935 Huang Ching joined student representatives in a secret meeting at Yenching called by the Yenching University Student Association on the night of 8 December. They planned the strategy for a daring mass street demonstration held on the following day. Its ultimate impact ended both the suppression of anti-Japanese patriotic activity and the urban isolation of the CCP.

Peking University (Pei-ta), the leading higher institute of the nation, had no student association, but 9 December made it possible to revive one. Huang Ching and others (Yao I-lin, Huang Hua, *qq.v.*), who had participated in '9 December', rapidly helped to organize Pei-ta and other student associations for subsequent protest activities. From Peking, propaganda spread all across the country. Demands for resistance, for political education, for military education of the masses, etc., led to an excitement which so infected the population that serious preparation for a war of resistance against Japan could no longer be avoided.

Huang Ching went to Yenan in 1937, to enter the Party school. With the outbreak of war he assumed the important post of secretary of the CC Shansi-Hopei-Chahar regional Party committee. By 1949 he was Party secretary of the greater municipality of Tientsin. Long a semi-invalid from illnesses contracted during a youth of strenuous hardship, Huang died prematurely in 1958. He was then a member of the CCP CC and vice-chairman of the State Planning Commission. At this writing his wife, Fan Chin, was still a deputy mayor of Peking.

Huang Hua (p. 51n.) was the party name of Wang Ju-mei, born in 1912 in an educated family in Kiangsu. He took a leading role in the 9 December (1935) student movement, became a national youth organizer, and rose to important posts in the Communist Foreign Ministry, as an ambassador and a negotiator. The author met Wang Ju-mei at Yenching (Christian) University in 1934. Wang was active among the student rebels at Yenching and conspicuous in patriotic anti-Japanese organizations then illegal. He joined the CYL in 1935 and the CCP in 1936. When the author went to North-West China he sent word to Wang to meet him there. On their journeys Wang met Mao Tse-tung, Chou En-lai, P'eng Teh-huai, Teng Hsiao-p'ing, and other leaders. Later he worked there and in Hankow (1938) as a youth organizer, recruiting many student volunteers. Among them were Kung P'eng and her sister Kung Pu-ch'eng, both of whom became officials of the Foreign Ministry.

At the Foreign Office in Yenan and Chungking (1939–45), as chief CCP information officer during KMT-CP mediation talks (1945–7), as director of foreign affairs of the Nanking military area (1949), and in charge of affairs of foreign residents of Shanghai (1952), he became outstanding among young diplomat-negotiators trained by Chou En-lai. He conducted the bitter terminal truce talks in Korea (1952); served as spokesman of the Chinese delegation, Geneva Conference (1954); headed the West Europe and African department, Ministry of Foreign Affairs (1954–6); directed the West European department of the ministry (1956–9); and became China's first ambassador to Ghana (1960–65). He negotiated a number of treaties and agreements with Ghana and the Congo, providing for trade, technical, and cultural cooperation. After Peking's wholesale recall of diplomats he was, in 1968, at Cairo, the only Communist Chinese of ambassadorial status west of Vietnam and Cambodia. Recalled to China in 1969, Huang Hua was sent to a commune and 7 May (re-indoctrination) Mao Tse-tung School, together with his wife, Li-liang, also a prominent Party leader. Emerging from the countryside he at once assumed important Foreign Office activities in liaison with the premier. English speaking and highly personable, he remained one of China's top diplomats. In 1971 he was appointed the CPR's first ambassador to Canada. The Huang Huas have three children.

Jen Pi-shih (p. 234n.) was born in Hsiangyin county, Hunan, in 1904, attended school in Changsha, and joined the Socialist Youth Corps in Shanghai in 1920. He studied at Oriental University in Moscow, 1920–22, and joined the CCP while there. In China, in 1927, he became secretary of the CYL, when he was also elected to the CCP CC. He was elected to the PB in 1930. In 1931 he entered the Hunan-Kiangsi-border soviet area, where he was chief of the military committee in Ho Lung's forces, and also political commissar. At the Tsunyi Conference Jen Pi-shih supported Mao against Po Ku. During the Long March, Ho and Jen Pi-shih sided with Mao Tse-tung against Chang Kuo-t'ao. Re-elected to the CC PB in 1945, he remained in Yenan with Mao Tse-tung during the Second Civil War. He died in 1950 of heart failure.

K'ang Sheng (p. 136n.), whose other party names were Chao Yung and Chong Wen, was in August 1966 (eleventh plenary session of the Eighth Congress) jumped to a PB position in the standing committee sixth below Mao. He was a vice-premier of the SC, head of the Party control commission, and among those officially described as 'leaders of the cultural revolution under the Central Committee'. From Yenan days K'ang Sheng had closely identified himself with cultural concepts set forth by Mao in his 'Talks at the Yenan Forum on Art and Literature'.

K'ang was born (*circa* 1903) Chang Shao-ch'ing in a gentry family in Shantung. While attending middle school at the CCP-organized Shanghai University he joined the CYL (1920) and CCP (1924–5), participated in Shanghai insurrections led by Chou En-lai (1926–7), and then worked underground. Sent to Moscow in 1932, he was, except for a brief visit to Shanghai in 1933, employed in the CMT under Wang Ming (*q.v.*) until he returned to China in 1937 with Wang Ming and Ch'en Yun. These three were lecturing at K'ang Ta ('Resist-Japan University') when the author first met them in Yenan, in September 1939. Elected to the CC secretariat in 1938, K'ang was criticized during the rectification movement (1942), but after self-reform replaced Li Wei-han as director of the Party school. Working closely with Lin Piao, director of K'ang Ta, he sharply dissociated himself from Wang Ming, who became the Party's personification of 'formalism' and imported dogmatism.

Elected to the PB at the Seventh Congress (1945), K'ang headed the CC Orgburo, led the Shantung Party committee (1949–54), was re-elected (alternate) to the PB (1956), spearheaded Party attacks on 'rightists' (1957) and became a secretary of the CC secretariat (1962) under Teng Hsiao-p'ing and P'eng Chen. In 1963–5 he participated in major 'line' talks led by Liu Shao-ch'i and/or Teng Hsiao-p'ing with foreign CP delegations to Peking seeking a Moscow-Peking reconciliation and also visited Rumania (1960). In 1964 he accompanied Chou En-lai to Moscow for talks (abortive) after the fall of Khrushchev. In 1965 he joined Ch'en Po-ta in an offensive against Liu Shao-ch'i and Teng Hsiao-p'ing as 'revisionists'. By 1967 K'ang Sheng appeared to be a possible successor to Teng Hsiao-p'ing as Party general secretary. While he remained in the PB no reconciliation with the USSR seemed likely. Re-elected to the CC and PB in 1969, K'ang Sheng was a member of the five-man PB standing committee, ranking just below Chou En-lai.

Kao Kang (Kao Chung-yu) (p. 183) was the chief target of a major Party purge in 1954, when he was accused of 'warlordism' and seeking to detach Manchuria as his 'independent kingdom'. Disgraced, he committed suicide. Born in Hengshan, Shensi, in 1891, he and Liu Chih-tan built the Party there, and its isolated Red base became a sanctuary for the Communists at the end of the Long March. The son of a landlord, he graduated from a normal college in Sian, joined the CCP with Liu Chih-tan, led a peasant insurrection in 1927, and maintained guerrilla war bases in the Shensi-Kansu-Ninghsia area thereafter. As leader of a Party committee consisting of Lin Piao, Li Fu-ch'un, Ch'en Yun, Hsiao Ching-kuang, and P'eng Chen, he entered Manchuria and organized mass bases for guerrilla operations which ended in PLA victory there in 1946. Elected to the PB in 1945, he was in 1949 political commissar for all Manchuria, and in 1950 secretary of the Party North-East Bureau and concurrently military commander. Chairman of the state planning commission in 1953, he was relieved of his Manchurian posts. Kao's deputy on the planning commission was Jao Shu-shih, secretary of the Orgburo of the CC. During 1954, when Kao and Jao were removed from office as 'anti-Party', the most articulate accuser was Liu Shao-ch'i. Five provincial governors and several regional party and army chieftains were also dismissed. After Kao committed suicide and Jao Shu-shih fell into obscurity, foreign reports suggested that Kao Kang may have had Stalin's backing in an attempt to overthrow Mao and set up a satellite state in Manchuria.

Ku Ta-chen (p. 197) was born in Kiangsi in 1903. He helped to form the Eleventh Red Army (1928), made the Long March, and held responsible posts throughout the Resistance War and civil wars. In 1967 he was a permanent member of the All-China Labour Union Federation, a member of the CC, and vice-governor of Kwangtung province.

Lan P'ing. See Chiang Ch'ing (Mme Mao Tse-tung).

Li Ching-ch'uan (p. 492) was for a decade the foremost Party personality with authority in Szechuan, Kweichow, and Yunnan, a vast territory with nearly 100 million inhabitants and numerous minority and frontier peoples, and embracing approaches to Tibet, Burma, Thailand, and Indochina. During the GPCR, frequent clashes, reportedly between Maoist Red Guards and Party authorities in those provinces, seemed aimed at Li. In April 1967, the official press announced his replacement. Born in Hua-ch'uang county, Kiangsi (*circa* 1905), in a peasant family, Li was one of Mao's students when he lectured at the Peasants' Training Institute, Canton (1924–5). He helped organize peasant uprisings, received some military training in Kiangsi, and became a political commissar in units led by P'eng Teh-huai. During the Long March he served for a year with troops of Chu Teh and Chang Kuo-t'ao when the two Red armies split. After their reunion in the North-West, Li took commands in the Mongolian border region, organizing guerrilla warfare (1937–47). During the Liberation War he held leading positions in Szechuan, from which developed an unusual degree of individual regional dominance. Re-elected to the CC in 1956, he entered the PB in 1958 and was named first secretary of the Party's South-West Bureau in 1961. His Party and administrative control in so important an area as Szechuan could hardly have been held without the support of Party Secretary General Teng Hsiao-p'ing (*q.v.*), a Szechuanese with a special interest there. Evidently Mao was unable to prevent his re-election to the PB in August 1966, but when Red Guards chose Teng Hsiao-p'ing as a main target Li's prestige was badly shaken. After Maoists took over the Kweichow provincial Party bureau in 1966, and denounced its old leaders as 'bourgeois reactionary', Red Guard posters reportedly demanded that Li be put to death. In May 1967, the official Peking press denounced Li as 'No. 1 Party power-holder taking the capitalist road in the South-West region', holding him responsible for a 'bloody tragedy in Chengtu' (the suppression of Maoist anti-Li Red Guards). An army reorganization completed in 1968 removed Li from all posts and he was in 1971 living in obscurity.

Li Chung-chin. See Chiang Ch'ing (Mme Mao Tse-tung).

Li Fu-ch'un (p. 88) was re-elected by the eleventh plenary session of the Eighth Congress to the PB in 1966, in the same rank (tenth) he held in 1956 (First Plenum). He was reportedly associated with the 'economists' (those advocating the use of material incentives as against ideological incentives). One of Mao's lifelong friends, and a fellow Hunanese, Li was born in Changsha in 1900, attended middle school there, joined the Work-Study Plan sponsored by the Sino-French Education Association, Peking, and went to France in 1918. In 1921, with Chou En-lai, Li Li-san, Lo Man (Li Wei-han), Ts'ai Ho-sen, and others, he helped form the Communist Youth League in France, which soon incorporated into the CCP. He worked in the Schneider munitions plants and a motor factory in Paris, and French workers first introduced him to Marxism.

Li left France in 1924, studied six months in Russia, returned to China, and became a member of the CC and PB in 1924. Director of Party political training in Canton, he was political director of Liu Po-ch'eng's Sixth Army in the Northern Expedition. After the KMT-CP split he became secretary of the Kiangsi provincial CP (1927–33). He made the Long March and, when the author met him in 1936, was a member of the CC and chairman of the Shensi-Kansu-Ninghsia regional Party committee (see RNORC). He held important posts in the Yenan government (deputy director, finance department, 1940–45) until, in 1945, he was sent to Manchuria with a Party committee headed by Kao Kang to organize economic and related affairs. In 1956 he was re-elected to the CCP CC: his main duties continued to be in finance and economics. In 1950 he became minister of heavy industry. After Kao Kang's dismissal in 1954, Li became chairman of the State Planning Commission, continuing in that job at this writing. Re-elected to the PB in 1956, he attended many intraparty conferences abroad and at home, especially concerning economic matters, and signed many trade agreements, as well as the China-Korea Treaty of Alliance (1961). Li Fu-ch'un and his wife (Ts'ai Chang, *q.v.*) were re-elected to the CC in 1966, and Li to the PB, but Li himself was attacked by wall posters for allegedly opposing a new Great Leap Forward economic policy. Paradoxically, Li Fu-ch'un was in 1967 elevated to membership in the standing committee of the PB, which normally had consisted of Mao and six vice-chairmen of the CC.

In 1968 Li Fu-ch'un was dropped from the PB. He was re-elected to the CC in 1969, however, and in 1970 was seen on the reviewing stand during the October anniversary.

Li Hsien-nien (p. 234) was born in 1905 in Huangan county, Hupeh, the son of a worker, and was himself a carpenter's apprentice. In 1966 he was re-elected to the CC and PB and was often mentioned in the press as prominent among leaders of the GPCR.

Li joined the Northern Expedition when it reached Hankow and soon (1927) became a Communist. A Red Guard guerrilla leader in Hupeh peasant uprisings, he rose to a regular command in the Red Army under Hsu Hsiang-ch'ien, and withdrew westward with Chang Kuo-t'ao and Hsu. In 1935, at Maoerhkai, he first met Mao Tse-tung. Party discipline requiring that he obey his immediate superior, Li stayed with the recalcitrant Chang during the Mao-Chang dispute. A year after Mao reached Shensi, Chang Kuo-t'ao moved his troops northward. His main forces were caught in an enemy encirclement near Sian and nearly destroyed, while Li Hsien-nien's Thirtieth Army, renamed the West Route Army, attempted to reach Sinkiang but again suffered very heavy casualties. Li got to Yenan in 1937, where he entered K'ang Ta ('Resist Japan

University') and studied for a year. In 1938 he was sent behind Japanese lines in Hupeh to organize guerrilla warfare. Starting with only a few rifles and old friends among peasants, Li built an army of 60,000 by 1941. During the civil war he became a field army commander. From victory onward he was the chief political and military person in his native province, Hupeh. In 1956 he was elected to the Party PB, after which he took a leading part in conferences, pacts, and trade agreements with Albania, Guinea, Mali, Tanzania, Ghana, North Korea, North Vietnam, etc., travelling to some of those countries and to Eastern Europe. Elected a vice-premier, PRC, in 1962, he was in August 1966 confirmed in his position in the PB. Re-elected to the CC in 1969, Li also ranked high in the PB. In 1971 he was the more active of Chou En-lai's two remaining vice-premiers and took a prominent part in planning and execution of China's post-GPCR diplomacy.

Li Hsueh-feng (p. 244n.) was born in 1907, in Shansi, the same province as P'eng Chen (q.v.), whom he replaced in 1966 when the latter was driven from his office as secretary of the Peking Party committee, a key post because its membership embraced many CC members and the highest administrative officials of the central government of the CPR.

Li Hsueh-feng joined the Party about 1926, had affiliations with Liu Chih-tan during early peasant insurrections, and was elected (*in absentia*) a member of the CEC of the provisional Central Soviet Government (1934). In the North China Bureau under Liu Shao-ch'i (1935–9) he was active during the Red Army drive into Shansi in 1935. He served variously as political commissar and Party secretary in Shansi, Chahar, Hopei and the Central Plains Bureau in the 1940s. Director of the CC Central Plains Orgburo in 1949, he then held responsible Party bureau posts in Central and South China 1949–52, until he became first deputy Party secretary of the Central-South Bureau in 1952. In 1956 he was elected a member (No. 71) of the CC. He was in the presidium of the NPC from its outset (1955) and in 1965 was a vice-chairman of its standing committee. In 1963 he became first secretary of the CC North China Bureau. In 1966 he entered the PB, where (as *de facto* mayor of Peking) he carried primary organizational and management responsibility for repeated Red Guard demonstrations, and for Party direction of the GPCR. In 1969 Li was re-elected by the Ninth Party Congress to the CC and as an alternate member of the PB, where he remained at this time of writing in 1971.

Li K'e-nung (p. 83) was still inhabiting the Foreign Office – as a vice-minister – when he died in 1963.

Li Li-san (p. 88), rehabilitated in the CCP in 1945, was still in the CC when the GPCR was formally launched in August 1966, and presumably remained a member at this writing.

Li was born in Liling county, Hunan, in 1896, in a landlord's family; his real name was Li Lung-chih. After graduating from middle school (1914) he went to Peking to join the Work-Study Plan established by the Sino-French Educational Association, and to study French. He reached France in 1918. With other Chinese students (Chou En-lai, etc.) he helped found the CYL, which merged with the CCP in 1922. Returning to China in 1922, Li was assigned to work with Liu Shao-ch'i in the organization of miners at Anyuan, Kiangsi, where Mao Tse-tung was also active. In Shanghai in 1923 he began to organize labour unions and in 1924 became chairman of the Shanghai Federation of Trade Unions and concurrently secretary of the propaganda section of the KMT. The same year he entered the KMT CEC to become a political instructor at Whampoa Academy, in Canton. In 1925 he and Liu Shao-ch'i led workers who launched the 30 May Movement in Shanghai.

Proceeding to Moscow, Li represented the All-China Federation of Trade Unions and was elected to the Trade Union International Committee. Returning to Shanghai in 1926, he was elected to the CCP PB and worked with Chou En-lai in preparing the 1927 Shanghai Uprising. In July 1927, after breaking with Ch'en Tu-hsiu's PB leadership (and authorized by a directive from Stalin) Li Li-san joined Chou En-lai and others in planning the Nanchang 1 August Uprising. Following its defeat he attended the emergency conference of the PB, held 7 August, where he was instrumental in electing Ch'u Ch'iu-pai to succeed Ch'en Tu-hsiu as CC general secretary.

Elements of Li's political career from 1927 onwards are summed up in Part Four, Chapter 6, note 3, and in biographical notes on the principals mentioned therein. For further details see an account by James P. Harrison: 'The Li Li-san Line and the CCP in 1930', *China Quarterly*, Nos. 14 and 15 (London, 1963); see also R N O R C.

After Li's removal from the PB following his 'trial' in Moscow by the CMT in November 1930, Li stayed on (probably involuntarily) to work there as a translator and editor in the Foreign Languages Press. In 1936 he was arrested as a Trotskyist but was released in 1938 and resumed his work. With Mao's support (at Stalin's suggestion) he was re-admitted to the CCP and at the Seventh Congress in April 1945 was elected (No. 16) to the CC. In the same year he left Moscow for Manchuria, to join Lin Piao's group there as a political adviser. In 1948 he was elected to the presidium of the Sixth All-China Congress of Labour, at which he delivered the opening address, in Harbin. Elected first vice-chairman of the All-China Federation of Labour, he was also director of its Cadres School until 1953, when he was dismissed for 'mistakes of subjectivism'. Meanwhile he had held numerous other important government posts, notably as Minister of Labour and director of the CC Industrial and Communications Work Department (1949–54). At the Eighth Congress of the CCP (1956) Li confessed to 'leftist opportunist mistakes' and was re-elected to the CC (No. 89). In 1962 he was briefly secretary of the CC North China Bureau. Li remained a symbol of Mao's 'forgivingness'. Although he took no prominent part in the GPCR he was not attacked as a revisionist nor were his past errors exhumed for vilification.

Li's first wife, Wang Hsiu-chen, a leader in the CCP CC women's department, was arrested in Shanghai in 1932 by the Nationalists, and disappeared. During Li's stay in Moscow he married a Russian.

Li Ta (p. 183) left the Party during the 1927 repression but took no counter-revolutionary action. He reappeared as a Communist collaborator during the Second World War, and became a member of the CPPCC of the PRC. In 1966 he came under heavy attack as a 'revisionist', during the GPCR, but the role assigned to him seemed largely symbolic, since he had no political power.

Li Ta-chao (p. 87) became, during his relatively brief life (1888–1927), which ended in execution by strangulation, the single most important Chinese radical political influence in his time, the first impressive Chinese interpreter of Marxism, and the first major contributor to a system or ideology which may be called Chinese Marxist thought. As librarian at Peking National University, Li Ta-chao gave Mao Tse-tung a job and first introduced him to serious Marxist study. To say that without Li Ta-chao there could have been no Mao Tse-tung may be an overstatement, but some of the main features of Mao's Thought are explicit or implicit in the writings of Li Ta-chao, which Mao implemented in action. As a co-founder of the CCP he provided a bridge between China's few Western-educated 'liberals' and the younger generation of intellectuals decisively influenced by the Russian Revolution. For a fascinating account of the range of Li's life and works – indispensable to a fuller understanding of the complexity of the Chinese revolution and of Maoist Thought – see Maurice Meisner's *Li Ta-chao and the Origins of Chinese Marxism*.

Li Teh (p. 105) was the Chinese Party name adopted by Otto Braun, born *circa* 1896. A German Communist sent to China by the Comintern, Braun so identified himself in print for the first time in an article published in *Neues Deutschland* (East Berlin), 27 May 1964. 'Li Teh' may have reached Shanghai late in 1932. Early in 1933 he called on the author in Peking, representing himself as a German newspaper correspondent named Otto Stern. In Pao An, where his role was clear, he never mentioned his real name, but he did speak of work undertaken as a revolutionary agent in South America and Spain. In 1928 he was arrested in Germany and reportedly 'sentenced to death', but he escaped and fled to Moscow. A soldier in the First World War, he received some further military training in Moscow. After serving as CMT representative on the underground military advisory committee in Shanghai, Braun entered Kiangsi in 1933, smuggled into the Red areas in a sampan where he lay covered with cargo for many days. As a Comintern delegate he held a position of extraordinary prestige in the CC revolutionary military council, and he bore a large share of responsibility for military practices followed in 1933–4. He was the only foreigner who made the Long March. After the Tsunyi Conference he was placed in a subordinate and advisory capacity under Mao. Li Teh left Yenan in 1939, on the only Russian plane known to have landed there during the Second World War. In Moscow until 1945, he entered Berlin with the Soviet Red Army. *Neues Deutschland* described him as a 'professor' and a China expert. Li's role in Kiangsi is further described in Part Four, Chapter 6, note 3. His article, *'In wessen Namen spricht Mao Tse-tung?'* ('For whom does Mao Tse-tung speak?') in *Neues Deutschland* (East Berlin), 27 May 1964, fully supported Moscow in the Sino-Soviet dispute. Otto Braun's Memoirs, which appeared in 1970, were given a critical analysis, as a source of history concerning the Kiangsi and Tsunyi periods, by Dieter Heinzig in *China Quarterly*, April–June 1971. See Bibliography.

Li *Tsung-jen* (p. 131) led his Kwangsi army in one of the Nationalists' few victories against the Japanese. He was 'elected' vice-president of China in 1947. Before 'President' Chiang fled to Taiwan (1949) he resigned, and General Li became Nationalist president. When Chiang Kai-shek later took back his title, on Taiwan, Li retired to the United States. In 1965 he returned to Peking, made his peace with Mao Tse-tung, and denounced Chiang Kai-shek as a puppet of American imperialism.

Liao *Ch'eng-yun.* See Ch'en Yun.

Lin *Piao* (p. 47) was in 1966 officially declared 'Chairman Mao's closest comrade-in-arms'. After the Eleventh Plenum of the CC (August 1966), Lin emerged as second only to Mao in the seemingly all-powerful standing committee, as first vice-chairman of the Party, first vice-chairman of the Party's supreme military affairs committee, minister of defence, and first vice-premier of the State Council. Lin was commonly regarded as effective leader of the People's Republic in case of Mao's death – having replaced, in effect, President of the Republic Liu Shao-ch'i.

Lin Piao was born in 1908. In 1936, at Pao An, Shensi, he gave the author the details of his early life which appear in the text (Part Three, Chapter 4).

When Generalissimo Chiang drove the rebels from Kiangsi, in 1934, Lin Piao led the breakthrough forces of the Long March. At Tsunyi, Kweichow, in 1935, he helped elect Mao to supreme command. He fought successful battles in Shansi and Shensi (1935–6) and took part in the occupation of Yenan in December 1936. During the resistance against Japan, Lin commanded Red Army (renamed Eighth Route Army) detachments in northern Shansi. His 115th Division delivered a smashing defeat to invading Japanese forces, a first proof that Chinese troops, properly organized and led, could be victorious against modern armies. Seriously wounded in 1939, he spent about two years convalescing in Russia. On his return he was briefly with Chou En-lai's 'liaison headquarters' in Chungking, and then became deputy chairman of the Party school in Yenan, of which Mao was chairman. He was elected to the CC in 1942.

Sent to Manchuria in 1945, Lin became commander-in-chief of Red forces there. To him, in 1946, Mao Tse-tung addressed his now celebrated 'general concepts' of military operations for renewed KMT-CP civil war. Lin held command of the main Communist forces in Manchuria. Within a year he entrapped the core of Chiang Kai-shek's American-armed and American-trained armies, capturing or killing a total of thirty-six generals. Following victory in Manchuria, Lin encircled Chiang's main forces in northern China. Peking surrendered to him without a battle.

In July 1950, Lin Piao was elected to the PB. Early in China's intervention in the Korean War, in November 1950, Lin Piao led the 'Chinese People's Volunteer Corps' in a counteroffensive which took General MacArthur's headquarters by surprise. Using 'human sea' tactics, Lin pushed the American and United Nations troops to near-disaster. Withdrawn from Korea, supposedly because of illness, he again spent some time recuperating in Russia. Marshal P'eng Teh-huai replaced him. A deputy chairman of the Party military affairs committee from 1950, and a deputy premier, he was re-elected to the PB in 1956; a year after he was promoted to the rank of marshal of the PLA.

In 1959 the Chinese Party bitterly debated future policy towards the

USSR. Obvious and bitter personal rivalry had developed between P'eng and Lin in which Mao himself was a protagonist. In the midst of their ideological dispute, Nikita Khrushchev cancelled his promise to supply China with a 'sample atom bomb'. P'eng Teh-huai was relieved as Minister of Defence, and Lin Piao replaced him. Lin Piao's reforms aimed at 'de-Russification'. 'Professional-officer-caste' mentality was fought, titles and insignia of rank were abolished, special officer privileges ended, the Yenan type of soldier-peasant-worker-student combination was restored, and the Thought of Mao Tse-tung superseded all other ideological texts. By making the PLA a 'great school of the Thought of Mao Tse-tung', Lin indoctrinated a leadership whose aid was decisive (1967) to Mao's triumph in the GPCR.

In 1965 Lin published a lengthy thesis on revolutions in the underdeveloped countries, entitled 'Long Live the Victory of the People's War!' Lin's article likened the 'emerging forces' of the poor in Asia, Africa, and Latin America to the 'rural areas of the world', while the affluent countries of the West were likened to the 'cities of the world'. Eventually the 'cities' would be encircled by revolutions in the 'rural areas', following the Thought of Mao Tse-tung. Lin made no promise that China would fight other people's wars, however; they were advised to depend mainly on 'self-reliance'. In 1966 the Chinese Party press referred to Lin's thesis as an integral part of the Thought of Mao Tse-tung. In 1964 Lin Piao had brought together a number of excerpts of Mao's writings in a little red book first used in the PLA. As *Quotations from Chairman Mao Tse-tung* it became the chief handbook of the Red Guards in 1966 and soon a world-wide best-seller.

Since 1956 a member of the presiding seven-man Party standing committee, Lin emerged as Mao Tse-tung's guarantee of armed support during the major *bouleversement* of 1966. One million Communist Party members, integrated in the army command, became the decisive ideological force in the national rectification movement known as the GPCR. Still the youngest member of the PB, Lin Piao seemingly held in his hands the fate of China in the event of Chairman Mao's death, and that such was Mao's intention was confirmed when, at the Ninth Party Congress, 1969, the new Party constitution named Lin Piao Mao's 'close comrade-in-arms and successor'. Second in rank under Mao in the five-man standing committee of the PB he was, in mid-1971, credited with winding up the GPCR, through army intervention, restoration of Party-army amity and unity, and recovered stability of administration. It seemed unlikely that Lin could 'replace' Mao – or that anyone else could – but the team of Chou, as chief administrator and executive, and Lin as consensus leader of the army, might provide a collective leadership in the event of Mao's demise.

Liu Hsiao (p. 217) was born in Shenking, Hunan, in 1911, in a family he described to the author in 1936 as 'middle landlords'. His father studied in Japan for two years, and was antireligious. Liu Hsiao began school at five. He attended a middle school run by the American Christian Reformed Church, in Shengchoufu, where he learned English and became a Christian. After graduating he went to Shanghai to attend a higher school. En route he met a radical Chinese Christian pastor who introduced him to Marxism. In 1926 he joined the Communist Party and took part in the Shanghai Uprising. He was then sent north of the Yangtze to teach and organize. His school was attacked, he fled to Shanghai, was arrested in the French Concession, and spent three years in jail. On his release he went to Red Kiangsi in 1931, and he became secretary of the Kiangsi CP CC in 1932. (For a detailed account of this period see *RNORC*, 'The Liu Hsiao Story', pp. 64–9.)

Liu made the Long March and in 1936 was chairman of the political department of the First Front Army. Throughout the Japanese and Liberation wars he continued to work in the General Political Department of the army, with special responsibilities in the Shanghai and Kiangsu underground, where he was secretary of the CCP. Elected to the CCP CC in 1945, he was appointed ambassador to the USSR (1955–63), and made contacts with East European and other Communist parties. Vice-Minister of Foreign Affairs from 1963, he took part in conversation between Chou En-lai and President Sukarno in Shanghai in 1964. In 1966 he was re-elected to the CCP CC and was prominently listed as a leader of the GPCR. In 1967 he became ambassador to Albania.

Liu Po-ch'eng (p. 225), popularly known as the 'One-eyed Dragon', was born in Szechuan in 1892, joined the CCP in 1926, rose to the rank of marshal of the army, and in 1967 was a member of the PB, a vice-chairman of the standing committee of the NPC, and a member of the all-powerful Party military affairs committee. His father was a strolling musician who saved money to give his son a basic classical education, but Po-ch'eng chose a military school in Chengtu, won a commission in the provincial army, and took part in the 1911 Revolution. In the course of many battles he lost an eye. After joining the CCP he was chief of staff during the Nanchang Uprising in 1927, a fiasco from which he escaped; he went to Russia and studied at Frunze Military Institute until 1930. Returning to China, he entered Kiangsi and became chief of staff of the Central Revolutionary Military Committee. He led part of the vanguard forces during the Long March, and then commanded the 129th Division, Eighth Route Army, at the start of the Resistance War (1937–45). After widely extending his guerrilla forces in North and Central China he commanded the Central Plains Army in operations coordinated with Ch'en Yi's armies which (1948) decisively defeated KMT forces north of the Yangtze. First elected to the CC in 1945 and to the PB in 1956, logically he should have been a key PLA supporter of Mao Tse-tung and Lin Piao during the critical Party struggles of 1966–7, but he took no noticeable responsibility. He was, of course, seventy-five years old.

Liu Shao-ch'i (p. 173n.) was elected chairman of the National People's Congress and government (replacing Mao Tse-tung in that role in 1959) but by 1966 he had become 'China's Khrushchev' and the major target of the GPCR and the Red Guards campaign.

Liu was born in 1898 in Ning Hsiang, Hunan, close to Mao Tse-tung's home, and graduated from the Hunan First Normal School, which Mao also attended. Son of a 'rich' peasant family, he turned radical under influences very similar to those described by Mao. In 1920 he helped Mao organize a Socialist Youth Corps in Hunan, and was recruited for study at the Comintern's Sun Yat-sen University in Moscow, where he joined the branch CCP. When he returned in 1922 he became secretary of the All-China Labour Syndicate. He organized workers in the Yangtze Valley, and at Anyuan, on the Kiangsi-Hunan border, led a successful strike of the miners' union. In 1927 some of these miners joined Mao Tse-tung's first Workers' and Peasants' Red Army. (But in 1967 attacks on Liu by the Maoist press for the first time accused Liu of following bourgeois-reformist policies when leading the Anyuan unions – thus establishing for him a history of forty years of revisionist thought.)

In Canton in 1925, Liu was on the executive committee of the All-China Federation of Labour. He helped organize Shanghai labour unions (1925–6) and general strikes, and organized the Hupeh League of Labour Unions. Underground labour organizer from 1927 onwards, he was a member of the CC but had differences with leaders Li Li-san and Wang Ming. He entered Soviet Kiangsi in 1932, as a member of Po Ku's PB. Liu participated in the 1934 retreat from Kiangsi but did not make the Long March. He was sent to try to reorganize the shattered Party underground in the White areas of North China, making his headquarters in Peking and Tientsin. In 1937 he rejoined the CC at Yenan, and in 1941 became political commissar of the New Fourth Army. After the Party rectification of 1942–3 (in which he supported Mao against

Wang Ming), Liu Shao-ch'i became a pivotal person in the PB and CC secretariat.

During the Resistance War, Liu headed the Central Plains Bureau and was supreme in the branch Party PB in the guerrilla areas of North China and Manchuria. Many of the millions of new Party members recruited during that period were trained under Liu's direction. First vice-chairman of the CCP CC (1945–66), he was acting Party chairman when Mao went to Chungking for talks with Chiang Kai-shek in 1945. At the Seventh Party Congress, in 1945, Liu asserted that Mao Tse-tung had made new and original contributions to Marxism-Leninism, and later declared that Mao's 'Asiatic Marxism' was 'of universal significance'. He was recognized as No. 2 in the Party, and his written works (esp. How To Be a Good Communist and On Inner Party Struggle) carried authority second only to those of Mao (until 1967). In 1949 he was vice-chairman of the Central People's Government, and from 1955 to 1959 was first vice-chairman of the NPC. In 1958 Mao retired as chairman of the CPG of the PR and Liu Shao-ch'i succeeded him. In 1961 Mao publicly indicated that Liu was his choice to follow him as supreme Party leader.

In 1966, after Mao's reappearance following a long absence from public view, supposedly a convalescence from a severe illness, a major Party purge was initiated under slogans of the GPCR. Following a meeting of the eleventh plenary session (Eighth Congress) of the CC CCP (August 1966), presided over by Mao Tse-tung, Liu's name dropped from second to eighth place in the PB. Lin Piao replaced Liu in the hierarchical rank and also became Mao's deputy leader of newly formed youth brigades called Red Guards (Hung Wei-ping). A 'main target' of the Red Guards was 'reactionary bureaucrats'. As chief administrator of the Chinese state superstructure, Liu Shao-ch'i was held personally responsible for alleged bourgeois, reactionary, and feudalistic atavisms in the Party and state bureaucracy, as well as for dangerous tendencies towards 'revisionism', 'economism' (material incentives over-zealotry), and softness on class-struggle and anticapitalist indoctrination. In 1967 the Maoist press denounced Liu's books as counter-revolutionary and described him as 'No. 1 among those in the Party in authority who are taking the capitalist road'. He was attacked for sabotaging the GPCR by sending in hostile 'work teams' (among them those led by his wife, at Peking University) to try to take control of the movement. Red Guard posters accused him of involvement in a February 1966 coup aimed at Mao's overthrow. Conspiracy charges were not pressed but for reference to details concerning an alleged opposition verging on conspiracy see P'eng Chen, P'eng Teh-huai, Lu Ting-yi, Lo Jui-ch'ing, and Mao Tse-tung.

In October 1968, in the last reported meeting of the CC before the Ninth Party Congress (April 1969), Liu Shao-ch'i was declared a scab, renegade and traitor, expelled from Party membership, and dismissed from all offices. (Constitutionally speaking, Liu could have been dismissed as Chairman only by the National Congress, but the GPCR had *de facto* superseded congressional constitutionality. A new constitution was to be adopted when the Congress next met.) In 1971 Liu's whereabouts were unknown but he was said to be under protective arrest.

Literature and propaganda concerning the Mao-Liu duel and revelations of the long history of 'struggle between two lines' had by 1971 become so voluminous that even a selected list of titles could not be included here. For a few guiding references, see Bibliography and BDRC.

Liu's first wife was killed by the KMT in 1933, during the Civil War. His second wife was Wang Kuang-mei (*q.v.*). See TOSOTR; see also Howard L. Boorman, 'Liu Shao-ch'i, a Political Profile', *China Quarterly* (London, May–June 1962).

Liu Shao-ch'i, Mme. See Wang Kuang-mei.

Lo Fu (Chang Wen-t'ien) (p. 114) nominally was general secretary of the PB from 1935 to 1945 (when the office was abolished), but by 1936, during the author's conversations with him in Pao An, he deferred to Mao as principal authorized spokesman of the Party. His Party power sharply declined after a Party rectification (*cheng-feng*) in 1942, aimed at Wang Ming and other Soviet-educated members.

Lo Fu was the only Chinese PB member who knew the USA first-hand. Born in 1900, in Kiangsu, he was the son of a scholar-official (Manchu regime) who became a prosperous businessman, able to send his son through engineering school in Nanking. Lo Fu then spent a year at the University of California (1921). On his return to China he taught school, worked as an editor, met Ch'u Ch'iu-pai and other left writers, translated Western classics under the pen name Lo Fu, was recruited to the CCP by Ch'en Yun, and studied at the Comintern's Sun Yat-sen University (1926–30). There he fell under the influence of Pavel Mif, the CMT delegate to the CCP. Chosen for the CC at the CCP Sixth Congress (Moscow, 1928), Lo Fu returned to Shanghai, became a PB member in 1931, and headed the Orgburo. As one of Mif's 'Twenty-eight Bolsheviks', Lo Fu opposed Mao Tse-tung's 'peasant line' and his leadership in Kiangsi. For details of his career during this period, see Part Four, Chapter 6, note 3; and RNORC.

Lo Fu was re-elected to the CC and PB in 1945 and was the CPR's first ambassador to Russia (1949–55), but he steadily lost place after the Sino-Soviet split. In 1966 he was dropped from the PB. In 1967 he was attacked by the GPCR press as an ally of P'eng Teh-huai and Liu Shao-ch'i. Lo Fu was not re-elected to the Ninth Party Congress CC.

Lo Jui-ch'ing (p. 137n.), former chief of staff of the PLA, was secretary general of the Party military affairs committee until his eclipse occurred early in 1966. In February, Red Guard wall posters accused him of involvement in a conspiracy (together with P'eng Chen, Liu Shao-ch'i and others) to seize supreme Party power from Mao Tse-tung in an alleged attempted coup.

Born into a gentry family in Szechuan in 1906, Lo Jui-ch'ing was close to his fellow Szechuanese, Chu Teh, Mao's military right arm during the whole Communist struggle for power. A graduate of the Soviet-financed Whampoa Academy, Canton, Lo joined the CCP in 1926, was a political officer under Yeh T'ing, and followed Chu Teh and Mao to Chingkangshan. At some period (1932–4?) he studied secret police and security techniques in Moscow and, briefly, at a CMT special Party services school in Paris. Director of Security Forces during the Long March, he was teaching at the Red Army College in Pao An when the author met him in 1936. Thereafter Lo was in charge of various branches of security and intelligence, continuing in that role as Minister of Public Security and commander of Public Security Forces (1949–59). Elected to the CC in 1945, he became a secretary of the CC secretariat in 1961, under Teng Hsiao-p'ing, and a vice-premier of the SC PRC in 1959. In 1966 Red Guard posters accused him of conspiring, with P'eng Chen and others, to seize power from Mao. Reportedly he attempted suicide. He was paraded before one mass meeting with Teng Hsiao-p'ing and Lu Ting-yi, in 1967, wearing a placard of self-denunciation; but no attempt was made to bring him to formal trial. In 1971 he was said by one authority in Peking to be still alive and under protective arrest.

Lo Jung-huan (p. 194) was born in Hungshan, Hunan, in 1902, and joined the CCP in 1921. He took part in the Nanchang Uprising and later was in the political department of the Red Army in Soviet Kiangsi. He was political commissar in Lin Piao's First Army Corps from 1932 throughout the Long March, and on into the War of Resistance, the Civil War (1948–9), and in Korea (1950). In 1955 he was named one of ten marshals of the PLA. After Lin Piao became Defence Minister in 1960, Lo Jung-huan headed the General Political Department of the PLA and was responsible for its security forces until his death in 1963.

Lo P'ing-hui (p. 201) was killed in combat in 1943.

Lu Ting-yi (p. 400) was born in 1904, in Wusih, Kiangsu, the son of a bourgeois family. He graduated from Chiaotung (Communications) University, Shanghai, and joined the CYL in 1922. He studied in Russia (1924–8) but did not collaborate with the 'Twenty-eight Bolsheviks'. He rose to high rank in the Party PB until 1966, when he was deprived of all his Party posts and identified as a collaborator of P'eng Chen (q.v.), foremost among anti-Maoists. He was until 1966 also a vice-chairman of the State Council. As director of the propaganda bureau of the Party CC he often acted as spokesman for Mao Tse-tung and other leaders. He wrote and edited many official press pronouncements and was also responsible for cultural and educational institutions. In 1966 Lu Ting-yi was blamed for rightist 'anti-Party' and 'black line' revisionist trends in the press and education. Dropped from the PB, he was replaced by T'ao Chu (q.v.), who was himself soon eliminated. In 1967 the official press accused Lu of having joined P'eng Chen in an effort, in 1962, to secure Mao's effective retirement. Attacks on Lu Ting-yi virtually ceased in 1968. In 1971 the author was told, in Peking, that he had not been expelled from the Party but was suspended and retired.

Ma Hai-teh (p. 428n.), an American named George Hatem, was born in Buffalo, New York, in 1910, the son of Syrian immigrants. He completed his medical studies at the University of Geneva and went to practise in Shanghai. In 1936 he volunteered to serve in the Red areas. Dr Hatem entered the Communist districts with the author, but asked him not to mention it when he left and wrote of the trip. That story, with an account of Dr Hatem's subsequent career, was related in TOSOTR.

Mao An-ch'ing (p. 485), Mao's second son by Yang K'ai-hui, was born in Changsha (circa 1921), and was hidden by friends when his mother was arrested. He was sent to Shanghai with his brother and later went on to Russia, where he was educated, reportedly as an engineer. On his return to China he worked as a Russian-language interpreter and translated some textbooks. Mao An-ch'ing and Mao's two daughters by Chiang Ch'ing were his only surviving children, Mao said in 1965. When the author asked Mao about reports that his son was an engineer, Mao replied that he did not know what 'they' had taught him in Russia and implied his disappointment that An-ch'ing had not been educated in China.

Mao An-ying (p. 485) was Mao's first son by Yang K'ai-hui, born in 1920. In 1930 he was arrested in Changsha with his mother, who was executed. Released, he was taken into hiding by other members of the family, who fled from Changsha. During the Second World War he studied in Russia. In 1948 he returned to China and for a few months worked on a commune in Shansi. Later he entered a higher Party school. Among the first of the Chinese to reach Korea during the intervention, he was in command of a division in the 'Chinese People's Volunteer Corps' when he was killed on 25 October 1950.

Mao Tse-min (p. 186n.), younger brother of Mao Tse-tung and Mao Tse-t'an, early followed them into the Party. In 1923 he worked with Mao and Liu Shao-ch'i in Hunanese labour organizations. When Mao was deputy director of the Kuomintang Peasant Movement Training Institute in 1925, Mao Tse-min was a student there. He participated in the Northern Expedition, joined Mao at Chingkangshan, took part in the Kiangsi Soviet struggles and made the Long March. In Pao An and Yenan he was, under Lin Tsu-han, deputy director of finance and economy. In 1938 he was sent to Sinkiang province to serve as a financial adviser to General Sheng Shih-ts'ai, who then followed a pro-Communist policy. When Sheng reversed himself, and initiated an anti-Communist purge, Mao Tse-min was arrested and in 1942 he was executed.

Mao Tse-t'an (p. 203) worked with his two brothers in organizing labour unions in 1925. During the Kiangsi Soviet period he specialized in 'building the economy'. He was criticized for sympathizing with the 'Lo-Ming line' – reliance on guerrilla tactics (Mao Tse-tung's) – during the 1933–4 era, when the Politburo adopted a strategy of 'meeting the enemy beyond the gates' and positional warfare. At the start of the Long March he was entrusted with the 'State treasure'. He was killed in action in 1935. Mao Tse-tung adopted and educated his children, as well as the children of Mao Tse-min.

Mao Tse-tung (p. 47). Part Four of this book, 'Genesis of a Communist', tells Mao's own story to the age of forty-three. I presented Mao with many questions concerning himself, the history of the Party, and his own leadership. The personal questions were used as a frame of reference; there were many flashbacks and flash-forwards, and various sidelong excursions elicited by further queries. I did extensive reorganization of my notes, and then gave the draft to Wu Liang-p'ing, who wrote a full translation. Mao read it over, corrected, reorganized, and amplified or condensed. The script was put into English again by Wu Liang-p'ing and myself, and then done into Chinese once more. Mao provided a revised text which Mr Wu and I rendered into the final English.

On my return to Peking from the North-West late in 1936 I quickly wrote up part of my notes. Early in 1937 I gave copies of my newspaper and magazine reports (about twenty-two articles) to some Chinese professors who translated and published them (semilegally) in a volume entitled *Chung-kuo Hsi-pei Yin-hsiang Chi*, 'Impressions of North-West China'. In July 1937 I gave the same professors a copy of the completed manuscript of *Red Star Over China*, which they smuggled to Shanghai (the Japanese had occupied Peking), where they organized a translation team to secure speedy publication. They were patriotic members of the National Salvation Association, to which I granted translation rights, with earnings assigned to the Chinese Red Cross. Their volume was called *Hsi-hsing Man-chi*, or 'Travels in the West'. It was the only authorized Chinese version of Mao's interviews.

Later on, various chapters and biographies were pirated from RSOC and reprinted in pamphlet form, in both English and Chinese. One of these, with the imprint of the 'Truth Book Co.', of Canton, in 1938 appeared under the title, 'The Autobiography of Mao Tse-tung', which omitted my own interpolations, questions and comments. In Hongkong, in 1949, the same company reprinted that English-language pamphlet as 'dictated by Edgar Snow' and 'revised' and 'annoted' by 'Tang Szu-chen', someone unknown to me. The 1949 pamphlet contained numerous footnotes in Chinese presumably intended to guide readers seeking to follow the English text. Some of the Chinese names and terms were given correctly, some were not, and the 'annoter' added a number of errors. (Mr Tang explained that 'tramped' meant 'trampled' in Chinese, that 'peach' meant 'pear', that 'militancy' meant 'military strength', and so on.)

A few American scholars evidently accepted the Canton piracy, 'The Autobiography of Mao Tse-tung', or other Chinese translations, as 'new sources', independent from RSOC.

In 1960, when I was in Peking, Mao Tse-tung told me that he had never written an 'autobiography' and that the story of his life as told to me was the only one of its kind. None is included in his official works. Mao added that he did not intend to write an autobiography.

At the end of the Long March all the archives of the Red Army were held in two dispatch boxes in Mao's cave. The details he related to me were almost entirely from memory and no man's memory is perfect. Besides unintentional (or intentional) omissions, he made a few mistakes in names and dates. For another thing, Mao spoke in a southern (Hunanese) dialect in which a northern 'Hu' becomes a 'Fu', a 'Shih' becomes 'Ssu', etc. The names of many Communist leaders now famous in China were then unknown, I did not always copy down every name in Chinese characters, and when it came to trans-literating – miles away from the Red areas, in Peking – I often failed to get a correct version even with the help of politically sophisticated Chinese. Benefiting from the research literature now available, I have been able to correct some errors, but it is not improbable that others still remain in this text.

Except for such minor corrections as are acknowledged above, or in footnotes, I have left Mao's personal recollections untouched, but in some annotations I have attempted to widen the perspective and sharpen the focus of his account of events. Biographical data here about Mao's co-workers and rivals may also help to illuminate certain happenings. For the reader's immediate convenience some highlights of Mao's career down to 1968 are summarized below.

Following the Sian Incident (1936) Mao moved his headquarters to Yenan. In January 1937, he became chairman of the directorate of K'ang Ta ('Resist-Japan University'), a key post in that transitional period. In the same year he wrote *On Practice* and *On Contradiction*, followed in 1938 by *On Protracted War*. Prior to publication all were delivered as lectures at K'ang Ta (he told me in 1960) attended by PB and CC members. In August 1937, at a meeting of the PB, enlarged by CC members (the Lochuan Conference), Mao's leadership as chairman was confirmed. Chang Kuo-t'ao, condemned for his 'rightism' and violations of PB orders, was invited to confess his errors. He did so only superficially; in the following year he voluntarily left the Red areas to work for Chiang Kai-shek. With his departure practically the last open knowledge of any serious challenge to Mao's supremacy vanished until some intraparty controversies were publicly exhumed in 1966–7.

During the decade 1939–40 Mao wrote more political essays and evolved his military concepts, many originally expounded first as lectures at K'ang Ta and the Party school of which he was president. (See Bibliography.) At the Seventh CCP Congress, in 1945, Mao was elected chairman of the CC and PB. After writing *On Coalition Government* he went to Chungking with Chou En-lai (August 1945) but failed to realize his ideas there. Civil war was resumed in June 1946, and Mao became PLA C-in-C, with Chu Teh as field commander. Retreating from KMT-occupied Yenan to the mountains of Shansi in 1947, Mao planned operations with Chou En-lai, Jen Pi-shih, Ch'en Yi, P'eng Teh-huai and others, then recovered Yenan and the whole North-West region in 1948.

In 1949, Mao's *On the People's Democratic Dictatorship* provided the framework for the provisional people's government (of various classes), set up in Peking, of which he became chairman. Late in 1949 he went to Moscow (his first trip abroad), where he and Chou En-lai negotiated the thirty-year Sino-Soviet treaty of alliance signed in 1950. Following the Korean War (in which Mao's full role has yet to be revealed) adoption of the constitution formally established the CPR, and in 1954 the NPC elected Mao chairman and chief of state. At the Eighth Congress of the CCP (1956) Mao was re-elected chairman of the CC and the PB; thus he became both the titular head of the governmental superstructure and the leader of the Party.

In 1957 Mao led China's delegation to Moscow's fortieth-anniversary celebrations of the October Revolution and there signed the manifesto of the Communist and Workers' parties of sixty-four countries. While in Moscow, Mao made a speech in which he proclaimed Communist world strategic superiority, which he described as a 'turning point' of an 'East Wind prevailing over the West Wind'. Tacit rejection of Mao's 'turning point' theses by Khrushchev – whose 'thaw' in the cold war was already well advanced – marked the beginning of the end of Sino-Soviet collaboration against US imperialism, which became an open split by 1960.

Meanwhile the CCP CC had carried through an agrarian revolution in accordance with Mao's *Outlines of Agrarian Reform Law*, which phased agriculture through various stages of land distribution, cooperatives, and basic collectivization. Major industry was nationalized and capitalism was transformed, with private ownership of small enterprises merging into full state ownership and operation. CC directives under Mao revolutionized the social, cultural, and political life of the country and introduced state planning. In 1957, Mao's *On the Correct Handling of Contradictions Among the People* (which recognized the continuation of class contradictions after a proletarian seizure of power) launched the brief-lived 'Hundred Flowers' period of free speech and free criticism – to reveal widespread Party and extra-Party dissatisfaction with the 'democratic dictatorship'. A drastic purge of 'rightists' soon followed.

Hard upon the 'rectification' came Mao's Great Leap Forward and the communes. Some experiments of the controversial GLF (such as backyard steel-making) were later acknowledged as errors. The communes were soon abandoned in the cities but they persisted, in form, in the countryside. Khrushchev ridiculed both the GLF and the communes as 'adventurism' and attributed China's food crisis and the 'disaster years' of 1959–62 to Mao's innovations.

At the Lushan Conference of the CC, in August 1959, Defence Minister P'eng Teh-huai was dismissed from office. It was known that he had opposed Mao's 'general line,' the GLF, communes, and 'politics in command' (vs 'economism' or pragmatism) and had sought to heal the break with the USSR. Not until a year after the launching of the GPCR (1966) and its attack on President Liu Shao-ch'i, however, did the Maoist press reveal something of the depth of the Party crisis of that period, and the ill-repaired split it had occasioned. Only at that time, also, did it become apparent that Mao had not altogether voluntarily retired from his post of chairmanship of the government in favour of Liu Shao-ch'i at the end of 1959. Evidently Marshal P'eng's dismissal (he was succeeded by Lin Piao) had been compensated for by some modifications in Mao's powers and policies, and loss of prestige within the CC.

China's partial economic recovery in 1963 and 1964, accompanied by Lin Piao's egalitarian army reforms and a 'socialist [re]education' campaign in the countryside and among youth, foreshadowed the GPCR, the Red Guards, and a renewed contest between what may be inadequately termed Party ideologues versus pragmatists, or revolutionary purists versus politician technocrats, in dispute over whether the Party machine would command the Mao cult or Mao would command the machine. Pragmatists could be seen as 'revisionists' of Maoist doctrine both at home and abroad, especially of its total irreconcilability with post-Stalinist Soviet doctrine, called 'Khrushchevism'. Achievement of the atomic bomb (October 1964) was acclaimed as a fruit of 'self-reliance' by the Maoists and China's hydrogen bomb, in 1967, was likewise a product of the Thought of Mao. In 1965 there were unprecedented demonstrations of adoration and veneration of Mao and other signs of a coming all-out counter-offensive against revisionists. No doubt the American armed intervention in Vietnam also helped detonate the raw materials of internal combustion in a struggle for power which broke fully into the open in China in 1966.

Circumstances under which Mao managed to put through a resolution at the eleventh plenary session of the Eighth Party Congress which launched the GPCR, later utilized to attack many leaders who voted for it, were paradoxical. Evidently the meeting followed attempts by a CC group at a coup intended either to secure Mao's effective retirement or at least to bring the Cult under their control. Those involved included the PLA chief of staff, Lo Jui-ch'ing, a vice-premier; Ulanfu, the Mongol leader who was the only non-Han vice-premier in the PB; Li Ching-ch'uan, Party and PLA leader in South-West China;

former defence minister P'eng Teh-huai; Wang En-mao, commander of the Sinkiang region; Mayor P'eng Chen, boss of the North China CC and high in the PB; Vice-Premier Lu Ting-yi, PB member and CC propaganda chief; and various other CC leaders later alleged to have had support from President Liu Shao-ch'i, first vice-chairman of the Party and Mao's designated successor, and Vice-Premier Teng Hsiao-p'ing, general secretary of the CC and the PB standing committee. Subsequent developments singled out Liu Shao-ch'i and Teng Hsiao-p'ing as prime targets of GPCR resolution. Yet at the CC meeting itself their supporters were sufficiently powerful to re-elect them to the PB, albeit in downgraded positions.

Evidently Mao had possessed strength enough in the CC to win sanction for the GPCR but not formally to attack and depose President Liu in a frontal assault on the whole Party-state bureaucratic administrative apparatus largely built up by Liu and by Teng Hsiao-p'ing. The alternative was to mobilize and indoctrinate millions of extra-Party youths, and Red Guards reinforced by the PLA, to overthrow key anti-Mao bureaucrats ('revisionists') regionally entrenched in power. In 1966 it became clear that Liu was the No. 1 target of the GPCR among 'the handful of those in the Party in authority who are taking the capitalist road'. But not until August 1967 did the Maoist press (seized from the revisionists by 'rebel revolutionaries'), having depicted Liu as 'China's Khrushchev', openly charge him and his accomplices with concrete acts of collusion with Marshal P'eng Teh-huai.

Now publication of excerpts from the 1959 CC resolution revealed that P'eng, Lo Fu and a few others who enjoyed the 'shelter of the bourgeois headquarters headed by China's Khrushchev' had 'viciously attacked' Mao's 'general line' at the Lushan (1959) meeting, calling it 'left adventurism' and 'petty bourgeois fanaticism'. According to P'eng the GLF was a 'rush of blood to the brain', 'a high fever', and the communes, 'set up too early', were 'a mess'. After P'eng's dismissal Liu himself had deplored the effects on Party unity, had repeated some of Peng's criticisms, and had called the economic crisis 'three parts natural calamities and seven parts man-made disasters'. What the farmers needed, he was accused of having told cadres, were the incentives of larger private plots and wider free markets. What small enterprise needed was less centralization and more freedom to produce for consumer demand. That was more or less (after 1960) what they had got. And what the country needed was 'open opposition both among the people and within the Party'. And that too was what the Red Guards had got – but open opposition to Liu Shao-ch'i, the man for material incentives, and not to Mao, who stressed motivations of service, class struggle, and revolutionary glory.

Now it was also revealed that P'eng Teh-huai had secretly written an 80,000-word book amplifying his critique, and had circulated it among army and CC leaders. Among those who attended the eleventh plenary session the book had probably been carefully read. Once the GPCR was launched P'eng's views must have found far wider circulation – not least in Szechuan, where P'eng apparently had found sanctuary and sympathizers. After more than a year of ceaseless Red Guard pressure (which Mao had insisted must eschew violence and win by persuasion alone – advice partly ineffective) evidently neither Liu Shao-ch'i nor Teng Hsiao-p'ing had offered satisfactory 'confessions' of error. Nor had P'eng Teh-huai or, as far as is known, any of the other 'top persons in the Party taking the capitalist road'.

In 1970 Mao indicated to me that his final breach with Liu came in January 1965 and that the two main causes were Liu's refusal to carry out a thoroughgoing purge of bourgeois elements in the Party bureaucracy and his continued efforts to reactivate the Sino-Soviet *entente*.

Not even to secure Russia's backing in the event of a Sino-American war would Mao compromise over ideological and national differences, as Liu and others may have sought to do. Nor would he compromise to preserve the unity and power of the Party at the expense of his own prestige – which he identified absolutely with China's survival. Indeed the GPCR aimed at no less than to destroy that Party bureaucratic power over which Mao's Thought could not command absolute authority. It sought to seize and place that power in the hands of persons and producers (especially youth) committed only to Mao, of those in the party committed only to Mao, and of the army over which – in so far as Lin Piao could command it – Mao's Thought reigned supreme. In this new 'three-way alliance' all but the Mao-dedicated among the managerial élite would be thrown out or downgraded, while a new ruling system – bypassing at least part of a whole generation of Party-trained aspirants to power – might emerge in real control of the means of production and administration.

In 1968 there was set up a network of 7 May schools of Mao Tsetung where in largely rural but some urban settings tens of thousands of Party cadres, many of high rank, were sent for re-education. Something like ninety per cent of the Party members had been suspended in 1966–7, but by 1970 Premier Chou En-lai told the author that all but about ten per cent had been or soon would be reinstated. By July 1971, all but three provinces had reconstituted provincial Party committees formed mainly around a nucleus of revolutionary committees which grew out of the three-way alliance mentioned above, which seized power from the old Party hierarchy during the GPCR. The Ninth Party Congress in April 1969 hailed the 'final victory' of the GPCR and Lin Piao proclaimed that henceforth anyone who criticized or opposed Mao Tse-tung Thought in any form or for whatever reason would be 'denounced and punished' by the whole nation.

In China's 3,000 years of written history the combination of Mao's achievements was perhaps unique. Others had ridden to power on the backs of the peasants and left them in the mud; Mao sought to keep them permanently erect. Dreamer, warrior, politician, ideologist, poet, egoist, revolutionary destroyer-creator, Mao had led a movement to uproot one fourth of humanity and turn a wretched peasantry into a powerful modern army which united a long-divided empire; provided a system of thought shaped by valid Chinese needs and aspirations; brought scientific and technical training to millions and literacy to the masses; laid the foundations of a modernized economy, able to place world-shaking nuclear power in Chinese hands; restored China's self-respect and world respect for or fear of China; and set up examples of self-reliance for such of the earth's poor and oppressed as dared to rebel. No wonder Mao refused to yield ground to those who sought to revise his success formula.

In December 1970 the author conversed with Mao in his Peking home for five hours, when he found Mao in good health but still 'not satisfied' with the results of the revolution. For a preliminary report of this conversation see *Epoca*, Milan, April/4 May 1971, ibid, 2 May 1971, and *Life*, 2 May 1971.

Mif, Pavel (p. 484) was Stalin's appointee to the CMT Far Eastern Department to replace Lominadze after the latter joined Syrtzov in an attempt to overthrow Stalin. Mif had been on the CMT 'China Commission' as early as 1925; as a teacher at Sun Yat-sen University in Moscow he helped to expel pro-Trotsky Chinese students there in 1927. He was made director of the university in 1927, when he also took over the CMT China desk and eliminated Earl Browder as chief of the CMT Far Eastern Bureau. Mif's role as brood-hen of his Chinese students sent back to take over the CCP leadership is briefly described in Part Four, Chapter 6, note 3. His influence waned after Mao's rise in 1935 but he continued to serve in the CMT until 1938, after which he became a joint editor of *Tikhii Ocean*, organ of the USSR Council of the Institute of Pacific Relations. Mif's real name was given as Mikhail Alexsandrovich Fortus, and his death put at 1937, by Dieter Heinzig. See Bibliography.

Nieh Ho-t'ing (p. 295n.) was born in Hu-yuan, Anhui, in 1908, in a family of small landlords. After primary school he studied one year in the Han-Mei (Chinese-American) Middle School in Anyuan, then graduated from a two-year teachers' training school in Anyuan. Involved in revolutionary student activity, he fled from an arrest order, to Nanchang, where he entered a military academy. In 1924 he joined the CCP and was sent back to Anhui, where he taught for a year and organized a Party cell. After April 1927, he took part in an Anhui uprising which failed. He participated in the Nanchang and Canton uprisings, and escaped to Hongkong. He worked underground in Shanghai (1928–9) and entered Kiangsi in 1930. As a Red division commander he was wounded, recovered in time for the Changsha victory, and fought throughout the Kiangsi campaigns. In 1935 he was deputy chief of the political department of the Red Army. In the war against Japan he organized large guerrilla forces in Shansi and Hopei. A member of the CC and of the National Defence Council, he seemed somewhat eclipsed after the dismissal of P'eng Teh-huai in 1959.

Nieh Jung-chen (p. 377) was in 1967 a member of the CC, a vice-premier of the State Council, vice-chairman of the National Defence Council, a member of the Party military affairs committee, and chairman of the Scientific and Technological Commission to which China's nuclear programme was entrusted. He was born near Chungking, Szechuan, in 1899, in a rich peasant family. He left Chungking Middle School to join the Work-Study group that went to France in 1920. He worked part time in the Schneider munitions plant, then entered a 'workers' college' in Belgium, studied natural science two years, and acquired some technical training as an electrician. In France he met Chou En-lai, studied Marxism under the French instructor who taught Li Fu-ch'un, and joined the CCP by way of the branch CYL in France. He learned French and some German and English. In 1924 he studied in the Red Army Military Academy in Moscow for six months, and in 1925–6 was secretary of the political department of Whampoa Academy. He participated in the Nanchang Uprising, as political commissar in Yeh T'ing's division, took part in the Canton Commune, and from 1931 was in the political department of the Red Army in Kiangsi. He made the Long March and in 1936 was chief of staff of the First Red Army Corps. During the Resistance War he became famous as an organizer of guerrilla forces in the Wu-T'ai Mountains, and after the

Liberation War was made one of China's ten marshals of the PLA. In 1966 he entered the PB as a full member, with duties of the highest responsibility, but his seat in the PB proved temporary. The Academy of Sciences of which he headed the nuclear sciences development came under attack in a late phase of the GPCR and Nien himself was criticized. In 1969 he was re-elected to the CC, however, and in 1970 was seated in a honoured position in the review of the October anniversary parade. He retained his important post as coordinator of nuclear science and operations.

P'eng Chen (p. 478), the dynamic former mayor of Peking, stood only twenty-ninth in CC precedence but was listed as ninth in PB rank before his seeming political eclipse in 1966. It was under Liu Shao-ch'i that P'eng rose to prominence in the Party for his work (1935-9) in the North China Bureau. Their close relationship persisted when, while P'eng was Peking Party secretary, and first deputy to Teng Hsiao-p'ing on the CC secretariat, Chairman Liu became the main target of the Red Guards among 'those in the Party in authority who are taking the capitalist road'.

Born in Shansi in 1899, in an impoverished gentry family, P'eng attended a normal school where he was infected by the May Fourth Movement. He drifted into radical company, studied Marxism in the CYL in 1922, helped organize railway workers, and was briefly jailed in Peking. He joined the CCP in 1926 but played no significant role until he began to organize students and teachers in the Peking-Tientsin area in 1935, at a time when Liu Shao-ch'i was chief of the bureau there (underground) and K'e Cheng-shih was his first deputy. In 1937 he visited Yenan and was assigned to work in Shansi and Hopei. From 1939 to 1942 he taught at the Party school in Yenan and, as a deputy director under Lin Piao, had special responsibilities for indoctrination in 'rectification' principles. Elected to the CC in 1945, he accompanied Lin Piao to Manchuria and served there (1946-9) as Party deputy under Ch'en Yun, after which he became a deputy secretary of the Peking Party committee (1949-66) and later first secretary and mayor. Re-elected to the PB in 1956, he was No. 2 under Teng Hsiao-p'ing in the CC secretariat, the operational arm of the PB.

P'eng began to emerge as CCP CC spokesman abroad when he denounced Khrushchev at Bucharest in 1960 for criticizing Mao and advocating coexistence with the USA. Subsequently he led various delegations abroad (1961-3). This work was climaxed (1965) by a long speech in Indonesia which bitterly denounced Russia and contained all the essential exhortations repeated later in Lin Piao's call for world revolution under Mao's banner – 'Long Live the Victory of the People's War !'

In Mao's 16 May (1966) circular P'eng was denounced and disgraced as a revisionist. He was also accused by the press and by Red Guard posters of planning a 'February [1966] coup' against Mao, but the charges rested publicly unsubstantiated two years later. Stripped of his posts in the spring of 1966 and succeeded by Li Hsueh-feng as Peking Party secretary, he was variously reported killed or a suicide. But in April 1967, he was recognized by a foreign visitor when seen (partly bald, of medium height, a briefcase under his arm) strolling through the Imperial Palace grounds of Peking, a stone's throw from Mao Tse-tung's residence. Official Peking press vilification of P'eng as a 'renegade', 'revisionist', 'counter-revolutionary', and 'anti-Party minister' continued throughout 1967 but no confession by P'eng was yet forthcoming.

Although P'eng was not publicly expelled from the Party he was heavily attacked during the Ninth Party Congress. By 1971 he was totally discredited and believed to be under protective arrest.

P'eng P'ai (p. 183), a member of the Central Committee, held views on the poor peasants as a 'main force' of the revolution very similar to Mao Tse-tung's. In the same month (November 1928) that Mao set up a soviet at Chingkangshan, P'eng P'ai led formation of the Hailufeng Soviet on the Kwangtung provincial border. Hailufeng was destroyed by KMT forces and P'eng P'ai was executed in 1929. See *TOSOTR*.

P'eng Teh-huai (p. 197) was deputy commander-in-chief of the Eighth Route Army, under Chu Teh. He successfully expanded guerrilla war against Japan (1937–45). As deputy commander of the North-West Border Area during the Second Civil War (1946–9), P'eng defeated KMT forces which invaded Shensi. In 1950 he succeeded Lin Piao as commander-in-chief of the Chinese 'Volunteers' in North Korea and held that position until the truce with the United Nations forces. As a marshal of the army (1955), a member of the PB, and Minister of Defence, P'eng was until 1960 the chief liaison between the PLA and the Soviet military advisers during the modernization of China's armed forces and basic construction of modern military industries.

As bitter Sino-Soviet ideological and strategic differences intensified during 1957–9, P'eng apparently favoured placating Russia to gain time and strength. He did not believe China was yet ready to 'go it alone'. He also opposed Mao's 'self-reliance' strategy and a return to Yenan guerrilla-style training in the army. In September 1959, P'eng was defeated in a fateful meeting of the Party and defence chiefs and was dismissed from his posts. Under Peng's successor, Lin Piao, Russian influences were extirpated from the army. (See RNORC and TOSOTR.) In 1967 the Red Guard and official press aired charges against P'eng Teh-huai as a counter-revolutionary who conspired with Liu Shao-ch'i against Mao as early as 1959.

During 1967–9 P'eng remained a principal target of Party polemics during the Ninth Congress. As the subject of Wu Han's *Hai Jui Dismissed from Office* (see Chiang Ch'ing), a play which by analogy attacked Mao Tse-tung for forcing P'eng from the office of defence minister in favour of Lin Piao in 1959, he was held guilty of collusion with reactionary and revisionist elements who all but overthrew Mao Tse-tung as supreme commander and Party leader. The author could learn nothing of his whereabouts when in Peking in 1971. For some documentation on the P'eng-Mao break see *The Case of P'eng Teh-huai*, Bibliography.

Po I-po (p. 478) rose steadily in the Party hierarchy, reaching the PB in 1956. He was re-elected in August 1966, but in 1967 came under attack by the Red Guards for alleged past sympathy with the policies of Chairman Liu Shao-ch'i.

Po's real name was Po Shu-ts'un and he was born in Tingshang, Shansi, in 1907, with a gentry family background. He joined the CCP in Taiwan in 1926 and later became a student leader at Peking University. He was arrested and imprisoned in Peking in 1933. Released in 1936, he may have been one of those Communists who recanted, in that year, on authorization of the regional Party leader (Liu Shao-ch'i), in order to secure their freedom – a crime for which Hsu Ping came under attack as late as 1967. Po worked as a political commissar in North China guerrilla areas throughout the Second World War and the Second Civil (Liberation) War. He specialized in financial and economic affairs and state planning from 1951 onward and held important supervisory powers over major industrial ministries down to 1967.

Po I-po was openly attacked in 1968 for sheltering Liu Shao-ch'i sympathizers in his ministries and favouring 'economist' ideas akin to Soviet revisionism. He was dropped from the PB and was not re-elected to the CC at the Ninth Party Congress. Eventual rehabilitation in the Party seemed possible.

Po Ku (Ch'in Pang-hsien) (p. 290) died in an airplane crash in 1946, but since he was general secretary of the Party, chief antagonist of Mao from 1932 to 1935, and responsible for policies that Mao in 1945 asserted had 'cost more Communist lives than enemies'', some knowledge of his career remains important to an understanding of Party history.

Born in 1908, the only son of a county magistrate, Ch'in Pang-hsien graduated from a Soochow technical school at seventeen, and then entered the CCP-organized Shanghai University, studied English, and joined the CCP. Sent to Russia in 1926, he studied four years at the CMT's Sun Yat-sen University, where, like his classmate Wang Ming (q.v.), he became fluent in Russian and in Marxist-Leninist doctrine. In 1930 he returned to China as one of Pavel Mif's 'Twenty-eight Bolsheviks', and helped Mif and Wang Ming discredit Li Li-san and put Wang Ming in the leadership, although Hsiang Chung-fa remained nominally general secretary. With the latter's execution by the KMT in 1931, Wang Ming (aged twenty-four) replaced him, and Po Ku (aged twenty-three) became Wang Ming's first deputy. Later that year Wang Ming returned to Moscow and became resident delegate on the CEC of the CMT. Po Ku was elected general secretary of the CCP CC and PB. In the protracted struggle between 'Moscow-oriented' and 'native' Marxists for dominance in the Chinese Party leadership (which reflected differences over the relative importance of the cities and the countryside in the conquest of power) Po Ku personified the former and Mao Tse-tung the latter. For a brief chronological digest of events of that struggle see Part Four, Chapter 6, note 3.

At the end of the Long March Po Ku continued in the PB, and in 1936 the author found him acting as chairman of the provisional North-West Soviet Government. In December 1936, he accompanied Chou En-lai to Sian during the Incident there. After the KMT-CCP truce of 1937 he became propaganda director in the Eighth Route Army's liaison mission in Chungking (1938–40), and then was first editor of the *Liberation Daily* in Yenan.

Po Ku's name was linked with Wang Ming's once more during the rectification movement (1942). By 1945 his dwindling influence was indicated in his decline to No. 44 position in the CC, to which he was re-elected shortly before his death. Po Ku was married to Liu Ch'un-hsien, also Moscow-trained, whom he divorced. He fathered seven children. For interviews with him, and his autobiography as told to the author, see RNORC.

P'u Yi, Emperor (p. 141), abdicated from the throne of the Ch'ing Dynasty in 1911, when the ancient empire collapsed and the first Republic was established. He was then five years old. After a brief attempt at a restoration by militarists, he fled in 1915 to the Japanese Concession in Tientsin. In 1934 he left Tientsin with Japanese officers who installed him in occupied Manchuria as puppet emperor of the puppet empire of Manchukuo. In 1950 he was seized by the Russians during their occupation of Manchuria. In 1950 he fell into the Chinese Communists' hands. After a long period of 'thought remoulding' he was a common gardener in the Botanical Institute when the author met him in Peking in 1960. By 1965 he was a member of the Academy of History – working on the archives of his imperial ancestors – and held a seat in the CPP CC. He had divorced his several imperial brides and, for the first time, married a woman of his own choice, a Chinese nurse. He had also written an interesting autobiography, *From Emperor to Citizen*, Peking, 1965 (*The Last Manchu*, NY, 1967), when he died in Peking, of cancer, in 1967.

Shao Li-tzu (p. 54), a native of Ningpo, Chekiang, remained with the Nationalists until after Pearl Harbour, when he favoured a coalition government between the Kuomintang and the Communists. He helped to form the CPP CC, which in 1949 represented a fusion of non-Communist but anti-Chiang Kai-shek 'united front' groups and parties, including a 'revolutionary Kuomintang'. In 1949 the CPP CC, with 662 delegates present (Communist-led), formally adopted a 'Common Programme' and an Organic Law for its own existence, to proclaim the People's Republic of China. In 1954 the Conference adopted a constitution and announced an election to be held to choose delegates to an NPC, to which it then transferred power. The CPP CC continued to exist also, however, to represent non-Communist elements. Shao Li-tzu remained one of its factotums. In 1967, at the age of eighty-eight, he still held minor government posts and frequently appeared at state functions.

Soong (Sung) Ch'ing-ling (Mme Sun Yat-sen) (p. 116n.), who married Dr Sun Yat-sen in Japan (1914), was a graduate of Wesleyan College, Macon, Georgia. She was born in Shanghai (*circa* 1895), the second of three sisters, of whom the youngest was Soong Mei-ling (Mme Chiang Kai-shek), in a family originally from Hainan Island. After the death of Dr Sun, his widow remained a member of the CEC of the KMT but continued to uphold a pro-Communist, or leftist, interpretation of his principles, and declined office in Chiang Kai-shek's government. In the CPR she held leading positions in women's organizations and in the fields of child care and education. In 1968 she was a vice-chairman of the NPC, an office she had held since the inception of the People's Republic. After the vilification of Liu Shao-ch'i (chairman of the NPC and chief of state), Soong Ch'ing-ling received foreign envoys on official occasions, as acting chief of state.

In 1971 Soong Ch'ing-ling retained office as vice-chairman of the

NPC. Her symbolic role as link between the Kuomintang and the CCP assumed new importance, as negotiations for a rendition to mainland China of Kuomintang-ruled Taiwan required some interim transitional formula for the peaceful assimilation of that island which might re-invoke past Kuomintang-Communist collaboration. For a profile of Mme Sun see *JTTB* but add important corrections given to the author by Mme Sun in Peking in 1971. These concern her family background. Her father, son of a trader in Haikou on Hainan Island, Kwantung province, was descended from the Hakka or 'guest people' who had migrated from the mainland centuries earlier. Hakkas included northern soldiers of the Sung Dynasty armies who were defeated by the Mongols, and as refugees in Hainan often were called Sung (or Soong).

A brother of Soong Ching-ling's grandfather emigrated to New York and established a business in Chinese goods. He had no children and when, as a boy, Ch'ing-ling's father arrived in New York, having been carried thither on an American sailing vessel, his uncle adopted his nephew and sent him to school. Through the help of a friend of his uncle-father, General Julian S. Carr, of North Carolina, young Soong was able to enter Duke University and later went to Vanderbilt in Tennessee. He was expected to become a missionary and indeed on his arrival in Shanghai he founded a Christian family and a printing company which published Bibles. He also helped Sun Yat-sen produce anti-Manchu underground literature, and Soong himself became a secret member of Dr Sun's *T'ung Meng-hui* revolutionary party, precursor of the Kuomintang. Soong Ch'ing-ling's mother was a direct descendant of Hsu Kuang-chi, a distinguished scholar of the Ming Dynasty who produced a still-valued Encyclopedia of Agriculture. The Shanghai suburb called Hsukuauchi (Siccawei, in Shanghai dialect) was named after him. Cf. also BDRC.

Su Yu (p. 217) was in 1966 among the few generals under the age of sixty who were veterans of the Nanchang Uprising, the 'birth of the Red Army'. Chief of the PLA General Staff (1954–8), when P'eng Teh-huai was defence minister, he seemed somewhat eclipsed after P'eng's dismissal in 1959. In 1966 he was re-elected to the CC and held a high position as a member of the Party military affairs committee.

Born in 1909 in Fukien, he attended the Second Hunan Normal School, where in 1926 he joined the CYL branch established by Mao Tse-tung. In 1927 he enlisted in Yeh T'ing's army, with about 1,000 other student members of the CYL-CCP, in time to participate in the Uprising. Two years later he led a division in the Fourth Red Army, and by 1932 was chief of staff of the Tenth Army. During the Long

March he stayed behind as chief of staff to Fang Chih-min. After Fang's capture and execution Su took command. His rear guard force later merged with Ch'en Yi's army, which in 1937 became part of the New Fourth Army, of which Su Yu was vice-commander. Thereafter, as Ch'en's deputy, his career ran parallel to Ch'en's until after the establishment of the CPR. Su held many important administrative and political responsibilities besides the military posts mentioned above.

Sun Ming-chiu (p. 431) was in 1964 reportedly a vice-admiral in the naval forces of the CPR.

Sun Yat-sen, Mme. See Soong Ch'ing-ling.

T'an Chen-lin (p. 195n.) was born in 1912, a native of Kiangsi. In the Party PB from 1956, he was a specialist in agricultural policies who came under Red Guard attack in 1966. A follower of Mao Tse-tung since the Autumn Harvest Uprising (1927), he supported Mao's military concepts in Kiangsi in opposition to the 'Twenty-eight Bolsheviks', and was a Long March veteran. He played a role in the Resistance War at the highest level of political and military command. During the Second Civil War he was a member of the Front Committee led by Teng Hsiao-p'ing, which directed all the PLA forces in eastern China. In 1966 he stood eighteenth in Politburo rank – a vice-premier and a member of the CC secretariat. Despite criticism by Red Guards he appeared in public with Mao in May 1967. T'an Chen-lin was dropped as a vice-premier and also from the PB. The Ninth Party Congress of 1969 did not re-elect him either to the CC or PB, and in 1971 he was said to have 'waved the red flag in order to defeat the red flag' – that is, surreptitiously opposed the complete dissolution of the Liu Shao-ch'i régime.

T'ao Chu (p. 492), a Hunanese born in 1906, joined the CCP about 1927 and after 1930 was active in the Oyuwan Soviet with Li Hsien-nien. He held responsible posts representing the CC in various armies throughout the Resistance War and the Second Civil War, and after 1949 became a leading Party secretary in South China. In 1962 he was vice-premier of the SC of the CPR and chief of the Party bureau in the Central-South region. At the eleventh plenary session of the Eighth Party Congress (August 1966) he was jumped from No. 95 rank in the CC to the fourth highest rank in PB membership, as published after that meeting. He emerged as chief among those responsible for carrying through the GPCR. By November 1966 he had been discredited as a 'pragmatist-revisionist' and had fled to obscurity in the South. Judging from attacks in Ch'en Po-ta's official press on T'ao Chu's two books, formerly used as training texts for youth (*Ideals, Integrity and Spiritual*

Life and *Thinking, Feeling and Literary Talent*), he had overemphasized the material rewards promised by communism and understated the importance of continued class struggle as taught by Mao. Perhaps more significant than the formal charges, Ch'en Po-ta took over T'ao Chu's tasks as propaganda-culture chief.

Teng Fa (p. 65) was a PB member at the time of his death in the airplane crash, April 1946, which also killed Po Ku, Yeh T'ing, and Wang Jo-fei.

Teng Hsiao-p'ing (p. 143), after 1956 general secretary to the CCP CC, became a principal target, during the GPCR, among 'those in the Party in authority who are taking the capitalist road'. He was born in 1904 in Chiating, Szechuan. After a rudimentary schooling he joined the Work-Study Plan and went to France in 1920. When the author met him at Yu Wang Pao, Shensi (19 August 1936), Teng said that he did not attend school in France but spent his five years there as a worker. He learned Marxism from French workers and became a Chinese member of the French Communist Party, from which he transferred to the CCP. In 1925 he returned to China by way of Russia, where he 'studied several months'. General Feng Yu-hsiang, commander of the Kuominchun ('People's Army'), was visiting in Moscow in 1926. Teng joined Feng's headquarters and became a dean of a training school Feng set up at San-yuan, near Sian. In 1927 he helped form a peasant army in Kiangsi. After the counter-revolution Teng worked in the Shanghai Party underground until 1929. He then formed the Seventh Red Army at Lungchow, Kwangsi. 'The Lungchow Soviet had relations with the Annamites [Vietnamese] who began the worker-peasant rebellion in 1930. French airplanes bombed Lungchow and we shot one down,' Teng told the author in 1936. Combined French and Nationalist forces destroyed the Lungchow soviet movement, as well as the Vietnamese forces, but the latter maintained ties with the Chinese guerrillas. With remnants of the Seventh Army, Teng made his way through Kwangsi and Kiangsi to Chingkangshan. With his followers reorganized as the Eighth Army, he took part in the capture of Changsha in 1930. From 1932 to 1934 Teng was in the political department of the Red Army and edited *Hung Hsing* (*Red Star*). In that period he supported the 'Lo-Ming line', which followed guerrilla tactics and strategy advocated by Mao Tse-tung, in opposition to the prevailing PB leadership. In 1935, at Tsunyi, he voted for Mao to lead the CCP PB.

During the Long March Teng Hsiao-p'ing was deputy commander and political commissar of Liu Po-ch'eng's Twelfth Division. He backed Mao Tse-tung in his dispute with Chang Kuo-t'ao at Maoerhkai, and he completed the Long March with Mao's columns. In 1936 he was Nieh Jung-chen's deputy as political commissar of the First Army Corps in Kansu.

At the start of the Resistance War in 1937, Teng became political commissar of the 129th Division commanded by Liu Po-ch'eng, with whose forces he was identified for the next twelve years. In 1943 Teng headed the general political department of the People's Revolutionary Military Council and entered the secretariat of the CC. At the Seventh Party Congress (Yenan, 1945) he became secretary of the CC and PB. Returning to the field with Liu Po-ch'eng, he served as chief of the General Front Committee, the supreme staff of all the PLA on the Central Plains, and was also political commissar of Liu Po-ch'eng's army of victory in Szechuan (1949). As such he carried out Mao's 'general strategic concepts' which led to the complete defeat of all Chiang Kai-shek's armies north of the Yangtze River. Teng became first secretary of the Party's South-West Bureau and concurrently a vice-chairman of the provisional government (1950–54). From 1952 to 1954 he was minister of finance and a member of the State Planning Commission. With formation of the NPC in 1954, he became a deputy premier and a deputy chairman of the National Defence Council. In 1956 the Eighth Congress of the CC restored the post of general secretary (which no longer carried the primary leadership role, however), and Teng was elected to that office. Teng wrote an introduction to the revised Party constitution of 1956 which included explicit warnings against 'cult of leadership' tendencies. Third in rank in the SC, Teng Hsiao-p'ing served as Acting Premier during Chou En-lai's absences from China (winter, 1963–4, and March 1965). At the August 1966 meeting of the CC, Teng was re-elected to the PB and listed sixth, as before, but was no longer vice-chairman of the Party or PB general secretary. Until December 1966, Teng Hsiao-p'ing and Liu Shao-ch'i both appeared on the stand with Mao to review the Red Guards, but after that became prime targets of wall poster attacks in Peking and elsewhere. Their followers in the Party and state apparatus were widely accused of sabotaging the GPCR and were driven from office by Red Guards (often with PLA help) in half a dozen major cities and provinces, but elsewhere they stubbornly clung to power. Teng's fate at this writing was undetermined.

Teng Tzu-hui (p. 197) during the Resistance and Second Civil wars resumed his ties in Fukien, where he was a veteran guerrilla leader, and carried out many responsible political, cultural, and military missions from 1937 onwards. Born in 1893, in Lungai, Fukien, he attended middle school in Amoy, studied briefly in Japan (1916), taught school, joined the KMT in 1925 and the CCP a year later. He was active throughout the Kiangsi Soviet period, notably with Chu Teh and Chang Ting-ch'eng. Often serving as deputy to directors of important tasks, and avoiding intraparty struggles, he remained a second-line though respected leader, who was re-elected to the CC in 1966. His standing unimpaired in 1969, he was re-elected by the Ninth Party Congress to the CC. Now (1971) nearing eighty, he belongs to the elder statesmen group, along with Chu Teh.

Teng Ying-ch'ao (Mme Chou En-lai) (p. 87) in 1956 ranked nineteenth in the list of CC members and was re-elected to the CC in 1966. She had continued her activities as a leader of women's organizations during and after the Resistance War and the Liberation War, and as a member of the NPC standing committee since 1955, but she played no conspicuous role in the GPCR as compared to her past prominence.

Born in 1903 in Hsinyang county, Honan, of the gentry (her mother tutored in the Yuan Shih-k'ai family), she studied at the First Girls' Normal School in Tientsin and then graduated from Peking Higher Normal School. A radical student, she was arrested in 1919 and briefly jailed. With Chou En-lai she helped found the Awakening Society (Chueh Wu She), and she joined the Work-Study Plan, with Chou and others, to go to France. A member of the Chinese CYL in Paris, she returned to China in 1924, joined the CCP, married Chou, was elected to the KMT CEC (1926) and was the only prominent woman participant in the Nanchang Uprising. In 1928 she went to Russia with Chou, and returned with him to China to do underground work (1928–31), until she entered Soviet Kiangsi, where she led the women's work department of the CC. She was one of only thirty-five women who made the Long March, during which she developed pulmonary tuberculosis and had to be carried on a stretcher. In 1937, while convalescing outside Peking, she was endangered when Japanese occupied the city. The author helped her escape to guerrilla territory. From 1938 onwards she played a leading role in the political organization of women both in China and internationally, frequently travelling with her husband. Mme Chou shared the danger and hardships of her husband's life in an extremely close relationship since their schooldays. Her urbanity and simplicity, mixed with patriotic and revolutionary ardour, won her nation-wide respect even among her enemies. Teng Ying-ch'ao was re-elected to the CC at the Ninth Party Congress (1969) and appeared at the reviewing stand in October 1970, but failing health is said to limit her Party activities.

Ting Ling (p. 145), born in Hunan in 1907, became China's best-known revolutionary woman writer. She studied at Peking University and Shanghai University, began to publish short stories in 1927, and married another noted writer, Hu Yeh-p'ing, who had joined the CCP in 1929. Ting Ling joined in 1931. Both were members of the semi-underground League of Left Writers, organized in Shanghai in 1929, and both were arrested by KMT authorities in 1933. Hu was the leader of a Shanghai ricksha-pullers' union and a CC member who supported Li Li-san and opposed Wang Ming. He was executed but Ting Ling was released in 1936, and went to Yenan the same year. There she wrote, taught, and published some articles which satirized the CCP, but were in sympathy with Mao Tse-tung's 'Talks at the Yenan Forum on Art and Literature'. In 1950 she was elected chairman of the Central Literary Institute.

Formally declared a rightist and 'anti-party' in 1957, Ting Ling refused to admit her 'mistakes'; she was expelled from the CCP and sent to a commune to undergo thought reform. *Sunshine over the Sangkan River*, which had won her a Stalin Award (1952), was withdrawn from sale in China, together with Ting Ling's other works. In 1960 the author was authoritatively told that Ting Ling was dismissed from the Party not because of her anti-Party literary works but because she had 'lied to the Party' about the circumstances under which she was released from prison in Nanking in 1936. For early data on Ting Ling see Snow, *Living China* (NY, 1937).

Ts'ai Ch'ang (p. 88), born in Hunan in 1900, a sister of Ts'ai Ho-sen (*q.v.*), received a classical education to a degree unusual for girls. She joined the Paris branch CYL with her husband, Li Fu-ch'un, and in 1924 became the first director of the women's department, CCP CC. She was one of thirty-five women on the Long March and the only woman member of the CC at the front in 1936. Re-elected to the CC in 1956, with the rank of No. 12 in the Party, she was also a delegate to the NPC from 1956, and chairman of the Democratic Women's Federation. A leader of the women's auxiliary of the Red Guards, she was re-elected to the CC in 1966 but played no conspicuous role in the GPCR after August of that year. Ts'ai Ch'ang was re-elected by the Ninth Party Congress to the CC but, like her husband, Li Fu-ch'un (*q.v.*), was thereafter seldom seen in public gatherings or featured as a Party leader.

Ts'ai Ho-sen (p. 88) probably had a greater influence than anyone else on Mao's thinking as a revolutionary 'internationalist'. The son of an intellectual family of Hunan, Ts'ai was among the first Chinese to join the Work-Study student emigrants to France in 1920, and perhaps the first Chinese to espouse the Communist cause there. Ts'ai Ch'ang, his sister, accompanied him to Europe. While in France he kept up a lively correspondence with Mao. After he returned to China, Ts'ai played a leading role in the CC during the 1925–7 period. At the time of his arrest and execution in 1927, by order of Chiang Kai-shek, he was a member of the Party PB. His wife, Hsiang Ching-wu, a fellow Hunanese whom he married in France, was an outstanding women's leader; she was executed in 1928.

Ts'ai Shu-fan (p. 399) was a trade-union leader and member of the CC at the time of his death (aged fifty-three) in an airplane crash, en route to the USSR, in 1958.

Tso Ch'uan (p. 234) was killed during the Patriotic War.

Tung Pi-wu (p. 136n.). Seven years Mao's senior, Tung was in 1967 one of two surviving Party founders in the PB, the other being Mao.

Born in 1886 in Huang-an county, Hupeh, in a large gentry family headed by scholars and teachers, Tung received a classical education and passed the imperial official (Confucian) examinations at the age of sixteen. He joined the Republican forces during the Hankow revolt of 1911 and became a member of Dr Sun Yat-sen's T'ung Meng Hui. In opposition to Yuan Shih-k'ai in 1913, he fled to Japan, joined Sun Yat-sen's inner circle there, and studied at the Tokyo Law College. From 1917 to 1920 Tung performed tasks for Dr Sun but gradually drew to the left in his thinking. Meanwhile he earned a living teaching in Hankow. In 1921, influenced by Ch'en Tu-hsiu and Li Han-chun, he journeyed to Shanghai, there to become a founder of the CCP. He then helped to organize the Hupeh provincial branch of the CP.

After the 'two-party alliance', Tung's liaison role became pivotal, for he was a veteran member of both the T'ung Meng Hui – precursor of the KMT – and the CP. In 1927 the counter-revolution caught his closest comrade, Li Han-chun, who was executed in Hankow. Tung himself narrowly escaped to Shanghai, disguised as a sailor. Next, in Russia, he spent four years at the CMT's Sun Yat-sen University. Not among the 'Twenty-eight Bolsheviks' (see Wang Ming, etc.), he became a Mao partisan and an important source of information about Sun Yat-sen University when he returned to China and went directly to Kiangsi, to become director of the newly organized Party school there. As an alternate member of the CC he supported Mao Tse-tung at the historic meeting at Tsunyi, in 1935. At the end of the Long March, Tung resumed his post as head of the Party school. A Party 'elder statesman', Tung played an advisory role in CCP diplomacy from 1936 onwards. He helped Chou

En-lai negotiate terms of the second united front at Nanking in 1937 and he was with Chou at CCP Chungking liaison headquarters 1938–45. As a member of the People's Political Council, a united-front consultative body set up by the Chiang Kai-shek government, Tung was the only Communist in a ten-member Chinese delegation to San Francisco in 1945 to establish the United Nations. Chang Han-fu (now Vice-Minister of Foreign Affairs) and Ch'en Chia-k'ang served as Tung's English-speaking secretaries.

Seventh-ranking member of the CC at the Seventh Congress, in 1945, he served in Chou En-lai's mission during negotiations for a coalition government (1945–7), mediated by General George C. Marshall. The first National Congress in 1954 elected Tung president of the Supreme People's Court. In 1959 he was elected vice-chairman of the People's Republic. In 1966 he was, however, dropped from eighth place in the PB to twelfth. The only high-ranking Communist to hold an imperial degree in the Classics, a loyal follower of the late Sun Yat-sen as well as Mao Tse-tung, widely respected among all classes in China, an extensive traveller abroad and held in high esteem among foreign Communists, modest, selfless and patriotic, Tung Pi-wu was a remarkably durable gentleman. At the Ninth Party Congress (1969) Tung Pi-wu was re-elected to the CC and the PB. In 1970 Chairman Mao remarked to the author that he and Tung Pi-wu were the lone survivors (in good standing) among the founders of the CCP in 1921.

Wang Ching-wei (p. 166n.) as a youthful rebel tried to assassinate the Manchu prime minister, Prince Kung, but the bomb he threw failed to explode. He was pardoned and became a hero, and, later, a rival of Chiang Kai-shek for leadership of the Kuomintang. In 1927 his Left Kuomintang government in Hankow collaborated with the Communists in a coalition formed after Chiang Kai-shek broke the two-party alliance. In a few weeks he also expelled the Reds and his régime soon disintegrated. In 1932 Wang was again Nationalist premier, at Nanking; in the same year he was ousted by Chiang Kai-shek. Returning to the Kuomintang in 1938, he once more quarrelled with Chiang. After accepting the post of premier of a puppet government sponsored by the Japanese, at Nanking, he died in disgrace in 1943.

Wang En-mao, a poor peasant born in Yunghsien, Kiangsi province (*circa* 1910), joined the Red Army in 1927 with his father and two brothers, was educated by the CP, and rose steadily as a combat commander. From the 1950s onwards Wang dominated North-West Party and military affairs. During the GPCR Wang commanded the vast Sinkiang military areas and the Army Production and Construction

Corps concerned with military installations. Attempts to extend the GPCR purge to Sinkiang caused sanguinary clashes, according to wall posters in Peking. Mao Tse-tung nevertheless was photographed offering a cordial handshake to Wang at a 1968 New Year's reception in the capital. He was, however, not re-elected to the CC in 1969.

Wang Ju-mei. See Huang Hua.

Wang Kuang-mei (Mme Liu Shao-ch'i) (p. 553) was a graduate of Peking University (Pei-ta) and a physics teacher when she met Liu shortly after the establishment of the PRC. She became his second wife, his first wife having been killed in Kiangsi. Mme Liu was a member of the CEC, All-China Women's Federation, and a delegate to the NPC from 1964. In 1964 she accompanied her husband on visits overseas. During the GPCR she led women's cadres at Tsing Hua University, but wall posters later attacked her for attempting to protect 'bourgeois' and 'revisionist' elements in the Party, and criticized her for wearing jewellery and patronizing fancy hairdressers. Allegedly her daughter denounced her and Liu before the Red Guards. She was evidently not in harmony with Mme Mao, deputy leader of the GPCR. Scorn and ridicule were her lot in accounts which appeared in publications advised by Mme Mao. The revolutionary committee set up at Tsing Hua subsequently accused Mme Liu of attempting to sabotage the GPCR's objective, (the removal of the pro-Liu Shao-ch'i president, Lu Ping, Party leader of the University), by bringing in work teams to 'attack all' for the purpose of smashing the 'rebels' along with the old régime, and replacing both with second-echelon Party cadres loyal to Chairman Liu. By 1971 Mme Liu had been dropped from all her former offices and called an American spy and renegade but without, as yet, undergoing any open trial.

Wang Ming (Ch'en Shao-yu) (p. 413) lost all his Party influence after 1942, but he remained important as a 'negative example' used to personify major leadership errors and issues underlying intraparty struggle and the Sino-Soviet split of the 1960s. He was leader of the 'Twenty-eight Bolsheviks' trained under Pavel Mif in Moscow when he became, at twenty-four, general secretary of the CCP and founded a PB régime which opposed Mao Tse-tung between 1931 and 1935.

Born in Anhui in 1907 to a prosperous gentry family, Ch'en joined the Socialist Youth Corps (later the CYL) while at middle school in Wuhan, then in 1923 enrolled in Shanghai University (established to train CP cadres). He was admitted to the CCP in 1925, and took the Party name Wang Ming. Sent to Russia to study at the CMT's Sun Yat-sen University (1925–7) he returned to China as interpreter for

Pavel Mif at the Fifth Congress of the CCP at Wuhan (July 1927). After the KMT-CP break he went back to Russia with Mif, who was made director of Sun Yat-sen University. He served Mif as interpreter at both the CMT and CCP Sixth congresses, held in Moscow (1928), and with Mif's help won leadership among those Chinese students at Sun Yat-sen University who became known as the 'Twenty-eight Bolsheviks'. They were at first a minority, who favoured Stalin against Trotsky. Most important were Po Ku, Lo Fu, Wang Chia-hsiang, Teng Fa, Yang Shang-k'un, and those elected to the CCP CC with Wang Ming, who himself (aged twenty-one) helped compose CMT directives sent to China.

In 1930 Wang Ming returned to China with Mif, then chief CMT delegate to the CCP, and helped him ease Earl Browder out of influence and out of China and then to unseat Li Li-san from PB leadership. At the Sixth Congress CC's Fourth Plenum, held underground in Shanghai in January 1931, Hsiang Chung-fa was confirmed as PB general secretary but, invoking Stalin's prestige, Mif manoeuvred Wang Ming into Li Li-san's place as head of the labour department and the PB's dominant figure. When Hsiang was executed later that year Wang Ming replaced him and put Po Ku, Lo Fu, and others in control of key PB organs. In the same year Wang was recalled to Moscow, where he became CCP resident delegate on the CEC of the CMT. As Pavel Mif's mouthpiece he published (1932) *The Two Lines*, in which he defined the current CMT line. In China, Po Ku succeeded him as general secretary of the CCP and the two worked together closely against Mao's 'peasant line' leadership in the rural soviets.

In August 1935, Wang Ming, reflecting Moscow's need for a broad united front against Hitler, called for a union of proletariat, peasants, petty bourgeoisie, and national bourgeoisie, to oppose Nazi-Fascism and Japan. In China, the CCP adopted the Moscow line in principle but with Mao's own interpretation, as already submitted in draft form at Tsunyi (January 1935). When Wang Ming returned to China (Yenan) in 1937, with Ch'en Yun and K'ang Sheng, he again made common cause with Po Ku, still in the PB. In his December 1937 thesis, 'A Key to Solving the Present Situation', Wang proposed a complete merger of the Red forces with the KMT, in opposition to Mao's united-front strategy, limited by the retention of separate CCP command of armed forces and territorial bases. Thus began the last chapter in an old struggle. In 1940, Wang Ming republished *The Two Lines* (his own and Mao's). Seeking to modify Mao's views, which had placed main reliance on an armed peasantry, Wang called instead for a thorough 'Bolshevization' (proletarianization) of the Party along orthodox Russian lines. Mao's response was the *cheng-feng* (rectification) campaign of 1942, when the entire Party was 're-educated' and brought into conformance with Mao Tse-tung's Thought.

In 1945 the official Party repudiation of Wang Ming was embodied in a long historical review signed by Mao and adopted at the opening of the Seventh Congress of the CCP: 'Resolution on Some Questions of the History of Our Party' (see Mao's *SW*, Vol. I). The document identified three infantile 'left' lines, followed in opposition to Mao's policies, and the most serious was that led by Wang Ming and Po Ku (1931–4). Mao blamed Wang's doctrinaire ideas – basically, the rigid application of foreign (Soviet) Marxist dogma to Chinese conditions – for 'the loss of more Communist lives than enemies''.

In 1951, to cap the climax, Ch'en Po-ta wrote 'Mao Tse-tung's Theory of the Revolution Is the Combination of Marxism-Leninism with the Chinese Revolution', in which Wang Ming was profiled for posterity as the archetype of 'slavish' mentality and blind following of foreign dogma in defiance of Chinese conditions and revolutionary practice (Mao's) based upon them. Despite this vilification, Wang Ming was re-elected to the CC in 1956, but his position as No. 97 in that ninety-seven-member body ironically honoured him only in the breach.

Wang Ming's prestige was already shattered even in 1936, when Mao ridiculed (to the author) the inaccuracies of Wang Ming's reports in *Inprecorr*. When the author first met Wang Ming in Yenan, in 1939, he was astonished by Wang's youthful appearance (he was then only thirty-two), charmed by his urbanity, and struck by marks of his sedentary life – he was a round little man, a head shorter than Mao – as well as by the mild contempt with which he was referred to by veterans of the Long March. Clearly Wang constituted no further threat to Mao, but perhaps the latter welcomed – *pour encourager les autres* – Wang's earnest and open espousal of his cause in order to expose and thoroughly eradicate any remaining tendencies in the Party to exploit borrowed Russian prestige in competing for internal power. In 1967 the Japanese press reported that Wang Ming had secretly returned to Russia with his wife.

Wang Ping-nan (p. 55n.), an assistant foreign minister in 1967, and one of China's most experienced diplomats, first came to prominence when he served as Chou En-lai's political secretary in Chungking (1938–45).

Wang Ping-nan was born in 1906, in Sanyuan, Shensi. His father was a rich landlord and a blood brother of General Yang Hu-ch'eng, who made Wang his protégé and sent him to Germany to prepare to become his secretary. In Berlin he became active among radical students, and there met the daughter of a conservative German family, a remarkable linguist who became his wife. When he returned to China in 1936, to work as Yang's secretary, he was also underground liaison between the CCP, Chang Hsueh-liang, and Yang Hu-ch'eng. He was in Sian before and during Chiang Kai-shek's captivity there, which he helped to bring about. In June 1936, he served as interpreter in an interview between General Yang and the author. After visiting in Yenan, where he first met Mao in 1937, he was sent to Shanghai and later to Chungking to the Eighth Route Army liaison headquarters of Chou En-lai (1938–47). During the KMT-CP 'peace talks' (1945–6), mediated by General George C. Marshall, Wang was secretary to the CP delegation. Subsequently he held important posts in the Ministry of Foreign Affairs and in 1954 was made general secretary of the Chinese delegation to the Geneva Conference on Indochina, headed by Chou En-lai. As ambassador to Poland 1955–64, he became China's senior diplomat in Europe and principal Chinese representative in United States-China ambassadorial talks held in Warsaw from 1955 until Wang's return to Peking in 1964. Wang also took part in the 1962 Geneva Conference on Laos and led important missions which resulted in significant political, economic, and military agreements between China and Poland, Germany, and other East European countries. Made a deputy minister of foreign affairs under Ch'en Yi in 1964, he was China's foremost expert on German and Polish affairs. He and Anna Wang were divorced in 1954 and both remarried. Their son, an engineer, remained in China.

Wang Ping-nan was one of several veteran diplomats who lost position during the GPCR. He was still incommunicado as late as early 1971. With the restoration of a moderation in state policy, and the re-election of former foreign minister Ch'en Yi to the CC in 1969, his return to official life seemed a likelihood.

Wang Shuo-tao (p. 337n.) was born in Liuyang, Hunan, in 1907, in a family of poor peasants, who somehow managed to see him through primary school. He was adopted by a more prosperous uncle, who sent him to middle school and, at twenty, to a state agricultural college. Through the influence of Chen Tu-hsiu's *New Youth* he turned to radicalism, joining the CYL in 1922. In Canton in 1923, he enrolled in the Peasant Movement Training Institute, where Mao Tse-tung was deputy director and P'eng P'ai a teacher. Under their influence he joined the CP and received instruction in Marxism and in 'principles of land revolution'. In 1926 he organized peasant unions in his native town. They took part in the Autumn Harvest Uprising (1927), and began confiscating land and redistributing property to the poor. After their defeat, Wang found his way to Mao Tse-tung's guerrilla forces. He was a political worker with P'eng Teh-huai's army when Changsha was captured (1930), and his wife was caught and executed there. At the end of the Long March he joined the Red Army expedition to Shansi in 1935, and became political commissar of the newly organized Fifteenth Army Corps. During the Resistance War Wang headed guerrilla detachments organized on the Hunan-Kiangsi border, where his Party deputy chief was Wang En-mao. Subsequently he became Hunan Party chief and governor (1949), a member of the CC from 1945, Minister of Communications, SC, 1958–64, and secretary of the CCP Central-South Bureau from 1964. In 1966 he held the important post of deputy chief of the General Political Department of the PLA and was a member of the CC group leading the GPCR. Following direct army intervention in the GPCR in 1967 Wang was replaced and thereafter came under attack. His position in 1971 was still obscure.

Wu Han (p. 523), a non-Party intellectual leader of the China Democratic League, who closely collaborated with the Communists from the 1930s onward, became a principal target of the GPCR when, in November 1965, he was attacked in official publications for his play, *Hai Jui Dismissed from Office*. The official Maoist critique was written by Yao Wen-yuan (elected to the PB in 1969) with the close collaboration of both Chiang Ch'ing and Chairman Mao. In the same month Chiang Ch'ing, Mme Mao Tse-tung, 'exposed' Wu Han's play as 'anti-Party' and 'opposed to socialism' in a Shanghai speech later described as the 'clarion call' which initiated the GPCR.

Wu Han was born in Yiwu, Chekiang, in 1909, in a middle-class family too poor to pay for his education at National (Tsing Hua) University, where Wu supported himself by tutoring until his graduation in 1934. The author first met him in that year, when he was already a lecturer at the university and one of the few faculty members who risked imprisonment by supporting the radical-patriotic student movement. After the Japanese occupation of Peking (1937) Wu went to Yunnan, where, as a historian and a scholar, he won intellectual prominence and was a founder of the China Democratic League. He helped form the CPP CC, in a united front with the CCP, working with Hsu Ping and Lo Man. After 1949 he held many offices in the Peking municipal government; e.g., he was one of the city's eight deputy mayors. As a 'democratic personage' Wu made a number of trips in Asia, Africa, and Eastern Europe, representing cultural and friendship groups. He was also dean of the arts and science department of Tsing Hua University, a national official of the All-China Federation of Democratic Youth, and, at the time of his fall, vice-president of the Peking branch of the World Peace Committee.

Mao's view of Wu's role in activities aimed at the downgrading of Mao Tse-tung's influence – if not his total removal from power, as some Red Guard wall posters of 1967 alleged – may have been accurately portrayed in a huge cartoon displayed in the Drum Tower in Peking. The cartoon lampooned twenty-seven leading Party members accused of revisionism, shown in a procession headed by Lu Ting-yi, former P B propaganda chief. Immediately behind Lu trotted Wu Han, wearing the uniform of an imperial messenger (yamen-runner), while at the tail of the procession, carried in sedan chairs, came Chairman Liu Shao-ch'i and Deputy Premier Teng Hsiao-p'ing, the big-game targets of the GPCR.

Wu Han's specialty as a Chinese historian was the Ming Dynasty. His controversial play, *Hai Jui Dismissed from Office*, dramatized the experience of a Ming official who dared to displease the emperor by criticizing some of his policies. The official was wrongfully dismissed but later vindicated as a patriot. Wu Han's play appeared in 1961, with the support of Lu Ting-yi and P'eng Chen, mayor of Peking. Five years elapsed before analyses in the Maoist press effectively exposed it as an allegorical attack on Mao. Wu had intended Hai Jui to be likened to P'eng Teh-huai, who was 'dismissed' as defence minister by Mao in 1959.

By 1967 the play was recognized as only one of the many 'big poisonous weeds' promoted by cultural 'revisionists' and 'those taking the capitalist road', led by Liu Shao-ch'i. Nothing better demonstrated the chasm that separated Western China experts from comprehension of Communist China than the fact that not one of them discerned the current political significance of Wu Han's play, and of the published Aesopian literature of the same nature, before these works came under counter-attack by the Maoists. Wu Han by 1971 came to symbolize the continuing bourgeois mentality inherited from the Kuomintang regime which had dominated the educational system prior to reforms instituted by the GPCR.

Wu Hsiu-ch'uan (p. 399) continued work in Soviet relations assignments and as CCP representative in many meetings of foreign CPs, and was mentioned prominently as a Maoist supporter during the GPCR. Wu was born in Wuch'ang, Hupeh, in 1909. He studied in Russia at the CMT's Sun Yat-sen University (1927–30) and on his return was a professor at Fu-t'an University in Shanghai. After 1949 his most dramatic appearance was at the head of Peking's delegation to the United Nations in 1950, where he berated (20,000 words!) the United States as an 'aggressor' in Korea. No. 62 in the CC since 1956, he held many assignments in Eastern Europe and at international party conferences.

Wu Liang-p'ing (p. 124) was born in Fenghua, Chekiang (1906), in a merchant family. He was in the CC from 1962, and became Minister of Communications in 1967. Wu graduated from Nanyang (Overseas) Middle School, studied at Amoy and Tahsia (Shanghai) universities, took part in the 30 May Incident, joined the CYL in 1925, and studied at Sun Yat-sen University (1925–9) in Moscow, where he joined the CCP branch. Later he travelled to Europe. Returning to Shanghai he worked in the underground and translated Engels' *History of Socialism, Anti-Duehring*, and *The Materialist Interpretation of History and Dialecticism*. He was imprisoned, 1931–2, in Shanghai, and then entered Soviet Kiangsi, where he worked in Lin Piao's political department. He has been mistakenly identified as one of the 'Twenty-eight Bolsheviks', but in Kiangsi was a Mao supporter. When the author met him in 1936 he was Mao's secretary and a member of the agit-prop department of the army. He spoke excellent English and Russian and knew some French. For an interview with Wu, see *RNORC*.

Yang Ch'eng-wu (p. 197n.) rose to membership (alternate) in the PB in 1966, replaced Lo Jui-ch'ing (his vilified former superior) as chief of staff of the PLA, and became a vice-chairman of the supreme Party military affairs committee.

A native of Fukien of peasant birth (1912), Yang joined the guerrillas when he was seventeen. He was largely educated by the Party and its army, especially under Lin Piao, with whose command he fought and/or studied continuously, 1932–8. After the Long March (during which he led a regiment), Yang was a student in the Red Army University at Pao An when the author met him in 1936. During the Resistance War he served under Nieh Jung-chen in Shansi, and acquitted himself so well that a Japanese commander once wrote to congratulate him. In the Liberation War he was deputy commander of group armies in Hopei, Shansi, and Chahar, and afterwards commanded the Peking-Tientsin garrison, where he was also PLA Party secretary until 1955. Elected an alternate member of the CC in 1956, he set up China's air defence command and its Party organization. He served as an infantry private for a year during the Great Leap Forward period. Becoming deputy chief of staff of the PLA in 1959, he accompanied Lo Jui-ch'ing on many of his missions until the latter's eclipse, when Yang succeeded him. Yang was eliminated in the army reorganization under Lin Piao in 1967, and in 1971 may have been still under protective arrest.

Yang Hu-ch'eng (p. 54) during the Resistance War offered his services to the Generalissimo. General Yang was put under house detention in Chungking, and towards the end of the war he was secretly executed.

Yang K'ai-hui (p. 107) came from a wealthy landowning family of Hunan. She was the daughter of Yang Ch'ang-chi, Mao Tse-tung's highly respected teacher at the First Teachers' Training School in Changsha. Hsiao Yu gives a sympathetic portrait of Yang K'ai-hui in his dubious memoirs, *Mao Tse-tung and I Were Beggars* (Syracuse, NY, 1959). Mao was a frequent visitor in Yang's home; in Peking he often dined with the family. Marriages were then arranged by parents; in many cases, the bride and bridegroom did not see each other before betrothal (as in Mao's first 'marriage'). Yang Ch'ang-chi obviously had advanced ideas about women's rights or he would not have provided a higher education for his daughter and permitted her to dine at the table with Mao and himself. Mao influenced Yang K'ai-hui towards radicalism – and marriage to himself, in 1920. She was then twenty-five. When arrested, in 1930, she refused to repudiate the Communist Party, or Mao, as the alternative to death. She was executed in the same year, at Changsha. Yang K'ai-hui bore Mao two sons, Mao An-ch'ing and Mao An-ying.

Yang Shang-k'un (p. 296) after 1936 became secretary of the CC in Shansi and chief of its united-front department (1937–43), then director of the general office of the CC (1943–59), until in 1956 he ranked forty-second among ninety-seven full members and ninety-six alternate members of the CC. Yet in 1966 Yang was accused of major duplicity and dimissed from all his posts.

Born in Szechuan, in 1903, in a middle-class family, Yang was influenced by the cultural renaissance (May Fourth Movement, 1919), joined a socialist youth group, and was sent to the CMT-organized Sun Yat-sen University in Moscow, where he entered the branch CCP. He returned to China with Wang Ming in 1927 and was considered one of the 'Twenty-eight Bolsheviks'. At the end of the Long March, when the author met him, he was acting director of the political department of the Red Army. As alternate secretary of the CC secretariat 1956–66, he held responsible positions in meetings with Soviet and other foreign Communists, especially after the Sino-Soviet split. In 1966 he was accused of utilizing such opportunities to conspire against Mao, and Red Guard posters alleged that he had tried to wire-tap Mao's conversations. In

April 1967, 'revolutionary cadres' of Peking reportedly demanded his execution, together with that of P'eng Chen, Liu Shao-ch'i, Lo Jui-ch'ing, and others. In 1970 Yang was reportedly in exile in Russia.

Yao I-lin (p. 478) was, as Minister of Commerce, the youngest member of the State Council. Born in Anhui in 1916, the son of a bankrupt bourgeois family which lived (he said) by periodically 'selling some article', he had his secondary education in Shanghai and Peking. He then enrolled in Tsing Hua University but left during his second year (1935) to devote full time to revolutionary activity.

When the author met Yao in 1935, he was a student leader working closely with Huang Ching and Huang Hua. Soon after Japan's seizure of Peking in 1937 he joined them in organizing guerrilla warfare in the countryside, working under the CCP CC North China Bureau, headed by Liu Shao-ch'i. Yao I-lin had no special training in commerce but learned, during his guerrilla days, how to manage a wartime economy. In 1950 he attended a cadres' school for trade, and in 1952 became vice-minister of commerce. As the official mainly responsible for the functioning of the rice-rationing system during the critical years 1959–61 he made a record of outstanding achievement. In 1960, aged forty-four, he was promoted to full minister of the Commerce Department.

Yao I-lin, also attacked by Red Guards under the leading cultural revolutionary group of the CC, was removed from office to undergo ideological re-indoctrination. He was held responsible for observing policies related to 'economism' and 'capitalist-roadism' attributed to Liu Shao-ch'i, particularly during the 'hardship years' (1961–3) after the GLF and the break with Russia. In 1971 he was, according to several of his former colleagues in Peking, soon to be 'cleared' for resumption of work.

Yeh Chien-ying (p. 84n.) became one of the ten marshals of the PLA and in 1966 was named one of 'the group leading the cultural revolution under the CC' and a member of the CC military affairs committee. That combination of roles reflected an early period when, already a general, Yeh studied at Sun Yat-sen University in Moscow (1928) and the following year 'learned about drama in Germany and France'.

Born in Kwangtung in 1897, in a merchant family, Yeh graduated from Yunnan Military Academy, became a district magistrate in Kwangtung, joined the KMT in 1922 and became an instructor at Whampoa Military Academy in 1923. In 1924 he joined the CCP. He commanded a division during the Northern Expedition. After participating in the abortive Nanchang and Canton uprisings he spent two years in Russia and Europe. After he returned to China in 1930 his Party history became closely identified with Chou En-lai. For a time he also headed a drama school in Soviet Kiangsi.

Yeh was on the revolutionary military council in 1934 when Chou En-lai replaced Chu Teh as its chairman and both Mao and Chu Teh were in opposition. Chou and Yeh planned, with Li Teh, the retreat which developed into the Long March. After the historic meeting at Tsunyi (1935), where Mao assumed Party PB leadership, Yeh backed Mao against Chang Kuo-t'ao at Maoerhkai. During the Resistance War he became (with Chou En-lai) a principal military liaison person in KMT territory (1938–45), where the author frequently interviewed him (see RNORC). He was said to have persuaded sixteen regimental commanders in the Shansi KMT armies to join the Reds. Chief of staff of the PLA in 1946, he was military commander and concurrently mayor of Peking in 1949, and from 1949 to 1955 was military and party chief in South China. He was also a member of the SC of the NPC from 1954 and a vice-chairman of the National Defence Council from 1962. Yeh retained his position on the PB during the GPCR and played an important role in coordinating army and political activity in the formation of revolutionary committees. In 1969 he was re-elected by the Ninth Party Congress to the CC and re-elected to the PB. Yeh was married to Tseng Hsien-chih, a Japanese-educated Hunanese, long a national leader in women's organizations. For an American general's opinion of Yeh as a military leader, see Evans Carlson's *Twin Stars of China* (New York, 1940).

Yeh T'ing (p. 135), a Whampoa cadet and commander of the Twenty-fourth Division of the Nationalist forces during the Northern Expedition (1926–7), was a principal leader of the Nanchang Uprising on 1 August 1927. After its failure Yeh retreated to Swatow, took part in the CMT's disastrous Canton Uprising in December 1927, and escaped to Hongkong. He withdrew from politics for a decade. In 1937 Yeh was authorized by Chiang Kai-shek to reorganize surviving Red partisans on the Kiangsi-Fukien-Hunan borders, to create the New Fourth Army. These partisans had formed a rear guard when the main Red Army retreated to the North-West in 1935, and one of their leaders, Hsiang Ying (Han Ying), became vice-commander of the New Fourth Army. In 1941 Chiang Kai-shek's troops ambushed part of the New Fourth Army, killed Hsiang Ying, and wounded and imprisoned Yeh T'ing. After Yeh's release in 1946 he died, en route to Yenan, in an airplane crash which also killed Teng Fa, Po Ku, and others.

Leadership in the
Chinese Communist Party

FROM the inception of the Chinese Communist Party (CCP) its constitution provided for the election of delegates to periodic congresses, which chose a supreme or Central Committee (CC). The CC itself decided when congresses should convene, but once a decade was a minimum. The GPCR interfered with plans announced to hold a Ninth Congress in 1966. It was not held until 1969.

Congresses of the CCP have taken place as follows:

>Founding Congress, Shanghai, June–July 1921
>2nd, Shanghai, July 1922
>3rd, Canton, June 1923
>4th, Shanghai, January 1925
>5th, Hankow, July 1927
>6th, Moscow, July 1928
>7th, Yenan, April 1945
>8th, Peking, September 1956
>9th, Peking, April 1969

The Seventh CCP Congress (1945) elected 44 full members to the CC and the Eighth Congress (1956) elected 97 full members and 101 alternate members. The CC chooses a Political Bureau (Politburo), the equivalent of a Party cabinet. The Eighth Congress CC chose 20 full members of the Politburo (PB) and 6 alternate members. The Ninth Congress elected a CC of 170 full members (100 alternates) and a Politburo of 21 full members and 4 alternate members.

From 1921 to 1935 the CCP followed the pattern of Stalin's Party, in which the General Secretary (of the CC and the PB) held chief responsibility for leadership. The term used in Chinese for 'General Secretary' was *Tsung shu-chi*. General secretaryship of the Party was held by the following:

Ch'en Tu-hsiu	1921–7
Ch'u Ch'iu-pai	1927–8
Hsiang Chung-fa	1928–31
Wang Ming (Ch'en Shao-yu)	1931–2
Po Ku (Ch'in Pang-hsien)	1932–5
Lo Fu (Chang Wen-t'ien)	1935–43
Teng Hsaio-p'ing	1956–69

A change in the significance of the title 'General Secretary' took place at an enlarged meeting of the PB (including CC members and army commanders) on the Long March at Tsunyi, Kweichow, in January 1935. At that time Mao Tse-tung won majority control of the PB. The Tsunyi Conference heard and accepted Mao Tse-tung's critique of Po Ku's mistakes, and Po Ku resigned as General Secretary. Mao now held the mandate of the Red Army and the Party to lead them on the Long March. Mao was already Chairman (*Chu-hsi*) of the Central Soviet Government, but the latter had disintegrated. The Tsunyi Conference simply transferred top authority to the Chairman, above the General Secretary. Lo Fu was named new General Secretary, but was subordinated to Mao, who was also named Chairman of the supreme Party revolutionary military committee.

Lo Fu was still General Secretary of the PB when the author visited Pao An in 1936, but Lo Fu referred (in English) to Mao as 'leader of the Party'. Mao was *Chu-hsi*. In a conference of the PB held in Lochuan in 1937, Mao was elected *Chu-hsi* of the CC and the PB. Lo Fu's title remained *Tsung shu-chi*. He was still called that when the author again saw Lo Fu in Yenan in September 1939. The position of General Secretary was formally abolished at the Seventh National Congress of the Party in 1945. Provision was then made for a Chairman and four Vice-Chairmen of the PB to constitute a standing committee. One of the Vice-Chairmen served as a recording secretary (*mi-shu-chang*). In 1956 the Eighth National Congress restored the title 'General Secretary', but the position carried less significance than formerly, although it was a job of top administrative coordination. In 1956 Teng Hsiao-p'ing was chosen General Secretary. In the official order of listing, after the Eighth CC's Eleventh Plenum (August 1966), Teng still appeared as fifth in rank under Mao Tse-tung – but by 1967 he was under heavy attack, together with Liu Shao-ch'i, from leaders of the GPCR, and it seemed likely that his career had come to an end.

Following is the order of rank of members of the Politburo after the eleventh plenary session of the Central Committee of the Eighth Congress of the CCP in August 1966, together with notations of official and unofficial action for or against them (see *Code,* next page), and a list of members of the Politburo after the Ninth Congress in April 1969.

Mao Tse-tung, *Chairman of the CCP Politburo,* 1935, to date

1966 (August) Members
Standing Committee

Lin Piao   P, M, LM
Chou En-lai   RR, ORG, LM
T'ao Chu   NM, RG
Ch'en Po-ta   P, ORG?
Teng Hsiao-p'ing   D, RG, LM
K'ang Sheng   P, ORG?

Others

Liu Shao-ch'i   D, RG
Chu Teh   D, ORG, LM, M
Li Fu-ch'un   P, ORG, LM
Ch'en Yun   D, LM
Tung Pi-wu   D, LM
Ch'en Yi,   D, ORG, M
Liu Po-ch'eng   RR, LM, M
Ho Lung   RR, LM, M, RG
Li Hsien-nien   RR, LM
Li Ching-ch'uan   RR, RG
T'an Chen-lin   RR, LM
Hsu Hsiang-ch'ien   NM, LM, M
Yeh Chien-ying   NM, LM, M
Nieh Jung-chen   NM, LM, M
Po I-po   P, RG
Li Hsueh-feng   NM, LM
Hsieh Fu-chih   NM, LM
Liu Ning-yi   NM
Hsiao Hua   NM, ORG, LM

1969 (April) Members
Standing Committee

Lin Piao (vice-chairman,   CC)
Chou En-lai (premier)
Ch'en Po-ta
K'ang Sheng

Others
(not necessarily in order of rank)

Yeh Chun (Mme Lin Piao)   NM
Yeh Chien-ying
Liu Po-ch'eng
Chiang Ch'ing (Mme Mao
   Tse-tung)
Chu Teh
Hsu Shih-yu   NM
Ch'en Hsi-lien   NM
Li Hsien-nien (first vice-premier)
Li Tso-p'eng   NM
Wu Fa-hsien   NM
Chang Ch'un-ch'iao   NM
Ch'iu Hui-tso   NM
Yao Wen-yuan   NM
Huang Yung-sheng   NM
Tung Pi-wu
Hsieh Fu-chih

Alternate Members

Ch'i Teng-kuei   NM
Li Hsueh-feng
Li Teh-sheng
Wang Tung-hsing   NM

Code

D   Demoted

RR   Retained Rank

P   Promoted

NM   New Member

RG   Repeatedly attacked by Red Guard posters

ORG   Occasionally attacked on posters, possibly by opposition Red Guards

M   Rank of Marshal of the Army

LM   Long March

Apart from members who had died, two from the 1966 list were in 1969 re-elected to CC but not PB: Ch'en Yi and Li Fu-ch'un. The following 1966 members were dropped from both PB and CC: Liu Shao-ch'i, Teng Hsiao-p'ing, P'eng Chen, P'eng Teh-huai, Ho Lung, Li Ching-ch'uan, T'an Chen-lin, Ulanfu (the only Mongol member), Chang Wen-t'ien (Lo Fu), Lu Ting-yi, and Po I-po. Ten among the sixteen new members had military affiliations.

Bibliography

BEYOND listing a few works directly related to the principal historical context of this volume, it would seem redundant to offer a general bibliography on China when so many already exist.

Primary sources on the 1921–37 period were virtually nonexistent when this book was written. Much has since been added by the work of foreign scholarship and research as well as by publications released in Peking. An early and basic bibliography of works in Chinese, Japanese, and European languages appeared in Benjamin Schwartz's *Chinese Communism and the Rise of Mao*. John Rue's *Mao Tse-tung in Opposition* contributed some new sources, in 1966, as did Jerome Ch'en's *Mao and the Chinese Revolution* (1965), and Stuart Schram's biography a year later. *The Chinese Communist Movement, 1921–27* (Stanford, 1960) and *The Chinese Communist Movement 1937–49* (Stanford, 1962) are bibliographies of materials in various languages prepared by Chun-tu Hsueh. Allan B. Cole compiled another guide to some basic literature in English in his *Forty Years of Chinese Communism*, published by the American Historical Association (Washington, DC, 1962).

Bibliographical notes compiled by Howard L. Boorman appear at the end of his essay, 'Mao Tse-tung : The Lacquered Image', *China Quarterly* (London, Oct.–Dec. 1963). The latter periodical contains many articles of special interest to students of the pre-1949 period of the Chinese revolution, as well as analyses of current information. In Paris the *Cahiers Franco-chinois* serves a valuable purpose. There are, of course, abundant Russian and Japanese historical works of which no listing is attempted here.

By 1971 many new sources on the pre-1937 revolutionary period had become available. Materials released by Red Guard publications were of varying degrees of authenticity, but many official Party documents also became available. A selected list has been added to the Bibliography.

1. American and European Books on Early Phases of the Chinese Communist Revolution

Bertram, James, *First Act in China*, New York, 1938. An eyewitness account of the Sian Incident.

Brandt, Conrad, *Stalin's Failure in China*, Cambridge, Mass., 1958.

Brandt, Conrad, Schwartz, Benjamin, and Fairbank, John K., *A Documentary History of Chinese Communism*, Cambridge, Mass., 1952.

Buck, J. Lossing, *Land Utilization in China*, Chicago, 1937. Dr Buck seriously contradicts some of the Communists' claims regarding the extent of tenancy.

Carlson, Evans Fordyce, *Twin Stars of China*, New York, 1940. Interesting first-hand impressions of Chinese Communist leaders in 1937–8 by the only American general who applied Communist guerrilla tactics in the training of American troops – 'Carlson's Raiders' of World War II. His China reports were read by President Roosevelt.

Chen Han-seng, *Landlord and Peasant in China*, New York, 1936. A Harvard graduate who lived in exile before the revolution, Dr Chen made reports on Chinese agrarian problems which influenced many scholars in China and abroad. He was in 1966 a specialist in Peking's Institute of International Affairs.

Ch'en, Jerome, *Mao and the Chinese Revolution*, London, 1965.

Chiang Kai-shek, *Soviet Russia in China*, New York, 1957. The Generalissimo gives his estimation of the strategic factors that favoured his Communist adversaries in China.

Chiang Kai-shek, Mme (Soong Mei-ling), *General Chiang Kai-shek: The Account of the Fortnight in Sian* ... (original title: *Sian: A Coup d'Etat*), New York, 1937. A popular version of the Incident, with extracts from the Generalissimo's diary.

Chow Tse-tung, *The May Fourth Movement*, Cambridge, Mass., 1960. A Chinese scholar traces the causes and the consequences of the cultural renaissance period, which Mao Tse-tung defines as the beginning of modern revolutionary China.

Clubb, O. Edmund, *Twentieth Century China*, New York, 1964.

Compton, Boyd, *Mao's China, Party Reform Documents, 1942–44*, Seattle, 1952. Important for several of Mao's texts which appear only in bowdlerized form in his *Selected Works*.

Dumont, René, *La révolution dans les campagnes chinoises*, Paris, 1954. Tends to support the Communists' main contentions concerning problems of land ownership, tenancy, and utilization.

Fei Hsiao-t'ung, *Peasant Life in China*, New York, 1939. Generally supports conclusions that a preponderance of poor and landless peasants in China presented a crisis solvable only by land redistribution and social revolutionary changes on a vast scale.

Hsiaso Tso-liang, *Power Relations Within the Chinese Communist Movement*, Seattle, 1962.

Isaacs, Harold R., The Tragedy of the Chinese Revolution, Oxford, 1961. The tragic view, as seen largely through Trotskyist lenses, of contradictions in KMT-CC-Comintern relationships during the 1923–7 period and 'the first revolutionary civil war'. (The operation was fatal but the patient lived.)

Johnson, Chalmers A., Peasant Nationalism and Communist Power, Stanford, 1965. Valuable for its Japanese sources.

Levenson, Joseph, Liang Ch'i-ch'ao and the Mind of Modern China, Cambridge, Mass., 1959.

Lindsay, Michael, North China Front, London, 1943.

Lin Piao (compiler), Quotations from Chairman Mao Tse-tung, Peking, 1966.

Mao Tse-tung, Red China: President Mao Tse-tung Reports on the Progress of the Chinese Soviet Republic, London (Martin Lawrence), 1934.

Mao Tse-tung, et al., Fundamental Laws of the Chinese Soviet Republic, London (Martin Lawrence), 1934.

McLane, Charles B., Soviet Policy and Chinese Communists: 1931–1946, New York, 1958.

Meisner, Maurice, Li Ta-chao and the Origins of Chinese Marxism, Cambridge, Mass., 1967.

Mif, Pavel, Heroic China, New York, 1937. By a Comintern instructor at Sun Yat-sen (Eastern Toilers') University in Moscow who taught China's 'Twenty-eight Bolsheviks'. The book is largely a propaganda exhortation.

North, Robert C., Moscow and Chinese Communists, Stanford, 1962.

Pischel, Enrica Collotti, L'origine della rivoluzione cinese, Turin, 1958.

Rue, John E., Mao Tse-tung in Opposition, 1927–35 (Stanford, 1966).

Schram, Stuart R., Mao Tse-tung, London, 1966.

Schram, Stuart R., The Political Thought of Mao Tse-tung, New York, 1963.

Schwartz, Benjamin I., Chinese Communism and the Rise of Mao, Cambridge, Mass., 1951, reprinted 1966.

Siao Yu (Hsiao Yu), Mao Tse-tung and I Were Beggars, Syracuse, NY, 1959. By the brother of Hsiao San, but much less credible. Amusing apocrypha.

Smedley, Agnes, Battle Hymn of China, New York, 1943.

Smedley, Agnes, The Great Road: The Life and Times of Chu Teh, London, 1958.

Stalin, Joseph, 'Leninism'. Selected Writings, London, 1943.

T'ang Leang-li, The Inner History of the Chinese Revolution, London, 1930.

Tawney, R. H., *Land and Labour in China*, London, 1932, reprinted in New York, 1964. A classical analysis by a noted Western economist of China's 'unsolvable' agrarian problems.

Trotsky, Leon, *Problems of the Chinese Revolution*, New York, 1932.

Trotsky, Leon, *The Third International After Lenin*, New York, 1936.

Wales, Nym, *Inside Red China*, New York, 1939.

Wales, Nym (ed.), *Red Dust: Autobiographies of Chinese Communists*, Stanford, 1952.

Wilbur, C. Martin, and Julie Lien-ying How, *Documents on Communism ...*, 1918–27, New York, 1956.

Yang Chien, *The Communist Situation in China*, Nanking, 1931.

2. Peking Publications on Revolutionary History
(Foreign Languages Press)

Ch'en Po-ta, *Notes on Mao Tse-tung's 'Report of an Investigation into the Peasant Movement in Hunan'*, 1954.

Ch'en Po-ta, *Stalin and the Chinese Revolution*, 1953.

Ch'en Po-ta, *A Study of Land Rent in Pre-Liberation China*, 1958.

Ho Kan-chih, *A History of the Modern Chinese Revolution*, 1959.

Hsiao San (Emi Siao), *Mao Tse-tung T'ung-chih-ti ch'ing-hsao-nien shih-tai* [Comrade Mao's Boyhood and Youth], 1949. Some sympathetic personal reminiscences. The author knew Mao in his schooldays in Hunan.

Hu Chiao-mu, *Thirty Years of the Chinese Communist Party*, 1954.

Hu Sheng, *Imperialism and Chinese Politics*, 1955.

Li Jui, *Mao Tse-tung T'ung-chih-ti ti ch'u-ch'i ke-ming huo-tung* [Comrade Mao's Revolutionary Activities], 1957. Not to be regarded as an official biography. The book was withdrawn from circulation in China.

Liu Shao-ch'i, *How to Be a Good Communist*, 1960, should be compared with original, entitled *Training of the Communist Party Member*, published in Yenan in 1939. See Compton, *Mao's China*, listed above.

The Long March: Eyewitness Accounts (Symposium), 1963.

Lu Hsun, *Selected Works*, 1957.

The Roar of a Nation, Reminiscences of December 9th Student Movement, 1963.

A complete list of other works published in French and English by the Foreign Languages Press, an official Chinese government organization, may be obtained from Guozi Shudian, P.O. Box 399, Peking, China. Among recent publications are dozens of reprints of polemical documents of the Sino-Soviet schism which throw some light on earlier difficulties in relationships between the Soviet and Chinese parties.

3. Works by Mao Tse-tung Published in China

Prior to 1960 three volumes of Mao Tse-tung's *Selected Works* were officially published, in Chinese, covering the period 1926–49. Unofficial English-language translations were issued by the International Publishers, New York and London, in four volumes. The latter covered the following periods: I (1926–37); II (1937–8); III (1939–41); and IV (1941–5). (These four volumes corresponded to Vols. I–III in Chinese.) In 1960, Vol. IV appeared in Chinese. In 1961 the Foreign Languages Press of Peking published, in English, a translation of the Chinese edition of Vol. IV, *Selected Works of Mao Tse-tung* (1945–9). English translations of Mao's *SW*, Vols. I, II, and III, were published by Peking, 1963–5; Vol. V of the *SW* was scheduled for publication in Peking in 1971.

In 1963 Peking brought out in English and other foreign translations a 408-page book, *The Selected Military Writings of Mao Tse-tung*. It contains Mao's work of that genre from 1928 through 1940. Seventeen pieces of Mao's poetry were translated in *Poems*, in 1959, and Mao's *Nine Poems* appeared in English in 1963. In 1966 a collection, *Quotations from Chairman Mao Tse-tung*, was published in Chinese first for the PLA and then for the edification of the Red Guards. Many foreign-language versions became available in the same year. By 1968 China had published 86,400,000 four-volume sets of *Selected Works of Mao Tse-tung*, in addition to 350,000,000 copies of *Quotations from Chairman Mao Tse-tung*, and more than 57,000,000 copies of Chairman Mao's poems. Those items reached 'hundreds of millions of Chinese workers, peasants, and soldiers' as well as 'revolutionary people in 148 countries and regions throughout the world', according to the official *Hsin Hua News*, 17 January 1968.

Since 1949 Mao had produced a steady stream of essays, reports, ideological statements, exhortations, and a few poems, but little had been published under his name. It was known that many of the treatises in the long series of exchanges in the Sino-Russian controversy were written or edited by Mao, as well as much of the abundant accusatory literature of the GPCR, which contains important revelations about early Party history and relations with Moscow. For example, late in 1967 Mao was officially revealed as the author of *Khrushchev's Phony Communism*, first printed in the Peking press anonymously in 1964. Three notable pamphlets by Mao published by FLP were: *On the Question of Agricultural Cooperation*, 1956; *Imperialism and All Re-*

actionaries Are Paper Tigers, 1958; and *On the Correct Handling of Contradictions Among the People*, 1959.

A significant work widely attributed to Mao, but not signed by him, is *Historical Experiences of the Dictatorship of the Proletariat* (in Chinese, 1955–6; English translation, Foreign Languages Press, 1959). Mao told the author that this essay precisely expressed his evaluation of Stalin and the role of a personality cult in the revolution. Other references are listed in the Notes and the Biographical Notes in this volume.

Many of Mao's speeches, essays, and polemical treatises were revised and edited before being included in his *SW*, as Mao himself acknowledged – a practice not unknown to public figures and statesmen from Caesar to Churchill. For the most part the alterations have resulted simply in improved clarity, but when possible, meticulous scholars consult the originals.

4. Additional Books and Articles Relevant to the Pre-1937 Period of the Revolution Available in 1971

Braun, Otto, 'Von Schanghai bis Jana', in *Horizont*, East Berlin, 1969. Nos. 23–4. Li Teh's version of events, 1933–7.

Chang Ai-p'ing, *Tsung Tsunyi tao Ta Tu Ho* (*From Tsunyi to the Tatu River*), Hongkong, 1960. An account of the Long March.

Chang Kuo-t'ao, *Wo-ti Hui-yi* (*My Recollections*), a series of articles in *Ming Pao Yueh-k'an*, Hongkong, 1969–70. Part of Chang's projected autobiography.

Ch'en, Jerome, *Mao Papers, Anthology and Bibliography*, Oxford, 1970. Includes both English and Chinese titles listed chronologically, 1917–67; letters, commemorative writings, and statements. Many are not to be found in Mao's *SW*.

Ch'en, Jerome, 'Resolutions of the Tsunyi Conference', 1935. *China Quarterly*, Oct.–Dec. 1969. Highly important.

Chou En-lai: for speeches, statements, and writings attributed to Chou during the 1930–5 period see bibliographical entries for Hu Chih-hsi, Jerome Ch'en, Dieter Heinzig, and Otto Braun.

Heinzig, Dieter, 'The Otto Braun Memoirs and Mao's Rise to Power', *China Quarterly*, Apr./June 1971. An analysis of some rather arcane events which led to Mao's assumption of Party leadership at Tsunyi, 1935, as suggested by the Otto Braun Memoirs. Cf. Jerome Ch'en, 'Resolutions of the Tsunyi Conference', below.

Hsiao Tso-liang, *Power Relations Within the Chinese Communist Movement*, 1930–4, Seattle, 1961. Based on documents examined in Taiwan.

Hu Chih-hsi, 'Hua Fu, the Fifth Encirclement Campaign and the Tsunyi Conference', *China Quarterly*, July/Sept. 1970. Analyses articles by 'Hua Fu' translated from *Revolution and War*, published in Juichin, (Soviet) Kiangsi, 1933–4. 'Hua Fu' is said to have been Li Teh (Otto Braun). See Dieter Heinzig, above, and Li Teh, BN.

Isaacs, Herald R., 'Documents on the Comintern and the Chinese Revolution', *China Quarterly*, Jan.–Mar. 1971.

Mao Tse-tung, *Selected Readings from the Works of Chairman Mao Tse-tung*, FLP, 1967. A compilation drawn mainly from Mao's SW but including a few important writings of the post-1949 period.

Mao Tse-tung, *Selected Writings by Chairman Mao*, Joint Publications Research Service, Washington, No. 50792. An English translation of Red Guard compilations, including lectures purportedly delivered by Mao at Yenan in 1937, in a book which the compilers assert was 'edited' by Mao in 1959. Whether Mao himself wrote *all* the materials included is doubtful. Two selections, 'On Practice' and 'On Contradiction' are substantially the same as the essays Mao edited for inclusion in SW.

Takeuchu, Minoru, *Mao Tse-tung chi* (Collected Writings of Mao Tse-tung), Vol. 3, Sept. 1931–Aug. 1933; Vol. 5, Nov. 1935–May 1938. Tokyo, 1970. With introductions in Japanese and text in Chinese, the volumes form part of a veritable encyclopedia of Mao's writings, the most comprehensive yet attempted.

Pien-cheng Fa-wei Wu-lin (Cheng-shou T'i-kang) (On Dialectical Materialism [Outline for Lectures]). Attributed by some western specialists to Mao Tse-tung, this relic is divided into three parts, each with subtitles, and consists of lecture materials originally separately stapled together and later bound by string into one volume. Cover date, Yenan, 1937. Subtitles include 'On Practice' and 'On Contradiction', which are undoubtedly by Mao Tse-tung. (In 1964 Mao told the author that he did not deliver any lecture or write any book or essay entitled *On Dialectical Materialism*.)

Schwarz, Benjamin I., 'The Legend of the "Legend of Maoism" ', *China Quarterly*, Apr./June 1960.

Shewmaker, Kenneth E., *Americans and Chinese Communists, 1927–1945, A Persuading Encounter*, Ithaca, NY, 1971. A useful résumé which incidentally demonstrates that the 'agrarian reformer myth' was demolished at birth by those later accused of having fostered it.

Thornton, Richard C., *The Comintern and the Chinese Communists, 1928–31*, Seattle, 1969.

Wilson, Dick, *The Long March*, London, 1971. A highly readable account based on old and new materials and some original research.

Wittfogel, Karl A., 'The Legend of Maoism', *China Quarterly*, Jan.–Mar. 1960; Apr./June 1961.

Clubb, O. Edmund, *Communism in China as Reported from Hankow in 1932*, NY, 1968. Early field studies by a US Foreign Service China language officer which refuted KMT 'red-bandit' propaganda.

Union Research Institute, *The Case of P'eng Teh-huai, 1959–1968*, Kowloon, Hongkong. Documents and excerpts of documents of a decisive split between Mao and his former defence minister, which awaits full authentication.

Index

MORE ABOUT PENGUINS
AND PELICANS

Penguinews, which appears every month, contains details of all the new books issued by Penguins as they are published. From time to time it is supplemented by *Penguins in Print*, which is a complete list of all available books published by Penguins. (There are well over four thousand of these.)

A specimen copy of *Penguinews* will be sent to you free on request. For a year's issues (including the complete lists) please send 30p of you live in the United Kingdom, or 60p if you live elsewhere. Just write to Dept EP, Penguin Books Ltd, Harmondsworth, Middlesex, enclosing a cheque or postal order, and your name will be added to the mailing list.

Note: *Penguinews* and *Penguins in Print* are not available in the U.S.A. or Canada

Also by Edgar Snow

RED CHINA TODAY
THE OTHER SIDE OF THE RIVER

In *Red China Today*, Edgar Snow returns to the country he described in *Red Star Over China*, and in a detailed and absorbing survey shows it developing under Communist rule through 'enormous difficulties' towards nuclear power.

For this new Pelican edition the author has substantially revised his 'vast, panoramic survey', which 'has the advantage of a long perspective and of a true knowledge of conditions in China in the past. His book can be recommended as much the most honest and sympathetically written account of what change in China means in actual relief of human suffering and not just in the material sense, but in relief from the misrule which China has suffered as far back as living memory goes. His book ranges far and wide in time and space, often recalling the past and analysing the present, interspersed with racy descriptions' – *The Times Literary Supplement*

Not for sale in the U.S.A. or Canada